Symbol and Sacrament

Louis-Marie Chauvet

Symbol and Sacrament

A Sacramental Reinterpretation of Christian Existence

Translated by
Patrick Madigan, S.J., and Madeleine Beaumont

A PUEBLO BOOK

The Liturgical Press   Collegeville, Minnesota

About the author:

Fr. Louis-Marie Chauvet has taught sacramental theology at l'Institut catholique in Paris since 1974.

A Pueblo Book published by The Liturgical Press

Design by Frank Kacmarcik, Obl.S.B.

This book was first published in French under the title *SYMBOLE ET SACREMENT: Un relecture sacramentelle de l'existence chrétienne* © 1987 by Les Éditions du Cerf.

Library of Congress Cataloging-in-Publication Data

Chauvet, Louis-Marie.
    [Symbole et sacrement. English]
    Symbol and sacrament : a sacramental reinterpretation of
  Christian existence / Louis-Marie Chauvet ; Patrick Madigan,
  Madeleine Beaumont, translators.
        p. cm.
    ''A Pueblo book.''
    Includes bibliographical references.
    ISBN 0-8146-6124-6
    1. Sacraments—Catholic Church. 2. Symbolism. 3. Catholic
  Church—Doctrines. I. Title.
  BV800.C5213 1995
    234' . 16—dc20   93-28746
                                                                      CIP

Contents

xiv

xvi

Introduction

Contemporary awareness of the diversity of sacraments and, more broadly, of the extreme heterogeneity of what makes up the "world" of sacramentality, has served to discredit the traditional treatises *de sacramentis in genere* ("of sacraments in general"). It does not, however, seem to have extinguished all interest in a study of the common traits of sacramentality. On the contrary, we see today an increasing interest in this topic, but from a perspective *unlike* that of the classic treatises. The numerous conferences and articles devoted to the themes of *ritual* and *symbol* over the past ten years could be mentioned as evidence of this. This curiosity does not seem to stem exclusively from theological students, but also from interested laypersons of all ages, catechists, campus ministers, and pastoral workers. At the same time, and from these same sources, at least in France, one notices an increasing desire to uncover the *marks* proper to Christian identity, among which the sacraments, of course, occupy a fundamental position. Today, however, we are profoundly conscious of the fact that the sacraments are far from constituting the sum total of Christian life; for example, they should not elbow aside Scripture or eclipse ethical engagement. We are determined to hold the sacraments within their rightful place — but also to demand that they *occupy* this place fully: neither the unique center of Christian life nor a mere appendage to it.

It appears that what is being sought through this manifest interest is ultimately a *theology of the sacramental*, that is, a theology which opens up a *sacramental reinterpretation*, initially modest but ultimately global in its potential extension, of what it means *to lead a Christian life. A foundational theology of sacramentality* — that precisely is what we are proposing to elaborate here.

Far from dissolving the distinct sacraments into the blur of a "general sacramentality," the theology we suggest bases itself upon them as *symbolic figures allowing us entrance into, and empowerment to live out, the (arch-)sacramentality which is the very essence of Christian existence.* Perhaps, in spite of appearances, this last statement is far from obvious. For what, actually, does it claim? That the sacramental celebrations place us in both the figurative order and the pragmatic order: whatever we are permitted to *see* there is given to us precisely that we may simultaneously *live* it. Revelation is immediate empowerment; it is empowerment that is emptied of its strength if it does not act as revelation.

Where do we get this? Not from ourselves. We cannot make sense of the sacraments if we attempt to start from rational deductions. We are simply trying to understand what we *already* believe, immersed as we are, through baptism and Eucharist, in *sacramentality.* It would be naive, not to say dishonest, to pretend that we are not always-already actively interested participants in sacramentality. What modernity has taught us is precisely the importance of taking into account, indeed taking as *decisive,* the *place* out of which we speak: the *place* of our individual desires; the social, cultural, or historical *place* we inhabit. Through all this, we attempt here nothing more than to articulate a sort of law of the symbolic order, which is valid over the entire territory we propose to cross. It is impossible to really comprehend anything without recognizing oneself as always-already involved in what one is trying to comprehend; this is the clearest description we can give of the method of our project.

Under the double aspect of revelation and empowerment we have just used to characterize the sacraments, we recognize something of what the Scholastic theory of sacraments attempted to capture with the categories of "sign" and "cause." However, our language is different. Furthermore, this change of language is not merely cosmetic, but constitutes a *fundamental revision of the terms with which we approach the problem:* those of language and symbol, and no longer those of cause and instrument. For it is only as symbolic figures that the sacraments can be *strictly* conceived as "expressions" (another concept with connotations different from those it has in current language) of the "arch-sacramentality" of Christian existence. The thoroughgoing reinterpretation of this last from the limited viewpoint of sacramentality will require such a radical overturn of the classical approach.

This overturn ultimately strikes at the unexamined presuppositions of *metaphysics* and its always-already onto-theological profile. Our study may aspire to rigor only to the extent that it is ready to confront such fundamental questions. This concern accounts for the important place accorded in our First Part to contemporary criticisms of metaphysics and, correlative with this, to the epistemological reorientation currently revolutionizing science, especially all disciplines directly connected with anthropology. The *theological* reflection proposed here can stand only if we have first made explicit the *philosophical* position which undergirds it. The first four chapters are a fundamental critique, opening the very possibility of the kind of theological discourse we propose here. They also have a direct bearing on our discussion of sacraments, for they set in place concepts or notions which will reappear regularly in what follows: language acts, expression, symbol, otherness, corporality, presence and absence, and so forth — notions which, for us, belong not to the realm of metaphysics, but rather to that of the symbolic.

It is in the symbolic order proper to the Church that the Second Part of our study (Chapters Five to Eight) situates the sacraments. We appreciate them as *one element among others* in this vast and yet coherent psychic structure which all together makes up Christian identity. We will unfold this structure as a series of connections between Scripture (the level of cognition), sacrament (the level of thanksgiving), and ethics (the level of action).

Within this whole, the sacraments occupy a *unique* place and exercise a *unique* function. The Third Part (Chapters Nine to Eleven) is centered on them as acts by which Christian identity is symbolized and which employ a ritual expression that cannot be "translated" into any other language, an "instituted" expression which, precisely as such, "institutes" the Church and the people who believe in it.

The approach taken here naturally reflects a particular understanding of the relations between God and humankind. In the Christian tradition, these relations inevitably revolve around the person of Jesus, the Christ. This understanding makes itself felt repeatedly throughout the first three parts of the work, but it is only in the Fourth Part (Chapters Twelve and Thirteen) that it is treated explicitly. To claim, following the Church's tradition, that

3

the sacraments are the privileged means of grace-filled communication between God and the believer — and such, in summary, is what they are — requires not only that theologians, seeking to make sense of what they believe, analyze the linguistic and symbolic mediation which constitutes this communication, but that they (following the same path of the symbolic) simultaneously examine precisely what one understands by the word "God." For what *sort* of God are we speaking of when we claim that God takes flesh in the sacraments, that through them God reaches into the very corporality of believers? It is this question that makes room for a Trinitarian Christology.

For this reason, our proposal for a fundamental theology of sacramentality, or for a reinterpretation of the whole of Christian life from the viewpoint of sacramentality, must be articulated according to two principal axes: the axis of *language and symbol* and the axis of the *LOGOS of the cross* — for it is only on the latter that a Trinitarian Christology can be built up. The second axis cannot be foreign to the first, nor may it exactly parallel it; but it will naturally be affected by it. For as we change our view of humanity, we necessarily and concurrently change our view of God as well. At the intersection of these two axes stand the sacraments, which knit the two together symbolically, while respecting their absolute distinctness.

Part One

From the Metaphysical
to the Symbolic

Critique of the Onto-Theological Presuppositions of Classical Sacramental Theology

1. *Our Initial Question*

The initial question of the present study may be formulated as follows: *How did it come about that, when attempting to comprehend theologically the sacramental relation with God expressed most fully under the term "grace," the Scholastics (and here we will consider only Thomas Aquinas) singled out for privileged consideration the category of "cause"?* Let us make explicit what underlies this question. On the one hand, *grace* can in no way be considered an object or a value. It is the paradigmatic case of something that is a *non*-object, a *non*-value; otherwise, it runs the risk of being negated in the very graciousness and gratuitousness which in fact constitute it. On the other hand, in Scholastic discourse, the category of *causality* is always tied to the idea of production or augmentation; thus, it always presupposes an explanatory model implying production, sometimes of a technical, sometimes of a biological variety (the germ cell in development), a model in which the idea of "instrumentality" plays a pivotal role. Clearly, there is an (apparently fundamental) heterogeneity between the language of grace and the instrumental and productionist language of causality. Our initial question must then be why the Scholastics chose this idea, apparently so inadequate and poorly suited to expressing the modality of relation between God and humankind in the sacraments.

Of course, this idea served only as an analogy. But were there not other analogies that would have been more appropriate? And if there were, why did these thinkers not search out a more suitable one? It surely was not due to a lack of ability or of philosophical and theological sophistication among the best of them! The only possible answer is found in the never explicitly recognized or criticized assumptions that lay hidden at the foundation of the way they set up their problem. The Scholastics were *unable to think otherwise;* they were prevented from doing so by the onto-theological presuppositions which structured their entire culture.

2. The Metaphysical and the Symbolic

We have spoken of onto-theological presuppositions. A second preliminary question immediately comes to mind: Is it valid or justifiable to assume the existence of such an "onto-theology," of such a "metaphysics"? The criticisms frequently directed hereafter against such a position — are they perhaps directed at a straw man?

To answer this, one must distinguish on the one hand the many concrete, diverse, and even opposed *forms* which the philosophical tradition inherited from the Greeks has taken over the twenty-five centuries of its existence, and on the other the *unconscious logic,* the uncriticized assumptions lying at the base of all these systems and giving to them all a kind of "family resemblance," discernible by studying their "genealogy." These are, as Martin Heidegger calls them, the "foundational ways of thinking" that aim at explaining the totality of being.

One would have to add immediately that *the truly great metaphysicians have continually attempted to go beyond the limits* of this metaphysics, and thus to overcome these inherent conceptual constraints. Like a conspiratorial wink, the *oion* ("such as") of Plotinus, the *quasi* ("similar to") of the Latin thinkers alert the hearers or readers that they should not be duped into thinking that they are in possession of a transcription of the real into language. For Thomas, the very notion of *esse* ("being") plays a critical role as a corrective to any reductive portrait of God to the extent that this *esse,* uncircumscribed or without limit, is not included in any "genus." Thus, the great thinkers have always known how to take a *step backwards,* a step of humble lucidity before the truth, a step which has protected them from falling into the deadly dogmatism of confusing their thought with the real. On occasion, they have even explicitly reflected on this disparity. But to ponder such a disparity is one thing; to take this disparity *as a point of departure and as a framework* for one's thought is another. This lack of interest in exploring the bias of their unconscious assumptions is what gives these thinkers a "family resemblance" and allows us to speak of *the* "metaphysics" or, better still, *the* metaphysical.

One could be more precise by saying that the *metaphysical* or the onto-theological framework (that is, the always-already theological outline of the metaphysical) does not designate a simple reality existing in a pure state. It is a *methodological* concept which we give ourselves, a concept showing a *tendency* or an attracting pole characteristic of Western thought since the Greeks; this attraction is characterized as the "foundational way of thinking" and therefore as the very impossibility of taking as the point of departure for thought the very distance between discourse and reality. This is to say, we suppose another possible tendency or attracting pole for thought, starting from and remaining within this disparity: this second way is that of language, or of the *symbolic.* We must specify here — it is all-important — that what we have just presented roughly as a tendency or a pole of attraction opposed to that of the metaphysical, proves to be not simply the reverse model of the metaphysical, therefore placed on the same ground, but in fact *another epistemological terrain* for our thinking activity.

Such a pair of methodological concepts (metaphysical-symbolic) seems to us to possess a *heuristic* value. These concepts are first of all working tools. The target of our criticism will thus be less the explicit *themes* treated in classical metaphysics than the unconscious and concrete *schemes* which constitute its implicit and unrecognized logic. Further, in proposing such a revision, we do not mean to suggest that we can simply pass magically from the metaphysical to the symbolic. We will have more to say about this later; let us simply indicate for the time being that the "symbolic" designates a process of approach never fully achieved, thus a transition to be done again and again . . . This is to say how little we have to do here with the mere substitution of a new conceptual system for an old.

I. SACRAMENTAL CAUSALITY
ACCORDING TO ST. THOMAS

1. *The Place of the "Treatise on the Sacraments"*
within the Summa Theologica

This treatise is located, as is well known, in the Third Part of the *Summa*, following Christology and soteriology. In fact, its position had already been set by the discussion in IIa-IIae concerning the *virtue of religion*, that is, the acts by which humans make contact with God: acts of interior devotion (q. 82) and prayer (q. 83); exterior acts mediated by the body in adoration (q. 84), by gifts proffered to God in offerings (sacrifices, oblations, tithes: qq. 85–87) or vows (q. 88), or, finally, by the use made of sacred objects in sacraments (a mere allusion) and by the use of the Name of God (oaths, solemn promises, invocations: qq. 89–91). As is evident, in this last subsection Thomas indicates the place that the sacraments could occupy; however, he adds, "It will be more fitting to discuss sacraments in the Third Part of this work" (q. 89, prologue). In other words, as elements of the Christian cult, or "exterior acts of devotion," the sacraments are considered to belong to "ethics." They are thereby the principal expression of our moral relation to God, a relation authentically Christian because it is brought into being by Christ, who directs the offering of a sanctified humanity toward God. This same line of interpretation has recently been followed, as we will see, by Karl Barth.

But this aspect of the sacraments is insufficient. For Thomas, it is not even the most important. The sacraments are not only the cultic expression of our thankfulness to God for salvation (justification and sanctification) already given; they are also, and even primarily, present mediations of this salvation, "channels" by which we profit from the grace acquired by Christ. "After the study of the mysteries of the Word Incarnate should come that of the sacraments of the Church because it is precisely from the Word Incarnate that they derive their efficacy"; such is the announcement which inaugurates the "Treatise on the Sacraments" in the *Summa* (III, q. 60, prologue). Thus, to a first movement of exterior worship, *ascending* through Christ toward God, there corresponds a second movement, one of justification and sanctification, *descending* from God through Christ toward humankind; and this second movement is, for Thomas, theologically primary. Thus, even if in one direction and according to their "religious" dimension, sacraments are signs which testify to the presence of a "faith which justifies" (III, q. 68, a. 8), in the opposite direction and according to their efficient dimension, they are the means by which God works the justification obtained by Christ for all humankind.

One may regret that Thomas insufficiently emphasizes, in the treatise contained in the Third Part of the *Summa*, the ascendant and ethical aspects of the sacraments touched upon in the questions relating to the "exterior acts" of the virtue of religion. This would have allowed him to achieve a better balance in a presentation which, stressing as it does the role of the sacraments in the sanctification of human beings, is too heavily weighted in favor of the "Christological-descending" aspect. This weakness highlights the central character of their efficacy; it also raises the question of the mode of this efficacy: sign and cause.

2. *The Major Innovations of the* Summa Theologica

It is generally recognized that Thomas' understanding of sacramental causality underwent several important changes between the composition of the *Commentary on the Sentences* (1254–1256) and that of the Third Part of the *Summa Theologica* (1272–1273). "While in the *Summa*, a sacrament in general (at least for the sacraments of the New Covenant) is a sign having this special character of causing what it signifies, in the *Sentences*, a sacrament is a cause (or a remedy) having this special character (and which strikes us as more arbitrary) of signifying what it causes." Further, in the *Sentences*, Thomas "grants only a disposing causality to grace," while in the *Summa*, its causality becomes "perfective."[1] We have here the three principal innovations the *Summa* introduces in this area.

a) The first change consists in the transition from the priority of the *medicinal* function of the sacraments to the priority of their *sanctifying* function. Almost the entire Scholastic movement between the twelfth and thirteenth centuries, and Thomas himself in his *Commentary on the Sentences* and *Contra Gentiles* (1261–1264), was under the influence of Hugh of Saint-Victor's (d. 1141) theory of the sacrament as a kind of "vase" containing a healing ointment of grace; it thus tended to view the sacraments primarily as remedies.[2] What is important to notice is how this medicinal analogy

1. A. M. Roguet, *S. Thomas d'Aquin, Somme théologique: les sacrements* (Paris-Tournai-Rome: Revue des Jeunes, 1951) 266.

2. Ibid., 260–265. Cf. A. Michel, "Sacrement," *DTC* 14/1 (1939), col. 529; P. Pourrat, *La théologie sacramentaire* (Paris: Gabalda, 1907) 35.

fits directly into the received theory of efficient causality — the healing agent is the cause of health — whereas, holiness is linked with final causality. This is precisely the aspect Thomas emphasizes, beginning with his first article on the sacraments in the *Summa:* "The medicine is the efficient cause of health. All terms derived from 'medicine' have a similar reference to this first and identical agency; this is why the word 'medication' expresses a causality. The major difference is that holiness, the sacred reality from which 'sacrament' derives its name, is a reality better represented as a formal or final cause. The word 'sacrament' should thus not make us necessarily think of efficient causality."[3]

b) This clear declaration of intention, from the very beginning of the "Treatise on the Sacraments," does not mean that Thomas intends to abandon the idea of efficient causality; it will return — and with what force! — in question 62, where the first article's main body begins with the following peremptory declaration, "It cannot be denied [*necesse est dicere*]: the sacraments of the New Covenant in some fashion cause grace." But still, by lowering the remedial function of the sacraments to a secondary position at the very beginning, the author intends to *subordinate the notion of causality to that of sign.* Even more: his intention is to fashion a definition of sacraments which makes no mention of causality. Of the four definitions of sacrament coming down to him from the Scholastic tradition,[4] it is that of Augustine that Thomas retains:

3. *ST* III, q. 60, a. 1, ad 1.

4. Here is a list of the principal definitions of *sacramentum* in the Middle Ages. *I italicize the four formulas retained by Albert the Great* and put the variant forms between parentheses (*IV Sent.* d. 1, a. 5).

(1) Augustine:

(a) "Sacrificium visibile invisibilis sacrificii sacramentum, id est sacrum signum" ("The sacrament is the visible sacrifice of the invisible sacrifice, that is, a sacred sign," *City of God* 10:5; PL 41:282). Albert, through Peter Lombard: *"Sacramentum est sacrae rei signum"* (*"The sacrament is the sign of a sacred thing"*).

(b) "Si enim sacramenta quamdam similitudinem earum rerum quarum sacramenta sunt non haberent, omnino sacramenta non essent" ("If the sacraments did not resemble in some way the things of which they are the sacraments, they would not be sacraments at all," *Ep.* 98:9, to Boniface; PL 33:363).

(c) "Sacramentum est in aliqua celebratione, cum rei gestae commemoratio ita fit ut aliquid significare intelligatur, quod sancte accipiendum est" ("There "the sign of a sacred thing" (*sacrae rei signum*). It is important to mention that the Scholastic tradition felt the need to complete this definition by adding to it the term "cause" or "efficacy": "sign . . . and cause of a sacred thing" (*signum . . . et causa rei sacrae,*

---

is a sacrament in any celebration where the commemoration of the thing done is done in such a way as to be understood as signifying something to be received in a holy manner," *Ep.* 55:2, to Januarius, *PL* 33:205).

(2) Isidore of Seville: Instead of the "sacrum signum" ("sacred sign") of Augustine, it is the "sacrum secretum" ("sacred secret") which dominates in his writings. This definition will retain its authority until the twelfth century.

"Sacramentum est in aliqua celebratione, cum res gesta ita fit ut aliquid significare intelligatur quod sancte accipiendum est. Ob id sacramenta dicuntur, quia *sub tegumento visibilium* (corporalium) *rerum virtus divina secretius salutem* (eorundem sacramentorum) *operatur;* unde et a secretis virtutibus et a sacris sacramenta dicuntur" ("There is a sacrament in any celebration where the thing done is done in such a way as to be understood as signifying something to be received in a holy manner. For this reason, the sacraments are so called because, *under the veil of the visible* [corporeal] *things, the divine power works salvation* [through these same sacraments] *in a secret manner;* hence, they are called sacraments owing to both their secret and sacred powers," *Etymologiae* 6:19; *PL* 82:255).

(3) In the ninth century:

(a) Paschasius Radbertus: "Sacramentum est quidquid in aliqua celebratione divina nobis quasi pignus salutis traditur, cum res gesta visibilis longe aliud invisibile intus operatur, quod sancte accipiendum est. Unde et sacramenta dicuntur a secreto, eo quod in re visibili divinitas intus aliquid ultra secretius fecit per speciem corporalem" ("A sacrament is something in any divine celebration which is given us as a pledge of salvation, when the thing visibly done effects, far inside, something other and invisible which must be received in a holy manner. Hence, the sacraments are so called from the fact that they are secret, from the fact that in the visible thing divinity more secretly effects, through corporeal appearances, something inside and beyond," *Liber de Corpore et Sanguine Domini, PL* 120:1275).

(b) Ratramnus: A definition very close to the preceding. See below, ch. 8, n. 15.

(c) Rabanus Maurus returns to Isidore's text: "Sacramenta dicuntur, quia sub tegumento. . . ." ("The sacraments are so called because under a veil. . . ." *De Clericorum Institutione,* 1:24; *PL* 107:309).

(4) In the twelfth century:

(a) Peter Abelard: "Est autem sacramentum invisibilis gratiae visibilis species, vel sacrae rei signum, id est alicuius secreti" ("The sacrament is the visible form of the invisible grace or the sign of a holy thing, that is, of something secret," *Epitome Theol. Christ.* 1 and 28; *PL* 178:1965).

P. Lombard); "efficacious sign of a sacred thing" (*signum efficax rei sacrae*, Duns Scotus). Thomas also completes it in the *Summa*, but *so as not to leave the genus of "sign"*: "the sign of a sacred thing in-

---

(b) Alger de Liège (in reaction against Isidore, by distinguishing "sacramentum" from "mysterium"): "In hoc differunt, quia sacramentum signum est visibile aliquid significans, mysterium vero aliquid occultum ab eo significatum" ("Here is the difference: the sacrament is a visible sign signifying something, but the mystery is something hidden signified by the sacrament," *De Sacramentis Corporis et Sanguinis Domini*, 1:4; PL 180:751).

(c) Hugh of Saint-Victor: "*Sacramentum est corporale vel materiale elementum oculis extrinsecus suppositum* (foris sensibiliter expositum), *ex similitudine repraesentans, ex institutione significans, et ex sanctificatione conferens* (continens) *invisibilem* (et spiritualem) *gratiam*" ("*The sacrament is a corporeal or material element offered to view from outside* [exhibited from outside in a sensible manner], *representing through similitude, signifying through institution and conferring* [containing] *through sanctification an invisible* [spiritual] *grace*," *De Sacramentis I*, p. 9, c. 2; PL 176:317). (On the substitution of "conferens" for "continens," see our text.)

(d) *Summa Sententiarum* (ca. 1140): "Sacramentum est visibilis forma invisibilis gratiae in eo collatae, quam scilicet confert ipsum sacramentum. Non est solummodo sacrae rei signum, sed etiam efficacia. . . . Sacramentum non solum significat, sed etiam confert illud cuius est signum vel significatio" ("The sacrament is the visible form of the invisible grace contained in it, which the sacrament itself confers. Not only is it the sign of the holy thing, but also its efficacy. . . . The sacrament not only signifies but also confers that of which it is the sign or significance," *Tr.* 5:1; PL 176:117). This definition shows clearly, doubtless for the first time, the precise point Scholasticism hoped to elucidate: sign and cause; this latter term will come in the following definition, from the Master of the Sentences.

(e) Peter Lombard: "Sacramentum eius rei similitudinem gerit, cuius signum est. . . . Sacramentum enim proprie dicitur quod ita signum est gratiae Dei, et invisibilis gratiae forma, ut ipsius imaginem gerat et causa existat" ("The sacrament bears the likeness of the thing of which it is the sign. . . . The sacrament indeed is properly so called because it is the sign of God's grace and the form of the invisible grace, so that it bears its image and stands as its cause," *Sent.*, IV, d. 1, n. 2; PL 192:839). Albert the Great: "*Sacramentum est invisibilis gratiae visibilis forma, cuius similitudinem gerat et causa existat*" ("*The sacrament is the visible form of the invisible grace, whose likeness it bears and as whose cause it stands*").

(f) Thomas Aquinas:
(1) early: the sacrament is "in genere causae et signi" ("in the genus of cause and sign," *IV Sent.*, d. 1, q. 1, a. 1).
(2) later: the sacrament is "in genere signi" ("in the genus of sign," *ST*, III, q. 60, a. 1).

sofar as it sanctifies human beings" (*signum rei sacrae in quantum est sanctificans homines*).[5] "Clearly," writes H. F. Dondaine, "Thomas seeks to avoid the appearance of logical equivalence resulting from definitions which put signification and causality on the same footing."[6] To arrive at that point, that is, to consider the sacraments in the first instance no longer "in the genus of cause and sign" (*in genere causae et signi*)[7] but only "in the genus of sign" (*in genere signi*),[8] it was necessary for Thomas to recognize that "causality is never a constitutive element of an essence."[9]

The importance of this altered perspective is considerable. Defined as signs, the sacraments bring about only what they signify, and that according to the manner in which it is signified. As a consequence, one could construct a sacramental theology only by beginning with the Church's *act of celebration*, that is, with the manner in which it signifies what it intends. In fact, this should be a *fundamental principle* of sacramental theology. One regrets that it has been too often forgotten over the long course of the centuries and that Thomas himself did not always develop it consistently — far from it. The Church could have avoided many false problems and deadlocks on the question of the real presence in the Eucharist (the words of institution taken in an isolated manner), on the theology of ordained ministry (the "we" of the Canon), and so on.

c) The "decision" (Dondaine) taken by Thomas in the *Summa* to understand the sacrament as a sign rather than a cause only casts into bolder relief the difficulty he discovered in doing justice to the phrase *in quantum est sanctificans homines* in any terms other than those of causality. Banished from the definition of sacrament — and we have seen this as a significant step — causality returns in force in the third question of the treatise, which considers "the principal effect of the sacraments, which is grace" (q. 62), a question following those on the "essence" (q. 60) and the "necessity of the sacraments" (q. 61). It is no accident that the *Commentary on the Sentences* affirms sacramental causality only with prudent qualifications, even if it does include this in the essence of the

5. *ST*, III, q. 60, a. 2. On this point compare H. F. Dondaine, "La définition des sacrements dans la Somme théologique," *RSPT* 31 (1947) 213-228.

6. Ibid., 223-224.

7. Thus, in *IV Sent.*, d. 1, q. 1, a. 1, ad 5:1.

8. Thus, in *ST*, III, q. 60, a. 1.

9. Dondaine, "La définition des sacrements," 227-228.

sacrament, while the *Summa*, on the contrary, leaving out all mention of it in the definition, affirms it afterwards "without adding the restrictions and precautions of the *Commentary*."[10]

The reason for this is that, in the meantime, a third theoretical innovation has occurred: Thomas has gone *from disposing causality to instrumental causality*, according to the title of an article by Dondaine.[11] These two types of causality make up the two principal types of "efficient causality." Thomas was always opposed to the theory, which has been labeled "cheap" or "easy," of *"occasional* causality" defended by the Franciscan school (William of Auvergne, Bonaventure, and Duns Scotus among others).[12] He is quite clear on this point, rejecting the thesis according to which the sacraments would be a kind of company scrip or IOU which could be cashed in for valid coin by the arbitrary fiat of the legislator. For "if we accept this explanation, the sacraments of the New Covenant would be nothing more than signs of grace, while it is the consistent teaching of the Fathers that the sacraments not only signify but also cause grace."[13]

Sacramental "occasionalism" sought above all to safeguard the free activity of God: God has linked the sacraments to grace only in virtue of a "divine pact" (*ex pacto divino*) of which God is the free author.[14] The theory of efficient causality, called "disposing," that Thomas, beginning in the *Commentary on the Sentences*, appropriated, following Alexander of Hales and his own master Albert the Great, was itself equally sensitive to and respectful of this sovereign liberty in the activity of God through the gift of grace; but it sought to connect this liberty with the efficacy of the sacrament itself. Thus, only God can give grace, which is the "ultimate

10. Ibid., 223.

11. H. F. Dondaine, "A propos d'Avicenne et de S. Thomas: de la causalité dispositive à la causalité instrumentale," *Revue thomiste* 51 (1951) 441–453.

12. L. Mathieu, "Introduction," S. Bonaventure, *Breviloquium* (Paris: ed. Franciscaines, 1967) 21.

13. *ST*, III, q. 62, a. 1.

14. For Bonaventure, "the sole cause of grace can be only God-in-the-Trinity. . . . It cannot possibly be the case that there might be some physical quality in the material rite that could produce supernatural grace. . . . If the sacraments dispose us to grace, it is because God intervenes in the rite through a particular assistance in such a way that the divine power itself is the cause of grace and brings about in the subject the faith and the devotion required" (Mathieu, "Introduction," 23–24).

effect" (*res tantum*) of the sacrament. The latter nevertheless retains its proper efficiency, which is primarily directed to what concerns the "first effect" (*res et sacramentum*: a "character" or "ornament of the soul," *ornatus animae*) that disposes the soul to receive grace. This "disposition," produced by the sacrament itself, is sufficient to elicit grace, which God (and God alone) then bestows necessarily, if the subject at least does not place any serious *obex* ("obstacle") in its path.[15] Thomas was following here a distinction of causalities proposed by Avicenna (d. 1037), the Arab philosopher whose works, translated into Latin in Spain in the middle of the twelfth century, were then exercising a notable influence throughout Europe: "the dispositive cause prepares the matter, the perfective cause affects the form" (*causa disponens praeparat materiam, causa perficiens influit formam*). Let us note in passing that this same distinction was applied in the *Commentary* to an issue in soteriology: there, the human nature of Christ is said to play a disposing role in relation to his divine nature, as concerns our salvation.[16] Bonaventure maintains the same: "The human nature of Christ gives grace by way of preparation; the divine nature actually bestows it."[17]

However, to Thomas this explanation appeared in the end insufficient to render justice to the old Scholastic adage according to which the sacraments of the New Covenant "effect what they represent" (*efficiunt quod figurant*). For a theory of the sacraments considered as the simple "material disposition preparing for the reception of grace" (*materialis dispositio praeparans ad susceptionem gratiae*, Guerric de Saint-Quentin) did not adequately explain how, in them, what is brought about is also exactly what is represented, or further, how, in them, "the reality signified and given" (*res significata et data*) is connected by divine institution with "the mode of signification" (*modus significandi*). In other words, the sacraments are not, in the last analysis, a play in which God assumes all the roles (or the only role); they are not a play for one actor. The "sign" (*signum*), as it is presented by the celebrating Church, is the *very mediation* of the gift of grace. The whole problem consisted in *harmonizing two categories as completely foreign to one another as are "sign" and "cause,"* and doing so in such a way that the type of sign under examination would have these unique traits: it

15. *IV Sent.*, d. 1, q. 1, a. 4, ad 1.
16. *III Sent.*, d. 13, q. 2, a. 1, ad 3.
17. Ibid., d. 13, a. 2, q. 1.

would *indicate what it is causing* and it would *have no other way of causing except by the mode of signification.* It is Thomas' great achievement in sacramental theology to have attempted to reduce, insofar as this could be done, the heterogeneity between sign and cause, all the while recognizing the impossibility of complete homogeneity.

The innovation in the *Summa* in this matter is that "St. Thomas abandons the Avicennian distinction in causality in favor of that of Aristotle and Averroes."[18] It is well known that very reliable translations and commentaries on Aristotle by the Muslim philosopher Averroes (d. 1198) were widely disseminated throughout Europe during this period. However, even if the Avicennian adage "the giver of the form effects; the preparer of the matter disposes" (*dator formae efficit, praeparator materiae disponit*) opened up the possibility of a double effect operating within the sacrament, it in no way illuminated whatever order might exist among the causes. The Aristotelian distinction, restored by Averroes, permitted such an elucidation: "the principal cause moves; the instrumental cause, being moved, moves" (*causa principalis movet, causa instrumentalis movet mota*). "It was in Aristotle and Averroes that St. Thomas was able to discover a means of explaining the communication between two agents with one subordinated to the other."[19] With this one stroke, the sacraments no longer have to be considered as merely pseudo efficient causes — only disposing — but rather as *true causes* in their own right, exercising their proper agency and leaving their mark on the final effect, even if this action is always subordinated to the action of God, who remains the principal agent. We may now distinguish a "double action" of the instrument in the following manner: if the bed does not resemble the ax with which it was made (instrumental cause), but rather the projected design of the artisan (principal cause), it is because the instrument "achieves its end not by its proper virtue but rather by the virtue of the principal agent." One cannot make a bed with a paint brush; rather, one needs a tool which can cut, like an ax, and thus leave its mark on the resulting product. Under this second aspect, an *instrument "thus exercises its*

18. Dondaine, "A propos," 441.
19. Ibid., 450.

proper function when it operates out of its own form (for example, the ax is able to cut something in virtue of its sharpness), while it is able to make a bed only in virtue of the artisan's idea. It accomplishes its instrumental role only when it exercizes its own proper action: it is only in cutting that the ax can make the bed. The situation is analogous with the corporeal sacraments. . . ."[20]

But how can a created instrument, even when operating in a subordinated status, participate in an act which is creative (and that *ex nihilo*) of grace? The theory of instrumental efficient causality was possible only because in the *Summa* Thomas, contrary to the *Sentences*, no longer considers the infusion of grace according to the model of a creation. More deeply, grace is no longer considered a concrete substance but only an accident, a mode of being which transforms a human being;[21] and *only beings, and not merely modes of being, may be said to be created by God*. Thus, nothing now keeps the sacraments from participating, admittedly in a subordinate status, in this production of grace, or prevents them from claiming, with total honesty, that they "contain and confer" grace, that is, that it is given *by* them, and even "in virtue of the action" (*ex opere operato*). There is nothing reifying in this: "Grace is contained in the sacraments as a function of a certain instrumental virtue *which is something in process and incomplete by nature*" (*quae est fluens et incompleta in esse naturae*).[22] Let us understand this: "In the instrumental cause, the form of the effect to be realized is not to be found in an achieved or permanent state but only as the final stage of a passing impetus imparted to the instrument by the principal cause. For example, a painting may be said to exist in the state of an exemplary idea in the artist's mind; it exists in the condition of form embodied in the concrete picture; what is in the paintbrush is only a 'virtue,' a temporary impetus impressed on this instrument by the artist which will have its intended result not in the instrument but beyond it, in the painting."[23]

To the extent that any sacramental theology employs certain representations to illustrate the relation between the action of God and the actions of human beings, and where, as in Christianity, this relation finds its preeminent instance or example in Jesus Christ,[24] any theology worthy of this name must find some way to

20. *ST*, III, q. 62, a. 1, c. and ad 2.
21. *ST*, Ia-IIae, q. 110, a. 2, ad 3.
22. *ST*, III, q. 62, a. 3.
23. Roguet, *S. Thomas d'Aquin*, 354.
24. This point will be developed in the fourth part of this work.

achieve a coherence between its *Christology* and its *sacramental theology*. We have indicated this when speaking of the *Commentary on the Sentences:* the intellectual scheme in the two domains is that of disposing causality. In the *Summa* it is, in both cases, a matter of instrumental efficient causality. While in the *Sentences* Thomas takes care not to attribute to the human nature of Christ a divine efficacy for our salvation, in the *Summa* the Aristotelian-Averroistic theory of communication between subordinated agents allows him to do full justice to the saying of St. John Damascene: "in Christ, human nature was like the instrument of the divinity" (*humana natura in Christo erat velut organum divinitatis*). According to Dondaine this formula is quoted a good forty times throughout the works of Thomas; but it is in the *Summa*, for the reasons indicated, that "he makes it an axiom of his Christology"[25] — to such an extent that the sanctified humanity of Christ, as "instrument of his divinity," "causes grace in us, both by merit and by a certain efficacy."[26] Here, as in the sacraments, it is a case of instrumental efficiency, but with a twofold difference: "Although at the disposal of his divinity, the humanity of Christ is not simply an instrument which could be moved without moving itself. On the contrary, it is a living and rational instrument which moves itself at the same time it is being moved."[27] Further, "the principal efficient cause of grace is God, for whom the humanity of Christ is a *conjoined* instrument (like the hand), while the sacrament supplies an instrument that remains *distinct* (like a stick moved by the hand). It is thus necessary for the salvific power to pass from the divinity of Christ through his humanity and finally through the sacraments."[28] One could not better express how closely sacramental theology is modeled on Christology. The sacraments remain the *sacraments of the Incarnate Word*, from whom "they derive their efficacy" and to whom they "are conformed by the fact that they join the 'word' to the sensible object, just as, in the mystery of the Incarnation, the Word of God is united to human flesh."[29]

25. Dondaine, "A propos," 452.
26. *ST*, III, q. 8, a. 1, ad 1. Cf. C. V. Héris, *S. Thomas d'Aquin, Somme Théologique, le Verbe incarné* (Paris-Tournai-Rome: Revue des Jeunes, 1927) 2:356–364.
27. *ST*, III, q. 7, a. 1, ad 3.
28. Ibid., q. 62, a. 5.
29. Ibid., q. 60, Prologue to the "Treatise on the Sacraments" and a. 6.

*The sacraments are thus appreciated as *prolongations of the sanctified humanity of Christ*. We will return to this point in the final section of this study.

II. THE PRODUCTIONIST SCHEME OF REPRESENTATION

To explain the specificity of the sacraments in comparison with other means of mediating God's grace, one must say that they effect what they signify. But according to what modality? For Thomas, only one is possible: causality. He underlines this conviction in the *Summa*. The terms chosen to explain this characteristic of the sacraments in question 62, entitled "The Principal Effect of the Sacraments Which Is Grace," are significant: sacraments *"cause* grace," they *"work"* or *"produce"* it, they *"contain"* it, they *"add to"* grace considered in general a "certain divine assistance." They are "necessary to produce certain special effects that the Christian life requires," they *"confer* grace," they derive their *"virtue of producing* [causativa] *grace"* from the Passion of Christ. The whole question is conceived according to the model of an *"instrument."* Of course, Thomas reminds us repeatedly that he is using this only as an analogy. This has been true from the first article of his treatise on the sacraments; for from the start he maintains that it is only *by analogy* that the sacraments can be grouped under the genus of "sign."

In this circumstance it is a case of an analogy "of attribution." In this type of analogy, the same term "sign" may be attributed to different objects according to different relations: just as, he says, health, which first belongs to a healthy body, may be attributed from a different viewpoint or with a different connection to what causes health, such as a remedy, or that which indicates its presence, such as a type of urine. Similarly, "holiness," which is attributed in the first instance to God or to humans insofar as they participate in the divine life, may be attributed, according to different relations, to what causes it or what indicates its presence; this is exactly the case with the sacraments. The same holds true a fortiori for such terms as "instrument," "containing," "producing," and so forth, and most centrally for "causality." If we dare to say that the sacraments "cause grace," it is only "in a certain way" (*per aliquem modum*, q. 62, a. 1). This kind of qualification ("in a certain way," "as if," *quodammodo*, *quasi . . .*) reappears frequently in Thomas. For the fact that it is an analogy forbids any "reifying" interpretation of these expressions, especially in a domain where "grace is found in the sacraments according to a certain instrumental virtue that is always in process and incomplete in its natural existence," that is, according to a mode that is closer to the way form is present in matter or its substrate than the (explicitly rejected) manner in which a physical liquid might be *"contained"* within a vessel.[30]

However, even when purified by the reminder that it is only an analogy, these terms all serve to build up an ever-present *scheme* of representation that we call *technical or productionist.* From this comes the question we posed at the start of this chapter: How did it come about that, when speaking about the gracious relation of God to humankind, Thomas restricted himself to this sort of representation? The answer suggested above pointed us in the direction of his unconscious (and uncriticized) onto-theological presuppositions. It is incumbent upon us now to explore and justify this thesis. We will do this by showing that, because of its distinctive metaphysical bent (in the sense discussed above), Western thought is unable to represent to itself the relations between subjects or of subjects with God in any way other than one according to a technical model of cause and effect.

1. *The Reduction of the Symbolic Scheme to the Technical Scheme*

Availing ourselves of the "Discourse on Grace" of Guy Lafon, we will begin with the *Philebus,* one of the late dialogues of Plato, which we take as a "typical reference" insofar as one may easily recognize there the "extraordinary influence which this type of thinking has exercised in the West."[31] This dialogue aims at insuring the victory of wisdom over pleasure by demonstrating that "it is not pleasure but intelligence which has the greater similarity and affinity with the Good" (*Philebus,* 60b).

One of the key moments in the demonstration occurs when Socrates distinguishes what is in a state of perpetual "arrival" or "process" (*genesis*), as opposed to "existence" (*ousia*) (53c–55a).

---

30. Ibid., q. 62, a. 3. Cf. the commentary on the *Physics* of Aristotle (IV, 4), where Thomas enumerates, following Aristotle, the eight ways in which one thing can be in another. Grace is present in humans in the way a form is present in its subject of inherence (fifth way). For the sacraments, it is a bit different: grace is present there in the way that something that is moved is "in" whatever moves it (sixth way), but not "as in a vase" (eighth way).

31. G. Lafon, *Esquisses pour un christianisme* (Paris: Cerf, 1979) ch. 3, "Discours de la grâce," especially pp. 77–88.

Pleasure belongs to *genesis:* it is in perpetual becoming, always looking to something else, always under the dominion of generation. It is infinite, that is to say, unbounded, limitless. Once it is attained, once it reaches its end or a condition of rest, it dies. The *Good,* on the other hand, and the wisdom which allows us to approach it, is of the order of measure, proportion, the order of what is sufficient to itself and rests in itself. It is "existence." This *ousia* which exists "in itself and by itself" is that toward which other things move and develop; and since "the entire realm of things in process is developing toward the entire realm of existence" and since every process develops toward an existence "which belongs to the class of the Good," we must conclude that pleasure necessarily falls outside the Good.

But for Socrates to reach this conclusion, he has to illustrate this broad distinction between *genesis* and *ousia* with examples capable of instructing Protarchus, his principal interlocutor. The first he uses is the case of men who find themselves infatuated with handsome youths. Which one of the two is in a condition of *genesis,* the *lover* or the *beloved?* Which one is in a condition of *ousia?* To overcome the obscurity in Protarchus' mind, Socrates leads him toward another example similar to the first but illustrating more clearly the distinction between process and existence. Protarchus says, "Are you asking me in effect, 'Does *shipbuilding go on for the sake of ships* or do ships exist for the sake of shipbuilding?'" Socrates answers yes and adds that although people provide themselves with material objects always with a view to things coming into being, this "becoming always takes place with a view to the being of this or that, so that becoming in general takes place with a view to being in general." Thus, in the final analysis, it is this *technological* argument of shipbuilding that allows Socrates to carry off the decision and to set in place as a general law that all process is for the sake of *existence.* At the same time, it is clear that the first example, that of love, is likened by Plato to cases similar to shipbuilding.

Here, however, we foresee the difficulty in this sort of reasoning: May one legitimately reduce the lover-beloved relation to that of shipbuilding-boat, merely in virtue of the common trait which seems to unite them in the relation of process to achievement? Is there not a major difference between them, so much so that the general relation of process to achievement is itself devalued? Ship-building aims at making boats; it builds them, that is all there is to it. The lover is similarly oriented toward the beloved, but he does not produce the beloved. He only causes the other to exist *as a beloved,* and thus as capable of making a *response in return;* he causes the other to exist — and this is a risk — as capable of not making a response in return. The boat is a finished product; but the beloved is precisely a product that is *not finished* — and is thus "infinite" in the sense of "indefinite," always in process; which is as much as to say that the beloved is *not a "product"* at all. *Because the beloved is a "subject," this person can never be simply reduced to an "achievement," but is always process, development — even a development without end.* This relation of *reversibility* or reciprocity within and through which each human subject exists (under pain of extinction as a human subject) — because one is only a subject in a condition of mutual and ever open exchange — means that the human may never be adequately understood according to the technical mode of causality (even if we add immediately, as a corrective, "but with a free will!").

However, this is precisely what seems *unthinkable* for Plato and what, in our eyes, characterizes the *metaphysical bent* of Western philosophy: a permanent state of incompleteness defies any logic and destroys any discourse; *any thought which would not come to rest in a final term,* a final significance, a recognizable and ultimate truth, such a thought, in his eyes, is *unthinkable.* "The infinite is the enemy; if humankind is to survive, it must be wiped out." And this in fact, as Lafon shows, is precisely the task to which Plato devotes his whole life. Furthermore, in a general way, according to E. Jüngel, this is "the characteristic premise of the ultimate idea of metaphysics which understands itself as theo-onto-logical . . .: its metaphysical *negative* evaluation of every impermanent condition." This results in "the concealment of the characteristic dignity of a 'passing' that is also a 'becoming.' Only the negative aspects of transience are emphasized."[32] True, Plato insists that pleasure has its rightful place in the ascent of the soul toward the Good; but it is always specified as a pleasure that is

32. Ibid., 79. E. Jüngel, *Dieu mystère du monde: Fondement de la théologie du crucifié dans le débat entre théisme et athéisme* (Paris: Cerf, 1983) 1:318.

"true and pure," one that is "almost of the same family" as wisdom, one that is "free of all suffering," a pleasure whose absence "would neither make us sad nor be noticed," thus an *ideal* pleasure, totally controlled by truth, measure, and proportion. In other words, of its original infinity, not much remains . . . The entire presentation is inspired by a *fundamental desire to eliminate as far as possible whatever pertains to a becoming without end, in favor of the Good described as achieved perfection,* self-sufficiency — as that which is perfectly measurable and proportioned. Everything is under the domination of "value," of calculation, of the cause that measures, of what is *"worth more,"* of what offers more advantages and greater usefulness: these are all distinctions of wisdom and intellect oriented toward the Good (*Philebus*, 11b-c). So completely is this the case that the only kind of pleasure one may tolerate is one that can enter into intimate accord with wisdom to lead humans toward the Good and happiness, a type of pleasure so true and good that there is room in this blend *"neither for joy nor for pain, but only for thought at its highest level of purity"* (*Philebus*, 55a).

Inasmuch as it is fully realized achievement, the Good must end by exterminating the interminable becoming. The argument proceeds at the expense of the infinite, which is entirely subordinated to the finite, since all "genesis" is subordinated to "existence." This subordination finds its very principle in *causality* (*Philebus*, 26e); and the fundamental ontological cause of the world (which accounts for all the "ontic" causes operating within the world) is conceived entirely according to the productionist paradigm of shipbuilding-boats, to which the case of lover-beloved is analogously likened. We have already raised objections to the just-mentioned reduction. Our objection comes down to saying (with Lafon) that there are "happenings, such as love, and joy, and pleasure, which do not produce existence or come to an end in the sense of a distinct term. There are many other realities of this nature and these all attest in one way or another to the presence of a symbolic order."[33]

Plato's discourse exacts, as a price, the reduction of the symbolic scheme of representation, by which subjects give birth to and modify themselves continually by their relations with other sub-

33. Lafon, *Esquisses*, 88.

jects, to the technico-productionist scheme oriented toward the finished product, the guaranteed outcome, the necessary first cause or the ultimate significance serving as the highest reason. Thus is set in place the *exemplar* of metaphysical discourse with myriad, and often opposed, variants. According to Heidegger, this exemplar always seems to be a *discourse* of the "foundation that gives an account of the base, explains it, and finally asks it to explain itself" (see below).

2. *Metaphysics: An Onto-theo-logic Based on Causality*

Exemplar of metaphysical discourse, we have just said, regarding Plato's *Philebus*. We must explain our point in more detail.

a) Metaphysics According to Martin Heidegger. Metaphysics was born in Greece simultaneously with the forgetting of what Heidegger calls "the ontological difference," that is, "the difference between being and entities."[34] We have forgotten that we have *forgotten* now for over twenty-five centuries, so difficult is it — perhaps in some ways irreversible, as we shall explain later — to wrest ourselves away from what seems to present itself as an incontrovertible datum: that is, that the entity is "that which is," and that being is "the being the entity is."[35]

This is because metaphysics "considers entities in their entirety, and speaks of Being . . . (from which springs) a continual confusion between entity and being."[36] Being is "defined as the *common trait of all entities* which, by that fact, become fundamentally identical due to the presence of this common property within them." Being is thus represented as the general and universal "something" or "stuff" which conceals itself beneath entities, which "lies at the base" of each of them (*hypokeimenon*), a permanent "subsistent being," *sub-stratum, sub-jectum,* and finally, as Descartes describes it, *sub-stantia.* On the basis of this confusion, metaphysics identifies being with the type of being of entities (their "being-ness"), forgetting the basic ontic-ontological difference in this confusion of ontic and ontological. And metaphysics believes itself to have produced an explanation of being, when in

---

34. M. Heidegger, *L'être-essentiel d'un fondement ou "raison," Q. 1,* 100.
35. Heidegger, *Le retour au fondement de la métaphysique, Q. 1,* 29.
36. Ibid.

fact it has only ontically reduced being to metaphysics' *representations*, utterly forgetting that nothing that exists "is."[37]

Because it must make some representation of being, metaphysics conceives it as the property common to the entirety of entities. But because it must conceive it as a "foundation-being" (*Grund*), it also allows itself to be ruled by a logic of "foundations," which requires a "foundational being." That is why, from the moment it is conceived as at the base of all entities, being necessarily and simultaneously "twins" into a unique *summit*; it refers to a first entity — the Good or the One (Plato); the divine (Aristotle); God in God's very self, absolute entity, "uncreated being" (*ens increatum*) (Aquinas); both "first cause" (*causa prima*) and "ultimate reason" (*ultima ratio*) (Leibniz); "beginning" and "end" (*arche* and *telos*) — that cannot be this without being "its own cause" (*causa sui*). Thus, from its inception with Plato, metaphysics appears to have been — indeed, such is its "defining trait" — "*an onto-theo-logic . . .* a kind of thinking which everywhere ponders the entity as such and justifies it within the totality of being as foundation (*logos*)." Inevitably this brand of "logic" understands being as a foundation, and equally necessarily as a "primordial thing, the *causa prima,*" also as "*ultima ratio,* the supreme reason for all things." Ultimately, "the being of entities, thought of as a foundation, must be understood — if one wishes to go to the bottom of the question at all — as a *causa sui.* This is equivalent to naming the metaphysical concept for God." Thus, through its status as a preliminary onto-theological interpretation of the relation of being to entities, metaphysics, far from preceding theology, proceeds from it in a fundamental, and not an accidental, way.[38]

The apprehension of this "something" of entities takes place by *analogy*, that is, by aligning (*ana logon*) them according to their order in a hierarchy (*taxis, ordo*), mounting to the unique summit. Although he thought Plato's speculations about Ideas unreasonable, Thomas did agree that Plato was correct in postulating the existence of a "first reality which is (Being and) Good by its very essence, and which we call God" and even that "it is because of

37. A constant theme in the work of this author.
38. Heidegger, *Identité et différence, Q. 1,* 294.

this first being, which by its essence is Being and Good, that any other reality can be called being and good, insofar as it participates in the former according to a certain formula of assimilation, even if deficiently and at a distance."[39] Analogy is as *congenital to metaphysics* as is the ontological substrate of entities and this substrate's twinning as the divine summit.

Because of its exclusive fixation on the being of entities, metaphysics is to be placed at the level of a "technique of explanation of reality by means of ultimate causes."[40] The god it posits appears only in the perspective of a *causality* working as a foundation. The entire discussion is distorted by the passion to master the truth. Such an ambition inevitably degrades the truth into an unfailingly available foundation, a substantial permanence, an objective presence. This need for a reassuring plenitude is symptomatic of a visceral *anthropocentrism*: the need to begin with the certitude of the self, with the presence of the self to the self, by which everything else in the world is ultimately to be measured. In this manner, everything "is ordered," everything is justified, everything has good reasons to be and to be there as present. From the notion of being-as-substance as present permanence to the notion of the subject-substance as permanent presence, it is the same logic at work, a logic of the Same unfolding itself: a utilitarian logic which, because of fear of all difference, of what is by its nature permanently open, and finally of death, reduces being to its own rationality and, unknowingly, makes of it the glue that bonds a closed totality.

Thus, in spite of the multiplication of schools and the frequent "reversals" which characterize the metaphysical tradition from its inception in Athens, it is nonetheless true, according to Heidegger, that there is a single source of thought, a single logic — that of a "foundation" — which has been generated over the centuries. "Metaphysics conceives the being of entities in two ways: in the deep unity of what is *most universal*, that is, what is indiscriminately everywhere, and at the same time in a unity which is foundational by reason of the entirety, that is, of what is *highest* and thus controls everything. Thus, it is a postulate that the being

39. *ST*, I, q. 6, a. 4.
40. Heidegger, *Lettre sur l'humanisme*, Q. 3, 80.

of the entity is conceived as the *base which founds;* that is why every metaphysics is, at its base and when building on this base, itself the Foundation that gives an account of the base, explains it, and finally asks it to explain itself."[41]

b) The Dichotomy between Being and Language. It is generally recognized that for the "split" (*chorismos*) which Plato locates between the sensible and the intelligible realms, Aristotle substitutes another split within the only world he deems to be real, separating off on the one side a super-lunary region characterized, if not by total immobility and changelessness, at least by an immutable regularity of motion, and, on the other side, a sub-lunary region where local motion takes place: generation, corruption, and death. Although this-worldly, Aristotle's philosophy is thus no less dualistic than that of his master; indeed, for Heidegger, metaphysics is of its *essence dualistic.*

This cosmological dualism is itself inseparable from a logical (and axiological) dualism. Whereas the pre-Socratic thinkers, according to Heidegger, were able to engage "nature" (*physis*) in its primordial bursting forth, and to conceive it preserving both the identity and the difference characterizing the "fold" (*Zwiespalt*) between *being* and *language*, Plato opens up a "rupture" (*Spaltung*) between the two: language no longer "gathers in" (*legein*) Being in its unconcealing pro-cession as well as in its re-cession; it is no longer the very place where the world happens; it is the world's reflection. Or rather, the things of this world are now no more than the shadows cast by the "ideal" realities represented by thought and objectified by language. While it is true that Aristotle turns against the thought of Plato in assigning priority to the "this" (*tode ti*) or particular substance, over the general "something" (*ti*), there remains upon the totality of his philosophy (as J. Beaufret has argued) "the shadow cast by Platonism, for which the foundation of being is the communitarian generality of the realm of 'idea' (*eidos*)"; and this tendency "will grow only stronger" in the later history of philosophy.[42]

Thus, being presents itself, in the final analysis, as the vis-à-vis of thought, rendered objective by the latter. Beneath the variety of

41. Heidegger, *Identité*, 292–293.
42. J. Beaufret, *Dialogue avec Heidegger* (Minuit, 1973) 1:111–112.

themes which have preoccupied the different metaphysical traditions, one can discern a common way of representing being as *"something facing human beings which stands by itself"* in relation to humans thinking and speaking (Heidegger). Language has ceased to be the place where humans are born at the heart of the real.

At the level of the sounds emitted, *language* is the conventional expression of a mental content which itself consists of images of exterior things; such, in general, is the way metaphysics conceives of language. For example, at the beginning of his treatise *On Interpretation*, Aristotle distinguishes three elements: (1) "the sounds emitted by the voice," (2) the "states of soul" of which the sounds are the "symbols" or "immediate signs," and (3) the "things of which these states are the images" (par. 16a). The *sounds* or "the words emitted by the voice" are "not the same for all people"; they are thus arbitrary and conventional, variable according to languages. The states of soul are to be understood as a *content* present, not in the words but in the minds of the speakers. This content, in contrast to the sounds, is "the same for everybody." For example, whether one says "horse," *cheval,* or *Pferd,* everybody forms the same mental image of what is enunciated by the different sounds. This representation is in turn "identical to the thing" of which it is the image, the external referent, which in this case is the four-legged creature in question. Commenting on this passage from Aristotle, Thomas sums up its point by saying that "according to the Philosopher, words are signs of ideas, and ideas are likenesses of things" (*voces sunt signa intellectuum, et intellectus sunt rerum similitudines*).[43]

Between Aristotle and Thomas, we find Augustine, notably in Book II of his *De Doctrina Christiana,* which T. Todorov considers "the first real work of semiotics"[44] in the sense that the theory of signs developed there encompasses not only words but also nonlinguistic signs, the latter being considered *quasi quaedam verba visibilia* ("as if they were some sort of visible words," II, iii, 4). "It is through signs that we come to know things," Augustine writes at the start of his treatise (I, ii, 2). "Indeed, a sign is a thing which, beyond the impression it offers to the senses, causes by itself something else to enter our thought" (*Signum est enim res, praeter*

43. *ST,* I, q. 13, a. 1.
44. T. Todorov, *Théories du symbole* (Paris: Seuil, 1977) 38.

speciem quam ingerit sensibus, aliud aliquid ex se faciens in cogitationem venire,
II, i, 1). In the case of words, the signifying "thing" (*res*) is evidently the
sound emitted by the voice; this sound is a sign in that "beyond the impression it makes on the senses, it causes, *by itself [ex se]*, something else
to enter our thought." Words (II, iii, 4), like the letters which are only
their copy (II, iv, 5), are not "natural signs" (such as smoke or the track
of an animal) but "conventional signs" (*signa data*). Their raison d'être "is
to give birth to and to transmit to a second mind that which is contained
in the mind of the person who uses the sign" (II, ii, 3). Thomas will later
say, "Speaking to another is nothing else than manifesting the concept of
the mind to that person" (*Nihil aliud est loqui ad alterum quam conceptum
mentis alteri manifestare*).[45] Of the fact that this "something else" (*aliud aliquid*, the words Thomas uses here for the concept) which the sign causes
to arise in the mind is or should normally be the *immediate and faithful
representation of the extra-linguistic reality,* Augustine has no more doubt
than does Aristotle or Thomas, even if he does not emphasize this viewpoint in *De Doctrina Christiana*: "Upon seeing tracks, we judge that an
animal has passed by . . . upon hearing a person's voice, we know how
he or she feels" (II, i, 1). And did Augustine not write, in Book XV of his
De Trinitate, that *"the word which resonates without is the sign of the word
which shines within"* (XV, xi, 20)? Apparently this "word of the heart"
(*verbum cordis*) is one which *"impresses itself* upon the soul with every object of knowledge." Like the "states of soul" of Aristotle, "it does not
belong to any language. . . . It is neither Greek nor Latin" (XV, x, 19).
"Preceding all the signs into which it may be translated, it is born of an
interior knowledge within the soul," a prelinguistic knowledge whose secret
source can be no other than the "interior Teacher" (*intus Magister*), the
Word of God himself (XV, xi, 20).

There are diverse theories of language within the metaphysical
tradition, but they all seem to rest on a relation between three
basic elements which one can present in the following manner:
(1) the word considered as a sound emitted by the voice and
entering into a purely conventional or arbitrary relation with (2) a
universal mental reality which it evokes, usually called the "concept," which is in a natural relation of similarity with (3) the extra-
linguistic thing of which it is the image. In contemporary terms,
(1) the linguistic signifier is in a *conventional* relationship with
(2) the signified, which itself refers back, in a *natural* fashion, to

45. *ST*, I, q. 107, a. 1.

(3) the referent. It is within the conventions of such a theory that Thomas elaborates his theory of knowledge.

One could briefly summarize Thomas' theory as follows. (1) The object imprints its image (2a) in the senses by its sensible "impressed species" (*species impressa*) — the particularity of the thing — and (2b) in the mind through its intelligible impressed species — the universal aspect of the thing. Through the abstractive powers of the active intellect, the mind constructs (3) the concept, which is the mental representation of the thing, or the presence of the thing itself in the mind by way of its mental representation, and which is called the "interior word" (*verbum cordis* or *mentis*). The concept is then transmitted to the outside by (4) the exterior word in a discourse which is a judgment.[46] To achieve clarity in this synthetic overview, we have distinguished four principal elements; but this presentation is misleading. For Thomas, there are only three truly distinct elements: the thing, the moment of intellectual activity (the formation of the concept), and the moment of judgment. The "impressed species" is not a thing-in-itself; if it were, the mind would not know the thing itself but only its "species," that is, that which each knower takes from it. Such an "Idealism" would be in direct and fundamental contradiction to the "Realism" Thomas professes because for him it is definitely the *thing itself that, through its mental representation, is "naturally" present within the mind*. It is the thing itself that we *attain* in knowledge. The species is not a material object (*quod*) but a formal object (*quo*); it is not an object of knowledge but a means or, rather, a principle of knowledge. It is that through which we attain the thing that has impressed itself upon the mind by its form. As for language, it is only the *instrument* for translation outside, a purely conventional translation, of what has, by contrast, been "naturally" formed in the mental representation.

Thomas' "realism," as is immediately evident, takes its point of departure from the conviction that the real is an object, an objective to *be reached*. This is the same metaphysical presupposition which governs the opposed theory, *nominalism*. The only difference is that, whereas nominalism states that we always miss our objective since the universals (transcendentals, genera, species), which always function as predicates, can be only "words" (*voces*) and not "things" (*res*), realism on the contrary confirms the success of our enterprise. In both cases, however, being and humans are equally imagined to be in a vis-à-vis, dialectically linked only

46. Cf. *De Veritate*, q. 4, a. 1–2; *De Potentia*, q. 8, a. 1.

by language; language itself is conceived as a purely *instrumental intermediary* which enables the two, with more or less success, to dialogue between themselves. According to Heidegger, throughout the whole tradition of metaphysics, language has ceased to be what it was at the dawn of pre-Socratic thinking: the *meeting place where* being and humankind mutually stepped forward toward one another.

c) Language as Instrument. Rather than considering language as the "mutual belonging together" (*Zusammengehörigkeit*) of "Being" (*Sein*) and the "human being" (*Dasein*), the metaphysical tradition views language as belonging exclusively to humans. An "animal having language" (*zoon logon echon*), a "rational animal" (*animal rationale*), the human being is an entity that has, among other *attributes*, speech. Humans have language, instead of being originally possessed and constituted by it (although we do not mean thereby to hypostatize language into another ultimate reality!). They use language as a necessary *tool for the translation* of their mental representations to themselves (thought) or to others (voice).

But "translator, traitor" (*traductor, traditor*): although an instrument of translation, language is simultaneously — alas! — an *instrument of betrayal;* for it can never exhaust the "what the presence of meaning wishes to say about itself" which, according to J. Derrida, characterizes the Augustinian sign.[47] When compared with this absolute primacy of the presence of meaning, that is, this interior word whose ultimate source is the Word of God illuminating the human heart, language always remains inadequate — by its very nature even, and not just because of the lies, the incompetence, or the distraction of the speaker. The ideal, impossible in this world, would thus be to *dispense with* language altogether — just as to dispense with the body — in order to benefit directly by the light of the immanent meaning. That is why language, as indispensable and precious as it may be and as magnificent as its literary masterpieces may also be, is for Augustine an *obstacle* to human self-realization. First of all, according to Augustine, language is a consequence of original sin which has so dried up the inner source of the direct knowledge of God that

47. J. Derrida, *La voix et le phénomène* (Paris: PUF, 1967) 37.

our first parents discovered they could no longer communicate with each other, except through the skill (quite imperfect) of language.[48] This is a significant statement because it implies that God could have created humans beyond any need for language . . . Without going that far, Augustine comes close to saying the same thing in another text, quoted and commented upon by Thomas to this effect, that "before [the fall], God perhaps spoke with Adam and Eve in the same way he communicates with the angels, that is, by directly illuminating their intellects with God's permanent truth."[49]

It is thus impossible for us to get by without language; however, we only consent to this condition reluctantly because language poses *an obstacle to this ideal transparency* of the self to itself, to others, and to God which seems *to constitute one of the fundamental presuppositions of the metaphysical tradition.* Beyond this resentment of the necessity of a mediation through language, we discern a further suspicion of the very *corporality* and *historicity* of humankind: such is the unconscious paradigm that seems to control the metaphysical way of thinking. For the decision to describe either the body or language as an instrument presupposes an anterior existence, at least of the logical order, of humanity in relation to its "tools"; it presupposes an ideal human essence that, since its fall and exile, has been thus imprisoned — "body-sign" (*soma-sema*) — in the empire of the sensible. In spite of all its variations, metaphysics has never departed from this original Platonism; but it is impossible, when working under such presuppositions, to develop a positive evaluation for either the body or language as the environment in which both the subject may come to life and truth may happen.

d) The Dichotomy between Subject and Object. The dualistic opposition between subject and object is in a sense as old as metaphysics since it is linked to that between being and language, as well as to the instrumentalist conception of language. But it is in the modern period, notably with Descartes, that this dichotomy becomes full-

48. *De. Gen. contra Manich.*, II, 31.
49. Augustine, *Super Gen. ad Litt.*, XI. *ST*, I, q. 94, a. 1. Cf. *De Veritate*, q. 18, a. 1–2.

blown. Heidegger discusses this in his *Holzwege:*[50] "The fulfillment of Western metaphysics commences with Descartes" (p. 129). For once Plato had conceived the "being-ness of the entity as *eidos* (*ad-spect, 'vision'*)," this determination announced the historical conditioning — still far in the future of course — of what was to come to completion in modern times (pp. 118–119).

Descartes' "I think" (*cogito*) corresponds to a certain *stage* in the development of metaphysics: that of science, of the "objectification of the entity," where "humans as calculators," have "all entities come before them" to extract from them an "explanatory representation" that will be "sure, that is, certain" (p. 114). Thus, it is "in the metaphysics of Descartes that, for the first time, the entity comes to be defined as the objectivity of the representation, and the truth as the certitude of this representation" (ibid.). Now, to this *objectivism* which tries to "stop and hold" the entity before the human being "in its aspect as an object (p. 118)," there corresponds, "as a necessary and reciprocal interplay," a *subjectivism* of the same scope and significance (p. 115). *For the first time the human being becomes a "subject"* [subjectum] — for the first time because up to then this word *subjectum* was never used for the "I," but only for the *sub-stratum (hypokeimenon)*, that is, "what lies before [*das Vor-Liegende*], which, as ground [*Grund*], holds all together in itself." But now, in becoming "the first and the sole *sub-jectum*," the human being becomes *"the unique center of reference,"* the entity "on which from now on every *other* entity is based" (p. 115). The world thus becomes *ob-jectum* "spread out in front of" the *sub-jectum* that the human being is, prostrate before the human being. The world becomes a "picture" *(Bild)*, or a movie which unfolds before humans' eyes, so that they may sovereignly and serenely pronounce their judgements of truth. Descartes' *cogito* is contemporary with this period of metaphysical development, when, as Paul Ricoeur describes it, "humans stage themselves, they cast themselves as the stage where the entity should from now on appear, present itself — in sum, become a picture." This radical Cartesian split between subject and object brings to the light of day "a movement belonging to the metaphysical tradition," where the subject-object relation now "obliterates the belonging of the human being [*Dasein*] and being" and "disguises the

50. Heidegger, "L'époque des 'conceptions du monde,'" *Chemins qui ne mènent nulle part*, French trans. W. Brokmeier (Paris: Gallimard, 1962). From now on I will quote from the collection *Idées*, published by Gallimard. Cf. P. Ricœur, "Heidegger et la question du sujet," *Le conflit des interprétations* (Paris: Seuil, 1969) 222–223. Cf. also below, ch. 2, n. 26.

process of truth as the uncovering of this ontological implication."[51] Descartes thought he could deduce the self starting from the *cogito*. But what kind of self could he reach except an *objectified I*, conceived after the manner of an Aristotelian substance, an I which finally is only the *representation of the ego* and which, to carry out its role as "unshaken foundation of truth" (*fundamentum inconcussum veritatis*), finally has to invoke as a guarantee the divine Absoluteness? A paradox thus arises; the opposition between subject and object is never as clear as when the *subjectum* harbors within itself, but in a status of "unequalled preeminence,"[52] the objective traits of the *hypokeimenon*: a paradox which brings into full light the impossibility of deducing the self from anything . . .

Everything hangs together. Metaphysics, in the course of its successive ages, has unfolded the historical destiny that was inscribed on it at its original forgetfulness of the ontological difference. The search for a foundation which both explains and justifies this base, which is the being of the entity, was necessarily accompanied by a representation of the relation of being to humankind as the dialectical relation of face-to-face, and no longer as the mutual belonging of one to the other. At the same time, this representation required the representation of being as *outside language*, and of language as a pure *instrument*. Metaphysics thus reveals itself, according to its most characteristic tendency, as the logic of a discourse which conceals the original moment of its own knowledge, forgetting, in the words of Maurice Merleau-Ponty, that "every relationship with being is simultaneously to take and to be taken,"[53] that the subject who does the enunciating is never completely separate from the linguistic subject of its statements — in short, that humans never utter their judgments from a distant height and with a sovereign neutrality, but rather start with a concrete language in which a universe is already structured into a "world," that is, from a place that is socially arranged and culturally organized.

51. Ricœur, "Heidegger," 227–228.
52. Heidegger, *Chemins*, 139.
53. M. Merleau-Ponty, *Le visible et l'invisible: Notes de travail* (Paris: Gallimard, 1964) 319.

3. The Onto-theological Representation
of the Relation between Humans and God

The metaphysical ontology which began in Greece exercised a decisive influence, in both its (neo) Platonic and Aristotelian forms, on Christian theology, the more so since the former was, as we have seen, theological from the beginning. As a consequence, the Christian God became identified with the Sovereign Good, the underived One, the unmoved Mover, the "Supreme Being" (*ens supremum*), ultimate Cause, in short, as Heidegger says, the "supreme value," which is the "most entity of entities."[54]

a) Analogy. It is possible for us to speak of God only by analogy. Analogy, according to Thomas (whom we take here as our guide), consists in an act of judgment (and not in a concept) which concerns the *relation* of humankind to God (but not the essence of God). When attributing to God such names as Goodness, Wisdom, and so forth, this judgment is valid as far as the "signified reality" (*res significata*) is concerned. In fact, from this viewpoint, these terms may be applied to God "with more propriety than to creatures, for it is to him that they are appropriate in the first instance." On the other hand, the judgment of analogy loses its validity in what concerns the "mode of signifying" (*modus significandi*), "which belongs to the creature."[55] For the Scholastic logicians and grammarians, these *modi significandi* determined the three major functions of terms in a proposition, and responded to these three questions: *quid?* (the Word is God: name of an essence), *quis?* (The Word is Son: name of a person), *quo?* (The Word is distinguished from the Father by the relation of sonship: name of a property or notion). If that is the reach of the "modes of signifying," one can understand why Thomas would go so far as to say, "On the subject of God there is one thing which must remain *completely unknown* [*omnino ignotum*] to humans in this life, and that is what God is."[56] Again, "We do not know what God is but only what he is not and what relation he maintains with everything else."[57] In saying such things, Thomas was in no way

---

54. Heidegger, "Le mot de Nietzche 'Dieu est mort,'" *Chemins*, 313.
55. *ST*, I, q. 13, a. 3.
56. *In Ep. ad Rom*, cap. 1, lect. 6.
57. *Contra Gentiles*, I:30.

an innovator; on the contrary, he was heir to a long onto-theological tradition which — notably among the Neoplatonists, in the treatise *On the Names of God* by Dionysius, and in many of the Greek Fathers — had attempted to express the incomprehensibility of God (John Chrysostom) and thus blazed the trail for negative theology.[58]

God must remain "completely unknown" to us because there is no concept which can encompass both God and humankind, no third term which would be common to both. *As a consequence, if a word such as "goodness," "in terms of what it signifies," may be applied, and "in the first place" (*per prius*), to God, it is by way of negation — but a full, super-eminent negation. This suggests that this kind of analogy is a *relation between relations*, specifically, that "God has the same relation with what concerns him as the creature has with what is proper to it." Thus, it is not a question here of an analogy of direct proportion or *attribution*, according to which a single reality (for example, health) would subsist with different relations in different terms (for example, a "healthy" remedy as the cause of health, and healthy urine as a sign of health). It is rather an instance of analogy *by proportionality*, according to which several realities may find themselves in the same relation — as old age may be to life what evening is to day. The first kind of analogy will not apply, because "the infinite and the finite may not enter into a proportion"; the second is re-quired, because "what the finite is to the finite, the infinite is to the infinite."[59]

Now, on what basis may we posit such a relation? The answer is provided in the quotation from the *Contra Gentiles* given above: about God, we know only "what [God] is not, and what *relation* [God] maintains with everything else." Similarly, in the *Summa*:

---

58. Plotinus: "We say what God is not, we do not say what God is" (*Enneads*, 5:3, § 14); Pseudo-Dionysius, *On the Divine Names*, especially 7:3: the manner of knowing God that is most worthy of God is "to know God through the way of not-knowing in a union that surpasses all understanding" (French trans. M. de Gandillac).

59. *De Veritate*, q. 23, a. 7, ad 9; q. 2, a. 11. In Thomas the relation between the two types of analogy concerning God is in fact more complex than what we are suggesting here. On this point, see the refined analyses of Jüngel, *Dieu, mystère du monde*, vol. 2, especially 78–85.

The validity of our analogies ''is determined by the relation the creature maintains with God as its principle and its cause.''[60] Thus, *before* the act of judgement, which is the analogy, there is posited a ''relation'' (*ordo*) of the creature to its Creator, of the effect to its Cause. True, this postulate was itself the object of a prior ''demonstration'' in the question ''Does God exist?'' But, as J. L. Marion has indicated, God's existence reappears as a question at the end of each of the five proofs Thomas gives of it. For after the first path leads to a first mover, the second to a first efficient cause, . . . the last to a final cause, Thomas has to add to each of these five conclusions, as an apparently completely innocent clause, ''and this *all* understand to be God,'' ''*all* call this God,'' ''what *all* say is God,'' and so forth. But the question is: Who establishes this equivalence between the final term to which the demonstration (and thus rational discourse) tends and the God which ''all'' are claimed to discover there? Even if ''all'' do, with what right do they? Who are these ''all,'' and how can they establish an equivalence which no theologian, no philosopher has been able to establish, but an equivalence these ''all'' build upon? When all is said and done, Thomas is appealing here to a support *outside the demonstration proper:* that of common agreement. ''Our effort at conceptual discourse must confess itself unable to generate this support since it reaches its ultimate result thanks only to a gratuitous ''that is to say'' lacking evidence in spite of its claim to evidence.[61]

Thus, in the final analysis, God is simply postulated, not *demonstrated*, by the discourse itself. Postulated outside of language, because Thomas, no more than his contemporaries, could ever imagine the non-existence of God. For that, he would have had to leave behind not only his social position as a religious and a theologian but, more than that, his desire, his entire culture, a culture saturated with evidence for the existence of God — a God who, as Jüngel notes, ''is, in any case, always conceived as the ultimate *cause* of all things''; who, in analogy, is always necessarily ''*presupposed* as the condition, itself unconditioned, of the world.''[62] To prevent this identification of the first mover with what ''all call God,'' it would have been necessary to show that the conclusion of the demonstra-

60. *ST*, I, q. 13, a. 5.
61. Ibid., q. 2, a. 3. J. L. Marion, *L'idole et la distance* (Grasset, 1977) 28–29.
62. Jüngel, *Dieu, mystère du monde*, 2:86–88. Chauvet's emphasis.

tion was already contained in the forgotten starting point of metaphysics: onto-theology. At that time, such an identification imposed itself irresistibly as a cultural imperative, that is, as one of the numerous assumptions which appear within any culture as so naturally self-evident that they are impervious to questioning.

This last remark discloses the human inability to get totally outside of language, culture, and desire. This fact should *also* be the object of our reflection; indeed, perhaps we should think about it *before all else*. But it is just this that onto-theology has never been able to think, for fear of seeing itself immediately defeated; thus, onto-theology had free rein to postulate a divine *ens supremum* as the capstone of the arch and absolute foundation for the totality of entities. It is precisely an essential trait of onto-theology, as Jüngel has demonstrated, to presuppose the "ontological priority of thought to language," overlooking the fact that every thought is "always already language."[63] It is precisely this oversight that has opened up for it both the possibility and the necessity of the doctrine of analogy: *before* language, and thus beyond culture and desire, the existence of a relation between the creature and God as to its cause and principle must be postulated — a datum that cannot be open to question (even in the question: "Does God exist?" [*An sit Deus?*]).

b) The Critical Thrust of Christian Theology. We cannot naively hope to get by without analogy. Whether we wish to or not, we cannot help but make use of it, whether in discussing the essential divine attributes (God is just, good, and so forth), or in using names that imply a relation (God is Father, Spouse, Word, and so forth). But the foregoing critique demonstrates also that we may not rely upon it either; as a "synthesis of opposites" (pro-cession and re-cession of God), the best it can "produce is an inevitably mediocre compromise," whose ambition, according to S. Breton, is a harmonious synthesis of the two languages of revelation, one positive and one negative, which nevertheless "belong to the human condition from which they have no way of exempting themselves."[64]

Rather, it behooves us to accept the language and the internal

63. Ibid., 47.
64. S. Breton, *Ecriture et révélation* (Paris: Cerf, 1979) 160.

conflict it presents us with: a conflict difficult to take o\
which we are constantly tempted to erase in order to in
domination over the world; a conflict, however, from w\
subject is born and sustains itself; a conflict outside of w.
in our imaginations, install our *subjecta* in the center of th̲ ̫υrld
and take our desire as reality . . . As a doctrine validating the
truth of our language about God, that is, guaranteeing the ade-
quacy of our judgments concerning the divine reality, *analogy
erases the internal conflict inherent to any discourse. However, this conflict cannot be resolved; rather, it must be managed — and precisely
through the mediation of language:* once we are able to say it, we are
able to live it as the ever-open place where the true nature of
what we are in our relations with others and with God may
become reality.

In thus locating the place of theology at the heart of the mediation by language, by culture, and by desire, that is, at the heart of
the lack which this mediation opens in every subject, we place
theology's *critical thrust* no longer in a prolongation of the negative onto-theology stressing the unknowability of God but rather
in the direction of the believing *subjects* themselves. Of course,
negative theology has forcefully emphasized the point that, in
order not to silence God, we must be silent about God. But this
must be done in an appropriate manner; otherwise, the silence
will be empty or at least so ambiguous that it will no longer be a
silence about *God.* The only appropriate silence about God is one
mediated by language, and even by a language whose superabundance and superlatives are as much required by the surpassing
transcendency to which the negation is carried as by the necessity
of never stopping on one or the other of the negations, as if — by
outbidding — it could finally be adequate to God.[65] That there is
no theological discourse which does not know an inescapable critical moment of negative theology and that the great tradition of
Dionysius, Eckhart, and Thomas Aquinas will always be an obligatory route of passage is absolutely evident. But this cannot mean
that the *primordial task* of Christian theology is to purify through
analogy the concepts that we use to express God — so that we
can reach "knowledge under the mode of unknowing" (Diony-

65. Cf. Jüngel, *Dieu, mystère du monde,* 2:52–62.

sius). In this case, moreover, the Bible, replete with anthropomorphisms, would at best present us with a sub-theology for
unsophisticated minds . . . This primoridal task consists, as
Jüngel suggests, in considering the gospel itself as a form of
analogy, that is, as a type of *parabolic* language whose distinctive
characteristic is "to insert human beings, insofar as they are summoned, into the being about which they are speaking."[66]

We agree with J. Ladrière that this comes down to regarding this language, where the hearers find themselves engaged, as a peculiar kind of
"language game" (Wittgenstein): a "hermeneutical" language which has
its own type of coherence and cannot be "translated" either into causative or explanatory language, notably scientific language, or into
metaphysical language (we shall explain this more in the next chapter).
As Breton has expressed this point with regard to Eckhart, the onto-
theological "basis language," even when overturned by a "metabasis language" in which negation predominates and sublimated by an "anabasis
language" which attempts to synthesize the first two, still perseveres
from end to end.[67] As Claude Geffré expresses it, "Whatever be the correction brought by the *via negationis*, the movement of thought inaugurated by Pseudo-Dionysius within Christian theology only makes more
apparent the power of human knowledge in its will to deal with the
divine through a concept of God as the supreme Entity."[68] Put another
way, negative theology, even in its most sublime moments where it transcends, through negation, the notion of being as cause, nonetheless remains viscerally connected to a type of language that is irremediably
causal and ontological. Because of this, it cannot take on the distinctive
idiosyncrasy of a "language game" that, characterized as it is by the predominance of the "illocutionary" (see below), happens only by touching
to the quick the subjects engaged in that game.

The critical thrust for Christian theology does not consist in the
apophatic purification of our concepts in order to express God but
rather in the *use* that *we* make of these concepts, that is, in the *at-*

66. Ibid., 102, 108.

67. S. Breton, "Les métamorphoses du langage religieux chez Maître Eckhart," *Dire ou taire Dieu*, RSR 67/3-4 (1979) 53-75. "The basis language, even
sublimated through the metabasis, continues into the anabasis language" (p.
73).

68. C. Geffré, *Le christianisme au risque de l'interprétation* (Paris: Cerf, 1983)
181.

titude, idolatrous or not, they elicit from us. As a matter of fact, the tradition has understood this point for a long time: the most sophisticated ideas may be corrupted into idols; conversely, the most earthy anthropomorphisms ("Lord, you are my rock!") may emerge as our most refined expressions for the radical otherness and holiness of God.[69]

If the present criticism of the productionist scheme of causality, which has traditionally dominated theological thinking, had no higher ambition than to intellectually purify one concept or to replace it by another which seemed more adequate, this game would not be worth the effort. But something much more serious is at issue. In showing why we must renounce, as much as this can be done, the scheme of "explicative" causality and embrace rather the symbolic scheme of language, of culture, and of desire, we set up *a discourse from which the believing subject is inseparable —* just as language is inseparable from being or *Dasein* from *Sein*. In theology as in philosophy, subjects can truly "grasp" nothing without at the same time recognizing themselves to be already grasped by it. Theological discourse, even in all its rigor, must therefore touch the quick of the subject. The critical thrust in Christian theology is precisely this in our opinion: to show the conditions which render possible a passage — a passage which must be *continually undertaken* — from the *attitude* of a slave toward a Master imagined as all-powerful, clothed in the traditional panoply of the attributes of *esse*, to the attitude of a child toward a God represented far differently because this God is seen always in the shadow of the cross, and thus to the attitude of a brother or a sister toward others.

---

69. A frequent theme, at least since Pseudo-Dionysius. Cf. *Hiér. cél.* II:3 (Sources chrétiennes 58, p. 85 and introduction, p. xxii). F. Marty has shown that, if Kant rejects dogmatic anthropomorphisms (that purport to say something about what God is), on the other hand he is keenly interested in "the symbolic anthropomorphisms which in fact concern the *language* and not the object itself" (cf. *Prolegomena to Any Future Metaphysics*, § 57). This symbolic anthropomorphism is in the last analysis "the humble face of a negative theology that has renounced to take pride in its negativity" (p. 195). F. Marty, *La naissance de la métaphysique chez Kant: Une étude de la notion kantienne d'analogie* (Beauchesne, 1980) ch. 3.

III. OPENNESS TO THE SYMBOLIC: MANNA

We asked ourselves at the start of the present chapter how it happened that, to express this relation which immediately strikes us as beyond all "value" because it belongs completely to the order of grace, Thomas did not try some route other than that of causality, for example that of symbol, the way of the non-value because it is the way of the never-finished reversible exchange in which every subject comes to be. But the *Philebus* of Plato demonstrated in a decisive fashion that metaphysics was born from the evacuation and execution of this second point of view. For whatever is without limits is, for it, beyond thought, defies all *logic*. The only logic possible is that of a *first cause* and of an *absolute foundation* for the totality of existents; that of a *center* playing the role of a fixed point;[70] that of a *presence*, faultless, constant, and stable, which, as Heidegger shows, requires a representation of time in which the present, as a fixed center, enjoys a disproportionate privilege. The ontic-ontological difference is forgotten; the "play" of being in time is overlooked. Rather, time has become functional and measurable: being is ideologically isolated in its role as foundation. Everything is accounted for; at least, the attempt is made. Humans imprison themselves in a *logic of the Same*.

Nourished by a secret desire for *transparence* of the self to itself, this logic produces a type of thought which is independent of the body and thus of death; that, at least, is its ideal. Thus did Plato-Socrates come to recommend, as we have seen, a style of life "where there is no place for either joy or sorrow, but only for thought at its highest possible degree of purity." It is this logic, based on an aggressive forcing of identity, that explains why the relation of the lover to the beloved is conceived on the model of the shipbuilding and why the relation of humans to God in the sacraments is *unavoidably* represented according to the technical and productionist scheme of instrumentality and causality — with every attempt being made to "purify" this scheme by the use of analogy . . .

It is our opinion, on the contrary, that the discussion of grace (since it is grace that the sacraments are ultimately about) requires another approach. Like the *manna* in the desert, which is perhaps

70. A. Delzant, *La communication de Dieu* (Paris: Cerf, 1978) 19–22.

its most beautiful biblical expression, grace is of an entirely different order from that of value or empirical verifiability. Its very
name is a question: *Man hu?* Its name is "What is this?" Its consistency seems to be that of a "something" which has all the traits
of "nothing": something "as fine as frost on the ground" which
melts in the sun. Further, the measuring of it resembles a "non-
measure": they gather it up — "some . . . more, some less"; but
when they proceed to estimate its quantity, they observe, contrary
to all logic of value, that "those who gathered much had nothing
over, and those who gathered little had no shortage;" finally,
those who, violating the Lord's command, wanted to store some
for the future saw that "it bred worms and became foul" (Exod
16:9–21). *Grace as a question, grace as a non-thing, grace as a non-value:*
How can we make sense of this pure sign which begins with a
question, other than by choosing the path of *symbol,* the path of
non-calculation and non-utility? This is, in any case, our primordial
question.

But may one simply decree, by a simple announcement, the
replacement of an onto-theological logic of the Same, where the
sacraments are controlled by their instrumental and causal system,
with a symbolic representation of the Other, where they are appreciated as language acts making possible the unending transformation of subjects into believing subjects? Is such a replacement
even possible? Are we able to think in any way other than the
metaphysical? If so, how? Such is the question which the next
chapter will take up.

Chapter Two

Overcoming Onto-Theology?

Can we think other than metaphysically or "onto-theologically"? Is it possible to simply scratch out, as with the tip of our pen, the whole way metaphysics approaches problems and with no further ado adopt another?

At first sight, the undertaking appears quite uncertain because our *mother tongue* itself, in its morphology and syntax — this language which, far from simply garbing the real in varied colors, constructs this real into a "world," that is, a world of sense — is permeated with the metaphysical logos.

None have struggled more vigorously than E. Levinas to liberate themselves from the Greek *logos* and to challenge the Greek tradition from the viewpoint of the Jewish; that is, to challenge Being (impersonal, anonymous, violent reducer of otherness to the totality of the same) with the Other (pure eruption and rupture bursting, through the "Face," the unifying pretensions and the ultimately totalitarian essence of the Greek *logos*). An impossible enterprise, declares J. Derrida: the question which underlies Levinas' discourse "cannot be posed without forgetting itself in the language of the Greeks;" but on the other hand, when forgetting itself, the question "cannot express itself except in the language of the Greeks."[1]

Our initial perplexity will change into a sense of impossibility if we observe that to pose the question, as we have done above, in terms of alternatives is to place the path we wish to explore on the same level as the one we wish to replace. When we do that, the failure of our project is a foregone conclusion: this "new" path will then be only the model opposite to the first, and equally

1. J. Derrida, "Violence et métaphysique," *L'écriture et la différence* (Paris: Seuil, 1967) 196.

metaphysical. We will have pitched our tent in a different location, but on essentially the same terrain. What we are considering here is precisely such a *change of terrain* — if it is true, as we will maintain, that the question here becomes inseparable from the *mode* of questioning, and the latter in its turn is constituted *by the questioning subject itself*: "It is the way which sets everything on its way, and it sets everything on its way inasmuch as it is a speaking way."[2]

I. OVERCOMING METAPHYSICS
ACCORDING TO HEIDEGGER

1. *Thinking Metaphysics, Not as a Fall but as an Event*

The "ongoing confusion between the entity and Being" that nurtures metaphysics must be rethought *not as a failing but as an event*, writes Heidegger in *What Is Metaphysics?*[3] For this confusion "cannot have its foundation in a simple failure of thought or superficiality of expression" (p. 29). In fact, metaphysics has always proceeded "from a revelation of being," but it has remained "unaware" of this revelation (p. 24).

The event (*Ereignis*) we must think about is this *destiny* "to which metaphysics seems chained without knowing it" (p. 30), a destiny which, according to *Overcoming Metaphysics*, is "a unique fatality, but perhaps also the necessary one for the West, and the price it had to pay to extend its dominance over the entire earth."[4] This dominance is achieved by technology, whose essence is the *"arraignment"* (*Gestell*), because it "obliges humankind to appoint the real as its stock-in-trade,"[5] to bring nature to reason, demanding that each thing "explain itself, that it make plain its reason."[6] Technology thus brings to completion the metaphysical stage of the world, a world viewed as a "picture" and "representation," which unfolded at the start of the modern period. From now on, Being is reduced to a mere "capital" always at the disposal of humankind, to a "reservoir of energy,"[7] "entrusted" to

2. M. Heidegger, *Acheminement vers la parole* (Paris: Gallimard, 1976) 183, 187.
3. Heidegger, *Le retour au fondement de la métaphysique*, Q. 1, 29.
4. Heidegger, *Dépassement de la métaphysique*, EC, 88.
5. Heidegger, *La question de la technique*, EC, 26.
6. Ibid., n. 1 (note of the translator from German to French).
7. Heidegger, *Séminaire de Zähringen*, Q. 4, 330.

the dominating subjectivity which "posits" (*stellen*) it and manages it for humankind's own service. But by the same token, we also see humankind conceiving itself as the center of the real, elevating to an exasperating degree its own subjectivity. To conceive this history as an Event is to read it ontologically as an *historic* destiny — a destiny which reveals the very essence of a human behavior that demands accounts, gives ultimatums, compels the real to adjust itself to human needs "from the perspective of what can be calculated";[8] a destiny which, as a consequence, is also that of Being: "The *Ge-stell* is in no way the result of human contrivance; on the contrary, it is only the final stage of the history of metaphysics, that is, of the destiny of Being."[9]

2. Overcoming Metaphysics: An Unachievable Task

For this reason, "overcoming" metaphysics is not a matter of discussion between different schools of philosophy. "One cannot shed metaphysics the way one gives up an opinion. One cannot leave it behind like a doctrine which one no longer believes and will no longer defend. . . . *For even vanquished, metaphysics does not disappear.* It comes back under another form and maintains its control, as in the distinction, still in force, between being and the entity."[10] Overcoming metaphysics then is no simple matter of crossing it out with one stroke of the pen as if it were an opinion, doctrine, or system to be refuted; rather, to do so one must reascend to the very source of its life, that is, to "the truth of Being," which is its *ignored* "foundation."[11]

Now, "Being — what *is* Being? Being is What it is; this is what the thought of the future must learn to experiment with and to express. "Being" is neither God nor a foundation for the world. Being is more distant than any entity and at the same time closer to humans than any entity. . . . Being is that which is closest. However, for humankind, this proximity remains that which is farthest."[12] Against all evidence of "good common sense," which "stubbornly clings to the exigencies of what is immediately use-

---

8. Heidegger, *Identité et différence*, Q. *1*, 268.
9. Heidegger, *Séminaire*, Q. *4*, 326.
10. Heidegger, *Dépassement*, EC, 81–82.
11. Heidegger, *Le retour*, Q. *1*, 24–25.
12. Heidegger, *Lettre sur l'humanisme*, Q. *3*, 101–102.

ful"[13] and pretends thereby to be able to summon Being by identifying it with its "eidetic" representations (and with its own "erotic" desire), Being manages to slip through this net as the *non-available*, the non-representable, the 'Incalculable.'"[14]

According to J. Lacan, the truth of the word of the subject emerges only in an "enunciation that denounces itself" and in a statement that renounces itself.[15] Levinas makes the same point, although in a different context: philosophical discourse is a thematic Statement that, ceaselessly trying to return to the primordial Speech which it translates and simultaneously betrays, requires an unachievable "unsaying."[16] Heidegger would accept these assertions, but for a different reason: it is Being *itself* that withdraws; that is what he wishes to indicate in crossing out the word ~~Being~~ in his *Contribution to the Question about Being* (1955). He explains it thus, "This crossing out counteracts this almost irreformable habit of *representing 'Being' as something facing humans which stands by itself* and only subsequently comes to meet humans."[17] This crossing-out marks the "non-being" (*ne-ens*) of Being — Being, which is neither the being-entity ("beingness") of entities, nor an arch-entity. Further, it marks Being's radical *annihilating* action, for "Being never ceases to hide within a difference which constitutes it.[18]

This erasure indicates, in other words, that the statement *es gibt Sein* ("there is Being") is not to be understood in the same way as *das Sein ist* ("Being is") — which would represent Being "too easily as an entity" — but in the sense of a gift; for Being, according to the *Letter on Humanism*, is the *gift of self in openness;* more exactly, "it at once bestows and withholds itself." And it is specifically "beginning with this essence of the truth of Being" that one must re-think the essence of humankind as "ecstatic ex-sistence." One recognizes here the famous Heideggerian *Kehre*,

13. Heidegger, *De l'essence de la vérité*, Q. 1, 162.
14. Postscript to *Qu'est-ce que la métaphysique?*, Q. 1, 79–83.
15. J. Lacan, *Ecrits*, 801 [missing further bibliographical information].
16. E. Levinas, *Autrement qu'être* (The Hague: M. Nijhoff, 1974) 8.
17. Heidegger, *Contribution à la question de l'être*, Q. 1. 232. "This cancellation," comments Derrida, "is the last writing of a period. . . . Insofar as it de-limits onto-theology, the metaphysics of presence, and logocentrism, this last writing is also the first writing." J. Derrida, *De la Grammatologie* (Paris: Minuit, 1967) 38.
18. J. P. Resweber, *La pensée de M. Heidegger* (Privat, 1971).

this "conversion" by which humans, renouncing to convoke and measure being starting from the awareness of self, now "decenter" themselves *from* themselves, and henceforth understand themselves only as always-already infused with the call of being. Such a conversion is unthinkable apart from a meditation on the "essence of *language*" as "correspondence to Being." The relation of humans to Being is essential and indissoluble: "Language is the house of Being where humans live and thereby ex-sist, belonging as they do to the truth of Being over which they keep watch." Since humans are thus conceived as the "shepherds of Being," they may no longer represent themselves as the "Rulers of all entities."[19] For they ex-sist only when spoken by language and thus only when summoned and convoked by Being which, in the mediation of language, attracts them as it withdraws and comes into their presence in the very move-ment that conceals it. This is what the erasure intends to show.

To overcome metaphysics is to ponder that very thing metaphysics ex-cludes and yet at the same time makes metaphysics possible, specifically, the truth of Being as the "Event which uncovers" and the truth of the entity as the "Arrival which takes cover" — the Difference maintained "by the strength of the Same," by *"the space between the two,* where the Event and the Arrival sustain one another in relationship, distant from one another and simultaneously turned toward one another." We must therefore consider the "Concilia-tion between the Event and the Arrival," which is nothing other than tracing the Difference "back to its essential origin": that of "the essence of being" as "the Play itself"; that of "being consid-ered as *starting from* the Difference."[20] For, it is precisely from this "Play" of being that metaphysics first arose; but the latter has dis-owned its playful origin by clinging to its representations: the dance of advance and retreat which being carries out, its move-ment of presence in absence, has been reduced to the presence of an available foundation; originally ec-static, temporality has been tamed into the solid permanence of a constant "now"; logical clarity has replaced the blend of light and shadow at the break-through of Being. To overcome metaphysics, one must perform this "step backwards," this jump into the difference, *advance by going back* toward this original place where metaphysics has its

19. Heidegger, *Lettre*, Q. 3, 104–109.
20. Heidegger, *Identité*, 2nd part "La constitution onto-théo-logique de la métaphysique," Q. 1, 299–300.

abode, the play of being in which it has been engaged from the very beginning. This is a test of conversion: Can we consent to leave the solid, reassuring ground of our represented foundation and the stable, fixed point in order let ourselves go toward this demanding *letting-be* in which we find ourselves out of our depth?

"The essence of metaphysics is something other than metaphysics itself. A thinking which pursues the truth about Being does not rest content with metaphysics; still, it does not *oppose* metaphysics. To express it in images, such thinking does not tear out the root of philosophy. Rather, it excavates the foundation and plows the soil."[21] We must not be misled by this "image": to avoid falling back into "metaphysical thinking," we must not conceive of the "root" or the "foundation" of metaphysics as something restricted to a single location, such as an object somewhere outside us; rather, it is everywhere, it lives within us. This is why Heidegger's philosophy is not just a "new" system, one more which would be added to those which preceded it. More properly, it is a certain manner of living within the metaphysical tradition, of *recalling* it, this time, however, by *thinking its unthought essence.* Heidegger's philosophy questions and overflows this tradition only in being nourished by it. Finally, why this forgetfulness by metaphysics, the forgetfulness of its origin? Why the forgetfulness of this forgetfulness, upon which metaphysics constantly feeds, even in its will to let itself be torn open from the inside by the unclosable question which confronts it? Such forgetfulness can assuredly not be accidental! That the history of being is the "history of the increasing forgetfulness of being" cannot be explained simply by incompetence of thought; rather, this is something which must necessarily be conceived as an "event." This "event" (*Ereignis*), finally, proceeds from being itself — we would prefer to say, from being's withdrawal. It is this withdrawal which we must think about. But to think about it is to ponder it as the characteristic manner by which being reveals itself, even at the very heart of the tradition which conceals it — for being does not speak to us except "from within a tradition."[22] To overcome metaphysics is

21. Heidegger, *Qu'est-ce que la métaphysique?*, Q. 1, 26.

22. Heidegger, "La constitution," Q. 1, 286. Also, the author continues, it is through a "step backward" that one progresses "from metaphysics to its essence" (which is not metaphysics).

nothing more than to reflect that "perhaps part of the essential destiny of metaphysics is that its own foundation eludes it."[23] The forgetfulness of being is thus contained within the destiny of being itself, and its "revelation" is marked by the very history of its "concealment." Such a forgetfulness, veiled by being, "belongs to the very essence of being."[24] Therefore, there is no other method for thinkers to overcome this forgetfulness than to "settle themselves and stand within it."[25]

Now we see it: the business of metaphysics is the very business of thought. Furthermore, it is the business of thinkers themselves, always questioned by metaphysics because they are *involved* in it. We may then ask ourselves, " 'To what extent does metaphysics belong to human nature'; to what extent is it 'linked to the unnoticed difference between being and the entity' and thus to the desire for 'objectivity,' which makes human beings represent each entity 'as an object for a subject' — beginning with the subject itself, which becomes the 'first object of an ontological representation'?"[26] What we have here is a *vast* and probably unavoidable *hermeneutics*, this circle where questioners pose questions only to the extent that they have already understood, by anticipation, the questioned — because the questioners are contained within the questioned. This circle is not vicious because it corresponds to the very nature of the ex-sistence of human beings, who cannot comprehend themselves except in relation to the tradition which lives within them but which in turn inhabits them only in order to

23. Heidegger, *Qu'est-ce que la métaphysique?*, Q. 1, 29.
24. Heidegger, "La parole d'Anaximandre," *Chemins*, 405. See the author's entire reflection on the translation of *on* and *einai* by "entity" and "being" ("Do we perhaps in thus translating correctly already begin to think incorrectly?" p. 402) and on *aletheia* as covering and uncovering, retreat and illumination of being (pp. 405–406).
25. Heidegger, Q. 4, 59.
26. Heidegger, *Dépassement*, EC, 83–86. See, regarding *ego cogito* of Descartes: "The original object is objectively itself. The original objectivity is the I *think* in the sense of I *perceive* which, prior to anything perceptible, lies before (*sich vor-legt*) and has already lain, that is, which is *subjectum*. In the order of the transcendental genesis of the object, the subject is the first object of the ontological representation. *Ego cogito* is the *cogito* in the sense of *me cogitare* ("to think myself," pp. 84–85).

open them to a future always-already anticipated in their reading of the past.

The task to be attempted, that of "overcoming," can never be the mere matter of an isolated, free decision; to want simply to *jump* outside metaphysics with one bound would be to naively condemn oneself to repeat it. This is a protracted task, never fully executed, which in fact progresses only by stepping backwards and which requires of the thinker a process of *conversion*. In this process, one learns little by little to *reverse the direction* of the tradition with which one lives and by which one is nourished. This is the easiest thing in the world because it consists in learning to "let go," but it is also the most difficult because it requires us to unmask the false evidence on which rests the eidetic representations of being, the first of which is this almost ineradicable habit of representing Being as "something facing humans which stands by itself" (see above). In thus unmasking the never-elucidated presuppositions of metaphysics, thinkers learn to serenely acquiesce (the *Gelassenheit* of letting-be) to the prospect of *never* reaching an ultimate foundation, and thus to orient themselves in a new direction — inasmuch as this is possible — starting from the uncomfortable *non-place* of a permanent questioning, which both corresponds to and guarantees being — if it is true that human beings are these "particular entities who hold themselves open to the opening of being."[27] We must give up all "calculating thinking," all "usefulness,"[28] and learn to think starting with this ecstatic *breach* that a human being is.[29] An unachievable task, a task whose very essence is its incompleteness.

27. Heidegger, *Qu'est-ce que la métaphysique?*, Q 1, 34, with the clarification that Heidegger makes concerning the "ecstatic essence of existence."
28. Ibid., 31.
29. O. Laffoucrière, *Le destin de la pensée et "la mort de Dieu" chez Heidegger* (The Hague: M. Nijhoff, 1968), 31. Humankind, according to Heidegger, "collides with the disconcerting arising of its question. It is this arising that it cannot fully account for. It comes to understand that it does not fully dispose of itself. . . . It reaches the point of seeing that if there is such a thing as a definition of itself, it is something completely different from what it had imagined; it is the breech."

3. A "Transitive" Way

To think is to be always on the way. But this way is not to be thought of as a path traced on the ground before us. *It is inseparable from us.* It is a *be-wëgender Weg*, a "way making its way," a "transitive" way: "It is the way which sets everything on its way *(der alles be-wëgende Weg)*"; and "that which sets everything on its way sets everything on its way inasmuch as it is a speaking way."[30] It speaks, in that it is open to the primoridal summons of Being, with regard to which all human speech is a listening and a response (see above). We only "address a word" *(an-sprechen)* to whomever we are speaking because we are "claimed" (same verb — *ansprechen*) by Being, to which we always-already belong. "We have truly *heard (gehört)* when we *become part (gehören)* of what is spoken to us."[31]

Thus, there is no treasure, no value to be discovered at the end of this way. Rather, the treasure is nothing else but the *work of journeying which takes place in ourselves*, the labor of giving birth to ourselves since it is *we ourselves* who are being plowed, turned over and who are bearing fruit by becoming different. Through this step, the "infinity" of the event, demolished by Plato, as we have seen, recovers its rights. It could not be otherwise — let us make no mistake about it: the infinity of *genesis* can be rehabilitated only within a perspective which understands this overcoming metaphysics as a task which is possible only through its permanent *non-completion.*

Such a way of thinking is not that of a rational and argumentative logic frozen in the knowledge of its objective representations. "Science, the rage to know, is the most implacable enemy of thinking."[32] This kind of thinking involves human beings themselves, for what is at stake is to think the truth about being — its "revelation" *(aletheia)* by tearing away "forgetfulness" *(lethe)* — in *Da-sein*, whose being is its "there" *(da)* and not simply its vis-à-vis. *Sein* and *Dasein* subsist in a relation of mutual belonging; this

---

30. Heidegger, *Acheminement*, pp. 183, 187; n. 2 above.
31. Heidegger, *Logos*, EC, 259–260. The same relation obtains between *gehören* and *hören* in the *Lettre*, Q. 3, 78. On the double meaning of *ansprechen*, see *Lettre*, 157.
32. Heidegger, *Que veut dire "penser"?*, EC, 157.

relation may become the object of reflection because being is never separate from language and language is "the house of being, in which humans live and thereby ex-sist."[33] To overcome metaphysics is thus to be always underway, "on the road," — "on the way toward language," *Unterwegs zur Sprache*.

4. *A Non-instrumental Conception of Language*

The reverse journey of metaphysics unmakes little by little what metaphysics had made. This journey does not dissolve it; rather, it unknots it. It unties it, to "re-connect" and "re-read" (*legein/legere-ligare*) it in another way. Transcending the congenital dualisms of metaphysics, thought unavoidably questions the instrumental representation of language. "Humans conduct themselves as if they were the masters of language, while in fact it is language that governs them." This statement is significant for Heidegger, for he wonders if it is not "precisely because humans have reversed this relation of sovereignty that they are pushed toward what is foreign to them."[34] For "when this relation of sovereignty is reversed, strange schemes enter the human mind. Language becomes a *means* of expression," only to fall quickly — a short step — "to the level of nothing more than a means of coercion." It is by one movement that humans, putting themselves at the center of the universe, imagine they dominate the world because they are the point of reference and see themselves as the masters of language: the explicative reduction of the world and the instrumental reduction of language go hand in hand. It is necessary, then, to rethink everything. "For, in the proper sense of the terms, *it is language that speaks*. Humans speak only to the extent that they *respond* to language by *listening* to what it says to them"; it is in this way that language "leads the being of a thing toward us."[35]

As a consequence, "where the word is lacking, there is no thing. Only the available word confers being on the thing."[36] Such a statement, absurd in the eyes of traditional metaphysics,

33. Heidegger, *Lettre, Q. 3*, 106.
34. Heidegger, *Bâtir, habiter, penser, EC*, 172.
35. Heidegger, "*L'homme habite en poète," EC*, 227–228.
36. Heidegger, *Acheminement*, 207.

cannot make sense unless one accepts it: "A word is not simply a handle, a simple tool for giving a name to something that is already there and represented; it is not merely a means for showing what presents itself by itself. On the contrary, *it is the word which bestows the coming-into-presence*, that is, being — that in which something can make its appearance as an entity."[37]

Language is neither primarily nor fundamentally a convenient tool of information nor is it a distributor of carefully regulated titles. More fundamentally, it is summons — *vocation*. There is a poem by Georg Trakl, "A Winter Evening:"

When it is snowing at the window,
When long rings the evening bell.

The "naming (of the snow, of the bell . . .) is a summons. . . . A summons to come into the presence, summons to go into the absence. The snow which falls and the evening bell which rings — now, here, in this poem — these are the things addressed to us through these words. They come into presence through the summons. However, they do not come to take their place among other things that are, here and now, in this room. But which of the two presences is the higher, the more real: that which spreads itself out before our eyes, or that which is summoned?"[38]

Language has, indeed, an instrumental *pole* of naming and labelling. This aspect of utilitarian designation makes language a tool of the greatest importance for humankind. But this first pole must be joined to a second, more fundamental pole. Indeed, so fundamental is this second pole that it is not to be understood as being simply opposite the first, to which it remains joined, but as belonging to a *different level*. At this ontological level, language is of an order completely different from that of the useful instrument that rhetoric exploited so well as a means of manipulation and power. Now, this power of words, so easily mystifying, gives evidence that language is capable of seizing us — *of trapping us*. Such a power shows that language is not a mere attribute of human nature. The metaphysics of the "animal having language" (*zoon logon echon*) or of the "rational animal" (*animal rationale*) is also to be

37. Ibid., 212.
38. Ibid., 22–23.

reviewed. Humans do not possess language; rather, they are possessed by it. *They speak only because they are always-already spoken;* and humans are human only "to the extent that they are those who speak."

That is why, continues Heidegger, "we speak when awake, we speak in our dreams. We speak continually, even when we are uttering no word and are only listening or reading; we speak even when, no longer really listening or reading, we immerse ourselves in work or give up and simply decide to do nothing."[39] This clearly shows that humans and language are inseparable. At the same time, this shows that it is impossible to treat language as "a simple instrument" which human beings, supposedly existing before it, would have created, just as they fabricated the spear or wheelbarrow for their own convenience. On the contrary, it is only in language — itself the voice of Being — that humans come into being. It is only within this matrix, that of a universe always-already spoken into a "world" before they arrive, that each subject comes to be. And it is this "word," this "Saying" (*Sage*), that continually speaks itself across all our pronouncements through the interpretation made by discourse.[40] It is this which permits the falling snow and the evening bell to come-to-presence for us in the poem.

The *poem*, moreover, only shows what is "at play" in all language, even banal everyday talk: "True poetry is not just a more elevated mode of everyday speech. On the contrary, it is *everyday speech* which is a forgotten poem, a poem *exhausted by its overuse*, whose summons is now barely audible."[41] The poetic metaphor — one ought to say "poietic" because it is a question of a word-action, a word which "makes" (*poiein*) the world — is not a sort of sickly excrescence on the healthy stock of language, as if its essence were the univocal designation of the real; no, such poetic metaphor is what brings language closest to its ultimate source: "Poetry," writes G. Bachelard, "casts language into a state of emergence."[42] Poetry is the human vocation. Human beings are

39. Ibid., 13.
40. Ibid., 133.
41. Ibid., 34-35.
42. G. Bachelard, *La poétique de l'espace*, 10 (quoted by P. Ricœur, *De l'interprétation: Essai sur Freud* (Paris: Seuil, 1965) 24-25.

essentially penetrated by a speech which constitutes them and is the speech of Being. They have to respond, to co-respond, to this call of Being — a call always ahead, beckoning them — to be attentive to its "silent voice" which puts them to the test. To become human is to learn to speak well, not in the sense of speaking well according to grammatical or aesthetic norms — this would be to remain shut within the value system — but in the sense of *letting oneself be spoken,* which "exacts much less a hasty expression than an appropriate silence."[43] Speaking is first of all *listening:* "mortals speak to the extent that they listen," and thus to the extent that they answer this "speaking word" which is always ahead, beckoning them.[44] Thus is brought about, within language itself, the coming-to-presence of what is summoned. This presence is not at all the simple factuality of "what lies before our eyes," therefore, not this frozen metaphysical presence of a subsisting entity, even if counterbalanced by an absence that one somehow represents dialectically, as, for instance, the relation of one side of a coin to the other. Rather, it is a true *"coming-to-presence,"* that is, a presence whose very essence is the "coming," the advent, and which is *thus essentially marked by the stroke of absence.* In sum, a signifying presence, a "human" presence. A presence which does not erase "the dawn-like trace of the difference," which "melts away as soon as presence is conceived as present-entity, and finds its provenance in a supreme present-entity."[45] Presence-as-trace; trace of a passing always-already past; trace thus of something absent. But still trace, that is, the sign of a happening which calls us to be attentive to something new still to come.

5. *"To Hold Ourselves in a Mature Proximity to Absence":*
Discourse on Grace

Such a meditation on language leads the thinker close to the poet. What we must think about from now on is the very thing the poet tries to name, that is, what attracts only as it withdraws: "What withdraws is present, and specifically in such a way that it

43. Heidegger, *Lettre, Q.* 3, 122.
44. Heidegger, *Acheminement,* 36.
45. Heidegger, "Pourquoi des poètes?" *Chemins,* 382.

attracts us."[46] That is why Heidegger has frequently brought poetry and thought together; although dwelling "on the mountains most distant from one another" — for one "speaks Being" while the other "names the sacred" — still they both "devote themselves to the service of language and spend themselves for it."[47]

It is from Hölderlin, the poet of the sacred, that Heidegger learned to think about our relation to the "absence of god." Obviously, this god of the living experience of the sacred can in no way be confused with that of traditional onto-theology — the First Cause, the Ultimate Foundation, the Supreme Entity placed on the summit of the hierarchy of entities. "Before this *Causa sui* humans can neither fall to their knees in fear, nor play instruments, sing, or dance." This, he explains, is why "atheistic thought, because it feels itself constrained to abandon the God of the philosophers — God as the *Causa sui* — is perhaps closer to the divine God. But this means that such a line of thought is more open to God than onto-theo-logic would like to admit."[48]

In opposing this "customary god" whose triumph has been assured by the onto-theology whose power Christianity has secured — simultaneously contributing to the "de-divinization" (*Ent-götterung*) and distress of present times — Heidegger does not mean either to opt for atheism[49] or to advocate an attitude of indifference toward the question of God, as if it were devoid of meaning. Rather, in view of the multiple manipulations to which the name of God has been subjected (and still is), he prefers to observe a respectful silence.[50] For "who is the god? Perhaps this question is too difficult for humans and posed prematurely."[51]

---

46. Heidegger, *Que veut dire*, EC, 159.

47. Heidegger, *Qu'est-ce que la philosophie?*, Q. 2, 37; "*L'homme habite en poète*," EC, 231; Postscript to *Qu'est-ce que la métaphysique?*, Q. 1, 83; *Acheminement*, 42.

48. Heidegger, *Identité*, Q. 1, 306.

49. Unless he does it like Levinas (*Autrement qu'être*, 30), who understands "atheism" as "a position anterior to both the negation and the affirmation of the divine," since the point at issue is the affirmation of the absolute autonomy of the Self — simultaneously both fuly independent and fully responsible — in conflict with any idea of the "participation" of this Self in whatever Principle (the One, Being, History, the Divine . . .).

50. Heidegger, *Identité*, Q. 1, 289.

51. Heidegger, "*L'homme habite en poète*," EC, 239.

It is only through the sense of "the truth of being" (which is not God), a sense which itself opens to "the essence of the sacred,"[52] that humans can let "the experience of the god and of the god's manifestation arise."[53] Now, this sense of the truth of being comes to humans in the simplest and most ordinary occurrences, "wherever humans open their eyes and ears, unbar their hearts, give themselves to the thought and consideration of a goal, ask for grace and give thanks,"[54] that is, wherever the empirical and utilitarian factuality of entities begins to crack open to let these entities appear as the play and gift of being, wherever an attitude of listening to the gift of the presence and a sense of human poverty and mortality are simultaneously born or reborn in humans. Wherever human beings have lost this taste for the gratuitousness of things, this sense of the basic dimension of things, which inspires humans with respect, there they close themselves in against all possibility of a bursting forth of salvation. "Perhaps the dominant trait of our stage of the world consists in the failure of our awareness of being uninjured (that is to say, 'saved')."[55]

Against the invading objectification of things by representation, calculation, and planning, the poet is the one who reminds us of the *Openness of being* in which we must maintain ourselves; thereby the poet opens us to the *Sacred*, which is the space of the play of being and of the risk of openness, where the gods may come near us. Thus, the poet brings to mortals "the trace of the gods who have fled into the opacity of the night of the world."[56] By doing this, the poet reveals the human vocation, continually forgotten: to hold oneself ready, to be constantly "on watch" in order to reserve a space for the possible arrival of the god, in a gracious attitude of letting be the gratuitousness of being and of letting oneself be spoken by it. There is, in Heidegger, a *discourse of grace* (in the deliberately ambiguous senses of "by grace" and "about grace"), which seems to sum up for us his entire approach. For Being, without either measure or calculation, without explanation or justification ("The rose is without a 'why?' It

52. Ibid., 133-134.
53. Heidegger's answer to a student on June 11, 1951. Translated by J. Greisch. Quoted in *Heidegger et la question de Dieu* (Grasset, 1980), 334.
54. Heidegger, *La Question de la technique, EC*, 25.
55. Heidegger, *Lettre, Q. 3*, 134. The "uninjured" is the "safe" (saved) — *das Heile* — in opposition to the "damned" — *das Unheil*.
56. Heidegger, "Pourquoi des poètes?" *Chemins*, 383-384.

blooms because it blooms"[57]) is pure grace, pure gift. More precisely: it is pure donation of "the given which gives only its donation but which, in thus giving itself, holds itself back and eludes us." This movement of donation can only be welcomed graciously in an attitude of "letting-enter-into-presence," where the accent falls not on the presence itself but on the letting as *"letting* the coming-into-presence."[58] The "event" (*Ereignis*) we must think about is precisely this "appropriation" (*er-eignen*) of what is freely given, which can come about only through an attitude of graciousness and "disappropriation" (*Ent-eignung*): "To the appropriation-*Ereignis* as such belongs the disappropriation."[59] The human mode of the *appropriation* of Being as play and grace is through the *disappropriation*, that is, the *Gelassenheit*. Charged with attending to the "revealableness" of Being by carrying it into language, the poet, allowing the word to speak, is touched by grace.

But how can *thinkers* express this event in their own way without destroying it by a "logical" approach that is disrespectful and finally impious? They must, in their turn, break habitual language in order to denounce, in their very speech, its calcified representations. This is what Heidegger does; he is not motivated by the desire to sound esoteric but by the necessity to show respect for the mystery of Being. Finally, it is necessary for thinkers to say something like this: "The poeticizing word is being-present close to . . . and for the god. Presence suggests: simple being-ready, wanting nothing, not counting on success. Being present close to . . . [suggests]: unalloyed letting the present of the god speak itself."[60]

Such an attitude requires constant vigilance, inasmuch as it must *convert our desire to master things* through an explaining science or a calculating will — to which the God of onto-theology is precisely the secret key. A thinking which abandons this God is perhaps more open to the "divine God" than one would normally believe (see above); it is the thinking which experiences the present ab-

---

57. Commentary on this maxim of Angelius Silesius in *Le principe de raison* (Gallimard, 1962), ch. 5, pp. 97–111.
58. Heidegger, *Q.* 4, 299–300.
59. Heidegger, *Temps et Etre, Q.* 4, 45.
60. Heidegger, *Débat sur le kantisme et la philosophie* (Beauchesne, 1972), 136.

sence of the gods. But "this absence is not nothing; it is the presence of the hidden plenitude of what . . . is" and what the Greeks, the Hebrew prophets, and Jesus named "the divine." It bears a "no more" which in itself is a "not yet," the "not yet" of the "hidden coming of its inexhaustible being."[61] The question of God can thus be thought about only by starting from this "*absence of the god*" which is "*not a deficiency*," as Hölderlin suggests.[62] Thought must here make a new path for itself, which "is at best a country path, one which not only speaks of renunciation but has already *renounced* the pretensions of a doctrine claiming authority or of a worthy cultural work or of a great achievement of the spirit."[63] Finally, what we must do is attempt to consider "the concern of the poet," which is this: "To be without fear before the apparent absence of the god, not to run away but, starting from this relation to the absent god, remain *in a mature proximity to the absence* long enough to safeguard the word which at the beginning names the High One."[64]

The *theism* of the customary god of onto-theology is obviously disqualified; this applies even to the "learned unknowing" of negative theologies.[65] The *atheism* of the death of God, which is just another way of masking the absence of God, is equally disqualified. Last, any *indifferentism*, which is a comfortable refuge against unacknowledged anguish, is disqualified. These are three forms of nihilism where "the presence of the absence is lost,"[66] three forms of the *death of the absence* of God. But the thinking on the question of God comes alive only insofar as it consents to the "distress" of this absence. In its role as "shepherd of Being" (and not "rulers of entities"),[67] humankind has the vocation to remain vigilant against the myriad ruses which would rob it of a *distress* it is only too eager to cast off. But such an "absence of distress is itself the supreme distress and the most hidden. . . . The absence

61. Heidegger, Postscript to *La chose*, EC, 220.
62. Heidegger, *Approche de Hölderlin* (Paris: Gallimard, 1962) 34.
63. Heidegger, EC, 221 (n. 61 above).
64. Heidegger, *Approche de Hölderlin*, 34.
65. Cf. J. Greisch, "La contrée de la sérénité et l'horizon de l'espérance," *Heidegger et la question de Dieu*, 184.
66. Heidegger, *Approche de Hölderlin*, 34.
67. Heidegger, *Lettre*, Q. 3.

of distress consists in this: one imagines that one has reality well in hand and that one knows what is true, without needing to know where truth resides."[68] Against this supreme distress — which is the lack of distress — the absence of the god, by maintaining the distress in which humans can live and the god can come forth, is "not a deficiency." Emptiness is not nothing; *the absence is precisely the place from which humans can come to their truth* by overcoming all the barriers of objectifying and calculating reason. This task is burdensome. Is there anything more difficult than to hold oneself in such a "mature proximity to the absence of the god," than *to agree to this "presence of absence"*? Moreover, this is a test that we do not choose for ourselves, embarked as we are on life, because the God whose absence we let die revives this absence within us as an excruciatingly painful wound.

II. THEOLOGY AND PHILOSOPHY

The itinerary of overcoming metaphysics, several of whose major moments we have just recalled in the thought of Heidegger, engages our theological interest. And yet, serious questions remain to be addressed. Notably this one, which is absolutely basic: Is it possible to situate a theology in the perspective of this thinking without "recovering" it and, finally, without betraying it in its most essential aspect?

1. *Philosophy and Theology According to Heidegger*

Heidegger's principal texts devoted to the question of God were gathered as an appendix to a work which appeared in 1980 entitled *Heidegger et la question de Dieu*.[69] The leitmotiv emerges clearly: Heidegger's Being is not God. As for the connection between philosophy as the thinking on Being and theology as the science of faith, Heidegger has never substantially wavered from his initial position of 1927: there can be no passage from one to the other.

Faith and thought therefore constitute *two irreducible worlds*. They even oppose one another as the wisdom of God and the folly of human beings. To have them encounter one another, whether for reconciliation or combat, is inevitably to reduce both to an ideol-

68. Heidegger, *Dépassement, EC,* 104.
69. N. 53 above.

ogy; just as any thinking which would attempt to make itself a "Christian philosophy" would be doomed, so any theology which would base itself on a philosophy would corrupt itself into an ideology of "the Christian view of the world." Its "God" would inevitably become (again) a "Supreme Value," losing "everything it has of the holy and sublime" and "falling to the level of a cause;"[70] such a God, once again "provable," would be "hardly divine," and the proof of this God's existence would lead to, "at most, a blasphemy."[71] Now, "believers and their theologians" are themselves the instigators of "this last blow struck against God" by scaling God down again, as "the entity of entities," to the level of a "supreme value." They have thereby set up a way of thinking and a language which, "viewed from the Faith, are the supreme instance of a blasphemy, once they are mixed with the theology of Faith."[72] For faith is unfaithful to faith when it thus flirts with philosophical ontology: "If I ever wrote a theology, something I am on occasion tempted to do, the expression 'being' should not appear there. Faith has no need of the thinking about being. When it does need it, it is no longer faith. Luther understood this. But today even his own Church seems to have forgotten it."[73] Thus, it is "exclusively within the bounds of revelation" that the theologian should stay.[74] This seems to have been the position of Heidegger to the end. Let the attentive reader take note.

2. Questions

But can one accept without question this understanding of the relation of thought to faith, of philosophy to theology? "Why reflect only on Hölderlin and not on the Psalms, on Jeremiah? This is my question," writes Paul Ricœur, at times "astounded" that Heidegger "seems to have systematically avoided any confrontation with the ensemble of Hebraic thought . . . which is totally foreign to Greek discourse."[75]

70. Heidegger, *La question de la technique, EC,* 35.
71. Heidegger, *Nietzsche,* 1:286.
72. Heidegger, "Le mot de Nietszche," *Chemins,* 313–314.
73. J. Beaufret, *Dialogue avec M. Heidegger* (Minuit, 1973), 334.
74. Ibid., 335–336.
75. P. Ricœur, Introductory Note to *Heidegger et la question de Dieu,* 17; *La métaphore vive* (Paris: Seuil, 1975) 397.

And above all, is such a separation between the world of thought and that of faith tenable? Why does it happen, asks G. Morel among others, that religious revelation, which is only "a particular case compared to the philosophical revelation," is never subjected by Heidegger to the same "radical and universal questioning" as is the thinking on Being?[76] Inversely, does not a theology closed within the circle which goes from faith to faith without ever venturing outside the "exclusivism of revelation," lest it "pervert itself," have a strong fideistic cast? Is there not here in any case, Morel again asks, a "strong contempt for theology," perhaps connected with an unacknowledged bad conscience, in the desire to enclose theology, under the pretext of respectfully safeguarding its otherness, in a *closed circularity?*[77] At the very least, there is a misapprehension here. And one finally understands why Heidegger, even if he was "sometimes tempted" to write a theology (see above), never got around to it . . .

a) The Theological Act: A Witness; Theology: A Hermeneutics. For us, however, the thinking on Being seems to open a path for theology. Not that we feel authorized to "baptize" the Heideggerian Being; it is something entirely different.

Is not Christian faith, as much as philosophy (although by a different path), a form of "madness"? Heidegger does recognize that if it is to be more than merely a "psychological crutch," faith "must expose itself constantly to the possibility of falling into unbelief" (see above). But the costs of such a risk cannot be calculated in advance, at least when theology is what it should be, that is, a *theological act.* At this point, theologians are not outside their work; rather, they make spectacles of themselves, they ex-pose themselves, they take risks, since they are required by their profession not to demonstrate anything by a calculating knowledge but to *give witness to that in which they know themselves to be already held.* If it is truly a witness that they bear, a witness demanding that they be receptive to both past tradition and contemporary culture and express themselves in the first person, with all the risks and perils this involves, then their "work" cannot be

76. G. Morel, *Questions d'homme: L'autre* (Aubier, 1977) 2:278.
77. Ibid., 61.

reduced to a science that seeks to explain everything, to ultimately respond to a "why?" — in short, to justify the world in order to justify their being in the world and inhabiting it as believing subjects. There certainly is a need for knowledge in theology as well as in philosophy, beginning with the "scientific" knowledge concerning the tradition. All the better if such knowledge is immense . . . But theology, as the theological act, begins with the abandonment of this knowledge *as* knowledge or these themes as themes. It begins when all of that opens to theologians a "country" for a "path of thinking" *which they themselves are* in their relationships with God and with others, relationships lived out in the Church. Is the *attitude* of those who attempt to think thus about their faith very different from that of those who try to think about the truth of Being?

Of course, some will say, but nonetheless you believe in God from the beginning. Now, "those who stand on the ground of such a faith may most certainly in some fashion follow the line of our questioning and participate in it; but they are not able to question authentically without denying themselves as believers, with all the consequences of such an act. They can only "go through the motions."[78] But *what kind of God* are we speaking about? Is the job of theology to strengthen the idea of "God" — in which case theology would be forever condemned to what Heidegger calls "onto-theology"? Or is it of another order? For if it is true, as we will argue, that in Jesus Christ God has revealed God's self as essentially human in God's divinity, then the faith-inspired understanding that one should develop in God's regard is never separable from our humanity where God continues to "take on flesh"; in other words, this "humanity" of the divine God *requires us* to be the place where it fulfills itself. It is impossible to "grasp" such a God, without being "grasped" there. Thus, in Christian theology, the question *"Who is God?"* cannot be separated from the question *"Who is it who speaks of this God?"* Thus, the question of God fundamentally belongs to a hermeneutical theology.

But what is the state today of such a hermeneutical theology? We know what criticisms have been recently directed against her-

78. Heidegger, *Introduction à la métaphysique*, 19.

meneutics by the "critical theory of ideologies" inspired by J. Habermas, by the theory of the "text" and the "reading" originating in structuralist circles and, more radically perhaps, in the "grammatology" of J. Derrida.[79] We are also aware of Ricœur's efforts to challenge these attacks. He has been able to do this, however, only by renewing the manner of posing the problem inherited from W. Dilthey, still visible in the work of H. G. Gadamer. This renewal has been so significant that one may speak of a "dislodgment of humanity from the center of a false subjectivity or of a renunciation of self consciousness." Because of this, adds C. Geffré, "those for whom the very word 'hermeneutics' has become a taboo should take note of this development, and not be too prompt to criticize a 'hermeneutics' always marked by the primacy of the subject, whether of a metaphysical or transcendental variety."[80]

For if, on the one hand, Ricœur refuses a reductionist structuralism which ends up diffusing meaning in the regulated "play" of differences between signifiers, on the other, he equally refuses an uncritical, romantic psychologizing hermeneutics according to which readers pretend to "think themselves back" so as to become contemporary with the author's intention and thus restore the original meaning or separate from a variety of languages a single, identical meaning. There simply is no ready-made truth lying "beneath" the text. That is why hermeneutics must give up the ambition of reaching the author's intention. From this viewpoint, hermeneutics returns to what is certainly the most fundamental requirement of the semiotic theory of the text and the reading.

It rejoins this requirement, without however identifying itself with it. For if there is no pre-given meaning to be discovered behind the text, neither is there the simple emergence of whatever effects are permitted by the structure and mechanisms operating within the text. "What there is to interpret in a text is a *proposal of a world*, of a world I might inhabit in order to project, among my myriad possibilities, the one that is most my own."[81] The *world of the text*, this world which the text proposes as possible, corresponds neither to the structure of the text nor to the intention of

79. We build upon the work of C. Geffré, *Le christianisme au risque de l'interprétation* (Paris: Cerf, 1983) ch. 2, "L'herméneutique en procès," 33–64. On Derrida, see ch. 4, n. 41.

80. Geffré, *Le christianisme*, 50.

81. We rely essentially here on F. Bovon and G. Rouiller, eds., *Exegesis: Problèmes de méthode et exercices de lecture*, Bibl. Théol. (Neuchâtel-Paris:

its author; it is rather that which the text, as a "work," unfolds before the reader as a possibility. "What in the last analysis I appropriate is a proposal for a world; this proposal is not *behind* the text, as a hidden intention would be, but rather *before* the text, as that which the work unfolds, uncovers, reveals. To understand is to come to understand oneself before the text."[82]

The text is a "work." But the work is what it is — and what it renders possible — only because it is a text, a text constructed according to the articulations that structural analysis sets into relief, and also according to an irrefutable historicity. There is no such thing as the meaning of a work apart from this "letter" of the text in the positivity of its structural articulations and inalienable historical otherness. In fact, it is just this *otherness* that creates potentialities, new possibilities for structuring the world.[83]

Thus, structural analysis, the critical theory of ideologies, and grammatology have all forced hermeneutics to respect this necessary mediation of the "letter" and to give up the traditional dualism between "comprehension" and "explication." "From now on," writes Ricœur, "*explication* is the obligatory route for *comprehension.*"[84] The same holds true for the distinction between a "positive" and a "speculative" theology: all empirical data — including, of course, the Scriptures — are already "constructed." The Christian text is constituted by the very history of its interpretations, and the history of Christianity is to be treated as a "text."

When understood in this way, hermeneutics has nothing to do with a "nostalgia for an origin identified with the plenitude of being and

---

Delachaux-Niestlé, 1975). Ricœur has contributed three important chapters: In "La tâche de l'herméneutique" (pp. 179–200), he retraces the history of hermeneutics in F. Schleiermacher, W. Dilthey, the early Heidegger (*L'être et le temps*), and H. G. Gadamer (*Vérité et méthode*, Seuil, 1976), and shows the necessity of renewing the hermeneutical approach of these thinkers. The major moments in this task of renewal are uncovered in "La fonction herméneutique de la distanciation," expecially around the notions of "discourse," "work," and the "world of the text" (pp. 201–215). The principles of philosophical hermeneutics set forth in the second chapter are applied to biblical exegesis in the third, "Herméneutique philosophique et herméneutique biblique" (pp. 216–228). The quotation is taken from p. 213.

82. Ibid., 214.

83. On the power-to-be and the possible, see especially R. Kearney, *Poétique du possible: Phénoménologie herméneutique de la figuration* (Beauchesne, 1984).

84. Ricœur, "La fonction herméneutique," 209.

truth'' which seems to be ''the secret motivation of onto-theological thinking,'' a motivation triggered by ''the megalomaniacal desire of a humankind denying its own finitude.''[85] In its role as hermeneutics, theology has the job, not of retrieving an original meaning but, on the contrary, of *producing*, starting especially from the text of the Scriptures, *new texts*, that is, new practices which *foster* the emergence of a new world. Its truth is always to be made; it resides in a future constantly happening. ''Thus, the Christian truth is not,'' Geffré emphasizes, ''an invariant core that is passed on from century to century in the form of a frozen deposit. It resides in a continual *advent* exposed to the risks of history and of the Church's interpretative freedom under the Spirit's inspiration. In regard to the content of the faith, it is manifestly inadequate to always speak of a rapport between some invariant core and variable cultural expressions. One must guard against the illusion of a semantic *invariability* which somehow subsists beyond all contingencies of expression; to believe this is to retain an instrumental and vehicular conception of language. Rather, one must speak of a *relation of relations*.''[86]

Accordingly, the well-known hermeneutical circle is not an abstraction outside time; it is the circle of life itself, in all its historicity, corporality, and mortality. The question ''Who is God?'' must then be posed in a *concrete* manner, and not starting from the generic onto-theological concepts of ''nature'' and ''person.'' That is to say it takes flesh for us not by descending from the theologies of the hypostatic union but rather by rising from the languages of the New Testament witnesses, which are historically and culturally situated. Certainly, we must begin with the language of the *cross* because it is in the One whom human beings reduced to less than nothing in his humanity that Paul was able to recognize para-doxically the indirect revelation (''para'') of the glory (''doxa'') of God: a ''madness'' from which ''the power of God'' breaks forth (1 Cor 1).

b) The Logos *of the Cross, between Jews and Greeks.* Heidegger refers to chapter 1 of the First Letter to the Corinthians, where Paul describes the ''wisdom of the world'' as a ''folly'' in the eyes

85. Geffré, *Le christianisme*, 81.
86. Ibid., 87.

of God; then he asks, "Will not Christian theology finally resolve to take seriously the Apostle's words and, as a consequence, to consider philosophy as a folly?"[87] But for Paul, if *the* Logos *of the cross* is "foolishness to Gentiles," it is also "a stumbling block to Jews" (1 Cor 1:23). This *Logos* is thus *neither Jewish nor Greek*. Following S. Breton here, we shall say that it can satisfy neither of the two major models of religious consciousness as Paul conceives it: neither the Greeks' wisdom, motivated by the principle of *reason* and the search for causes, nor the Jews' demand for signs, motivated by the principle of God's good *will*. In the Word of the Cross two excesses thus coincide: "the 'beyond' of thought is also the 'beyond' of will and self-will."[88] Let us explain more fully.

Thomistic exegesis, of course, rejects the possibility of measuring faith according to the standards of reason; but "reason" as the basis for faith, not as its support, is challenged here. In the end, this "humiliation, far from crushing reason, makes it, through the audacity of a transgression, step across the threshold of its own house" (p. 28). This is so much the case that *analogy* can reconcile Jews and Greeks and "interpret the energetic negation of Paul as preeminence. At bottom, the folly of God is only the excess of a 'super-wisdom' " (p. 29). At the other extreme, the *Bultmannian* exegesis interprets the "incomprehensibility" of God only at the level of personal existence, and no longer at the level of theoretical thought. If it interprets the negation of the cross as the radical negation of the *Logos,* it has "nothing specific to say concerning the break with Judaism" (p. 47). But to reject a "God-as-object" or "super-object" only to replace it with a "God-as-existence" or an "Absolute Thou" is not to escape the sphere of oppositions; it is to favor one or the other of the terms and not to see that the paradox of the Cross demands that we overcome the two alternatives. For "the Cross opens up another space, an elsewhere which cannot be expressed in either of these languages, even if we are condemned to speak them by turns" (p. 47).

How, then, can we think about the message of the cross, this "thing that the cross pro-poses," concretely: "the God who reveals God's self in Christ crucified" (p. 78) and who is other than the kerygmatic or theological representations of God, out of which, however, we cannot extract God like a gemstone from its matrix? Must we conceive of God in the same vein as the "Uncreated Nothingness" of the negative theologies?

87. Heidegger, *Introduction à la métaphysique,* 19.
88. S. Breton, *Le verbe et la croix* (Paris: Desclée, 1981) 9. The references between parentheses on the following pages refer to this work.

But "Paul's theology is of a completely different order" (p. 109). It "takes exception to any theology inspired by the ontology of transcendentals . . . in order to mark the 'most real being' of religions and philosophies with the sign of contradiction" (p. 110). It does not aim at "the elaboration of new divine attributes reversing the former ones" but rather "at the necessity of a *mutation of attitude*" (p. 116) in the direction of "a critical vigilance which makes language supple so that we may no longer fall victim to its traps" (p. 114) and which distances itself by changing levels. For the one thing on which Paul insists "is the impossibility of saying, in one or the other of the language-objects at our disposal (Hebrew or Greek, for example), the *'Thing'* his heart is set on" (p. 116). However, it is precisely this impossibility which is shown, in speech, by the effort of stepping back in order to choose "the least inadequate expression." And it is in this humble stripping away of a language always on the point of self-destructing that the *trace* of "the liberating presence of the very thing we sought" is disclosed (p. 114).

If from its very origin this message of the language of the cross, which is also "the cross of language" (p. 48), necessarily demands to be set forth in discourses, it nevertheless exercises a "critical function" that "converts the work of necessity into liberty" (p. 120). In the middle of the "inevitable drifting" that, in these discourses, ends by making into "constituents of another world" what are in fact only determinations of "this world," the cross reminds us that what is expressed here is *less what God is than the "history of our attitudes" and of the becoming "through which" we say God* (p. 119).

Paul's kerygmatic language is no exception to this law, even when he attempts to say things which constantly subvert it. Thus, coming from "the conditions of his milieu," a certain "mode of thinking" is imposed on him which, because of the "mental attitudes of the age," manifests itself in the "dominating image of the dominator." It is precisely this representation of God that he seeks to overturn by the counter-image of the *slave* (pp. 148–149). The kenotic hymn in Philippians (2:5–11) has itself been the object of two opposite kinds of inadequate exegesis. The first one, following the most common patristic and medieval tradition, considered any change in God so blasphemous that only the *human* nature of Christ was subject to kenosis (the doctrine of the "interchange of the properties" [*communicatio idiomatum*] came as a logical corrective to this thesis, to justify that "one person of the Trinity suffered"). Further, when we say that "God touched us," the relation is real (from our side); but it can be only metaphorical when we say that God is touched by us. Therefore, such a theology "remains faithful to the extreme limit of onto-theology — I want to say, of a metaphysics of being, understood as containing, in its eminence and in its eternal immobility, the infinite integrality of infinite perfections'' (p. 137).

The second kind of exegesis, proper to some more recent theologies stressing the "becoming" of God, seems to err in the other direction. In place of the unchangeable "omniperfection" which would isolate God in "a transcendence of egoism" and thus deprive him of his most attractive attribute — Love, which never comes without suffering (p. 138) — this substitutes the "sublime theater" of the kenosis of God in Jesus. This is an emptying by free will, but at the same time necessary; God is not free to not be free. Thus, the "kenotic drama" of sacrifice leaves untouched in the end the prestige of the divine essence: such a free willing to love, giving up all claim to possession, seems redolent of "the Plotinian formula according to which the One, in its capacity as 'cause of itself,' makes itself what it wishes to be" (pp. 140-141). It is still an "eminent self" which presides at this willing to will (p. 169). Thus, these theologians who stress the suffering of God are, in the last analysis, moving on the same ground as the preceding group — whereas, "the real issue, from the beginning, should have been to find another space" (p. 149).

Another space: because, in elevating "the figure of the *Doulos* ['slave'] to the dignity of an absolute," Paul renders "the very idea of a divine SELF" outmoded — if it is true that the slave, no longer existing either for him- or herself or by him- or herself, has no more being than to "have no being at all." As a consequence, to conceive "true 'becoming' " is not to detach the divine kenosis from that which is carried out in *us*, as the introductory verse of the hymn suggests: "Let the same mind be in you that was in Christ Jesus, who . . ." (Phil 2:5). It is our "soul" itself which, "in expelling from itself the glories that it used to offer to the Most High, undergoes a diminishment that conforms it to 'the form of a slave' in order that it may realize its strength" (pp. 151-152). Thus, the cross-founded message of Paul touches us to the quick — to the quick of our desire, urged to conversion. The theological message can find no way to "say" itself *outside of our being grasped by it*. It is our *corporality* which has the responsibility of becoming the very place for this message. Theological discourse, as we said above, is a *theologoical act*, a witness where we can take nothing without recognizing ourselves as being taken.

However, Paul's crucified Word is conjugated together with John's "Word of Glory" which, while belonging to biblical Judaism, also contains an indisputable "Hellenic coloring" (p. 166). In any case, "from the very beginning, Christianity was forced to speak *Greek and Hebrew*" (p. 171). In spite of Paul's double "No," Christianity was very soon "led into more or less conjunctive compromises" between the two (p. 170). Such was *inevitable*, to the extent that the credibility of the message exacted an apologetic reading of an innovating present by projecting it into a past that somehow "prefigured" it and where the old covenant was called upon to step aside in favor of the new. One sees that it was impossible from the start not to reclothe the "naked god" on the cross and thus to refrain from "bestowing on him the existence that he did not have." At the same time, moreover, the cross does not dispense us from this "very human necessity." It does not demand that we take leave of our world but rather that we no longer remain prisoners within it: the Johannine Logos teaches us "that the faith, in its very faithfulness, pronounces its word of intelligence" in a kind of "determining judgment," while the Pauline *logos*, in a "reflecting judgment," "pronounces a judgment on the chain of determinations that reduces their pretention to eternity without removing their service" (p. 181). Here is a difficult balance between archeo-logy and an-archy . . .

This kind of equilibrium does not represent a compromise of the two extremes in order to reach some sort of mean. If theology cannot express the message of the cross, it must nevertheless begin its thinking with that message. This *empty place*, this void somehow omnipresent, continually requires theology to take a step backwards, a step which both disenthralls it from itself and reopens it. In fact, this leap is not only or even most basically a simple intellectual criticism of our permanent condition as image-makers; it is *ourselves, in our corporality, that it involves*, as we indicated above. The most sophisticated subversion of our theological categories would still be idolatry if this were not part of a conversion of our desire and ethical practice. The cross cannot cast its shadow on the creations of our mind unless it simultaneously extends itself over the work of our hands. That is what we mean by a theological act, if it is authentically a *discourse that witnesses*. This is why, Breton emphasizes, "the God who exceeds all forms of being, of wisdom, and of power . . . solicits from us this body of world and humanity, without which God cannot come among us in *truth*. It is precisely because God is nothing of what is, that God must *become*. Further, the path of this 'becoming' goes necessarily by way of the faces of others . . . 'I was hungry, and you gave me to eat' (Matt 25:31–46). . . . What a bizarre condition for this god, who seems to obtain a Self only by the help of these little ones, 'the least' who do not really exist and whose essence seems to consist solely in the possibility of being such a face. The one who is most distant, could that one also be the one who is closest?'' (pp. 190–191).

c) A Homology of Attitude. If such is the theological task, is it not, in its own order, as much a *''folly''* as the *''thinking on being''*? Is not the *''Logos* of the cross,''* J. L. Marion asks of Heidegger, also *''a logos* foreign to onto-theo-logic?''[89] And if there is no passage from Being, even crossed out, to God, even crucified, are not theology and philosophy *homologous,* not in their ''object'' but in their *approach*? In both activities, are we not grasped in the same type of ''gracious'' *attitude* characterized by a *way* which is always ''making its way'' (*er-wëgend*), always transitive, or else by *birth pangs,* a ''per-laboration'' (compare Freud's ''working through'' *Durcharbeitung*), whose fruit is not an object (in this case, a wisdom exterior to us) but *our pro-duction of our own selves as subjects*? This is a labor that involves not only the *eidos* and its representations but also the *eros* and its desire to extend its control over all that is. This amounts to the slow work of apprenticeship in the art of ''un-mastery,'' a permanent work of *mourning* where, *free of resentment,* a ''serene'' consent to the *''presence of the absence''* takes place within us little by little. In gospel terms, this is a work of conversion to the presence of the absence of a God who ''crosses himself out'' in the crushed humanity of this crucified One whom humans have reduced to less than nothing and yet where, in a paradoxical light, faith confesses the glory of God.

The crucified ~~God~~ is not crossed-out ~~Being~~. The kenotic erasure visited upon God by the cross represents less the ''non-entity'' than the *non-other*. The me-ontology indicated here is not of the same order as negative onto-(theo)logy but of the order of *symbolism:* it is in disfiguring Jesus to the point of removing from him all otherness, in reducing him to a non-face, a non-subject, an ''object'' of derision (cf. Isa 52:14), that humans have made of him a *me-on* (''non-being,'' cf. 1 Cor 1:28), which is what Paul expresses culturally under the figure of the slave.

That the non-face of the crucified One be the ''para-doxical'' trace of Divine Glory, that the face of God show itself only by erasing itself, that we think of God less in the metaphysical order of the Unknowable than in the symbolic and historical order of

89. J. L. Marion, *L'idole et la distance* (Grasset, 1977), 37.

the unrecognizable — quite clearly this is the "folly" which theologians attempt to express through their discourse. Here is also manifestly what from the start keeps this discourse from closing in on itself, demands that it struggle upstream from what it has said toward a word that always exceeds it and thus provokes it to a continual *disavowal* in which it compromises itself by a word of witness.

It is thus a question of "holding ourselves in a mature proximity to absence" or, as Levinas puts it, to *"hold ourselves in the trace of the Absent."* To hold oneself there, one must unfold a discourse that keeps permanently alive in itself the wound of an Otherness which, always beyond our grasp, nonetheless leaves its trace in the humble call of the neighbor; a discourse where, as Levinas again writes, "an invisible God signifies not only an unimaginable God but also a God *accessible* through justice."[90] Such is the "hidden God" (*Deus absconditus*) with which Christian theology deals, a study which must also be a "staurology" or "science of the cross": the study of a God whose divinity is effaced in a crushed humanity *to the point of* "requiring of us this body of world and humanity without which God cannot come among us in truth" (see above).

If it is true, as Derrida maintains, that "we live in the difference between Jews and Greeks that is perhaps the unity of what we call history,"[91] then it makes sense for our theological discourse to at least try to "speak God" from the middle of this irreducible difference inscribed in history. A discourse where the Being of the Greek Logos is overlaid by the Other of the Jewish *Dabar* (the "creative word of God," which, contra Levinas, can never be without the first); a discourse where ontology and concept, although unavoidable, are transcended into a symbolism and an ethical practice which nevertheless never exhaust them; a discourse which from the first thinks that research vain which looks for a compromise or for a "middle way" to neutralize the difference between the two. Is this not a "folly"?

If philosophy is, in the words of Breton, "the service of an unavailability that eludes knowledge but yet is indispensable," then is there not between philosophy and theology an "affinity" which

90. E. Levinas, "Totalité et infini," *Autrement qu'être*, 51.
91. J. Derrida, "Violence et métaphysique," *L'écriture et la différence*, 227.

has less to do with their content than with their *attitudes* and consists in their "availability toward an *unavailability* which specifies them both in an original manner?"[92] We agree that this is their connection. And such a *gracious* homology of attitudes is more important than a simple exchange of contents because it involves the very word spoken by the subjects and their respective labors of genesis.

Heidegger never admitted that theology could be the place, in its own order, for such a work. However, is not the Heideggerian consent to deprivation, to patience, to listening, against all forms of closed dogmatism or idolatrous domination — is not this an echo of an "authentic" religious and spiritual experience? Is not such an attitude of "graciousness" the "way" which *also* constitutes theology . . . at least if it is true that theology cannot be disconnected from the *believing subjects* who are required to give place to the crucified God whom they profess and are thus *themselves questioned* in their very act of asking questions about God? Such a theological "way" *cannot* be concretely added to the philosophical "way," as one adds two different numbers. This is because the thinker and the believer are but one subject; and even if one must distinguish the two in speech, one should never forget that it is always the concrete *integrity* of the subject which must eventually be considered. This is precisely what has led us to understand the two approaches or the two attitudes as homologous and thus, without building a foot-bridge between the Heideggerian Being and God, to reject a fundamental divorce between the philosophical and theological ways of thinking.

III. THEOLOGY AND PSYCHOANALYSIS

Overcoming metaphysics, notably as the attempt to surmount the subject-object dichotomy and thus as the recognition of the impossibility of any "taking" without simultaneously being "taken," is characteristic, as we said above, of a certain period in the historical unfolding of Being. Our entire society bears this mark. First of all, there are the sciences themselves, which are the object of an "epistemological revolution" which participates in the

92. S. Breton, "Comment envisager aujourd'hui une recherche philosophique qui tienne compte de la foi?" *Revue de l'Institut Catholique de Paris* 9 (1984) 30–34.

annihilation of the metaphysical way of thinking. As a matter of fact, against the illusions and pretensions of positivism, the so-called *exact sciences* are now seeing themselves as also afflicted with this *"devaluation"* that Heidegger and Levinas (each in his own way) announced. From now on it is impossible, even in this realm, not to recognize that observers themselves are "caught" in what they naively thought to be their self-assigned task: "to catch," in a purely "objective" manner, in a discourse "without a subject" (see below).

But it is certainly within the domain of the *social sciences* that the constant interference of subject with object is most clearly discerned. This is true in sociology, in ethnology, in history; it is true also in linguistics: as J. Kristeva asks, "Since they are inside of it, how can one separate the linguistic reality from what the speaking subjects think of it, from what they know of it?"[93] The same is a fortiori true of *psychoanalysis,* which constitutes the most distinctive symptom of the present time.

1. *The Problematic Status of Psychoanalysis*

How can one make a scientific theory of what not only cannot be reduced to a relation of involvement between an observing subject and an observed object but in the concrete is an *interaction* of one subject *as* a subject with another subject *as* a subject? In this domain, the observable objects (dreams, failed actions, slips of the tongue, rephrasings of speech) become scientific "objects" only in the framework of the therapy itself, that is, in the act where the patient's desire to be cured *intersects* the analyst's desire. Moreover, the analyst-observer, like his or her eventual "observations," belongs equally to the realm of the observable, caught, as he or she is and must be by his or her own desire, in the process of transference, unable to see without being seen and allowing the process of transformation begun in his or her own analysis to go on unceasingly.

Thus, the situation of psychoanalysis is a strange one. It cannot make a science and must not make a philosophy of its obscure specific object (the unconscious), as C. Castoriadis points out;

93. J. Kristeva, "Du sujet en linguistique," *Langages* 24 (1971) 107–125. Quotation on p. 115.

rather, it aims at "a dialectical and *problematic elucidation.*"[94] Dealing with an object which is *"meaning, incarnate meaning, each time a singular* meaning," thus with an irreducible individuality, it cannot, however, function without a science-like *theoretical* formalization, thus without postulating the non-singularity of the singular individual it encounters in the therapy, without postulating, as a consequence, the theoretical reducibility of this singularity whose transformation, by transference, nevertheless proves to be each time a unique case.[95] But for all that, it is not a phenomenology; it cannot be because of its essentially *practical* orientation and its specific object: psychic reality. Even if it attempts to express itself in formulas similar to those of the sciences (the *"mathemes"* of Lacan), analytic discourse nonetheless cannot be a *science* of the unconscious: it would then ignore the *subject* of the unconscious. On the other hand, even if it turns to *philosophical* questioning, it still can never be a speculative knowledge: the subject would no longer be that of the *unconscious.*

In his work *Lacan and Philosophy,* A. Juranville shows clearly this *problematic situation* of analytic discourse. In contrast to "metaphysical discourse," postulating "that there is a total truth" and pretending to bring to that truth an appropriate response, and at the other extreme to "empiricist discourse," postulating "that there is no truth," "philosophical discourse" affirms that there is "total truth and partial truth," while "analytic discourse" declares that "there is only partial truth."[96] But, at the moment when it can articulate only the *partial* truth of the signifier, analytic discourse sees itself led, Lacan asserts, toward the demand for a *total* truth, which it cannot enunciate, however, "without destroying itself as a discourse which sets the therapeutic situation in place and puts it into effect."[97] Without this requisite for total truth (which is not really its mission to pronounce), analytic discourse could not justify the therapeutic goal of the cure through the process of sublimation. Of course, such a process is never achieved. From this point of view, neurosis is "irreducible." At best one can transform it into a "good neurosis"[98] by under-

94. C. Castoriadis, *Les carrefours du labyrinthe,* 58.
95. Ibid., 39.
96. A. Juranville, *Lacan et la philosophie* (Paris: PUF, 1984) 11–16.
97. Ibid., 438.
98. J. Lacan, *Séminaire XXIV* (11/16/76), quoted in Juranville, *Lacan,* 409. On the "good neurosis," see Juranville, *Lacan,* § 62, pp. 428–437.

going (and this is sublimation) the test of "melancholy," that is to say, by learning to consent "to find oneself alone in the ordeal of the real."[99] For the real or the "non-world"[100] is nothing else than what puts the "world" in question, what comes to fracture it — the pure *lack*, whose symptom is the trace in us but which the signifiers constantly rush in to mask by filling up its space.[101] Consequently, "the real is the impossible."[102] And the test of the Oedipus complex is not just the *prohibition* of pleasure but its very *impossibility*. The impossible belongs to the very nature of the "Thing," that is, the primordial object of desire (whose place is currently taken by object *x*).

Under these conditions, one cannot be surprised that analytic discourse tends to point toward philosophical discourse. For, as Juranville asks, is the Lacanian test of melancholy anything but "the presence of the *question about being*, insofar as it remains impossible to resolve?"[103] Such is the paradox of philosophical questioning: it rises from a desire for knowledge — even total knowledge; but contrary to certain suggestions of Lacan, who likens philosophy to metaphysical discourse, that is, to the "teacher's discourse,"[104] this desire becomes the possible place for philosophical questioning only if all knowledge as a response is radically put in doubt and held to be impossible: "The question has value in itself, not for the knowledge to which it might lead but because of the *test of non-knowledge* that it supposes,"[105] a test connected to the fact that the being that is questioned is the "being inasmuch as it is encountered first in the person who is doing the questioning."[106]

Provided it does not lapse into a "psychologism of the depths," psychoanalysis shows by its very history that it is *struggling to give birth to philosophy*. With his themes of Eros ("love"), *Thanatos*

99. Juranville, *Lacan*, 428.

100. Ibid., § 8, pp. 39–41.

101. Ibid., p. 85: "What makes of the real world a world excludes from it the presence of the real as such." P. 192: "It is the fantasm that supports the world both for and by the subject, because it renders the world 'interesting' in rediscovering among its various elements the object *x*."

102. Ibid., 85.

103. Ibid., 439–440.

104. Ibid., 356.

105. Ibid., § 12, pp. 56–59.

106. Ibid., 64.

("death"), and other forms of *Ananke* ("fate"), did not Freud already point analytic discourse toward certain philosophical *boundaries?* Lacan shows this well in the fact that he rejects any "medicalistic" reduction of psychoanalysis and reinterprets the Freudian dynamic by placing it "in the domain of the word." His great concepts of "Truth," the "Other," the "Real," the "Lack," the "Thing" constantly overflow into philosophy. Making the questions of philosophy its own, analytic discourse does not have to treat them in a philosophical way but according to its own methods. That is to say, its responsibility is to uncover the *concrete psychological processes* in which they are *embodied.*

2. Analytic Discourse as a Major Social Symptom
of the Historical Unfolding of the Question of Being

The interest which analytic discourse awakens in us comes precisely from the fact that it gives a *body* to philosophical questioning by connecting it from end to end to these bodies which we are, as we mentioned above with Heidegger, without being able to answer the philosophical questioning on its own ground. Again, following the remarks of Juranville, let us say that if humans have never been unaware of "the presence of the un-thought at the deepest level of thought," from now on, analytic discourse forces this truth upon them in the most radical manner.[107] The fact that such a truth imposes itself is characteristic of a certain historical *period*, that is, of the concrete manner in which the historical unfolding of the question of Being takes place (Heidegger).

Among the diverse periods of history, each of which is marked by a specific existential mode of philosophic thought, the present is characterized by the possibility of successfully enduring the test of melancholy, that is, of "undergoing the presence of the question of being, as a question without solution."[108] To endure the world as "flawed," truth as "partial," knowledge as wanting is not to enter into the end of history (as Hegel interprets it) but to finally end the process of entering into history. Since history's direction is set by the flight from the test of melancholy, the *"end of the entrance of the social world into history"* is at the same time the end of this flight because of the destruction of traditional struc-

107. Ibid., 481.
108. Ibid., 439.

tures.[109] Where tradition imposed the evidence of a know-how for living which prevented a full experience of this bereavement, the contemporary *de-traditionalization*, with its "crisis in sacrifice," obligates each of us to denounce the alibi of the "sacred" and to assume the trial of mourning by taking up our own responsibility within history.[110] In this perspective, the emergence of the "analytic discourse," denouncing the "political discourse" of the ruler and the "learned discourse" of the professor (encouraging an exclusive devotion to the "great masters" of the past), constitutes the *"social symptom"* of the present age.[111] This emergence shows that the time has come when it is possible to renounce this flight from the test of melancholy in order to accept this "loss of mastery" for which philosophical discourse has long fostered the desire but which it has avoided, by a thousand stratagems, carrying to its fulfillment. However, this opportunity is at the same time the drama of our era: neurotic regression becomes more likely as the difficulties of assuming this grief become more clearly visible.

Among the symptoms that "all is not right" in the historical world, analytic discourse gives people the most to think about. Today, it is the most provocative problem and *"the viewpoint from which all the other discourses examine themselves."*[112] Philosophical discourse cannot ignore this "partial truth" the analytic discourse proclaims, just as the latter cannot maintain itself, as we have seen, without aiming at a "total truth" which only philosophy can articulate while it simultaneously assumes the partial truth which analysis imparts. Thus, analytic discourse, with its "partial truth" (that which cannot become part of any system) is the "good symptom" for philosophy, "the symptom whose truth does not plug the hole of the real." But analytic discourse cannot be this without philosophy because the sublimation implied by the analytic work can be understood only with philosophy. Thus, the *conflict* between the two discourses is both *"irreducible"* and *"the condition for the truth"* in each.[113] By the very distance between them, philosophy and psychoanalysis represent the internal contradiction from which arises the human subject.

As a discourse that takes into consideration the human characteristic of being-body — its enfleshed signifiers, its "living words" (*logoi embioi*) — analytic discourse knits together concrete corporality with the philosophical questioning of humans as always *unter-*

109. Ibid., 441.
110. Ibid., § 67, p. 465–469.
111. Ibid., § 68, p. 469–474.
112. Ibid., 471.
113. Ibid., 484.

wegs, always "on the way" toward the word that goes ahead of them. Against all metaphysical escapes, analytic discourse declares that *the* truth does not come to anyone except as *his or her* truth, that is, through the incessant labor of passage through mourning, deprivation, absence. But philosophy reminds analysis that the latter would be an imposture if each of us, in trying to fashion our *own* truth, did not at the same time respond to *the* truth which is always beckoning us.

IV. TOWARD SACRAMENT

Such is our position. The path of theological thought on a crucified God keeps us in an attitude of "folly" that is homologous to the path of philosophical thought on Being, although there is no passage from one to the other. Lacan's theory, which sees psychoanalysis as an attempt at problematic elucidation of its "impossible" object, gives this mode of thought an anthropological density which embodies it in us. For is not the "folly" of such a line of thought finally that of a mourning to be endured, a mourning that pierces through our bodies? It is a "folly" because we must accept the death of the illusion *everything in us desperately wants to believe, that is, the illusion that we can somehow pull ourselves out of the necessary mediation of symbols,* situate ourselves outside of discourse, and apprehend reality directly, without passing through cultural tradition or the history of our own desire — in short, that we can take our "That's self-evident," our "It goes without saying" as reality. *It is precisely these judgments, seemingly so "reasonable," that never cease to delude us.* These supposedly evident data, as an almost inevitable consequence, lead thought to represent Being as "something facing humans which stands by itself"; similarly, they arouse our desire to attain the "Thing" under the many disguises of its substitutes. In regard to these data, we must take the opposite tack, by an unstinting labor, since they belong to the initial proclivity of reason and to the very constitution of desire.

This "path of the word," used by Christian theologians confronted with a crucified God, is thus a path of ongoing genesis — a path that, far from being external to their condition as "witnesses," leads directly through them. It thus *demands* that they give to this Jesus Christ to whom they pledge allegiance a human body: the body of sons and daughters and a body of brothers and sisters.

For, just as this "body of God" in humanity had, within the chosen people, an historical reality in Jesus of Nazareth, it also has a reality — no less scandalous in some respects — in the *Church*. A reality as irreducible to a simple subsisting-entity as is the human body; thus a reality like that of the body which the indwelling word constantly opens up, but also an incontestable reality concretely determined as an institution.

The *sacraments* are the most distinctive representations of this institution. How are we going to avoid stumbling against their scandalously empirical consistency as the symbolic place where God becomes enfleshed in our humanity? What a challenge! Is it not folly? A folly so difficult to sustain that believers are constantly tempted to domesticate it into human wisdom: the sacraments then become the principal means by which the institution serenely displays and thus perversely manipulates (in good faith, by the way — out of habit) the emblems of its legitimacy and social domination. In any case, a "folly" which gives us much to ponder from the theological viewpoint . . .

The sacraments thus force us to confront *mediation* — mediation, *by way of the senses,* of an institution, a formula, a gesture, a material thing — as the (eschatological) place of God's advent. And so, we find ourselves in the end sent back to the *body* as the point where God writes God's self in us . . . This announces the reflection of the next two chapters: "Mediation" (Chapter Three), "Body and Symbol" (Chapter Four).

Mediation

I. THE UNAVOIDABLE MEDIATION
OF THE SYMBOLIC ORDER

1. *No Speech, No Humankind*

"*What is most immediate is the last thing we can express,*" so much so that "the human characteristic is to begin at the end."[1] A conversion is necessary if we are to begin with the "beginning." To begin with the beginning is to question what seems to impose itself upon us with absolute certainty, that we are in contact with the "real" (the world, other people, ourselves).

For, contrary to this initial "it goes without saying," "what appears most natural to us may be only the most habitual of a long habit which has forgotten the non-habitual which is its source."[2] Reality is never present to us except in a mediated way, which is to say, *constructed* out of the symbolic network of the culture which fashions us. This *symbolic order* designates the system of connections between the different elements and levels of a culture (economic, social, political, ideological — ethics, philosophy, religion . . .), a system forming a coherent whole that allows the social group and individuals to orient themselves in space, find their place in time, and in general situate themselves in the world in a

1. E. Ortigues, *Le discours et le symbole* (Aubier-Montaigne, 1962) 13–14.
2. M. Heidegger, *Chemins qui ne mènent nulle part*, French trans. W. Brokmeier (Paris: Gallimard, 1962) 22.

significant way — in short, to find their identity in a world that makes "sense," even if, as C. Lévi-Strauss says, there always remains an inexpungible residue of signifiers to which we can never give adequate meanings.[3]

Between sensation and perception there is a margin: the stone that violently hits the head provokes an identical *sensation* of pain in the animal and in the human being, but the *perception* of the stone is of another order. What is perceived by humans is not only the physical reality that affects the senses but the "semiological layer" in which this event is embedded by the culture. That is why "what perception conveys to me is not directly the tree that is in front of me but *a certain vision* which the tree provokes in me and which is *my response* to the call of the tree."[4] All human perception "projects into the world the signature of a civilization."[5] The water I perceive is never reducible to a purely "natural" thing, unless I perform a chemical analysis on it (and even that is qualified); it is inevitably apprehended to some degree as *expressing* my culture and desire. From the landscape which I take in, I notice only a few aspects — those which elicit a response within me and are relative to the changing forms of my desire and to the values of the socio-cultural system to which I belong, values which I have interiorized to such a degree since infancy that they now appear entirely "natural." *The perceived object is always-already a constructed object*; and that is true in all domains, from sexuality (human sexuality is of a different order from simple biological reproduction) to cooking: eating for us is not simply a matter of absorbing a certain number of calories but of consuming foods that are socially hallowed, so that the meal is the preeminent place for the nourishment of the social body . . .

"[Thus,] apart from the natural sciences (and even there it is not self-evident), linguistic activity is never confronted with a physical universe that is heterogeneous to it but rather with a *world always already filled with signification*, always already ordered, always already socially fitted out."

3. C. Lévi-Strauss, "Introduction à l'œuvre de M. Mauss," in M. Mauss, *Sociologie et anthropologie* (Paris: PUF, 1973) xlix.

4. B. Parain, *Recherches sur la nature et la fonction du langage* (Paris: Gallimard, 1942) 61.

5. M. Merleau-Ponty, *La prose du monde* (Paris: Gallimard, 1969) 60, 97.

Certainly material reality has an existence independent of the awareness human subjects have of it; but it is not with *that* universe that infants are initially confronted; it is rather in a world *inhabited* by other humans that they make their way. . . . The same thing is true for adults: the acts of getting dressed, eating, residing, moving, working, suffering, finding enjoyment — all these plunge us continually into a world filled with symbolic reference points."[6]

There is no emergence of subjects without the *subjugation* of each of them to this *law*, this cultural agreement which is the symbolic order. Apart from that, there are only regression into the imaginary and neurosis because one fixates on bits or fragments of the world, which — now "de-symbolized," that is, torn from the symbolic network within which they take on meaning — become "in-significant." Having lost their direction, subjects are lost as well. It is in the symbolic order that subjects "build" themselves; but they do this only by building the world, something that is possible for them insofar as they have inherited from birth a world already culturally inhabited and socially arranged — in short, a world already spoken. The symbolic order consequently appears as a *set of building blocks.* Just as children learn to build their connection to the real by building houses or machines with Legos or Meccanos, the symbolic order is *the mediation through which subjects build themselves while building the real into a "world,"* their familiar "world" where they can live. Or again, it is similar to contact lenses which cannot be seen by the wearers since they adhere to their eyes but through which all their vision of the real is filtered. Therefore, the real as such is by definition *unreachable.* What we perceive of it is what is constructed by our culture and desire, what is filtered through our linguistic lens. But our perception has become so accustomed to this lens and this lens adheres so tightly to our perception that, almost as a reflex, we take the cultural for the natural and our desires for the real.

What is true for the symbolic order is clearly and in the same way true for language. *Subject and language build themselves up in tandem.* "We never discover humans apart from language, and we never catch them in the act of inventing it. . . . It is always humans speaking that we encounter in the world, always humans

6. F. Flahault, *La parole intermédiaire* (Paris: Seuil, 1978) 84–85.

speaking to other humans; and language gives us the very definition of a human being."[7]

Like the body, language[8] is not an instrument but a *mediation;* it
is *in* language that humans as subjects come to be. Humans do
not preexist language; they are formed in its womb. They do not
possess it like an "attribute," even if of the utmost importance;
they are possessed by it. Thus, language does not arise to translate after the fact a human experience that preceded it; it is *constitutive* of any truly *human* experience, that is to say, significant
experience.

That is why, writes B. Parain, *"no one is silent.* This is our first datum;
we have to begin from this." For, "our words create beings; they are
not content to manifest sensations." When the farmer, occupied in har-
vesting his potatoes, cries out, "Look, a beetle larva!" "the purpose of
his exclamation is not to verify the existence of a beetle larva. . . . He in
no way doubts the existence of all the other things which surround him,
and you would surprise and confuse him if you made such a distinction
between the beetle larva of which he speaks and the sun of which he
does not speak but which, nevertheless, makes him open the collar of his
shirt or take off his sweater." The meaning of his words is for him not a
"recognition of existence" but the cry of alarm before a "menace," that
of the thousands of beetle larvae which threaten to wipe out his crops. It
is his *entire cultural world* that is set into motion by this exclamation.
Moreover, this could have taken the more modest form of a "Look!" or
even a sigh or simply a mechanical, unthinking gesture of rejection of the
beetle larva through which, nonetheless, the farmer would still be
spoken-speaking, just as he continues to be when noticing that the potatoes are not too spoiled, when catching the voices of farmers in a nearby
field, when wiping his brow, when straightening up to relieve a crick in
his back, or when feeling himself growing older . . . Language is always
present, affirming something other than the simple recognition of exis-

7. E. Benveniste, *Problèmes de linguistique générale* (Paris: Gallimard, 1966)
1:259.
8. "Language" is understood here first from the concrete implementation
of language as such, but also from the "quasi-languages:" "supra-language"
made up of gestures, mime, and all artistic endeavor; "infra-language" of the
archaic impulses of the unconsious, to the extent that they are human only if
they function "continually . . . toward and within language" without which
they would only be instinctual animal reflexes or still-born psychotic experience.

tence, something else "which perhaps is the essential. Essence is in the word 'essential.' Light, sadness, the wind — would they exist without the words of our language? Would there not be in their stead only vibrations, the collision of atoms, moments inseparable from my duration, clouds racing across the sky, trees groaning in the wind, a breath of air, all disappearing as soon as appearing — in fact, not really appearing?"[9] This is also the profound conviction of the later Heidegger: "When we go to the fountain, when we pass through the forest, we always pass through the name 'fountain,' the name 'forest,' even if we do not pronounce these words, even if we do not think about language."[10]

2. Language, Creative Expression

a) The Word, Creator of the "World." We have quoted from Heidegger's commentary on these two lines by Stefan George:

"Thus sadly did I learn this: resignation;
Where the word fails, no thing is there."

"Only the word confers being on a thing. But how can a simple word do such a thing, lead something into being? Rather, things happen in the reverse order. Take, for example, sputnik. This thing — supposing it is a thing — *is* independently of its name, which was given it later. . . . And yet! This 'thing,' whatever it is, however it is, is it not what it is in virtue of its name? Of course! The hurry, the push to hurry . . . , thanks to technology — speeds in whose 'space' only modern machines and devices can be what they are — if this hurry had not spoken to humans to the point of obligating them and placing them under an injunction, if this injunction to hurry had not challenged humans by taking possession of them, if the word of this compulsion to hurry had not spoken — then there would not be any 'sputnik.' There is no thing where the word is lacking."

But to accept this is to recognize that we no longer have control over things; it is to recognize that *the "word" precedes us,* that we are not its masters. This demands a *"resignation,"* a true mourning for this desire to be all-powerful, a desire that makes us believe that we can reign over a real that we have well in hand. "By renunciation, the poet lets go of the desire to have something already exist even if the word is still lacking." At the same time, he

9. Parain, *Recherches*, chs. 1 and 2 (quotes from pp. 14, 26, 28).
10. Heidegger, "Pourquoi des poètes?" *Chemins*, 373.

or she experiences — for it is truly a *test* — that "only the word makes a thing appear and thus come into presence as the thing it is."[11] To speak is thus *accepting to be forbidden the pretension of controlling things by "the representative power of the word"* in order "to let the thing come into presence as a thing" through the word.[12]

Language *creates*, creates "things." This idea is absurd from the viewpoint of traditional metaphysics, which sees language only as an attribute that humans possess and as "an instrument for bestowing a name on something that is already there, already represented" or as a simple "means for displaying what presents itself by itself." This is precisely the view of language we must give up. "On the contrary, it is the word alone that permits the coming into presence, that is, being in which something can make its appearance as an entity."[14] The task of the poet is to manifest the very essence of language, always misunderstood; language is "voca-tion," an invitation addressed to entities to come into presence while remaining in their absence — the creation of the universe as a "world." This is the distinctive *activity*, the primordial human activity; in this *poiesis* — and let us remember, all language is of its essence "poietic," all language is a "forgotten poem" — language kills entities as simple facts spread out before our eyes in order to resurrect them as signifiers of humans and for humans. It is in language that the "world" becomes for us a world that speaks; it speaks in both senses of the word "speak," transitive and intransitive: it speaks us and it speaks to us. The linguist confirms this: "Reality is *produced all over again* by language," to the point that "the 'form' of thought receives its configuration from the structure of the language."[14]

b) The Concept of "Expression." Heidegger finds fault with the "pseudo-realism" of common sense which always presupposes a substantial content "behind" the expression-accident: "First and before all else, talking is expressing oneself. Nothing is more common than to represent language as exteriorization; this representa-

11. Heidegger, *Acheminement vers la parole* (Paris: Gallimard, 1976) 148–149, 152.

12. Ibid., 218.

13. Ibid., 212.

14. Benveniste, *Problèmes*, 25.

tion presupposes from the start the idea of something interior that exteriorizes itself. But to make of language an exteriorization is precisely to remain on the outside, all the more so in that one explains the exteriorization by referring to this supposed inner realm.'' Such a model totally misrepresents the existential constitution of the human being, which ''expresses itself . . . not at all because, as an 'interiority,' it would be separated at the very start from something 'exterior' to it but because, as 'being-in-the-world,' it is always-already 'outside itself' by the very fact that it understands.''[15] E. Levinas makes the same point: ''Language does not exteriorize a representation already existing within me — it offers to share a world that until then was only my own''; it is the ''offer of a world.''[16]

To express oneself is not to give an exterior covering to a human reality already there interiorly, especially not in the sentimental and romantic sense of the ''need to express oneself'' heard so frequently today . . . For *there is no human reality, however interior or intimate, except through the mediation of language or quasi-language that gives it a body by expressing it.* Expression, writes E. Ortigues, is ''an act that is for itself its own result. In effect, it produces nothing beyond its own manifestation. It 'takes to the boards,' as one says of an entertainer who goes out to play in public, on the stage.'' Whether the expression be verbal, facial, or gestural, it ''indicates an act of presence which acts itself out for itself, as a walking-in-place from the interior into exteriority and from the exterior into interiority.'' It is ''the process by which the differentiation of the interior and the exterior'' takes place, but in such a fashion that ''it would not suffice to say that the expression is the exterior, supposing an interiority acquired somewhere,'' because the two moments of interiority and exteriority of this process of differentiation ''flow into one another: *to exteriorize oneself consists precisely in differentiating oneself interiorly.*'' In other words, every ''impression'' can take form (a human, significant, form) only in the expression that accomplishes it, and every thought ''forms itself by expressing itself.''[17]

15. Heidegger, *Acheminement*, 16.
16. E. Levinas, *Totalité et infini*, in *Autrement qu'être* (The Hague: M. Nijhoff, 1974) 149.
17. Ortigues, *Discours et symbole*, ch. 2 ''L'expression,'' 27–28.

All of the above should remind us of the phenomenological project of M. Merleau-Ponty: "In attempting to describe the phenomenon of language and the intentional act of signification, we will have the opportunity to leave behind definitively the classic subject-object dichotomy."[18] For the connection between consciousness and language is intrinsic; the word is not "a simple device for stabilization, or the envelope and clothing of thought." To the contrary, word and thinking are so well "wrapped up in one another" that "the expressive operation realizes or effects signification and does not limit itself to a translation." In short, there is no thinking "which would exist for itself before its expression."[19]

From another viewpoint, this time theological, against the magical distortions of sacramental rites when thought of as tools by which the subject can manipulate the divine omnipotence, A. Vergote also assails the misunderstanding of the process of expression. This misunderstanding is due to the fact that one confuses the act of expression at the moment it happens with the split — that a retrospective reflection perceives in it afterward — between "an initial, hidden intention and a subsequent, public expression." One inevitably thinks in terms of cause and effect, but such a scheme is not really applicable here. For "the act of authentic expression has neither a finality outside itself nor a hidden motive. . . . The *expressive sign is the very flesh of the intention which is born by taking significant form.*" The amorous expression, for example, is "pure manifestation — provided that love and its expression are not a chance unity of interior and exterior. That is to say, the expression, insofar as it is manifestation, effects what it signifies: love invents its expression and the expression creates the love."[20] There is no love apart from the expression which we give of it, which we give of it to one another, or rather which "this something" gives us, from the most archaic impulses — if it is true that, as something distinct from a simple animal instinct, these impulses belong to the unconscious and that "language is the condition of the unconscious"[21] — to the final consummating

18. M. Merleau-Ponty, *Phénoménologie de la perception* (Paris: Gallimard, coll. Tel, 1945) 203.

19. Ibid., 212–214.

20. A. Vergote, *Interprétation du langage religieux* (Paris: Seuil, 1974) 207–208.

21. J. Lacan, Discussion in December 1969, quoted by A. Lemaire, *J. Lacan* (Brussels: P. Mardage, 1977) 190, 365.

act, through the gamut of smiles, kisses, and words. In short, (quasi)linguistic expression is the necessary mediation of all human reality: "Every human situation, every experience common to several people wherever they may be, is a reality that, in its constitution, its advent, its realization, implies language. . . . *Every human reality has language for its catalyst.*"[22]

3. *How the Subject Comes to Be through Language*

But where does this creative power of language come from? Evidently not from some mysterious force within it, a sort of quasi-divine mana. If Heidegger sees here a manifestation, dimly outlined, of the invitation by Being (always linked to the *Logos*) to the human being, linguistics and psychoanalysis attempt to show us the concrete process of this invitation. The reason for the rapid detour which we propose to make through these two disciplines consists in this: they permit us to elucidate in a concrete manner two points which will be important in our later reflection on the connection between God and humans in sacramental theology (and Christology). First, how are we to understand the *communication* between God and humans, while at the same time preserving their radical *difference* (the scheme of difference-otherness)? And second, how are we to understand that there is no truly human *life* except one radically crossed by *death* (the scheme of initiation)?

a) A Linguistic Viewpoint.

— *The Threefold Structure of the Personality*

According to E. Benveniste, the personal pronouns (or the verbal inflections which take their place) form a class of words "that are unlike all other signs in language." In effect, they refer "neither to a concept" (there is no "concept" of I which would encompass all the particular I's who utter themselves at a given moment) "nor to an individual" (one and the same term cannot pick out one particular individual and at the same time refer indifferently to any other individual). More precisely, as J. Lacan says, the linguistic I "designates the subject of the enunciation. . . . It does not signify it."[23] I thus can refer only to a reality that is "exclusively linguistic," that is, to "the individual act of discourse in which it is pronounced" and of which "it designates the speaker only while the speaker speaks." It is precisely in this fundamental mediation

22. Ortigues, *Discours et symbole*, 202–203.
23. J. Lacan, *Ecrits*, 800.

by the linguistic subject that existential subjectivity has the possibility of emerging.

Now, every discourse is "dependent upon the I who states itself there."[24] This accounts for the fact, as Ortigues and Benveniste have both remarked, that *"the I is a unique case."* For "even where the word I is not pronounced, the reference to the person who is speaking is a permanent condition of meaning for the entire discourse because nothing has meaning that does not concern humans conscious of their presence in the world as speaking and acting subjects."[25]

On the other hand (and here appears the separation that we wish to show from the linguistic point of view), the I that is the condition of every discourse has two "values" at the same time: as the "content of the pronouncement," it is the subject of the verb; as the "author of the pronouncement," it is the subject of the discourse. Moreover, this I is not conceivable without a YOU, the reversible partner of the I, so that "to be whole, the category of person requires the reversibility of the relationship" between the I and the YOU in the discourse.[26]

Besides, this I-YOU linguistic relation is itself possible only through the mediation of a *third*. As the "condition of the integrity" of the category of person, "the reversibility of the relationship between the I and the YOU" would deteriorate into a dual relation of mirror images if it did not develop under the influence of a third agent — the social and cosmic world. If speaking is to say (oneself) to someone, this act of enunciation is possible only through a statement in which one says something about something, and necessarily under "the category of the object," that is, of the *non-person*. But that is precisely the status of IT, the linguistic support of the "non-person." This impersonal IT is the linguistic mediation that permits the I (in its relation with the YOU) to open itself to the universal: it situates subjects under the authority of the *Other-that-cannot-be-appropriated* (see below), the Neutral (*ne-uter*, "neither the one nor the other") that renders possible every symbolic exchange, that is to say, every advent of one in its relation to the other. If it were not driven by the IT toward the Other, the linguistic I would not be able to posit itself, and consequently, the existential subject could not even exist.[27] That is to say, this I is not possible except as *open*, barred from its own interiority, a fact that confers upon it its unique status of having a twofold value, as represented (in the statement), as present (in the act of stating).

24. Benveniste, *Problèmes*, 261–262.
25. Ortigues, *Discours et symbole*, 152–153.
26. Ibid., 153.
27. Ibid., 153–154. Benveniste, *Problèmes*, 265.

— The Scheme of the Difference-Otherness in the Symbolic Order

The preceding analysis is rich in consequences since it leads us to fundamentally revise the traditional representation of the difference. In effect, the linguistic YOU, inasmuch as it is reversible with the I, has a status that can appear paradoxical: on the axis of contradiction, it occupies the position opposite the I, from which, as a consequence, it is *the most different;* but it is also *the most similar* to the I since it designates the interlocutor *insofar as* he or she is capable of taking in his or her turn, and in his or her own name, the same linguistic I as the one who is speaking. This paradoxical position is rendered possible by the third agent, the IT, the social and universal Other under which both the I and the YOU abide and which permits them, spoken as they are by the same culture, to "understand one another."

Consequently, the "difference" can no longer be represented according to the (meta)physical scheme of *distance-separation.* It is certainly impossible to do away with this spatial scheme of representation since, according to Kant, it is a priori and belongs to the primary symbolism, impossible to reject, that comes to us through our bodies. But thinking is precisely learning to do away with seemingly obvious facts. Now, according to the traditional representation, difference is the more firmly established as the two terms are farther apart from each other, to the point where, at the limit, one can define one term by what the other is not. One knows the significance of this "evidence" concerning the relationship between humans and God . . . According to this reasoning, difference can only be considered a negative; like the *genesis* of Plato's *Philebus,* with which it is linked, it cannot be imagined as the place of truth. On the contrary, it can be represented only as an *obstacle* to truth, a barrier to this ideal transparency of oneself to oneself, to the other, and to a world, a transparency to be reconquered; it can be represented only as the expression of our finitude conceived to be the consequence of a primeval fall or of original sin. By the same token, otherness can be attributed only to a tragic *alteration* of the fallen self.

Now, if what is most different (I-YOU as opposite and radically other) is also what is most similar (YOU as the reversible of the I), then the anthropological difference should not be conceived as a distancing which attenuates or even cuts communication but rather as an *otherness* which makes it possible. Such is the distinctive trait of every human difference that nothing is more similar to the I than the YOU in its very difference; that, as a subject, the "one" is possible only through the "other" recognized precisely as "my counterpart — the other similar to me." The original difference out of which every subject arises is thus no longer understood, with resentment, as an obstacle — inevitable perhaps but still relatively reducible — to the truth but as *the very place where truth is brought about.*

b) A Psychoanalytic Viewpoint.

— The Subject Split in Two

The subject does not arise except as cleft in two because of the threefold structure of the linguistic subject outside of which the subject cannot develop. The Freudian-Lacanian brand of psychoanalysis shows this in another way.

According to what Lacan has called the *"stage of the mirror,"* there develops within the infant between the ages of six to eight months, when it begins to notice its *self* in the mirror, an initial kind of identification crucial for its structuring as a subject. With this discovery, the *infant* abandons the view of its body as a collection of unrelated parts. While this primary identification with an "ideal unity" perceived in the mirror is salutary, it also is alienating: it is the stage where "the infant who strikes says it has been struck, [where] the one who sees someone fall, cries"; "the slave identifies itself with the despot, the actor with the spectator, and the seduced with the seducer."[28] If it remains thus, the captive of its mirror image, the infant cannot advance to the condition of a subject: like Narcissus, it is doomed to drown in the water-mirror in which it wants to rejoin its ideal image.

The situation will not be resolved until the infant can see itself in the mirror as a subject, that is, as forming a symbolic unity *of an order other* than its reflected body. But to *see itself* this way, the infant must *hear itself* named by another, it must hear itself represented by a name, its name. It is through this identification with its proper name, or with the pronoun I, that it emerges as a subject. It is from this symbolic capacity to recognize itself in those things *representing* it that the infant derives its possibility to accede to subjectivity. These signifiers (but also all the other possible signifiers in the symbolic order because a signifier is by nature diacritical,

---

28. Lacan, *Ecrits*, 113.

that is to say, makes sense only in relation to other signifiers) play a double and paradoxical function: they constitute the mediation for the *advent* of the subject, to the extent that the subject is represented in them; but also, and simultaneously, they constitute the mediation of the *exclusion* of the subject, to the extent that the latter is *only* represented in them. Thus, it is through a break with the immediate image that access to true subjectivity begins: "The subject mediated by language is irremediably divided because it is excluded from the signifying chain at the same time that it is therein 'represented.' "[29] Language breaks forever the imaginary coincidence of the self with itself. It puts the real at a distance. But it is precisely this lack, this lack-in-being, that saves the subject. Such is the *Law*, the law of *language*, the law of culture, *which anchors the subject by dividing it:* "It is by its partition that the subject proceeds to its parturition."[30]

There is no access to the symbolic order without this primoridal division by language whereby the subject becomes capable of recognizing itself in the representations of itself. From now on, this "splitting" (*Spaltung*) "occurs with every intervention of a signifier, namely, from the subject of the enunciation to the subject of the statement."[31] This "crack," out of which the subject is born and maintains itself, initiates, as this "crack" deepens, the dialectic of its *alienations:* the distance between the (I) of the enunciation and the "I" of the statement leads the first (I) to constantly disguise itself (the reason for putting it here between parentheses) as the "I" of its discourses, to calcify itself in its social roles, to dramatize itself, and thus to hide from itself its own lack, in short, to confuse itself with the illusory image of its conscious self.

Thus the human situation is contradictory. On the one hand, what divides human beings — that is, the world of signifiers, first of all their names, but also everything that belongs to language or the symbolic — is the very thing that makes them human; but on the other, what divides them is also the place of their alienation. The *imaginary* is the psychic agency that tends to deny the lack, to erase the difference, to fill up the distance separating humans from the real. Thus a deceptive agency, which, however — and this must be emphasized — plays, even in its enticing aspect, a positive role in the structuring process of the subject (the stage of the mirror) and provides a goad indispensable for all future "progress."

29. Lemaire, *J. Lacan*, 123.
30. Lacan, *Ecrits*, 843.
31. Ibid., 770.

The truth of the subject, as we see, *depends on its psychic consent to the lack which constitutes it and which language opens within it.* This is the law, the law of difference, which access to signifiers imposes. This law goes together with that of symbolic deprivation, that is to say, of the deferment where the young child sees itself enjoined by the parent-depriver (symbolic representative of the culture) to defer the immediate attainment of the coveted object (cf. Freud's Oedipus complex). That is why the prohibition against incest is "the only one among all the rules that has a universal character" and thus does not constitute simply one rule among others but rather constitutes, following the expression of Lévi-Strauss, *"the fact of the rule"* itself.[32] For such is the law from which the human community arises: a law of deprivation to force a *disconnecting* from any relation with the immediately coveted object, a disconnecting begun as soon as there is language with the *placement of the real at a distance.*

—*Death and Life: The Scheme of Initiation*

To become someone, someone "among others" (according to the title of a work by D. Vasse), we must renounce to be everything, to have everything, and right away. This work of *mourning* finds in the Oedipal experience its decisive structural moment; but it is never fully achieved or achievable, so true is it that "there is for each of us, always, a child to kill off, the mourning to go through again and again for this representation of plenitude" — that of the "miraculous child being continually reborn," the imaginary fruit of the "nostalgia for the regard of the mother who has made of this child an extreme splendor."[33] *To reject this death is to forfeit one's life.* "One can place the analytic procedure under the evangelical adage: those who would gain their lives must lose them, but they who consent to lose them will gain them." Of course, qualifies Vergote, "it is only with a certain hesitation that one makes discourses that appear to verge on the rhetorical"; however, "clinical experience shows that human beings gain their lives only by paying a heavy price to death." Through this fact, psychoanalysis "rediscovers the fundamental law of the *scheme of initiation.*" This is a scheme of regeneration through a symbolic

32. C. Lévi-Strauss, *Les structures élémentaires de la parenté* (Paris: PUF, 1949) 10.
33. S. Leclaire, *On tue un enfant,* 11–12.

death which is at work in all rites of initiation, a scheme which seems to be universal: the conviction that death inhabits and mediates life — here is a "law written at the very heart of existence."[34] The subject's conquest of its liberty and truth is never achieved once and for all. It is effected by an *unending process* of costly "working through" (*Durcharbeitung*, Freud). However, there is no objective treasure to be gained at the end of this labor. *The treasure is nothing but the slow self-change whereby the subject succeeds in producing fruit as a result of the painful plowing and tilling of the field of its desire.* The treasure is never separable from the very process of killing our primary narcissism, that is to say, our imaginary omnipotence and right-to-enjoy-everything. The truth of the subject is the *path* itself: "it is the way which sets everything on its way," as we said above, following another approach, Heidegger's.

4. *Human Truth: Consent to the Presence of the Absence*

Thus, it is only through a *breach* that a subject comes to birth, and it is in this breach that it maintains itself. Its truth can be produced only by consenting to this absence which constitutes it.

To consent to this presence of the absence is to consent to *never being able to leave mediation behind* — mediation of the symbolic order that always-already precedes human beings and allows them to become human because they start from a world already humanized before them and passed on to them as a universe of meaning. It is impossible to seize the "real," which is by its very definition what humans fail to reach. But the psychic agency of the imagination, on the basis of the primary narcissism, is bent on making each of us believe the contrary; and each one of us is consumed by such a strong wish for omnipotence and domination over things that it is as if we were possessed by an irresistible need to believe in this fantasy and thus to believe in ourselves. The truth of the psychic subject, always open to the question of Truth, takes place through mourning: mourning for the imaginary coincidence between the (I) of the enunciation and the "I" of the statement, mourning for the correspondence between the subject

34. A. Vergote, in X. Léon-Dufour et al., *Mort pour nos péchés* (Brussels, 1976) 73-74.

and the ideal Self, mourning for the hope of ever recovering original beatitude or (which is the same thing) of ever discovering the complete fullness of meaning. It is precisely in the radical loss of this "paradise" and in the consent to the absence of the Thing that the possibility for the subject to cor-respond to the Truth emerges.

Traditional wisdom calls the self-important person a liar. Beyond the psychological level and the moral judgment explicit in this statement, psychoanalysis attests that this delusion is the lot of each of us. Further, this theatrical dramatization of the self as *"full of itself"* is only the reverse of the eidetic representation of entities as ontologically *firmly anchored*. This dramatization goes hand in hand with culpability, that is, the irrepressible desire to justify one's own existence, to base the world of meaning which permeates us upon an ultimate signified object, to give an ultimate reason for things — in short, to find a "foundation that gives an account of the base, explains it, and finally asks it to explain itself" (see above).

Finally, the subject exists only in a permanent becoming, in a *never-finished* process where it has to learn, at its own expense, to be bereaved of its umbilical attachment to the Same, to renounce to win back its lost paradise, its own origin, and the ultimate foundation which would explain its existence. Its task is to consent to be in truth by accepting the difference, the lack-in-being, *not as an inevitable evil but as the very place where its life is lived*. This is what is necessarily implied by reassigning humans to the symbolic order or to the mediation of language. In any case, this is what analytic discourse leads us to think.

II. SYMBOLIC EXCHANGE

The condition of being always on the way, which is the fate of the human subject, is not an aimless wandering in a desert waste without landmarks. In fact, there is the basic law, eminently "objective," of the symbolic order. This law is made concrete in a process, the process of symbolic exchange, which is properly structured and structuring in that it contains the *rules of the game* without which play cannot begin for lack of mutual understanding. This process is of interest to us primarily because it furnishes us with a model, one among others no doubt, for understanding the distinctive way in which the subject comes to be in its relations with other subjects. The outstanding characteristic of this process is that it functions *outside the order of value*. Because of this, it opens for us a possible path by which to theologically conceive this "marvelous exchange" (*admirabile commercium*) between God and humankind which we call *grace*.

1. In Traditional Societies

In his celebrated work *Essai sur le don*,[35] M. Mauss has studied a type of exchange which regulates the network of relations between groups and between individuals in several traditional societies (Native Americans of the Pacific Coast in Canada and Alaska, native inhabitants of Polynesia and Melanesia), and traces of which we still find in archaic Roman law, ancient German law, and so forth.

a) Outside the Order of Value. Let us simply recall two important traits of this type of exchange. First of all, it is a *total* social fact touching exchanges in all domains (food, women, men, festivals, and so forth) and at all levels of society (pp. 163-164). Second, it concerns exchanges of the *symbolic* order, for "it is something different from the merely useful that is passed around" (p. 267). Certainly the useful is not absent. Thus, the Melanesians understand "haggling" (*gimwali*); they are even very hard bargainers. But the haggling is only one moment, clearly differentiated linguistically and socially from the "general symbolic exchange" (*kula*), which, contrary to the principle which controls exchanges in the marketplace (the *gimwali*), has nothing to do with the realm of "value": the use value (for example, a sack of grain = x days of food or x calories) or exchange value (one sack of grain = so many harpoons for fishing, according to the barter system, or so much cash, according to the money system).

It is impossible to understand these societies as long as one does not recognize that the *principle* which regulates general exchange is of a *completely different order* from that of the marketplace or of value. That is why, according to G. Duby, the "barbarians" of the Frankish and Merovingian periods, despite "the precariousness of

35. M. Mauss, "Essai sur le don," in *Sociologie et anthropologie*, 143-279. We will quote from this edition in the following pages.

their existence," nevertheless carried out the "apparently useless destruction of all the riches they had acquired." They were addicted to pillage, and with "an avidity that seemed insatiable"; but this was only to be able to "give more lavishly." Their leader's treasure was not viewed as capital, but rather as "an adornment" in which "the entire tribe" could take pride. Finally, "the entire society was criss-crossed by the infinitely diversified networks of the circulation of riches and services set in motion by what I have called obligatory generosity. That of dependents toward their patrons, that of parents toward their daughter-in-law, that of friends toward the one giving a feast, that of the nobles toward the king, that of the king toward the nobles, that of all the rich toward the poor, and finally that of all the people toward the dead and toward God. *These are certainly exchanges, and they are innumerable; but they have nothing to do with business.*"[36]

This system of "obligatory generosity" confers on the sack of grain or golden object that one exchanges a reality of an order other than that of utilitarian value. It is given "for nothing" — nothing from the viewpoint of this kind of value — but with the understanding that a third party will give you "for nothing" the produce of fishing, harvest, craftsmanship, or plunder. Outside of this logic — for it is truly a logic, and not, as Lévy-Bruhl said in 1910, a kind of "pre-logic" of "inferior societies" supposedly arrested at an infantile stage — one cannot understand how these people allow themselves the luxury — insane in our Western eyes — of squandering all their "possessions" frivolously in order to throw a party or to keep up with their equals, while at the same time living day-to-day in a state of "privation" and "precariousness."

b) *Obligatory Generosity.* We have just put between quotation marks the terms "precariousness," "privation," and "possessions." We thus raise an absolutely fundamental problem, that of *language.* Mauss has posed this enormous question very well: "The terms which we have used — present, gift — are not in themselves completely exact. We find no others; this is the best we can do. These concepts from economics and law which we like

36. G. Duby, *Guerriers et paysans, vii-xii siècles: Premier essor de l'économie européenne* (Paris: Gallimard, 1973) ch. 3 "Les attitudes mentales."

to oppose to each other — liberty and obligation; liberality, generosity, luxury and thrift, interest, utility — need recasting" (p. 267). Nothing in our languages, in our institutions, or indeed in the totality of our culture can give a name to the reality in question. One gives *without counting*, but this "gift" is *obligatory*, for "to refuse to give would be equivalent to declaring war, that is, to refusing alliance and communion" (p. 162). Reciprocally, one cannot refuse the "gift": "A clan, a family, a party, a guest are not free not to ask for hospitality, not to receive gifts" (pp. 161–162). *Every gift received obligates in its turn*. It is impossible to take what is offered without returning, usually to a third party who, in turn, will offer the return-gift to a fourth, and so on. Thus, riches circulate endlessly from top to bottom, reaching all levels and all domains.

There is much evidence that these "free" exchanges are "obligatory," that this "generosity" is "mandatory," that this "liberality" pushed to the extreme of not wanting even to seem to desire a gift in return is really quite "interested," (p. 201). But "their notion of 'interest' is only a rough analogue to the interest that drives us" (p. 271). It has to do first with the desire to *be recognized as a subject*, not to lose face, not to fall from one's social rank, and consequently to compete for prestige.

2. *In Contemporary Western Society*

This detour through the system of symbolic payments in traditional societies would be of no interest for our topic if it did not *reveal our own archaisms*, largely unconscious, as Mauss has indicated. The fact that we find traces of them in our Indo-European languages, notably in the vocabulary of exchange ("give-take," "buy-sell," "loan-borrow") and the vocabulary of "hospitality," is, as Benveniste has shown,[37] already an indication of this. A slight indication, however. For in our societies, so many centuries of metaphysical tradition, technological civilization, and the dominance of business values have passed, enshrining the notion of equivalence, that by an almost historic fatality, our languages have forgotten the original ambivalence of our vocabulary of exchange.

37. Benveniste, *Problèmes*, 316–318. *Le vocabulaire des institutions indo-européennes*, vol. 1 *Economie, parenté, société* (Paris: Minuit, 1969), sec. 2 "Donner et prendre," pp 65–121, and ch. 10 "Achat et rachat."

This is why it is difficult for us to recognize that the fundamental system of "obligatory generosity" and "mandatory gratuitousness," organized according to a process of gift—reception—return-gift, continues to pervade our exchanges. We have trouble recognizing that it is nevertheless *what allows us to live as subjects and structures all our relations in what they contain of the authentically human.* At least if it is true that what makes us live is not of the order of the useful, but of the order — like love — of "graciousness," of super-abundance — that which is thrown into the bargain . . .

The *gift* is without doubt what, among our institutions, best resists the imperialism of "value" (on the condition that it is not reduced to an object of utilitarian value, as sometimes happens in current wedding registries, for example). J. Baudrillard sees there "the closest illustration" of symbolic exchange, insofar as "it cannot be dissociated from the concrete relationship where the exchange takes place, from the transferential pact that it seals between two persons. . . . Thus, to speak correctly, it has neither utility value nor commercial value," but only "the value of symbolic exchange." Because it is some object which "one lets go as if it were a part of oneself," it becomes a signifier that "grounds both the presence of one to the other and their absence from one another. From this comes the ambivalence of all elements of symbolic exchange (glances, objects, dreams, excrement): as a medium of relation *and* distance, the gift is always a sign of love and aggression. . . . Thus, the structure of exchange (cf. Lévi-Strauss) is never that of mere reciprocity. These are not two simple terms, but two *ambivalent* terms which are exchanged, and the exchange establishes their relation as *ambivalent.*" In contrast to the *sign-object,* which refers "only to the absence of the relation," the *symbol-object* (such as the gift) establishes the relation "in the absence." This opposition finds its support in the general theory Baudrillard proposes. According to him, there exist four distinct logics of value: (1) a functional logic of *utilitarian value,* based on usefulness (for example, the automobile as a means of rapid transportation); (2) an economic logic of *exchange value,* based on equivalence (the automobile as equal to so much money); (3) a differential logic of *sign value,* based on a code of difference (the automobile as sign of a certain standing or social position); (4) finally, a logic of *symbolic exchange*, based on ambivalence. Now, all this is bisected by a "single large opposition," which passes between "the whole field of *value* (that of the first three logics) and the field of *non-value* (that of symbolic exchange),[38] more precisely, between the third, which represents the completed stage reached by the first two, and the last.

The entire work of Baudrillard tends to show that our "contemporary consumer society" is characterized by a stage where "the merchandise is immediately produced as a sign, as sign-value, and the signs (the culture) as merchandise."[39] What accounts for the *value* of things is not their usefulness, but *the sign that arises out of this usefulness* and thus, imaginatively, duplicates the "real." Production is determined only by the ideological needs that it creates; placed under the sign of growth for the sake of growth, without any other goal or referent than the sign of prestige, power, progress which it gratifies in us, production lives only from its own reproduction as an encoded value-sign.

What we are sold is less the thing than the *idea* of the thing. We are sold less a return to nature through vacationing than the idea of nature, of "naturality." It is actually impossible to return to the "nature" of ancient societies; our system can at best create only a duplicate of it as a *sign*.

Thus, everything is done and undone in our society *according to the code* which parodies and duplicates itself by simulating itself. Mirroring the "system of fashion," recently analyzed by R. Barthes, where, beyond the beautiful or the ugly, the useful or the useless, one "abandons meaning, without however surrendering the spectacle of signification."[40] Mirroring the entire contemporary culture which, thinking and pronouncing itself "cultivated," can do nothing but give itself as a spectacle for itself. Duplication is what counts. Everything functions in what Baudrillard calls *"the order of semblances"*; the system has no referent but the code that rules it. It is the reign of the *available object*. One can have anything. Further still, one is urged to have everything. But one can give back nothing. Society gratifies human beings with its gifts, offers them all the "security" possible so that they may be completely assured of not losing anything from their hoards of valuables by theft, fire, sickness, accident — even beyond death (life insurance). But society snatches away at the same time — and

38. J. Baudrillard, *Pour une critique de l'économie politique du signe* (Paris: Gallimard, 1972) 61–63, 144-153.
39. Ibid., 178.
40. R. Barthes, *Le système de la mode* (Paris: Seuil, 1967).

it is a heavy ransom to pay — the right to give a return-gift. Symbolic exchange, organized on the basis of the reversibility of the exchange, is neutralized: work, leisure, comfort, security, information, physical and psychic health, scientific knowledge, "culture" — all is given *unilaterally* to better insure submission to the ruling code. And if the "lack" reappears, then the theories about the unconscious are there, available, usable like all the rest, to fill it up again with a "knowledge" which allows all persons to dream "analytic" dreams, to live through the "Oedipus thing" — cultural gadgets that each one can pick up and use right in his or her own home.[41]

From these few reflections we see that to dream of returning to the "marvelous" time of sailing ships or oil lamps would be the worst of illusions; no traditional society ever experienced itself as particularly "happy." The mythic "golden age" is always located, by definition, somewhere else . . . But this totalitarian reign of the code does not necessarily herald the apocalypse, as is attested by the numerous *counter-discourses* that, through the multiform desires for a "return" — a return to "nature," to "festival," to the "sacred," to "history" — rebel, and not just at the margins of society, against the stifling of symbolic exchange. As deceptive as they may be, these "returns" are still, at the level of representation, an *authentic reclaiming of the symbolic*. They prevent the system, by the very efforts they force it to make to maintain its mastery over them, from becoming congealed; by unlocking it, they supply the oxygen which guarantees its survival but which also prevents our contemporaries from asphyxiating. Is there a contradiction here? Of course! What human society does not live by its internal contradictions? Our consumer society cannot live without denouncing itself — thereby secreting its own antidote.

No more than our ancestors, can we today allow the "lack" which constitutes us to be filled. That is why this lack, masked by the reign of "value," necessarily *haunts* us — like death, which, however, everything today hides from us. But is not that precisely our possible salvation? For "it is precisely in this extreme danger" that "the possibility of salvation rising up on the horizon" can best show itself.[42] We may extend Heidegger's meditation on the historical destiny of metaphysics reaching its climax in humanity making use of technology to humanity making use of signs, with

41. J. Baudrillard, *L'échange symbolique et la mort*, in *Pour une critique*, 103–105.
42. M. Heidegger, *La question de la technique*, EC, 44.

"sign" understood as "the apogee of merchandise."[43] For is not *metaphysics* as a logic of representation and of value brought to its *full realization* in the human use of *value-sign*, where the referent is nothing but the code of representations that governs the system — if it is true, at least, that "the culminating stage of merchandise occurs when it imposes itself as a *code*"?[44]

3. *Business Exchange and Symbolic Exchange:*
Two Poles and Two Levels

As predominant as it is today, the logic of the value-sign, which is that of the marketplace, cannot smother that of "non-value," which is that of symbolic exchange. Both are present in *every* human society, but in variable proportions, with the traditional societies and our current consumer society being the extreme cases. These two logics are thus to be understood as *two poles*, the tension between them being constitutive of every human society.

But these two poles in dialectic tension belong to *two different levels* of exchange. The logic of the marketplace (under the form of barter or money) is that of value; it belongs to the regime of need which seeks to satisfy itself immediately through the possession of objects. The logic of symbolic exchange is of another order. For what is being exchanged through yams, shells, or spears, as through a rose or a book offered as gifts in our own culture, is more and other than what they are worth on the open market or what they may be useful for. It is more and other than what the objects are in themselves. One is here outside or beyond the regime of usefulness and immediacy. Rather, the principle which rules here is one of *super-abundance. The true objects being exchanged are the subjects themselves.* By the intermediary of these objects, the subjects weave or reweave *alliances*, they *recognize* themselves as full members of the tribe, where they find their *identity* in showing themselves in their proper place, and in putting others in their "proper place." As a consequence, what is transpiring in symbolic exchange is of the same order as what is transpiring in language, if it is true, as F. Flahault writes, that "every word, as important as its referential and informative value may be, arises also from an

43. J. Baudrillard, *Pour une critique*, 259.
44. Ibid.

awareness of 'who I am for you and who you are for me' and is operative in this field."[45] In both cases, it is a matter of a reversible recognition of each other as fully a *subject*.

The difference of "level" between the principle of the marketplace and that of symbolic exchange is thus clear. As with the gift, what one exchanges in this latter case has no currency on the open market. It is beyond all business, *"thrown into the bargain,"* that is to say, without price, "gracious." For the symbolic essence of the gift is precisely characterized not by the worth of the object offered — this can be practically nothing in terms of usefulness or commercial value, and yet the "nothing" offered is received as a true gift — but by the *relationship of alliance,* friendship, affection, recognition, gratitude it creates or recreates between the partners. *It is subjects who exchange themselves* through the object; who exchange, *under the agency of the Other,* their *lack-in-being* and thus come before each other in the middle of their absence deepened by their exchange, in the middle of their difference experienced radically as otherness because of their exchange. We are no longer in the realm of need and the possession of objects, but in that of "desire" connected with the "request" for the Other. Thus, in spite of undeniable differences,[46] it is *our own archaic dimension* that is revealed to us, written large, by the traditional systems governing total exchange. Today as yesterday, what gives us the possibility of becoming and of living as subjects is this process, unconscious until recently, of gift-reception-return-gift that structures every significant relationship, that is to say, every "human" relationship, between partners — a process which is the very process of language.

---

45. Flahault, *La parole,* 50.

46. The difference between our gift and the obligatory generosity of traditional systems is that the only obligation which we assume in accepting an object as a "gift" is, at the minimum, the return-gift of a word of "thanks" (without which the object is acquired as a value-object, but not received as a gift), while in traditional societies the receiver is obliged to give in return other goods, and *to a third party,* since the entire system functions that way, beginning with the distribution of necessary foodstuffs. This difference is clearly not negligible, for it gives rise to almost diametrically opposed economic and social systems.

4. Graciousness and Gratuitousness

To consider the grace of God theologically, and more specifically sacramental grace, in the order of symbolic exchange, has for us the immense advantage of situating it from the start in the area of non-value. We indicated this above regarding the manna in the desert: grace is essentially that which cannot be calculated and cannot be stocked. It is "beyond the useful and the useless," according to the expression of A. Delzant.[47] It belongs to what is "thrown into the bargain" and to super-abundance. Therefore, it is "*graciousness.*" This concept designates here that which cannot, by definition, become the object of a *calculation*, of a price, of haggling.

But this concept of graciousness expresses only one dimension of grace. There is a second which it does not show: the *precedence* of God's gift which, according to theological tradition, grace also implies. We must then complement the concept of "graciousness" with that of "*gratuitousness.*" This is an equally precious word because it indicates that we are not at the origin of our own selves but that we receive our selves from a gift that was there before us. A free gift, which can in no way be demanded and which we can in no way justify.

To be theologically Christian, then, a study of grace *must unite the two concepts* we just distinguished. To limit oneself to the aspect of gratuitousness would be evil. For to weigh someone down with an avalanche of free liberalities made "without desire of return" is to deprive that person of the inalienable right of response that every recognition of a human being as a subject demands; it is thus to alienate that person, not to recognize that person as "other." The subject can only die, asphyxiated, if it becomes the "object" (that is exactly the word to use!) of free generous gifts which it cannot reciprocate.

We said above that every gift obligates; there is no reception of anything *as a gift* which does not require some return-gift as a sign of gratitude, at the very least a "thank you" or some facial expression. Which is to say that by the very structure of the exchange, the gratuitousness of the gift *carries the obligation of the return-gift of a response.* Therefore, theologically, grace requires not

47. A. Delzant, *La communication de Dieu, par-delà utile et inutile: Essai théologique sur l'ordre symbolique* (Paris: Cerf, 1978).

only this initial gratuitousness on which everything else depends but also the *graciousness of the whole circuit,* and especially of the return-gift. This graciousness qualifies the return-gift as beyond-price, without calculation — in short, as a response of love. *Even the return-gift of our human response thus belongs to the theologically Christian concept of "grace."*

This is an important reversal for the Christian understanding of our relationship with God. A single example: While it is true that the baptism of infants obviously attests to the gratuitousness of grace, on the other hand, this baptism cannot be held to be an exemplary model of this grace without the risk of distorting it; for in fact, the more it worked in competition with the free response of the person the more it would be "grace." Augustinianism did not always escape this trap . . . One does not affirm God at the expense of the human person; the wholeness of grace is never so well attested as when one takes into account the freedom of the human return-gift it solicits. Not able, as a consequence, to be extricated from this process of exchange where it is perceived as a "gift," grace cannot be treated on the model of an "object" or "finished product," even if a spiritual one. Grace must be treated as something outside the boundaries of value, according to the symbolic mode of communication, and in the first place communication of the word. Rather than being represented as an object-value that one would "refine" through analogy, the "treasure" is really not separable from the *symbolic labor* by which the subject itself bears fruit by becoming a believer.

Two important points emerge from this chapter. First, the truth of the believing subject in its relationship with God can come about (like that of any subject) only through *mediation,* of which the sacraments constitute the major symbolic expression, as we will see. Second, because it is contemporary with mediation and not anterior to or dissociable from it as an instrument, the subject is *always giving birth* to its truth as a believer, which is the truth of its relationship with God. This truth effected, not by "amassing" spiritual values, but by a symbolic work whose process is nothing other than that of *symbolic exchange* or of verbal communication between subjects. It is thus in the wake of linguistic mediation and its symbolic efficacy that we understand the sacraments, and the grace of which they are the "expression."

Chapter Four

Symbol and Body

The way we have approached the problem up to now leads us to speak theologically of the sacraments not as instruments but as mediations, that is to say, as expressive media in which the identification and thus the coming-to-be of subjects as believers take place. This is why:

To the extent that, as we will see in the first section of this chapter, the distinction between *"sign"* and *"symbol"* turns, according to us, on whether the subjects *as such* are taken into account (in a symbol) or not (in a sign), we will be led to theologically think of the sacraments in terms of symbol rather than sign.

To the extent that, among other things, such a symbolic occurrence is characteristic of what one calls *"language acts,"* we will be led, in the second section, to take the sacraments as *acts of symbolization* putting into effect the *illocutionary* dimension of language acts, according to which they effect (execute the "performance" of instituting) a *relation of places* between the subjects and thus an identification of these subjects with regard to others within this particular "world" we call the Church.

To the extent that this interpersonal dimension may be most clearly seen in *ritual* language acts and that this ritualism is constitutive of the liturgical expression, we will be led — this will be our third section — to ponder the *symbolic efficacy* of this type of expressive mediations and to critically situate the sacramental grace in this perspective.

These first three sections thus enlarge the point made in the preceding chapter: symbol, and especially ritual symbol, is the very epiphany of mediation in its most contingent and most culturally determined aspects. Thus, we are led back from the symbol to the *body*, for the body is the primordial and arch-symbolic form of mediation, as well as the basis for all subjective identification. Then, this will lead us to theologically consider the sacraments, which engage precisely the bodies of believers, as the exemplary symbolic representations of the corporality of the faith. *From the symbol to the body*, therefore, there is one approach to mediation which unfolds itself in fidelity to the fact that language is constitutive of human nature and to our perspective of the overcoming of metaphysics.

I. SIGN AND SYMBOL

Previously, we distinguished two logics which are at work in the exchange of goods: that of the marketplace and value, based on the objects in themselves, and that of symbolic exchange, before or beyond the realm of worth and based on the relations between subjects as such. We said that in their very principles, these two logics reflect *two different levels*; however, they are concretely connected yet subjected to the dialectical tension between *two poles*. It is these two levels and these two poles that we will now meet again with our distinction between sign and symbol.

In the concrete world, sign and symbol are always mixed together. It is impossible to say unilaterally that "this object is a sign" and "that object is a symbol." As with concepts like "metaphysics" and "the symbolic," the value of these two concepts of "sign" and "symbol" is first of all *methodological*; their distinction plays a *heuristic* role in allowing us to discriminate between complex empirical realities. These two concepts thus have only a *relative* value in this work; it is their mutual relationship of differences, as we are going to explain, that makes them useful for our study. In other words, we do not pretend to define the absolute "essence" of the symbol; we claim only to point out several aspects which distinguish it from sign, in a purely "formal" way. But it will soon be evident — and this is the principal benefit of our exercise — that because it is governed by a different principle, the symbol cannot be understood as an offshoot of the sign, as if it were only a more "aesthetic" or complex realization of the latter.

1. *Two Levels of Language*

a) The Ancient Symbol. The Greek verb *symballein* signifies literally "to throw together." If one construed it transitively, one would translate it, according to the context, as "gather together," "hold in common," "exchange," (*symballein logous* — "to exchange words"); intransitively, as "meet" or "converse." The substantive *symbole* designates the joint at the elbow or knee and, more generally, the whole idea of conjunction, reunion, contract, or pact. The ancient *symbolon* is precisely an object cut in two, one part of which is retained by each partner in a contract. Each half evidently has no value in itself and thus could imaginatively signify anything; its symbolic power is due only to its connection with the other half. When, years or even generations later, the partners or their descendants come together again to "symbolize" their two portions by joining them together, they recognize this act as the expression of the same contract, of the same alliance. It is thus the agreement between the two partners which establishes the symbol; it is the *expression of a social pact based on mutual recognition* and, hence, is a *mediator of identity.*

The semantic field of the word "symbol" has been extended to every element (object, word, gesture, person . . .) that, exchanged within a group, somewhat like a pass-word, permits the group as a whole or individuals therein to recognize one another and identify themselves. In a similar way, the bread and wine of the Eucharist, the water of baptism, the paschal candle, the "Lamb of God who takes away the sins of the world," the priest wearing the liturgical vestments, the genuflection before the altar, and so forth are mediators of Christian identity. These words, gestures, objects, people *transport us immediately into the world of Christianity to which they belong;* each one of them, because it belongs to the order of Christianity, immediately "symbolizes" our relation with Christianity. Like every group, the Church identifies itself through its symbols, beginning with the formulation of the confession of faith, called appropriately the "Symbol of the Apostles."

b) "The Symbol Introduces Us into a Realm to Which It Itself Belongs." According to E. Ortigues, this is one of the distinctive characteristics of the symbol in its difference from the sign: "The symbol does not refer, as does the sign, to something of another order than itself; rather, its function is to introduce us into an order to which it itself belongs, an order presupposed to be an order of meaning in its radical otherness."[1] The sign "relates to something other than itself" because it implies "a difference between two orders of relations: the relations of sensible signifiers, and the relations of intelligible signified meanings" (p. 43). By contrast, the symbol introduces us, as the several Christian examples mentioned above show, *into a cultural realm to which it belongs* inasmuch as it is a symbol, a realm which is "of an order completely different from that of immediately experienced reality" — a "symbolic order" which "necessarily supposes an initial break, a power of heterogeneity which situates it beyond immediate life" (p. 210).

— The Phoneme

The symbol begins with the initial *rupture of the immediately given;* it finds its rock-bottom expression in the *phoneme.* "A phoneme is a symbol." First, because, signifying nothing, it does not refer us to anything else of another order than that to which it itself belongs; second, however, because it introduces us into the world of meaning: to be recognized as a phoneme, it presupposes a human convention that snatches it from the simple state of being "noise" and places it within a chain of signifiers destined for communication, that is to say, in the human, and no longer the animal, realm. To notice the difference, in the middle of the virgin forest, between a "ba," a "be," or an "ah" and no matter what animal cry or sound of the forest is to *recognize* a human presence, to *renew our alliance* with humanity. The social pact of the symbol begins, at the origin of language, with the phonemes.

But this pact or convention has this unique characteristic, in contrast with every other pact, *it was never the object of a decree* on the part of human society because the latter only comes into existence simultaneously with language. The phonetic symbol thus introduces us into the *primordial* space, where every convention, every rule of the game, the very possibility of communication have their foundation. It is the device that, by introducing always recognizable differences into a scale of natural "sounds," converts them into a cultural system of communication. At this intra-linguistic level, the symbol shows "the function of negativity es-

1. E. Ortigues, *Le discours et le symbole* (Paris: Aubier-Montaigne, 1962) 65. The references between parentheses in the text pertain to this work.

sential to all language: that is to say, it corresponds, inside the very *Logos*, to what the action, work, or operation is that transforms the natural datum, and by the same token, denies it or refuses to accept it as it is" (p. 186).

The symbol is thus the *witness of the internal structuring of every system of language*. It is in this sense that one can speak of a *logico-mathematical* symbol: empty of all representative content, pure figure of the rule of language that mathematicians have developed for themselves, the variable *x* has no precise "meaning"; its "meaning" goes no further than the rule of the game itself (p. 174).

In both these cases, that of phonetic and of mathematical symbol, "the *internal* connection of language to language is the raison d'être of the symbolic function." There, where the sign is like "a centrifugal power oriented toward the present expression and the genesis of objective forms of thought," the symbol is like "a centripetal power which presupposes in its internal law of formation the genesis of possibilities of recognition between subjects." *Thus, the symbol marks the very limit of language; it testifies to its "structure as such"* (p. 65). It manifests the *law that controls it internally*. It is the primary agent of every subjectivity, for every subject initiates itself *within* language.

The interest in our going back to the rock-bottom expression of the phonetic symbol (we leave aside the particular questions raised by the logico-mathematical symbol) is twofold. First, because "b" is a phoneme only through the discrete traits that differentiate it from "p," "g," "k," and so forth, we notice that a simple element becomes a symbol only through its *relations* with all the other elements of the system. By itself, isolated, this element can signify virtually anything. As in neurosis, the object then functions imaginatively; instead of replacing it in the ensemble, where it would find its coherence, one attends to it as to a focus, and this detail, in itself "in-significant," develops into an idée fixe to which one reduces all the rest. "One and the same term can be imaginary, if one considers it absolutely, and symbolic, if one considers it as a *differential value*, correlative with other terms which limit each other reciprocally. . . . One cannot isolate a symbol without destroying it, allowing it to slip away into the ineffable world of the imagination" (pp. 194, 221).

Second, like a piece from a broken vase, a symbol retains its value only through the place which it occupies within the whole. This place is indicated by its neighboring and complementary symbols, obtained by putting the different pieces together into a kind of "mental collage." This is what allows us, for example, to say upon the discovery of a shard of porcelain in the street, "Ah, a vase . . ." It seems then that an element becomes a symbol only to the extent that it *represents the whole* (the vase), from which it is inseparable. That is also why *every symbolic element brings with itself the entire socio-cultural system to which it belongs.* It is by this indirect form of reference that the symbol becomes the agent for recognition and identification between subjects as such.

— *The Symbol Properly So Called*

We find again the same two traits which we have just mentioned in what Ortigues terms "symbols properly so called": religious or political symbols, mythic or poetic symbols . . . First, it is only insofar as it is *correlative* to other elements constitutive of the ritual sequence in which it is located that a ritual element functions as a symbol. More generally, to the extent that a ritual relates to an ensemble of religious representations, with the latter linked to a coherent network of economic, social, political, and ethical values that we call culture, one may, as V. Turner has shown in his analyses, recognize within the ritual symbols "stock units" of inventory of normative values, beliefs, social roles within the community — "stores of information on the dominant structural values within the culture."[2]

Second, *it is the entire symbolic order to which it belongs* (or at least an entire part of it, correlative to the rest) *that a symbol evokes.* Thus, for example, the forked branch with its bark removed that the Ndembu of Zambia call "chishing'a" and which they use in a hunting ritual is (as Turner has shown in his analysis of the origin of its name, the substance of which it is made, and the object itself) like a symbolic "precipitate" of their language (the root of the word and its diverse meanings), their kinship system and social relations, the ethical values which govern their behavior, and the representations of their ecological environment. So true is this that "the Ndembu consider the 'chishing'a' less a knowable object than a *unifying force which brings together* all the powers inherent in

2. V. Turner, *Les tambours d'affliction: Analyse des rituels des Ndembu de Zambie* (Paris: Gallimard, 1972) 12, 16.

the activities, objects, relations, and ideas it represents."[3] This symbol, "properly so called," takes the people into the ritual, religious, social order to which it belongs; this is why all Ndembu perceive their culture there, in a manner largely unconscious, and so *recognize themselves*, "find their bearings," identify themselves there in their relations with their kinfolk, with the ancestral tradition, with the universe which surrounds them and which they inhabit as their world. This symbol is thus *a mediation for mutual recognition between subjects and for their identification within their world*. Further, its intimate bond with the world of subjects is so strong that it ceases to function, *here and now*, as a symbol the moment one steps back and adopts a critical attitude towards it.[4]

One understands why the symbol eludes, in its very essence, the system of "value" (except, to be sure, in its formal contours, without which one could not distinguish it from the other elements with which it forms a system). Thus, following the superb passages Heidegger has written on the *work of art*, any *utilitarianism*, whether it be of the technical, cognitive, or even "aesthetic order," is *banished*, for example, from the peasant woman's shoes painted by Van Gogh: this picture does not "communicate any knowledge whatsoever"; it "causes the very budding-forth."[5] It in

3. Ibid., 204–207. Emphasis mine.

4. Cf. T. Ushte and R. Erdoes, *De mémoire indienne* (Paris: Plon, 1981). After having noted that "from birth to death, we Indians are held in the folds of the symbol as under a blanket," Tahca Ushte adds, "It is strange, because *we don't even have any word* for 'symbolism' and yet symbolism pervades us to the depths of our being" (pp. 118–123). There really is nothing "strange" there: as soon as it becomes the object of critical reflection, the symbol deteriorates. It "adheres" so strongly to the cultural world of the group that it functions all the better when one does not identify it as such in a particular semantic category. Such is the ethnological observation of E. de Rosny: "To speak of the rite or of the symbol is to isolate it, look at it from a distance, demystify it a bit: it is an intellectual and desacralizing operation the danger of which was felt by my partners. . . . The use of the word 'rite' or 'symbol' presupposes a tactical withdrawal, typical of language, that risks impoverishing the very meaning of the action that it covers." E. de Rosny, *Les yeux de ma chèvre: Sur les pas des maîtres de la nuit en pays douala (Cameroun)* (Paris: Plon, 1981) 285.

5. M. Heidegger, "L'origine de l'œuvre d'art," *Chemins*, 47–48. The references between parentheses in the text pertain to this edition.

no way serves to illustrate shoes-as-products, it rather "shows us the *truth* of *this* pair of shoes" (p. 36).

For "in the dark intimacy of the hollow of the shoe is written the fatigue of the steps of labor. . . . Through these shoes pass the silent appeal of the earth, its tacit gift of grain maturing, its secret refusal of itself in the dry fallow land of a winter field. Through this product pass anxiety over the scarcity of bread, the silent joy of having once again overcome need, the anguish over an imminent birth, the shiver before a menacing death. This product belongs to the earth, and it is sheltered in the world of the peasant woman."

And as the peasant woman takes them off in the evening, searches for them at dawn, or passes them by, she "knows all that," without having any need to consciously think of it: for *all that is symbolically "gathered together" in her shoes*; through them the peasant woman is, thus, "welded to her world' (pp. 34–35).

Such is the "essence of art: the truth of the entity putting itself into effect." This has nothing to do with any "imitation" or "copy" of the real, with truth as the "conformity" (*adaequatio*) of traditional metaphysics (p. 37). In opposition to this truth-as-exactitude, which bends everything to its "indiscrete calculation" (p. 50), the work of art, like all symbolic work, shows what the truth is: not something already given beforehand to which one only has to adjust oneself with exactitude, but rather a "making-come-into-being" (p. 48), an "advent" (p. 52) which, like a "fugitive glimpse," gives itself only in simultaneously "holding itself back" in a sort of "suspense" to the person who, against every utilitarian tendency, knows how to respect the "vacant place" where it discloses itself (pp. 58–59). No real peasant's shoe is more *true* than the one in Van Gogh's painting. The symbol *touches what is most real* in our world and allows it to come *to* its truth.

— *The Witness of the Vacant Place*

The symbol cannot carry out this task except in its role as witness to the founding faith of humanity: the law of distance, of lack, of otherness, of the "vacant place" where the real belongs to an order different from the immediate data or the available value. This is why, as Ortigues writes, "the symbol exists efficaciously only where it introduces something more than life; something like an oath, a pact, a sacred law"; something which, like language, "obliges us to integrate reference to the dead (the ancestors, the gods, the absent) into the pact which forges the bond among the living."[6] It is in its role as *witness to this vacant place* of the Other that the symbol gathers together entities into a significant world and, within this world, "imposes a law of reciprocal recognition between subjects." Such a recognition of subjects in their world and between themselves requires that the symbol be the mediator "of a *third term* by overcoming a fascinating, 'imperialistic' dual relation where consciousness loses itself in its imaginary double."[7] It is true that "the whole problem of symbolization is in this transition from the dualistic opposition to the threefold relation":[8] precisely the problem of language, which the symbol carries, as if to the "second power," the problem of the identification of subjects in their relation to the world and between themselves.

c) Value and Non-Value.

— *The Sign as Value of Knowledge*

To treat a word as a sign, on the intra-linguistic plane, is to define its *value* as a relation of difference, whether this be a paradigmatic one between this word and all the other words of the lexicon or a syntagmatic one between this word and the other words of the statement. If we move past the strict intra-linguistic appropriateness of a word, determined by its "discrete" traits, we also treat the word as a sign when we inquire, in a more general way, if it is indeed able to evoke the extra-linguistic referent which it intends. It is the value of the *statement*, insofar as it says something about something, that is being measured here. One thus approaches language under the aspect of *information*, estimating the accuracy of the understanding it furnishes. The ideal of language in this perspective is to move toward the maximum of exactitude and thus of univocity and equivalence: scientific language, which aspires to be a discourse without an author, constitutes the model underlying this ideal.

— *The Symbol as Mediation of Recognition*

To treat words as *symbols*, on the other hand, is to become

6. Ortigues, *Le discours et le symbole*, 66.
7. Ibid., 198–199.
8. Ibid., 205.

primarily interested, not in the thing enunciated and in its value, but in the *enunciation* and in the subject who through the enunciation speaks itself to another subject. If the fact of "saying something about something" is evidently not indifferent, it is to the act "of someone who says it to someone" that attention is now directed. For, on this level, the first function of language is not to designate an object or to transmit information — which all language also does — but first *to assign a place to the subject* in its relation to others. The symbol stands on the side of the subject who produces itself in producing it, who places itself upon the stage in putting it to work. The effects of meaning that the symbol produces (in a relation, as Paul Ricœur says, not "of meaning to the thing, but of meaning to meaning")[9] are to be understood as *effects of the subject* — either a group subject or an individual subject, a "broadcasting" subject or a "receiving" subject: the subject recognizes itself in the effects, identifies itself with them.

If, wandering down the streets of Beijing in the middle of a crowd where, as the only American or even the only Westerner, I feel lost, I suddenly distinctly hear the signifier "kid," which I identify immediately as a signifier in the English language, distinct by at least one phoneme from "lid," "squid," "bid," my first reaction is not to interest myself in the meaning of "kid" — insofar as it is distinct from the signified objects of the same paradigmatic class of animals like "nanny," "billy," "goat" and, of course, from all the signified objects of the mineral and plant classes — I do not say to myself in this circumstance, "Look, they're talking about a 'kid' . . . " but rather, "Ah, what luck! Another American here . . . " My reaction would have been the same if I had heard "bloom" or "thanks," or again — a supremely symbolic term — "shit" . . . The meaning of these words has hardly any relevance in this circumstance. The effect immediately produced is the *recognition* of "America" present here, the *link* symbolically renewed with "American-ness" and not the understanding that the word brings me in its capacity as a sign. Hearing a person-speaking-English immediately introduces me into the linguistic community to which "kid," "blossom," or "shit" belong; that identifies me as a member of this community, with all that is intrinsically linked to it by way of culture, historical tradition, culinary customs, "the green hills of Vermont," the "blue Pacific."

9. P. Ricœur, *De l'interprétation: Essai sur Freud* (Paris: Seuil, 1965), 25–27.

The same sort of analysis can be applied, on a *non-linguistic* plane, to the national flag or a postcard of the Washington Monument. One can take both as simple signs; one can ask: What is the historical meaning of the blue and the red in our three-colored national flag? When and how was the Washington Monument built? These are questions that belong to the order of "knowledge," information, utility, value. But most often, that kind of thing makes little difference to us. The simple sight of an American flag flying somewhere at the far ends of the earth *renews* my bond with my native land and identifies me as an American, just as that of the postcard showing the Washington Monument renews my connections with "Washington-ness." For, in a sense, this monument *is* Washington, just as the three-colored flag *is* the United States. Of course, they are this to different degrees, taking account of circumstances (for example, the raising of the flag on the Fourth of July) and the connection between the flag and the cultural world of each person (for example, anyone who would trample the flag before aged veterans would commit a sacrilege in their eyes; such an attack against the mother-country would wound them as much as any blow directed against them personally). There are many words, images, and material objects whose denigration *affects us* like a personal insult.

In all these cases the symbol maintains us in the order of recognition and not of cognition, of summons or challenge and not of simple information; it is *the mediator of our identities as subjects within this cultural world it brings with itself, whose unconscious "precipitate" it is.*

— *Three Major Traits of the Symbol*

The examples we have just given permit us to discern three major traits that we think characterize every symbol:

1) If the symbol has necessarily a distinctive, formal "value," if, even from this formal point of view, one must consider it as the interior witness which renders possible any culture as a coherent system of values, still its function is not, like that of a sign, to refer to a "something else" (*aliud aliquid*) that always stands on the plane of value, measure, calculation: a cognitive value of representations with regard to the real, an economic value of possessions with regard to what the group may have at its disposal, a technical value of objects with regard to the work to carry out, an ethical value of behavior with regard to the norms of society, and so forth. The primary function of the symbol is to *join* the persons

who produce or receive it with their cultural world (social, religious, economic . . .) and so to *identify* them as subjects in their relations with other subjects. The symbol thus ties the cultural pact where all mutual recognition occurs. At the same time, the symbol attests this law of the *lack* (law of the Absent One, of the Other, of the Ancestor . . .) which founds every human society and every individual in it as a subject. All these are things which, by their very definition, fall outside the realm of "value."

2) *The symbol thereby accomplishes the primordial function of language of which it is the interior witness:* this is primarily a function, not of information about the real (an instrumental perspective), but of "information of the real" on which it bestows the significant "form" of a "world" in rescuing it from its natural state by placing it at a distance; not primarily a function of naming or distributing labels, but of *summons or challenge,* of coming-to-presence; not primarily a function of *representation* of objects, but of *communication* between subjects. Of course, language also plays, and necessarily so, an informing, naming, representing role. This is why the sign pole always exists in relation to its symbolic pole. But the symbolic function is primary and belongs to another level from that of the sign. *It is the symbolic that, in language, makes the real speak:* speaking for human beings because speaking about human beings, and even speaking "human beings." At the same time, it is the symbol that makes human beings speak: "Therefore, human beings speak, but only because the symbol has first *made* them human beings."[10]

3) The difference between sign and symbol thus appears as *homologous* to the difference which exists between the principle of the value of something as an object, which governs the *market-place,* and the principle "beyond value" of the communication between subjects, which controls *symbolic exchange.*

d) *Symbol and Reality.* If it is accurate to say that sign and symbol go back to two levels that are different in principle, *then it is no longer possible to think of the second as simply a derivative of the first.* Yet this is the presupposition that has governed the tradition of Western *rhetoric,* as T. Todorov has shown in his work *Théories du*

10. J. Lacan, *Ecrits,* 276.

symbole.[11] Such a presupposition was also intrinsically linked to the *metaphysics* of language-as-instrument aiming at restoring, in as *univocal* a manner as possible, the "real" perceived in its "natural" state, and then simply adjusting itself to the "real" as to a norm.

According to this approach, a symbol can be considered only as a *more complex sign* (polysemous by nature); the more complex it is the more distant it is from the norm. By an "intentional change" (p. 75), it *clothes* things with more beautiful ornaments, it decorates the truth with jewels, not, as Augustine emphasizes apropos of Christ, "to refuse to communicate it, but rather to arouse the desire for it all the more by just this dissimulation."[12] For "the more things appear veiled with metaphorical expressions, the more they are attractive once the veil is lifted."[13] Interpretation is therefore an "undressing. . . . For in classical hermeneutics, the length of the process, or even its difficulty, increases its worth — as long as one is certain of arriving in the end at the body itself" (p. 75).

Thus the symbolic expression does not in any way affect *the body of the truth, which remains always the same.* Such is "one of the most persistent paradigms of Western culture" since antiquity. More precisely, since "thought is more important than its expression" (p. 116), it can be detached from this expression, so much so that, throughout all of traditional rhetoric, "the existence of the figure rests on the firm conviction that two expressions, one with and the other without an image, express," as Du Marsais put it in the eighteenth century, "the same stock of thought" (pp. 122–123).

The *German Romantics* are going to revolutionize this model. "As language raised to the second power," writes Novalis, the symbol is not "a means to an end" but "the end in itself" (p. 207). Its *"auto-telism"* (p. 246) renders it *"intransitive"*: it does not refer back to an "idea" which would be exterior to it or preexist it. That is why, Schelling goes so far as to say, symbolic figures "do not simply signify, but rather are the thing itself," just as Mary Magdalene in the gospel story "does not simply stand for repentance, she is living repentance itself" (p. 246). Noteworthy in this context is Goethe's remark: the symbol "is the thing, without be-

---

11. T. Todorov, *Théories du symbole* (Paris: Seuil, 1977). The references between parentheses in the text pertain to this work.

12. Augustine, *Sermon* 51:4-5. Quoted by Todorov, *Théories* 75.

13. Augustine, *De doctrina christiana* 4:7, 15. Quoted by Todorov, *Théories*, 76.

ing the thing — and yet in spite of that, the thing" (p. 239). The entire tradition of the classical ideal in art is at the same time attacked; no longer is it a question, as Diderot still thought, of imitating either nature or some ideal model "which artists possess in their minds" (p. 146). From now on the accent falls squarely on artists "*pro-ducing themselves*" in the process of producing their works, and no longer on art as reproductions of predetermined models.

This romantic revolution is certainly not without its risks. In stressing too one-sidedly the expressive over the representative function, one is in danger of sinking in the swamps of an exacerbated subjectivism, in the quicksands of the "unutterable" and "touching," in the vaporous mysticism of some para-psychological or para-religious esotericism — where everything is eventually held up by a pseudo-theory of "symbol for symbol's sake" or "art for art's sake." One protects oneself against such risks only by reminding oneself that *"there is no such thing as a pure symbol."*

Symbolization is thus neither a simple *ornament* nor a degeneracy of language. On the contrary, it unfolds the *primary* dimension of language, its essential "vocation," by which "human beings never perceive water in a state of 'pure' reality, that is, a state non-significant for themselves. The water which I look at is always either deep, clear, pure, fresh, or stagnant; its reality is to be immediately a metaphor for my entire existence."[14] My existence is not simply "like" water; "the 'like,'" continues A. Vergote, "does not establish a transposition from the water into its symbolic signification" because the comparison establishes a connection that stays exterior to the reality evoked.

But the relation here is global and internal — to such an extent that we recognize in ritual baths, notably those used as part of an initiation ceremony involving a symbolic death and rebirth, the highest manifestation of the "reality" of water. Water never comes so close to its "truth" as when it functions as both sepulcher of death and bath of rebirth: the fundamental metaphor of human existence.

Far, then, from being opposed to the "real," as the reigning logic of signs would have it, *the symbol touches the most real aspect of ourselves and our world*. It touches us to the quick. From this comes the risk of drifting in the direction of romanticism, of the

---

14. A. Vergote, *Interprétation du langage religieux* (Paris: Seuil, 1974) 64.

"touching"; but this risk is also the bearer of a profound truth. For "is it not in what makes us speechless, in this anxiety which constricts our throat, that we renew contact with the living sources of language?"[15] There are circumstances — bereavement for example — where words, powerless or out of place, can do nothing but yield to "body language." The rose offered, the kiss exchanged, the simple silence filled with a presence express better than any discourse the uncrossable chasm that separates me from the friend in distress — "I cannot put myself in your place . . . I am not you" — and simultaneously, in this breach of *otherness* that they show, the truth of my *presence* to this person — "I am with you." Perhaps mutual presence is never so real as in this moment when, through the grace of a symbolic gesture, the insurmountable gulf, the radical lack which renders it impossible for one person to take the place of another, is represented. This gesture unfolds the very essence of every language, as if lifting it to its second power: it brings about communication, alliance, the recognition of two subjects in the very act where, with death in the background, they recognize each other as most "other"; and death ceases thereby to be simply a fatal biological necessity. Tamed by this symbolic gesture, it becomes "human"; it reveals its "truth": not simply an inevitable happening about which we could talk together, as we do about an exterior object that would affect us only when we speak of it, but rather the very thing that allows us to sustain each other and resides permanently in the most vital centers of our lives.[16]

2. The Two Poles of Every Language

The fact that sign and symbol, like exchange in the marketplace and symbolic exchange, belong to two different principles, two different logics, two different levels does not mean that we could choose one to the exclusion of the other; for the two hold concretely together.

a) The Symbolic Claim to "Re-cognition" in Every Discourse of "Cognition." Every discourse can be read on two different levels: either

15. Ortigues, *Le discours et le symbole,* 33.
16. Notice the remarkable developments concerning the relations of death with *l'entretien* in G. Lafon, *Le Dieu commun* (Paris: Seuil, 1982).

on the level of symbol, as a language of "recognition," foundation of the identity of the group and individuals, and agent of cohesion (successful or not) between subjects within their cultural world, or on the level of sign, as a language of "cognition," aiming at delivering information and at passing judgments. *Myth* represents the most typical example of the first, so much so that, as C. Lévi-Strauss has shown, bringing together into play ("symbolizing") the diverse cultural codes, from that of kinship to that of cooking, from which the group unconsciously lives, myth constitutes the foundational language that permits the group to recognize itself, identify itself, find itself a significant place in the sun. And this language makes of individuals subjects who are part of a "we" that is social and common: all recognize themselves in the myth. *Scientific discourse*, on the contrary, is typically representative of the language of cognition, all the more so in that it aims by its very methodology to be a discourse without an author.

However, it would be a grave mistake, as F. Flahault has remarked — and positivism is an illustration of it — to believe that speaking subjects, *men and women* of science, are somehow absent from their "objective" discourses; that they do not seek to be recognized by their "peers" as well, to occupy positions among other persons, to discover a *human* dimension to their research. For in effect, "it is not in the content of their words that something that transcends them takes place, but in the fact that their words are *recognized* as relevant to science." Moreover, what satisfies them, as they read their papers, is "to occupy the place of this unshakable authority, to be this unassailable 'one' or impersonal 'researcher,' or simply 'it' ('it was discovered that,' 'one found out that,' and so forth), to sit majestically on this guarantee of the truth that 'scientific achievement' is."[17]

From this comes the "point of honor" among scientists, as P. Bourdieu has remarked, of "multiplying the signs of distancing

17. F. Flahault, *La parole intermédiaire* (Paris: Seuil, 1978) 220–221. In our society, many propositions are held to be "scientific" only inasmuch as "science plays the role of the ancestors," notes D. Sperber, *Le symbolisme en général* (Paris: Hermann, 1974) 113. See the interesting analysis the author proposes on this phenomenon in terms of "symbolic knowledge" (pp. 97–125).

themselves from the representations of common sense"[18] and of laying claim to an elevated social status by these marks of "distinction." For "the attempt to maximize information yield is the exclusive goal of linguistic production only by exception; and the purely instrumental use of language that it implies normally enters into contradiction with the goals, often unconscious, of symbolic gain"[19] or again with the preservation and increase among the interlocutors of their "symbolic capital, that is to say, of the recognition, institutionalized or not, that they receive from a group."[20]

Everyday language is also constantly caught between sign and symbol. The most banal conversation on the vagaries of the weather, in spite of its impressive and confident appearance, usually has little scientific information to transmit. Although it is less apparent, the symbolic pole involved in *speaking when there is nothing to say* is more important; this is so because it is important that everyone have someone to speak to: communication has a value in itself; it is the social recognition of one's "presence" that is claimed here.

This is why a few lines, or just a signature, on the back of a postcard can symbolically function as powerfully as a long letter to (re)seal a friendship.

One could also give a thousand examples from the *extra-linguistic* domain: the most casual and ordinary handshake may reacquire its symbolic power for alliance and for recognition and gratefulness in certain circumstances. The same wine from the same cask can be used to simply slake one's thirst or to add something special to a celebration where one wishes to express the happiness of being together, the joy of being reconciled, or the mutual respect between guests. And the most worn-down shoe, pitiably abandoned on the sidewalk, can lose every aspect of utilitarian value as a fabricated object to become a symbol for all the misery in the world. Our days are filled with such symbolic readings: they do not cease to speak within us. Steadily, and most often without our thinking of it, these renew the connections between our world and those of others; they claim for us a significant place; they demand a recognition of "who I am for you and who you are for me." In the last analysis, is it not this symbolic "bread" of the word that gives us life and holds us together?

18. P. Bourdieu, *Ce que parler veut dire: L'économie des échanges linguistiques* (Paris: Fayard, 1982) 145, n. 10.

19. Ibid., 60.

20. Ibid., 68.

b) The Necessary Place of "Cognition" in Every Symbolic Expression.
If in every informational discourse there is at play a symbolic
negotiation for position, conversely, every symbolic expression
tends to be taken into a discourse of *cognition* where something is
said about something amenable to being ratified by a *judgment of
value.* With perhaps the exception of its rock-bottom expression,
the phoneme, a "pure symbol" does not exist; at least not at the
level of the "symbol properly so called."

We need a minimum knowledge if Van Gogh's painting of the peasant
woman's shoe is to exercise its power of symbolization. Thus, it is probably indispensable to *know* what shoes are and what they are habitually
used for and also what peasant life used to be like, if the symbolic separation between these shoes as a simple product of manufacture and their
pictorial representation is to strike us: in one sense they are the same
thing, but in another sense they are completely different. Further, for
these objects to speak to us symbolically, it is no doubt helpful to know
the painting is a work by Van Gogh: it is something from his life, which
was so often miserable, that is here turned into a metaphor, just as his
personal agonies were transposed into twists of color, paint, and space
that so clearly characterize his style in other paintings. No less helpful for
the symbolic appreciation of the painting is to realize that the depiction of
such "ugly" or banal objects is characteristic of a new era of painting in a
culture revolting against its traditional aesthetic canons and the legitimate
tastes, of the baroque period for example, and that such a painting is the
expression by Van Gogh, not as an individual isolated abstractly from his
world, but as a member of a concrete society whose conventional norms
he reflects even in his opposition to them and to the reigning academic
style. Of course, this knowledge about Van Gogh and the appreciation of
his place in the history of painting do not produce the viewer's aesthetic
enjoyment. The proof of this is that any encyclopedia, or even a simple illustrated dictionary, can furnish us with most of this knowledge; but at
this level the work is no longer art, it is simply a fine plate of illustrations
in color that are useful and informative for the reader. Nevertheless, as
we have just seen, *such knowledge is not totally foreign to the symbolic effects
produced by the work.*

To have no knowledge of these things would be to find oneself in the
situation of Amazonian Indians who knew nothing of the world of Euro-
peans: neither shoes, nor peasant life, nor any image from the West — a
fortiori, something put into a frame and shown in a museum. Not only
would the picture say nothing to them, but they would not even "see"
it. No more than, as A. Malraux says, "if Delacroix — a hundred years

ago — could have seen the works we show today," specifically those of Sumerian art, "he would not have *seen* them"; for, if the nineteenth century had discovered them, they would not have yet "become visible as works of art," so much did the aesthetic canons of the time, ruled by "beauty," pose obstacles to such an unveiling.[21]

Thus, the symbolic experience is not sufficient unto itself. *Every symbol tends toward a discourse of cognition*, a discourse of truth which is the ambition of all language. A symbol about which one could say nothing would dissolve into pure imagination. If then we have denounced classical rhetoric for having reduced the symbol to a sort of "aesthetic" excrescence on the sign, it is not to replace it with the theory of the Romantic philosophers, even if their contribution has been decisive in other respects. Pure "autotelism" and the absolute "intransitivity" of the symbol, like "art for art's sake," are exclusively the product of Romantic ideology. It remains for us then to recognize the simultaneous existence of two levels and two poles in language.

II. THE ACT OF SYMBOLIZATION

1. *Analysis*

In analyzing the very act of symbolization, we are evidently going to meet again the fundamental traits already mentioned; but this will also give us the opportunity to add several refinements which seem important to us. Let us imagine an incident that illustrates the nature of symbol, specificaly here the ancient symbol. During the Second World War, there are two secret agents who do not know each other but are supposed to cooperate in an act of sabotage. The Office of Strategic Services passes on to each one half of a five-dollar bill cut irregularly so that only the other's half will fit perfectly. This symbolic act can be broken down into six elements:

1. First there is the *act of joining* the two pieces of the bill. The symbol exists only in the act. It does not subsist in the order of "ideas," but of "actions." This "action" is eventually a gesture, as in this case. But more deeply, this symbol has a goal of practicality and achievement, as we will see in number 6.

21. A. Malraux, Preface to A. Parot, *Sumer* (Paris: Gallimard, 1960) xi.

2. The two pieces of paper are necessarily *distinct*. This truism does not need to be mentioned except to remind us that we symbolize only distinct elements (this will have more serious consequences later when we say the sacraments symbolize Christ and the Church).

3. Each of the two halves has value only *in relation to the other* (compare the pieces of a broken vase): half of a five-dollar bill is ordinarily not worth two fifty. In other words, taken in isolation, each one of them can only "regress toward an ineffable imaginary realm" (Ortigues) and signify pretty much anything at all.

4. *The monetary value of the bill is of no consequence.* A one-dollar bill would do as well as a hundred-dollar one — or even a torn piece of newspaper. The efficacy of the act of symbolization is not dependent, except accidentally in certain cases, on the *commercial* or *utilitarian value* of the object used. We have already insisted on this point when we spoke of symbolic exchange. The same is true with regard to a gift: a "nothing at all" — nothing as far as its commercial or utilitarian value — can be very effective symbolically! The symbol is by its nature *outside the realm of value*. What is important is not the utility of the object, but the exchange that it permits between the subjects.

This accounts for the *drifting* away from its original meaning that has occured to the term "symbol" in our Western languages: "the more a thing is 'symbolic,' the less important it is" or "the less real it is." For example, why actually pour the water which runs over the forehead of an infant being baptized? Three drops, that is all that is necessary since "it is symbolic"! And how can one not think here of the "symbolic dollar" paid by way of damages and interest? Such a drift in language is perfectly understandable because it is rooted in the fact that the performance of the symbol is not connected to its value or to its economic, practical, cognitive, moral, or even "aesthetic" utility.

Now, if the few dollars I give to buy a calendar from the Boy Scouts or cookies from the Girl Scouts is "symbolic," it is not because it is such a paltry sum, but because this purchase constitutes for me an *effective mediation to renew my connections* with these organizations in which I wish to have a stake without being a member or active participant and because this effectiveness is not essentially a function of the size of my contribution. As in the (essentially symbolic) example of the gift, we notice here that the symbol, far from drifting away toward the "unreal" (except in the sense of identifying the "real" with commercial value), on the contrary touches *the most real part* of our identity.

5 and 6. The act of symbolization is simultaneously *a revealer and an agent*. It is the revealer of identity: the two secret agents recognize one another as partners. It is an agent: *through* recognizing each other as partners, they become bound together in a common "we," running the same risks of being taken prisoner and exposed to the same danger of death. The symbol is an agent of alliance *through* being a revealer of identity.

We can truthfully speak here of the *efficacy* of the symbol, an efficacy which touches reality itself. The whole question is to know *what reality* we are speaking about. If we represent it on the model of a *hypokeimenon*, a "substrate," an ontological "substance," then such an efficacy becomes unthinkable. But as we have explained, we are not dealing with such unprocessed reality. It is a reality always already culturally processed, speaking only because spoken, that happens to us; and this reality is *the most real*.

2. *The Performance Dimension of the Act of Symbolization*

a) Narrative and Discourse. The act of symbolization, we have noted, carries out the essential vocation of language: to bring about an alliance where subjects may come into being and recognize themselves as such within their world. Now, this description corresponds well enough to what J. L. Austin calls *language acts*.[22] Every language act is a process, that is, something which sets the system (phonemes, morphemes, lexemes, syntax) to work. E. Benveniste distinguishes two general types within this process: one is the historical *narrative*, governed by the third person and the past tense (even where the first person and the present tense may be incidentally used); the other is the *discourse*, governed by the first person in relation to the second person and the present tense.[23] This discourse is not concerned with the text of the enunciation as such but with *the act of enunciation*. For this act, this "setting the discourse into motion," is *unique every time* because each time it posits the "I" and in the present tense. As with the "I" (and

22. J. L. Austin, *Quand dire, c'est faire* (Paris: Seuil, 1970).
23. E. Benveniste, *Problèmes de linguistique générale* (Paris: Gallimard, 1966) 1:ch. 19, especially 242–243.

thus reciprocally the YOU), this "axial present of the discourse" is always at least "implicit"; it is "reinvented each time a person speaks because it is, in the literal sense, a new moment, one which has not yet been lived."[24]

b) Declarative and Performative. But this presupposes that something is said about something. This saying something about something requires that all language have a *declarative* function, as Austin calls it — for example, a description: "I wagered" or "she wagers"; but the act of saying this "to someone" requires another function in which communication between subjects is primary and which belongs to the *performative* as a language act, that is, as an act really changing the position of the subjects by the very fact of the act of enunciation. "I wager" is not just information or a description of performance, like "I wagered" or "she wagers"; "I wager" *constitutes the performance itself:* I am now obligated toward my interlocutor by my wager.

Declaration and performance activate two different *functions* of language: the first is its declarative function; the second, its communicative or "allocutive." However, neither ever exists in a pure state; they always subsist in dialectical tension as the two *poles* of language. "It is a fact that performative utterances always say something at the same time they do something," Austin remarks.[25]

Thus, "I wager" contains a minimum of information, even if the accent falls on the performative aspect. In the same way, "I order you to close the door": this statement presupposes the fact that there is a door and that it is open; but of course, as a language act, it "signifies" to the other his or her subordination (real or simply desired), it puts the other in his or her place (as we say), it instates or reinstates, it creates or reinforces the authority of the speaker over the other. On the other hand, "It's a nice day today" seems to be a pure declaration; but the information thus transmitted is so obvious that, unless the other person is mentally impaired, something else is most likely being communicated — the pure and simple request to establish a connection with someone. This request by the other, so disguised and encoded that we respond to it half-

24. Ibid., 2:73-75, 1:252-255.
25. Austin, *Quand dire, c'est faire,* 144. The references between parentheses in the text pertain to this work.

automatically without even thinking about it, is not fully performative and yet is akin to it. More precisely, it reflects what Austin calls the *illocutionary* dimension of language.

c) *The Locutionary, the Illocutionary, and the Perlocutionary.* According to Austin, every discourse, every language act, has in fact three dimensions, of differing importance in each case. The *locutionary* dimension consists in "the production of a sentence having meaning and a referent, these two elements corresponding roughly to the traditional meaning of the term." Distinct from this "act *of* saying something" is the "act effected *in* saying something" and designated by the *illocutionary* dimension of the language act ("act" understood here in the strongest sense of the term). In its turn, the "act effected *by* saying something" is distinct from the external effect produced "*by* the act of saying something (this 'by' has here an 'instrumental sense') and constitutes the *perlocutionary* dimension of the language act" (pp. 119, 136). The expression "language act" fits the illocutionary in a particular way, inasmuch as the illocutionary designates an action that is strictly intra-linguistic, whose achieved expression is found in the class of performative verbs in the strict sense, such as "I promise you," "I bet you," "I commit myself to you," "I order you" . . . : the *relation between the subjects* is not the same after as it was before.

One can see how the illocutionary dimension is susceptible of various *degrees* of meaning in its usage, from the most explicit level, as in the strict or formal performative statements ("I take an oath," "I take you for my spouse") to the most implicit, as in the example given above of the most obvious information, "It's a nice day."

Between these two there is an intermediate illocutionary level that is semi-explicit, as in an interrogative sentence. For example, "What time is it?" presupposes "I am asking you to tell me the time" or again "I am making you stop what you are doing to answer me." A request of this type in effect so changes the situation between subjects that a failure of the addressee to respond to the question clearly formulated would be interpreted as a personal insult, a wounding attitude ignoring the presence of the one making the request, a symbolic murder. From this it follows that "to make a locutionary statement in general is by that very fact (*eo ipso*) to make an *illocutionary* statement as well" (p. 112) so that "every act of authentic discourse contains the two aspects at the same time" (p. 149).

What the illocutionary carries out in the language act itself, the *perlocutionary* achieves as a *consequence* of the latter; for it designates the effect of the language act "on the feelings, the thoughts, the behavior of the audience or the speaker or still other persons." There are some verbs that are strictly perlocutionary, such as "convince," "persuade," "frighten"; others, according to the circumstances, may be perlocutionary or illocutionary or both, such as "command," "order," "threaten." "I order you to close the door" certainly has a perlocutionary intention (for the door to be closed), but this could be a pretext for the speaker to manifest (illocutionarily) his or her authority. More generally still, "a perlocutionary act may always, or almost always, be elicited, with or without premeditation, by almost any statement, and notably by what appears to be a purely declarative sentence" (p. 120): a piece of information given to someone may make him or her give up a project; the suspicion may even be this precise perlocutionary effect was desired by the speaker, though hidden beneath the statement's apparent neutrality (see the statement of Mary to Jesus at the marriage feast at Cana, "They have no more wine," John 2:3).

d) Distinctive Traits. Austin is the first to recognize that the proposed distinction is, as a matter of fact, not very clear in a number of cases. In real life, the three dimensions are often mixed up with one another. It seems that several traits should be kept in mind.

1. First, there is the distinction between the *intra*-linguistic illocutionary effect and the *extra*-linguistic perlocutionary effect. The sentence "I order you to close the door" affects primarily either the intra-linguistic (the relation between the superior and the subordinate) or the extra-linguistic (the door is closed or not; or the sentence might engender a feeling of fear, irritation, or pleasure in the one hearing it).

2. The illocutionary, and even more the performative, is not concerned with the true or the false, but with the happy and the unhappy, that is to say, in the last analysis with the *legitimate* or the illegitimate. "I bet you" can be an empty performative act without effect if the *circumstances* are defective — for example, if I omit to shake hands in the manner required to seal a wager or if I am not qualified to place a bet of this kind . . . In the same way, "I take

you for my spouse'' is without effect if one of the two partners is already legally married to someone else.

3. Thus, even if ''it is difficult to say where the conventions begin and leave off'' (p. 126), one can still say that ''illocutionary acts are *conventional*'' while ''perlocutionary acts are not'' (p. 129). The performative function thus depends, not only on the internal conditions of the language, but also on circumstances attending the statement — notably, the existence of a recognized *procedure;* its correct execution; the legitimacy of agents, locations, and times . . .

4. This last trait shows two things. First, the paradigmatic examples of illocutionary acts are to be sought in the verbal or gestural language acts of *rituals;* or rituals are stagings which unfold the illocutionary-performative dimension of language. Second, as Bourdieu and F. A. Isambert have stressed, the ''illocutionary force'' of this language is not to be sought in a ''magic power of words'' or some ''verbal mana,'' but rather in *''the consensus that validates them.''* Thus, an ''I promise'' has value only as a pact between my partner, myself, and the collectivity which governs the conditions for the validity of promises[26] or as a ''relation between the properties of the discourse, the properties of the one who pronounces it, and the properties of the institution that authorizes one to pronounce it.''[27] The power of words in the illocutionary act, notably as a performative ritual manifestation, resides in the fact that they are not pronounced by an individual as an individual, but rather as the proxy of the group, as the *representative* of its ''*symbolic capital.*''[28] Thus, this shows clearly what is going on in all language: a relation of places between subjects, a recognition, an identification, within a social and cultural world.

5. An entire *hierarchy of degrees* exists at the level of *ritual.* For example, social codification appears strongly in an ''I baptize you'' or ''I confirm,'' uttered by the presider at a meeting acting in his or her capacity and within the confines of a negotiation rite. The correctness of the procedures (legitimate agent, proper formula and gestures, and so forth) plays a major role in such ceremonies.

26. F. A. Isambert, *Rite et efficacité symbolique* (Paris: Cerf, 1979) 194.
27. Bourdieu, *Ce que parler veut dire*, 111.
28. Ibid., 107–109.

By contrast, in an "I bet you" uttered among chatting friends, the reference to the absent Third (the social Other under whose jurisdiction alone a bet can be made) is now only implicit.

At these different levels we are in the order of ritual (in the broad sense) and, even more obviously, in the order of the *"illocutionary which alone breaks the duality between saying and doing"*[29] and brings about symbolically, on the sole basis of the statement, a transformation in the relations between the subjects, under the authority of the social Third (the law) to which they necessarily refer — and refer in an explicit manner in the great instituted rituals. "It is only within this framework that the performative takes on meaning. . . . It has all the characteristics of a rite, and its performance is exactly of the order of symbolic efficacy."[30]

III. THE SYMBOLIC EFFICACY OF RITES

1. *Several Examples of Symbolic Efficacy in Traditional Rites*

Whether this be in the shamanistic ritual of giving birth among the Cuna Indians reported by Lévi-Strauss, in the "distress" Ihamba ritual among the Ndembu studied by Turner, or finally in the Esa healing ritual among the Douala of the Cameroun chronicled by E. de Rosny, symbolic efficacy always takes place within the *socio-cultural order*.

a) C. Lévi-Strauss. In the first case, a pregnant woman finds herself unable to give birth. Without touching her body or giving her any medicine, the shaman succeeds, through a long incantation, in stimulating the birth process. What he sings is a myth, the story of a violent combat, woven together from a thousand incidents, between, on the one side, the shaman and the sacred images (*nuchu*) representing the good, protective spirits and, on the other side, Muu, the power responsible for the formation of the fetus, who, with its daughters, has taken possession of the "soul" of the future mother. Now, in the local thinking, the "path of Muu and the residence of Muu are not a mythical voyage and residence, but literally represent the vagina and uterus of the pregnant woman, which the shaman and the *nuchu* explore and in whose deepest recesses they fight their victorious battle."[31] The mythic song thus constitutes "a

29. Isambert, *Rite et efficacité symbolique*, 94.
30. Ibid., 99.
31. C. Lévi-Strauss, *Anthropologie structurale*, 207.

psychological manipulation of the sick organ."[32] But such a manipulation is possible, emphasizes Lévi-Strauss, only because "the sick person believes in it and is a member of a society that believes in it. Protective spirits and hostile spirits, supernatural monsters and magic animals, all belong to a coherent system which establishes the indigenous conception of the universe. The sick woman accepts them or more exactly, she has never doubted them. What she does not accept are the *incongruent* and arbitrary pains which, as such, constitute an element *foreign to her system* but which, through the invocation of the myth, the shaman *relocates within a coherent whole.*"

This point is capital; for, it is not only because she knows and understands the connection between the myth and her bodily condition that the woman in labor is effectively cured. This kind of knowledge does not suffice: for us, to know the connection of cause and effect between germ and sickness does not cure anyone because such a relation is "exterior to the patient's mind." On the other hand, for the Cunas, the relation between the powers evoked in the myth and the sickness "is interior to this same mind, conscious or unconscious": "it is a relation of symbol to the object symbolized. . . . The Shaman provides the sick person with a *language* in which states, unformulated and otherwise impossible to formulate, may be immediately expressed. And it is this accession to verbal expression (which permits the person to assimilate an actual experience of pain, otherwise anarchic and inexpressible, into an ordered and intelligible form) that releases the physiological processes."[33]

One sees it clearly: if the *"perlocutionary" extra-linguistic effect* of giving birth is rendered possible, it is *by the mediation of an "illocutionary" intra-linguistic effect.* The symbolic efficacy of the myth consists in manipulating an element foreign to the cultural system of the patient and her group, incongruent in relation to her "world," thus literally "unsayable" and unthinkable, for the purpose of "restoring it to its place within an ordered and coherent whole."

b) V. Turner. We have another illustration of this same type of phenomenon in *The Drums of Affliction* by V. Turner. Kamahasanyi is truly physically sick; he is afflicted by a "shadow," persecuted by a malevolent spirit. Turner shows that, as a matter of fact, he has become sick because he is in an untenable social situation due to a contradiction between his

32. Ibid., 211.
33. Ibid., 218. Emphasis mine.

position in the village and his position according to his kinship. The long Ihamba ritual performed for him culminates in the extraction of a tooth from his body. This tooth is the major *symbol* for the socio-cultural animosity between Kamahasanyi and his fellow tribesmen. It is as though the tooth were the concentrate of this feeling. The ritual permits the sick person, among other things, to speak out without being contradicted. Its aim, in fact, is to give him the possibility of expressing his rancor against those (especially his relatives on his mother's side) who "have a tooth [bear a grudge] against him." In any case, as Turner notes, after the final sequence where the "sorcerer" extracts a human tooth from the body of the sick person, "I had the feeling that what they were in fact taking from this man was the *animosity of the village*." The sick person is physically healed. But it is also, and at the same time, the entire group that is healed, for "an explosion of friendly sentiments suddenly broke out among the entire village community. Those who had nursed hostile feelings toward one another ended by cordially shaking hands."[34]

Here again the *somatic* efficacy is rendered possible by the *symbolic* efficacy of language, which the ritual provides both to the sick person and to the group and which allows for the resetting of an incongruous element into a coherent pattern. *Everything returns to order.*

c) *E. de Rosny.* "In what consists the healing of the *nganga* (good sorcerers)?" asks de Rosny. "As far as I can tell, it is to be understood by the title of the last story, 'Returning to Order.'"[35] The story to which the author refers is about one of the numerous rituals of healing he analyzes in his work; it is the Esa ritual performed for Kwedi. "Two months ago [Kwedi] suddenly could not see, could not walk, could not hear. The loss of her means of communication was the sign of the most complete abandonment. Each day Loe (the nganga) gave her good medicines which put her back on her feet, but they did not cure her. The essential remained: *to correct her disturbed relations with her universe.* The best way to achieve this return to normal would be again through the efficacious use of rituals. Towards this goal, Loe succeeded in achieving the general mobilization of the forces upon which Kwedi's life depended. That was the price for a healing, and it

---

34. Turner, *Les tambours d'affliction*, 192–193.
35. de Rosny, *Les yeux de ma chèvre*, 296.

was worth an entire night's work."[36] Here again, the cure is obtained by means of the symbolic effect of the ritual which, as a concentrated code of the socio-cultural system of the group, allows the incoherent element to "return to order" and "normal" relations between the sick person and her "world" to be restored.

Moreover, this author goes further in this direction than the preceding ethnologists. After years of patient and sometimes dangerous work among of the Douala and their nganga, he ended by asking one of them, Din, to initiate him into their "vision."

Now, what did he finally "see" after long months of ritual preparation? *"The vision is the revelation of the violence between people.* It takes tremendous personal strength for me to face the reality in its brute form. Without initiation, without teaching, this vision would overtax our psychological powers or hurl us into the maelstrom of violence. Society is organized to conceal from its members the violence which can break out at any moment between them. This is a dangerous revelation for society; that is why the nganga is a disturbing personality."[37]

To become a nganga is to learn to see the violence that rules relations between people, and to manage it; further, violence is disorder — disorder of which sickness is a species. For in all indigenous societies sickness is seen as more than a simple biological event; it is a *cultural disorder,* the effect of a violence done by some malevolent spirit, an ancestor, or relative who is persecuting a member of the group. Consequently, physical healing requires that the social source of this affliction be uncovered, as in Kwedi's case. It requires that a ritual be carried out, a ritual conducted by a qualified agent who has learned to look at the violence, to "steel himself or herself" against it, and thereby to master it. This ritual restores the incongruent element (the disease) *to the social order* by providing it a language; it reestablishes the disturbed relations between the sick person and his or her universe. It is this symbolic work that the nganga is charged with carrying out, and it is through his or her efforts that the effective cures are obtained.

These three examples show us the same thing: the ritual "acts on the real by acting on the representations of the real."[38] If there is actually a physical healing — an extra-linguistic perlocutionary effect — it is *by the intermediary of a symbolic efficacy,* of the illocu-

36. Ibid., 279. Emphasis mine.
37. Ibid., 354–355.
38. Bourdieu, *Ce que parler veut dire,* 124.

tionary order, that it is obtained. The ritual acts performatively: from the sole fact of its enunciation by an "authority" recognized as qualified to carry it out, it restores the health of the sick person through reestablishing his or her troubled relations with the members of the community and with the culture of the group. The alliance thereby triumphs over violence. Like the piece from a broken vase, the element, incongruent as long as it remains isolated, is "restored to its place within a coherent whole" (Lévi-Strauss); everything "returns to order" (de Rosny); the ritual reestablishes "the health of the social body" (Turner).[39]

To wish to give this symbolic efficacy "an explicative power analogous to that of a physical law which explains phenomena" would clearly be to follow a "wrong lead," as Isambert emphasizes. For the symbolic efficacy is a function, "of the consensus created around the representations, on the one hand, and of the symbolic connection between the representations and what is at issue, on the other." *Therefore, it cannot be identified with the scheme of cause and effect* (as if, for example, it were a species in the wider genus of psycho-somatic activity, whereby the spirit acts directly on the body). For *the effect here is itself a "symbolic effect,"* distinct from other effects — physical, for example — which "can be taken only as secondary effects." This is a fundamental distinction, which allows us not to confuse symbolic efficacy with its most spectacular physical effects and to understand that the ritual may often intend "other effects than the healing of the body. These are the effects which spiritual religions seek."[40]

2. Symbolic Efficacy and Sacramental Grace: First Sketch

Christianity belongs to those religions which one may call "spiritual" and which seek in their rituals effects other than the purely corporeal. Designated by the generic term "grace," these effects are found beyond the realm of value (compare, the manna). By this fact, the communication of grace is to be understood, not according to the "metaphysical" scheme of cause and effect, but according to the symbolic scheme of communication through language, a

39. Turner, *Les tambours d'affliction*, 302.
40. Isambert, *Rite et efficacité symbolique*, 83–85.

communication supremely effective because it is through language that the subject comes forth in its relations to other subjects within a common "world" of meaning. It is precisely a *new relation of places between subjects*, a relationship of filial and brotherly and sisterly alliance, that the sacramental "expression" aims at instituting or restoring in faith.

However, if this kind of symbolic work is to be correctly placed within the purview of *intra-linguistic* efficacy, it cannot, as far as God's grace is concerned, be reduced to this socio-linguistic process: this would be to transform theology into nothing more than a peculiar form of anthropology and to diminish the absolute otherness of God. We must say, then, that "sacramental grace" is an *extra-linguistic* reality, but with this distinction, in its Christian form it is comprehensible only on the (intra-linguistic) model of the filial and brotherly and sisterly alliance established, *outside of us (extra nos)*, in Christ. Despite grammar, which should never be taken at face value, "grace" designates not an object we receive, but rather a symbolic work of *receiving oneself*: a work of "perlaboration" in the Spirit by which subjects receive themselves from God in Christ as sons and daughters, brothers and sisters. We will develop in its proper place (Chapter Eleven) this perspective which we can only sketch here.

IV. THE SYMBOL AND THE BODY

Our approach of returning human beings to the field of language is accompanied from end to end by the body, the *body-being*. This approach has repeatedly sent us back to the *contingent mediation* of a language, a culture, a history as the very place where the subject comes to its truth. Of this reality outside of which the subject can only lose itself in its imagination, the body is the primordial expression. It is easy to see that this fact is of fundamental importance for a theology of *the sacraments* because the ritual symbolism which constitutes them has the body for its setting. Now, according to Church tradition, the most "spiritual" communication of God (that of the Holy Spirit itself), and thus the truth of the believing subject, takes place through this language, eminently sensory and bodily. The sacraments accordingly teach us that *the truest things in our faith occur in no other way than through the concreteness of the "body."*

1. Language as "Writing"

a) On Significant Matter. The concept of *writing* seems to us to be a valuable aid in reflecting on what is at issue in the concept of "corporality." There is no language except through the mediation of a given, particular, and limited *tongue.* Now, as soon as you have a language, you have *material,* phonetic material. This is not raw phonetic material — that would be only noise — but *significant* phonetic material, made significant thanks to a cultural delineation. For language to come into being, it is necessary that the sounds emitted by the voice stop being simple noise or unintelligible rumblings and become phonemes. They become so by the *recording of differences* culturally recognized as pertinent: "a" is not "o," and "b" is not "p." This simple delineation does not suffice all by itself to give meaning to phonetic material — "a" does not mean anything — but it is sufficient to make this material belong to the world of sense.

The material thus delineated as significant is a *given.* It is a radical given that *precedes* each person and *is law* for each person, as it is for the group as a whole. This law is an institution, a convention so profoundly cultural that the marking off of sounds into phonemes is as diversified as the different linguistic groups. However, it has this unusual characteristic, that no one person ever sat down one day and decided to be its creator. Consequently, we are dealing here, as we have emphasized above, not with one institution among others, but rather with the original "space" out of which every institution was born. If language is that which institutes, we must recognize that it is so *only because it itself is already instituted.*

Thus, in its significant *materiality,* language represents the unavoidable law and poses the primordial stumbling block against which every fantasy desire for self-possession, for sweeping away all mediation and all contingency, for advancing to immediate and transparent presence of the self to the self, must shatter. Language *resists* in the same way that *matter* resists. And it is easy to forget this resistance. To counter this temptation, the recognition

141

of language as a "writing" is important. "There has never been anything but writing," J. Derrida insists.[41] Obviously, this proposition escapes absurdity only if the concept of "writing" designates not just the convenient tool that humans invented at a certain point in their history, but a component of all language.

41. J. Derrida, *De la grammatologie* (Paris: Minuit, 1967) especially chs. 1 and 2. In availing ourselves of Derrida's concepts of "writing" and "trace," we are not giving up *hermeneutics* whose general contemporary outline we have described in ch. 2. For we do not consider that Heidegger's deconstruction of metaphysics leads to the rejection of every philosophy of meaning. Derrida criticizes Heidegger for not having carried the ontico-ontological difference to its limit, specifically to this "difference" or "production of the difference" which, without being the "origin," would however be "more 'original' " (Ibid., 38). Even if it is true that with Heidegger "the meaning of being is not a transcendental or trans-epochal signification" (p. 38), the German philosopher does not remain any less, through his very act of climbing back toward the origin — even if this origin is impossible to name as such — a prisoner of metaphysics; for in effect, he continues to pose the question of meaning; but, "each time the question of meaning is posed, it can be so only within the metaphysical enclosure" (*Marges de la philosophie*, 239-240).

As we have developed it, hermeneutics does not appear so congenitally linked to metaphysics and onto-theology as Derrida assumes. If, then, we have criticized the metaphysical understanding of "wishing to express the presence of meaning" that is supposedly hidden *behind* the text, this is not to yield to a pure emergence of the effects of meaning on the sole basis of the structural play of differences between the signifiers. The notion of a *"world of the text"* in Ricœur appears to us to express, on the one hand, the necessity of respecting the *body of the letter* in its irreducible positivity and otherness and, on the other, the *proposal of a "world"* that the text, such as it is, opens to the reading subject: the "meaning" thus proposed by the text is not already there "under" the text, that is to say, in the "wishing-to-express" of the author, whose intention I could uncover by a correct method; rather, it is "the world proper to *this* text," it is "the way of being-in-the-world unfolded *in front of* the text." Hence, to "understand is to *understand oneself in front of the text*"; to interpret is to *"expose oneself to the text,"* instead of reducing this latter to the (central) subjectivity of the author or of the reader. "As a reader, I find myself only in losing myself."

By emphasizing in this way the importance of stumbling against "the thing that is the text," that is to say, against the distancing that "writing" imposes, Ricœur seems to us to criticize in his own fashion the "metaphysical logocentrism" that Derrida vigorously denounces. "Thanks to the distancing achieved by *writing*, appropriation no longer has to have the character of a particular empathy with the author's intention. In fact, appropriation is exactly the op-

Derrida understands the concept of "writing" in the fundamental sense of *"the enduring institution of a sign."* For "every writing stroke is essentially a testament";[42] it is a sign meant to endure in the absence of the writer. But is this not the case with every linguistic sign, including the phonetic? The phonemes "a," "b," "k" disappear as soon as they are produced by the voice; but they are no less continually present as points of reference within the same phonetic system which has extracted them arbitrarily, conventionally, from the midst of a sequence of noises. Consequently, according to Derrida, all language signs are *"written, even those which are phonetic.* The very idea of institution — and thus of the arbitrariness of the sign — is unthinkable before the possibility of writing and outside of its horizon" (p. 65). The *"arch-writing"* of which he is here speaking, in contrast to the "popular understanding of writing" which could "impose itself historically only by the *masking of arch-writing,"* can obviously "never become the object of any science" (p. 83). Rather, it implies "the agency of the instituted trace," the mark "where the difference appears as such" or where the origin of the world presents itself "as the irreducible absence in the presence of the trace" (p. 68). In short, what is at work here is the *trace of the unavoidable priority of the law.*

b) The Logocentric Repression of the Body of the Written Trace. Such an understanding of language as (arch-)writing is, according to Derrida, *"an assault on metaphysics itself."* For metaphysics has always, from Plato (*Phaedrus*, 274–279) down to F. de Saussure himself, considered writing as merely the reduplication of the spoken word — a derivative product, a mere covering of language — in short, a convenient instrument, a practical mnemonic device. Now, it is no accident that metaphysics has been biased in favor of the voice over the letter: the letter presents itself as a mute body and opaque material; the voice is lithe, limber, subtle, incapable of be-

---

posite of this contemporaneity and congeniality; it is understanding through distance, understanding at a distance" (quotations taken from P. Ricœur, *Exegesis*, 213–215). See J. Greisch, *Herméneutique et grammatologie* (Paris: éd. CNRS, 1977).

42. Derrida, *De la grammatologie*, 100. The references between parentheses in the text pertain to this work.

coming frozen into matter because it vanishes as soon as it is born. The voice is understood as the *effacement of significant matter* because it is what is closest to ourselves. It has an immediate proximity to the soul, thus also to our sense of being and the ideality of meaning, while writing seems to "provoke a fall into the exteriority of meaning" (p. 24).

The metaphysical tradition is *logocentric* or "logo-phonocentric." Its unexamined presupposition — attainment of the ultimately real and a totally transparent presence to oneself — has led it to conjure up exteriority, materiality, and the body as so many *obstacles*, certainly inevitable but partially vanquishable, to the truth, up to the final sloughing off of the body which, in death, will insure the triumph of the immortal soul. "All dualisms, all theories of the immortality of the soul or of the spirit, as well as all monisms, spiritualistic or materialistic, dialectical or simplistic, are the one theme of a metaphysics whose whole history is oriented toward the deletion of the trace. The subordination of the trace to the full presence, summed up in the *logos*, the abasement of writing beneath the word fantasizing its own plenitude, such are the attitudes required by an onto-theology determining both the archeological and eschatological meanings of being as presence" (p. 104). *To the benefit of this fullness of presence, logocentrism represses the body and censures the letter.* Derrida writes elsewhere, "The history of metaphysics is the system of logocentric repression which developed to exclude or debase, to push out or to push under, as a didactic and technological metaphor, as servile matter or excrement, the body of the written trace."[43]

To prefer the *phone* ("voice") as closer to the interiority of the self, to the sense of being as presence, to the spirituality of the soul, is to wipe out the trace of significant matter, to erase it to the point of forgetting it — and to forget that one has forgotten it. It is to attempt the imaginary retrieval of the innocence and omnipotence of the lost paradise — this paradise from which we would have been expelled by our entrance into the world, a fall into exteriority and mediation (a theme already present in the Orphic myth). In attacking the logocentrism of metaphysics, Derrida seeks

43. J. Derrida, "Freud et la scène de l'écriture," *L'écriture et la différence* (Paris: Seuil, 1967) 294.

to unmask the unexamined oversight that governs it: that of the unavoidable law of the mediation of matter, the body, history — in short, of the mediation of the letter. For "the letter insists," according to J. Lacan's observation apropos the unconscious: language must be approached "literally," that is to say, in its significant materiality and density. "Language is a subtle body, but still a body. Words are caught in all the physical images that captivate the subject."[44] This is why there is no subject outside of this concrete *"imprint"* in matter, significant and subtle, yes, but quite sensible — the imprint of a given language, of a particular culture, of a unique body. Against traditional logocentrism and its visceral reaction against all exteriority, one must respond that the "outside" is the mediation of the "inside" of the subject; there is no "dualistic competition" between the two. *"The outside ̶i̶s̶ the inside."*[45] The crossing-out of the ̶i̶s̶ seeks to bring out the *trace* which rules out both a confusion and a separation of the two; it indicates a space "between the two" that is always moving, always vacillating — that of the "difference," that is to say, of "the production of the 'differing' — both deferment and difference"[46] — which marks the interminable process of signification through which the subject comes to be.

The lesson that we draw from the statement "There has never been anything except 'writing' " is not fundamentally a new one for us because it is but another variation of the *consent to mediation* which, as we have amply illustrated above, is the fundamental human task. However, it has the considerable advantage of showing us the ruses, as subtle as the subtlety of phonetic matter, by which we unconsciously attempt to hide both the concrete firmness and resistance of this mediation. For everything in us is bent on undermining this stumbling block, denying our limits, or — the same thing — not admitting their existence except as a necessary evil of which it would be better to rid ourselves. Now, against this megalomaniacal desire to "exclude or debase the body of the written trace," the understanding of language as arch-writing enjoins us not only to recognize the unavoidable requirement of media-

44. Lacan, *Ecrits*, 301.
45. Derrida, *De la grammatologie*, 65.
46. Ibid., 38.

tion, but also to grant it its *concrete resistance* and thus to literally accept the statement made above: *the most "spiritual" happens through the most "corporeal."* "Grammatology" returns us to the body.

2. "Body Am I"

a) A Body as Speech. Like language, the body is matter, matter significant from the first, that is, culturally instituted as speech. Outside of language, outside of culture, the body would be only an object or an instrument — indispensable certainly, in spite of its limits — which the soul would make use of to speak itself: humans would have bodies the same way they have language. Calling this traditional instrumentalist conception of language into question has immediate consequences for our understanding of the body. Humans do not ex-sist except as *corporality* whose concrete place is always their *own bodies.* Corporality is the body's very speech.

According to M. Merleau-Ponty,[47] thought is "in no way interior" because "it does not exist outside of the world and outside of words" (p. 213), because, like the painting of an artist, "language is not the illustration of a thought already formed, but the taking possession of this thought itself" (p. 446). This word is "a gesture and its significance an entire world" since "it is always at the interior of a world already spoken and still speaking that we ourselves think" (p. 214). Language "does not express thoughts anterior to itself, but is itself the subject's taking up a position within the world of its meanings" (p. 225) — meanings "already at our disposal because they are the results of earlier acts of expression" (p. 213) — in short, it is the body which speaks, this body — my body — that is "made of the same flesh as the world."[48] All this requires, according to the explicit program of the author of *The Phenomenology of Perception,* the definitive overcoming of the classical dichotomy between subject and object" (p. 203).[49]

47. M. Merleau-Ponty, *Phénoménologie de la perception* (Paris: Gallimard, coll. Tel, 1945) 230. The references between parentheses in the text pertain to this work.
48. M. Merleau-Ponty, *Le visible et l'invisible: Notes de travail* (Paris: Gallimard, 1964) 302.
49. One could go farther in this direction in wondering, with Frank Tinland:

Is it any surprise, finally, that culture or the symbolic order takes root in human beings as bodies? For their bodies in fact place humans in the world in a very particular way. The body is *the primordial place of every symbolic joining of the "inside" and the "outside."* It seems to us this is what E. Levinas means when he envisions the body "as the regime of the separation" that allows us also to "overcome the very otherness of what [we] must live by." Such is the distinctive "economy" of human beings: the body is the human "way" of inhabiting the otherness of the world as a home, a familiar dwelling.[50] The body is the *binding*, the space in the middle where both identity and difference are symbolically connected under the authority of the Other.

The navel is a good representation of this *liminal* position of the body, at the frontier between me and the non-me under the authority of the Other. This umbilical scar is the *trace* of the inaugural sewing up of the child in its "sack of skin" and thus of its delivery into the autonomy of a place which nobody else can occupy; but it is also the trace of a primordial opening maintained in the apertures (first of all, the eyes and ears) through which it communicates with the exterior and especially with the others-who-are-bodies, that, as both closed and open, permit it to experience every communication with the universe as a speaking one. One sees why, as Vasse has emphasized, this connection of identity and difference lived out corporally through the closing-opening of the body asks to be symbolized primordially by the sphincteral function, which is a living metaphor for it (whereas the navel is a kind of dead metaphor for it), so that the subject can elude psychosis and structure its psyche "normally."[51]

b) The Sub-ritual Schemes of Primary Symbolism. The selfhood of the subject requires a break with "sameness." This rupture, whose decisive moment we have just referred to as the instant of

---

"What is the essence of a human being as an organism . . . [or] bodily structure?" It would then seem that "a living being whose feet were different would also manifest different forms of consciousness," a statement that obviously does not imply a simplistic naturalism that would hold that the feet somehow produce thought . . . F. Tinland, *La différence anthropologique: Essai sur les rapports de la nature et de l'artifice* (Paris: Aubier-Montaigne, 1977) 30, 27.

50. E. Levinas, *Totalité et infini*, 89, 142–143.

51. On all this see D. Vasse, *L'ombilic et la voix: Deux enfants en analyse* (Paris: Seuil, 1974) ch. 2, "Les trous du corps et sa clôture."

our delivery into the world and toward others, runs through our bodies. The body is also attended by a whole series of *sub-ritual schemes* that belong to the *primary symbolism:* the vertical scheme of above and below, the horizontal schemes of left and right (in space), of before and behind (in time as well as in space). These corporal schemes constitute the primary mediations of every possible identification: to identify oneself is to differentiate oneself, and for this reason every significant creation, beginning with that of the world, takes place through a separation (see Gen 1).

Nothing can become significant for us without becoming invested by the body with the primordial schemes that are inherent in it. For that matter, there is no religious experience, as "spiritual" as it may be, that is not undergirded by the upright posture; as Vergote has shown in a study, God is invariably represented according to the primordial symbolism of height (majesty, absolute-power, lordship, and so forth) or depth (hidden source of existence "more intimate to me than myself," [*Intimior intimo meo*], and so forth).[52] There is no ethical sensitivity that is not characterized by a left-right differentiation (variable according to culture); there is no historical sense that is not structured by the scheme of "in front-behind" or "before-after."[53] Every feeling of power or domination, on the intellectual or moral as well as on the physical level, experiences itself, speaks itself, thinks itself through the primordial scheme of the upright posture of our bodies, just as every sort of assimilation, from intellectual effort to the amorous embrace, experiences itself, speaks itself, thinks itself through the primary scheme of feeding, with all of its inherent ambivalence between an amorous adoration and a destructive aggression: one can "love someone to death," and one can be "consumed" by a "devouring" need for reading or ideas. We could give many other examples of these sub-ritual schemes, such as that of being "soiled" in relation to any feeling of sinfulness or guilt,[54] that of a gesture of sharing in relation to any difference, that of an open hand in relation to any gift,

52. A. Vergote, "Equivoques et articulation du sacré," *Le sacré: Etudes et recherches,* Colloque Castelli (Paris: Aubier-Montaigne, 1974) 471–492.

53. We uncover here the well-known Kantian schematism — with this difference, and this a capital one, that it is never "pure," for it is always-already invested with the particularity of a desire as well as a language and culture.

54. On the primary symbolism of *impurity,* see P. Ricoeur, *Finitude et culpabilité,* vol. 2 *La symbolique du mal* (Paris: Aubier-Montaigne, 1960) ch. 1, "La souillure." On that of the sharing gesture, see M. Jousse, *L'anthropologie du geste* (Paris: Gallimard, 1974) 1:201–230.

exchange, or offering . . . These are not "secondary phenomena" which would come merely to color, according to different "temperaments," a supposedly pure and innate set of schemes; rather, as Vergote has noted, these indicate an *existential topography which is constitutive of the internal structure of the human being.*[55] As G. Bachelard has put it, "The hand also has its dreams."

Leib bin ich, ganz und gar, und nichts ausserdem ("Body am I, entirely and completely, and nothing besides"). This saying by Nietzsche is to be taken literally. It does not simply say, as Y. Ledure remarks, that "I am utterly and entirely body, and nothing besides," for this would be to make the body a mere attribute bestowed on an "I" which exists, logically and grammatically, before it. To take the *Leib bin ich* to the letter [literally] is to notice that this "letter" causes *grammar to explode* — and thus, at least by implication, *metaphysics.* "In a healthy reversal, the proposition 'Body am I' gives us to understand that body — in the third person — assumes the function of subject of a verb in the first person," to the point that "there is no longer the slightest interstice between the body and the 'I.'"[56]

c) Corporality: A Body of Culture, Tradition, and Nature. This person-body, this distinctive body that each person is, is body speaking and spoken. The concept of *corporality* seeks to express this symbolic order which holds that the human being does not have a body, but is body. What kind of thing is the I-body? Necessarily my *own body*, irreducible to any other, and yet, in the midst of its difference, recognizing itself to be similar to every other I-body. It is a body irreducible to any other because it is the place of "living words" (*logoi embioi*),[57] of living significations, proper to each person, depending upon the history of his or her desire, each history unique and unrepeatable; a body at the same time linked to others from its beginning and structured by a culture, if only through the model of identification that parents inevitably project on their offspring and have themselves received from their own parents. And so, this unique body is "speaking"

55. A. Vergote, *Interprétation du langage religieux* (Paris: Seuil, 1974), 112.

56. Y. Ledure, *Si Dieu s'efface: La corporéité comme lieu d'une affirmation de Dieu* (Paris: Desclée, 1975) 44–45.

57. C. Castoriadis, *Les carrefours du labyrinthe*, 36.

only because it is already spoken by a culture, because it is the recipient of a tradition and is tightly bonded with a world.

Thus, each person's own body is structured by the system of values or symbolic network of the group to which each person belongs and which makes up his or her *social and cultural body*. It is equally and simultaneously spoken by an historic *tradition* whose foundation is always more or less mythic and of which it is, often unconsciously, a kind of living memory. Finally, it is in permanent dialogue with the *universe* which, by projection of itself, it "anthropomorphizes" (the macrocosm becomes something like its own larger living body); and conversely, by introjection of the universe — "*intus*-susception" as M. Jousse describes it[58] — it "cosmorphizes" itself (it becomes a microcosm). From this is derived, as a permanent source of symbolism, this exchange with its "body" of the world (the macrocosm), notably in the alternations of day and night, the cycle of the seasons, and in the fundamental oppositions of earth-sky, water-fire, mountains-abysses, light-shadow, and so forth. The I-body exists only as woven, inhabited, spoken by this *triple body* of culture, tradition, and nature. This is what is implied by the concept of *corporality*: one's own physical body certainly, but *as the place where* the triple body — social, ancestral, and cosmic — which makes up the subject is symbolically joined, in an original manner for each one of us according to the different forms of our desires. The selfhood of the subject as corporality thus occurs at the juncture of the "being-in-the-world" (Heidegger's *in-der-Welt-sein*), the "being-with" (Heidegger's *Mit-sein*), and "historicity." Each one of us is what he or she is only to the extent that each one "retains" in one's self and "extends" to others this triple body of which each is, as it were, a living memory.

It is because being-there is existentially *"being-in-the-world"* that its "primordial mode of being" is "to find itself always-already 'outside' yet next to an entity"; and it is precisely "in being 'outside' yet next to the object that being-there is in truth 'at the interior' of itself."[59] In the same way, it is because this

58. Jousse, *L'anthropologie du geste*, vol. 2 *La Manducation de la parole* (Paris: Gallimard, 1975) second part (on *intussusception*).

59. M. Heidegger, *L'Etre et le temps* (Paris: Gallimard, 1964) 85.

"being-in-the-world is a *being-in-the-world-with*" that every being-there "has already revealed others in its being-there."[60] Finally, it is because, as Heidegger says elsewhere, Being is tradition (*es gibt Sein*) that being-there is *memorial*, "memorial-thought-in-Being," a living memorial that, of course, "is fundamentally different from a mere recall understood in the sense of the past that has 'passed away.' "[61] This is why only "expression" allows the subject to differentiate itself interiorly. The subject is not in the body as the stone is in the peach; it is body as the onion is in its layers. "Everything is in the skin," as P. Valéry used to say. Selfhood is "skin offered" to otherness (Levinas). "The outside ✗ the inside" (Derrida).

d) The Body as Arch-symbol. The living body is indeed, in the expression of D. Dubarle, "the arch-symbol of the whole symbolic order."[62] For it is in it that the within and the without, myself and others, nature and culture, need and request, desire and word are joined together. The word exists only as primordially written in the body, and by this very fact, ontically in discourses and statements. Of course, it is before we get to these statements, or in the "blank spaces" between them, that the word is spoken; but it is still necessary to have these discourses and statements to provide a "place" in their blank spaces from which the word may rise up.[63] Any word which seeks to be expressed in a kind of transparent purity is an illusion; no word escapes the necessity of a laborious inscription in a body, a history, a language, a system of signs, a discursive network. Such is the law. The law of mediation. The law of the body.

That is why "revelation" — Christian as well as Jewish — "could become the word of God only by an 'exodus' into the

60. Ibid., no. 26, pp. 150, 155.
61. M. Heidegger, *Lettre sur l'humanisme*, Q. 3, 108–109.
62. D. Dubarle, "Pratique du symbole et connaissance de Dieu," *Le mythe et le symbole* (Paris: Beauchesne, 1977) 243.
63. See, in this sense, the entire work of J. P. Resweber, *La philosophie du langage.* "By its very nature absent, the *word* renders itself present in and through *discourse*" (p. 6), which characterizes "the way the subject speaks, its turn of expression, the style of locution, while the *statement* designates the matter of the language constituted by the words used and by the things designated" (p. 43). Emphasis mine.

of writing."[64] We will show that, to find the Spirit, one 〟t first grasp the Letter. *The anthropological is the place of every possible theological.* And the sacramental — can it be anything else but the arch-symbolic space for this economy?

V. OPENNESS: THE SACRAMENTALITY OF THE FAITH

This perspective opens for us a theological understanding of the sacraments as expressions of the "corporality" of the faith. They are not the only ones, certainly (see the Church's use of the Scriptures and its ethical practice). But they constitute the major symbolic expression of faith.

In effect, in the sacramental celebrations, the faith is at work within a ritual staging in which *each person's body* is the place of the symbolic convergence — through gestures, postures, words (spoken or sung), and silences — of the triple body which makes us into believers. First, the *social* body of the Church with its symbolic network of values so distinctive that this network structures an original interpretation of history, life, and the universe — a different interpretation in any case from the one that a Muslim, Buddhist, or atheist would make. Second, the *traditional* body which dwells within this group called the Church and which supports the whole of the ritual, notably through references to the words and deeds of Christ attested by the apostolic witness of the Scriptures. Third, the *cosmic* body of a universe which is received as the gracious gift of the Creator and from which symbolic elements (water, bread and wine, oil, paschal candle, ashes . . .) are recognized as a "sacramental" mediation of the inscription of God by the Spirit. The sacraments are thus made of significant materiality: that of a body which cannot experience them without submitting itself to them through a program already specified, a gesture duly prescribed, a word institutionally set; that of a communal "we" presided over by a minister recognized as legitimate; that of a regulation by the living apostolic tradition referring itself to a collection of Scriptures recognized as canonical; that of the manipulation of elements and objects which each person is not free to choose according to his or her convenience.

64. S. Breton, *Ecriture et révélation* (Paris: Cerf, 1979) 118.

1. *The Sacramental Stumbling Block*

In their significant materiality, the sacraments thus constitute an *unavoidable stumbling block* which forms a barrier to every imaginary claim to a direct connection, individual and interior, with Christ or to a gnostic-like, illuminist contact with him. They represent the indefeasible mediations, beginning with the Church, outside of which there is no possible Christian faith. They tell us that the faith has a body, that it adheres to our body. More than that, they tell us that to *become a believer is to learn to consent, without resentment, to the corporality of the faith.*

Now, this is precisely the most difficult and onerous task there is. It suffices to observe how easily *we stumble against the sacraments* — from the moment, at least, when the faith seeks to live itself as the adoration of the Father "in spirit and truth" (see John 4:23-24) and does not allow itself to fall asleep in the securities of the institution and the drone of habit. Then they strike us full blast. We stumble against them more than against the Word. Of course, the Word presents itself as "Writings" and even as "the letter"; thus, with the immense cultural detour that Scripture today requires of believers, it also exercises this same function of "stumbling block." But the metaphysical logocentrism that possesses us is determined to erase, as far as possible, the empirical density of the letter in its historical consistency through the direct appeal to a "spiritual" sense which the letter supposedly contained in advance in an atemporal and ahistorical manner. Within this perspective, the Word of God can easily reascend very close to the evanescent subtlety of an exterior breath and in its immateriality become an echo of the interior breath of the Spirit of God and of the interior Word it causes to resonate within us. Then the Word appears totally adequate to whatever is "spiritual" in the faith.

It is not the same with sacraments: Do they not cause the faith to fall into *exteriority*, into an *institution*, into the *body*? Must we not "submit" ourselves to them and go through the multiple sensible elements which make them up? One then feels the impulse to justify them, bring in arguments of appropriateness, offer reasons for them. But why all this, unless Christianity — in spite of the corrections required by the Incarnation of God in Jesus and the promise of the resurrection of the flesh — has never completely recovered from suspicion with regard to the body? Having found in the onto-theological structure of metaphysics its fundamental manner of thinking, Christianity fully embraced logocentrism with its idealistic presuppositions of transparent presence and fullness of truth, presuppositions to which all forms of "mediation" are unacceptable obstacles. It would be a good thing to purify oneself from them. Under such conditions, the sacraments can be thought of only as *remedies* or, at least, *concessions* that divine Providence, by a wise pedagogy, has made available to human nature which cannot accede to the intelligible without passing through the sensible. It is obvious that such an appreciation has as *its principle the conviction that, ideally at least, things should be otherwise* . . .

One stumbles, then, on the sacrament, as one stumbles on the body, as one stumbles on the institution, as one stumbles on the letter of the Scriptures — if at least one respects it in its historical and empirical materiality. One stumbles against these because one harbors a nostalgia for an ideal and immediate presence to oneself, to others, and to God. Now, in forcing us back to our corporality, the sacraments shatter such dreams. And because of the essential corporeal and ritual mediation which constitutes them, the sacraments do this precisely in a still more radical manner than do the Scriptures (we will give a fuller development of this point in our chapter on ritual). They thus indicate to us that it is in the most banal empirical details — of a history, an institution, a world, and finally, a body — that what is most "true" in our faith thrives.

2. *The Arch-sacramentality of the Faith*

Just as empirical writing is the phenomenal manifestation of an arch-writing that constitutes language as the place where the human subject comes into being, so the sacraments can be appreciated as the empirical manifestation of the *"arch-sacramentality"* *that constitutes the language of faith,* which is the place where the believing subject comes into being. This arch-sacramentality is a *transcendental condition for Christian existence.* It indicates that *there is no faith unless somewhere inscribed, inscribed in a body* — a body from a specific culture, a body with a concrete history, a body of desire. Baptism, the first sacrament of the faith, shows this well: the plunge into water, together with this "precipitate" of the Christian Scriptures, which is the mention of the names of the Father and the Son and the Holy Spirit, is a metaphor for being plunged into the body of signifiers — material, institutional, cultural, and traditional — of the Church: assembly, ordained minister, sign of the cross on the forehead, book of the Scriptures, confession of faith, remembrance of Jesus Christ and invocation of the Spirit, paschal candle . . . All these are symbolic elements that are inscribed on the body of every baptized person, his or her *scriptural body* on which they are bestowed as a testament. *One becomes a Christian only by entering an institution and in letting this institution stamp its "trademark," its "character," on one's body.*

The faith thus appears to us as *"sacramental" in its constitution,* and not simply by derivation. Our existence is Christian insofar as it is always-already structured by sacramentality, better still, as it is *always-already inscribed in the order of the sacramental.* It is thus impossible to conceive of the faith outside of the body.

*
*　*

Any theology that integrates fully, and *in principle,* the sacramentality of the faith requires a consent to corporality, a consent so complete that it tries to *think about God according to corporality.* We have already announced this necessity for a new kind of thinking about God to insure the coherence of our own discourse, and we have sketched the direction in which this must lead us, toward the historical stumbling block of the Cross. Our approach to the question of the inescapable mediation by symbol and the body that we have just expounded only reinforces this same imperative. We will honor this commitment in the last section of this work.

Part Two

The Sacraments in the Symbolic Network

of the Faith of the Church

Introduction:
A Fundamental Theology of the Sacramental

In conformity with the way we have been looking at the problem so far, the question that will guide our theological discourse cannot be "Why have sacraments?" We give up in principle the ambition to return to the origin of things, to give a reason for everything. Rather, we take our point of departure from the undeniable fact that we are, as the Church, *people who practice* certain common rituals called "sacraments" — notably baptism and the Eucharist — and that we find ourselves always-already embarked into sacramentality. Thus, the question that guides our theological reflection is the following: *What does it mean for the faith that it is woven together out of sacraments? What does it mean, then, to believe in Jesus Christ if such a belief is structured sacramentally?*

Taking this question seriously leads us to develop not only a theology of the sacraments of our faith but, at a more primordial level, *a fundamental theology of the sacramental* or *of the sacramentality of the faith.* Obviously, we cannot omit to reflect on the individual sacraments, especially baptism and the Eucharist; rather, we will consider these as paradigmatic expressions of a sacramental dimension of the faith which extends beyond them and which constitutes the condition of their having any meaning.

From this perspective, and against the custom that has prevailed since the rise of the Scholastic "treatises," sacramental theology cannot be viewed as just another sector in the field of theology; it is rather, as the Fathers recognized,[1] a *dimension* that recurs throughout the whole of Christian theology, a distinctive way of looking at it. It is not completely encompassing since it provides a

---

1. See, for example, the way in which St. Irenaeus refers to the confession of baptismal faith at the beginning and end of his *Demonstration of Apostolic Predication* (Sources chrétiennes 41 and 170), as well as to the Eucharist in *Adv. Haer.* IV:17-18 (Sources chrétiennes 100, pp. 575-615).

perspective from a distinctive angle; still, it fully deserves to be called, from our viewpoint, *fundamental* theology. For it is the *entire* field of theology — from creation to eschatology, from Trinitarian speculations to practical ethics, from Christology to ecclesiology . . . — that is to be rethought according to this constitutive dimension of the faith we call "sacramentality."

Of course, the sacraments are *only one element among others* within the particular epistemological configuration of the faith; as such, this element functions correctly in Christianity only in relation to the others with which it forms a system. It is only by isolating it (which amounts, we agree with E. Ortigues, to causing it to regress toward the "ineffable imaginary realm") that one could be tempted to think that God resides there.

We will begin, therefore, by situating the sacraments within the vast ecclesial whole within which they find their coherence. We name this totality "the structure of Christian identity." We will *describe* this structure in Chapter Five. Following that, Chapters Six and Seven will propose a reflection on the *relations* between the elements of the structure thus made clear: relations between sacrament and Scripture on the one hand, between sacrament and ethics on the other. Later we will need to show the *process* according to which these concrete elements function; this we will do in Chapter Eight, in the context of the process of symbolic exchange which we have already discussed.

Chapter Five

Description of the Structure of Christian Identity

I. THE STRUCTURING OF FAITH
ACCORDING TO THE STORY OF EMMAUS

"Structure" is defined by the *Dictionary of Critical and Technical Vocabulary in Philosophy* (A. Lalande) as "a whole formed of coordinated phenomena, such that each depends on the others and could not be what it is without its relation to them." The description of the elements and their relations with each other furnishes a "model" of the structure in question. It is *one* model of the structure of Christian identity that we propose here.

1. *Luke 24*

How does one become a believer? How does one pass from non-faith to faith? This is the basic question which underlies the story of the appearance on the road to Emmaus (Luke 24:13-35). Now, this story, typically Lucan, is constructed along the same principal axes as the two stories which flank it: the message received at the tomb (24:1-12) and the apparition to the Eleven (24:36-53). Those receiving the message or the apparition in all three pericopes are in a condition of non-faith: the women at the tomb are "perplexed" (v. 4), Cleopas and his companion have their eyes closed (v. 16); the Eleven are "terrified" (v. 37) and "disbelieving" (v. 41). In all three cases this negative condition is linked to the desire to find, to touch, or to see the body of Jesus: the women "did not *find* the body" (v. 3), while Peter saw nothing but "the linen cloths by themselves" (v. 12); likewise, in the Emmaus story, "they did not *find* his body," and the text specifies that, while the disciples have indeed run to verify the women's story, still "they did not *see* him" (v. 24). As for the appearance to the Eleven, precisely what the Risen One enjoins his disciples to "see" (twice) and to "touch" are the marks of his death (v. 39). It is thus noteworthy that vision and touch in all three cases are fixed on the *dead body* of Jesus; it is no less noteworthy that again in all three cases (for even in the third case, seeing and touching are not sufficient to make someone accede to faith: "they were disbelieving and still wondering," as verse 41 makes clear) the resolution of the situation is achieved only through two factors: first, an appeal to memory ("remember . . ." [v. 6], "slow of heart to believe all that the prophets have declared" [v. 25]; "these are my words that I spoke to you . . ." [v. 44]); second, an opening of the Scriptures to reveal the plan of God ("must be handed over . . ." [v. 7]; "was it not necessary that . . ." plus the interpretation of all the Scriptures [vv. 26-27]; "everything . . . must be fulfilled" plus a rereading of all the Scriptures [vv. 44-45]).

The passage to faith thus requires that *one let go of the desire to see-touch-find, to accept in its place the hearing of a word,* whether it comes from angels or from the Risen One himself, a word recognized as the word of God. For the desire to see, analogous here to the desire to know, and the desire to find, analogous here to the desire to prove — can only lead us to fail to recognize the risen Lord because they direct us back toward his dead body. The story of Emmaus makes this lesson explicit. It is all the more striking in that the passage is arranged in exactly the same way as two other Lucan stories: the baptism of the Ethiopian eunuch (Acts 8:26-40) and the first account of the conversion of Saul (Acts 9:1-20).

2. *Three Key Texts*

These three stories describe the journey necessary to the structuring of the faith, that is, they show us how becoming-Christian comes about. We are now clearly in the *time of the Church,* symbolized in our three stories by the road which leaves Jerusalem and leads to Emmaus, Gaza, and Damascus. The theological meaning of Jerusalem for Luke is well known; it is the place of the death of Jesus, the place of his resurrection appearances — Luke mentions no appearances outside Jerusalem — and the place of the promised Spirit's outpouring. Jerusalem is the paschal focus toward which the entire third Gospel converges, as well as the Pentecostal cradle from which the Church expands outward to "all of Judea and Samaria, and to the ends of the earth" (Acts 1:8; see Luke 24:47).

In this time of the Church, the Lord is no longer visible. Luke insists on this point: resurrected, Jesus is the "Living One" (see Luke 24:5) — a divine title — he lives in God, as the account of the ascension clearly emphasizes. However, the *Absent One* is present in his "sacrament" which is the Church: the Church rereading the Scriptures with him in mind, the Church repeating his gestures in memory of him, the Church living the sharing between brothers and sisters in his name. It is in these forms of witness by the Church that Jesus takes on a body and allows himself to be encountered. Such an interpretation is one of the keys for unlocking these three texts: the *Church* is never mentioned as such, but it is everywhere present in a veiled fashion; if it seems omitted from the text, it is because it alone constitutes its authentic "pre-text."

Behind the traits of the Risen One performing, on the road to Emmaus, a "hermeneutics" (*dihermeneusen*) of the *Scriptures* in relation to his own messianic destiny (Luke 24:25-27), is it not possible to discern *the Church* and its Easter kerygma? In casting the Lord Jesus himself in the story, Luke is indicating that each time the Church rereads and announces the death and resurrection of Jesus "according to the Scriptures," it is he himself who speaks through it; it is his mouthpiece, his "sacramental" stand-in. So much is this the case, as Acts 9:5 shows, that to persecute the Church is to persecute the Lord Jesus himself. There is no opening of the eyes and mind to the recognition of the Crucified One as the Messiah and Lord without the Church as the guide in such a rereading of the Scriptures, without the pattern of interpretations it provides: "Do you understand what you are reading? . . . How can I, unless someone guides me?" (Acts 8:30-31).

Neither is there any possible access to faith, according to our texts, without what will later be called the *sacraments* of the Church. The breaking of the bread at Emmaus, the baptism of the Ethiopian eunuch, the imposition of hands to call down the Holy Spirit on Saul, all characterize the passage from non-faith to faith.

These ritual gestures are not mere accessories, but structuring elements of the faith. It is at the moment of the breaking of bread (Luke 24:31), the moment of the imposition of hands (Acts 9:17-18), that the eyes of the disciples on the road to Emmaus in the one case, and of Saul in the other, are opened. And there again the gestures of the Risen One, described with the same four technical verbs used in recounting the Last Supper (he "took," "said the blessing," "broke" the bread, and "gave" it to them), inescapably call up the image of the *Church* as it celebrates the Eucharist. Moreover, it is possible that the deliberate use of the imperfect (*epedidou*, "and he was giving it to them") instead of the aorist (*epedoken*, "he gave it to them") tense is an indication of the continued action of the Lord Jesus at each Eucharist. In the same way, to speak of a "breaking of bread" at Emmaus is a "revealing anachronism; it is a phrase taken from the Christian liturgy," showing that "the story is intended to be understood in the time of the Church" (v. 14a). We no longer see the Lord Jesus; however, as Luke shows his audience, we are invited to recognize him in the ritual gestures the Church continues to carry out in his name; like the miraculous deeds performed by the apostles through their "faith in the name of Jesus" (see Acts 3:6, 16), the ritual gestures made by the Church in his memory are in fact his own gestures.

In the last analysis, faith can exist only if it expresses itself in a life of *witness*. It is well known that the resurrection stories in the Gospels are constructed according to a threefold plan: first, an initiative by the Risen One that imposes itself on the witnesses;[1] second, the recognition by a "faith that has eyes" (*oculata fide*, in the beautiful phrase of Thomas Aquinas) of the Risen One as the same as the Crucified One, but living henceforth in a completely altered state — as a "spiritual body" (*soma pneumatikon*), says Paul; third, the sending of the apostles into mission. This last trait means that no one can claim to truly recognize Jesus as the living Lord unless one announces him at the same time: there is no possible reception of the gift of the good news of the resurrection

---

1. See especially, in this sense, the "divine passive" (*passivum divinum*): "he showed himself" (*ophtē*) — used 13 times in Luke against 22 in the NT as a whole; used 4 times in the ancient confession of faith of 1 Cor 15:3-8.

without the return-gift of Christian witness. This witness is not a purely extrinsic consequence of faith, but constitutes an *intrinsic moment* in the very process of structuring faith. As the use of the verb *anistemi* may suggest — used elsewhere, it is true, in the ordinary sense of "to get up," as in Luke 24:33 apropos Cleopas and his companion (*anastantes aute te hora*) — the recognition of the resurrection of Jesus cannot truthfully take place without provoking the re-surrection of the disciples into witnesses. In any case, the road which at "that same hour" leads the two disciples to the Eleven in Jerusalem (Luke 24:33-35) just as quickly leads them out of town again toward "all nations" (24:47); this same road also leads Paul, after "several days . . . with the disciples in Damascus," out to announce in the synagogues that Jesus "is the Son of God" (Acts 9:19-20); the same journey continues for the baptized Ethiopian, whose faith leads him off in joy toward Gaza (Acts 8:39): all three show how closely missionary witness belongs to the very structuring of the Church and its faith.

At the beginning of Acts, in his first two summaries of the activities of the first Christian community in Jerusalem (Acts 2:42-47; 4:32-35), Luke loves to emphasize that this witness requires equally the word and a life lived in "community" (*koinonia*). This term indicates not only a unity of hearts engendered by faith in the same Lord,[2] but also the active manifestation of this unity in the concrete exercise of sharing material goods. The latter, as J. Dupont has made clear, does not designate "a juridical transfer of properties; rather, each one remains the owner of what he or she possesses, but the affection each has for the brothers and sisters leads him or her to place these at their disposal."[3] The ideal attempted here is not that of voluntary poverty, but that of charity for brothers and sisters: "one abandons one's goods not out of the desire to be poor, but precisely so that there will be no poor in the community."[4] And it is also possible that Luke, indirectly dependent ("at an earlier stage than that of this redaction") on Deu-

---

2. See the theme of the "being-of-one-mind" (*homo-thymadon*) that is repeated 4 times at the beginning of Acts (1:14; 2:46; 4:24; 5:12) as one of the major characteristics of the first community.

3. J. Dupont, *Etudes sur les Actes des Apôtres* (Paris: Cerf, 1967) 508.

4. Ibid., 512.

teronomy 15:4, and directly on a "very ancient" Christian tradition, gives to this concrete sharing of goods a major theological significance. "The fact of not finding indigents among their number took on the importance of a sign: the promise to Moses was being accomplished in their midst; they were the messianic community become fully realized in the present."[5] In any case it is significant that Luke devotes practically half of his first summary and three quarters of his second to the concrete practice of the brotherly and sisterly *koinonia:* as a sign of the realization of the messianic community, the *koinonia* is a *testimony rendered to the risen Christ.* Such an ethic of "to each as any had need" (Acts 4:35; see 2:45) seems, for the author of Acts, to constitute one of the principal dimensions of missionary witness: the announcement of the risen Messiah requires *the concrete sign of the realization of the messianic community,* specifically, sharing with the most destitute among the brothers and sisters. Moreover, is not the brother or sister, according to the theology of Acts 9:5 ("I am Jesus, whom you are persecuting") or of Acts 5:14 (where the expression "added to the Lord" seems to suggest, according to the note in the *Traduction oecuménique de la Bible,* "a sort of identification between the Lord and his own") a kind of "sacrament" of the Risen One (see also the theology of the last judgment in Matthew 25:31-46)?

Luke in effect asks his audience, "So you wish to know if Jesus is really living, he who is no longer visible before your eyes? Then give up the desire to see him, to touch him, to find his physical body, for now he allows himself to be encountered only through the *body of his word,* in the constant reappropriation that the *Church* makes of his message, his deeds, and his own way of living. Live in the Church! It is there that you will discover and recognize him." Thus, Luke sees the Church as the fundamental sacramental mediation within which alone the believing subject can emerge. However, such a consent to the sacramental mediation of the Church does not come easily; it requires a complete about-face. This is what the story of Emmaus is particularly meant to show.

5. Ibid., 510.

3. The Story of the Disciples on the Road to Emmaus

Jerusalem-Emmaus-Jerusalem: this topographically round trip is for us the symbolic support of the turn-around, the "transformation" that gradually takes place in the disciples' hearts during the telling of the story; a passage from non-recognition to recognition, from closed eyes to opened eyes, from giving up the mission to taking up the mission and at the level of the group as such, a transition from a state of breakdown ("Peter went to the tomb by himself," as verse 12 shows) and thus of death to a resurrection of the group as the Church.

In the first section of the story (vv. 13-17, up until their first stopping on the road), the two disciples have in effect abandoned their mission; in turning away from Jerusalem, they are also in effect turning their backs on their previous experience with Jesus. They talk between themselves, each a sort of mirror-image of the other, tossing back and forth the same expression of a definitive postmortem on the failed mission of their Master. Consequently, their eyes are "kept from recognizing him"; their spirits, like their eyes, are shut. For that matter, everything is shut. They have allowed themselves to be sealed up together with the dead body of Jesus in the constricted place of his death, the sepulcher, whose mouth has been blocked with a huge stone. Their past is dead; in any case, it has no future.

"They stood still, looking sad." This stop, which concludes the first part of our account, begins a second sequence (vv. 18-30), which ends, like the first, with another topographical note, "so he went in to stay with them." This sequence, centered on the exchange of words between the two disciples (acting as one) and Jesus, is divided into two parts: in the first (vv. 18-24), the disciples do the speaking; in the second, Jesus. In relation to the first section, the whole of the second is characterized by a transition from a dualistic relation to a triangular relation: instead of speaking to each other, in a closed circle, they open themselves to this stranger who has joined them. They break out of their closed conversation to address someone who listens to them. This act of directing a word to a Third who becomes a witness to their consternation lifts a little the heavy stone on their tomb. A thin ray of light penetrates through this tiny crack; their desire awakens anew as they relate to this third person how their hopes have been dashed. Then, however, "reality" intrudes again with its undeniable evidence: "Jesus of Nazareth," the "prophet," is really dead, and God has not intervened on his behalf. The resolution of this situation seems impossible as long as Cleopas and his companion keep the initiative in the discussion and thereby remain in a position of knowledge; for they know all there is to know about Jesus of Nazareth. But their understanding is a misunderstanding; it reaches only as far as events. It is the same with the women and the disciples who went to the tomb and did not find the body: they observed that the tomb was empty, "but they did not see him." What were they expecting to see anyway, to touch, to find at the tomb if not a *cadaver*? Prisoners of this illusory compulsion to see and to know, by which they wish to avail themselves of an all-powerful mastery over the object of their desire, they remain buried in the tomb of their own misunderstanding.

However, faith requires an act of dispossession, a reversal of initiative; Instead of holding forth with self-assured pronouncements *on* God, one must begin by listening to a word as the word *of* God. The reference to the *Scriptures as a third agency* plays a role that is of capital importance here. In allowing Jesus to open the Scriptures for them, the two disciples begin to enter into an understanding of the "real" different from what they previously thought evident. For suppose the "reality" of the plan of God and the destiny of Jesus were different from what they were convinced they were. Suppose the Scriptures disclosed a reality about God which they had never suspected because it directly contradicted the most authoritative doctrines. Suppose, finally, it was true that he who had just passed through death had now entered into glory. Let us be quite clear about this: the stumbling block for a Jew was not that God could resuscitate someone, for a majority of Jews at the time of Jesus did in fact believe in a final resurrection of the dead; nor was it that God could resuscitate someone before the day of general resurrection, for there was widespread faith in the traditions according to which the prophet Elias, Enoch, and Esdras had been "taken up" . . . Rather, it centered on a more radical point: Could God still be God, our God, the God of our ancestors, if he raised up *someone who had been justly condemned* to death for having blasphemed against the Law of God given to Moses, that is, against God himself? Could God contradict himself? Could it be, as Paul puts it, that someone who had died cursed by God — for the Law (Deut 21:23) declares that "anyone hung on a tree is under God's curse" (see Gal 3:13) — would later be recognized as in fact God's blessing on all the nations? What kind of God would allow his own Christ to die, and then, in raising him up, vindicate him against his own Law? Could it be, finally, that God himself rolled such a rock of scandal away from the mouth of Jesus' tomb? One gets an inkling of the depth of the necessary conversion; for the two disciples it is a question of accepting the possibility that the word of God, according to the Scriptures, *has come to "deconstruct" their best established evidence* concerning the "reality" of God.

168

The relation between Jesus and the Scriptures could only be, in their eyes, the same as his relation to the tomb: a relation of death. For them the Scriptures played the role of a tombstone inscription backing up the funeral oration they had pronounced at the grave of the "dearly departed one," their feelings of loss all the more intense in that they had expected from him the liberation of Israel. The circular connection between the three places of the *body* of Jesus, the *tomb*, and the *Scriptures* was complete and closed: over the dead body rose the "memorial tomb" (*mnemeion*) crowned by the verdict of "put to death according to the Law" (or "according to the Scriptures"), which guaranteed the verdict's religious legitimacy.

But now, their eyes begin to "open" when the Risen One, appealing to their memories, "opens" the Scriptures to them (the same verb is used, *di-anoigo*); the "abbreviated word" (*verbum abbreviatum*) of the Scriptures ("was it not necessary . . .") is the place from which his corpse is re-membered in a new fashion. "Were not our hearts burning within us?" they will say to each other when remembering in retrospect, after the breaking of bread, what took place earlier on the road. That is, they begin to *see* the Risen One while *hearing* him "raise himself up" from the Scriptures: *he lives there where his word is heard*, there where people witness to him "according to the Scriptures." "There," that is to say, in the *Church*. As we have said, behind the traits of the Risen One, it is the Church, with its kerygma --this "abbreviated word" of the entire Scriptures — which is visibly if subtly outlined: Luke intimates that each time the Church announces the Easter kerygma, it is the "sacrament" of his word. The risen body of Christ is recognized first in his scriptural "body," itself re-membered and joined to his ecclesial body.

Afterwards, the two disciples are sufficiently shaken from their previous convictions that their desire, initially fixated on the "need" — the need to know and be reassured — is transformed into a *request* — a request that is addressed to the other in his full otherness, a request for presence: "Stay with us." Jesus has ceased to be an "object" come to satisfy — by integrating himself into their system — their need for an explanation; he has become a subject whose presence is desired for itself . . . But the presence of the other is precisely, by its very definition, elusive. The Stranger is not yet recognized in his radical strangeness.

It is not outside, on the road, but *inside,* around the table, that the two disciples have the decisive experience of their encounter. In this third sequence (vv. 30-32), the Risen One brings to completion the initiative he has taken: his "word" becomes flesh in the shared bread. At this point, their eyes are opened; what they see allows them to understand what is truly at issue, specifically, the Eucharist *of the Church* — as we mentioned previously with regard to the four technical verbs used in the account of the Last Supper and repeated here. Their eyes open on an *emptiness* — "he vanished from their sight" — but an emptiness full of a presence. They open on the emptiness of the invisibility of the Lord each time the Church breaks bread in memory of him; but this emptiness is penetrated by his symbolic presence because the disciples have just realized that whenever the Church takes bread, pronounces the blessing, breaks, and distributes it — it is he, the Church's Lord, who continues to take the bread of his life given for others; to direct to God the thanksgiving prayer; to break the bread, as his own body was broken, to achieve unity for us all; and to give it saying, "This is my body." In the time of the Church in which our story takes place, Jesus the Christ is absent as "the same"; he is no longer present except as "the Other." From now on, it is impossible to touch his real body; we can touch it only as *the body symbolized* through the testimony the Church gives about him, through the Scriptures reread as his own word, the sacraments performed as his own gestures, the ethical witness of the communion between brothers and sisters lived as the expression of his own "service" (*diakonia*) for humankind. From now on, it is in the witness of the Church that he takes flesh, and especially in the reenactment of his very words, "This is my body . . ."

"That same hour," Luke tells us, Cleopas and the other disciple rise up and return to Jerusalem. The recognition of Jesus' resurrection brings about *their own "surrection"*: his Easter has become their Easter; the same people have become different. Their return to Jerusalem is the symbolic analogue of the transformation that has taken place in them: their "demobilization" has been turned around into a "mobilization," and the dispersion of the group into a renewed communion. For it is the entire group of disciples that, having passed through death, *is now reborn as the Church*. It bursts forth from the Easter words, "he is risen," an announcement supported above all, according to Luke, by the testimony of Simon (v. 34). The two companions first receive the testimony of the Eleven; later they join their own witness to that of this founding group. The Church thus appears as the community of those who, having encountered the risen Lord, give witness to this fact, but who also compare their testimony with that of the founding group to verify the apostolic authenticity of this testimony.

4. *The Trial of Faith or the Consent to Loss*

We believe we can extract an entire theology of the "sacramentality" of the Church from the Lucan texts we have just looked at. This is not the only theology in the New Testament. It is characteristic of what E.

Käsemann calls "precatholicism," that is, the stage of "transition between primitive Christianity and what is called the ancient Church, a transition characterized by the dying away of the expectation of the imminent second coming" and the transfer of the theological "center of gravity" from eschatology to a "great Church," with the accent more and more on "the sacramental presence of Christ in the Church for the world," as one sees it especially in the deutero-Pauline writings.[6] We are thus made aware that our own thesis on the structure of Christian identity is *relative* to a certain stage where the Church is sufficiently institutionalized to be perceived theologically as the "universal sacrament of salvation" for the world (*Lumen Gentium*, no. 48). This theology is *not the only possible one; it is not even the most ancient.* However — is it necessary to say this? — the most ancient is not necessarily the most theologically pertinent . . . In any event, it was probably inevitable that as the parousia was more and more delayed, eschatological enthusiasm was more and more tamed; to balance the "already," the "not yet" inevitably opened up space for a theology of the sacramentality of the Church, which was the only one that could be adapted to the in-between time whose duration was revealing itself to be more and more indefinite. For are not the sacraments precisely an adaptation to the in-between time?

a) The Symbolic Mediation of the Church. As we have seen, to the question posed by his audience (which is also that of our audience, and of every believer), "If it is true that Jesus is alive, how is it that we cannot see him?" Luke answers with "the Church." The passage to faith requires an acceptance of the Church, for it is in it that the Lord Jesus allows himself to be encountered. However, such a consent is a true trial. Our three key texts, and especially that of Emmaus, reveal with exemplary clarity the path that must be followed if such a passage to faith is to be accomplished. This presupposes the acquisition of a competence, recognized as given on the initiative of Christ or the Spirit, a competence in willing, in knowing, in being able to accede to the symbolic order proper to the Church and to its rules of procedure, especially to the pattern formed by its interpretation of Scripture, its liturgical celebrations, and its ethical engagement. We attempt to illustrate all this in the diagram of the *structure of Christian identity* given on the following page.

6. E. Käsemann, *Essais exégétiques* (Neuchâtel: Delachaux-Niestlé, 1972), ch. 13 "Paul et le précatholicisme," 256–270.

Later, we will give several useful clues for the interpretation of this diagram. For the moment, we stress but two points. First, we have here one model (among many other possible ones, no doubt) for the structure of Christian identity: the double arrows indicate that within this structure, each element, as in a jigsaw puzzle, takes on "value" only by its relations, of difference and coherence, with those elements which surround it. Therefore, the whole is primary, not the isolated elements taken by themselves. The first benefit of our effort is, as we mentioned above, to situate the sacraments *within a whole* where everything holds together: the symbolic order proper to the Church.

Second, this diagram illustrates well the fundamental sacramental mediation of the Church. We will develop this a little further on. The important thing for now is to reflect on what the diagram suggests, that is, that the faith requires a *renunciation of a direct line*, one could say a gnostic line, to Jesus Christ. It is impossible to truly recognize the Lord Jesus as living without giving up this illusory quest — an ambivalent psychic impulse, viewed here under its negative aspect of misleading enticement — which irresistibly leads us to desire to see, touch, find, that is, finally to

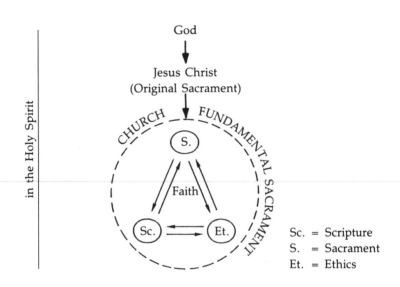

prove, Jesus. For, exactly like the women or the di
to the tomb, what could we see, what are we *expecti*
to know, if not the corpse of Jesus? Of course, we ou
no longer in the same situation as the first witnesses; \
perfectly well that Jesus is no longer visible. But in this
everything that touches the most vital parts of our existei   ar
intellectual convictions are far from being determinative; our
desires are often stronger. Our imaginations never cease their efforts to conceal what the experience of the real demands of us:
"Of course I know, but still . . . " Everything resides in this "but
still" that rises up like a psychic denial of what we nevertheless
"know." And it is on the foundation of these denials that we
often build up our evidence; we are constantly covering over the
true with the likely.

But access to faith requires an acceptance of the angels' message
given to the women at the tomb: "He . . . has risen." The tomb
is *empty of the dead body* of Jesus, as a "real object" to be observed; it is *filled with a "sign to be believed"*: the word of angels —
the word of God! — "He . . . has risen."[7] Coming to faith requires taking seriously this word from which the Church is born
and which structures it according to its threefold manifestation in
Scripture, sacraments, and ethics.

b) Three Forms of the Same "Necrotic" Temptation. But such a
renunciation of finding Christ in order to consent to his symbolic
body of the word, which is the Church, requires as a price that
we renounce our ambition to capture Christ in our ideological nets
or in the ruses of our desire. Each one knows the innumerable
subtle ploys making up the strategy of desire, perhaps nowhere
more so than in the religious domain, for it is this sector that directly touches the meaning we give to our lives. Under desire's
enticing aspect, our imagination feeds our illusion that we can
somehow heal the breach that constitutes us as subjects. In the religious domain, this tendency takes on myriad forms, which we
may reduce to three typical temptations, each centered around one
of the principal elements of Christian identity.

7. L. Marin, "Les femmes au tombeau: Essai d'analyse structurale d'un
texte évangélique," *Langages* 22, pp. 39–48. Text reprinted in *Etudes sémiotiques*
(Paris: Klincksieck, 1971) 221–231.

...e first is a closed system of *religious knowledge* which in practice functions as a way for the psyche to negate the otherness of God, the absence of the Risen One, the unmanageability of the Spirit. Of course, one protests against such a negation: "We all know well . . ." Yes, we all know well, but "all the same . . . !" The second form of this temptation is sacramental "magic," which A. Vergote, trying to avoid the ambiguities of this term and a certain pejorative connotation, calls instead *"sacramental imagination."* One has recourse to ritual to obtain either an essentially natural benefit or a spiritual effect such as the pardon of sins or some other divine grace, "without the interior disposition being put into consonance with the expected effect."[8] Here again it is useful to point out that the conscious negation of this process does not necessarily impede its effective psychological functioning. The third form is a *moralism*, understood as pharisaism in behavior by which one desires to obtain leverage over God. One can say loud and clear that God can never become subject to human beings, that our good works give us no "rights" over him; one can even recall the lesson Jesus gave to those who complained about what they considered a divine injustice — the workers in the vineyard who came at the first hour or the older brother in the story of the prodigal son — without ceasing for a moment to bridle beneath the surface at God's justice endured with resentment or even experienced as persecution. In this domain as well, we know only too well; but all the same! Only, this "all the same" is vigorously repressed.

These are the three major forms — each with a thousand possible variations — of the imaginary capture of Christ, the reduction of the gospel to our ideology, the subordination of its message to our desire or our established convictions. These are three different methods, most often subtle, for killing *the presence of the absence* of the Risen One, for erasing his radical otherness. *Three different ways*, expressed another way, *to convert him, the "Living" One, into a dead body or an available object.* No one in Christianity is exempt from the danger of this *necrotic* tendency — which obviously is not without connection to neurosis. This illusory and fatal capture of the Living One begins or comes to fruition — with every gradation possible between the two thresholds — from the moment we allow ourselves to *isolate* one or the other constituent of the ecclesial faith. For, as our diagram of the structure of Christian identity shows, faith lives only *in taking "all-together"* (sym-bolize) the

8. A. Vergote, *Religion, foi, incroyance* (Brussels: P. Mardaga, 1983) 302–303.

three elements of the structure. It is their proper symbolic connection that allows faith to remain sound.

The triple temptation mentioned above consists precisely in isolating one or the other of the elements of the structure, and thus in *exaggerating its importance* to the detriment of the other two. After that, following a well recognized mechanism in neurosis, the element in question becomes a point of fixation for the psyche. One chews over and manipulates the object in every way, without being able to come off it. One always comes back to the *same* thing on which one has focused so exclusively that it has become a quasi-substance. Salvation can come only from reinserting the element into the structure taken as a whole where it finds its coherence.

For example, the principle "Christ-in-the-*Scriptures*" can be put forward in so unilateral and exclusive a manner that one no longer respects the symbolic otherness of the Risen One. Erasing the historical and cultural concreteness of the letter, one levels everything under the rubric "Word of God," identified with the Scriptures in an immediate manner and without any interpretive hermeneutics. Even with their principle "Scripture alone" (*scriptura sola*), the reformers themselves did not fall into this trap. Nevertheless, it must be admitted that they favored this tendency and that this first form of temptation is rather typical of *traditional Protestantism*.

Similarly, the principle "Christ-in-the-*sacraments*" can also be used to minimize the symbolic otherness of the Risen One. An invocation of the phrase "in virtue of the action" (*ex opere operato*), poorly understood — joined to a scheme of cause-and-effect and to a representation of the sacraments as channels or, even more, as containers of grace or else as instruments for the injection of a germ — has tended to obscure the fact that their efficacy is the same as that of the Word, and is thus no more automatic than that, symbolic, of communication by word. We have here another way of controlling the Risen One, different from the first, but no less (and no more, perhaps, if we look closely) heavy with consequences. This hypertrophy of the sacraments is obviously a typical temptation of *Roman Catholicism*. A veritable malady of sacramentality, pastoral sacramentalism, with its unavoidable tendency to approach the sacraments as magic, has been the price we have paid.

More contemporary and *trans-confessional* is the third form of this temptation: that which so exaggerates the value of ethical activity as a criterion for authentic Christian truth that the principle "Christ-in-the-*brothers-and-sisters*" no longer permits Christ to be recognized in his radical otherness. This (neo-)moralism appears in two major forms, with very different goals. In its more *mystical* form, the service of the neighbor for the love of Christ may at times be so lived that Christ serves only to furnish a pretext for a condescending generosity toward others, an alibi to make us feel good about ourselves. Nietzsche's sarcastic comments on this topic are well known. When the image of "Jesus-Christ" is thus pasted over the faces of others, the symbolic distance between ourselves and Christ, as well as between ourselves and others, is no longer respected; it is only ourselves we are loving, behind the mask of Christ, in the other.

In its more *political* form, this moralistic tendency, while justly denouncing an orthodoxy that would like to stay "pure" and would thereby avoid practical social action, so accentuates the urgency of engagement in the service of justice that precisely this "orthopraxis" tends now to become the criterion of orthodoxy. The faith thereby risks being reduced to a way of acting in the world — it certainly is that, in some respects — and the reign of God, to another form of this world — again, something that is partially true. We are well aware of the impact of this temptation on the contemporary Church. We also recognize, as the diverse theologies of liberation show, the difficulties of theological judgment we encounter when we attempt to evaluate them, as we must, "in the particular situation."[9]

The good health of the faith requires that it rest on the *tripod* of Christian identity; to attempt to stand on only one or two of these legs means that we risk tipping over. With that said, the image of the tripod is deceptive in that it represents something static. It is normal for the dynamic of the life of faith to entail, according to the times and cultures and the personal history of each person, shifts in the center of gravity as one accentuates now one, now

9. See *Théologies de la libération: Documents et débats*, foreword by B. Chenu and B. Lauret (Paris: Cerf-Centurion, 1985); J. Doré, ed., *Jésus et la libération en Amérique latine* (Paris: Desclée, 1986).

another element. Immobility is not a good sign either in Christian life or in human life . . .

c) A Task Never Fully Achieved: Consenting to the Presence of the Absence. It remains that Christian identity is structured by the symbolic articulation of the three elements mentioned. Would not the *Scriptures* be a dead letter if they were not attested as the Word of God for us today, preeminently in the Church's liturgical proclamation, and if they did not urge the subjects who receive them to a certain kind of ethical practice? Of what value would the liturgical and *sacramental* celebrations be if they were not the living memory of the person whom the Scriptures attest as the crucified God and if they did not enjoin their participants to become concretely, by the practice of *agape*, what they have celebrated and received? Who would think of describing any ethics as "Christian" (whose scope, moreover, is the same as that of any human ethic of individual or collective service to others) if it were not lived out as a response to the love first directed toward us by God, including the gift of his only Son (John 3:16), which the Scriptures reveal to us, and if it did not return to the theological vitality of its source in the reception of this first gift in the sacraments?

To give up the hope of finding the lost body of Jesus by consenting to meet him, alive, in the symbolic mediation of the Church thus requires a good joining of the three elements in their mutual differences. Without this, one would become fixated on one or the other and enclose oneself imaginatively in it, insisting that Christ resides there. Now, as risen, Christ has departed; we must *agree to this loss* if we want to be able to find him.

To agree to this loss, as we said, is equivalent to consenting to its symbol: the Church. This is a very difficult task, and for two opposed reasons. Those who reject the Church in order to find Christ by themselves misunderstand — at least in the characterized forms of this attitude, for every shade of nuance is possible — its sacramentality. But those who live too comfortably in the Church also misunderstand it: they are then in danger of forgetting that the Church is not Christ and that if, in faith, it is recognized as the privileged place of his presence, it is also, in this same faith, the most radical mediation of his absence. This is why to consent to the sacramental mediation of the Church is to consent to what we called above, echoing Heidegger, *the presence of the absence of God*. The Church radicalizes the vacancy of the place of God. To accept its mediation is to agree that this vacancy will never be filled. The openness of each of the three elements of our structure to the other two and the impossibility of identifying one with the others or of forcing them together into a single block are, for us, the trace of this irreducible vacancy. But it is precisely in the act of respecting his radical absence or otherness that the Risen One can be recognized symbolically. For this is the faith; this is Christian identity according to the faith. *Those who kill this sense of the absence of Christ make Christ a corpse again.*

In other words, the task of becoming a believer is as *unachievable* as that of becoming a subject. This was already our conclusion at the end of our reflection on the connections between philosophy, in Heidegger's sense, and theology; we spoke there of a "homology of attitude." The present chapter has spelled out the concrete modality, for the believer, of the consent to the absence, that is, the Church as the symbolic body of the word of the Risen One.

5. *An Extension of Our Model*

The model we have proposed needs to be grasped in a more extensive sense than a strict understanding of the three elements allows.

For example, the term "Scripture" encompasses everything that concerns the *understanding of the faith*, starting with those glosses in the margins of the Bible which we call theology.

It thus applies not only to the Scriptures themselves, but to everything pertaining to the understanding of revelation: basic catechetical instruction and the present-day propositions concerning the on-going formation of Christians, as well as the corpus of patristic, medieval, and contemporary theologies. While indispensable, this dimension of *knowledge* is by itself insufficient for someone to become a Christian. One can be in possession of an excellent knowledge of Christian theology without, for all that, recognizing oneself as a Christian. And the concrete truth of people's relations with Christ is not measured by the depth of their theological knowledge . . .

A second dimension, that of *recognition*, is no less necessary; it is a question of living symbolically what one is attempting to understand theologically.

Under the term "sacrament" we place everything that has to do with the celebration of the Triune God in the *liturgy*. First, of course, the two paradigmatic sacraments of baptism and the Eucharist; but also the other five; and further still, even celebrations which are not strictly sacramental, whether in a small group or large, whether in a gothic cathedral or in an ordinary room. Prayer is partially included in ritual activities, but only partially because the line between prayer and ritual is "always a moving one."[10]

The third element of our model seems at first to have a rather large extension. Simply put, the element "ethics" includes every kind of *action* Christians perform in the world insofar as this is a testimony given to the gospel of the Crucified-Risen One and this conduct, as J. B. Metz has emphasized, concerns not only interpersonal "moral *praxis*" but also the collective "social *praxis*."[11]

Our structure Scripture-Sacrament-Ethics thus appears as homologous to a more fundamental *anthropological structure*: cognition-recognition-praxis. The first two terms indicate "the antithesis between *thinking* and *living*" in which C. Lévi-Strauss sees "the opposition inherent in the human condition between two inescapable servitudes": on the one hand, the necessity of "introducing divisions" in order to be able to conceive

---

10. Vergote, *Religion, foi, incroyance*, 258; R. Bastide, *"Le sacré sauvage" et autres essais* (Paris: Payot, 1975) ch. 9 "L'expression de la prière chez les peuples sans écriture," 125–150 (LMD 109 [1972] 98–122).

Following the "provisional definition" that Bastide proposes, prayer "is a communication which can take place through objects, gestures, words, and most often a combination of all three, between persons and supernatural powers, within a relation posed as asymmetrical" (p. 142). It therefore always has something of the ritual about it, so much so that a division occurs, not between prayer that is spoken and rituals that concern primarily the unspoken, but "between the 'ceremonial' complexes," some of which are prayer, that is, communication with the divinity always joined to a "feeling of dependence," and others which are not. If not every cultic activity is prayer, on the other hand, "prayer is always a cultic activity" (p. 138). Hence, the shifting of the boundary between prayer and ritual. Whether it be of petition or praise, whether it be mystic or extremely "ordinary," whether it be experienced through silent awe of the body or through words or gestures, prayer is always an expressive and performative behavior of communication of humankind with God, a behavior that requires the assimilation of ritual actions which are sometimes so interiorized that they are no longer conscious. It is thus primarily subsumed in our diagram under liturgy, although it exceeds the latter and differs from it in certain respects.

11. J. B. Metz, *La foi dans l'histoire et la société* (Paris: Cerf, 1979) 73–74.

the primordial chaos as a "world" (from which comes the *myth* as "an agency for classification"); on the other, the reverse obligation of "recovering the continuity of living" or the permanence of identity (from which comes the *ritual* and its "meticulous patching up" which seeks to "fill up the empty spaces").[12] It is in *acting* — which, according to Heidegger, is not primarily the "producing of an effect whose reality is valued according to the utility it offers," but rather an "accomplishment"[13] whose essence is of the ethical and not of the technological order — that this double and antithetical servitude finds its practical resolution.

Every human subject is born from the possibility of conceiving a world, of celebrating it, of acting in it. The discursive logic of the *sign*, the identifying challenge of the *symbol*, the world-transforming power of the *praxis* (to the benefit of everyone): these three elements coalesce and form a structure. The structure of Christian identity that we proposed turns out to be the restatement, albeit a new one, of this fundamental anthropological structure.

II. REMARKS ON THE FUNCTION OF THE CHURCH IN OUR DIAGRAM

As visualized above, the structure of Christian identity requires several remarks.

1. *A Viewpoint of Identity*

Our diagram illustrates a viewpoint of identity and not one of salvation. It does not mean "outside the Church, there is no salvation," but rather "outside the Church, there is no *recognized* salvation." This is why the circle indicating the Church is formed not by a solid but by a broken line. We are dealing with an open circle — open to the *reign* which always exceeds the Church; open to the *World*, in the middle of which it is charged with being the "sacrament" of this reign. While open, the Church still has borders that distinguish it from other religions; these are the *reference points* for her identity which the broken line also represents. Without these particular marks, it obviously could not be the "sacrament" of the reign.

12. C. Lévi-Strauss, *L'homme nu*, 600–603.
13. M. Heidegger, *Lettre sur l'humanisme*, Q. 3. 73.

Our broken line thus illustrates the *paradox of Christian identity*. On the one hand, to be a Christian is to be part of the Church because at a minimum it is to make one's own the Easter proclamation "Jesus is the Christ," a confession which constitutes the Church and becomes visible in each person's baptism. But, if to be a Christian is to enter into a well-defined group, it is also to free oneself from every parochialism in order to open oneself to the universal. The paradox of *the Church* is precisely that it is never more faithful to its particular marks than when it in some sense forgets them to open itself to this reign, larger than itself, which grows in the World. It is in this sense, and in this sense alone, that the Church can be called the "sacrament" of God. It is difficult to take on such a paradoxical identity, hence the twofold permanent temptation for all Christians. The first is for Christians to recoil into their particularity, where the Church is represented as coinciding with the reign and thereby becomes again a closed circle — the "club" of those who may possibly be saved. At the end, opposite this Church without a reign is the reign without a Church, that is, the Church so bursts open toward the universality of the reign that, giving up all its distinguishing marks, it also loses its function as the sacrament of the reign.

2. *Diversity of Circuits of Identification*

Our second comment concerns the term *identity*, which we often use here. That the Church is the mediator of every access to Christian identity will come as a surprise only if we overlook the eminently *institutional* nature of every identification; identification is a process that necessarily involves social institutions (family, school . . .) and the interiorization of norms passed on from these.[14] Now, the feeling of belonging to the Church passes, especially today, through *very diverse circuits:* childhood memories — a kind Christian grandmother, the fragrance of incense, the Christmas creche — a special mass on television, a pilgrimage to a place of devotion, the affective impact of a liturgical celebration — be it traditional, such as a first communion, or innovative — or simply — a rather common experience today, it seems — the feel-

14. D. Hameline, "Identité psychosociale et institution," *Lumière et Vie* 116 (1974) 31–41.

ıf living authentic gospel values by participating in the
ggles for human liberation. Moreover, the identification with
u₁ᵤ Church is now more and more *partial:* "There are some things
one hangs onto, some things one lets go, some things one doubts,
some things one leaves in suspense. One does not leave the
Church, but one day one notices that one is outside on one point,
inside on another."[15] This continues to such an extent that the
threshold for a rupture seems to withdraw indefinitely and the notion of heresy becomes, in practice, more and more elastic. One
could say that today the general tendency is the reverse of what it
was formerly: to remain attached to the "reality" (*res*) — the
gospel continues to exercise a considerable attractive power — but
without the "sacrament" (*sacramentum*) — ministries, dogmas, and
sacraments . . .

A general model neither can nor should attempt to enter into
detail on the various *empirical variations* of which it is trying to render a theoretical account. Its only claim must be that these variations do not contradict it; if they did, we would have to alter our
basic hypothesis and seek a more pertinent model. Such is the
case with our diagram: it does not imply that Christian identity is
in direct proportion to the degree of people's dogmatic orthodoxy
or to the conformity of their ritual observance with the prescriptions of authority (for example, the regular participation at Sunday
liturgy) or to the adherence of their ethical practice to official
norms. It does imply that the emergence — never complete — of a
subject as Christian is always linked to the confession of Jesus as
the Christ "according to the Scriptures"; to the ritual expressions
of this confession, where one moves from a general discussion of
Jesus as Christ and Lord to a personal acceptance of him as the
Christ and Lord for oneself — baptism or the desire to receive it is
here the first obligatory stage — and finally to a certain manner of
living and acting strongly informed by the gospel.

3. *The Priority of the Church in Relation to Individual Christians*
Our third remark touches on the fundamental mediation of the
Church. One advantage of our diagram is that it shows that the

15. Y. Congar, "Sur la transformation du sens de l'appartenance à l'Eglise,"
Communio 5 (1976) 41–49.

recognition of Jesus as Christ and Lord cannot take place, as we observed above, through a personal contact with him, but on the contrary requires acquiescence in the mediation of his symbolic body, the Church. Hence the Apostles' Creed: "I believe in the Holy Catholic Church." Of course, one does not believe *in* the Church as one believes *in* Jesus Christ. The difference is important and has been recognized since the first centuries. One places one's faith only in God; the Church does not believe in itself. However, it is only in the Church that one confesses Jesus Christ — at the very least in making one's own the Easter kerygma from which the Church sprang: as Fr. de Lubac puts it, "The faith is ecclesial in its modality (if one may speak this way), and theological in its object and in its principle."[16] The gospel is *by nature communal.* To believe is to be gathered together from the start by him whom we confess to be our common Lord. This is manifested not only in the meal of the Lord where, as Paul indicates in 1 Corinthians 11, it is impossible to attempt to truly discern his Eucharistic body without discerning his ecclesial body, but also (and already) in the first sacrament of Christian life: for in effect all "put on" the same Christ through baptism; that is why it creates this "new human being" where the differences between Jew and Greek, slave and free, man and woman are eschatologically abolished (Gal 3:26-28; Col 3:10-11). It is equally manifested in the liturgical prayers, which are always cast as *we:* we give you thanks, we offer you, we beseech you, and so forth. From the linguistic viewpoint, this *we* does not designate a sum or aggregate of individual *Is,* but rather "a complex moral person."[17]

If the acting subject in the liturgy is the *ekklesia* as such, this is not because it is following a democratic ideal — although the rediscovery of this primary theological truth was probably linked with the cultural valorization of democracy — but rather *because and insofar as* the assembly is the body of Christ who presides over it (see our reading of the Emmaus story in this sense) and who exercises in its midst and on its behalf his unique and untransmissible priesthood (see Heb 7:24-25). It is on the recognition of this "sacramentality" of the Church, the concrete mediation of the

16. H. de Lubac, *Méditation sur l'Eglise* (Paris: Aubier, 1953) 25.
17. E. Ortigues, *Le Discours et le symbole* (Paris: Aubier-Montaigne, 1962) 156.

presence and action of the risen Christ, that the fact of the celebration by the *ekklesia* as a body, as a constituted body one could say, is founded.

The Church is thus primary in relation to individual Christians. Fr. de Montcheuil has a concise and felicitous expression for this, "It is not Christians who, in coming together, constitute the Church; it is the Church that makes Christians."[18] One could find no better way of expressing that there are no Christians "before" the Church and that the Church is not simply the sum total of individuals who are already Christians. The *celebrating assembly*, beginning with the baptismal and Eucharistic assemblies, is the first place for the manifestation of this Church. This does not mean that we are less the Church in other assemblies or during our "dispersion" during the week but that the identity of the Church as the Church of Jesus Christ, animated by the diverse charisms of the Spirit, *manifests itself* primarily, on the plane of the sacramentality of the Church where we are placing ourselves, in this type of assembly.

It is also well known that in the New Testament the term *ekklesia*, before designating the Church spread throughout the world, means first the *local assembly* of Christians. This is not simply a portion of the unique Church of Christ, but rather its *integral realization* in the particularity of a group and culture. Vatican II, in presenting the local Church as the highest manifestation of the Church of God,[19] has effected, we know, a veritable "Copernican revolution"; from now on "it is no longer the local church which orbits around the universal Church, but it is the unique Church of God that is equally present in each celebration of the local Church," so much so that one is led to "think of the Church now as a communion of Churches."[20] Granted, the local Churches, of whom the council said that "in and from such individual churches there comes into being the one and only Catholic Church," for the most part designate dioceses; nevertheless, it is also each legitimate Eucharistic assembly that renders "truly present" the Church of Christ, according to number 26 of *Lumen Gentium*.[21]

18. Y. de Montcheuil, *Aspects de l'Eglise* (1948) 51.
19. *Constitution on the Sacred Liturgy*, no. 41.
20. H. M. Legrand, "La réalisation de l'Eglise en un lieu," *Initiation à la pratique de la théologie* (Paris: Cerf, 1983) 3:150–151.
21. *Dogmatic Constitution on the Church*, no. 23. Legrand ("La réalisation de l'Eglise," 146) explains that "among eight uses of *ecclesia localis*, four designate

From this perspective it is significant to note that according to the New Testament, *"it is the convoked (ek-kaleo) assembly which gives its name to the (Christian) group, and not the group which gives its name to the assembly."*[22] In other words, no better way was found to designate the nascent Christian phenomenon than to call it by the term which seemed to characterize it best, a "convoked assembly" — compare already the *Qahal Yahweh* of the desert, translated most often in the Septuagint by *ekklesia*, at times also by *synagoge*.

Moreover, one can observe with F. Hahn that while the cultic terminology of the Old Testament is "consciously avoided" in the New for designating the worship of the Christian community, "the only notion that reappears with a definite regularity" to express this notion is "assemble" (*sunerchesthai*) or "come together" (*sunagesthai*) — four times alone in 1 Corinthians 11:17-34 and twice in 1 Corinthians 14, besides Acts 4:31, 14:27, and 20:7. "The 'coming together' of the Christians is the distinguishing characteristic of Christian worship."[23] In short, the coming together in the name of the Lord Jesus was perceived as the chief mark of Christians, the fundamental sacrament of the risen Christ. Christians are people who get together. Throughout the first centuries, this idea was vigorously asserted: "To go to the *ekklesia* on Sunday always signified 'joining with the assembly' or 'making the Church,'" so much so that for the early Church Fathers, as P. M. Gy has noted, there is "an identity between participation in the *ekklesia*-assembly and belonging to the Church."[24]

4. To Receive the Church as a Grace

Our fourth remark follows theologically from what we have just said: the ecclesial institution is to be received as a grace.

This statement obviously presupposes that one distinguishes *the institutional Church*, the object of the "I believe in the holy church" (*credo sanctam ecclesiam*), which is to be recognized as a gracious gift of God in that it is, in its very visibility, the sacrament of the reign that is coming, and the *organization* which such an institution necessarily has to give itself and which is completely relative to the ambient culture and remains "always in need of re-

---

the diocese, a fifth the diocese in its cultural context, two a consolidation of dioceses, and the last, unique in the texts of Vatican II, refers to the parish."

22. P. Grelot, "Du sabbat juif au dimanche chrétien," LMD 124 (1975) 17.

23. F. Hahn, *Der urchristliche Gottesdienst* (Stuttgart, 1970) 34.

24. P. M. Gy, "Eucharistie et 'Ecclesia' dans le premier vocabulaire de la liturgie chrétienne," LMD 130 (1977) 30.

form" (*semper reformanda*). It is true that currently there are vigorous debates between the Churches and within each one over the question of distinguishing what, in the organization, belongs or does not belong to the institution. Moreover, it is true that it would be easy to show from history, or even from the current situation, how the "grace" of the institutional Church has been manipulated; the appeal to the "Mystery of the Church" always risks becoming a form of mystification.

The fact remains that beyond the often prickly problems of organization, the recognition of the institutional Church as the "fundamental sacrament" of the reign always requires a conversion — either because believers, too comfortably ensconced in the institution, forget that it is *only* a sacrament and overlook the distance between it and Christ or because their critical suspicions toward the institution result in their not seeing that it *is* indeed a sacrament. A too serene compliance with the Church is no less questionable than a resentment toward it. In the first case, the institution serves as a comfortable refuge; its dogmas and rituals serve as excuses ("sacrificial" as we will later call them) dispensing the believer from the obligation to assume positively the absence of Christ in favor of his presence, imaginarily "complete" in the Church. But one can find this same denial of *the presence-of-the-absence* of Christ in the second case, although from an opposite viewpoint. For is not the resentment which one feels toward a Church tolerated only as a necessary evil, a Church endured and dragged as a ball-and-chain, a symptom of this "gnostic" desire for the immediate contact with Jesus Christ we described above and of an ultra-metaphysical way of thinking that, counter to what we called consent to the corporality of our condition, is constantly reinforced by the preference granted a priori to interiority and transparency?

It is precisely as a consequence of our symbolic journey of respect for the presence-of-the-absence that we understand the *credo sanctam ecclesiam* here, that is, the institutional mediation of the Church as a *gift of grace*. The twofold temptation described above only further highlights the difficulty of receiving the Church as a grace, a difficulty from which no one is ever definitively protected. Oscillating as we always are between the "forbidden" extremes,

our balance in this domain can always be precarious. In ˎ
tion with its crucified God, can the Church ever be anythinɤ
than a sort of *"transitional space"* (in Winnicott's sense of "traɪˎ
tional object")?

5. *Pastoral Openness*

Without a doubt, the reflection proposed throughout this chapter is heavy with pastoral consequences. We will mention only one, the most fundamental in our eyes; and because we are dealing with sacramental theology, we will do so apropos the liturgy.

The assembly of Christians gathered in the name of Christ (Matt 18:20) or in his memory is, as we said, the first sacramental representation of his presence. At the same time, it is the first stumbling block for faith, for such a representation is also the radical mark of his absence. It is not at all self-evident that it is he, the living Lord, who presides over the assembly; that the assembly is the "holy Church" even while it is made up of sinners, the "body" of Christ even while its members are divided among themselves, or the "temple of the Holy Spirit" who makes all things new even while its members are imprisoned in the chains of their habits. In other words, such an affirmation is positively scandalous. Now, it is the basic point of this chapter's reflection to show that the *concrete path for becoming-Christian comes up against the obstacle of this very first scandal.* The other scandals concerning the faith — one thinks, for example, of the Eucharistic presence — can easily become "false scandals" masking the real one or excuses for secretly turning ourselves away from the real one. For this true scandal is that God, by the gift of the Spirit, continues to raise up for himself a body in the world — the body of the Risen One in its humiliated condition marked by the wounds of his death. The true scandal is ultimately this, the path to our relation with God passes through our relation with human beings and most especially through our relation with those whom the judgment of the mighty has reduced to "less than nothing."

Now, it is precisely in the liturgical assembly that we first see and experience symbolically this very first scandal for faith. Why go to the trouble of joining a praying community on Sunday when we could stay home and watch Mass on television? It can seem so much easier to feel close to Christ and to "give ourselves entirely to God" in the comfortable silence of our own homes than in a church where we must often close our eyes and, heads between our hands, cover our ears to free ourselves from being disturbed in our conversations with God.

And yet, according to one of the most ancient traditions of the Church,[25] the sacramental manifestation of the "first day of the week"[26] as the *memorial day* of the death-and-resurrection of the Lord is primarily linked with the coming together of Christians. As the first sacramental representation of the Risen One, this *ecclesia*-assembly shows that the truth of the bond with him not only requires that we not ignore *the presence of others*, but on the contrary demands that we make our *way* through them. It shows the nature of the Christian task that is inaugurated eschatologically at baptism: to form this "new human being" for whom Christ died, giving his life for the reconciliation of Jew and Greek in a single body (Eph 2:15-16; Col 3:10-11). If it is precisely this baptismal task, which is an unremitting one, that it makes undeniably apparent, then the Sunday *ecclesia* denounces as illusory this *individualism* by which we would believe ourselves to be more Christian the more we achieve immediate contact with God in the silent conversation of meditation. Meditation, of course, has its place in an authentic Christian life; we do not wish to belittle it but to situate it in its rightful place.

Theologically, that place is secondary. The first, properly Christian attitude as we arrive at the Sunday assembly is not to turn inward, concentrating on ourselves and God, heads buried in our hands to avoid the disturbing presence of others. As praiseworthy and even necessary as this recollection might otherwise be, theologically it should be subordinated to a reverse attitude of "de-centration": that is, of a *deliberate taking cognisance of others* in their diversity, and in recognizing them as *brothers and sisters*.

Such is the significance of the encompassing circle of the Church in our diagram. This circle makes visible on paper what we see and live sacramentally in the liturgy, that is, *the task of becoming-Christian:* learning to unmask the forgetfulness which everything in us wishes to forget — the forgetfulness of the humanity of the divine God revealed in Jesus and thus the forgetfulness of the fact that alliance with him can be lived only in the mediation of alliance with others, and not in an imaginary direct contact with him that presupposes his "full" presence. In directing us toward this alliance with others as the privileged place where the body of Christ comes into being, *the liturgical assembly constitutes the funda-*

25. See Grelot, "Du sabbat juif," 33-34.
26. B. Botte, "Les dénominations du dimanche dans la tradition chrétienne," *Le Dimanche*, B. Botte et al. (Paris: Cerf, 1965), 7-28; J. Daniélou, "Le dimanche comme huitième jour," *Le Dimanche*, 61-89.

mental "sacramental" representation of the presence of the absence of God. To consent to this absence and thus, simultaneously, to be willing to give back to God this body of humanity that he expects from those who claim to belong to Jesus Christ, constitutes, as we have stressed, the major trial of becoming-Christian. The liturgical assembly is certainly not the exclusive place where this test occurs, but it is the principal *symbolic* place. One begins to get a sense of the pastoral work to be done in this direction. But at the same time one perhaps senses the powerful role that the liturgical assembly itself can play in such a pedagogy of the faith.

The Relation Between Scripture and Sacrament

After having worked out the structure of Christian identity, we are now ready to reflect on the connections between the sacraments and Scripture (Chapter Six) and between the sacraments and ethics (Chapter Seven). We will then propose a model of how this structure functions (Chapter Eight).

We will proceed in this present chapter through three major steps: first will be an attempt at an historical understanding of the relation between the Bible, as it evolved, and the liturgy, first of Israel and then of the early Christian communities. The second part, basing itself upon a phenomenological reflection on the process of producing the Bible, will attempt to see the liturgy as the "place" of Scripture. The third will show in what sense one can speak of a sacramentality of Scripture, and inversely, in what sense Scripture opens up sacramentality from the inside.

I. "THE BIBLE BORN OF THE LITURGY"

This first section borrows its title from an article by P. Béguerie.[1] Such an assertion is to be understood on two levels. At the level of *facts*, it claims that among the multiple sectors of Israelite activity, that of worship played a decisive — which does not mean an exclusive — role in the development of what would gradually become the canonical corpus of its Scriptures. A few exploratory probes, which obviously stand in need of much commentary, will permit us to verify, at least partially, the effective consistency of such a statement. On the basis of these few indications, which we consider significant, we will be able to propose at a second level an *interpretation* of this liturgical rooting of the Bible, in both its

1. P. Béguerie, "La Bible née de la liturgie," LMD 126 (1976) 108–116.

Jewish and Christian parts, an interpretation that will make this appear not merely accidental, but essential.

1. *The Jewish Bible and Liturgy*

"The Bible was born of the liturgy, from its very beginnings, from the most ancient texts of the holy book."[2]

a) The importance of the "high places" and "sanctuaries" as places of pilgrimage *from the time of the conquest* is well attested in the texts that will become the Bible: Shechem, Gilgal, Shilo[3] . . .

It is around these sanctuaries that the patriarchal traditions, the oldest and the more recent, are transmitted and amalgamated. The priests of these sanctuaries are the guardians and the interpreters of the laws recognized by the tribes; they watch over the preservation and transmission of the oral traditions which will become regrouped and mixed little by little into larger cycles. The Bible is thus born out of the "liturgical" activity (in a wide sense) of these cultic centers[4] where the tribes were able to fashion and reappropriate their collective memories and to identify them as issuing from a single eponymous ancestor — a "wandering Aramean" (Deut 26:5) — from whom they inherited their confession of faith in Yahweh, the one God, who was responsible for their unity.

b) If we grasp the problem from the other end, that is, not from its origin but from its term, we observe the same decisive function of the liturgy. The canon of the Scriptures is in effect the result of a *selection* among multiple traditions, first oral, later written. The current Biblical corpus has conserved perhaps no more than ten percent — a number which has no other value than to indicate the order of magnitude we are dealing with, since a precise estimate is obviously impossible. The texts which the Bible retains "have survived *because of their use in the liturgy.*

2. Ibid., 109.

3. R. de Vaux, *Histoire ancienne d'Israël* (Paris: Gabalda, 1971) 1:160-179: the ancient sanctuaries of the patriarchal period (Shechem, Mambre, Bersheba, Hebron, linked to the wanderings of Abraham to which will be added later the traditions concerning the clan of Isaac; Bethel and Shechem, where the memories of Jacob were transmitted) are revived in this period. But they are supplanted by new ones: Gilgal (traditions concerning the crossing of the Jordan), Shechem (this time as a high place symbolizing the unity of the tribes), Shilo (meeting point for the tribes of central Palestine during the period of the Judges) (Ibid. [1973] 2:26-32).

4. Thus was the Decalogue "marked by its cultic usage." J. Briend, "Une lecture du Pentateuque," *Cahiers Evangile* 15 (1976) 32-33. Along the same lines, see Briend, "Lectures du Décalogue," *Catéchèse* 98 (1985) 95-96.

And the content of the writings, the reason for their peculiar grouping, come equally from their use in the liturgy."[5] This is true even for the most recent writings; in the Judaism that emerged after 70 C.E., one reads the book of Ruth at Pentecost, the Canticle at Passover, Qoheleth for the feast of Tents, and Esther at the feast of Purim.[6] As with many others, these texts would not have entered into the canon if they had not had a liturgical function. "The biblical corpus was built up primarily in connection with a communal proclamation and listening."[7] Such is the law, by the way, that P. Beauchamp has formulated on this subject: *"That is canonical which receives authority from public reading."*[8] By its very constitution, the Bible is made for public reading; this is the reason, as we will see, why "ecclesiality" belongs to it not accidentally but essentially.

c) In the third place, we may observe that if Passover, Pentecost, Tents — *the three great annual feasts of pilgrimage* (Deut 16; Exod 23:13-19) — have been kept in the Bible, it is because they have undergone, through a liturgical memorial, a *reconversion into history.* Derived from pagan rituals of fertility, pastoral or agrarian, they have been systematically reinterpreted, sometimes to the last detail, in connection with the founding events read as the "history of salvation" on the part of Yahweh "creating" (Isa 43:1) descendants of Abraham as his people. Thus, at Passover, the blood of the lamb, the unleavened bread, the bitter herbs are connected with the Exodus from Egypt; at Pentecost, the offering of the firstfruits of the harvest, with the Covenant and the Law given on Sinai; at the feast of Tents, the booths made of branches, with the wandering in the desert (Exod 23:14-16; Lev 23). This rereading as history was obviously not the result of an intellectual operation, but of a living experience, that of a confession of faith, in which the liturgical memorial played an essential role.

d) Our fourth point is that it is particularly significant that *the great founding events of Israel* (precisely because and to the extent they are recognized as foundational) are presented to us in the Bible *through liturgical recitations.* In a note introducing section 12:1-13:16 of Exodus, the *Traduction oecuménique de la Bible* observes that this complex "does not present itself as an account of the departure from Egypt, but as a collection of *liturgical* texts (coming from traditions of different periods), that shows how the *memorial* of this departure from Egypt is to be celebrated." The best way to show the importance of a past event is to recount it in the way liturgy memorializes such an event in the present. Liturgical practice

5. Béguerie, "La Bible née de la liturgie," 109.
6. J. A. Sanders, *Identité de la Bible: Torah et Canon* (Paris: Cerf, 1975) 140.
7. I. H. Dalmais, "La Bible vivant dans l'Eglise," LMD 126 (1976) 7.
8. P. Beauchamp, *L'Un et L'Autre Testament* (Paris: Seuil, 1976).

establishes the "text" of the text, the "meta-text," the margin which surrounds it, the page on which it is written. *The authentic point of departure for the story is the celebrating assembly in its present reality.*

We can make analogous comments apropos the section concerning the *Covenant on Sinai* (Exod 19–24). It is an impressive liturgy, with first (19:10-25) the washing of the vestments, the drawing of the sacred enclosure, the sounding of the horn, the separation of the priests, the great ritual symbols of fire and smoke at the time of the theophany, the terror of the people who withdraw to a respectful distance while Moses plays the role of intermediary (20:18-21); then the gift of the Law (the Decalogue, ch. 20, and Code of the Covenant, chs. 21–23); and finally the rites of the conclusion of the Covenant (ch. 24): a "liturgical" reading of the Law, ratification by the people, a covenantal sacrifice on an altar of twelve standing stones with aspersion of blood (Elohist tradition) and a communal meal (Yahwist tradition). Here again, the liturgy is not simply an external setting for the story; it is rather its place of origin, always contemporary.

The story of the *wandering in the desert* is no exception to this primordial hold of the liturgical memorial. The people are accompanied by the cloud, a sign of the presence of Yahweh, who guides them and stays in their midst, when he comes to take up residence, during their stops, in the first of his "temples," that of the Tent of Meeting (or Tabernacle). "Israel, in the Priestly tradition, is not an armed populace . . . but a people vowed to the worship of the Lord."[9] The *conquest of Canaan* also begins as an immense liturgical procession at the crossing of the Jordan (priests, Levites, Ark of the Covenant, the setting up of the twelve standing stones, and so forth, Joshua 3–4). All this ends with the solemn celebration of the renewal of the Covenant on Mounts Ebal and Garizim, which look down on Shechem, the chief sanctuary of the league of the twelve tribes, in Joshua 8:30-35, repeated again in more developed form in Joshua 24. Even the *discourses using the intimate form of address* in Deuteronomy probably also had their origin, as the *Traduction oecuménique* indicates, "in certain liturgical ceremonies where in effect all Israel was assembled to hear, as a single person, the law of its God"; moreover, it explains that "it was probably when this teaching (about the Law of the Covenant) broke out of its liturgical framework that the intimate form of address, more appropriate to a community, was abandoned in order to challenge the Israelites with the more formal you (*vous*), that is, as so many individuals, each responsible for her or his own conduct."[10]

9. *Traduction Œcuménique de la Bible*, Introduction to Numbers, 257.
10. Ibid., Introduction to Deuteronomy, 332.

Thus, the great foundational moments of Israelite identity are *recounted in liturgical terms*. If the liturgy is not apparent in the text itself, it is because it is its pre-text. One does not tell the liturgy; one liturgically tells the story that one memorializes. The "liturgification" of the telling of stories about the early times is the best way to manifest their continuing foundational role in the identity of Israel.

e) If *covenantal liturgies* appear as such only at four moments in the history of Israel, it is because these four are particularly significant insofar as what is at issue is either the establishment of a *communal* identity for a people (at Sinai [Exod 19–24]) or the restoration of this identity at three periods of crisis. First, at Shechem, at the time of the conquest and occupation of Canaan, the Covenant with Yahweh also establishes a covenant among the tribes (Josh 24; Deut 27). Second, under Josiah, a century after the fall of Samaria, when Judah is threatened as much by polytheism as by Assyrian pressure, the solemn renewal of the covenant in Jerusalem (2 Kgs 22–23) succeeds in restoring both the religious and the national identity: a single people, a single God, a single Temple. Third, after the return from the Exile, the people, without a king, dominated politically by the Persian empire, endangered within by idolatrous practices and intermarriage with their pagan neighbors (Ezra 9–10; Mal), is saved from the disintegration gnawing at its vitals by the reform of Ezra, its culminating point the renewal of the Covenant in the Temple (Neh 8).

Numerous anniversaries of this type, according to J. A. Sanders,[11] took place each year throughout all of Israelite history. The specific celebrations of the Covenant that the collective memory finally selected and preserved in the holy book should be understood as *archetypal:* within the canonical corpus, they are the marks of the religious and national identity of the group of tribes which form this original people which is the "people of Yahweh." The purpose of these covenantal liturgies reaches beyond — it is obvious — their episodic character; it concerns the essential dimension of the Bible, which is the confession of faith in Yahweh and, through this mediation, the very identity of Israel.

We certainly do not wish to claim here that the liturgy is the exclusive place of the birth and the production of the Bible! This, moreover, is one of the recurring themes in the work of P. de Vaux: "Worship does not create tradition; it recalls it,"[12] which, however, does not contradict the fact that the traditions recited on the occasion of a feast "were profoundly influenced by this cultic

---

11. Sanders, *Identité de la Bible,* 48.
12. De Vaux, *Histoire ancienne d'Israël,* 1:178; see pp. 307, 380.

usage."[13] The liturgy did not produce the traditions themselves, but — under the obvious influence of multiple political, economic, and social factors — it left its imprint upon them and played a *decisive* role in their being preserved as the "Word of God." And that is especially true insofar as Israel found in the liturgy the primordial location of its identity: the confession of faith in Yahweh, the one and only God, a confession of faith of which the Bible is essentially the meandering unfolding through the events of history. In this perspective, worship was for Israel much more than simply one sector of empirical activities among others; it was the principal *catalyst* of an identity which would later find its "official edition" in the canon of the Scriptures.

2. The Christian Bible and Liturgy

a) Christian Hermeneutics of the Scriptures. The Christian Bible is nothing else than a rereading of the Hebrew Bible in the light of the death and resurrection of Jesus Christ, or the rereading of these as accomplished "according to the Scriptures." As attested by this Christian hermeneutics, to believe that Jesus is the Christ of God and that he is living is to believe that he speaks in the Scriptures proclaimed in his name in the assemblies of the Church or to believe that the Scriptures speak of him. Thus, from its very beginning, the Christian Bible is thus nothing else than a variation of the traditional techniques of carefully searching the Scriptures, employed in the midrashic or targumic commentaries. It is a tissue of citations, explicit or implicit, from written and oral traditions of the Old Testament, reread as accomplished in Christ. This explains why Christian revelation consists in the joining of both testaments. This connection which both separates and connects the two is just the visible manifestation of one that is present in the New Testament itself, replete as it is with the Old.[14]

About 95, Clement of Rome cites as Scripture only texts from the Old Testament; it is for them that he reserves the expression "the sacred

13. Ibid., 380.
14. On the origin of the designation of "Old" and "New" Testaments in the second century, with a semantic slide "from the theological register" of covenant "to the literary register" of testament, see A. Paul, "L'inspiration et le canon des Ecritures," *Cahiers Evangile* 49 (1984) 44.

word" (*ho hagios logos*). But he does so with this fundamental difference, that the "Lord" (*Kyrios*) who speaks there is the Lord Jesus himself.[15] It will comes as no surprise that in addressing the Corinthians, he explicitly quotes Paul's letters at least three times (without counting the multiple implicit references), letters which, according to 1 Thessalonians 5:27 and Colossians 4:16, were intended to be read in the assembled *ecclesia* and exchanged between the different churches. This intention explains the fact that the customary epistolary opening and closing formulas have been transformed "liturgically" and that these letters probably had "from the very beginning a liturgical character."[16] Whatever the case, in quoting these, Clement of Rome does not yet refer to them as "Scripture." As for the Gospels, the "words of the Lord Jesus" that he reports seem to go back to "a collection of 'sayings' (*logia*), either oral or already committed to writing, but not to a precise gospel." And it is probable, continues A. Jaubert, that at a time when anything written was immersed in a culture still largely oral, the liturgical milieux played an important role in the choice and the tenor of texts quoted by Clement.[17]

The influence of these milieux on the way what was going to become the Christian Scriptures was transmitted is less surprising when one recalls that the first Christian communities inherited the *synagogue experience*. For the Law and the Prophets continued to be read in the Christian assemblies; and one continued as well to "actualize" them through the traditional techniques of targumic homilies or midrash, "stringing together like pearls the biblical texts which referred to a common theme or linking texts together with a common key word or a play on words based on simple assonance."[18] This sort of loose commentary was most likely influenced also by the various oral traditions which, at the time of Jesus, sometimes traced their origins back to Moses himself, so much so that "toward the end of the first century C.E., Judaism professed as a dogma that both the written Law and the oral Law had been revealed to Moses on Mount Sinai, the oral Law completing and explaining the written Law with the aim of rendering it intelligible and contemporary for each generation."[19]

15. A. Jaubert, *Clément de Rome: Epître aux Corinthiens*, Sources chrétiennes 167 (Paris: Cerf, 1971) 52, 62.

16. E. Cothenet, "Saint Paul en son temps," *Cahiers Evangile* 26 (1978) 21.

17. A. Jaubert, *Clément de Rome*, p. 52 and the scriptural index.

18. C. Perrot, "La lecture de la Bible dans les synagogues au premier siècle de notre ère," LMD 126 (1976).

19. A. Paul, "Intertestament," *Cahiers Evangile* 14 (1975), 7. Moreover, one should not forget that "the average religious culture of the Jews," fashioned

In the building up of the new Bible, three major kinds of charisms were determinative, according to C. Perrot: glossolalia, prophecy, and teaching.[20] First were the *"glossolalists,"* Christian prayers, specialists in blessings or thanksgivings (before the Christian prophets assumed this role, as the *Didache* already shows),[21] speaking *to* Jesus as they would to God in the name of the community. Second were the *Christian prophets* or homilists proclaiming, in their targumic homilies, the words of Scripture as words *of* the Lord Jesus to his community or as words of God about his Christ. Third were the *doctors* or "didascalists," the new scribes charged with packaging the *logia* of the Lord into stories and discourses, constructions which became the Gospels that Justin calls "the memoirs of the apostles" (1 Ap 66 and 67). Even this third charism, that of the doctors, was linked to the liturgical assembly, first by its origin, for it found its root there, especially in the activity of the homilist-prophets, and by its end, for their work of compilation, organization, and rewriting aimed at producing accounts which could be proclaimed as the Good News in the assemblies.

The Christian assemblies, Eucharistic and baptismal, seem to have functioned empirically as the *decisive crucible where the Christian Bible was formed.* Such, at any rate, is the "profound conviction" of Perrot: "The Christian meal is the place par excellence where the evangelical composition of history was crystallized. The gospel read in the Eucharistic celebration was born out of this celebration itself," although the author admits that he is not forgetting that there were "other places contributing to the Christian discourse."[22]

---

in the synagogues, was nourished "not by the letter of the Old Testament alone" (the majority did not understand Hebrew and could not read), "and assuredly not by the discussions and quibbles of the doctors. They lived from this living tradition rooted within Scripture, the inheritance of post-exilic Judaism." (R. Le Déaut, *Liturgie juive et Nouveau Testament* [Rome: Pontifical Biblical Institute, 1965] 68–69).

20. C. Perrot, "L'anamnèse néo-testamentaire," *Revue de l'Institut Catholique de Paris* 2 (1982) 21–37.

21. *Didache* 10:7. "Let the prophets give thanks as much as they wish." The *Apostolic Constitutions* (a compilation of earlier texts, about 380 in Antioch) transforms this text in a significant manner: "Let your presbyters give thanks" (VII, 26:6). These presbyters have already long replaced the "prophets," and they are no longer permitted to improvise their public prayer.

22. C. Perrot, *Jésus et l'histoire*, 293.

b) The Accounts of the Last Supper. The foregoing is especially true for the *accounts of the Last Supper*. They exemplify what we said above about the liturgical accounts of the great founding events of Israel. They are presented as stories about what Jesus did the night before he died, but in fact what they narrate directly is the way the Church re-enacts the last meal of the Lord. We have here a *"liturgical formula,* solidly fixed from a very early date and become familiar through worship,"[23] a formula that Paul may have received, according to an Antiochene tradition, as early as his first stay in Antioch about 43, before he "handed it on" to the Corinthians the way he "received" it (1 Cor 11:23). Now, the marks of Christian liturgical practice are deeply embedded in the ordered succession of technical verbs for the Jewish breaking of bread, in the parallelism between the formulas for the bread and the cup, in the formula of distribution "for you," in the already ritualized theological introduction, "the Lord Jesus, on the night he was delivered up. . . ." These marks, erased from the surface of the text, reveal the authentic pre-text: one does not tell the Church's liturgy; one liturgically tells the story one is commemorating to show how to commemorate it and thus to make it present again for each generation. *The true source of these accounts of the Last Supper is the liturgical ecclesia.* So much so that in virtue of their constitutive liturgical "pre-text," these *stories about* Jesus, condensing in the extreme the *oral gospels* (moreover, these are all that Paul tells us about Jesus "according to the flesh"), function in effect as *speeches by* Jesus himself, that is, as proclaimed gospel; the remembrance becomes an official memorial, and the narration of the story becomes the official proclamation, evangelical — that is the meaning of the "you proclaim" (*kataggellete*) of 1 Corinthians 11:26—or kerygmatic, of "the Lord's death until he comes."

The introduction of these accounts of the Last Supper, initially independent, into the passion narratives (the most ancient redactional units in our Gospels) seems to have taken place at the moment when the latter were expanded into their "long" forms. Now, such an insertion provides a major key to our understanding of the production of the Christian Bible: the Gospels would never have been born if he about whom they testify had left only

23. J. Jeremias, *La Dernière Cène* (Paris: Cerf, 1972) 108.

the beautiful memories of a "dearly departed one." For, in fact, they were born out of a faith in him as alive and thus out of the faith that his death was "for our sins" (1 Cor 15:3), "for us"; his victory, attested by his resurrection, is the victory of God himself. Now, the liturgy is the primary place *for this confession of faith.* This faith was lived globally in the living symbolic experience of baptism and the breaking of bread before being developed into theological discourse. The confession of Jesus as *Lord* goes together with that of Jesus as *Savior.* This is especially clear in the pre-Pauline hymn to Christ in Philippians 2:6-11; "the *Sitz im Leben* of this confession is the liturgical doxology."[24] In singing this hymn, the community adores Christ in the same way it adores the Lord God; before him it "bends the knee" and stands with hands extended and upraised (see Tertullian, *Apol.* 30:4 and ancient iconography), acclaiming the Crucified One of Golgotha as Lord. This confession of faith acted out shows straightaway the *"for us"* of the death and resurrection of Jesus. It shows that it was a soteriological motive which gave rise to the Christological confession and, following the remark of W. Pannenberg, that "all the Christological ideas had, so to speak, soteriological motives."[25]

c) The Priority of Liturgical Practice. This *priority of symbolic practice* in the liturgy in relation to the properly theological elaborations allows one to understand why "it is quite likely that the missionary discourses on the one hand and the formulas of the confession of faith on the other have a common or related origin in the milieu of liturgical tradition."[26] The milieu that transmitted the soteriological "for" concerning the death of Jesus seems to have been the one in which arose the "cultic" tradition that produced our accounts of the Last Supper and probably also Mark 10:45 (". . . and to give his life as a ransom for many").[27] This is why, as J. Guillet notes, it is probably "in repeating and transmitting in its Eucharistic liturgies the words and gestures of the Lord" that the

24. W. Kasper, *Jésus, le Christ* (Paris: Cerf, 1976) 253.
25. W. Pannenberg, *Esquisse d'une christologie* (Paris: Cerf, 1971) 37.
26. J. Guillet, *Les Premiers Mots de la foi* (Paris: Centurion, 1977) 97-98.
27. X. Léon-Dufour, "Jésus devant sa mort à la lumière des textes de l'institution eucharistique et des discours d'adieu," *Jésus aux origines de la christologie* (Louvain, 1975) 165-166.

Church was led to "discover and proclaim that Christ died for all human beings."[28]

A confession of faith in act, the liturgical practice of the first Christian communities seems to have functioned as the catalyst allowing the different factors (doctrinal, apologetic, moral, liturgical) and the diverse agents (the Christian communities themselves with their concrete problems, internal and external; their various ministries of government, prophecy, teaching, prayer, and so forth) to *come together* in order to flesh out little by little these Gospels confessed as the gospel of the Lord Jesus.

"That is canonical which receives authority from public reading," we said above apropos the Jewish Bible. It appears that this is no less true for the Christian Bible. The formation of its canon was progressive; if there were waverings concerning certain books during the second and third centuries, they "are minimal." At any rate, continues P. Grelot, a canon (in Irenaeus' meaning) "existed in practice from the time the local churches read in their assemblies certain texts in which they recognized the authentic legacy of the apostles." For "the essential criterion (for the establishment of the canon) was always the *venerable customs* of the communities." And these customs were primarily determined by the *liturgy:* "The assembly in the Church remains the place where the books are preserved, read, and explained, just as it had been the place where they evolved."[29]

II. THE LITURGICAL ASSEMBLY: THE PLACE OF SCRIPTURE

From the empirical level where we have been operating until now, we pass to a *phenomenological* reflection in which we will show according to what processes the liturgical assemblies provide a place for the Jewish and Christian Scriptures.

1. *A Phenomenological Analysis of the Process That Produced the Bible*

a) This Production Results from a Relation between Three Principal Elements. We call "*canon I*" or the "*instituted* tradition" the

28. Guillet, *Les Premiers Mots*, 35.

29. P. Grelot, "Aux origines du Canon des Ecritures," *Introduction à la Bible: Nouveau Testament*, vol. 5 *L'achèvement des Ecritures* (Paris: Desclée, 1977) 156–177; quotations are from pp. 169–177.

corpus, first oral, then written, which already functions as a practical canon of the traditions in which a clan, a tribe, or a group of people recognize and identify themselves. In its final form, this canon 1 corresponds to the *canonical Bible*. In its earlier stages, it includes those *"Bibles before the Bible,"* that is — according to the times, the places, the genealogical affiliations, for some clan or group of clans, some tribe or group of tribes — such "documents" as the Yahwist (J), Elohist (E), Deuteronomic (D), and Priestly (P) or, still earlier, the cycles of Abraham, of Isaac, of Abraham-Isaac, and again of Jacob-Israel — cycles where traditions of distinct origins were integrated.

"Canon 2," or the *"instituting* tradition,"* designates the *hermeneutical process* of rereading-rewriting canon 1 in relation to constantly changing historical situations. It is this process that, varying according to the conjunction of political, economic, and cultural factors, amalgamates the ancient traditions into "cycles," into the history of such-and-such a "house" (for example, the house of Joseph), into "documents," and at last organizes these into "books" which will themselves ultimately be classified under the three great categories (Law, Prophets, Writings), according to the act of recalling in which "each generation finds itself before a task that is always the same and always new — to understand itself as Israel."[30] As Sanders emphasizes, *this hermeneutics, "although not written, is itself also canonical."*[31]

The author illustrates this point with many examples. Most especially he shows the hermeneutical process by which the *exclusion of the period of the conquest of Canaan* (and of the David-Solomonic monarchy) *from the Torah,* that is, from the archetypal history of its origins which was to serve as a paradigmatic reference for Israel to identify itself throughout history, was brought about by the Deuteronomic school (itself linked in its origins to levitical circles), and later by the Priestly school. For it is certainly a case of deliberate exclusion, since the ancient confessions of faith (Deut 26:5-9; Josh 24:2-13 already more developed; cf. Ps 136) include at least a reference to the conquest as belonging to the proto-history. Between the fall of the Northern Kingdom in 722 and the reform of Josiah in

30. G. Von Rad, *Théologie de l'Ancien Testament,* 3rd ed. (Geneva: Labor et Fides, 1971) 1:109.

31. Sanders, *Identité de la Bible,* 159–160.

621, linked to the "discovery" of the "book of the Covenant" (Deuteronomy in a shorter earlier form), one observes the establishment, for reasons of political history as well as for the religious reform desired by levitical circles (for the most part refugees from the North after 722), of a process of "mosesization" of the mystical triad "David-Zion-Jerusalem" that ruled the Yahwist circles of the South. But did Moses not die just *before* the entrance of the people into Canaan (Deut 31–34, in a later redaction)? We see the process: "because it is a question of *identity*,"[32] one invokes a *new authority* (Moses) to be able to continue to understand oneself as Israel in a novel historical situation; and this reference implies a new delimitation of the history of the origins whose memory insures Israel's identity. Thus, Deuteronomy "drives a wedge" between the traditions of the time in the desert and those which narrate the entrance of Joshua into Canaan. As a consequence, the Torah could conclude with the death of Moses and be entirely attributed to him. During the time of the Exile, the Priestly circles will reinforce this process begun by the Deuteronomists. This is understandable: it was the price Israel had to pay, now that it had lost all its territory, to be able to continue to recognize itself as Israel in a situation that otherwise would seem to contradict the memory of its foundational past.[33] Thus, the "pheno-text" (the apparent text, canon 1) was woven secretly by a hermeneutical "geno-text" (hidden and creative text, canon 2). This hermeneutical process is obviously *canonical, even if not written.*

In the process of producing the Bible, the relation between the instituted tradition and the instituting tradition depends on a third element: *the events recognized as foundational.* As the very early confession of faith in Deuteronomy 26:5-9 shows, the faith of Israel rests primarily on such events proclaimed as saving acts of Yahweh.[34] This is why this confession cannot be subsumed under the literary genre of prayer or of a creed understood as a finely tuned theological synthesis of beliefs (likewise, the fabric of our Christian

---

32. Ibid., 120.

33. Ibid., first part, 25–78.

34. Von Rad, *Théologie de l'Ancien Testament*, 112. Deut 26:5-9 may be a "creed that shows all the signs of great antiquity" and could have been elaborated "before the Yahwist and Elohist traditions." However, not everyone shares this opinon since one can see equally well in this passage the very characteristics of the Deuteronomic circles; thus L. Rost, "Das kleine Credo," *Das kleine Credo und andere Studien im Alten Testament* (Heidelberg, 1965).

creed is also narrative), but only under that of a *narrative pure and simple*.[35] These bare facts doubtless contain a theology, if only in virtue of their selection made among many other possibilities. However, they remain embryonic on the level of theological discourse as such. In the last analysis, the Hexateuch is nothing more than the theological unfolding of these bare foundational facts. "In other words," as Sanders writes, "the Yahwist collection of traditions concerning the origins of Israel is in some way Psalm 78 or chapter 15 of Exodus written large, just as the Hexateuch as a whole is equivalent to 1 Samuel 12:8 or Deuteronomy 26 or again Joshua 24, written large."[36] As a matter of fact, the Bible as a whole can be understood as the transcription into capital letters of this fundamental confession of faith.

b) The Meta-historical Functioning of the Events Recognized as Foundational. The connection with the founding events deserves some reflection. If the "Law" is composed first of all of stories, and only secondarily of legislative codicils, this is because these stories from the proto-historic period that the Torah covers *act as the law* for the identity of Israel. Hence their unusual status. For — as we sketched above — the Torah ends, at the conclusion of Deuteronomy, at the frontier formed by the Jordan and is placed under Moses' authority, an authority confirmed by his death just before this frontier is crossed. Thus, the frontier of the Jordan and the death of Moses have a metaphorical significance: they separate irreversibly the *historical types* of the proto-historic period from all the future history of Israel. By this metaphorical separation, they are lifted out of their status as simply ancient events and promoted into *meta-historical archetypes of Israel's identity* in the future.[37] *The original proto-history becomes thereby origin-giving meta-history*, that is to say, always contemporary. Thus, for Israel, to live is to *relive the journey of its origin* by replunging itself into these memories again and again with each generation. As Deuteronomy 26:1-11 clearly shows, the *liturgical assembly*, where all Israel, gathered as a one person at the "place chosen by Yahweh" (the Temple of Jerusalem), recites its creed ("My father was a

35. Von Rad, *Théologie de l'Ancien Testament*, 113.
36. Sanders, *Identité de la Bible*, 47.
37. Beauchamp, *L'Un et L'Autre Testament*, 57-71.

wandering Aramean. . . .''), is the privileged place for this
memorial, the place where Israel is restored or confirmed in its
identity.

The same thing happens with *Christians*, but with this irreducible difference, that the metaphorical barrier which separates them
from their origins is that of the *resurrection* of Jesus from the dead.
For them, to live is to relive the founding journey of Jesus, their
Lord, (and through him of the people of Israel because this journey has a Christian meaning only as accomplished ''according to
the Scriptures''). And it is also in the liturgical memorial they
make of him that their identity as Christians is established in a
decisive manner — especially in their telling their creed, this practical creed which is the story of the Last Supper (that too, just a
simple story!) told in memory of him. In passing, one notes the
central importance of this concept of ''memorial''; we shall return
to this later.

2. The Connection of the Book to the Social Body

What is at issue in the process of producing the Bible, which we
have just analyzed, is finally the *very essence of every text* in its relation to its author and to its reader — to the reading social body.
Therefore, the present development places the preceding reflection
within a larger context and opens a more fundamental perspective.

a) The Semio-linguistic Theory of the Text. Let us begin by recalling
briefly several basic points of the semio-linguistic theory of the
text as it has been developed notably by R. Barthes.[38]

This theory of the text runs counter to certain presuppositions of
the *classical theory*. In effect the latter holds that, on the side of the
author, to write is to deposit in a text the meaning present in the
thought of the person writing and, on the side of the reader, to
read is to decode the meaning thus deposited by the author in
order to be able to reproduce it. This presupposes, first, that truth
transcends historical contingency in a universal and eternal manner; second, that the same body of truth can be expressed under
historically different forms, which is as much as to say that the
language and socio-cultural situations of the author and the reader

38. R. Barthes, ''Texte (théorie du),'' *Encyclopédie Universelle* 15.

are only accidental coverings for the translation (or for the betrayal) of the truth; and third, that the difference between, on the one hand, what the text says and, on the other, what the author wants to say or what the reader understands can be reduced to a simple accident, to some extent inevitable no doubt, but largely avoidable by improving the technique or method.

Against these assumptions, which are those of the classical metaphysics analyzed in the first part of this book, the semiolinguistic theory holds that every text is written or read, not from a neutral place that sovereignly transcends all socio-historical determinations, but from a "world" already spoken, socially arranged, and culturally constructed. Thus, *"every text is an intertext"* (Barthes). To write is to read or at least to quote other earlier texts, and to read is to trace a "passive writing" over the text (T. Todorov, above). Everything is interpretation. This does not mean that all interpretations are equal; a reading which can handle more aspects of the textual material is more faithful than another.

This leads us to distinguish "decoding" and "reading." *Decoding* is a technique of analysis, whether it be historical-critical, semiotic, or "materialist" . . . As necessary as decoding is for the reading to be faithful to the text, such a decoding is only a *preliminary* step in the service of the reading, for *reading* is the symbolic act of producing a *new text*, an original word, on the basis of the rules of the game decoded from the texts. It is reading that allows the reader to speak. A human activity, it engages the reader as a subject, with his or her "world," causes the same text to inspire different interpretations in different readers. In a certain sense, the difference between decoding and reading is the same as the one between a course on the exegesis of a text — or a semiotic analysis of it — and a homily based on that text. If biblical technique as such does not disappear from the homily in order to set free a word from the preacher but by so intruding silences the hearers, there is a confusion of genres and a dictatorship of exegesis; conversely, if under the pretext of "inspiration," the preacher says anything at all because of a failure to do the preliminary work of decoding, she or he betrays the text and cheats the hearers.

The *failure to master meaning* which results from this theory of texts is not due to a simple accident, as unfortunate as it is inevitable. It is linked to the constitutive split of the subject in the symbolic order and language. The "difference" is thus appreciated, *not as an obstacle to be overthrown* or a resistance to be overcome, *but as an otherness to be assumed,* an assumption which goes together with the emergence of the subject: this non-coincidence is the very place from which the word arises.

b) *"The Reader Is Essential to the Writing Itself."* The preceding reflection leads us to make this statement by S. Breton in *Ecriture et Révélation* our own.[39] Every piece of writing supposes the process of setting words down on some material, which is followed by a reverse movement of retreat. Thus the writer goes away from her or his product; she or he can disappear, leaving it behind as a *testament.* And such is the fate of every piece of writing: not able to come into being as writing except by becoming other than its author. This "death" of the author, celebrated throughout M. Blanchot's *Livre à venir,*[40] is the condition for the very existence of the book. Trace of the author's passage, effect of this "singular homeopathy" (p. 62) by which the author dies in her or his work in order to affirm through it her or his victory over death, the book becomes for the author something that detaches itself from her or him and finally is no longer the author. It is delivered over to the reader who, as Mallarmé says, now becomes its "operator." This is so true that the very being of a book depends on its history and the multiple readings of which it is the object and that "the operation of reading, far from being foreign to it, is *essential* to its very constitution" (p. 34). The same also goes for oral discourse. Thus, *"since the reader is essential to the writing itself,* understood no longer as a fixed reality but as an "actualization," *one can no longer reduce the reader to the condition of an "accident"* or a chance "addition." The judgment, individual or social, that is exercised during the "listening-reading" inscribes itself in the very texture of the text, from which it is impossible to dissociate it" (p. 40). Breton, following the *Rhetoric* of Aristotle, emphasizes that

39. S. Breton, *Ecriture et Révélation,* 40. We refer to this work in what follows.

40. M. Blanchot, *Le Livre à venir,* Coll. Idées NRF (Paris: Gallimard, 1959) 334: "The book is without an author because it is written after the speaking author's disappearance."

the reception of a speech not only provides the rules for the discourse, it also determines and constitutes it (p. 39). This is why
one must "reverse the usual perspective. In the relation 'reading-
writing,' it is the writing that — in what used to be called its
ontological truth — must adapt itself to a normative 'reading,' in a
never ending movement toward conformity. This reading does not
determine the writing's effective content in its materiality, but
prescribes to meanings the general guidelines which they can and
must follow" (p. 70).

Obviously *there are books, and books.* In their plurality, books
share a "scriptural space" divided into two large regions (p. 28):
on one side, books requiring *hermeneutics* (revelatory books of
different religions, philosophic books, books of literature or poetry), on the other, disciplines of *knowledge* (formal and empirical
sciences, human sciences). Of course, the line between them is in
fact not as clear as it might seem: let us remember that even in
the case of a discourse without a subject, such as that of physics,
the author-subjects, with their "worlds," their social standing,
and their claims upon our recognition, are not absent at all. Still,
it remains that it is the first category of books and everything that
concerns the meaning of life which have given rise to reflection
upon the relation between the book and the reading social body.
This is not by chance, for this relation systematizes the "circularity" of this human existence which, confronted with questions
about its origin, about death, meaning, salvation, constructs such
works as a response. Thus, among the diversity of books, including those of the first category, an *empirical gradation* exists in the
relation of the body of readers to the book. And this gradation
goes hand in hand with the gradation of its "canonicity."

This *canonicity* is in effect a constitutive process of the text: the
more the social body recognizes itself in a text, the more the text
manifests its essence as a text, in the sense explained above. Such
a recognition functions as a practical canon — expressed or unex-
pressed — of the values and norms of the group. There are *varying degrees* of this recognition: there are works which are "required
reading," whether because of certain prizes (Nobel, Pulitzer, and
so forth) or a new fashion, temporary or more enduring (the
"process philosophers," Whitehead, and so forth), or rather because of a venerable tradition (the "great authors" of literature).
To say that one must have read these texts is also, partly, to indi-

cate *how* one must read them. At this point, a *second level of canonicity* appears, intermediate between the implicit preceding level and the explicit level. It is established by being taught or discussed in the schools and the "orthodoxies" which provide normative interpretations of a text or of an entire corpus. For example, Plato's text has historically existed only in the ways the philosophical schools have read it, and those readings have not always been in agreement. These traditions of interpretation belong to its very nature as a text. For every text "needs, to support itself, a social body or a common subjectivity that decides upon its semantic essence" (p. 84).

One reaches a *third level of canonicity*, this one completely *explicit*, when a corpus of texts is officially the subject of a global orthodox interpretation; this is the case, although diversely realized, with the "holy books" revered by different religions. The more one approaches this explicit degree of canonicity, the more it becomes clear that its reception by the reading group is constitutive of the text. This canonicity is linked to the fact that the social body recognizes itself, consciously or not, officially or not, in the text. It experiences the text as exemplary of its identity. Magisterial canonical sanction is nothing else but the decisive social expression of this process: an authority, recognized by the group as legitimate, officially validates this recognition and thereby entrusts the text to the group as its authentic *"exemplar."* In availing ourselves of J. Kristeva's distinction between "geno-text" and "pheno-text",[41] we may say that the definitive setting of the canon of "holy books" is the ultimate unfolding, at the level of the pheno-text, of a process of canonicity constitutive of the geno-text, a process which manifests the essential relation of the reading body to the text. This process is at work in every text, but particularly in the *myths* and in the *books held sacred* by various religious groups. So true is this for myths that a story invented by someone at the beginning becomes a myth only when it loses its author and so becomes the collective coded expression of the identity of the group which "believes it."[42]

41. Barthes, "Texte."

42. P. Smith, "Mythe: Approche ethno-sociologique," *Encyclopédie Universelle*, 11:528. The myth does not function unless it gains acceptance. Thus, we are "inclined to recognize as myths only the myths of others."

c) The Bible: "The Community Writes Itself in the Book It Reads."
The sanction of canonicity unfolds in the community's process of
writing itself "into the book it reads" (p. 70) — a process constitutive of every text, but particularly powerful in the sacred texts.
Book and community are recognized as inseparable. The book is
nothing without the community, and the community finds in the
book the mirror of its identity. The norm is thus not the Book
alone, but *the Book in the hand of the community.* The Church thus
represents the impossibility of *sola scriptura.*

Our theory of the text and of reading entails what we showed
above about the genesis of the Bible, following Sanders: "Hermeneutics, although unwritten, is also canonical." This implies
that "believing communities that today find their identity in the
Bible are canonically obligated to carry on this approach and to
continue research within *our* contexts, just as the primitive communities did in theirs."[43] Fidelity to the Bible consists in reliving,
in ever-changing situations, the same process that brought about
its production. The geno-text is the norm of fidelity to the pheno-
text. It is a question of drawing something new out of the old.
Only on this condition does the "inspiration" of the Bible have
meaning: it inspires a new word. *The (re-)reading of Scripture is an
integral part of Scripture; access to meaning is constitutive of meaning,
and reception belongs to revelation itself.* Neither from the text alone,
nor from the reader alone, but from the always unpredictable encounter between the two does biblical truth — a symbolic truth —
arise.

The canonical Bible is the fruit of a "reading" (*lectio*) operating
simultaneously as a "selection" (*selectio*). We saw this at the level
of its empirical genesis: the social, political, and religious *lectio-
selectio* led to the elimination of numerous oral traditions which, in
themselves, were no less "worthy" of being included than the
ones which were finally retained. The liturgy played an important
role in this principle of selective reading, as also in the hermeneutics which determined the internal organization of the Book, on
the one hand, into Torah-Prophets-Writings, on the other, into
Old and New Testaments. Thus each book, each part, finally each
Testament of the Bible becomes a "something" (*aliquid*), that is,

43. Sanders, *Identité de la Bible,* 159–160.

"something else" (*aliud quid*) than the rest from which it differentiates itself while at the same time remaining joined to it. The
principle of "*selection*" is complemented by a principle of "*integration*": in Christian reading, "all the parts of the book eventually
converge toward the unity that is Christ whose truth, spread out
everywhere, becomes particularized without fragmenting itself in
each of the 'sectors' where it is found."[44] In the last analysis, it is
this hermeneutical principle of selective inspiration and integrative
convergence that is at the heart of the Christian Bible. The Bible
exists, as the Bible, only in the hands of the *ecclesia*. Of course,
such a principle does not justify everything that the Church has
made of the Bible in manipulating it, consciously or not, for its
own benefit. For our canon 2 has meaning only in relation to
canon 1. And the Church itself has not always been faithful in its
interpretation of the meaning of the data of canon 1 to which it
necessarily referred itself . . .

3. *The Reading of the Book in the Liturgical* Ecclesia,
the Place of the Bible's Truth
   In line with our previous reflection, we find it worthwhile to
compare what we have said about the essence of a canonical text
such as the Bible with what we call the "Liturgy of the Word."
The latter is constituted by a relationship between four major elements: (a) texts are read from the *canonically received* Bible (the
possible use of other texts, as inspiring and pedagogically effective
as they sometimes are, always remains in the service of the biblical texts); (b) these written texts, relating a past experience of the
people of God, are proclaimed as the living Word of God *for today*; (c) they are proclaimed to an assembly (*ecclesia*) which recognizes in them the *exemplar of its identity*; (d) the assembly is under
the leadership of an ordained minister who exercises the symbolic
function of *guarantor* of this exemplarity and, for us Christians, of
the apostolicity of what is read.

   The second of these four elements requires some explanation. We will
do this from three points of view: theological, anthropological, and ritual.

44. Breton, *Ecriture et Révélation*, 69. Cf. R. Le Déaut, "Principes et règles de
l'exégèse juive ancienne," *Introduction à la Bible: Nouveau Testament* (Paris:
Desclée) 1:112–113.

Theologically, we find in the homily Jesus gave at Nazareth, according to Luke 4:21, the essence of the reading from the Scriptures condensed: "Today this scripture has been fulfilled in your hearing." Of course, Luke is speaking of the homily; but the homily has no other goal than to make clear the *relevance* already present in the reading itself. Have we not had the experience of a reading so well proclaimed that the homiletic exposition of this relevance was already half done before it was even begun?

Besides, the claim to relevance of these readings as the Word has a particularly significant *anthropological* support: the voice. The voice in effect bases itself upon the Book; it maintains it as a *writing* whose essence, like that of all writing, is that of a testament, one that refers us to the inescapable otherness of an irretrievable origin, that is, to the "inaccessible place" of the Father. But at the same time, the Book, of its very essence, is meant to be read, and read publicly. "That is canonical which receives authority from public reading," as we emphasized previously. The reading voice thus belongs to the biblical text as such. This is why, as Beauchamp remarks, "the writing and the voice put limits on each other": the writing prohibits "the occupation of the place of the first writing, that of the Father," and the voice complies with this prohibition; but at the same time, drawn as it is to the voice's present by its very essence, the writing "also says that there is more to be written." Thus, the voice expresses the hermeneutical process of rendering the Bible relevant, without which it would be a dead letter. In their intrinsic relationship to the text, writing and speaking "cooperate by writing the book within the book."[45]

It is precisely this dynamic relationship which the *ritual* sequence of the Liturgy of the Word shows. It is dialogic by nature: the psalm constitutes the assembly's response to the first reading; whereas, besides the *alleluia* and the performative phrase "Praise to You, Lord Jesus Christ" addressed as "an acclamation to the Word of God" heard in the gospel, the prayer of the faithful, sealed in ancient times with the kiss of peace,[46] concludes the Liturgy of the Word. Thus, all the ritual symbolism unfolded in the course of the Liturgy of the Word manifests an intention of communication between the founding past and the present.

The relationship between the four elements of the Liturgy of the Word we have just referred to proves *homologous* to that between the four constitutive elements of the biblical text as the Word of

45. Beauchamp, *L'Un et l'Autre Testament,* 191–192.

46. Justin, 1 *Ap.* 65; Hippolytus, *Apostolic Traditions* 18 and 22; Tertullian, *De Or.* 18: "The kiss of peace is the seal of the prayer" (that is, the prayer of the faithful).

God. In effect, (a) canon 1 designates, as we indicated, the instituted traditions, oral and later written, and finally the biblical corpus as such; (b) canon 2 represents the hermeneutical process instituting the rewriting in relation to the present; (c) the community is the agent in this process; it "writes itself into the book that it is reading"; and finally (d) this dynamic internal to writing renders itself visible in the institutional act of canonical sanction uttered by an authority recognized as legitimate by the group (for Christians, an "apostolic authority"). Thus, the complex formed by the four elements of the Liturgy of the Word may be understood as the visible, "sacramental" manifestation of the complex formed by the four elements which went together in the production of the Bible. So true is this that *the liturgical proclamation of the Scriptures is the symbolic epiphany, the sacramental unveiling, of their internal constituents.*

In the wake of Heidegger's meditating thought on the unveiling of the essence of the pitcher,[47] we may say that the Bible unfolds its essence in the liturgical proclamation that is made of it. This unfolding takes place in the differentiated coming together of a sort of quadripartite whole: *the writing* (canon 1) laid down there, flat, as a testament of the earthly history of the believing people; the *voice* which, in proclaiming the writing from the pulpit, bestows life on it and lifts it from its prone position as a "dead" text (canon 2); the *community* of persons who are nourished by the proclaimed word; and finally, the whole thing, validated by the ordained minister as the authentic Word of *God* to his Church (apostolic tradition). In this perspective the Bible never comes into its truth as Bible as much as when it is read within the celebrating *ecclesia.* The latter is the premier sacramental milieu for the *a-letheia* (truth as uncovering) of the former; it reveals the Bible's invisible ecclesial essence, always in danger of being forgotten (*lethe*). Therefore, we can say in a completely literal sense that *the liturgical assembly* (the *ecclesia* in its primary sense) *is the place where the Bible becomes the Bible.*

47. See Chapter Ten.

III. THE SACRAMENTALITY OF SCRIPTURE

1. *Scripture Is Sacramental Not by Derivation but in Essence*

We had to take a long detour to show the ecclesiality of Scripture. Of course, we are not totally ignorant of this dimension; but our custom of individual and mental reading (whereas the ancients always read at least half aloud, thus showing, by this bond between the interiority of the writing and the exteriority of the voice, the irreducibly social essence of a text), together with our habit of individual technical work on the Bible, too easily leads us to consider this ecclesial dimension nonessential. Consequently the manifestations of this dimension seem to emerge not from the very essence of the text as an expression of its internal constituents, but rather simply from factors initially foreign to it. This a priori characteristic of our society scarcely permits us to discern in the proclamation of the Scriptures in the midst of the Christian assembly anything but one means among others for their presentation. One could say that one thereby reduces the ontological to the ontic. Granted, the public reading of the Scriptures in the assembly is only *one of the activities* to which they give rise for the believing subject and for the Church; however, if one attempts, as we have, to think through the essence of this biblical text as text, what presents itself initially as only one activity among others proves to be of a *different order* from the others and should not be grouped with them.

a) The Traditional Veneration of Scripture. It is in exactly the same perspective that we now speak of a *sacramentality of Scripture.* Sacramentality is not an accident; it is a *constitutive* dimension of Scripture. It has a long tradition within the Church.

One recalls the famous passage from Origen's *Homily* 13 on Exodus: "You who participate regularly in the divine mysteries, you know with what respectful precautions you keep the body of the Lord once it is given to you, lest a few crumbs fall and some part of the consecrated treasure is lost. For you hold yourselves culpable (and in that you are correct) if, by your negligence, some of this treasure is lost. But if you justly take such precautions with regard to the Body of our Lord, can you expect that neglect of the Word of God deserves a lesser punishment than neglect of his Body?" As Tertullian had already said, basing himself on the discourse on the bread of life in John 6: "The bread is the living

Word of God, come down from heaven." Similarly, St. Ambrose apropos Scripture: "Eat this food first, to be able to come later to the food of Christ, to the food of the Body of the Lord, to the sacramental feast, to this cup where the love of the faithful becomes inebriated."[48]

We could multiply quotations from the Fathers supporting this position; it is obviously one of the strongest Church traditions, developed in a particularly vigorous way by Origen. For him the Eucharistic body of the Lord can be understood only in relation with both his ecclesial "body" and his scriptural "body," the whole constituting the symbolic mediation of the body of our Lord Jesus, historical and glorious.[49] This is why for him the broken bread refers as much to Scripture as to the Eucharist: "If these loaves had not been divided, if they had not been broken into pieces by the disciples — in other words, if the letter had not been broken piece by piece — its message could not have reached everyone" and the assembly would not have been satiated.[50]

Vatican II reflects this tradition faithfully: "The Church has always venerated the divine Scriptures just as she venerates the Body of the Lord, since from the table of both the word of God and of the body of Christ she unceasingly receives and offers to the faithful the bread of life, especially in the sacred liturgy" (*Dei Verbum*, no. 21). Christians need "to receive nourishment from God's Word at the twofold table of sacred Scripture and the Eucharist" (*Presbyterorum Ordinis*, no. 18). It is clear that the expression "bread of life" is applied as much to the Scriptures as to the Eucharist, and the expression "Word of God" as much to the Eucharist as to the Scriptures, so much so that the veneration directed toward Scripture is almost put, as with Origen, on the same footing as that toward the Eucharistic Body of the Lord. The sumptuous decoration of lectionaries, the processions with candles, incense, singing, and the acclamations at the gospel are traditional expressions of this veneration. *Such a ritual symbolization is the concrete mediation where the theology of Scripture as the sacramental temple of the Word of God is embodied. Lex orandi, lex credendi:* we are talking here about an authentic "theological lo-

---

48. Origen, *Homily on Exodus* 13:3, Sources chrétiennes 16, p. 263; Tertullian, *De Or.* 6; Ambrose, "Expos. ps. 118," vv. 15, 25, CSEL 62, p. 345.

49. H. de Lubac, *Histoire et Esprit: L'intelligence de l'Ecriture d'après Origène* (Paris: Aubier-Montaigne, 1950) 355-373.

50. Origen, *Homily on Genesis* 12:5, Sources chrétiennes 7, p. 211.

cus," always timely even if, because of our current cultural sensibilities and our distrust of anything which smacks of triumphalism, the pomp displayed in the liturgy, a relic in many respects of European court etiquette, has yielded to a greater simplicity.

b) *The Letter, "Tabernacle" of the Word.* It is in its very historical *reality* as *letter*, and a canonically *closed* letter, that Scripture is recognized as the "tabernacle" of the Word of God: "The Spirit is discovered only if the Letter is not avoided."[51] This is an important point in our view, for the sacramentality of this Writing goes together with respect for the letter as letter, that is, with respect for its *concrete social and cultural delimitations.* Each time, it is singular historical destinies that mediate God's revelation: this person (Abraham), this people (Israel), this particular Jew (Jesus) . . . And the letter is the socio-historically conditioned deposit of this revelation. God's revelation requires such a deposition in an empirical "scriptural body." By the same token it resists every attempt at an "idealist" reduction of the letter that would, by appealing to a "spiritual" sense understood as a timeless truth, erase the historical contingency under the pretext of better revealing the "Word of God." Instead of searching for the Spirit in the letter itself, such interpreters have already located it a priori outside the letter, which serves only as a springboard toward an *aliud aliquid* (or a *res*) that would already be secretly pre-contained in it.

We know that such a temptation is always present; the *logocentrism* that characterizes the metaphysical tradition is secretly animated by the desire to blunt *the letter's resistance as the indication of an irreducible socio-historical otherness.*

As a consequence, one is tempted to read in the letter only the shadow projected by the full light which is yet to come or "types" already foretelling the full truth of Christ. As a matter of fact, we have easily superimposed the pairs of terms "sensible and intelligible," "shadow and light," "appearance and reality" — metaphysical pairs which are atemporal and ahistorical by nature — onto time and history ("before and after" Jesus Christ). Such a reading of "salvation history" is but the projection of the vertical model of metaphysics onto the horizontal axis of time.

51. P. Beauchamp, *Le Récit, la lettre et la corps* (Paris: Cerf, 1982) 8.

Of course, the Fathers and the medieval theologians did not read Scripture only in the three senses of allegory-typology, tropology-ethics, and anagogy-eschatology, but also in a first, called the literal, sense. But, as Beauchamp remarks, *"littera* does not mean 'literal sense,' but just the letter. And if we accept this, what a difference it makes! Once one allows the meaning of a text to intervene, one prefers the 'equivalent' to the letter. . . . Thus the 'literal sense' itself becomes allegorical, if we understand this word according to its etymology: to say something else."[52] But, the letter resists. It resists, for example, seeing in a life "full of days" anything more than this-worldly satisfaction, which, by the way, has nothing "materialistic" about it and whose eminently "spiritual' meaning we would be wrong to misperceive, since what is at issue is the fulfillment of God's promise to favor those who are faithful to his word. It resists, for a long time at least, every attempt to read any notion of "eternal life" into the Bible where "immortality" will be recognized much later than in Greek thought. It resists, here again at least for a long time, reading about a liberation from "eternal" death in Exodus. Why did these biblical authors so long resist saying what others had already accepted in spirit? "However, it is this very resistance which deserves our respect because it is the substance of Scripture and another name for what we call history."[53] Here history has an irreducible "theological pertinence."[54]

c) The Division of the Letter into "Figures": Idol and Icon. Nevertheless, one may ask oneself whether this respectful incensing of the letter-as-sacrament is not liable to drifting dangerously toward idolatry. First we have to determine what sort of thing this term "idolatry" stands for; it is a fuzzy notion which has been used to concoct the most diverse mixtures — provided that it is always somebody else's position that is called idolatrous . . . We can at least agree with J.-L. Marion that the *idolatrous* attitude does not reside either in "some priestly fraud" or in "the stupidity of the masses" which would purely and simply identify a god with its image, but in *"the subordination of the god to the human conditions for experiencing the divine."*[55] This definition has the advantage of diagnosing the possibility for idolatry's residing in every religious sys-

---

52. Ibid., 61.
53. Ibid., 66.
54. P. Gisel, *Vérité et histoire*, ch. 1 "La question du Jésus historique ou la pertinence théologique de l'histoire."
55. J. L. Marion, *L'idole et la distance* (Grasset, 1977) 23.

tem (and in every person), no matter how anti-idolatrous it claims to be: for example, there is conceptual idolatry in any closed discourse on the subject of God; there is ethical idolatry (pharisaism, Pelagianism, and so forth) in every pretention to have rights over God because of proper conduct; there is psychological idolatry in the reduction of God to certain experiences (especially the most "intense") that one claims to have had of God, and so on. These are as many ways, more or less subtle, for us to put our hands on the divine, to permanently place it at our disposal, to have it enslaved (and at the same time to be enslaved by it). In each instance, the potential idolatry that slumbers in each one of us seeks to assure itself concerning the divine by blunting its radical otherness. This is precisely the process of idolatry: to attempt to blot out the difference between God and ourselves.

The veneration of the letter swings toward idolatry whenever the writing is viewed as static, and no longer as a witness of a past and *different* era and as a representative of another, future, era, that is, whenever the present becomes everything, the immediate now encompassing everything. Whatever "God" is discovered in the letter is thereby subordinated to the moral, socio-political, or ideological assumptions of the present. The so-called "Word of God" is manipulated to serve as their transcendent justification.

The icon, by contrast, "conceals and discloses what it rests upon: *the separation* within it between the divine and its representation of the divine." Instead of trying to eliminate the otherness of God, it "preserves and emphasizes" the non-visibility of precisely what it presents to the eye.[56] Of course, the conventions in the use of certain esthetic elements of the icon codified in the Eastern Churches (geometrical structures: triangles, squares, circles, halos, and so forth; systems of perspective, especially inverted perspective; a symbolism of colors and of light; and so forth)[57] no doubt aim at representing the invisible "prototype"; but they do so according to a complex code whose elements are precisely recognized as

56. Ibid.
57. E. Sendler, *L'icône, image de l'invisible: Eléments de théologie, esthétique et technique*, DDB, 1981.

manifesting the irreducible distance between us and what they depict.[58]

The duration of the iconoclastic dispute — and the murderous acrimony to which it gave rise for more than a century in the East (recognizing the importance of the political issues involved) — together with the difficulty the Second Council of Nicea experienced in finding concepts that would adequately justify the veneration of icons and yet clearly distinguish it from idolatry,[59] are significant: from icon to idol is but one step; the borders of each are so close to one another that one could easily make a mistake here if one did not take precautions; however, this short step spans an abyss . . .

If the Scriptures are sacramental in the concreteness of their letter, they are so from an iconic perspective. The letter, in effect, can be the mediation of the revelation of God only to the extent that, as Beauchamp emphasizes, it forms *figures*. For the letter is not revelatory except as a witness after the fact of something that has been completed; but this retrospective comprehension can be maintained only by a "could be" which states itself quasi-imperatively as a "must be": "the figure converts memory into desire."[60] This is so much the case that the letter arises as figure — and thus as a sacramental mediation of revelation — only *by splitting itself in two*: a witness to the "has been" of the creation, the Exodus, or the manna, it is at the same time a witness to the "must be" of a new creation, a new exodus, a new manna, and so forth. As figure, it is an *in-between*, a passage, a *transit toward something other than itself, something else which is the other side of itself*. "The Jordan is the Jordan crossed by Joshua, then by Elijah; this is what it is for John the Baptist; and because of this, it awaits Jesus."[61]

58. See especially the very precise theological work of C. Von Schönborn, *L'icône du Christ: Fondements théologiques élaborés entre le premier et le second Concile de Nicée* (325-787) (Fribourg, Switzerland: éd. Univ., 1976).

59. See the distinction between the *latreia* or *latreiotike proskynesis*, adoration owed to God alone, and the *timetike proskynesis*, veneration of honor rendered not to the image as such but to the person whom it represents (see *Denz.-Schön.*, 600-603). Unfortunately, the adherents of the Latin rite in the Carolingian empire did not grasp this distinction for lack of an adequate translation (Council of Frankfort [794]).

60. Beauchamp, *Le Récit, la lettre et la corps*, 48.

61. Ibid., 42.

In the last analysis, it is the identity and difference of *the two Testaments* which for Christians is at issue in this symbolic separation; their difference is attested at the very point of their connection. As the ultimate juncture between heaven and earth, God and humankind — which it both radically separates (nothing is less divine than this crucified human who is "less than nothing") and strangely brings together (nothing is more divine than this disfigured less-than-human who says, "Whoever has seen me has seen the Father") — the *cross* is "the final letter that puts the seal on all the others," the precipitate of the book, "as if Jesus was crucified on this book,"[62] he whom the Church confesses to have "scripturally died for our sins" (according to the *de re* and not only the *de dicto* modality that affects this statement from 1 Corinthians 15:3, as Breton has pointed out).[63]

Thus, because the letter is always in transit (and this is true even within the Old Testament itself, as well as in its relation with the New), it takes on the *iconic status* of separation. It is Word in the present only insofar as it is a letter stretched between the past it recounts and the future it announces. Consequently, it resists any gnostic claim to a full presence. Like the icon, it preserves the radical otherness of the divine Word that it nevertheless offers to our hearing. It is the present of God that it testifies to: a present in the present. But, as with the Eucharist, this present happens only in an eschatological memorial which maintains the separation or the "difference." The extent to which the first Christian communities were tempted by a (semi-)gnostic "enthusiasm" is well known; they "were constantly in danger of putting their savior on a par with the lords and saviors of the salvation-mystery religions," and thus of "reabsorbing history, that is, the truth of the Cross, into myth." Although he "refuses to appeal to the memory of Christ according to the flesh, following the Judeo-Christian tradition," Paul still vigorously refers himself "to the

<hr>

62. Ibid., 92–93.

63. Breton, *Ecriture et Révélation*, 122. Thus, "It is written: 'You shall adore the Lord your God,' " is a modal proposition *de dicto*, where the mode bears directly on the proposition itself, while "Christ died for our sins according to the Scriptures" is a modal proposition *de re*, "where the mode forms an integral part of the proposition itself," so much so that one should better translate it "Christ *scripturally* died for our sins."

memory of the Crucified One, in opposition to an incipient gnostic development."[64] Hence the importance of the "announcement of the death of the Lord" in the Christian ritual meal. In thus placing in relief the historical stumbling block of Golgotha, Paul is continuing the very gesture to which the entire Book is a witness: the Eucharist is indeed the precipitate of the Scriptures.

2. The Sacraments: Precipitate of the Scriptures

The concreteness of the rituals corresponds to the concreteness of the Scriptures as documents and as a canon duly closed. Like the Scriptures, the rites exist only as received from a tradition that none can manipulate at their whim. They are witnesses to an anteriority or to an unrecoverable origin that is legislative for the group as a group and for the individuals within it. To the resistance of the letter, the rites add that of the body; *the letter-as-sacrament precipitates itself into the body-as-sacrament* in the expressive mediations of the rites: gestures, postures, objects, times and places, people with different roles . . .

From the table of the Scriptures to the table of the sacrament the dynamic is traditional and irreversible. Traditional in that, from the time of Emmaus, one sees the distinctively sacramental moment preceded by a scriptural moment; irreversible in that this pattern is not at all arbitrary: we never pass from the table of the sacrament to that of the Scriptures. This traditional fact is less banal than it seems, as the three following observations will show.

a) Evangelization and Sacramentalization. First on the pastoral level, the liturgical dynamic of the two tables poses numerous and painful questions concerning the sacramentalization of the poorly-evangelized (when they are not simply non-evangelized). Without being able to elaborate in detail these problems which are as complex as they are important, let us merely mention that sacramentalization has Christian relevance, in our own time as in Luke's, only as a step following a *prior* evangelization. This does not mean that one can rest content with this simple chronological understanding. For in effect, every liturgical act is also an act of evangelization — even if, of course, evangelization must have its larger domain outside the liturgy; the latter itself must then always be

64. Perrot, "L'anamnèse néo-testamentaire," 33–36.

evangelized to remain authentically Christian. In the second place, just as the breaking of the bread at Emmaus allows the previous evangelization on the road to "take hold" in a decisive manner, so the liturgical and sacramental expressions of the faith are a *constitutive* dimension of evangelization itself. Hence the contemporary insistence on a catechetical program that is "sacramentally structured."[65]

b) Word-Scripture and Word-Sacrament. The dynamic of the two tables shows us that it is always the Word that deposits itself in the sacramental ritual as well as in the Bible. In more rigorous terms, it would thus be better to speak, safeguarding the *sacramental essence* in each case, of a liturgy of *the Word under the mode of Scripture* and of a liturgy of *the Word under the mode of bread and wine*. This remark is not directed at the practice of calling the reading of the Scriptures the "Liturgy of the Word," but at the dangers that have accompanied it. We think especially of the *false dichotomy between Word and Sacrament*, a modern dichotomy largely due to the Reformation, afterwards reinforced by the Enlightenment and, more recently, by the faith-religion opposition. As a reaction against the sacramental "inflation" of the Middle Ages (a rough approximation), the return to the "Word" was a healthy theological development — always on the condition that we do not overshoot the mark and oppose the "Word" to the sacraments.

That the sacraments are always in a sense sacraments of the Word in the Spirit reminds us that their effects are no more automatic or "magical" than Scripture's. Besides, it will always be *under the mode of communication by word* (it being understood, as we showed in the first part of this book, that the word exists only as inscribed in the body) that we must understand the communication of God in the sacraments.

As is clearly shown in the baptismal formula, the sacrament is the *precipitate of the Christian Scriptures.* For the Church, the formula "In the name of the Father, and of the Son, and of the Holy Spirit" is indeed like a concentrate of all the Scriptures. Joined to the sign of the cross as the distinctive mark of the Christian, this

65. R. Marlé, "Une démarche structurée sacramentellement," *Catéchèse* 87 (1982) 11–27.

formula functions moreover as the symbol par excellence of Christian identity, a symbol which insists on being inscribed in the body, that is, in the fabric of life. In being joined to water or to bread, the Word precipitates into sacrament. St. Augustine expresses as much in his famous saying: "The Word approaches the element and a sacrament results" (*Accedit verbum ad elementum, et fit sacramentum*). The word we speak of here can be understood on three levels: the *Christ-Word* (he is the subject working in the sacrament, not its minister), the *Scriptures* which are read in the celebration, and finally the *sacramental formula* itself, pronounced "in the person of Christ" (*in persona Christi*).

It is worth mentioning in this regard that level 2 (the reading of the Scriptures) is the mediation that assures the coherence of the connection between the Christ-Word (level 1) and the sacramental formula pronounced in his name (level 3). Thus, it is important to respect, in the liturgical celebration itself, the *concrete* sacramental mode according to which Christ speaks. Now, he speaks according to *certain readings* of Scripture, appropriate to Lent for example, but not according to others. Without taking into account this concrete scriptural sacrament, one celebrates a timeless Christ and endorses the semi-gnostic Christianity that Paul (and others) struggled against. The same Christ who takes on flesh in the Eucharist does so according to different "forms" in which he has spoken earlier in the Scriptures. This principle, faithful both to the letter of the Scriptures and to the very nature of every liturgy, seems to us too often ignored. The liturgical and theological movement which proceeds from the first table to the second signifies concretely that the "this is my body" should be pronounced against the background of the Scriptures proclaimed on such-and-such a Sunday of Lent or during Easter time or on the feast of All Saints . . . A Eucharistic prayer which lacks any reference to the readings is seriously deficient; one certainly wants to celebrate a sacrament of the Church, but in such a way that the Church can "veri-fy" itself (make itself true) in *this* assembly, on *this* Sunday, where one has read *these* Scriptures . . .

c) Chewing the Book. We have already alluded to the manna several times. We have indicated its non-value status and have seen in it an eminent figure of God's gracious gift. The manna of

Exodus 16 is the test of powerlessness and dispossession: one receives it from heaven day by day without being able to store it up. According to the very letter of the Book, this test is the figure of another test: "By feeding you with manna . . . in order to make you understand that one does not live by bread alone, but by every word that comes from the mouth of the Lord" (Deut 8:3, taken up by Jesus, himself submitted to the test, according to Matt 4:4 and par.). The Word is difficult to swallow: the accounts of the callings of the prophets testify to this (Exod 3; Isa 6; Jer 1; Ezek 2–3). Ezekiel has this bitter experience when he, obedient to the voice of Yahweh, *eats the Book* filled with oracles of woe. This indigestible food so fills his belly that his prophetic words are pronounced as the Word of Yahweh himself (Ezek 2:8–3:4). And it is just when *the word takes over the prophet's body*,[66] when his body becomes a living parable, that he can most truly say, "It is not I who speak, but Yahweh." Such is perhaps the "major trait of biblical prophecy," that "no person is as present in that person's word as the one who says, 'Thus speaks another,' that is, God."[67] However, for those who chew it and become familiar with it to the point of being possessed by it, this hard Word becomes "as sweet as honey" (Ezek 3:3). The visionary of Revelation has the same experience: the book that he eats, at the order of the voice from heaven, is bitter in his stomach but has the sweetness of honey in his mouth (Rev 10:8-10).

The word that Jesus gives to eat is equally bitter, according to *the discourse on the bread of life* (John 6:22-71). This word is so "difficult" that "many of his disciples" can no longer listen to him and abandon him (6:60-66). This "scandal" (6:61) is truly difficult to endure. As a catechesis on faith in Jesus as the Word of God, this discourse brings to light a *double scandal*, concerning the celestial origin of Jesus and concerning his passage through death. The combination of Psalm 78:24 and Exodus 16:15 ("he . . . gave them the [bread] of heaven"), which this discourse exploits according to

66. We are speaking here of the prophet's own body or of his familial body (Isaiah and his sons, 8:18) or of his conjugal body, living (Hosea and his wife, 1-3), dead (the widowhood of Ezekiel, 24:15-27), or never realized (the celibacy of Jeremiah, 16:1-9).

67. Beauchamp, *L'Un et l'Autre Testament*, 76.

the method of midrash, against the background of Exodus and Wisdom literature, highlights this double scandal. On the one hand, how can this Jesus, whose mother and father are well known to us (6:42), pretend to be the Word-Bread-Manna "that came down from heaven"? On the other hand, if he really is what he claims to be, then how can God allow him to undergo death, since he affirms "the bread that I will give [that is, "give over"] for the life of the world is my flesh" (v. 51)? How can God not snatch his Messiah from his enemies and secure his triumph? If the first difficulty, concerning the *identity* of Jesus, was already hard to digest, the second, on the manner of realizing his *mission*, was quite simply impossible to swallow: God would no longer be God! As the various Jewish exegeses of the fourth Servant poem (Isa 52:13–53:12) indicate, the interpretation of the figure of the suffering Servant as a Messiah identified with a single person was practically unthinkable. In the Jewish milieu in which Jesus lived, the Servant was always interpreted as a collective figure, especially with reference to Israel ground down by the Exile, then remaining true to its faith in the face of the persecution of Antiochus IV, and finally loaded with honors. Now, this interpretation "made possible the application of this text to *every* suffering just person." It is probably by this roundabout way, Grelot surmises, that the figure of the suffering Servant was applied by the first Christian communities to Jesus, the unique Just One, and was later expanded to include in this same hermeneutics the very messiahship of Jesus.[68] In any case, the fact that the Messiah of God would have to undergo death could become conceivable only by means of such a long detour. For the Jews, however, this remained an insupportable scandal (see 1 Cor 1:22-25).

It is this scandal that is the background for the discourse on the bread of life. There should be no mistake here: the Jews' question "How can this man give us his flesh to eat?" (v. 52) does not concern the onto-theological approach of the "how" of what will later be called transubstantiation. The issue is of a wholly different order, much more radical, the same as at the time of the Exodus: belief or unbelief. The story of the multiplication of the loaves and

68. P. Grelot, *Les Poèmes du Serviteur: De la lecture critique à l'herméneutique* (Paris: Cerf, 1981), 137, 183–189.

the discourse on the bread of life in John 6 are written with Exodus as a background: the Jews "murmur" against Jesus (v. 41) just as they murmured against Moses and against God in the desert at Mara and at the time of the sign of the manna (Exod 15:24; 16:2, 7, 12); in the same way, they "complain among [them]selves" as the people did in their accusations against Moses and against God (Exod 17:2; Num 20:3). Faith in Jesus is at the heart of this discourse. The question of verse 52 now takes on its proper dimensions: *What kind of God would he be*, if he allowed his envoy from heaven to die?

Even if verses 51-58 focus on the mystery of the Eucharist (and there is no need to imagine a later interpolation here, as Bultmann does), it is still true that the discourse on the bread of life is not a discourse on the Eucharist as such, but rather a *catechesis on faith* in Jesus as the Word of God who has undergone death for the life of the world. But this catechesis is expressed *in Eucharistic language*, characterized as it is from start to finish by the theme of *eating*. This is a more effective device for speaking of the Eucharist than a treatise that would take the Eucharist as its formal object. For chewing the Eucharist provides John with a privileged symbolic experience of what the faith is all about. Faith is chewing, slowly ruminating over the scandal of the Messiah crucified for the life of the world (as the verb *trogein*, used in verse 54, suggests because it designates the act of carefully chewing one's food which was prescribed for the Passover meal). The thoughtful chewing of the Eucharist is precisely the *central symbolic experience* where we encounter this bitter scandal of the faith until it passes through our bodies and becomes assimilated into our everyday actions.

However, by being spoken within a context of ritual repetition, which by its nature tends to wear down the sharp edges of the gospel message, the scandal of the Messiah crucified for the life of the world ends by being something that almost goes without saying. Integrated within a surrounding Christian culture, domesticated as a more or less established religion, rendered acceptable by a "theory of redemption," the "word of the cross" slowly loses its unassimilable and useless sharp edge as the "God's foolishness" to become again human wisdom. Precisely because it counteracts such a weakening of faith, the symbolic experience of the chewing, the rumination, and the ingestion of the Eucharistic bread as the body of the Lord is irreplaceable for us. In thus experiencing concretely the *consistence* and *resistance* of this compact food, we experience symbolically the resistance of the mystery of the crucified God to all logic. Such a mystery is essentially recalcitrant to every attempt, however unavoidable, at domestication by reason — and for its "own reasons."

Before our own (necessary, however) discourses, a word is given us to hear in the Eucharist. Following Augustine's distinction, of which much was made in medieval Scholasticism, between sacramental chewing and spiritual chewing, the first is useless if it does not lead to the second, that is, we must "eat and drink in order to share in the Spirit."[69] Such a spiritual chewing by way of sacramental chewing is possible, according to a theme frequently expounded by the Fathers, only if one has first eaten the Book or ruminated on the Word according to the Spirit. In the sacraments, as in all other ecclesial mediations, it is always as *Word*, bitter and sweet at the same time, that Christ gives himself to be assimilated. Such a proposition opens up from within any sacramentality that would be tempted to close in upon itself: the efficacy of the sacraments cannot be understood in any other way *than that of the communication of the Word*, a Word that communicates itself only because it is carried to us and in us by the Spirit (that is why, by the way, it should be customary, as J.J. von Allmen emphasizes, for "an epiclesis to precede" the reading of Scripture.)[70]

It is clear that the dynamic which moves from the table of the Scriptures to that of the sacraments is not simple or commonplace. We will develop this in the next chapter: *It is written that the letter wants to take over the body of the people. The sacrament is precisely the great symbolic figure of what is thus written.* The sacraments allow us to *see* what is said in the letter of the Scriptures, to *live* what is said because they leave on the social body of the Church, and on

---

69. Augustine, *Tr. 26 on the Gospel of John*, sec. 11 and *Tr. 27 on the Gospel of John*, sec. 11, DDB, Bibl. aug. 72 (1977) 509, 561.

70. J. J. Von Allmen, *Célébrer le salut: Doctrine et pratique du culte chrétien* (Paris: Cerf-Labor et Fides, 1984) 140. The beautiful epiclesis of the liturgy of the Reformed Church of France which the author quotes in this regard (p. 146) should cause some reflection among Catholics.

the body of each person, a mark that becomes a command to make what is said real in everyday life. Thus, they are the symbols of the integration of the writing into "life," the transit of the letter toward the body. Only on this condition can the letter be vivified by the Spirit; only on this condition does it emerge as Word. But this leads us toward the third element of our structure of Christian identity: Ethics.

Chapter Seven

The Relation Between Sacrament and Ethics

Between "life" and "cult," between "prophecy" and "priest-hood," between the "intention" and the "institution," there exists *an authentic evangelical tension.* Therefore, it is not self-evident that a religion which proclaims "worship in spirit and truth" (John 4:23-24) should develop ritual forms of worship. *For the "sacred" is not Christian by definition,* even though faith cannot pretend to do without it.

This is the question underlying this chapter: How can we avoid the temptation to oppose ethical practice and ritual practice without yielding to the reverse temptation to reduce the tension that must remain between them? The first temptation is the more threatening today: "life," prophetic engagement, sincerity of intention, the urgency of evangelization, all these get high marks of positive approval and gain prestige as signs of "authenticity," while the rituals, the "priesthood," the institution, and sacramentalization are burdened with all the sins of the world — co-optation, alienation, suspect archaisms . . . Such an *opposition* is naive anthropologically and untenable theologically. However, the opposite temptation must also be criticized. It is easy to simply let oneself forget the evangelical *tension* between ritual practice and ethical practice and, overly confident in the ritual (as well as hierarchical and dogmatic) system of the institution, act as if the rites were natural to Christianity. Was the Church really that healthy when in all serenity it overdid sacramentalization? And is it really that unhealthy, as one sometimes hears today, simply because it conducts its ritual practice in a manner that some find less comfortable? Is it not this uncomfortable tension between the sacramental pole of the institution and the ethical pole of verification that holds the Church evangelically upright and in good health under "the law of the Spirit"?

We will proceed by first reflecting upon the status of cult in Judaism. Following that, we will show the relation of similarity and difference which exists between the Christian cult and the Jewish, from which it was born. This will lead us, in a third step, to develop a more global theological reflection on the tension that characterizes the relation between Sacrament and Ethics.

I. THE HISTORIC-PROPHETIC STATUS OF THE JEWISH CULT

Even traditional societies, which are said to be "without history," have their history . . . and their sense of history rooted in the succession of generations and the stories. At the same time they do not seem to experience time as history, in the sense we will give this further on, to the extent that they do not even have any word for it.

In the Bantu culture, for example, as a study by A. Kagamé has made clear, awareness of the passage of time "rests on three factors" of an essentially cosmic and cyclic nature: the alternation of night and day, the seasons as determined by the sun, and the months according to a lunar calendar. Does a cyclic view of time then result? Not exactly. Their image of time "resembles a *spiral* pattern, giving the impression of an open cycle. Every season, every generation to be initiated, every fourth dynastic name, all come back to the same point on the vertical, but at a higher level."[1]

1. *Faith in a God Who Intervenes in History*

The Bible makes a dramatic break with the pattern of this "spiral" notion of time structured by great cosmic cycles. From the very beginning it prizes events perceived as moments of the *advent of unexpected newness.* This new representation of time, where tomorrow is not founded on the eternal recurrence of the Same, corresponds to what we understand as "history." At the same time, Judaism casts into relief the prophetic dimension of events:

1. A. Kagamé, "Aperception empirique du temps et conception de l'histoire dans la pensée bantu," *Les cultures et le temps* (Paris: Payot-Unesco, 1975) 114, 125.

they open a new future, itself propelled toward a meta-historical eschatology that draws today forward and gives the key for reading the past. The myth about the origins becomes thereby the bearer of the myth of a new genesis of the world and of humanity propelled toward an *eschaton:* it is from the *Omega* that we read the *Alpha.*

This is why the first place of God's manifestation is not the creation as such, but *history.* "The faith of Israel," writes G. Von Rad, "is entirely founded upon an historical theology. It understands itself as based on historical facts, shaped and modeled by events in which it discerns the intervention of Yahweh's hand."[2] In fact, as certain psalms especially indicate, the creation of the world is understood in a fashion parallel to the creation of Israel as the people of God at the time of the Exodus and is perhaps even dependent on this event. In any case, it is no accident that the verb *bara,* reserved for the creative action of God alone, is used at the creation *of Israel* (Isa 54:5). K. Barth has correctly emphasized this: biblically speaking, the creation of the world presupposes the Covenant. It is the God of Israel, the God of history, the God of the Covenant who creates the universe.[3]

At the same time we must be on guard against a one-sided point of view which, notably in certain Protestant circles, has contested Scholastic onto-theology where the unity of the creation of the universe and the history of salvation is almost lost from view. If Barth is correct in emphasizing that creation itself is part of the order of grace, it is at the risk of misunderstanding the proper consistency of the world whose very essence would have meaning only in relation to redemption.

Having posted this very important qualification, it remains true to say that the *historical theology* of which Von Rad speaks is characteristic of the Bible. Indeed, we notice from the very first word of the Bible something very singular when compared to the cosmogonic myths of traditional religions. *Bereshit:* not "at the beginning (God created) . . . ," but, as the note in the *Traduction oecuménique de la Bible* (TOB) indicates, "in *a* beginning (when God

2. G. Von Rad, *Théologie de l'Ancien Testament,* 3rd ed. (Geneva: Labor et Fides, 1971) 98.
3. K. Barth, *Dogmatique,* 3:1.

created) . . ." "What appeared essential to the narrator of Genesis," A. Néher writes in this regard, "is not what there was at the
beginning, but rather that there *was* a beginning. . . . 'Time' itself
is primordial here. Creation was manifested by the appearance of
a 'time.'. . . In a beginning, time was set in movement, and since
then history advances irresistibly."[4] The divine word is before all
else the *creator of history,* and each new word of God makes a new
event-advent arise. It is no surprise that to A. Heschel the Jews
can appear as "the builders of time."[5]

Biblical time is most appropriately thought of, not as the time of
metaphysical Being, but as that of the *historical Perhaps* and thus
as that of the *symbolic Other* in connection with human liberty
snatched thereby from *Ananke* or blind *Fatum;* it is a risky time,
but capable by this very fact of giving birth to the unheard-of, instead of simply reproducing the always-expected of the eternal
recurrence of the Same. Biblical time is precisely the history of the
difficult accommodation, the often unhappy marriage, the covenant always needing to be restored, between the project of God
and that of a free humanity. There is here, no matter how one
looks at the question, a decisive rupture with the a-historical
myths of traditional religions.

2. The Jewish Cult, an Historic-Prophetic Memorial

a) The Memorial. It is precisely to the degree that its identity is
founded on its relation to a God who has entered history that Israel, in its cult, is sent back to its responsibility within history,
and more precisely to its responsibility towards others. Theologically, it is the concept of *memorial* that best expresses the historical
and prophetic essence of this cult. This term, as is well known,
comes from the root ZKR ("remember"). *Zikkaron* or *azkarah* are
often translated in the Septuagint by *mnemosunon* or *anamnesis.*[6]

4. A. Neher, "Vision du temps et de l'histoire dans la culture juive," *Les
cultures et le temps,* 171–174.
5. A. Heschel, *Les bâtisseurs du temps* (Paris: Minuit, 1960).
6. X. Léon-Dufour, *Le partage du pain eucharistique selon le Nouveau Testament*
(Paris: Seuil, 1982) 131: "neither *mneia* ('mention,' 'anniversary'), nor *mnema* or
mnemeion ('emblem,' 'commemorative monument,' 'tomb'), nor *mneme* ('the
faculty of memory,' 'a psychological type of remembrance')" the term
"anamnesis" has the dynamic sense of "the act of recalling to memory,"

The semantic scope of the notion of memorial is always determined by the liturgy, either explicitly or implicitly.[7] Of course, its semantic scope of remembering God and reminding God based on God's action in the founding events goes much beyond the area of strict ritual and in fact encompasses *all the identifying activity of Israel,* beginning with the overall production of the Bible. However, it is especially in *ritual* activity that this anamnestic process comes about.

The paradigm for this is the memorial of *Passover.* On the seventh day of the feast of Unleavened Bread, a day to which the priestly ritual of Exodus 12:1-20 has united that of Passover, the father of each family is commanded: "You shall tell [it says literally, you shall *haggada*] your child on that day, 'It is because of what the LORD did for me when I came out of Egypt' " (Exod 13:8). The Mishna comments, "From generation to generation each one should recognize himself or herself as having come out of Egypt" (Pes 10:5). Although the word "memorial" is not used, the same perspective is present in the "Deuteronomic fiction" where Moses proclaims: "The LORD our God made a covenant with us at Horeb. Not with our ancestors did the LORD make this covenant, but with us, who are all of us here alive today" (Deut 5:2-3). The intent of these texts and of many others is clear: they mark "the insertion of those who are remembering into the very event the celebration commemorates."[8] This is how the psalmist makes the faithful who remember contemporary with what happened in the

---

where by contrast *mnemosunon* ("memorial monument"), such as the twelve steles arranged as a memorial at the crossing of the Jordan (Josh 4:7), has a more static sense.

7. See M. Thurian, *L'eucharistie: Mémorial du Seigneur, sacrifice d'action de grâce et d'intercession* (Neuchâtel: Delachaux-Niestlé, 1963), pt. 1. "Memorial" designates a commemorative stele, the pectoral insignia of the high priest (Exod 28:12-29), the sounding of trumpets (Num 10:10), the feast of Passover (Exod 12:14; 13:9), the name YHWH (Exod 3:15; Hos 12:6), the smoke of the holocaust either as such (Lev 2:2) or in a spiritualized sense (prayer, almsgiving: Sir 35:1-9; Acts 10:4; or again the people of Israel in exile considered as the choice portion consumed on the altar, a fragrance pleasing to God: Bar 4:3).

8. J. J. Von Allmen, *Essai sur le repas du Seigneur* (Neuchâtel: Delachaux-Niestlé, 1966) 24.

past under David: "We," the psalmist has them say, "it is we who have found the ark" (Ps 132:6). This is equally how the psalmist shows "in what way a 'liturgy of Zion,' which leads the faithful all around the city in order to have them meditate on the meaning of memories recalled by the monuments and walls, which makes the pilgrims 'see' this past history ('as we have heard, so have we seen,' Ps 48:8), causes them to relive this history, renders them participants in the ancient events." If the exiles who weep "by the rivers of Babylon" are afraid of "forgetting Jerusalem" (Ps 137), it is because the living memory of the promises attached to this city is the concrete refutation of their present — death — and the pledge of a new future.[9] The memory of the past thus makes the present move; it puts back on their feet, in view of a new beginning, those who are prostrate in the silence and oppression of exile.

Of course, there is memory and memory. There is the memory that is nothing but the simple act of the *memorization* of static events one pulls out from the past the way one takes some yellowed photos out from the back of a drawer. Such a memory, imaginatively idealizing the past as "the good old days when things were so much better," is counter-productive; instead of mobilizing energies to take on present tasks, it plunges one into the lethargy of a dream-past. Shrunk to the size of an anecdote, this past, from which one has washed away whatever there was of suffering, struggle, promise of a future, has no more history: it is a *simple memory*, as J.-B. Metz has said, *that has been robbed of its future.*[10]

But there is also the memory that is a living act of *commemoration*. It is in this act of *communal* memory a people or a group regenerates itself. The past of its origins is snatched out of its "pastness" to become the living genesis of today. This today is thus received as "present," as a "gift of grace." It is thus a process of revivification, where the memory of sufferings experienced, of oppression undergone, and of the fight undertaken to liberate oneself play an essential role: tomorrow will be better than yesterday; and the present is full of this living hope. Every *project* con-

9. L. Monloubou, "Le mémorial," *L'eucharistie dans la Bible, Cahiers Evangile* 37 (1981) 11–13.

10. J. B. Metz, *La foi dans l'histoire et la société* (Paris: Cerf, 1979) ch. 6.

cerning the future seems rooted in the awakening of such a *tradition:* humanity has a future only because it has a memory. Totalitarian governments know this well; their strongest weapon is rubbing out the collective memories of the groups they oppress, beginning, where this is strategically possible, with their language. For a group sees its identity being erased insofar as it loses its collective memory or insofar as this memory is no longer the anticipatory carrier of a possible new future. "Revolutions" show this: whenever it is declared that the future is realized, whenever it is declared that eschatology is fully present, it is urgent to invent a new utopia under pain of dying.

In its Passover memorial, Israel *receives its past as present,* and this gift guarantees a *promise* of a future: the "today" of Deuteronomy is in essence this recollection-rereading (*re-legere*) of the past anticipating the future. Deuteronomy is ruled by the future perfect tense.

b) Memorial, Rite, and History: Deuteronomy 26:1-11. It is precisely in the future perfect that the account of the offering of firstfruits begins in Deuteronomy 26:1-11:[11] "When you will have arrived in the land that the Lord your God is giving you as a heritage, when you will have taken possession," here is what you, Israel, will do (Deut 26:1). We have here a remarkable example of what P. Beauchamp calls *deuterosis,* that is, this bending of a writing back upon itself, this sort of bubble created in the middle of the text, where the Law demands imperatively that one observe the Law, where prophecy declares that the word of God consists in what God says, or Wisdom announces, "The beginning of wisdom is this: Get wisdom" (Prov 4:7).[12] What Moses is telling us here, in the deliberate fiction of a bubble which takes us back to the time of the first law — whereas, in fact, we are (since Israel has been in possession of its land for a long time now) in the time of the second law (*deutero-nomos*) — is precisely that this land is to be always conquered — or rather always received. In any case this is the essential intention of this discourse which is organized as follows:

11. The translation of the quotations from Deuteronomy 26:1-11 in this section and the next is based on the French text.
12. P. Beauchamp, *L'Un et L'Autre Testament* (Paris: Seuil, 1976).

A-(1-3a): Level — "HISTORY TO BE LIVED"
The STORY is in the form of a prescription, written in the informal "YOU" (French "TU"), in the FUTURE tense ("When you will have arrived in the country that the Lord your God is giving you as a heritage . . . here is what you will do . . .")
B-(3b-4): Level — "RITUAL TO BE PERFORMED"
A ritual DISCOURSE, written in "I," in the PRESENT tense ("I declare today . . . that I have arrived . . ."
+ the giving of the offering to the priest)
C-(5-9): Level — "MEMORIAL-CONFESSION OF FAITH"
DISCOURSE in the form of a STORY of origins, written in "WE," in the PAST tense
("My father was a wandering Aramean . . .")
B'-(10): Level "RITUAL TO BE PERFORMED"
RITUAL DISCOURSE, written in "I," in the PRESENT tense ("And now, behold, I bring the firstfruits of the soil you have given me, Yahweh"
+ a gesture of presentation of gifts and prostration)
A'-(11): Level "HISTORY TO BE LIVED"
a STORY in the form of a prescription, written in the informal "YOU" (French "TU"), in the "ETHICAL FUTURE" of sharing with those who own nothing, who are
• the levite (an internal representative of the vocation of Israel)
• the alien in the land (external representative)

Let us recall at the outset that this story is a response to a very specific historical situation in which Israel, now sedentary, is interested in the fecundity of its soil and flocks and is consequently tempted to invoke the Baals of the Canaanites, divinities of fertility and vegetative growth. Can the God of history also be the God of nature? This is the question to which our text responds by showing that the God of the Exodus, the God who has made Israel "come into" the land, the land given them, is also the one who will make it possible for Israel to make food "come forth" from the soil that God is giving them (see ch. 8).

Section C is the heart of this text. Its literary form is that of a *story of origins*, from the wandering Aramean down to the arrival in this country "filled with milk and honey," and, in between, the slavery in Egypt, the cry of the people to Yahweh, "the God of our ancestors," and the liberating intervention of Yahweh "with a strong hand and outstretched arm." However, the *original* events of the past are related as *originating*, that is to say, as the foundation of Israel's present identity: the epic deed of the Exodus is simultaneously event and advent. This is possible to the extent that the story functions as a *discourse*, thanks, on the one hand, to the verbal-gestural ritual in the first person in the present tense (the collective "I," in which all Israel is represented as a single person) which frames it, and on the other hand, to the pronoun "we" which meshes the story with the present of the narrator and allows it to become a liturgical confession of faith. Let us note that this confessing "we" is possible only within the ritual context in which it expresses itself. The section B-B' which frames the story of the origins and permits it to become a discourse in "we," all the while recognizing the ineradicable empirical otherness of the past of the origins, snatches it out of its pure anecdotal "past-ness" to reveal its power as a *founding present:* hence the ritual gesture of oblation, which acts out what the memorial describes — today, Yahweh gives the promised land to Israel. The ritual is the symbolic operation which allows Israel to identify itself as the people of Yahweh and to live in fidelity to this identity.

This same ritual gesture exercises an equally decisive function with regard to the level of "history to be lived" (A-A'), especially with regard to the ethics prescribed in verse 11. The symbolic act of dispossession by which Israel enters authentically into posses-sion of the land, *insofar as it is* the promise of Yahweh (for the ob-ject to be received, as section A shows clearly, is the land, not as raw material, but as material bearing the stamp of the Word of Yahweh who promised it, as "opened" by the Law), demands to be "veri-fied" in the ethical action of sharing with those who have nothing.

This status of non-possession is, in effect, the element common to the two categories of people, "the *levite* and the *alien in the land* who are among you." However, they are dispossessed in different ways. The levites are so by vocation; whereas, the aliens "have a social status intermediary between Israelite citizens and slaves: they are free, but may not own land and must rent out their serv-ices (Deut 24:14). In practice, they are assimilated to the indigent, widows, orphans, and all the poor."[13] In contrast to the alien, ex-

13. L. Derousseaux, "Le droit du pauvre dans un peuple de frères: Ex 22, 20-26," *Assemblées du Seigneur* 61 (Paris: Cerf, 1972) 6.

terior to Israel itself, the levite represents what is interior, what is at the innermost heart of the nation. Levites have a particular identity: their tribe did not receive its own territorial property, but only several cities; as a consequence, since revenue from sacrifices in the Temple is insufficient, they are thrown on the public's generosity (Deut 18:6-8). Thus, they remind Israel, from deep within itself, of its identity: even after having entered into possession of the land, Israel can live as Israel only by continuing, generation after generation, to receive it from Yahweh's gracious hand.

The ritual gesture of the offering of firstfruits, an authentic *sacramentum* or *visibile verbum* (as Augustine would say) of the memorial-confession of faith which it frames, is the "expression" (in the strong sense that we have recognized in this concept) where the identity of Israel is brought forth in the very act of enunciating itself. As long as it was in the desert, under the dispensation of the *manna*, that is to say, of the *pure non-thing sign*, of non-possession, of pure expectation, Israel had to live from the grace of God or from heaven alone (without land and without its own work). But this desert dispensation was transitory: the divine promise was leading Israel toward a land. This is exactly why, as Joshua 5:12 notes, "the manna ceased on the day they ate the produce of the land." But once in possession of the land, the temptation to forget the lesson of the desert was strong, that is to say, the temptation to appropriate the *land* as a *pure non-sign thing*, as mere possession without dispossession, as mere attainment without need for expectation: Israel therefore risked living only from its own land, forgetting heaven from which had come the manna, and thereby falling into disgrace. Against this temptation, Deuteronomy continually brings to mind the *"today" of the gift of God* and announces in the imperative mode: "Israel, remember . . . . Do not forget." *The offering of firstfruits is the figure where object and sign, non-possession and possession, attainment and expectation, heaven and earth, God's grace and the human work intersect each other.* It is the figure of the history Israel must live to be true to its identity: in the desert the dispensation of manna was only a step toward this promised history; but the occupation of the land without the memory of the manna would transform this history into a pagan affair.

As a symbolic figure from the account of the origins — a simple narration of unadorned facts recognized as foundational events, as we remarked above — which it proclaims as a memorial, the ritual of the offering of firstfruits brings home to Israel *its responsibility within history*. In the last analysis, verse 11, to which the whole text leads, enjoins Israel to be as non-possessive toward others as God was toward it when it possessed nothing. Recognition of God and thankfulness toward God shown by the offering of the symbolic representatives of the land can be true only if they are veri-fied in recognition of the poor: it is in the ethical practice of sharing that the liturgy of Israel is thus accomplished. The rite is the symbolic representation of the conjunction between love of God and love of neighbor in which Israel will soon discern, as the scribe questioned by Jesus testifies (Luke 10:26-27), not only the central double commandment, but also the very principle of the whole Law.

c) A Crisis in Ritual. Such a stress on the historic practice of the "liturgy of the neighbor" (E. Lévinas) inevitably brings about a *crisis in ritual*. As the true knife of sacrifice, the Word in effect sacrifices the first naiveté concerning ritual: Israel can no longer be, as the pagan religions are, in tranquil possession of its own cult. The ap-peal to ethical responsibility creates in contrast to pagan religions a break with consequences, cultural as well as religious, so impor-tant that they continue to foster the behaviors and judgments of our contemporaries concerning liturgical practice, as well as our own theological questioning.

The crisis in ritual was provoked especially by the *prophets*.[14] Lis-ten only to Amos 5:21-27, Hosea 6:6 (compare Matthew 9:13 and 12:7), Isaiah 1:10-17, Jeremiah 7:1-28, Micah 6:6-8, Psalms 50:12-15 and 51:18-19, Sirach 34:24-35:4, and so on. All these roundly cen-sure cultic formalism. They all castigate a cult where God is given only lip service. They all demand that the heart be in harmony with what the cult expresses and that the latter lead to the prac-

---

14. The connections between the *prophets* and worship are complex. "For some, the prophets are linked to the cult; for others, they are in direct oppo-sition to it; and between these two extreme positions, every possible grada-tion is represented." J. Asurmendi, "Isaïe 1-39," *Cahiers Evangile* 23 (1978) 55-57.

tice of what is right and just — justice and judgment are the two foundations of the throne of God (Pss 89:14 and 97:2) — toward the widow, orphan, and stranger. The ritual memory of the liberation from slavery in Egypt? Yes, but in view of the liberation of the slaves every seventh year. Circumcision of the flesh? Yes, but in view of circumcision of the heart. The offering of firstfruits? Yes, but in view of respecting the goods of others, of sharing with the most destitute, of showing respect for workers . . . Sacrifices? Yes, but in view of the sacrifice of the lips toward God and of acts of kindness toward others.

It is clear: the historic-prophetic dimension of the Jewish cult as a memorial breaks the simple mythic circularity and the spiral cosmic recurrence of ritualism lived in its first naiveté. True, Judaism remains in a dispensation of symbolic naiveté: on the one hand, its calendar also conforms to the cosmic cycle of days, months, seasons, and years; on the other, this cyclic dimension — whether it be cosmic or whether it rest upon the great anthropological seasons of the group, according to its successive generations, or of individuals, according to the decisive stages of their lives — remains constitutive of ritual symbolism. But there is history and thus the engagement of the existential responsibility of Israel in the coming-to-be of this new exodus where God, through Israel — "for salvation comes from the Jews" (John 4:22) — would free humanity from every form of slavery. It is according to this *second naiveté*, a critical one, that Israel must live its liturgy.

II. THE ESCHATOLOGICAL STATUS OF THE CHRISTIAN CULT

1. *Eschatology*

The announcement of the resurrection of Jesus and of the gift of his promised Spirit marks the inauguration of the "last days" (Heb 1:2): the future has already begun. This is why, as the ancient anaphoras show, in the recalling — the anamnesis — of the *second* coming of the Lord Jesus, as well as of his death and resurrection, the Christian memory is eschatological: it is memory of the future.

"Eschatology": this is surely the most characteristic difference between Christianity and Judaism. However, it still causes difficulty for many Christians. Because of a slippage of meaning, it frequently evokes only the "not yet" of the parousia, itself interpreted too literally in connection with the image of the "return" of Christ. As a consequence, eschatology tends to awaken only the notion of a faraway future, more or less postponed to a month of Sundays, to a beyond which has no other connection with history than to mark its end. One too easily forgets that the eschaton is the final manifestation of the resurrecting force of Christ from now on transfiguring humanity by the gift of the Spirit. In a word, one too easily forgets that it is a *moment constitutive of the Pasch of the Lord*; it speaks the future of his resurrection in the world.

Of course, the Risen One remains marked with the wounds of his death: in raising him from the dead, God has not restored him to what he was "before" the incarnation; it is in his very humanity, with the death that is constitutive of it, that he has been trans-figured. This is why, if the gift of the Spirit, poured out over all flesh at Pentecost, inaugurates the participation of humanity and the universe (Rom 8:18-24) in the Pasch of the Lord, the resulting "sacramentality" of history and the world remains *tragic*. The world continues to experience itself as not yet redeemed; "in hope we were saved" (Rom 8:24).

Still, eschatology says that one cannot confess Jesus as *risen* without simultaneously confessing him as *resurrecting the world*; it says that one may never isolate Jesus as "something facing humans which stands by itself" and that, here also, we may "understand nothing, without being ourselves understood." And so, far from simply putting history between parentheses as a simple prelude to a meta-historical beyond that alone would have the true weight of reality, eschatology requires present history as the very place of the eschaton's possibility. To devalue history is also and necessarily to devalue eschatology. The eschatological dimension of the Christian cult thus implies a return to the historic-prophetic dimension of the Jewish cult whose heir it is.

2. Jesus and the Cult

a) The Criticism of Sacrifices in the Jewish and Hellenistic Milieux. "I desire steadfast love [mercy] and not sacrifice" (Hos 6:6, quoted in Matt 9:13; 12:7). "These people . . . honor me with their lips, while their hearts are far from me" (Isa 29:13, quoted in Mark 7:6-7; Matt 15:8-9). The Temple is the "house of prayer" (Isa 56:7) and not a "den of robbers" (Jer 7:11, quoted in Matt 21:13 par.). Jesus is a severe critic of cultic formalism; in this he is in no way innovative, he is merely repeating the *message of the prophets*. Nor does he innovate, it seems, in summing up the Law in the double commandment of love for God and neighbor (Matt 22:34-40). According to Luke 10:27-28, it is actually a scribe who speaks thus and is then approved by Jesus. In Mark 12:28-34, it is Jesus himself who sums up the Law in these terms; the scribe, however, is not satisfied in being bested but rather goes one better: "You are right, Teacher; you have truly [spoken] . . . this is much more important than all whole burnt offerings and sacrifices." As one can see, the prophetic criticism of cultic formalism had created a powerful current within Judaism itself. We find this current again at Qumran, where without refusing the sacrifices that would be offered by a legitimate priesthood and in a purified Temple, they prefer "the offering of the lips" over the flesh of holocausts (1 Qs 9:3-5). This same current is also found in Philo and, more radically, in the Baptist's followers (see below), the Mandeans, and "the entire Judeo-Christian milieu, of the sectarian type, known from the Clementine writings (*Recognitiones* 1:37-55) and the Gospel to the Ebionites: 'I am come to destroy the sacrifices,' Jesus declares in this last writing."[15]

If this critical current was at first rooted in prophetism, it nonetheless shared in a much larger cultural movement of *Hellenistic* origin. There are multiple witnesses to this fact, reported especially by R. K. Yerkes,[16] from Isocrates in the fifth and fourth centuries B.C.E. ("Carry out your duties toward the gods as your ancestors taught you, but be convinced that the most beautiful sacrifice, the most noble deed, will be to show yourself the best person and the most just" [Nicocles, 20]) down to Seneca, the Stoic, in the first century C.E. ("Good people please the gods with their offerings of bread, but bad people do not escape their impiety even if they pour out a river of blood" [*De benef.* I, 6, 3]). And the Hermetic literature frequently praises "spiritual sacrifice" (*logike thusia*) alone, that of a pure heart and of the prayer of "thanksgiving" (*eucharistia*), at the expense of ritual sacrifices which are banned because God needs nothing.

It is precisely at the confluence of this dual criticism, prophetic and Hellenistic, that we find, at the time of Jesus, Philo of Alexan-

15. C. Perrot, *Jésus et l'histoire*, 144.

16. R. K. Yerkes, *Sacrifice in Greek and Roman Religion and in Early Judaism* (London, 1953) 115–196.

dria. His "eucharistic" vocabulary has been carefully studied by J. Laporte.[17] God has no need of anything (*Spec. Leg.* I, 293); and so, if God commands us to offer something, it is to teach us piety (*Her.* 123). Thus, Philo does not minimize the value of the ritual sacrifices offered in the Temple in Jerusalem. He even holds them in high esteem, inasmuch as they are prescribed by the Torah. However, at the top of the hierarchy of sacrifices he places the "eucharistic sacrifice" (*tes eucharistias thusia, Spec. Leg.* I, 285). This belongs to the category of "peace sacrifices" (*zebah shelamim*) described in Leviticus 3 and 7, communion sacrifices in which the best parts of the victim (fat, kidneys, and liver) were burned on the altar; part of what remained was given to the priests and the other part returned to the person making the offering, who then consumed it with family and friends.

Among the "three particular kinds of communion sacrifice — the sacrifice of praise (*todah*), the spontaneous sacrifice (*nedabah*) offered out of devotion outside any prescription or promise, the votive sacrifice (*neder*) to which worshipers have committed themselves through a vow"[18] — the *zebah todah*, which probably corresponds to the "eucharistic sacrifice," occupies an eminent place for Philo. According to H. Cazelles, *todah* is the substantive of a verb (*yadah*) that one finds only in the causative mood and which can be translated as "make eucharist."[19] Moreover, during the second century c.e. when the Jew Aquila wants to translate anew the Bible into Greek in a way that seems to him more faithful to the Hebrew than the Septuagint, he translates the *zebah todah* of Psalm 50:14-23 not as *tes aineseos thusia* ("sacrifice of praise," or, according to the Aramean, as the TOB indicates, "the praise as sacrifice"), but by *tes eucharistias thusia* ("sacrifice of thanksgiving").

For Philo, this ritual "eucharistic sacrifice" has value in God's eyes only if it expresses the attitude of the heart, and so *the offering of good interior dispositions* exceeds in value all sacrifices (*Spec.*

---

17. J. Laporte, *La doctrine eucharistique de Philon d'Alexandrie* (Paris: Beauchesne, 1972).

18. R. de Vaux, *Les institutions de l'Ancien Testament*, vol. 2, *Institutions militaires, institutions religieuses*, 4th ed. (Paris: Cerf, 1982) 294.

19. H. Cazelles, "Eucharistie, bénédiction et sacrifice dans l'Ancien Testament," LMD 123 (1975) 10-17.

Leg. I, 271–272). It is this offering that truly makes the eucharistic sacrifice real: the true oblation is the soul united to God (*Quaest. et sol. in Exodum* II, 71–72). Moreover, all this has far-reaching consequences concerning the required spiritual disposition: "It is proper to criticize one's own motives for rendering thanks and so choose the best, for it is more worthy to give thanks for the love of God than for a motive of self-interest." (*Spec. Leg.* I, 283).[20]

One understands better why in some Jewish circles, more critical of the priesthood and Temple sacrifices than Philo but as imbued as he by the current of the spiritualization of sacrifices, the "eucharistic" accent *shifts from the animal victim toward the prayers.* Thus, the *zebah todah,* the bloody sacrifice of communion, was at its origin "accompanied by an offering (*minhah*) of unleavened cakes and raised bread"[21] and also by prayers, especially the psalms of thanksgiving. Now, at the time of Jesus this sacrifice had become so strongly spiritualized in certain circles critical of the Temple (the Baptist's followers, among others) that the entire sacrificial weight was transferred from the victim — who had disappeared because they disapproved of bloody sacrifices — to the psalms of thanksgiving, with the vegetable offering eventually remaining the only symbolic ritual support.[22] The "eucharistic" sacrifice thus became essentially a *"sacrifice of the lips"* (see Hos 14:2), that is to say, a confession of faith expressed in thanksgiving toward God who saves his people. Such is the *zebah todah,* the *aineseos (eucharistias) thusia* that Hebrews 13:15 recommends as an offering to God through Jesus, the unique high priest: "Through

20. "The method (according to Philo) consists in exactly dividing the thanksgiving, as the priest divides the victim with the help of a sacrificial knife (*Spec. Leg.* I, 210–211). First, they should not attribute to themselves, out of forgetfulness, the benefits which come from God. . . . No more should they make God the cause of any evil whatsoever. . . . Finally, they should divide the thanksgiving in a logical manner, going from the general to the particular while evoking the works and gifts of God. . . . Each should render thanks, even the person of average virtue, 'according to the power of his or her hands,' and following the value of the gifts received." Laporte, *Doctrine eucharistique de Philon,* 66.

21. De Vaux, *Les institutions,* 2:295.

22. C. Perrot, "Les repas eucharistiques," *L'eucharistie,* Profac. (Faculty of Theology of Lyon, 1971) 89–91. Cazelles, "Eucharistie, bénédiction et sacrifice," 11–12.

him, then, let us continually offer a sacrifice of praise to God [Ps 50:14-23], that is, the fruit of lips [Hos 14:2] that confess his name." *Thus, "to make eucharist" is in the first place to confess God as savior; and this confession of thanksgiving has an immediately sacrificial connotation.* In this perspective one understands that the ritual proclamation of "the Lord's death until he comes" (1 Cor 11:26) "corresponds exactly to the *todah*"[23] and that it could have marked for the first Christian communities *"Christ's substitution of the Christian meal for the ancient todah."*[24] In this, the first Christian communities continued in the prophetic tradition and agreed with the circles within contemporary Judaism which were critical of Temple sacrifices and which we have just mentioned.[25]

b) Jesus' Attitude. Jesus, this "disciple of the Baptist" (C. Perrot), was clearly part of this current critical of Temple sacrifices. Like every pious Jew, he probably recited the morning prayer, noon prayer, and evening prayer each day;[26] he went to *synagogue* regularly ("as was his custom," Luke 4:16 says) on the Sabbath. He also frequented *the Temple* (there are eleven references in the Gospels, compared with fourteen for the synagogues). The fact that he is never presented as praying there, but only as teaching, is perhaps the mark of a post-resurrection Christological intent. J. Dupont is categorical here: when Jesus was in the Temple, it "goes without saying" that he prayed with his fellow Jews.[27] However, it seems doubtful whether he ever participated in *sacrifices* as such. In overturning "the tables of the money changers and the seats of those who sold doves" in the Temple, he achieved, according to Perrot, much more than a simple

23. Léon-Dufour, *Le partage du pain eucharistique,* 57.
24. C. Perrot, "Le repas du Seigneur," LMD 123 (1975), 44.
25. See in this sense the *'abodah* prayer: initially it accompanied the sacrifices offered in the Temple; in the time of Jesus it had passed into the synagogue liturgy of the "eighteen benedictions" where it is Israel and its prayer that are presented to God as a sacrifice (text translated in L. Bouyer, *Eucharistie* [Paris: Desclée, 1966] 80). In his *Dialogue with Trypho,* Justin (ca. 150) only confirms what already belongs to Jewish tradition: "That the prayers and eucharists made by worthy persons are the only sacrifices, perfect and pleasing to God, I also affirm" (117:2).
26. J. Jeremias, *Abba: Jésus et son Père* (Paris: Seuil, 1972).
27. J. Dupont, "Jésus et la prière liturgique," LMD 95 (1968).

"purification" of the Temple. As Mark 11:16 — "and he would not allow anyone to carry anything [object] through the Temple," (where "object" or "vase" probably designates "Temple property") — (suggests, he was directly attacking the sacrifices as such: "he stops the process of cultic sacrifice."[28]

Was his attitude always so vigorous and abrupt? "It is difficult to say," concludes the same author. He sends the leper he has just cured to show himself to the priests and to offer the prescribed sacrifice (Mark 1:44). If "the children are free" from paying the Temple tax, at the same time, "so that we do not give offense to [these people]," he pays the tax anyway (Matt 17:24-27) (p. 150). And if, before presenting one's offering at the altar, one must be reconciled with one's brother or sister, at the same time this does not dispense one from this ritual obligation (Matt 5:23-24). It is true that Matthew, for whom "not one stroke of a letter will pass from the law" (5:18), may be suspected of having added that . . .

Nevertheless, we know that the very first Judeo-Christian communities continued to go to the Temple (Acts 3:1) and that the question of what behavior to adopt with regard to the prescriptions of the Law provoked an internal conflict which almost degenerated into a schism (Acts 15). Does this authorize one to conclude that Jesus would never have contested the sacrificial cult of the Temple? Not necessarily. "Once the Temple was destroyed, Luke could return to being, without great danger, a 'man of the Temple' to better root the new religion in the Israel of all times (Luke 1:5; 24:53)" (p. 145). Perhaps in the last analysis we must see in Jesus' attitude on this matter "a certain compromise" (p. 145). In any case, it remains *rather unclear* for us — just as his attitude toward a *direct overture toward the Samaritan "heretics"* (Matt 10:5-6) *and toward the pagans,* in spite of the numerous signs directed toward the latter, is much less clear than one used to think. On this point again, his attitude seems to have been "a little contradictory" (pp. 121–126).

In both cases (sacrifices and openness to pagans) Jesus *does not seem to have given clear instructions.* In line with the prophets he challenges cultic formalism, thus sharing, by the way, in the views of certain Pharisaic rabbis: that the Sabbath is for humankind and not humankind for the Sabbath; that worship is agreeable to God only if the heart is in harmony with what the worship expresses; that reconciliation is a major condition for purity of heart . . . These maxims were not rare, if not exactly cur-

---

28. Perrot, *Jésus et l'histoire*, 146-147. The references in the text that follows refer to this work.

rent, at his time.[29] However, his personal "authority" and the "novelty" of his message and attitudes (he pardons sins, he goes to eat in the houses of sinners, he cures lepers . . .) were already such that his condemnation to death for "blasphemy" (against the Law of Moses, thus against God himself) supposes that he also found fault with the Temple cult in a *new* way. As a matter of fact, he himself seems to have pronounced words *with regard to the Temple* that were decisive for his condemnation — the Temple functioning here as the symbol of Jewish religious and national identity. These words so embarrassed the first communities that they placed them on the lips of "false witnesses" and, depending on the milieux, gave them a more or less radical tone, from the pure and simple suppression of the Temple, according to the Hellenistic viewpoint which Luke expresses in Acts 6:13-15, to the eschatological reconstruction of this Temple, of which Matthew 26:61 speaks, and between these two extremes the substitution for this Temple of one "not made with hands" (Mark 14:58); as for John, who associates this saying with the prophetic deed of purifying the Temple and who places it, probably correctly, in the mouth of Jesus himself,[30] he gives these words a clearly paschal exegesis: "but he was speaking of the temple of his body" (2:19-22).

Jesus' attitude toward the Temple and the Jewish priesthood can be approached on the historical level only if one combines two criteria, described by E. Käsemann and taken up again by Perrot: the criterion of *difference* allows us to hold that the words of Jesus against the Temple could come neither from Jewish circles nor from the Christian communities, which appeared much embarrassed by them; the criterion of *coherence* places these words within the whole of the message and attitude of Jesus and allows us to think that they are in harmony with this whole. In any case it is difficult not to put these words into relation with Jesus' "often conflictual attitude, the novelty and strangeness of his actions, the radicalness of his call, the insistence he puts on the place and meaning to be given to his own person."[31] This hermeneutics of "historical retrodiction" allows us to depict the Jesus of history without foundering in the illusions of historicism since we never forsake the Easter community which, constitutive of the very essence of the gospel text, is the obligatory mediation of our own discourse. In this perspective, the words of Jesus against the Temple, words probably authentic but whose exact tenor we will never

29. C. Dodd, *Le fondateur du christianisme* (Paris: Seuil, 1972) 80-85; K. Schubert, *Jésus à la lumière du judaïsme du premier siècle* (Paris: Cerf, 1974) 41-69.
30. H. Cousin, *Le prophète assassiné* (J. P. Delarge, 1976) 47-50.
31. Perrot, *Jésus et l'histoire*, 66-67.

know, announce *an intensification of the prophetic criticism* of cultic formalism and *a new status for worship as such.* But this newness could not manifest itself until *after Easter.*

In sum, it seems that Jesus may well have announced the advent of a new cultic dispensation but that he may not have given clear guidelines to his own people on this point. As a result, the various Christian currents could afterwards appeal to one or the other of his words or attitudes, some more "conservative" and others more "liberal," to justify their own conduct with regard to the Temple. Reinserted within the whole of his message and within the perspective of his resurrection, these contradictions were to be progressively resolved in favor of newness, a newness whose radicalness will little by little be understood at the same level as our confession of him as the "Christ," "Lord," and finally "Son of God."

3. *The Easter Tear*

It is, then, after Easter that the newness appears as the first communities work out a reading of the death and resurrection of Jesus "according to the Scriptures." The promise made to the ancestors is declared fulfilled by the gift of the Spirit, received from the Father and poured out by the risen Christ (Acts 2:33). Now, in the eschatological fever of the time, this gift of the Spirit was eagerly awaited, among the Baptist's disciples and the community at Qumran for example, in connection with the forgiveness of sins. The daily ritual baths practiced at *Qumran* expressed the ideal of an interior purification and the expectation of a radical purification to come (Rule 2:25-3:12). As a final preparation for the end of time, John's baptism for the forgiveness of sins was experienced as the prelude to the messianic baptism in the Holy Spirit and fire (see Luke 3:16). Whatever its possible relationship with Qumran, the *baptist* sect "marks a very clear step beyond the Essenes. It believes in the imminent arrival of a Messiah, the founder of a kingdom where, according to the prophet Ezekiel, the Spirit of God would be given to humankind in a cleansing of pure water that would render it capable of following the commandments and thus of attaining a justice that had been until then constantly transgressed."[32] There is every reason to think that the prophecy of Ezekiel 36:24-28, on the aspersion with pure water and the gift of the Spirit to change Israel's heart of stone into a heart of flesh and

32. H. Cazelles, *Naissance de l'Eglise,* 95.

thereby render Israel capable of walking according to the Law, was quite popular during this period. And that of Jeremiah 31:31-34, to which Ezekiel makes allusion, was probably no less popular: God would make a new covenant by writing his law on the very hearts of his people so that all might faithfully put it into practice and gain true knowledge of him.[33]

a) The Metaphor of the Tear. In announcing the resurrection of Jesus and the gift of the Spirit, it is the fulfillment of these prophecies of Ezekiel and of Jeremiah the first converts were proclaiming. With the inauguration of the eschatological Reign of God, something radically new had arisen within history. One of the great metaphors for this newness in the New Testament is the *tear.* First, the heavens are *torn apart* on the occasion of the baptism of Jesus, thus permitting the Spirit to descend upon him (Mark 1:9-11; cf. Isa 63:11–64:1). Later, exactly as the new wine of the gospel can only cause the old wineskins of the Law to burst, so it is impossible to repair the old garment of the Law by stitching a new patch on it because "the patch pulls away from it, the new from the old, and a worse tear is made" (Mark 2:21-22). "Are you the Messiah . . . ?" asks the high priest during the trial; "I am," Jesus answers; then, in a ritual gesture, "the high priest tore his clothes" (Mark 14:61-63). More striking still is the mention, by all three Synoptics, of the complete tearing ("in two," says Luke 23:45; "from top to bottom," note Mark 15:38 and Matthew 27:51) of the Temple curtain at the moment of Jesus's death: the Holy of Holies is thereafter empty; the temple of the presence of God is now the body of the Risen One (John) or the community

33. Ezekiel, who was a priest in Jerusalem, "remembers here (36:25) the ritual purifications of the Temple; and the symbolism of water as the source of life and of purification is at work here to the full (see ch. 47)." But this purification is accompanied by a "complete change": through the gift of God's own Spirit, God makes the person endowed with a new heart and spirit into "a new creature," finally capable of "putting into practice the laws and customs of the Lord" (36:27). "Jeremiah also arrived at the same conclusion." In both cases, moreover, the oracle continued into a covenant formulation: "you will be my people and I will be your God. . . . We are very close to the saying of Jesus according to John, 'No one can enter the kingdom of God without being born of water and Spirit' (John 3:5)." J. Asurmendi, "Le prophète Ezéchiel," *Cahiers Evangile* 38 (1981) 52-53.

of the faithful (Paul). By both the tearing of the heavens and the tearing of the Temple curtain a new status for cult, inaugurated by the pascal and pentecostal fulfillment of the promise, is theologically expressed.

In Jesus, Christ and Lord, the religious fabric of Judaism has been torn. Something radically new has arisen within it, what one will finally call "the redemption of the world." This newness, moreover, will not be easy to express, for it will be necessary to show that what one is announcing is really "according to the Scriptures." Now, the question which arises for these first Christians, who think themselves Jews through and through, is huge: If Jesus of Nazareth is the Christ of God; if in raising him from the dead and allowing him to pour out the Spirit of the promise, God manifested him as the salvation offered to all humankind, *then what becomes of the two great divine salvific institutions of the Mosaic covenant: the Law and the Temple?*

Paul, as we know, asked himself this question primarily with regard to the *Law:* as the expression of the divine will, the Law remains good and holy; but as a means of salvation, it becomes a curse, for justification takes place, not through the Law, but through faith in Christ. As radical as his subversion of the Law is, equally as surprising is his silence about the *Temple.* However, did not the fulfillment of the Scriptures need to be theologically demonstrated by as much attention to sacrifices and priesthood (on the priesthood, Paul is completely silent) as to the Law?

One would have to wait until the Letter to the *Hebrews* for this problem — a major one, from this viewpoint — to be squarely tackled. The task was difficult; it required a theologian of great ability, endowed with "a barely believable audacity," in the opinion of A. Vanhoye.[34] For it required nothing less than skipping over the priesthood of Aaron to rejoin that of Melchizedek, who having no genealogy thus permitted the author to speak of an "eternal priesthood"; it further required subordinating the priesthood of Aaron and the sons of Levi to Melchizedek's by means of the subordination of Abraham (and thus all his descendants, Aaron and Levi especially) to Melchizedek to whom he paid

---

34. A. Vanhoye, *Prêtres anciens, prêtre nouveau selon le Nouveau Testament* (Paris: Seuil, 1980).

tithes. The result of this eminently rabbinical exercise — which was dangerous for all that because it risked reviving among its audience a nostalgia for the splendors of the Temple — was that the author of this letter, by applying to Christ the term "priesthood" or "high priest," brings about a *transmutation* every bit as radical and subversive with regard to the priesthood and sacrifices as Paul's with regard to the Law. For if one applies the term "priesthood" to Christ, one can then apply it to no one else; there is no common measure between Christ's "priesthood" and the Aaronic priesthood which is abolished by him because it is accomplished through him. It is thus the entire Jewish system which through its symbol, the Temple, is rendered obsolete as a means of access to God: the Holy of Holies is empty. Christians have no other Temple than the glorified body of Jesus, no other altar than his cross, no other priest and sacrifice than his very person: *Christ is their only possible liturgy.*

b) A Theological Difference. Theologically, the Christian cult is simply *of another order* than the Jewish cult whose heir it is. Certainly the difference is not to be sought in the *moral* domain: we have already seen how many pious Jews in Jesus's time were conscious of the ethical demands, as much interior (purity of heart, uprightness, a sense of thanksgiving) as exterior (reconciliation, the pursuit of justice, sharing with the less well off . . .), that their worship made if it was to be pleasing to God; the prophets had long since hammered home this point. The difference is of the *theological* order. More precisely, it is founded entirely upon the rereading of the whole religious system, a rereading imposed by the confession that Jesus is the Christ. Thus, all rests on Easter and Pentecost. In a word, the difference is *eschatological.*

We may read it in the perspective of the Pauline theology of justification by faith. Of course, the upheaval of his life as a zealous Pharisee because of his conversion to Jesus as Lord does at times add a polemical note to his way of speaking. Now, "the theme of the Covenant remained a pregnant one during the first century." The Law was then understood "at once as the divine revelation and the human response to God within the framework of the Covenant, without being in any way separated from the gratuitous gift of the Covenant and without being distorted into some sort of religious falsification that would calculate how to acquire merits.''[35] The caricature of a narrowly legalistic Judaism at the time of Jesus can no longer be sustained. And one will have to tone down certain suggestions Paul himself makes about the actual attitude of Jews, especially in Pharisaic circles.

It remains that according to a genealogical regression we can establish in this domain as in many others, Jewish *thought* about the Law, thematized in its theological expressions of the first degree, does not entirely coincide with the Jewish *way of thinking* about the Law, whose structure is more fundamental than its themes. The historical corrections brought to the first degree do not invalidate the criticism that Paul attempts, at the second degree, of Jewish thinking about the Law. It was necessary that the question of the Christian difference, which was inevitable, be raised in order to bring to consciousness this way of thinking — up to then not thought through as such. As Paul shows, this difference depends *entirely* on the proclamation of Jesus as the Christ: it is He who is the revealer of the difference.

Of course, because the Law is a gift from God, the fulfillment of its precepts is only a response to God's initial call. Still, it is indeed *through* the exercise of the "works" of the Law, especially cultic ones, that Jews claim to be justified, it being understood that these merits are in no way automatic since they require an authentic purity of heart whose quintessence is, so to speak, the very "eucharistic" attitude which Philo has described (see above). Paul precisely does nothing more than develop this eucharistic emphasis. But he does so not only in reference to the moral obligations required as a response to the blessings of God; he does it theologically and eschatologically in reference to *Christ* and the gift of the *Spirit*. It is this which changes completely the reading of the cultic system. For Christians' thanksgiving is *Christ himself*, and no longer their own faithful execution of the Law or the uprightness of their grateful hearts. The very principle of justification is different from what it is in Judaism: it is identified with Christ, the unique subject who has fully accomplished the Law, inscribed as it was by the Spirit in his innermost being. Consequently, to be a Christian is to live under "the law of the Spirit" (an expression

35. Perrot, *Jésus et l'histoire*, 153.

that "summarizes Jeremiah 31:33 and Ezekiel 36:27," as the note in the TOB on Romans 8:2 indicates); it is to have "the Spirit of God dwell[ing] in [us]," that is, to share in "the Spirit of Christ" (Rom 8:9). The *new modality* of justification is to be understood starting from and in connection with this *new* Christo-pneumatic *principle:* no longer the practice of the works of the Law (which would call into question this very principle) but *faith* in Jesus as Christ and Lord. Paul, as we see, is within a perspective of the fulfillment of the religion of the ancestors, at least that aspect of it which seems to him the most "spiritual"; but this very fulfillment, in that it is proclaimed in the Pasch of Jesus and the gift of the Spirit, cannot be accomplished without a tear.

c) A New Cultic Status. Consequently, where the spirit of the Law always consisted, finally, in hoisting oneself up towards God by one's own fingernails, that is to say, by accomplishing works (which in the realm of ritual prescriptions required the presence of a priestly caste between the people and God), the law of the Spirit reverses this perspective. It is no longer a question of *"ascending"* to God — granted, as a response to God's previous "descent" to us through the Covenant and the gift of the Law. From now on it is a question of *welcoming* salvation from God's self, fundamentally bestowed as a grace *"descended"* upon us in Jesus, the "Christ," God's "Son" (Rom 1:1-4, etc.). Jesus has finally sealed, in his Pasch, and especially in its culmination, the gift of the Spirit, this new covenant announced by Jeremiah and Ezekiel and consisting in God's writing God's law directly on the human heart (Jer 31:33) and in the gift of God's own Spirit (Ezek 36:26-27). Thus, we no longer have to lift ourselves toward God through the performance of good works, ritual or moral, or through the intermediary of a priestly caste, but we have to welcome salvation *in our historical existence* as a gift of grace: in effect, we are all "now justified by his grace . . . through the redemption that is in Jesus Christ" (Rom 3:24). What an overwhelming reversal for Paul!

The gospel cannot be used as a patch to mend the old garment of the Law. Such a repair is impossible, a tear is inevitable. The gospel radically *subverts* the existing system; it attacks it decisively at its very root. Obviously, the cultic status is as radically transformed. Because from now on God directly rejoins God's people

— the Gentiles as well as the Jews — in the risen Christ and by
the gift of the Spirit, and no longer through the twofold institution of salvation that was the Law and the Temple (sacrifices and
a priestly caste), *the primary worship of Christians is welcoming in
their daily lives this grace of God through theological faith and charity.*

We may illustrate this Christian difference by the following
diagram:

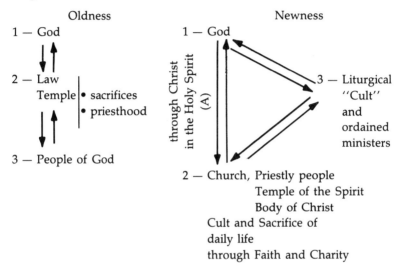

We will explain later why we give the titles "oldness" and
"newness," and not "Old Testament" and "New Testament," to
our two diagrams. Right now, let us stress that these have no absolute value, but only as related one to the other. The same elements can be found in each, but the fact that they are located
differently causes a modification in the system. In the second, the
cult (and the Law) is no longer in an intermediary position. According to the direction of rotation (A) indicated on the outside,
the cult acts as a *symbolic revealer* of what enables human life to be
authentically Christian, that is to say, the priestly act of an entire
people making their very lives the prime place of their "spiritual"
worship; according to the direction of rotation (B) drawn on the
inside, it acts as a *symbolic operator* making possible this priestly
and sacrificial act that is "pleasing to God" through Jesus Christ
and in the Holy Spirit. Thus our element "Sacrament" is posi-

tioned as a symbolic practice which simultaneously *comes from* (direction A) and *sends us back to* (direction B) the element "Ethics": it is above all in the everyday that the Risen One is encountered. It is corporality itself that is the fundamental mediation for Christian liturgy, as the cultic vocabulary of the New Testament makes clear.

4. *The Cultic Vocabulary of Christians at the Beginning*
The remark has often been made that the sacred and cultic vocabulary used in the Old Testament — *latreia, leitourgia, thusia, prosphora, hiereus, naos, thusiasterion,* and so on — never designates in the New Testament the liturgical activities of Christians or the ministers who preside over them. Of course, if these words are employed to indicate Jewish or pagan rites and ministers, in what concerns Christianity itself, they are used only in relation to *Christ* on the one hand (for he accomplishes and thus abolishes both the cult and the priesthood of the old covenant) and to the Christians' *daily life* on the other (insofar as, invested with the Spirit, it is a participation in Christ). It is this second aspect, strictly dependent upon the first, which we have already discussed, that interests us here.

a) *The New Testament.* According to Romans 12:1, the offering of the "body," that is to say, of the entire person, constitutes the *thusia zosa hagia* ("living and holy sacrifice") that is pleasing to God. Paul borrows from the Greeks (doubtless, as we have seen, through Jewish currents that had made it their own) the expression *logike latreia* ("spiritual worship") to designate this "living and holy sacrifice." We have here, as Käsemann notes, a "key expression . . . that was first used in the more enlightened Hellenists' polemics against the 'unreasonable' cultic offerings of popular religions." However, as verse 2 shows, Paul transforms it in connection with the eschaton inaugurated in the Pasch of Christ. For "in an eschatological time, nothing is profane any more, except what human beings themselves profanize or demonize," so that because of the change in the "lordship" of the world, "the doctrine of cult necessarily coincides with Christian ethics."[36]

---

36. Käsemann, *Essais exégétiques,* ch. 2, "Le culte dans la vie quotidienne," 17–24. However, *'abad* or *'abadah* is translated in the Pentateuch of the Septuagint by *latreuein-latreia* if it is a question of a non-priestly religious service; by *leitourgein-leitourgia* if this service is reserved to ministers consecrated to this office. But the fact that Paul elsewhere employs these latter terms for the

In 2 Corinthians 9:12, the collection organized by Paul among the Christians of Greece and Asia Minor to aid the brothers and sisters in Jerusalem suffering from famine (see Acts 11:28-30), a collection which is gathered during the Sunday assemblies in Galatia and at Corinth "on the first day of every week" (1 Cor 16:1-2), is regarded as a *leitourgia* ("liturgy") which causes an overflowing of "eucharists" ("thanksgivings") to God. What is more, the share of the Philippians in this same collection is the *thusia* ("sacrifice") that is pleasing to God, a fragrant offering" (Phil 4:18). This last expression is applied in Ephesians 5:2 (where it also refers to the holocaust that lies smoldering on the altar [Exod 29:18]) to the death of Christ interpreted as a sacrifice, "he who gave himself up for us, a fragrant offering and sacrifice to God."

Such is also the spiritual sacrifice spoken of in the last chapter of the Letter to the *Hebrews*. We said above that Hebrews attempts a Christological reading in exclusively priestly terms. Priesthood, however, applies only to Christ. Eternal, exclusive, untransmissible (see 7:24), nevertheless all who have become "partners of Christ" participate in it (3:14). In any case, this is the implication of Hebrews 10:14: "By a single offering he has perfected for all time those who are sanctified." Now *teleioun-teleiosis* ("to perfect-perfection"), which designates this fulfillment or this act of "rendering perfect" is applied first to Christ (5:9). And especially, as Vanhoye makes clear, this Greek verb or its substantive is used in the Septuagint to translate the ritual act (filling the hands) that "in the Pentateuch serves to designate the consecration of the high priest."[37] Thus, those who are sanctified by Christ are at the same time "made priests" by him; their *teleiosis* is their participation in his own consecration. This is also why, it seems, this letter presents Christians as *proserchomenoi*, "those in procession" who "advance toward God," more exactly toward the celestial sanctuary that Christ, the unique High Priest, has opened to them. Of the eight New Testament uses of *proserchomai* in the sense of "draw near to God," seven are found in Hebrews, and the eighth confirms this cultic sense because it is found in 1 Peter 2:4 ("Come to him, a living stone") in which the theology of a priestly people is explicit. According to J. Colson, this verb *proserchomai* is "a technical term in the Old Testament designating the entrance of the priest into the Temple for his ministry and his approach to the altar for offering his sacrifice."[38] The life of the Christian community is thus presented as a long priestly liturgy.

"sacrifice" of the daily life of Christians leaves scarcely any doubt as to the priestly background of Rom 12:1.

37. Vanhoye, *Prêtres anciens*, 196.

38. J. Colson, *Ministre de Jésus-Christ ou le Sacerdoce de l'Evangile* (Paris: Beauchesne, 1967) 133.

It comes as no surprise, then, that in its last chapter Hebrews comes to speak of the exercise of this priesthood of all Christians. This priesthood manifests itself in two ways: on the one hand, in the "sacrifice of the lips" (the profession of faith), in thanksgiving (for God's saving us in Jesus, see above); on the other, by that of good deeds and mutual aid among those in the "community" (*koinonia*), "for such sacrifices are pleasing to God" (see Heb 13:15-16). Here we meet again the same liturgical-sacrificial vein apropos the concrete exercise of charity among brothers and sisters through the sharing we found earlier in the collection taken up by Paul.

This current of a spiritualization of priesthood and sacrifice into the confession of faith and the practice of charity develops further with Paul into a missionary perspective. "To be a minister [*leitourgos*] of Christ Jesus to the Gentiles in the priestly service of [*hierourgounta*: sacrificing as a priest] the gospel of God, so that the offering [*prosphora*] of the Gentiles may be acceptable, sanctified by the Holy Spirit" (Rom 15:16): this is how Paul expresses the grace God has given him. His "priesthood" is his missionary activity; the sacrificial knife by which the pagans become a spiritual sacrifice is the gospel! There is the same kind of metaphor, against a cultic background, in Philippians 2:17 concerning his eventual martyrdom: "Even if I am being poured out as a libation over the sacrifice [*thusia*] and the offering [*leitourgia*] of your faith, I am glad and rejoice with all of you." The Philippians' faith is the liturgical sacrifice over which Paul is ready to spill his blood, just as one poured out libations of wine, water, or oil on the Jewish (Ezek 29:40; Num 28:7) or pagan sacrifices (see also the same expression in 2 Tim 4:6). As for the metaphor of the sacrifice with a pleasing fragrance, it recurs in Paul with this missionary perspective in 2 Corinthians 2:4-16: God accepts as an offering with a pleasing fragrance the apostolic action of one sent to make Christ known in all times and all places.

The proclamation of the gospel as spiritual *latreia* (Rom 1:9) or as priestly activity is developed in 1 Peter 2:4-10; more precisely, it is a question of proclaiming the "wonders of God" (*mirabilia Dei*, v. 9). The theme of a priestly people, present in Exodus 19:6, Isaiah 61:6, and 2 Maccabees 2:17, is rather poorly exploited in the New Testament. One finds it in Philo, who distinguishes two degrees: "the high-priest, who sacrifices for the entire nation, exercises the universal priesthood that the nation accomplishes in the midst of humankind" (*Spec. Leg.* II, 164).[39] Such is exactly the perspective of Exodus 19:5-6 and Isaiah 61:6. "In opposition to the pagan nations who, in spite of their belonging by right to Yahweh,

39. Laporte, *Doctrine eucharistique de Philon*, 130.

live far from his protective presence, the people of Israel enjoy the privileged position of priests who alone may enter into the holy place."[40] In a word, God says to Israel, "You shall be in relation to the other nations as the priests are in relation to you." It is in this perspective of *election,* different from the Christological-priestly perspective of Hebrews, that 1 Peter must be placed. Moreover, this is the reason all the terms are collective — *genos* ("race"), *ethnos* ("nation"), *laos* ("people"), *oikos* ("house"), and even the neologism created by the Septuagint to translate priesthood as a class: *hierateuma.* Thus, "this entire passage puts the accent, not on the particular dignity of each baptized person, but on the communitarian mission of the Church, as the parallelism between verses 5 and 9 indicates."[41] This priesthood — the Church — is charged with offering *thusias pneumatikas* ("spiritual sacrifices"), and especially the confession of faith (v. 9) and, as the exhortations which follow addressed to various sorts of Christians show, their ethical conduct as well which, even without words (3:1), should nevertheless testify to the Word. More exactly, such a "universal priesthood" of the people of God "has little to do with the question of ministries *within* the Church," but has to do with "the ministry *of* the Church in the world"; the Church is charged with "a substitutive, mediating, vicarious function," and its spiritual sacrifice is "to be the presence of God in the world and the presence of the world before God."[42]

The expression "spiritual house" (*oikos pneumatikos*) used in 1 Peter 2:5 reminds us of a theme frequently exploited by Paul. Indeed, the Church is the new *naos* ("temple") of God (there are forty-five uses of *naos* in the New Testament, against sixty-nine uses of *hieron,* which is invariably reserved for the Temple in Jerusalem). Christians are individually the temple of the Spirit in their bodies (1 Cor 6:19), but especially, according to a viewpoint also found in certain contemporary Jewish writings (from Qumran, for example), they are such collectively (1 Cor 3:16; 2 Cor 6:16 [cf. Ezek 37:27 and Lev 26:12]; Eph 2:21-22). As we said earlier, the Holy of Holies is now empty; the "body of Christ" which the Christians constitute (1 Cor 12:27) is the new temple, made up of "living stones," where God has chosen to make his home through the Spirit in the midst of humankind.

b) The Second Century. Throughout the entire second century the New Testament position was faithfully maintained on this point. If Clement of

---

40. E. Cothenet, "La première épître de Pierre," *Le ministère et les ministères,* 141.

41. Ibid., 143.

42. Von Allmen, *Essai sur le repas du Seigneur,* 93.

Rome, in a formal discourse (Cor. 40–44), and if the *Didache* (13:3) and Irenaeus (*Adv. Haer.* IV, 8, 3) incidentally refer to the priesthood of the Temple while discussing the ministers of the Church, in all three cases this is a *comparison of functions* and is not intended at all to represent the ministers of the Church as *sacerdotes* ("priests"). As M. Jourjon states, Clement "believes that those in charge (the ministers in the Church) are to the Church what the priests and levites were to the people of God" because God wished that there be an "order" (*taxis*) in the Church just as there was one under the old covenant.[43] An examination of the whole letter further rules out going beyond interpreting this text as a simple comparison: weaving together anti-sacrificial quotations from Scripture (notably Psalms 49 and 50), its aim is to lead the "dissidents" at Corinth back into obedience to their bishops and presbyters, an obedience which, as a humble confession of their sin, constitutes precisely the "eucharistic" sacrifice pleasing to God (Cor. 18; 52). As Jourjon writes, "The true sacrifice really is not one," and the very term "sacrifice" is for Clement "a *metaphor* for what transpires within the Church through faith, obedience, and humility."[44]

Chapter 14 of the *Didache* testifies to this same *"farewell to sacrifices."* What the Church carries out on the Day of the Lord in gathering for thanksgiving and the breaking of bread is a "sacrifice" ("your sacrifice," the text says twice) inasmuch as it is the fulfillment of the "pure sacrifice" announced by Malachi 1:11. Here again it is through humility of heart, expressed in *Didache* 14:1–2 by confession of faults and reconciliation between brothers and sisters (see Matt 5:24), that the assembly accomplishes the prophecy of Malachi: "Everything seems to indicate it is by the confession of faults and the forgiveness of brother or sister that the Sunday assembly, whose aim is thanksgiving through the breaking of bread, is constituted a sacrifice."[45]

Thus the anti-sacrificial course plotted by the New Testament is firmly maintained. It will be so throughout the entire second century, with a heightened polemical note among the Apologists.[46] This is evident, on the one hand, in that the ministers of the Church are never referred to as *hi-*

43. M. Jourjon, "Remarques sur le vocabulaire sacerdotal de Ia Clementis," *Epektasis*, Mélanges J. Daniélou (Paris: Beauchesne, 1972) 109. See also A. Jaubert, *Clément de Rome: Lettre aux Corinthiens*, Sources chrétiennes 167 (Paris: Cerf, 1971) 80–83.

44. M. Jourjon, *Les sacrements de la liberté chrétienne selon l'Eglise ancienne* (Paris: Cerf, 1981) 147, 11–14; Jaubert, *Clément de Rome*, 173, n.

45. Jourjon, *Les sacrements*, 15, see also 74–75.

46. Significant in this regard is the way in which Mal 1:10-11 is quoted. Justin (*Dial.* 41:2) stresses the negative side of this; whereas, the *Didache* (14:3)

ereis or *sacerdotes* nor the Eucharist as a *thusia* in the absolute later sense of the "sacrifice of Christ," and on the other, in that the theme "God has no need of sacrifices" is frequently used. This theme, which appears in the Letter of Barnabas (ch. 2), in Justin (*Dial.* 41, 70 and 117), in Irenaeus (*Adv. Haer.* IV, 17-18), in the Letter to Diognetus (3, 4), in Clement of Alexandria (*Paed.* III, 89-91), and so forth, is illustrated by an *anthology of anti-sacrificial biblical quotations* which, according to P. Prigent, goes back at least to a Judeo-Christian, and perhaps simply to a Jewish, source.[47]

It is only at the beginning of the third century that the terms "sacrifice" and "priest" will be used to describe in a precise manner the Eucharist and the ministers who preside over it, first with Tertullian, though still in a tentative manner,[48] more strongly with Cyprian[49] — who is well aware, as later Augustine will also be, of similar anti-sacrificial anthologies[50] — until finally these terms impose themselves powerfully in the fourth century.

c) Theological Import.

— Subversion

We witness, then, in the New Testament an unquestionable change of course in cultic vocabulary. Certainly, this transformation had already begun in various currents of contemporary Judaism (for instance, Qumran, Philo, the Baptist's followers . . .) and had its sources especially in the prophetic oracles. Besides, it is historically probable that in favoring the spiritualization of worship, the first Christian communities desired, as did analogous currents within or on the fringes of *Judaism,* to put some distance between themselves and the more official forms of Judaism. It is also probable that it was necessary for them to clearly distinguish themselves from the *pagan mystery cults:* C. Mohrmann has

---

mentions only the positive aspects, while Irenaeus (*Adv. Haer.* IV, 17, 5) maintains both dimensions.

47. P. Prigent, *L'épître de Barnabé,* Sources chrétiennes 172 (Paris: Cerf, 1971), nn. of pp. 82–91.

48. Tertullian applies *sacrificium* to the Eucharist in an absolute sense in *De Or.* 19, 1 and 4, and *sacrificare* in *Ad Scap.* 2; the priest is *sacerdos* in *De exhort. cast.* 11, 2.

49. Cyprian. See especially his famous *Ep. 63 to Caecilius.*

50. Cyprian, "Ad Quirinium" 1, 16 (CSEL 3.1, pp. 49–50); Augustine, *The City of God* 10:6.

demonstrated the tendency among Christian writers of the second and third centuries to "avoid words which in one way or another might be associated with contemporary pagan cults";[51] however, at the very beginning, the pressure to do so would have been much less. But we cannot limit ourselves to these remarks. As probable and understandable as this break with the traditional sacrifices might have been historically, it should nonetheless be studied at a properly theological level.

For the fact of the "farewell to sacrifices" is too widespread in the New Testament and afterwards for us to avoid interpreting it on any other level than the *very level* of the eschatological tear which is at work, according to the unanimous witness of the apostolic Church, in the event of Easter-Pentecost, with all the consequences this has for the Law (Paul) and the Temple (Hebrews). In other words, the theological hermeneutics of what we have called the change of direction of cultic vocabulary should be consistent with the Christological and pneumatological hermeneutics attested in all of the New Testament. The inescapable conclusion, we would argue, is an undeniable *anti-sacrificial and anti-priestly subversion*. We will have occasion later on to explain in what sense the door was left open for a possible retrieval of this vocabulary of the sacred by Christianity. But this later development should not lessen the theological import of this event: the status of "priesthood" and "sacrifice" is new with the very newness of *Jesus Christ* and of the fulfillment of the promise by the *gift of the Spirit*. From now on, the new priesthood is the priesthood of the people of God. The temple of the new covenant is formed by the body of Christians, living stones fitted together by the Holy Spirit over the cornerstone that is Christ himself. And the sacred work, the cult, the sacrifice that is pleasing to God, is the confession of faith lived in the agape of sharing in service to the poorest, of reconciliation, and of mercy.

— *Ritual Memory and Existential Memory*

Thus, the *ritual* memory of Jesus' death and resurrection is not Christian unless it is veri-fied in an *existential* memory whose place

51. C. Mohrmann, "Sacramentum dans les plus anciens textes chrétiens," *Etudes sur le latin des chrétiens*, vol. 1 (Rome, 1958) 233–244, vol. 3 (Rome, 1965) 181–182.

is none other than the believers' bodies. Paul himself testifies this, principally in a baptismal perspective (1 Cor 4:10); the fo\ Gospel, principally in a Eucharistic perspective. We know that _ Gospel introduces the story of the washing of feet at the very moment we would expect the account of the institution of the Eucharist: "I have set you an example, that you also should do *as* [*kathos*] I have done to you" (John 13:15). "The comparison with the anamnesis is inescapable," comments X. Léon-Dufour: "Do this in memory of me." For this Johannine *kathos* "is causal rather than merely exemplary . . . as if Jesus said: 'In acting this way, *I give you* power to act in the same way.' " This *kathos*, we would say, has the value of a *sacramentum* — that is to say, of a gift on the part of Christ — and not simply of an *exemplum*. This is why, "according to John, the community is founded and maintains itself as much by mutual service as by Eucharistic worship: the 'share with' of John 13:8 corresponds to the 'sharing in' of 1 Corinthians 10:16." It is finally "Jesus himself who, through his disciples, fulfills the service which must characterize them."[52] To wash one another's feet is to live existentially the memory of Christ that the Eucharist makes us live ritually.

It is precisely because the ritual memory sends us to the existential memory that the sacraments in general, and the Eucharist in particular, constitute a *"dangerous memory,"* in the words of Metz. It is dangerous for the Church and for each believer, not only because the *sequela Christi* ("following of Christ") leads everyone onto the crucifying path of liberation (as much economic as spiritual, collective as personal), but because this "following of Christ" is "sacramentally" the *location* where Christ himself continues to carry out through those who invoke him the liberation for which he gave his life. The ritual story at each Eucharist, retelling why Jesus handed over his life, sends all Christians back to their own responsibility to take charge of history in his name; and so they become his living memory in the world because he himself is "sacramentally" engaged in the body of humanity they work at building for him.

52. Léon-Dufour, *Le partage du pain eucharistique*, 287–288. The author refers to O. de Dinechin, *"Kathos:* La similitude dans l'évangile selon saint Jean," RSR 58 (1970) 195–236; 333, no. 8.

III. THE LETTER, THE RITE, AND THE BODY

1. *Reversal of the Sacred*

For the Jewish category of "sacralization" (the setting apart from the profane) the "sanctification" of the profane is substituted to the point that in the wake of the New Testament, the prime location of liturgy or sacrifice for Christians is the ethics of everyday life sanctified by theological faith and charity. In the same perspective, for the Jewish category of "intermediary" between God and humankind (the intermediary of the Law and the sacrificial priesthood) that of *"mediation"* is substituted, that is to say, a milieu in which the new communication of God with humankind made possible by Christ and the Spirit takes place; and this milieu is corporality itself.

The anti-sacral subversion at issue here should not be confused with that "desacralization" which one has heard praised in recent decades and is nothing but the fallout (crystallized in the uprising of French students in May 1968) of an ideology that opposes "faith" and "religion" — two interesting concepts for sure when used to effect a critical discernment in the act of belief, but which lose their value as soon as one pretends to apply them to different categories of believers. If there is indeed something radical in the criticism New Testament Christology and pneumatology raise with regard to cult, it does not bear *in any way on sacredness as such, but only raises questions about its status.* In other words, the sacred is in no way denied but *turned around.* For faith in Christ does not add up to the sacred, no more than an operator in mathematics is added to the numbers it adds or multiplies. In its capacity as operator, faith indicates what *kind of relation* is established in Christianity between religious and sacred manifestations and everyday ethical behavior: a *critical* relation, for faith turns this sacredness around in order to assume it in a Christian way, this sacredness without which, however, it could not even exist. It qualifies the sacred with a critical exponent that directs it back toward sacramental ethics.

The symbolic system of Christian identity does not derive its originality from the supposition that it would render its members "better than" Jews, Muslims, or others. Its difference is theological — Easter and Pentecost, or eschatology — not moral. This difference, we have emphasized, is in *continuity* with biblical prophetism and certain Jewish currents contemporary with Jesus that we have mentioned. However, because of the eschaton inaugurated — according to the New Testament's hermeneutics — in the resurrection of Jesus and the gift of the Spirit, there is a *rupture* even with regard to those currents most critical of institutional and nationalistic Judaism. As is readily comprehensible for historical reasons, the realization of the importance of the tear grew only relatively slowly, especially in the Judeo-Christian milieux. This explains the "conflict of hermeneutics" one finds even within the first communities. This conflict, more or less erased in the final redactions of the New Testament texts, is itself canonical; it expresses canonically the impossibility of pretending to adequately grasp the mystery of Jesus Christ.

2. The Transition from the Book to the Body

As we have noted, it is corporality that is the primordial location of the Christian liturgy insofar as it is invested with the Spirit that is poured out over all flesh by the Risen One. We concluded the preceding chapter by remarking that our element Sacrament acts as a symbol *for the passage from the letter toward the body.* Such a passage is written in the Scriptures. That the community "writes itself" into the Book it is reading is an indication that this Book, in its very essence, seeks to permeate the whole volume of the social body of the people. Such, by the way, is exactly the thrust of the prophecies of Jeremiah 31 and Ezekiel 36 in the perspective of the new covenant: *the Book, through the action of the very Spirit of God, will become one with the body of the people.* According to Christian hermeneutics, Jesus, "scripturally dead" (see above) for the many, "crucified on the book" (Beauchamp), has been the unique subject who, anointed by the Spirit (Matt 3:16 par.), has fully incorporated the Book. Baptized into his death so as to live from "the Spirit of him who raised [him] from the dead" (Rom 8:11), his disciples have as their task to learn little by little to incorporate into themselves this Book, rewritten as gospel.

Where the pagan religions have tended to favor, though not exclusively of course, cosmic signs of *seeing* as manifestations of the divinity, Judaism has tended to favor (again, not exclusively) signs of *hearing*. For the God of Israel does not tolerate graven images. To see God is to die; one can barely stand to gaze upon God's back (Exod 33:18-23). God has no image, only a Name — a name that humans are eventually forbidden to pronounce. God's mediation of revelation is the word so that fidelity to God consists essentially in the "receptive listening" (*hyp-akoe*, "obedience") to God's Law. Israel was by no means unaware of the cosmic signs of theophanies, still less of the ethical practice through which the Word insisted on penetrating the body.

But Easter and Pentecost give this last trait a new meaning. If the Christian difference favors the sign of *living*, this is not due to a mere refinement of "practical reason" that would discover in "ethical acting" (such as the Kantian maxim to "never do to others what you do not want done to yourself") the truth of this religion and of all religion. Moreover Rabbi Hillel declared, apropos this maxim, already well known, "It contains the whole Torah; the rest is only commentary."[53] Here again it is the eschaton that requires Christians to favor *living* — if not, incidentally, at the thematic level of their "pheno-text," at least at the structural level of the genuinely Christian genesis of their discourse. For the resurrection of Jesus and the gift of the Spirit specify *corporality* as the eschatological place of God. God wants to assume flesh, the flesh of the Christ, by the Spirit.

For us, this is the theological import of an ethics lived as the prime place of a liturgy pleasing to God. The body is henceforth, through the Spirit, the *living letter* where the risen Christ eschatologically takes on flesh and manifests himself to all people. The place of God's revelation is the existence of humankind as the place where the letter of the Book is inscribed — the letter, the very last one, of the cross — through the Spirit: "You yourselves are our letter, written on our hearts, to be known and read by all; and you show that you are a letter of Christ, prepared by us, written not with ink but with the Spirit of the living God, not on tablets of stone but on tablets of human hearts" (2 Cor 3:2-3).

We have shown previously that the proclamation of the Book in the celebrating *ecclesia* is the sacramental manifestation of the

53. Babylonian Talmud, Shabbat 31 a, quoted by Perrot, *Jésus et l'histoire*, 144.

Book's very essence. We can appreciate now more clearly the implications of this statement: it is the essential connection between the Book and the social body of the Church, where it seeks to be inscribed, that is symbolically represented and (at the same time, taking account of the nature of "symbolic expression") effected in the liturgy. The element *"Sacrament"* is thus *the symbolic place of the on-going transition between Scripture and Ethics, from the letter to the body.* The liturgy is *the powerful pedagogy where we learn to consent to the presence of the absence of God, who obliges us to give him a body in the world,* thereby giving the sacraments their plenitude in the "liturgy of the neighbor" and giving the ritual memory of Jesus Christ its plenitude in our existential memory.

3. A "Third" Naiveté

Therefore, there is even less reason for an explicit cult in Christianity than there was in Judaism. If for Judaism the cult can be practiced only through a second critical naiveté, in Christianity it may be practiced only with what we can call a *"third"* naiveté. It is still a naiveté, for every symbolic action "embraces" the whole of the subject, rather than directing itself solely to its brain. But it is a naiveté modified by a critical coefficient which, because of Easter and Pentecost, comes to reinforce the prophetic criticism of cult or, according to Christian hermeneutics, to proclaim the fulfillment of this criticism through the gift of the Spirit.

Thanks to this gift of the Spirit through the Risen One, the transition from the letter to the body is from now on eschatologically possible. Such a passage from Church to Ethics, symbolized by Sacrament, opens us to the study of the process by which the structure of Christian identity functions. This will be the subject of the next chapter.

Chapter Eight

How the Structure Functions:
The Process of Symbolic Exchange

A structure is not something that comes ready-made. The one
we have proposed indicates only that Christian identity is based
on the same fundamental "pattern" (to use the semioticians'
term): like a piece of clothing, one cannot put it on if one puts
one's head through the arm hole . . . But if one is assured of fidelity to the basic cut of the model, individuals may clothe themselves in Christianity in the manner which suits them; the style of
the sleeves, the length of the garment, the color, the material are
open to almost limitless variations. Some become Christians following a pilgrimage; others, because of the witness of some other
Christian's life; still others, at the reading of a Gospel passage
that knocks them over . . . The diversity of paths to the faith is
extreme. Nevertheless, within this diversity the structural process
functions fundamentally according to the same rules of the game.
It is this process we are going to examine now. We shall start
with the process of symbolic exchange.

Let us begin by recalling certain elements of this process. Either
falling short of or surpassing the realm of utility, symbolic exchange, as we said in chapter three, occurs in the order of non-
value, hence its major interest to us in thinking through the
gratuitous and gracious relation that is effected between humankind and God in the sacraments. We have illustrated this process
through the example of the gift and, more fundamentally still,
through that of the word. The word should not be treated as
merely one example among others but as the very archetype of
what happens between subjects and within any subject. It is in
language that symbolic exchange, along with the subject, takes its

origin; and because of this one best understands how, although "*gratuitous,*" it is also "*obligatory.*" Every gift received obligates. This is true of any present: as soon as the offered object — anything whose commercial or utilitarian value does not constitute its essence as a gift — is received as a present, it obligates the recipient to the return-gift of an expression of gratitude. As a true *sacramentum* of mutual alliance and gratitude, the present is a visible word; in fact, it is precisely because it is a word that it is a present. For every word "received" as such imposes an obligation. To refuse to answer the person who is speaking to us is to refuse to receive this word as a gift, to break the alliance by short-circuiting the communication. To involuntarily fail to answer is to overlook the proposed alliance because of a distraction which psychoanalysis might perhaps show to be not as innocent as it first appeared. Our response need not be a verbal one: a nod of the head, a look conveying our interest in what is being said will often suffice as a return-gift. Conversely, the ways of negating the other as other and of breaking off communication are as varied, and perhaps even more subtle. However, every language act, as we have stressed, has an illocutionary dimension which makes it, explicitly or not, a word given, in which it is always ultimately oneself that one gives, oneself that one surrenders and "ex-poses" to the risk of being misunderstood. Such is the bread of the word which enables us to live as subjects.

Availing ourselves of the diagram of A. Delzant, we may represent this process of symbolic exchange in the following manner:

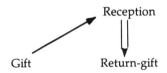

Gift and Reception, occupying the two poles of the *axis of contradiction,* are in opposition. Those who give lose some of their possessions; those who receive increase their own. This is as true, although in a different way, of an exchange of words as of goods; in a different way, we said, for in an exchange of words, it is by losing oneself that one gains oneself. Now even in this case, or rather in an exemplary way in this case, the two interlocutors occupy extreme positions on the axis of contradiction: we have seen that nothing is more different from (but also more similar to) an "I" than a "You," for the "You" is simply the reverse of the "I." Hence, Reception and Return-gift are aligned along the *axis of implication*. We know why: every acceptance of a gift as a gift necessarily obligates one to a return-gift. Starting from this process of symbolic exchange, we are going examine how Christian identity functions, starting from the Eucharistic prayer. Then we will verify our analysis by testing it against a specific theological theme, a Eucharistic one also: "sacrifice."

I. EUCHARISTIC PRAYER NUMBER 2

Our intention here is not to dwell on the directly observable elements that make up the Eucharistic prayer — dialogue, thanksgiving, Sanctus, first epiclesis, and so on — but rather to uncover the principle which transforms these elements into a Eucharist or which assures the Eucharistic nature of the whole. To do this, we propose a narrative analysis of the text.[1]

1. *Narrative Analysis*

Every text, even one whose literary genre is not narrative, has a narrative aspect. The text comes to an end, in principle, when the *narrative program* which has launched it is fulfilled (or judged to be so). It is easy to see the narrative program that sets the text of the Eucharistic prayer in motion: as the priest announces it in the imperative mood in the initial dialogue ("Let us give thanks to the Lord our God") and repeats it using an impersonal "it is" which functions as a sort of optative mood ("Truly, it is right and just for us to give thanks"), it is clearly a case of "we," the *operating subjects*, bestowing the *object*, "thanks" (or "glory"),[2] on the *receiving subject*, "God" — in this case, God the Father. One can easily verify that this program is declared accomplished in the final doxology, where "through [Christ], with him, in him," the ecclesial

1. Modeled on the same pattern as Number 2, the other Eucharistic Prayers of Vatican II would provide globally the same result.

2. In our current language, to "give thanks" and to "give glory" are practically equivalent (which was not true originally).

"we" renders to God the "almighty Father" and "in the unity of the Holy Spirit, all glory and honor . . . for ever and ever." One can represent this principal narrative program (NP) according to the following diagram, which we will continue to use:

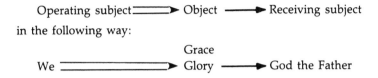

Operating subject ═══⟹ Object ──▶ Receiving subject

in the following way:

                     Grace
We ═══════════⟹ Glory ──▶ God the Father

From the narrative viewpoint, if the carrying out of such a program of thanksgiving happened by itself, there simply would be no text. The fact that there is a text signifies that at the outset we are not *competent* to carry out such an *action*. In sum, it is not natural for us to render thanks to God in a Christian manner. To carry out the Eucharist requires that the Church first gain this competence. It is precisely the text that allows the ecclesial subject *to gain* this *competence*. This text thus makes the assembly follow an itinerary which, by means of certain *"transformations,"* has for its goal the assembly's conversion: it is not God but we ourselves who are changed by the Eucharistic prayer: all the transformations are expressed as the differentiated work of the God-in-three-persons.

Between the initial dialogue which announces the principal program and the final doxology which concludes it, the narrative character is fed by three narrative programs (NP 1, NP 2, and NP 3). The first is given its character by verbs of thanksgiving and glorification: it includes the initial thanksgiving and Sanctus.[3] The second is given its character by a verb of petition addressed the Father ("Lord, you are holy indeed. . . . Let . . ."): it includes the entire sequence that depends upon this request, that is, the epiclesis over the gifts, the story of institution, and the anamnesis. The third is also given its character by another verb of petition

3. Besides, NP 1 of Eucharistic Prayer No. 4 includes after the Sanctus the entire history of salvation. Moreover, this was also the case in the early Antiochene anaphoras, such as that attributed to James of Jerusalem (see A. Tarby, *La prière eucharistique de l'Eglise de Jérusalem* [Paris: Beauchesne, 1972]) which served as a model for Eucharistic Prayer No. 4.

("May . . ."): it includes the epiclesis of communion over the assembly as well as the various petitions added to this epiclesis, the mementos of the living and the dead and the final eschatological supplication.[4]

In *NP* 1, the ecclesial "we" *gives thanks* to God for what God has accomplished through God's living "Word," God's "beloved Son, Jesus Christ." Creation is simply mentioned; and what we routinely call "salvation history" is entirely focused on Jesus in his incarnation, death, and resurrection. Whether it is strictly limited to the event Jesus Christ or even, as in some prefaces proper to a certain Sunday or feast day, to a relatively limited aspect of his mystery or whether, on the contrary, it is broadly spread out to cover various "stages" of salvation history, as in the ancient Antiochene anaphoras or in our own Eucharistic Prayer Number 4, it is always the *biblical past reread Christologically* that is recounted in this sequence. We here render thanks to God for having saved us in Jesus Christ. What NP 1 presents is what God *gives* us, Jesus Christ as an *historical* (born of the Virgin Mary and crucified) *glorious body.* Thus:

NP 1: God (the Father) ══════▶Historical-glorious body ──────▶We
                                    of Jesus Christ

In *NP* 2, the ecclesial "we" *entreats* the Father to send the Spirit of sanctification to transform the bread and wine into the *body and blood of Christ.* But fulfilling this program presupposes that Jesus delivered himself as sacramental body and blood at the Last Supper: this is shown by the story of the institution. The anamnesis, with its principal verb "we offer you" ("we thank you" is equal to "we offer you in rendering you thanks," according to the anaphora of the *Apostolic Tradition* of Hippolytus, of which our own Eucharistic prayer is simply an adaptation with the addition of an initial epiclesis and the mementos), does no more than express the effective *reception* of Jesus Christ as sacramental body and blood. We have then in this NP 2 three narrative sub-programs that may be represented in the following manner:

4. The same remarks apply to NP 2 and 3 with regard to Eucharistic Prayer Nos. 3 and 4.

(1st epiclesis): God + Spirit ⟹ Sacramental body-blood ⟶ We
        (co-subjects)

(Nar. of Inst.): Jesus ⟹ Sacramental body-blood ⟶ Disciples
(= presupposition)

(Anamnesis): We ⟹ Sacramental body-blood ⟶ God

Before the program of petition (NP 3) begins, the third of these sub-programs marks the completion of the first. This one seeks to obtain Jesus Christ, through the Spirit, under the mode of sacramental body and blood: the anamnesis declares this realized, but — an important point to which we shall return — in an act of oblation, that is, of dispossession.

The entire NP 2 may be written thus:

NP 2: God + Spirit ⟹ Sacramental body-blood ⟶ We
                of Jesus Christ

NP 3 is also one of *supplication,* but in an eschatological perspective strongly evident in its conclusion. This supplication is of its nature essentially *ecclesial:* making itself the object of its own petition, the Church begs the Father to send the Spirit over it so that it may *become what it has just received* in NP 2; and what it has received will be ritually completed in Communion. What has it just received? The sacramental body of Christ. What object does it now seek? To become the *ecclesial* body of this same Christ. NP 3, in its first sub-program (the epiclesis of communion) can be diagrammed thus:

NP 3 a: God + Spirit ⟹ Ecclesial Body ⟶ We
                of Jesus Christ

NP 3 concludes with an *eschatological* supplication (NP 3 b). The object sought here is in effect "eternal life" in company with all those who "have lived in your friendship" (Eucharistic Prayer No. 3), the saints "of all times." Thus, what is requested is participation by the ecclesia here assembled in the reign fully realized. This sub-program is consequently an expansion of the first into an eschatological perspective; it is a question of transforming oneself from now on into the ecclesial body of Christ (NP 3 a), but in the hope of what has not yet been achieved, the reign of God:

NP 3 b: God ⟹ Life eternal ────────➤ We
(= ecclesial body
even in the Kingdom)

Between these two sub-programs, the intercessions for the living and the dead add nothing essential. They only develop in a concrete manner the ecclesial and eschatological perspective of the "already-not yet" that characterizes NP 3: the intercession for the living is centered on the "already" of the Church of NP 3 a, that for the dead is oriented toward the "not yet" of the reign of NP 3 b.

The *final doxology* marks the fulfillment anticipated by the Church here and now of the announced principal narrative program, a fulfillment that will, however, be completely achieved "for ever and ever" only in the reign. We may note that the completion of this performance by "us" requires a competence which demands that God alone can be the operating subject in each of the three programs. It is God, the text tells us, who makes us able to celebrate his own glory. But he does so only if we are active, through our discourse of prayer, in expressing to him our thanksgiving and requests. And the basic Christian petition, that from which all others derive, is it not, here as in Luke 11:13, the petition for the Spirit?

2. The Symbolic Process Characteristic of the Eucharist

The process of symbolic exchange that determines the eucharistic character of our text requires, to be seen clearly, three prefatory remarks.

a) Three Keys to Reading.

— The Status of the Story of the Institution

It is certainly a case here of a *story* related in the third person. This "it" is the *deixis* ("mark") of the non-person, of absence. Clearly, the story is told in *the past*. But this story in the third person and in the past tense is framed by a discourse of prayer in "we" and "you" in the present tense. From the literary viewpoint, this abrupt change of register creates the effect of a *hiatus* that nothing justifies — unless it is something not written in the text but nevertheless constitutive of it because it is its authentic "pre-text": the ritual action. Only this, in fact, allows us to understand what seems at first sight to be literarily incoherent.

Particularly significant in this regard is the brusk transition from the "[*You*] do this in memory of me," which concludes the story and is addressed to the disciples gathered around Jesus at the Last Supper two thousand years ago, to the "*we recall*" (Eucharistic Prayer No. 4) that begins the anamnesis. Only ritual action permits us to understand this change. We seem to hear again the Jewish memorial ritual of which we spoke earlier: "*We* cried to the LORD, the God of our ancestors . . ." (Deut 26:7); "Not with our ancestors did the LORD make this covenant, but with *us*, who are all of us here alive today" (Deut 5:3). "It is because of what the LORD did for *me* when *I* came out of Egypt" (Exod 13:8). In fact, it is indeed this ritual action of living com-memoration that allows the contemporary Church to recognize itself as addressed by this "you" of the past.

Moreover, this "you," like what comes before it ("take," "eat"), is a *quotation from Jesus.* Now, every quotation acts on the two levels and the two polarities we have uncovered in every language act: one quotes a passage not only because of its intrinsic informative content, but also because of its author. In certain cases, as here, this second, symbolic, aspect takes precedence over the first and bestows on it its real importance: just as one summons a witness to appear in court,[5] one quotes someone in a text because he or she is "somebody" in society because he or she is "canonically" recognized as an "authority." However, the process is ambiguous: one may avoid compromising oneself by getting behind this "monument." And because one quotes to support one's own position, it is relatively easy to manipulate the quotation, even without changing its material content, by the mere selection of various passages. Since dead or absent persons are not there to represent themselves, it is easy to exploit them by hauling them

5. See R. Barthes, *S/Z* (Paris: Seuil, 1976) 29. The author remarks that the verb *citar* in the language of bullfighting designates "the stamp of the heel, the arched back of the torero which summon the bull to the banderillas. In the same way, one calls the signified to appear."

into court as supporting witnesses for the particular thesis one is presenting.

Now, the substitution of the "we" of the present for the "you" of the past shows that this trap set to ensure the Church's hold over Jesus through the use of such quotations has been sprung: it is the Church that sees itself *subpoenaed by Jesus to testify,* summoned by Jesus to comply. By invoking the witness of Jesus, it is the Church who is convoked by him. Far from having a grasp on him, the Church finds itself in his grasp. This wordplay, where as in the theater (or even in the "theater" of everyday life) a speech is directed to someone other than its apparent addressee, is of capital importance here: the transition, at the end of the story of the institution, from "you" to "we" is the explicit manifestation of the veiled status of this story itself. We have already said this in effect: even within the New Testament itself, this is a *liturgical* narrative where the Church confecting the Eucharist is glimpsed behind the person and actions of Jesus at the Last Supper. *This story by the Church about Jesus in the past* functions in effect as *the words of the Lord Jesus to the Church in the present.* This is why the Church, through its gestures as much as through the priest's "liturgical" tone of voice — a tone different from what would be suitable for the narration of an "interesting story" — does what the story announces; it performs it. It performs it as a story to allow it to take place as speech, simultaneously recognizing itself as caught in the net of the meanings it casts, to the point of immediately substituting the "we remember" of the anamnesis for the "(you) do this" of the quotation. The Church is thereby "acted" and "caught." This story is its recitative: it is convoked by him whose witness it invokes, and in calling to him, it spells out its own name.

As we shall see below, ritual language is of the pragmatic order. This is why the Church does not present here a simple theological discourse about its identity. Through the primordial language of symbol, the Church *lives its identity by manifesting it.* What else does it do in this story of the institution but submit itself to the lordship (that it symbolically proclaims) of this Jesus of Nazareth, to whom it refers itself in a language that effects what it says? What else, but clearly express through an act that it can be the Church only *by receiving itself from him,* its Lord, *in a radical depen-*

dence (which is, moreover, the condition of its liberty)? Because it is a symbol, the story of the institution of the Eucharist is also the story of the institution of the Church: the story introduces the Church "into the order to which the symbol itself belongs," that is, into the order of this Christological dependence that constitutes the Church's identity.

— *The Anamnesis Discourse and the Offering*

The prayer of anamnesis renders explicit what is at stake in the story of institution we have just set forth. What is at stake? The fact, as we have just noticed, that the story effects the acted out confession of faith of the Church recognizing that its existence is dependent on Jesus, its Lord. Now, this is exactly what the anamnesis unfolds in its principal verb, "we offer you." This is an important point: at the very moment when, according to our narrative analysis, the Church is in the process of *receiving* the bread and wine as the sacramental body and blood of its Lord — behold, it *offers them* . . .

Moreover, this paradox has a long tradition. The oblation of the anamnesis, probably without being primitive (see *Did.* 9–10; the third-century anaphora of Addai and Mari), is clearly expressed in the anaphora of Hippolytus, and later on in the most important anaphoras of the fourth and fifth centuries. Set in motion by the participial phrase "calling to mind . . . ," the anamnesis continues with a principal clause in the present tense: "we offer you" (*prospheromen, offerimus,* Roman canon, James in Syriac and James in Greek, *Const. Ap.* VIII, Serapion). Unless, as in the anaphoras of Basil and Chrysostom where the principal clause contains verbs expressing praise and thanksgiving, the offering is the object of a second participial phrase; but here it is no less prominent, developed as it is into the powerful formula *ta sa ek ton son prospherontes (tua ex tuis tibi offerentes,* "offering to you your own gifts from what is yours").[6] This last formula shows clearly that through its

6. The Greek and Latin texts of these anaphoras are in A. Hanggi and I. Pahl, *Prex eucharistica* (Fribourg, Switzerland: Ed. Universitaires, 1968): James in Greek, pp. 248–249; James in Syriac, p. 271; Basil, pp. 236–237; Chrysostom, pp. 226–227. K. Stevenson, "L'offrande eucharistique," LMD 154 (1983) 81–106. The author indicates several exceptions. The Alexandrian tradition, especially, often employs in the anamnesis the verb "offer" in the perfect tense: "we have offered" (anaphora of Serapion, *Prex eucharistica,* 130–131); "we have

offering in the anamnesis, the Church confesses its radical dependence on God as Creator (the bread and wine are the firstfruits of
creation, which they represent metonymically) and as Savior in
Christ (this bread and this wine are offered as "sacraments" of
the body and blood of Christ).

The anamnesis is thus the fundamental place of the Church's offering.
The anamnesis unfolds, as we have seen, the status of the story of
the institution — a story of which the Church is, literarily, a development. It expresses the Church's reception — in the present
and as a present — of Christ as sacramental body. We have here a
paradox: this *reception* is effected by means of *oblation*. As in Deuteronomy 26:1-11, *the Christian mode of appropriation is through disappropriation:* the mode of "taking" is by "giving" — "giving
thanks." Because grace is outside the order of value, it is in rendering to God God's own grace, Christ Jesus given in sacrament,
that the Church receives it. This point is important: considered in
the sole context of the anamnesis, the gift of God, received by the
Church in the verbal-ritual memorial that it makes of it, requires
the return-gift of an offering in thanksgiving; however, considered
within the whole of the Eucharistic prayer, this same gift implies a
return-gift other than this ritual oblation in the anamnesis. This
return-gift will be expressed in NP 3 as that of practical ethics.
Within the whole of the process of exchange that the entire Eucharistic prayer sets in motion, the anamnestic oblation does not
occupy the position of return-gift, but that of reception. We have
just given the reason for this: the appropriation of this non-object
that is "grace" can occur only under the mode of disappropriation.
In other words, the process of symbolic exchange with God cannot stop with this cultic offering, as if liturgical practice could render us free and clear in God's eyes. The cultic offering is only the
symbolic representation of a return-gift yet to be "veri-fied" elsewhere: in
the here and now.

---

presented" (anaphora of Mark and anaphora of Basil, Primate of Alexandria).
This is an indication of their antiquity, according to Stevenson ("Offrande,"
88), and shows the power of the tradition of offering at this point in the
anamnesis. See also the synoptic table of several early anamneses and
epicleses in L.-M. Chauvet, "Histoire de la liturgie eucharistique," *Agape:
l'eucharistie, de Jésus aux chrétiens d'aujourd'hui* (Paris: Droguet-Ardant, 1981)
346-351.

— The Return-Gift of Ethical Practice (NP 3)

This return-gift to be "veri-fied" elsewhere than in the ritual is precisely the object of NP 3 which only develops what is already implied in the ritual oblation of NP 2. For the "we offer you" of the anamnesis is not a simple declarative or informative sentence, but a language act that is self-implicative. Because of this, rendering to God what God gives us is to dispossess ourselves not only of something but of our very selves. In other words, the "objective" offering of Christ by the Church puts the Church into an attitude of *subjective* offering. Such is, according to the celebrated formula of Augustine, what is expressed "in the sacrament of the altar, well known to the faithful, where it made clear to the Church that *itself is offered* in what it offers" (*City of God*, 10:6). This again is a symbol in the strongest sense of the term: "This sacrifice is the symbol of what we are" (Sermon 227).

This is just what NP 3 carries out, where the assembly petitions God, through the Spirit, to become in its present historical existence and forever the body of him whom it receives in the sacrament. Receiving, by offering it, the sacramental body of Christ (NP 2), it begs to *become his ecclesial body*. This gathering into a single body through the Spirit — the operative agent of unity in the Church, according to tradition and in the spirit of 1 Corinthians 12 — has an immediate *ethical* implication. For, to become historically and eschatologically the body of him whom they are offering sacramentally, the members of the assembly are committed to live out their own oblation of themselves in self-giving to others as Christ did, a self-giving called *agape between brothers and sisters*. Scholastic theology emphasized this with force: if the "first effect" (*res et sacramentum*) of the Eucharist is the body and blood of Christ, its "ultimate effect" (*res tantum*), that is to say, the grace that it intends for its participants, is the theological charity that is lived out in charity between brothers and sisters. Thus, the *sacramental rendering-thanks* seeks to be enfleshed in the *living-in-grace* among brothers and sisters.

This ethical dimension is not simply an extrinsic consequence of the Eucharistic process; it belongs to it as an *intrinsic* element. As our study of the cultic vocabulary of the New Testament shows, it is also the fundamental location of the Christian liturgy: it is precisely ethics that must become authentically "Eucharistic." Grace is always bestowed as a task; and the sacramental body, as an injunction to give to the Risen One this body made of the world that he requires of us. We here verify concretely what we said before: *it belongs to grace, in its very graciousness, to integrate into itself the free human response.*

b) How the Structure Functions. Taking account of the results of our narrative analysis and the keys to reading we have provided, we may represent the Eucharistic process by the following diagram:

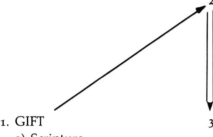

2. RECEPTION
a) Sacrament
b) Sacramental body of Christ
c) Reception under the mode
of oblation or thanksgiving
d) Present

1. GIFT
a) Scripture
b) Historical and glorious
body of Christ
c) Gift from God:
giving grace
d) Past

3. RETURN-GIFT
a) Ethics (agape)
b) Ecclesial body of Christ
• already now
• in the Kingdom
c) Return-gift of living-in-
grace between brothers and
sisters
d) Eschatological future
• already
• not yet

— *The Eucharistic Process*

The diagram can be understood in the following manner. The position of "gift" is specified as "*Scripture.*" This corresponds, in effect, to an NP that is none other than a Christian reading of the Bible — focused strictly on Jesus Christ in Eucharistic Prayer Number 2, more varied in other Eucharistic prayers which recall momentous events of salvation history. This is the gift of God, the "founding event" which launches the Church's Eucharist: the "*grace-bestowing of God,*" who "spoke to our ancestors in many and various ways by the prophets, but in these last days . . . has spoken to us by a Son," Jesus Christ (Heb 1:1-2), "born of a woman, born under the law" (Gal 4:4), who died and was raised up. This gift, where God extends God's grace, is thus finally expressed, in the Christian reading, in the *historical and henceforth glorious body of Christ.* This gift is recounted as something irreversibly *past.* It is not primarily for our own history that we are giving thanks, but for a history that is radically other and past; but in relating this during the ritual anamnesis, we show that we recognize this apparently other history to be our very *own.*

The position of *reception* is specified as *"Sacrament."* The fact that, according to the structure of the diagram, this position is contradictory to the preceding position corresponds, on the one hand, to the general economy of every symbolic exchange where, even at the level of a communicatory language act, sender and receiver are in the most radical linguistic difference (see above) and, on the other, within this general economy, to the *denial* of the simple "pastness" of what is being recounted in NP 1 as irreversibly past. The text affirms that the same Jesus Christ, formerly given by God as an historical body raised up from the dead, is *today* received by us as *a sacramental body,* God's present. Like the manna in the desert, we do not receive the grace of God like a graspable "object"; only those receive it who open their hands anew each day. This is why *oblation* is constitutive of reception. Just as Israel receives its land only when it offers it back through the firstfruits which symbolize it (for this land is not simply a thing, but is marked by the sign of the word that gives it), so too Christians do not appropriate God's gift except in dispossessing themselves of it through the oblation of giving thanks.

The position of *return-gift* is specified as *"Ethics."* This position is necessarily implied by the position of reception. This ethics is that of the "though many we are one body in Christ" (*multi unum corpus in Christo,* Augustine) symbolized by the reception of the one bread shared among all as the Eucharistic body of Christ. It consists essentially in the agape between brothers and sisters. But because it is rooted, through the Spirit, in the sacrament, it has a *theological* dimension that specifies it as distinctly Christian. According to the Johannine *kathos* ("as"), mentioned in the previous

ɪr to Matthew 25, it is thus the very agape of God in
ɪt is at work eschatologically in this agape between
ɪnd sisters. Thus, the sacramental reception of the free
ɡ·--- ɪtowing" of God in the symbolic "giving thanks" of the
oblation needs to be verified in a *living-in-grace* among brothers
and sisters. The moment of "Sacrament" then appears as the
symbolic expression that shows simultaneously what makes practical ethics into a "liturgy" or the "Eucharistic sacrifice" which
God (as revealer) asks of us and which God (as operator) makes
possible. Moreover, that this ethics of justice and mercy is the
return-gift where the truth of the "sacrament" is carried through
conforms to a long and solid patristic tradition: according to this
tradition, the Church is the *corpus verum* ("real body") of Christ
insofar as it is the *veritas* ("true reality") of his *corpus mysticum*
(that is to say, of his "body in mystery," his sacramental body, as
it was understood until the middle of the twelfth century). Unfortunately, this *veritas* was forgotten in subsequent centuries; we
shall come back to it. This "becoming the ecclesial body" in the
"already now" also has an aspect of the "not yet." Thus, if on
the one hand our NP 3 stresses the ethical return-gift, it simultaneously indicates that the reign to come is never the result of human
effort or at the end of humanity's process.

— *The Process of Christian Identity*

*All of this process of "becoming eucharist" expresses all of the process
of Christian identity.* Again, this does not mean that access to faith
always comes about according to a *chronological* progression which
begins with the Scriptures, passes through the Sacraments, and
culminates in Ethics. It means that this access always requires a
structural relation between these three elements, a relation that
functions according to the *process* indicated. (1) Whatever its concrete modalities may be, coming to faith is always founded
primarily on an affirmation that, "in fulfillment of the Scriptures,"
Jesus is the Christ freely offered by God for the salvation of all. (2)
Of course, the reception or the welcome accorded to this affirmation depends on the personal faith of the subject. But this faith is
never simply a human achievement: it itself is a gift from God.
Besides, it cannot be reduced to a simple change in anyone's subjective, individual opinion since it is the personal acceptance of

the universal and apostolic faith of the Church. It is this double dimension, of free gift and of belonging to the Church, that the *sacrament* manifests — beginning with baptism. (3) Finally, without the return-gift of an *ethical* practice by which the subject "verifies" what it has received in the sacrament, Christian identity would be stillborn. Moreover, ethics draws its Christian aspect from its quality of a "liturgical" response (see the "liturgy of the neighbor") to the initial gift of God. Consequently, just as the liturgy itself must become the object of an ethical reinterpretation to become fully Christian (see ch. 6), so also, and conversely, an ethics which is not reinterpreted liturgically, that is to say, as a theological response to the initial grace from God — as generous as it might be — would lose its Christian identity (1 Cor 13:1-3).

3. Function of the Element "Sacrament": A Point of Passage

The process of becoming eucharist is thus only a particular modality of the process of Christian identity. One easily discerns here the function of the moment "Sacrament." We shall express this in two propositions: the sacrament is only a point of passage, but it is fully that.

As *only* a point of passage, the sacrament has neither its origin nor its end within itself; it is neither the point of departure nor the point of arrival. The point of *departure* is the gift from God. Faith itself, which is never simply a logical result of our own intellectual or moral efforts, is a gift — a gift which is no doubt offered to those who desire and search for it and which, once received, opens up a new field of investigation undreamt of at the outset: "You would not seek me if you had not already found me" (Augustine). The point of *arrival* is the "missionary liturgy" of ethical practice where the reception of the gift of God is verified. Moreover, our very word "Mass" preserves traces of this missionary and ethical perspective. "Today there is no longer any doubt concerning the basic meaning of this word: *missa = missio = dimissio.*" Now, *dimissio* is a technical Roman term that denotes the breaking up of an official meeting.[7] Thus, "it was possible to name the worship by what brings it to a conclusion, by what has to happen when it is finished: implicitly one understands the en-

7. J. A. Jungmann, *Missarum solemnia*, 1:218.

tire worship, therefore, as a prelude to a missionary sendoff"; the worship charges those who have celebrated it "to do and be what they have been instructed to do and be."[8] Lacking this obligatory return-gift, the circuit of exchange would have been broken: one would not have received the gift as a gift; one would simply have acquired certain new (perhaps quite elevated) ideas about God or enhanced one's religious cultural baggage.

The fact that the moment "Sacrament" is only a point of *passage* shows that one cannot conceive of this covenantal exchange with God as paying off a debt toward God through performing certain ritual acts. Moreover, this debt, a debt of existence, is not something that we can *pay off:* we are insolvent and if we insist on thinking in these categories, we delude ourselves with imaginary notions, as we will see. This debt is not to be paid off, but *to be assumed symbolically in our ethical relations with others here and now.* The "giving thanks" of the ritual offering — our moment "Sacrament" — is precisely only a symbol which allows us to see and to live this covenantal ethics with others as the concrete mediation of God's covenant with us. The latter is veri-fied in our practice of the "living-in-grace" among brothers and sisters in which we become toward others as (according to what we say about God throughout the Eucharist) God is toward us.

This last point shows that although the sacrament is only a point of passage, it is an *obligatory* point of passage. Perhaps we must remind ourselves that such an obligation is not to be understood from a perspective of salvation, but from one of *identity.* And we must remind ourselves that even from this second perspective, this obligation does not imply that every believing subject has in fact received the sacraments but that his or her Christian identity, because it is made possible only within the Church, has at least an implicit reference to baptism and the Eucharist. Inasmuch as they are *structural elements of Christian identity,* the sacraments are not optional affairs.

4. *Judaism and Christianity*
One may wonder whether the process delineated above is in-

---

8. J. J. Von Allmen, "Célébrer le salut," *Essai sur le repas du Seigneur* (Neuchâtel: Delachaux-Niestlé, 1966) 55.

deed distinctive of Christianity. One could easily have the impression that, obviously apart from references to Jesus, it could be applied equally well to *Jewish identity*. This is what we are going to verify. This will lead us at the same time to take into account our previous distinction between "oldness" and "newness" in order to uncover the Christian difference.

  a) Jewish Identity: The Story of the Offering of Firstfruits (Deut 26:1-11). If we return to the story of the offering of the firstfruits (Deut 26:1-11), it is easy to show that we are dealing here with the *same kind of interaction* between Scripture, Sacrament, and Ethics as we uncovered with regard to the Eucharistic Prayer. However, here the text is more complex than in the Prayer. Each of the five sections discerned in the preceding chapter (I.2.b) functions according to the process of symbolic exchange in the following manner (translation based on the French text):

A — • Gift from God: "the land which Yahweh your God *gives* you."
  • Reception by Israel: "when you shall have arrived" (lit., "when you will *come*") . . . "and you will have taken possession . . ."
  • Return-gift by Israel: "you will set apart the fruit of the soil . . ." (lit., "you will take the firstfruits that you will have *made come* from the earth").

B — • Gift from God: "this land that Yahweh swore to our ancestors to *give* us."
  • Reception by Israel = its word of recognition: "I declare today that I have arrived . . ." (lit., "that I *have come* . . .").
  • Return-gift by Israel: the transmission of the basket to the priest and its placement before the altar.

C — • Gift by Israel: "we have cried to Yahweh, the God of our ancestors."
  • Reception by God: "he has seen our misery."
  • Return-Gift by God = the departure from Egypt and the gift of the land: "Yahweh *made us come* into this place and *gave* us this land."

B' — • Gift by God: the land "which you *have given* me, Yahweh."
  • Reception by Israel = the word that recognizes this gift: "and now, behold I bring you (lit., "behold that I have *made come* forth") the firstfruits of the harvest that you *have given* me, Yahweh."
  • Return-Gift by Israel: setting down the firstfruits and prostration before Yahweh.

A' — • Gift by God: "all the happiness that Yahweh your God *has given* you."

- Reception by Israel: not shown as such in the text, but presupposed by the previous sections and by its implication, the return-gift.
- Return-Gift by Israel: "you will be joyous with the levite and the alien who are among you."

Two verbs appear in each of these five sections: "to give" and "to come." Now, it is noteworthy that each is located in a particular position in section C: there, the operating subject of the verb "to cause to come" is God, while it is Israel in all the other sections; and if "to give" always has God as its subject, in C this gift is located in the position of the return-gift, while it occupies the position of initial gift in the other four sections. Section C has thus a particular place within the text: if Israel can "make to come [forth]" the fruits of the earth and if it must "make them to come" to the Temple as the offering of firstfruits, it is because Yahweh has first "made *it* to come" into this land (C); and if, in C, God "gives" the land in response to the cry of the oppressed people, this same gift can be found in other sections in the initial position. That means that *section C*, which contains the memorial, although at the center of the text from a literary viewpoint, *in fact acts as the true point of departure for the entire narrative.* Arranged around the liberating deed of Yahweh and the gift of the land, the founding events related in the memorial are the true catalyst for the story. That, in fact, is what the beginning of the text (section A) shows, where Yahweh's gift of the land puts in motion all that follows, that is, all that God prescribes for Israel to do as a response to God's gift.

This premier gift of God is received by Israel in the liturgical act of the narrative recited as a memorial. The *reception* is thus represented in our text by the quotation marks themselves which follow the "you will say," that is, by the liturgy which is initiated by these words and is, as we have said, the authentic "pre-text" of our text. Now, this liturgy unfolds in the two ritual sequences (B-B') which surround the memorial-story. The ritual word, in the first person and in the present, is perfectly explicit: "I declare today that I have come into the country . . ." (B), and "And now, behold I bring you . . ." (B') are the formal acknowledgment of the present reception of the land. *The ritual thus brings about in the present what the memorial proclaims to have happened in the past:* it is indeed to "us" — "all of us here alive today" (Deut 5:3) — that the land was given. By using the same verbs "give" and "come," the Deuteronomic redactors wish to show that "the liturgical process renders each Israelite contemporary with the divine history of the past since Yahweh gives fertility today just as he formerly gave the land itself. . . . To come into the sanctuary carrying firstfruits is to identify with the entrance of the people into the land of Canaan in the past."[9]

The gift of the land by God to the "we" of the people and in the past tense (C), received in "I" and in the present tense by Israel in a liturgical act of words (B-B'), enjoins a response on the part of Israel. This command is expressed in "you" and in the future tense. It involves all the prescriptions A-A', that is, the very history of Israel once it has "come into" the land: to "make to come" its fruits from that soil, to come to the Temple and to bring these fruits to offer there, and finally to share its prosperity with the levite and the alien in the land. The *return-gift* is thus *obedience* to the word of God which, through Moses, has the force of law. This law shows that the object of the gift is not simply a piece of earth, but a land as the *object of a promise*, as bearing the stamp of the Word: a land marked by the Other. God does not give simply soil to cultivate, but rather a nation to construct, a neighborhood to build, where concern for the Other lived out in concern for others and, more specifically, for the destitute must have a major place. Thus is initiated in this text the unfolding of the letter into prefiguration, of which we spoke before: according to Christian hermeneutics, the promised inheritance will be Christ and, in him, a new covenantal relation among peoples rendered eschatologically possible by the agape poured out in their hearts by the Holy Spirit (Rom 5:5). In any case, it is already this concern *to be toward others as God has been toward it* that constitutes the beginning of the return-gift required of Israel in our text (section A').

In this story, at the distinct levels of discourse interconnected in complex ways, the register of the prescription, like a double exposure, serves to intensify the play of internal symbolic exchange; this whole process can be expressed thus:

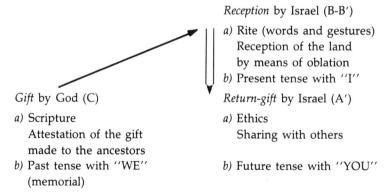

Reception by Israel (B-B')

a) Rite (words and gestures)
   Reception of the land
   by means of oblation
b) Present tense with "I"

Gift by God (C)

a) Scripture
   Attestation of the gift
   made to the ancestors
b) Past tense with "WE"
   (memorial)

Return-gift by Israel (A')

a) Ethics
   Sharing with others

b) Future tense with "YOU"

9. F. Dumortier, "Le Dieu de l'histoire devenu le Dieu de la nature: Dt 26, 4-10," *Assemblées du Seigneur* 14 (Paris: Cerf, 1973) 24-25.

The process by which Israel identifies itself as the Israel of Yahweh is patterned in a way *identical* to that which characterizes Christians. The confession of faith-memorial which relates the founding events as acts of the saving Yahweh is, we have shown, a kind of summary of the Scriptures: these are only the development, written large, of the former. The role of this confession of faith in the text is analogous to that of "salvation history" related as the *gift* of God in NP 1 of Eucharistic Prayer Number 2. As for the *reception*, it also is effected under the mode of oblation: the land is received as a gift of grace only through the offering of thanks. The "sacrificial" disappropriation is, for Israel as for the Church, the condition for the appropriation of God's gift. This ritual offering, where Israel shows its recognition of God as God and its gratitude to God, is itself only a point of passage, the symbolic representation of a *living-in-grace* where the liturgical giving-thanks must be veri-fied. Far from constituting the final return-gift that would pay off its debt to God, the ritual commissions Israel to take charge of history. Far from discharging Israel from its responsibility in history and placing that responsibility on a God who would serve as a heavenly alibi, it directs Israel toward the "liturgy of the neighbor," beginning with the "poor." It is through the exercise of sharing with others in real life that Israel's ritual sacrifice arrives at its truth and Israel as such at its identity. As should be clear, Deuteronomy 26:1-11 is a text replete with Eucharistic meaning.

b) The Christian Difference: "Oldness" and "Newness." In view of all this, where is the *Christian difference?* It does not appear in the process of symbolic exchange, which functions in both cases according to the same fundamental mechanism. The difference (which, as we know, is eschatological), does appear in our *diagram of oldness and newness* from the preceding chapter. In that chapter, we specified without further comment that "oldness" and "newness" are not to be purely and simply identified with the Old and New Testaments. For newness already cut across the Old Testament: let us recall especially the prophets, the summary of the Law that the scribe gives Jesus, the followers of the Baptist, many Pharisaic rabbis, Philo, and so on. Moreover, according to the Church, is it not Christ himself who spoke through the Scriptures, and did not the Spirit "speak through the prophets"? Thus, our term *"oldness" does not designate the Old Testament as such, but what led this Testament to become "old" by condemning the newness in Jesus Christ.* This term refers to whatever led to the smothering of the newness, which ran across it and worked through it. Even though, as we will explain later, the Old Testament was a progressive exodus from the "sacrificial," that is, from the realm of "works" as means of salvation, it became imprisoned within the "sacrificial." Who did this? No one in particular and no one deliberately . . . No official decision by someone in power, royal or priestly, could have provoked such a deviation. It comes from much farther back: it is not in the power of any one person because it is *the work, unacknowledged, of all,* as the death of Jesus allows us to understand if we indeed accept to understand his death as "for all" and read it as a suit between God and human-kind without searching for scapegoats (the Jews or their leaders) who would exonerate the rest of us or who — the same device, but more subtle — would make us guilty only in the "interior" order. To say it another way: oldness represents the Law, not as letter (we realize that the Spirit is not found without the letter), but as imprisoned in the letter even while the prophetic current (and not only the prophetic current) had endlessly called for the (re)vivification of this letter and had finally heralded a new era where the law would be written on the human heart by the Spirit of God.

Conversely, *"newness" is not the Church as such, but Jesus Christ.* He alone has fulfilled all newness. The Church is always in danger of reducing the gospel to the oldness of a document in which the Spirit would be extinguished, of a ritual which would again become a "good deed" and a "means of salvation," of a corps of ministers who would be priestly intermediaries between humans and God. This is to say that the law of the Spirit places on the Church the labor of an unceasing "pass-over" from the oldness that threatens it to the newness it proclaims accomplished in Christ. It must carry out this genesis for itself by turning to the One it confesses to be the New Human Being. It also has the simultaneous mission of making this genesis happen in humanity.

Thus, the transition from oldness to newness does not coincide with the historical succession of the time of Israel and the time of the Church. It is first of all on the *paradigmatic,* not the chronological, plane that one must consider the relationship of the two testaments: the first, inasmuch as it finally smothered the newness of the Spirit whose bearer it was, is the exemplary figure of what oldness produces; the second, insofar as it proclaims the fulfillment of this newness in Christ, is the exemplary figure of what will be, according to God's promise, the new humanity already in the process of arising. Now, the hinge that both links and distinguishes one from the other in our biblical canon represents, *from the viewpoint of the Bible itself*, the task enjoined on *all humanity* taken collectively, as on each one taken personally.

According to the Bible, what is at work for Israel is representative of what must be at work for all the nations: the blessing of Abraham is concluded with the blessing of the nations ("in you the families of the earth shall be blessed") according to the promise of Genesis 12:3, repeated in Genesis 18:18 and 22:18, renewed to Isaac (26:4), then to Jacob (28:14), and declared accomplished in Galatians 3:8 and Acts 3:25. This refrain from the Yahwist source is formulated differently in the Priestly tradition, but its harmonics are equally universal: the blessing of humankind, created "male and female" in the image of God in Genesis 1:27-28, is repeated to Noah and his sons (9:1-7) and is accompanied by a covenant with all of humanity through Noah (9:9-17). Still, it is always through Abraham's descendants that this divine blessing reaches the peoples. The Psalms insist on this: what happens to Israel is to be preached to the most distant nations: "Say among the nations, 'the Lord is King!'" (Ps 96:10). The nations themselves recognize the Lord and praise God because of what God accomplishes for Israel: "Praise the Lord, all you nations! . . . For great is his steadfast love toward us . . ." (Ps 117). So that, if "yes, it is in Philistia, in Tyre, or in Nubia that a person was born," then one can say of Zion, "in her, every person is born" (see Ps 87:4-5). In any event, this is the way in which, from the biblical viewpoint, humanity's process of becoming is enacted in that of the chosen people.

Election is a particular choice, but it is not the exclusion of others. It is simply the condition of every love, for there is no love without a choice. Those who under the pretense of loving everybody pretend not to love any one person in a special way can love no one; they can only close themselves in narcissism. The lover who elects one particular person for accompaniment through life does not harden the lover's heart with regard to others; the love of the chosen, well lived out psychologically, liberates the lover for an agape much richer in both depth and extension. Such is the *"difference"* in the symbolic order, as we have emphasized: it is not exclusion or competitive rivalry (compare the Oedipus conflict); it is the mediation of communication and of covenant (compare the symbolic emergence of the "other which is similar" in the language act in I-YOU). In the symbolic order, there is no universality except in the concrete mediation of the particular.

In an exemplary way through its letter, the Bible tells us, especially in the pattern it assumes through its symbolic division into "Old" and "New," that *every person* finds him or herself in the situation of the "old human being" and every person is in the process of becoming the "new human being." Not only every person, but *humanity* as such. According to biblical revelation, humanity can come to its truth only by dying to the oldness that dwells in it — the violence that it imposes on others and that finds its fundamental alibi in "God" — and by bringing about an "Easter" conversion from the sacrificial to what we will call the "anti-sacrificial." *The Church,* "sacrament of the coming reign," is specifically charged with *producing in the world and for the world the pattern of this passage* to which we are collectively and personally called. But it can produce this pattern only on the condition of *ceaselessly conforming itself to it.*

Thus, to return to the problem that led us to develop this reflection, the Christian difference does not appear in our process of identity because the elements which constitute its mechanism do not show the Christological and pneumatic *eschatology* as such. But it is precisely eschatology that, within this same process of identification, constitutes Christian uniqueness. To see this Christian uniqueness in our diagram of the process of identity, we must remind ourselves that the "object" placed into circulation in the exchange is *Christ* himself and that he comes to us in his threefold body, through the Spirit: he is the gratuitous gift announced in the Scriptures, the inheritance promised (see Rom 3–8); he is the object sacramentally received in the Church's "giving thanks," the entire liturgy of Christians; he is the object entrusted to the ethical responsibility of believers — by the "spiritual sacrifice" of their agape, he raises up a body for himself within humanity. This "object" does not change the structure of the game itself. But, and this is what our diagram "oldness-newness" shows, it demands *another reading* of this structure; and this changes everything . . .

II. TESTING OF THIS HYPOTHESIS:
THE ANTI-SACRIFICIAL STATUS
OF SYMBOLIC EXCHANGE IN CHRISTIANITY

The reflection we propose here aims at testing, by investigating a particular theme, the soundness of the process of Christian identity delineated earlier. There are two reasons for choosing the theme of sacrifice: On the one hand, this theme is explicit in the Eucharistic Prayer we have analyzed and we thus assure the unity of this chapter. On the other, we think it uses an important anthropological and religious pattern, equal only to the initiatory pattern.

"Sacrifice" is a term that has a bad reputation in many Christian circles. Among the terms belonging to traditional Catholic vocabulary, it is without doubt one of the most *suspect* today. All by itself it calls up symbolically an entire "world," a world of a past not all that remote when, through the medium of the catechism and the Christian model proposed there, it functioned as the cardinal notion of the Church-as-institution (and also, in parallel fashion, of society). One has only to glance at the old *Baltimore Catechism* to get a sense of its importance: the variety of linguistic symbolisms in New Testament soteriology has been reduced to the single theme of sacrificial expiation; as a consequence, the Mass (a propitiatory sacrifice), the presbyterial ministry (sacrificial priesthood), and the ideal of Christian life (sufferings offered in sacrifice with Jesus in reparation for the sins of humankind) are presented almost exclusively according to this one model.[10]

---

10. *Catéchisme à l'usage des diocèses de France* (Tours: Mame, 1947) par. 96: "Yes, Jesus Christ has truly ransomed all humankind because by his life, suffering, and death he has merited for them forgiveness of their sins and the graces necessary to gain heaven." A note adds, "Jesus Christ could suffer because he was a human being, but his suffering and death have an infinite price because he was God." After having emphasized in par. 97 that "to ransom us, Jesus Christ suffered a cruel agony," a note adds, "But the greatest suffering of Jesus Christ during his passion was to feel himself crushed by the great number and horror of our sins and by human ingratitude." We had lost sight of the feudal context of German law where Anselm's theory of "satisfaction" was born, a context within which this theory is understood in a much more sophisticated way, as W. Kasper has shown in *Jésus le Christ* (Paris: Cerf, 1976) 332–333.

If it is appropriate to criticize this model of Christianity, we must be on guard against judging it according to a more recent cultural sensibility — it is a golden rule in history to never judge the past by the cultural values of the present — and against too hastily denigrating what we have only recently — and perhaps equally uncritically — eulogized. The temptation is the more dangerous for many Christians in that they have accounts to settle with their past. Let us then try to see the matter clearly guided by our own way of approaching the problem.

1. *The Basic Principle:* In Sacramento, *the Sacramental "Representation"*
One fundamental sacramental principle must be set out from the start: *if the death of Jesus is expressed theologically in terms of sacrifice, its sacramental representation as a memorial will also necessarily be expressed in terms of sacrifice.* Sacrifice-in-memorial, sacrifice-in-sacrament: the hyphens we place here suggest that Christ-giving-his-life "sacrificially" comes to us only in the sacramental memorial that the Church makes of him. According to Augustine's formula, Christ, who was offered (sacrificed) once for all, is offered "everyday in sacrament" (*quotidie in sacramento*). This expression should not be translated "in *the* sacrament," in which case one might think that the truth of the offering might be found "inside" the *sacramentum*, as the pit is found inside the flesh of a peach, or that it might be found "behind" the sacrament, as if concealed by a veil; rather, it should be translated "in sacrament" or "sacramentally." What is at work here is a modality *de re* analogous to what Augustine says about the annual Christian Easter or about the Eucharistic body of the Lord: Christ was raised long ago. Why, then, does no one accuse us of being liars during each Easter solemnity when we affirm, "Today Christ is risen"? Because what happened long ago happens to us each year (and even each Sunday) "through the celebration of the sacrament" (*per celebrationem sacramenti*).[11]

Unfortunately we have lost sight of the force of this symbolic language that allowed Augustine to say: "Because you are the body of Christ and his members, it is your own mystery that lies on the altar, it is your own mystery that you receive. . . . Be what you see, and receive what you

---

11. Augustine, *Ep.* 98, 9, to Boniface (*PL* 33:363)

are." We have already quoted this and other similar passages, such as "This [Eucharistic] sacrifice is the symbol of what we are."[12] In this symbolic language Augustine in no way confuses Christ and the Church — one symbolizes only elements that are distinct — but he shows what is at stake in the *sacramentum:* the indissoluble marriage of Christ and the Church, the impossibility of saying the one, as a simple object ("something facing"), without also saying the other. The *sacramentum* illustrates precisely the *symbolic conjunction* of the two. The Augustinian language here is thus not a simple wordplay which by its ornamentation would aid in entering spiritually the depths of the mystery or add a touch of festivity to austere theological discourse. This language reaches to the very essence of language, its po(i)etic essence. If there is wordplay, and there always is, it is because language is itself essentially play. In this perspective, such language is *theologically rigorous* in that it is the most appropriate to the mystery it is trying to convey. Christ in "sacrifice" comes to us only through the expressive mediation of the *sacramentum.* To attempt to look for him "behind" is, as we have said, to attempt to discover the onion by peeling it.

Now, this symbolic language was to appear later on as insufficiently "realistic." The decisive moment in this evolution came, as is well known, in the middle of the eleventh century with the denial of the Eucharistic presence by Berengar of Tours — a denial perhaps less radical than it first seems if one understands it, as one should, as a reaction against the Eucharistic ultra-realism that was almost universal at the time. In effect, the "flesh of Christ" (*caro Christi*) was seen as adhering so closely to the *species* (of bread and wine) that the true miracle was how God maintained a visible "veil" (*tegumentum*) to keep the true body of Christ hidden. Such a representation was understandably favorable to a veritable flowering of Eucharistic miracles.[13] The soil had been long prepared for such a blossoming, notably due to the success of the sacramental theory of Isidore of Seville. The identification of "sacrament" (*sacramentum*) with "sacred secret" (*sacrum secretum*)[14] led to an understanding of the sacrament as a "veil" (*tegumentum*) which hides a secret reality — the reverse of Augustine's view (*sacrum signum,* "revealing sign"). The first great Eucharistic controversy, which was between Paschasius Radbertus and Ratramnus in the ninth century, was fed by the

---

12. Augustine, Sermon 272 (*PL* 38:1246–1248); Sermon 227 (*PL* 38:1099–1101).

13. E. Dumoutet, *Corpus Domini: Aux sources de la piété eucharistique mediévale* (Paris: Beauchesne, 1942) pt. 3. See our reflection on the Eucharistic presence of Christ in ch. 10.

14. See. ch. 1., n. 4.

same theory of *tegumentum*;[15] but the theory was developed in various directions around the central distinction between *figura* ("figure") and *veritas* ("truth"). Paschasius, starting straight from faith, said that the words of Jesus according to John 6, "I am the bread of life . . ." could be only a *veritas*; Ratramnus, starting from our mode of cognition, saw in these same words only a *figura*, for a figure is a veiled way of designating a reality, while the *veritas* designates a reality in an unveiled way.[16] The Eucharistic *tegumentum* thus obliged Ratramnus to emphasize the function of *figura*. Moreover, he did not deny the Eucharistic presence: Christ is "really" (*vere*) present there, but *in figura*, not *in veritate*. Ratramnus was still unaware of any opposition between "figure" and "truth"; however, the current was already running in such a direction. As an indication, King Charles the Bald asked Ratramnus to answer his question: Is Christ present in the Eucharist *in mysterio an in veritate* ("in mystery or in truth")?[17]

Such an alternative could be stated only through dialectics, of which Berengar was one of the great practitioners.[18] Now, as Father de Lubac has shown, in the hands of this dialectician the sacramental symbolism of the Church Fathers disintegrates. For Berengar there can be no middle ground between figure and reality. The "really in figure" of Ratramnus has become for him unacceptable. In his eyes "mystery" and "reason" are opposed. Where Augustine could say "the more mystery, the more

15. Ratramnus: "Corpus et sanguis Domini propterea mysteria dicuntur, quod *secretam* et reconditam habent dispositionem, id est aliud sint quod exterius innuant, et aliud quod interius invisibiliter operantur. Hinc etiam et *sacramenta* vocitantur, quia *tegumento* corporalium rerum virtus divina *secretius* salutem accipientium fideliter dispensat" ("The body and blood of the Lord are called mysteries because they have a *secret* and hidden ordering: what they show externally is one thing and what they effect internally is another. Hence, they also are called *sacraments* because the divine power, hidden by the veil of corporeal things, gives salvation in a more secret way to those who receive it with faith.") *De corp. et sang. Dom.*, 47–48; *PL* 121:147; cf. Paschasius, *PL* 120:1275.

16. On this point, see E. Martelet, "Histoire d'un écart grandissant," *Résurrection, eucharistie et genèse de l'homme* (Paris: Desclée, 1972) 131–160, especially 138–144.

17. *PL* 121:129 C.

18. "It is the mark of a great heart," writes Berengar, "to use dialectics in all things. For to use dialectics is to use reason so that those who do not do so, although made in the image of God according to God's reason, show contempt for their own dignity and are not able to be renewed from day to day according to the image of God." Quoted by P. Vignaux, *Philosophie au Moyen Age* (Paris: A. Colin, 1958) 23.

reason," Berengar "constantly separates what tradition united. . . . In his mind, every symbolic inclusion is transformed into a dialectical antithesis."[19]

A serious trauma in the conscience of the Church, the Berengar affair also had important consequences; as an immediate effect, it provoked in 1059 the imposition on the heretic of an ultra-realistic confession of faith in the presence of Christ in the Eucharist.[20] In the long run and more importantly, if the great Scholastic thinkers of the thirteenth century reacted against this sensual ultra-realism thanks to the subtle Aristotelian concept of "substance" — a concept that was not available during the preceding era — they nonetheless remained so profoundly anti-Berengarian that they accomplished what de Lubac has called a *"deadly dichotomy"* between the Eucharistic body and the ecclesial body. The Berengarian trauma had the effect of creating a substantial displacement in the traditional approach concerning the threefold body of Christ: where the Church Fathers had seen his ecclesial body as the *veritas* of his mystical Eucharistic body (his body in mystery or in sacrament), theologians now emphasized the link between his Eucharistic body and the true body born of Mary, dead and risen, so that there would no longer be any ambiguity concerning the reality of Christ in the bread and wine. The Church is no longer perceived as the *veritas* of the body that it receives "in mystery": it is now no more than the "reality signified but not contained" (*res significata et non contenta*). The *veritas* is contained in the Eucharist itself, which is the *corpus verum*, the Church becoming after that, in the second half of the twelfth century, the *corpus mysticum* in a sense that will be taken in the thirteenth century in an absolute way, that is, without any relation to the Eucharistic mystery. The Augustinian perspective, which still had defenders at the start of the twelfth century, such as Alger of Liege in his evocation of the Eucharistic "co-corporality" and "co-sacramentality" of Christ and the Church,[21] is thereafter ignored.

What one thus gains in "realism," at least according to the metaphysical representation which one at that time has of the "real," especially in the Aristotelian concept of substance, one loses in symbolism. This has two consequences: First, the ecclesial body, while it remains the ultimate

---

19. H. de Lubac, "Corpus mysticum," *Histoire et Esprit: L'intelligence de l'Ecriture d'après Origène* (Paris: Aubier-Montaigne, 1950) 260–266.

20. D-S 690: the body of Christ is touched and broken by the hands of priests and chewed by the teeth of the faithful *sensualiter, non solum sacramento, sed in veritate* ("in a sensible way, not only in sacrament, but in reality").

21. PL 180:794

finality of the Eucharist, is *expelled from the intrinsic symbolism* of the latter, to which it so intimately belonged with Augustine — leading to a more law-based than communion-based or sacrament-based ecclesiology and culminating in the thirteenth century in the conception of the Church as the *corpus mysticum* without any connection to the Eucharist! Second, there was general agreement with at least that part of the formula of 1059 that declares Christ present in the Eucharist "not only in sacrament but in truth" (*non solum sacramento, sed in veritate*). So shall it be in the thirteenth century and, against the Reformers, at the Council of Trent.[22]

Finally, where the Church Fathers said Christ is truly present and truly offered in sacrifice in the Eucharist *because* he is so "in sacrament" (in mystery, in figure, in symbol), from this point on one says Christ is truly present and truly offered there, *although* (necessarily) also in sacrament. This sacramental understanding, where the real is presupposed as something "behind" the

---

22. If the Council of Trent is more nuanced on this level, since it affirms once that Christ, "present under the sacramental mode, is there for us in all the truth of his being," it is still very marked by this perspective: this formula has scarcely any weight compared with the four *contineri* ("to be contained"), the three *esse* or *vere esse* ("to be" or "to truly be") having "the body and the blood of Christ" for their subject, and the three *existere* ("to be present") having "Christ" for their subject, which we see in chapters 1, 3, and 4 and in canons 1, 3, and 4 of the "Teaching on the Eucharist." The fact that Trent rejected — barely, it is true — the expression *conversio sacramentalis* ("sacramental transformation"), the only one that could have opened a true path of dialogue with the Reformers, stems from the same logic. This is not dictated only by the anti-Protestant stance of the council. Its origin is much older: according to the way "sacramental representation" had been conceived for a long time, the *"real"* was presupposed to be necessarily beyond the sacrament. Thus, in the thirteenth century, Bonaventure emphasized that "it is absolutely necessary that in this sacrament the body of Christ be contained [*contineri*] not only figuratively but also in truth [*non tantum figurative, verum etiam veraciter*], as the oblation that is appropriate to this time" (the "time of revealed grace"), although before this he had clearly affirmed that "in each of the sensible species the entire Christ is contained totally, not in a limited way, but sacramentally [*sacramentaliter*]" (*Breviloquium*, p. 6, c. 9, 3; c. 9, 1). *Sacramentaliter* is thus insufficient in his eyes to express *veraciter* ("really," "truly"). For his part, Albert the Great wrote, "Our [Eucharistic] immolation is not only a representation [*repraesentatio*], but a true [*vera*] immolation, that is to say, an oblation through [*per*] the priests' hands of the reality immolated" (*IV Sent.*, d. 13, a. 23).

sacramental, has survived until today.[23] Obviously, it is fundamentally dependent upon a metaphysical ontology.

This analysis shows us the importance of the question of *"sacramental representation."* It justifies our initial affirmation: if the reality of Christ comes to us in no other way than through its ex-

23. For example, the way in which M. Lepin translates Augustine in his celebrated work *L'idée du sacrifice de la Messe d'après les théologiens depuis l'origine jusqu'à nos jours*, 2nd ed. (Paris: Beauchesne, 1926) is telling. Let us give two particularly significant examples, in the sense that they come from texts quoted throughout the Middle Ages and into our own times as "authoritative texts" (*auctoritates*) for sacramental theology.

(A) *Augustine:* *"Res ipsa cuius sacramentum est. . . ."*
= "The reality itself of which it [the Eucharist] is the sacrament. . . ."
Lepin: "The reality itself of which this sacrament is the symbol" (p. 75).
(B) *Augustine:* *"Cujus rei sacramentum quotidianum esse voluit ecclesiae sacrificium: quae, cum ipsius capitis corpus sit, se ipsam per ipsum discit offerre."*
= "He wished to make the sacrifice of the Church a daily sacrament of this reality, for the Church, being the body of which he is the head, learns thereby to offer itself through him."
Lepin: "Of this truth he wished that a figure be contained in the daily sacrifice where the Church, as the body of its Chief, learns through his example to offer itself" (p. 79).

Obviously, in adding a second term each time ("symbol" in A, "figure" in B) to *sacramentum*, Lepin removes reality from *sacramentum* as he understands the term. He converts it into a "by-itself," hidden inside or behind the symbol or figure that comes to clothe or hide it; whereas, according to Augustine, this "reality" cannot be dissociated from its sacramental "expression." For this expression, the *res* in question, is not Christ taken in isolation, but, as we will see later, the *Christus totus*, head and members, the *multi unum corpus in Christo*, or, as Augustine says in the sentence immediately preceding passage A, "the society of his body and his members which is the holy Church." Since we are encompassed by the Church, we cannot separate it from the *sacramentum* in which it comes to us. It is this same misunderstanding of the patristic symbolism that, at the same time (1926), led as discerning an historian of dogma as J. Geiselmann to speak of the "a-metabolist character" (although not "anti-metabolist" as with Berengar) "of the Augustinian conception of the sacrament" (*Die Eucharistielehre der Vorscholastik* [Paderborn, 1926] 281). This whole movement of semantic displacement in the understanding of *sacramentum* and "sacramental representation" seems to us to be linked with the *desymbolization of Christ and the Church* as a reaction against Berengar: Is not the relation of Christ to the Church in the Eucharist in the thought of Peter Lombard a "secondary matter" (Lepin, *Idée*, 157)?

pressive mediation and if we can talk about it only *because and insofar as* it is sacramental ("in sacrament," "in symbol," "in memorial"), the sacramental representation of the sacrifice of Christ must itself be necessarily called a sacrifice. But this depends on a preliminary question: Can one talk about the life and death of Jesus as a sacrifice?

2. The Life and Death of Jesus: A Sacrifice?

The interpretation of Jesus' death as a sacrifice is not, in the New Testament, either the earliest (which does not mean it has less theological relevance than others) nor even the most important. X. Léon-Dufour has shown that Paul, for example, develops his theology of the cross around *three major symbolisms*, none of which has to do with either sacrifice or cult: the judicial symbolism where, in the context of a covenant relationship, all stand under a judgment of condemnation but are justified through the obedience of one person, the new Adam; the political symbolism, where human beings, *under (hypo)* the domination of sin, the Law, and death, are ransomed or freed through Christ and thus pass from the status of slaves to that of free sons and daughters; finally, an inter-personal symbolism, where human beings, in a state of enmity with God, are returned to a condition of covenant and peace with God, thanks to the reconciliation brought about by Christ who died *for (hyper)* them.[24]

None of these languages has either the cult or the sacrifices of the Temple as a background. While Paul does use, on five occasions, sacrificial language to express the soteriological significance of Jesus' death (see above), nevertheless, it is not a major theme with him. However, as we have shown, the various Pauline symbolisms are themselves crossed by the *two major axes* of reinterpretation of the death of Christ taking place "according to the Scriptures": the *Law* and the *Temple*. Paul is primarily interested in the first; the Letter to the Hebrews, essentially in the second.

We mentioned above the "barely believable audacity" the author of Hebrews demonstrates in his sacerdotal Christology and sacrificial soteriology. We judged this to be an authentic transmu-

---

24. X. Léon-Dufour, *Face à la mort: Jésus et Paul* (Paris: Seuil, 1979), ch. 5, especially pp. 182–197.

tation or subversion of the Old Testament cult. We indicated that the *teleiosis* ("action of rendering perfect") in the Pentateuch and its translation in the Septuagint designate the rite of consecration of a high priest through filling his hands. Now, as A. Vanhoye notes, the priestly consecration of Jesus, the Son, and that of an Old Testament high priest take place according to *reverse* movements. The latter in effect, "chosen from among mortals" (Heb 5:1), could exercise his function as mediator between God and human beings only by being separated from them according to an ascendant movement of separation and purification that placed him in the position of an intermediary. The priestly consecration of Jesus, on the contrary, coincides with his descendant movement of *kenosis* ("emptying," see Phil 2:7) or of intimate solidarity with human beings (Heb 2:17-18) even to death (4:15-16). It is this solidarity with humankind, freely consented to in a "docile listening" ("reverent submission") to the Father and filially offered in a prayer of supplication mixed with tears (5:7) that has made him "perfect" as the *Son*-in-humanity (5:8-9) and has constituted his "ritual" consecration as the only priest for eternity (7:24). His glorification marks the acceptance (5:7) of his "sacrifice," which is nothing other than the filial offering of his very weakness. Thus did he become in his person the unique mediator of our passage toward God. Participating, contrary to the usual intermediary, in the two extremes he unites, Christ thereby offers us direct access to God (9:24). His priestly "liturgy" (*leitourgia*, 8:6), offered "through the eternal Spirit" (9:14), abolishes in one stroke both the ancient priesthood as an institution for salvation and, as Paul underscored, the Law ("for when there is a change in the priesthood, there is necessarily a change in the law as well," 7:12). It is thus the entire Jewish religious and national system that becomes obsolete as a means of salvation.

Now, this sacrificing of the sacrifices cannot be restricted only to Jesus' *death*, which has meaning only in the logic of his *life* of giving. His dying-for is the ultimate expression of his living-for. He did not come to suffer and die, but to announce by his life — even up to death as the price for his fidelity — the good news that the reign of God is near, a reign of grace and mercy offered to all, and to thereby restore both God and human beings to liberty, that is, to destroy the barriers behind which the "oldness" of humankind had imprisoned both by abusing the very authority of God recognized in the Law.

Jesus' priesthood and sacrifice were exercised *existentially, and not ritually*. His sacrifice consisted precisely in bringing about this "newness," by which worship is embodied in life itself through faith, hope, and charity. In other words, the sacrifice of his life consisted in his refusal to use God to his own advantage. At least this is how we may interpret the *triple temptation* in the desert, whose placement in the Synoptics as an epigraph to his missionary ministry shows that it influenced his whole life during which, as the New Israel, he took up without falling the fundamental temptation to which Israel had succumbed: precisely that of using God, of "tempting" God through a kind of flattery ("for you are protected by God . . ." as Satan insinuates to Jesus), and thus of forgetting that God is God (see Matt 4:1-11 and his references to Deut). This is also what his scandalous *cry from the cross* — "My God, my God, why have you forsaken me?" — means, where in dying as the "Abandoned of God" (J. Moltmann), he lives out to its very end the trial of not using his God and Father, who nevertheless is so close to him. This is also what is suggested by the Christological hymn of Philippians 2:6-11: in contrast to Adam ("made of earth") whose sin, compassing the sins of all humanity, is to wish to be "like a god," Jesus, the New Adam, "though he was in the form of God, did not regard equality with God as something to be exploited."

He lived and he died in *reversing the fundamental sin* of Israel, which is also the paradigmatic sin of humankind. In effect, the sin of humankind is to live its relation with God according to a pattern of force and competition, a pattern whose typical representative is the *slave* trying to seize for him or herself the omnipotence of the *master* and to take the master's place. Here, according to the well-known Hegelian "master-slave" dialectic, we are dealing with an absolutely fundamental reality.[25] We also know that ac-

---

25. Remember that the moving force of this dialectics is "the struggle for recognition." In this struggle, Hegel, in the formula of J. Hyppolite, intends "essentially to show that the master reveals his or her real nature as slave of the slave and the slave as master of the master." The master makes the slave work and reserves gratification for him or herself. But to be gratified by a thing is to depend on it. To work on it, on the other hand, is to make the

cording to Freud, the child's advance toward its identity as a subject is possible only through a "mourning" or psychic "sacrifice" of the idealized parent, which is no other than its own idealized double. If, following the overcoming of the Oedipus complex proposed by J. Lacan (see above), we substitute the utter impossibility of the Thing (the primordial object of desire) for its mere prohibition under the form of the maternal object of complete satisfaction, we only radicalize the law which enjoins the transcending of this master-slave dialectic and competition in order for the subject to live: it all comes down to learning this difficult consent to "de-mastery," to absence, to "mutilation" in place of our illusory domination of the real that locks us into neurosis and thus leaves us enslaved.

Such an acquiescence to "de-mastery," always to be repeated, echoes Heidegger's meditative call for a "letting-be." It also evokes E. Jüngel's request for an *"end to any guarantee"* in his book *Dieu, mystère du monde (God, Mystery of the World)*. When Descartes, at the beginning of the modern era, developing openly a postulate which was that of the whole metaphysical tradition, establishes the necessity of God to guarantee the continuity of the *Ego* certain of itself in the act of the *Cogito*, he necessarily makes this God into a Master whose slaves human beings are — happy slaves because it is in God that they find the certainty of themselves and of their world; but these slaves are also the masters of the master (see Hegel): a God necessary to humankind is always a God at our disposal; a God necessary to humankind is always an all-powerful master, but in the end dependent on humankind (1:170-193). It is clearly impossible to let such a God be God. To conceive God appropriately in a theological way, we must learn to acquiesce to a God who is no guarantor of our certitudes.

---

thing dependent on you. Thanks to the resistance things present to the slave who works on them, the slave's consciousness becomes educated and elevated. The slave thus progresses in the consciousness of self and eventually comes to surpass the master. In the meantime, the slave remains a slave, and the master cannot progress in consciousness of self without getting out of this situation of domination expressed by reference to the slave. Thus both pay for the situation, and we will have to wait for other models of human relationships to make historical progress possible. J. Hyppolite, *Genèse et structure de la Phénoménologie de l'esprit de Hegel* (Paris: Aubier-Montaigne, 1946) 166–167.

We do not come to ourselves if we do not renounce ourselves and thus abandon the attempt to found ourselves on ourselves. This "sacrificial" letting-be seems to us to open a way to express theologically the significance of the life and death of Jesus "for all humankind," a way at least as fruitful as that of ritual sacrifice or of feudal justice exacting compensation. In particular, it allows us to understand better why the Bible, in its constant concern to respect the radical difference or holiness of a God whom it nevertheless proclaims to be close to what is most human in humankind, sees the primordial sin in idolatry, that is, in the reduction of God to the conditions of our experience of God, a reduction that is nothing more than the imaginary projection of ourselves into God. At the same time it allows us to read in a non-ritualistic manner the ritual interpretation which tradition has made of Jesus' death as sacrifice: the "sacrifice" of his life given unto death is that of the *consent to his condition as Son-in-humanity and as Brother of humanity*. In accordance with the psychic pattern of filiation (about which, in contrast to that of slavery, we shall say more in our last chapter), such a consent requires two things of Jesus: the renunciation of the will to possess himself, that is, the recognition of his *dependence as a Son* with regard to the Father; and, an obligatory corollary to the relation of filiation, the consent to his *human "autonomy,"* and thus the rejection of the temptation to use God to unburden himself of the full human responsibility he had to assume. In other words, his sacrifice is having agreed to serve God, and thus humankind, instead of having God, and thus humankind, serve him, however right and just his cause; having renounced to appropriate divinity, to "play" at being God, to make himself god in God's place, and thereby to have himself worshiped by humans; having allowed God his Father to be God and having fully accepted to become human; having preserved his filial trust in the Father in the most bewildering events accepted as the expression of the mission entrusted to him, even up to the incomprehensible silence of the Father who, allowing him to die, did not intervene to save him. *The sacrifice of Jesus is thus his "kenosis"* — the movement which is exactly the reverse of Adam's sin — where he consents to taste humanity to its extreme limit, death experienced in the silence of a God who would not even intervene to spare the Just One this death.

Such a sacrifice — we would call it "anti-sacrifice" — is more akin to the initiatory pattern of "dying to live" or of "the one who loses, gains"[26] than to the strictly sacrificial pattern. If it is true that the language of sacrifice gained authority as early as the New Testament because of the reinterpretation of the Temple system in relation to Christ, still, outside this perspective, this language is *in no way necessary* to express the meaning of Jesus' life and death. This is only *one* symbolism among other possible ones. Consequently, we do not accord it any particular privilege. However, it is still true — on condition that it be related to the other symbolisms with which it forms a network whose interstices, never filled, reflect the irreducibility of the mystery to its expressions — that the sacrificial symbolism should have *its place*; nothing more than its place, but certainly all of its place. From the *New Testament* viewpoint, it alone could thematize in a coherent way the "according to the Scriptures" seen in the light of the Temple. Moreover, from the *ritual* viewpoint, it would be naive to believe or lead others to believe that the act of eating and drinking what is presented as the body and blood of Christ, however "spiritualized," would not awaken a certain archaic sacrificial symbolism, with all its ambivalent phantasms of destructive aggressiveness and amorous assimilation: being human, the faith of Christians cannot pretend to bypass this elemental symbolism![27] The necessary demythologization in this area — what we have just performed — cannot be carried to a complete jettisoning of the myth without foundering, like Bultmann, on the new myth of a faith without mythic residue . . . Thus, we may interpret Jesus' life and death as a "sacrifice" ("anti-sacrifice," in the sense we will make clear). In fact, we would favor this line of interpretation when speaking of the Eucharist because it takes place on the ritual plane where we eat and drink the body and blood of Christ. We are, therefore, dealing here with a "sacrifice-in-sacrament"; but a quite singular sacrifice . . .

26. In this sense, see A. Vergote, "La mort rédemptrice du Christ à la lumière de l'anthropologie," X. Léon-Dufour et al., *Mort pour nos péchés* (Brussels: Fac. Univ. S. Louis, 1976) 70–83.

27. J. C. Sagne, "L'interprétation analytique du rite de l'eucharistie," *L'eucharistie*, Profac. (Faculty of Theology of Lyon, 1971) 153–164.

3. The Thesis of R. Girard[28]

This sacrifice is so singular that according to R. Girard, we should not speak at all of "sacrifice," even from Jesus' viewpoint; it was Christians who, beginning with the Gospels, made a sacrificial interpretation that had in fact been denounced by Jesus himself. In mentioning Girard here, we are aware of the favorable and unfavorable reactions his works have provoked. His thesis has elicited *grave reservations*, at the epistemological level ("an ontology of violence," in the estimate of A. Simon), the biblical (a reduction of all the biblical sacrifices to the same model: the scapegoat, and in the end a reconciling lynching), and the theological.[29]

28. R. Girard, *La violence et le sacré* (Paris: Grasset, 1972); Girard, *Des choses cachées depuis la fondation du monde* (Paris: Grasset, 1978).

29. A. Simon in *Esprit* (Nov. 1973) 515-527. *Biblically*, the peremptory affirmations concerning the prophets' criticism not simply of cultic formalism but indeed "of the very principle of sacrifice" are difficult to sustain from the historical viewpoint. One remains confounded by his assurance (the prophetic texts are "too numerous and too explicit to allow the slightest doubt" (Girard, *Des choses*, 473, n. 54]), all the more so because the author cites not a single exegete in support of his blunt assertions.

On the plane of *theological hermeneutics*, it is difficult not to be severe here. From its beginning (especially with the sacrificial scenario of the passion in the Gospels), the Church supposedly made a sacrificial interpretation of Jesus' fate, thereby betraying him in what the author considers to be the thrust of Jesus' message. One must wonder, theologically, about the kind of Church that would have been *unfaithful* to Christ *from the outset* . . . and consequently about the Gospels themselves since they were born out of the faith of this Church. And one must also wonder how Girard so clearly knows how it was with the "real" Jesus, inasmuch as there is not a single sentence in the Gospels that is not already a theological interpretation by this Church, which supposedly misunderstood the essentials of his message. At the very least we have here a methodological defect with regard to the very essence of the Gospel texts.

The author recognizes that the Church, like civil society, cannot live the message of absolute non-violence or radical non-sacrifice since it is not possible to live in common, either in a religious or civil society, without the mechanism of victim sacrifice. Thus, *the basic question* is: Is the impossibility for the Church to live under a non-sacrificial regime responsible for a fundamental betrayal by the Church of the gospel of Christ, a gospel which in this case would be only the announcement of a trans-historical eschatology? In other words, is the "not yet" truly constitutive of the gospel of Christ? Does the gospel take history itself into account? Is "becoming" essential to Christian existence or not? Does the reign of God appear within history, or

However, these very serious reservations cannot conceal the interest of Girard's highly coherent thesis. In particular it seems to us that it raises two crucial issues: first, *sacrifice* and second, the denunciation by *Jesus* of its specious elements.

Sacrifice is a process by which a group unburdens itself onto a scapegoat of both its internal violence, the result of a "mimetic rivalry" which threatens its existence, and the guilt inspired by this violence. Because this mechanism functions at its best when the group is unaware of what is really at stake (otherwise it must undergo a "crisis in sacrifice" — as in our own societies), it is fundamentally connected with a process of *nonrecognition of responsibility*. In its strict sense, this process is religious and ritual.

---

only outside history? Why should we presuppose that Jesus could not reconcile his effective announcement of the imminent arrival of the reign with the possibility of a lapse of time, even relatively short, after his death? If he could not, he would have been mistaken, and further this would not be consistent either with his parables about the growth of the reign (even refashioned by the Christian communities) or especially with his eschatological discourse at the Last Supper where, as Léon-Dufour among others points out, he attests that the group of his disciples will continue to exist a certain time after him ("Jésus devant sa mort à la lumière des textes de l'institution eucharistique et des discours d'adieu," *Jésus aux origines de la christologie* [Louvain, 1975] 160–161, n. 27). This debate ultimately concerns the *connection between history and eschatology*, and simultaneously the Church, the Church which is *only* "sacrament" of the reign already coming, the Church-as-institution especially with its sacrament of the Eucharist. In the last analysis, Girard appears too "Christian" to really be Christian . . .

For, as B. Lauret asks (in *Lumière et Vie* 146 [1980] 43–53), "how does one not be a Christian" if one follows Girard all the way to the end? With Girard does not Christianity become only "the refined flower of a cultural metaphor of which Jesus is the moral example, or even the revealer"? Does not this Jesus appear too much as just "the human being who would be the example for a society that would have left behind mimetic violence to engage in social relations exclusively dominated by love," as just the illustration (yet dramatic in its consequences for himself) of a God reduced to a "Principle": that of the prohibition of all violence? Girard's Christology has a certain "gnostic smell" about it. It looks simply like the key to an anthropology. This, we know, is a recurring temptation in the history of the Church, already present in Arianism; during the Enlightenment and the ascendancy of liberal theology, it found form in the attempt to conceive "religion within the limits of mere reason," reducing the mystery of Christ to the simple ideal of a universal morality.

Because it has a real symbolic efficacy in allowing the group to gain reconciliation through "purgation" (*catharsis*) of the violent impulses which threaten it from the inside, its benefit is projected onto a divinity in a world "out there." And so this *"god"* acts as a *sacralized alibi* (obviously unacknowledged as such) *which dispenses human beings from assuming their responsibility in history*, from confronting the real causes of their divisions, and thus from laboring ethically toward a reconciliation among themselves.

This religious process may convey itself in rites that are not immediately sacrificial, each ritual finally coming down to that of sacrifice, as understood by Girard. Further, this sacrificial process disguises itself within what may appear as non-religious: every literary work (especially theatrical), every social institution (notably the judiciary) or political institution (leaders' rivalries, on the national or international planes . . .) are substitutes for this sacrifice insofar as they allow the group to expel its violence, pinpoint the legally guilty, and manage the internal tensions which threaten the social fabric. It is in this way, according to the author, that the gospel texts (especially the passion narratives) produced by the first Christian communities transformed what is essentially the non-sacrifice par excellence, the death of Jesus, into a sacrifice by pointing out a guilty party: the Jews.

Now, Jesus came to unmask this sacrificial process "hidden since the foundation of the world." He was able to do this because the Old Testament, which may be regarded as a *"progressive exodus away from sacrifice,"* had opened a path in this direction. Contrary to the myths of various religions, the Bible is unique in this, God takes the part of the sacrificed victims (and from the very beginning as the story of Abel testifies) and as a consequence, instead of "blessing" a group that is cheaply reconciled by the use of a sacralized victim, God charges the group to take in hand its ethical responsibility toward such victims: the immigrant, the slave, the orphan, and so on. This Exodus-inspired reversal is particularly manifest in the prophets and culminates in one of the Songs of the Suffering Servant (Isa 52:13–53:12), even though the sacrificial process has not yet been completely abolished, the Servant remaining the expiatory victim of a God still seen as a judge. Against this biblical background, Girard develops, in our estimation, an especially felicitous interpretation of the texts containing maledictions against the Pharisees (Matt 23:29-36; Luke 11:49-53; John 8:43-44), the texts of Jesus' passion and Stephen's martyrdom (Acts 7:51-58), the parable of the murderous tenants (Matt 21:33-46 par.), and so on. All by itself the saying from Psalm 118:22, "The stone that the builders rejected has become the chief cornerstone," applied to Jesus, summarizes the substance of his reading of these texts.

One could present his views synthetically as follows: Christ revealed a nonviolent God in the sense that God is not motivated by the desire for punishment or revenge. If there is violence in Jesus, it is a kind that is non-sacrificial: in unmasking the violence of humankind with the aim of pushing this violence to its *end*, he pushed it to its *limit*, even to its paroxysm; he became its victim because people experienced his exposure of what ought to have remained hidden as intolerable. One may thus see in Jesus "simultaneously the most extreme violence and no violence at all since it deprives humans of all sacrificial aid." For the reign of God he announces is that of *"absolute nonviolence,"* that of "perfect reciprocity": this is precisely why he *"has"* to die, the victim of a world always violent. At the same time, "the gods of violence are completely devalued by the announcement of a God of love: the machine is thrown out of kilter, the old scapegoating no longer works." From now on all sacrificial worship is prohibited; Christ takes away humankind's last ritual crutch. From now on it must achieve reconciliation without sacrifice, or die." Salvation consists precisely in humankind's renouncing to unload its task of reconciliation here and now by projecting it onto a god: such a god is only an alibi humankind unknowingly gives itself to manage at lesser cost its guilt by projecting it onto a victim unanimously designated guilty. Christ is thus "the universal revealer" who preaches *"the absolute responsibility of humankind in history:* 'You want your house left to you? OK, it's in your hands.' " Put on the spot, humankind must now assume its ethical responsibility, giving up the image of a punishing deity who would lend a transcendent justification to its ingenious strategies by which it may continue to believe itself innocent.[30]

30. The quotations from Girard in the preceding paragraph are taken from "Discussion avec René Girard," *Esprit* (Nov. 1973) 553-556.

4. The Anti-Sacrificial

a) An Obligatory Third Term. There are grounds for doubting
whether this thesis of the sacrificial process is the only key for understanding rituals, religions, and finally societies themselves.
There are also strong reasons for questioning whether Jesus is the
universal revealer of this unique key, that is, whether Christology
is ultimately only an answer to the author's anthropology. Otherwise, how is it that not everybody is Christian? Thus, our interest
in Girard's thesis should not be taken to indicate an unconditional
acceptance — far from it; but it does seem to us to touch on a fundamental point, the *tension* that characterizes the relation between
cult and ethics under the Christian dispensation (in the wake of
Judaism). Girard interprets this as an *opposition:* there is either a
sacrificial regimen with ethical abdication or an ethical regimen of
responsibility. We have stressed in the preceding chapter that this
tension should be neither erased nor transformed into an opposition. There is in Girard's thesis a lack of recognition of the
Church's eschatological nature. The non-sacrificial reign of perfect
reciprocity may be lived only in practice *outside history;* it is thus
not able to accommodate itself to the ''in-between times'' condition of the Church and its sacraments.

This is why such a choice between sacrifice and non-sacrifice
does not appear tenable to us. We require a *third term* which we
call *''anti-sacrifice.''* This ''anti-sacrifice'' is not the denial of the
sacrificial pattern that dwells in all of us. Such a denial, in effect,
would spring from the same pattern of representation as the affirmation of the sacrificial it seeks to fight. Like any ''eschatological''
or ''gnostic enthusiasm,'' it is only a back-handed way of filling
this ''presence-of-the absence'' (of God) that we have such a hard
time enduring without resentment. Ultimately, it is only an avatar
of the metaphysics of the transparence of self to self which dis-
regards the radical contingency of historicity and corporality.

The anti-sacrificial regimen to which the gospel calls us *rests*
upon the sacrificial, but it does so to *turn it around* and thereby to
redirect ritual practice, the symbolic point of passage that structures Christian identity, back toward ethical practice, the place
where the ritual practice is verified. But the passage from sacrificial oldness to gospel newness, represented by the relation of the

ents, a relation which itself expresses the difficult task
ion that is incumbent upon every society and every
ing, is never fully achieved. And the Church, which is
? anti-sacrificial law of the Spirit, is always in danger of
sliding back toward the sacrificial, that is, of again subjecting both
God and humankind to its own very "worthy cause" through a
closed dogmatic system, either moral or ritualistic . . .

 b) *The Temptation to Return to the Sacrificial.* Such a temptation is
easy to identify throughout all of history. What is not at issue
here *as such* is the application of the *vocabulary of the sacred* (sacrificial and sacerdotal) to the Eucharist and the ministers who preside
over it, an application which began in the third century.[31]

However, sacerdotalizing the ministers was not without its *risk*
of regression toward the sacrificial. The first danger was to gradually recover the Eucharist-sacrifice and the priests-*sacerdotes* as new
mediators between God and humankind. Such a backsliding was
historically difficult to avoid completely, especially after the empire
became officially Christian in the fourth century and the Church
became an established institution seeking to win the pagan world
for Christ. The bishop and then the priests in the countryside,
when presiding over the Eucharist and other celebrations, appeared to new converts from paganism to be playing a role comparable to that of pagan priests. This development became less
avoidable as the clergy began to effectively replace the civil
"ministers" in both the religious and social "service" of the city
and as, following the barbarian invasions during which the
Church remained the only minimally solid organization capable of
taking in hand the multiple tasks normally the responsibility of
the civil power, it began to exercise an ever more predominant
role in society.

The direct result of this first danger, a second lay in the temptation to *use* the priestly status of the ministers: first by an *exclusive*

31. The "sacerdotalization" of the ministers is legitimate as long as it
respects the radical transmutation of "priesthood" that Hebrews effects. On
this condition, it is even rich in significance: in virtue of the person's ordination (and not of the person's baptism, by which one belongs to the "priesthood of all believers"), the minister is the "sacramental" expression of the
identity of the Church as a community where the unique and exclusive
priestly activity of Christ takes flesh.

utilization where, from being included in the ordained ministry, the "priesthood" ended up being perceived as itself an all-inclusive totality, sufficient unto itself to define itself;[32] later, by a one-sided focusing on the *cultic* activity of priests, to the point that "in the Middle Ages, the majority of priests simply ceased to exercise the ministry of the word at all — in general, they would not have been capable of doing so — and further they seemed to have almost no awareness of any responsibility to evangelize."[33] And finally, by a *confiscation of the baptismal priesthood* of the entire people of God by the priests — a confiscation which, it is not out of place to note, does not respect even the "difference of nature" between the baptismal priesthood and the priesthood of the ministers, a difference which, however, was constantly emphasized at the time.[34]

Practice evidently played as important a role as theory in this affair. Consider for example the multiplication of Masses said in order to redeem the many months or years of fasting imposed on sinners according to the graduated penance system of the high

---

32. This is why the title "ordained ministry" remains preferable to "priestly ministry" or "ministerial priesthood" which characterizes too exclusively the ministry through one of its dimensions. All the more should the *absolute* use of "sacerdotal" in reference to priests be carefully avoided.

33. P. M. Gy, "Evangelisation au Moyen Age," *Humanisme et foi chrétienne* (Paris: Beauchesne, 1976) 572.

34. St. Thomas' *Summa Theologica*, for example, very nearly ignores the *priesthood of all baptized Christians*. While he does make an allusion to it in III, q. 82, a. 1, it is to emphasize that the union of the "laity" with Christ is only "spiritual," that is, it operates only "through faith and charity" and not "through a sacramental power." This agrees with what he has said about the baptismal "character" as a "configuration to the priesthood of Christ": it gives the faithful only "the power to *receive* the other sacraments of the Church," in contrast to the "character" of priestly ordination which "commissions certain people to transmit the sacraments to others" (III, q. 63, a. 6). The first is a "passive power"; the second, an "active power" (Supp. q. 34, a. 2). We do not deny that this kind of theology has something important to say about the difference between the baptismal priesthood and the "ministerial priesthood." But it says it in a way that mirrors, justifies, and reinforces the progressive nibbling away at the assembly's liturgical activity in favor of the clergy's, which the history of Eucharistic practices abundantly illustrates.

Middle Ages[35] or, since the penalties not satisfied in this world were to be satisfied in the next, the Mass funds set up (through financial bequests, of course) for such and such a dead person: the new geography of the next world, established in a precise way from 1175 on with purgatory added as a "third place," evidently contributed to the growing success of this practice.[36] This multiplication of "ransom Masses" entailed a multiplication of the *ordination of "Mass priests"* and thus an inflation of the sacerdotal corps carrying out the roles of *intermediary* and *intercessor*. The swarming of these *Mass priests*, commissioned exclusively with the function of ransoming and expiating through Masses, is without a doubt one of the most visible social effects of this powerful current. There is no doubt that such a practice often distorted and even betrayed the dogmatic theory of the Church; one should not confuse the one with the other or even with many a theology. It is true, however, that at least at the level of the most common representation and practice, the emphasis had shifted to the sacrificial, the anti-sacrificial being retained only in certain treatises, and lived by an "elite."

5. Sacrifice of Expiation and Sacrifice of Communion

The sacrifice of *redemption or expiation* is more liable to drift toward a mercantile notion of exchange than is the sacrifice of *communion*, which promotes the appreciation of existence as a gift. However, it would be wrong to imagine that the Christian "antisacrificial" viewpoint could assume the sacrifice of communion to the exclusion of the sacrifice of redemption. For, as M. Mauss has recently written, "There is no sacrifice where the idea of ransom, or something contractual, does not enter in some way."[37] The

35. Thus the *Penitential "a"* of Vienna explains that "priests may celebrate for themselves no more than seven Masses per day, but at the request of penitents they may say as many as necessary, even more than twenty Masses per day." The text is in C. Vogel, *Le pécheur et la pénitence au Moyen Age* (Paris: Cerf, 1969) 30.

36. J. Le Goff, *La Naissance du purgatoire* (Paris: Gallimard, 1981) 166–173, especially 437–439.

37. H. Hubert and M. Mauss, "Essai sur la nature et la fonction du sacrifice" (1899), M. Mauss, *Works*, vol. 1, *Les fonctions sociales du Sacré* (Paris: Minuit, 1968) 304–305.

anti-sacrificial demarcation does not pass between the pattern of expiation and the pattern of communion but between a *servile* attitude and a *filial* attitude with regard to the entire sacrificial order.

Nevertheless, the dimension of communion is primary in Christianity, as is shown by the early connection between *todah* ("sacrifice of praise") and *eucharistia*. Consequently, if the dimension of *"propitiation"* (understood as "reconciliation" or "pardon"), so strongly underlined with regard to the "sacrifice of the Mass" at the Council of Trent against the Reformers, is indeed constitutive of the Eucharist, it is *within* its nature as a "sacrifice of thanksgiving" (inadequately emphasized by Trent) that this is to be understood. *It is in giving thanks,* in giving back to God God's own Grace, Christ given in sacrament, that *we are given back to ourselves,* that is, placed or replaced in our status of sons and daughters and thus reconciled.

One sees what is at stake in what we call the *anti-sacrificial:* not the negation of the sacrificial or of a part of it (its dimension of reconciliation), but *the task to convert all the sacrificial to the gospel in order to live it, not in a servile, but in a filial (and hence in a brotherly and sisterly) manner.* This is precisely why the realization of this intimate association, based on our common filiation, by the ethical practice of reconciliation between human beings, constitutes the premier place of *our* "sacrifice." That is what the anti-sacrifice of the Eucharist shows us and enjoins us to do.

6. *A Eucharistic Ethics: Irenaeus and Augustine*

According to the famous passage of St. Irenaeus in *Adversus Omnes Haereses* IV:17-18, the oblation is the major teaching moment where we learn to make our own the very attitude of Jesus, that is, to pass from the Adamic attitude of slaves, imaginatively considering the divine power as a booty to be plundered, to the attitude of *sons and daughters,* content to allow God alone to be God and to acknowledge ourselves as God's creatures, the gracious fruit of God's paternal love. "There were sacrifices among the [Jewish] people, there are also sacrifices in the Church," writes Irenaeus. But, he adds, "their nature has been changed." For the Eucharistic offering of the "firstfruits of creation" is, in the very *dependence* on God which it attests, "the distinctive mark of *freedom*": offered as thanksgiving, it shows that "God needs nothing'' and awaits only one thing from us, that we "express our gratitude to God." It is thus not for God, continues Irenaeus, following the Christian apologists of the second century and in the wake of Philo as well as numerous Jewish currents (see above), that God requests an oblation, but for *us: "It is we ourselves who need to offer God* the goods that we consecrate to God." For it is by recognizing that of ourselves we have nothing to offer and that we can offer nothing to God that does not come from God as a gift (see the *ta sa ek ton son prospherontes* ["offering to you your own gifts from what is yours"] of the early anaphoras), that we cease to be "sterile and ungrateful"; from being *"a-charistoi,"* we become *"eu-charistoi."* We turn from being ungrateful to being gracious; and becoming gracious toward God requires that we become gracious toward others. To recognize what God is doing for us, to recognize what God has ultimately done in the gift of the Son who "recapitulates" in himself all the Father's gifts and who constitutes the "pure offering" sacrificed "every place" (Mal 1:11), is to be urged *to be toward others as God is toward us.* The Eucharistic oblation thus teaches us how to "serve God" instead of how to make him serve us; it teaches us what is involved in the passage from being slaves to being a sons and daughters and through that to being brothers and sisters to others; in transforming us into sons and daughters with the Son, it gives us each other as brothers and sisters. This is why, as Irenaeus keeps insisting, using seventeen anti-sacrificial quotations from the Bible, the sacrifice that is pleasing to God is nothing else but, in imitation of Christ, *obedience to God's word* and the practice *of justice and mercy toward others.* Such is the anti-sacrificial pasch which, in communion with the Pasch of Christ, the Eucharist presents to us symbolically and enjoins us to live out ethically.

There are similar echoes of these words that come to us from the equally celebrated passage of St. Augustine in the *City of God* (X:5-6). "We must believe that God has no need of animals or of any earthly or corruptible thing, or even of human justice: all that honors God profits humankind, not God." And like Irenaeus, Augustine backs up his statement with a dozen biblical quotations. He then explains the precise function of the Eucharistic *sacramentum:* it is the *"visible sacrifice, that is, the sacrament or sacred sign of the invisible sacrifice."* Now, what is this invisible sacrifice? It is the obedience and love with which Christ delivered himself over to the Father and to humankind, offering with himself all humanity whose brother he had become. In communion with him, it is also *our* own lives given to others through the exercise of mercy. For *"it is mercy that is the true sacrifice."* Or again, this true invisible sacrifice is the practice of the "love of God and of neighbor" which summarizes the entire Law and which, Augustine makes clear, was signified by the sacrifices of the Temple; in sum, it consists in "every work carried out to establish ourselves in a holy society with God."

Now, this "holy society" is realized first of all in the *Church*.[38] Inasmuch as it is the body of Christ where all, according to the variety of the Spirit's gifts, are members of one another, the Church is the very place of communion with God and with others. This masterly passage of Augustine culminates in the presentation of the *Church as the "universal sacrifice" offered to God through Christ*. And the Eucharist is the *sacrum signum* of this universal sacrifice: "Such is the Christian sacrifice: that we who are many form a single body in Christ [*multi unum corpus in Christo*]. This is what the Church accomplishes in the sacrament of the altar, well known to the faithful, where it made clear to the Church that it itself is offered in what it offers." Thus, the Eucharist is the revelation of the accomplishment of this "true sacrifice" which is the *becoming-Christians in the Church-as-the-body-of-Christ*. This becoming takes place in the act where, offering Christ "in sacrament," Christians are themselves offered "through him, with him, and in him," in the words of the doxology of the Eucharistic Prayer. The sacramental sacrifice is that of "the whole Christ" (*Christus totus*), Head and Body.

Thus presented, this sacrifice is indeed "the symbol of what we are" (Sermon 227). It is impossible to say here "Christ" without at the same time saying "the Church": the Eucharist is the *sacramental sym-bolization of both*. The Christian sacrifice manifested in the

38. It is a matter here of the Church as *societas sanctorum* ("society of saints") and not as simple *communio sacramentorum* ("communion of sacraments"). This is an important distinction developed during the controversy with the Donatists, who belonged to the second but not to the first. See Y. M. Congar, "Introduction," *Traités anti-donatistes de S. Augustin*, vol. 1, Bibl. aug. 28, DDB, pp. 97–115.

sacramentum is not Christ taken in isolation, but the ecclesial *unum corpus* that must live "in him." In this way does his sacrifice become our sacrifice, and his Pasch our own pasch. It is impossible to conceive the first theologically without its symbolic involvement with the second in the sacrament. The term "symbol," we have pointed out, expresses the difference between the symbol and what it symbolizes; it also expresses the prohibition of thinking about the one outside its relation to the other — in this case, the impossibility for the one to become a sacrament outside its relation to the other. One thereby rejects any conception of Christ's sacrifice which, under the pretense of "realism," would be carried out at the expense of the truth of the participants' sacrifice in their mutual relations as members of the same body of Christ. The *sacramentum* cannot effect in truth a relation with Christ without simultaneously effecting, in truth also, a relation with others, a relation which seeks to become enfleshed here and now in the practice of reconciliation between human beings. The "anti-sacrifice" of the Eucharist, far from serving us as an alibi, puts us on the spot. It is the great symbol of the "exodus away from the sacrificial" of which Girard has spoken.

In spite of their differences of culture and sensibility, Irenaeus and Augustine meet in their doctrine of the Eucharist. Both present it as the great *pedagogy* where humans *"learn to serve God"* (Irenaeus), where the Church, the body whose head is Christ, *"learns to offer itself through him"* (Augustine). To be precise: in both cases, this pedagogy does not belong to the category of a simple *exemplum* exterior to us, but to that of *sacramentum* where Christ himself is the first agent. Through the Eucharistic oblation we learn to take on this "anti-sacrificial" attitude of him who was fully our Brother because he became fully Son. We learn there to acknowledge ourselves as *from others and for others* by recognizing ourselves to be *from God and for God.* Such is the condition for our coming into freedom. As the sacrifice of freedom, the Eucharist gives us back to ourselves and to others (its dimension of reconciliation) in the very act where we give ourselves back to God in offering God our filial thanksgiving (its [always primary] dimension of "sacrifice of thanksgiving").

The grace of the Eucharist is finally our own becoming *eucharistic people,* that is, our becoming sons and daughters for God and brothers and sisters for others, in communion with the Son and Brother whose memory we celebrate here. This grace is given to us as a *task*; it enjoins upon us the obligation of *renouncing God as an alibi*, which our desire never ceases to fabricate, in order to give flesh here and now to the crucified God who, by taking away our "ritual crutches," wishes us to be free within the house he leaves to our *responsibility*. The practice of the twofold commandment of love toward God and toward neighbor, with its socio-political implications, is the "true sacrifice," the most important liturgy which we learn from the Eucharistic anti-sacrifice.

CONCLUSION. RISKS AND OPPORTUNITIES OF THE VOCABULARY OF SACRIFICE

There is no doubt that the word "sacrifice" is one of the most treacherous in the Christian vocabulary. A. Vergote has powerfully criticized from the anthropological viewpoint the theologoumenon of a punishing God sacrificing his Son in our place, and has uncovered its questionable, not to say frankly unacceptable, character in authentically Christian theology.[39]

The "Strike, Lord, strike!" addressed to God hurling his rage on his Son in order to save us, in the sermons of Bourdaloue and Bossuet,[40] must be called by its name, a perversion of God. We know where this psychological need for a punishing God comes from — no necessity to go over it again. Let us simply make clear that from the Freudian viewpoint religion is essentially a management of guilt, as J. Gagey has emphasized;[41] and to wish that it were not so, under pretense of having reached one's "majority" as a mature and critical adult, is to only reinforce (naively) what one wishes to deny. Let us add further that the God who is "all love," to whom one sometimes appeals as a reaction against this vengeful God, can be no less perverse, although more subtly so: when "love," under the pretext of forgiveness, can no longer forbid *anything*, when it is itself no longer structured by a law and thus by prohibitions, this excess of love, to which one can never respond adequately because it can be consummated only by demanding more and more, risks being experienced imaginatively as an unpayable debt; one is then trapped in an infernal circle from which there is no escape, for the admission of the

39. A. Vergote, "La mort rédemptrice."
40. For example, Bossuet, "Sermon sur la Passion de Jésus-Christ" (March 26, 1660), ed. J. Calvet, *Oeuvres choisies* (Paris: Hatier, 1921) 101–108.
41. J. Gagey, *Freud et le christianisme*, especially ch. 9.

truth — that this supposed "love" is in reality a persecution — is the object of the most powerful taboo.[42]

However it may be with this last remark, the language of sacrifice requires that pastorally it be used with *care*. At the same time, for the reasons given above, it remains *ineradicable*. As symbolically representing the whole of Israel's activities and cultic institutions, it even appears theologically *precious* to us. From the perspective of "Scripture," it expresses the fulfillment of the Old Testament's worship in Christ through critical overcoming. From the perspective of "Sacrament," it constitutes, through the rites of oblation and communion, a particularly pregnant symbol of the identity that unites believers as sons and daughters of God and brothers and sisters in Christ. From the perspective of "Ethics," it lets believers make a "liturgical" reading of their practice of justice and mercy. Properly understood, this (anti-)sacrificial language thus reveals one of the constitutive dimensions of Christian identity. And its Eucharistic "expression" reveals in an exemplary way the process by which Christians come into the truth of their identity.

42. M. Bellet, *Le Dieu pervers*, 15-49.

Part Three

The Symbolizing Act

of Christian Identity

Our second part has located the sacraments as one element among others in the whole epistemic configuration of the Church. The next step is to make clear theologically the originality or "specificity" of this element — what is its difference with regard to the other elements. This will be the object of this third part.

We will do so in three major stages. First (Chapter Nine), we will investigate the particular mode of expression which constitutes the sacraments: rituality. After this, we will approach them from the angle of the dialectic between the instituted and the instituting. If the sacraments are the most "instituted" of the Church's types of mediation (Chapter Ten), they are also, in their capacity as operative symbolic expressions, the most *instituting* (Chapter Eleven). We will thus have occasion in the course of our study to look at a certain number of classical sacramental questions: from the institution of the sacraments by Jesus Christ to sacramental grace.

Chapter Nine

The Sacraments: Acts of Ritual Symbolization

THE RADICAL INVOLVEMENT OF THE CHURCH IN THE SACRAMENTS

How shall we understand the originality of Sacrament with regard to Scripture and Ethics, which are also ecclesial mediations of our relation to God? First of all, our theological reflection up to this point rejects as misleading any attempt to see in the sacraments anything "more" or "other than" what is contained in the Scriptures. "One finds oneself at a dead end when one tries to see this difference as quantitative, as if the sacrament gave us more than the Word," J. J. Von Allmen correctly observes.[1] In our opinion, the difference is in the *sacramentum* itself, that is, in the mode of mediation put into play.

K. Rahner has endorsed this approach. He writes that a sacrament is *"an act by which the Church fulfills itself in an unconditional involvement."*[2] The German theologian develops this thesis starting from the question of the efficacy of God's action in the various forms of the Church's proclamation of the Word. All this leads him to a fundamental conviction: the gift of God's salvation is no more linked to the distinctly ritual and sacramental announcement of the Word than to its announcement under the mode of the Scriptures or under the mode of ethical witness. This is why *"the concept of* opus operatum [*'efficacious action'*] *does not suffice by itself to mark the distinction between a sacrament and other events [of grace]."*[3] Or again, as the same author has written more recently,

1. J. J. Von Allmen, "Célébrer le salut," *Essai sur le repas du Seigneur* (Neuchâtel: Delachaux-Niestlé, 1966) 166.
2. K. Rahner, "Parole et eucharistie," *Ecrits théologiques*, vol. 9, DDB (1968) 78. See Rahner, *Eglise et sacrement*, DDB (1970) 35-39.
3. Rahner, "Parole et eucharistie," 72.

the *opus operatum*, that is to say, the efficacious Word of God, and the *opus operantis*, that is to say, "free, personal, ethically religious human activity," "are not to be distinguished as an action of God's grace in humankind on the one hand, and as a purely human achievement on the other." For "even free human action — where it is not sinful — is also an event of grace." If the two notions mentioned above are distinct, it is "as *institutional* history — explicit, endorsing ecclesial visibility in the sacraments" — and "as the purely *existential* salvific activity of human beings under the grace of God."[4] Thus, one cannot deduce the originality of the sacraments — their "specific difference" — from the sole criterion of efficacy.

No more can one deduce it from the requisite *degree of faith*, as if the *ex opere operato* ("in virtue of the action") offered the receiver a "bargain price" on grace. The fact that God always offers God's self in the sacraments because God is their operating agent (the positive signification of *ex opere operato*), or further that neither ministers nor receiving subjects, by reason of their degree of faith or holiness, can be the source of God's gracious gift or make it necessary (the negative signification of *ex opere operato*) does not render the sacraments "automatically" more efficacious: they cannot accommodate themselves any more to a lack of faith to bring about a communication of the subject with God than can the reading of the Scriptures or service to others. The notion of *validity* is only the transcription of the preceding affirmation that God alone is their operating principle into the domain of the administration of the sacraments: the Church is only their custodian, not their owner. As for the notion of (subjective) *efficacy*, it only serves to underline what Augustine said apropos baptism, "each receives according to one's faith." Faith is not the measure of the gift, but of its reception. The sacraments "become efficacious only by joining with human liberty in its act of welcoming."[5]

Under such conditions the originality of the sacraments comes only from *the Church*, which radically involves itself and puts into play its whole identity. We thus agree with the perspective of Rahner. However, the theological affirmation of the Church's *radi-*

4. K. Rahner, *Traité fondamental de la foi: Introduction au concept du christianisme* (Paris: Centurion, 1983) 475. Our emphasis.
5. Ibid., 460.

cal involvement needs to be more closely verified in the facts, that is, in the concrete texture of the mediation which constitutes the sacraments. This mediation is *ritual.* We have no intention of deducing the above theological assertion from an anthropological study of ritual. Its theological relevance can be ascertained only within the coherent whole of the Christian faith. But in sacramental theology we are in the order of symbolic expression from the outset, so much so that the "reality" of what is effected cannot be separated from the *sacramentum* where it takes on flesh, as we highlighted in the last chapter with the principle of *in sacramento.* Thus, if it is correct to say that the sacraments derive their unique character from the radical involvement of the Church that celebrates them, this fact needs to be verified in their concrete, that is, ritual modality.

After having first (I) set into relief the fundamentally practical law of all rituality, we will propose (II) a theological interpretation of some of its principal components, an interpretation pertaining to the radicalness of the Church's involvement in the sacraments, which constitutes one of the principal themes of this chapter. Afterwards (III), we will emphasize the essential connection between rituality and the whole human being as corporeal; and finally (IV), we will propose a review of the chapter's contents from the perspective of the corporality of faith. Let us add that the reflection we will set forward in Chapter Eleven on the distinctiveness of the "language game" that takes place in ritual could have, and perhaps in certain respects should have, found a place in the present chapter. We have, however, chosen to postpone it and place it within the context of a reflection on operative symbolic expression, which is more closely akin to it.

I. THE FUNDAMENTAL LAW OF RELIGIOUS RITUALITY: A SYMBOLIC PRACTICE

Numerous explanations of terms would be necessary here to delimit the object of our present reflection. We would have to explain the extension of the notion of "rite" into ethology and anthropology;[6] the various notions of "rituality," "ritualism," and

6. See J. Huxley, ed., *Le comportement rituel chez l'homme et chez l'animal* (Paris: Gallimard, 1971). "Rituals" in the animal kingdom, such as courting

"ritual";[7] the various degrees of rituality — from insane rituals, through rites of interaction, to fully formalized rituals.[8] Further, we would have to explain the typology of instituted religious rites: rites of passage of the "seasonal" kind (socio-tribal) or of the "mystery" kind (joining together into a "brotherhood" or "sisterhood"); rites of the conferring of power (investiture rites); rites of upkeep or "daily" rites, either of "purification" (exorcisms, expiatory sacrifices) or of "communion" (invocations, sacrifices of communion); and so forth.

Like most other words which end in "urgy," such as "dramaturgy" or "metallurgy," "liturgy" is a *practical activity*. Such is the *fundamental law* of rite. Because of its great significance for liturgy in general and for our subject in particular, it is worth going into this point in some detail.

1. *The Pragmatic Essence of Ritual Language*

Inasmuch as they are rituals, the sacraments are not primarily of the cognitive order, the order of "-logy," but of the practical order. Of course they do communicate information in the areas of doctrine and ethics; but they do not operate at the discursive level proper to theo-logy.

---

displays, marking territory, and preparing for or ending combat, are considered "adaptive formalizations" of behavior (p. 23) which permit a conservation of energy in the on-going adjustments of ethos which group life requires. Human rituals also perform this function, of course. But anthropologists, more aware of the rupture "culture" constitutes with regard to "nature," are less prepared than ethologists to speak of animal "rituals." Thus L. De Heusch ("Introduction à une ritologie générale," *L'unité de l'homme*, Centre de Royaumont [Paris: Seuil, 1974]) entitles the first part of his contribution "L'animal cérémoniel et l'homme rituel" ("The Ceremonial Animal and the Ritual Human," pp. 679–687) because "ceremony comes before language, but ritual comes after" (p. 687).

7. "*Rituality*" is a constitutive dimension of humankind. "*Ritualism*" designates a deviant and more or less pathological development of this dimension, notably in the direction of repetitive compulsion and obsessional neurosis (Freud), and even in the direction of "rubricism." A "*ritual*" is a sequence of programmed rites (following an oral tradition or liturgical books).

8. We can distinguish *three degrees of rituality*. Degree 3 is that of "*instituted rituals*," such as signing a treaty, taking an oath on the Bible, being married by a civil authority or in church; they always have a performative kind of ef-

Every religious ritual is of its essence so practical that it always presents itself as intending to initiate or restore communication with God, with the gods, the spirits . . . and it does this *through the simple fact* that it is carried out according to the social norms of legitimacy and validity. Every religious ritual thus purports to work *ex opere operato* in some fashion. Deeds have priority over words; or rather, *that which is truly said is that which is done.* So much is this the case that how something is said is more decisive than what is said, the content being largely determined by the context of the pronouncement. This is to say that ritual language must be treated within the framework of *pragmatics,* and not just semantics.

Now, according to the theory formulated by L. Wittgenstein on the variety of "language games," and taken up later by J. Ladrière (see ch. 11), liturgical language has this specific character: it unfolds the self-implication that is constitutive of the language of faith. Liturgical language stages this self-implication as such, ac-

---

ficacy. But below this third level, which alone interests us here, there is a second level which includes the *"interaction rites"* studied by E. Goffman (*Les rites d'interaction* [Paris: Minuit, 1974]); these are modes of behavior we have learned socially (codes of cleanliness, good manners, decorum, apparently "spontaneous" behavior to avoid losing face or causing someone else to lose face in a conversation, on the bus, in the bank or the classroom, according to the circumstances of place, time, and people involved . . .) At a still more basic level we find the rites of degree 1: rites more or less *compulsive or superstitious* (spitting on the hands before beginning to fell a tree or lift a heavy object, not stepping on the cracks in the sidewalk, making the sign of the cross before a game . . .), rites Freud described as subject to a compulsion of repetition in which he discerned the work of the death wish: even though eventually aware of their irrational character, the subject still feels a real frustration of he or she omits them. E. H. Erikson and J. Ambrose locate the origin of rituality in the preverbal experience of infants (in Huxley, *Comportement rituel,* 139–158 and 170–175). Between the various degrees of rituality, for example between the mother-nursling relation and the Eucharistic celebration, the same fundamental process of ritualization is at work, while admittedly formalized in very different ways (Erikson, "Ontogénie de la ritualisation," *Comportement rituel,* 142). We will go no further into this aspect; we have raised it here only to draw attention to the fact that rituality, unlike learning to read or walk, for example, is *not accidental* to humans; one can develop into a full subject without knowing how to read or being able to walk, but one cannot do so without ritualization.

cording to a pragmatic pattern that cannot be dismissed as merely accidental. In its diverse expressions (thanksgiving or supplication, confession or wish . . .) its unity is assured by its *illocutionary modality*, a modality that is crystallized in the efficacy of the sacramental formulas. *The symbolic "operating power" is part of the very "textuality" of the liturgy:* it belongs to its very essence as text or to the specificity of the language game which is proper to it.

This is why rites do not countenance either didacticism or moralism. Wordy explanations or sermons by which one purports to save rites in reality hinder them from operating on their proper level; this remedy is poison. And, moreover, these speeches, often wishing to free liturgical rites from "magic," risk arising from an alternative all-powerful magic: the magic of the word which believes it can change the world by its own mana. Is not the magic word, as L. de Heusch says, itself a "device-discourse"? Magicians "turn technology into language in the same way they turn language into technology."[9]

The illusion is all the easier for us Westerners in that formed by twenty-five centuries of logocentrism, we "spontaneously" direct our attention to the "ideas" the rite evokes, rather than to the "work" it does. We must therefore rid ourselves of an a priori deeply rooted in our culture and recognize that ritual is by its nature *less mental than behavioral.* It functions *at the level of the signifying* and the patterns it forms, *and not primarily at the level of the signified* and ideational "contents." Moreover, this is why the practice of solemn proclamation is often more efficacious than the content of the pronouncements themselves. The basic law of liturgy is, "Do not say what you are doing; do what you are saying."

Some will argue, "The Mass is a gathering." Agreed! But for that notion to go over, it makes much more sense to manage the space for the celebration so that the participants can see each other (instead of staring only at rows of backs), rather than talk oneself hoarse descanting on the importance of the Sunday assembly. "The altar is the table of the Eucharistic meal." No quarrel! But then let its arrangement and decoration evoke a table, and not a sacrificial stone or a depository for papers, chant books, reading

9. De Heusch, *Unité,* 701.

326

glasses, and other mismatched objects. Someone rejoins, "The Eucharist is a sharing." Of course! But then let the priest begin, when he breaks the host for the sharing in the one body of the Lord, by not consuming all by himself the bread that he has just broken!

Rite primarily functions before and beneath the advent of meanings. It is what deprives us of our desire for mastery and of our power. And this is why, in a culture whose foundation is a long metaphysical and technical tradition of the critical "inspection" of the real (see ch. 2), the required *dispossession of mastery* is so difficult for us to accept with serenity — unless we embrace (the reverse temptation) the esoteric symbolism of certain forms of parapsychology that are currently fashionable. One is in prayer as soon as one simply assumes the ritual position of kneeling; one is there as if at square one, before anything is said or even if the prayer will eventually have no other content than "Lord, I am speaking to you" or, even more, when it has no other content than the body itself in prayer, the body-as-prayer. The rite of readings from the Bible in the assembly starts well before the proclamation, "A reading from the prophet Isaiah"; it begins as soon as the assembly sits down and the reader stands up and takes the book or moves to place himself or herself before it. It is this specific kind of functioning that explains why a family, although deeply grieving over the loss of a loved one, is not offended (although exceptions are becoming less and less rare) by the fact that the priest ritually proclaims during the funeral, "Let us give thanks to the Lord our God."

2. Ritual Language in Our Culture

All this obviously does not mean that one should not be concerned about the theological quality of statements made in the liturgy and their level of credibility to the participants. In fact, even within the limits in which these statements are understood by the hearers,[10] which is the main factor in determining the significance of what is said, this theological quality remains one of the components of the liturgy's functioning. More importantly, it *is more and more a part of contemporary culture for people to demand to understand*

10. The expression is from J. Y. Hameline, "Aspects du rite," LMD 119, 108.

what is said; if they do not understand, they suspect mystification. That behind this request there may be a certain amount of illusion, even a large degree of pretention and a new form of naiveté (all the more dangerous for one's claiming to be no longer naive because one is "over eighteen"), is not sufficient reason to refuse to hear such a request which is here expressed collectively. Contemporary liturgy should *integrate this demand for intelligibility,* lest it fall victim to what A. Vergote calls the phenomenon of "desymbolization," that is, a rupture and isolation from the ambient culture. Granted, in honoring such a request, the liturgy risks drifting into the logomachy we have criticized above; but "suspicion" is such a characteristic trait of contemporary culture that our celebrations must sufficiently speak to the "brain" in order to speak to the "heart."

The *post-Tridentine* reform and, perhaps even more, the Ultramontane current of the second half of the nineteenth century created a liturgical ethos strongly oriented toward the all-powerful divine majesty and the humble respect appropriate for Christian people in its presence: propriety and decorum demanded that the people — awed by the liturgical pomp of the richly embroidered priestly vestments, the gold of the ciboria, the elevation of the throne — respond with a humble submission to the ceremonial, numerous external signs of respect, strongly interiorized attitudes of adoration and repentance, a "sacred" silence alone suited to the holy place . . . The reform of *Vatican II,* itself of course the expression of a much larger and more profound cultural mutation, engendered a completely different ethos: calling the Christian people to a "full, conscious, and active participation,"[11] it gave rise to a true revolution — whose full extent the council fathers probably did not realize. Where the "sacred" barrier of Latin had served as a protective screen, the use of the vernacular (so intelligible that its first effect on the congregation was to make them understand they did not understand . . .) as well as rites made more meaningful by being significantly simplified and carried out in full view of the congregation require that from now on we "go and see." As a consequence, the relationship of Christians with their liturgical celebrations lost its first innocence; it became more critical and awakened the suspicion, right or wrong, that they finally saw unveiled the mechanism behind the functioning of the ritual, a mechanism of which they had been ignorant until then. Such an unveiling typically brings with it what R.

11. *Constitution on the Sacred Liturgy,* no. 14.

Girard calls a *crisis in sacrifice*,[12] which is easy to observe today: from the moment the cultural unanimity of the group bursts open and a suspicion of mystification — lodged first by an "elite" (often supported by priests, traditionally agents specializing in worship) — if not openly admitted, is at least breathed in by everyone with the very air of the times, a crisis in ritual is inevitable.

To allow our Christian rites their opportunity to function in the symbolic mode that is proper to them, it is absolutely necessary to take into consideration these fundamental characteristics of our culture. Of course, being a *symbolic* action and thus not aiming, like technological action, at bringing about a transformation of the world, but at working upon the subjects in their relations with God and with one another, the efficacy of rites is never under our control; symbols, by their nature, escape us. But still, their mode of functioning is at least partially regulable. In this sense, if we do not take into consideration the "values" of the ambient culture which nourish the projects of our contemporaries, in particular critical suspicion and the demand for intelligibility, we take away from our rites their chance of functioning symbolically. This also means that calling upon certain archaisms, either psychological or social, which are effectively put into play through ritual activities, is itself suspect. When we call upon such archaisms, we risk looking for an imaginary refuge in an idealized past which, under the excuse of being "inexpressible," is only a neo-romanticism in danger of sliding toward any of the many forms of theosophy and endorsement of the occult which batten on the uncertainties of our age. We are thus forewarned about this "unmasterable" power of symbols; we have mentioned it and we will have occasion to discuss it further.

These various reflections do not call into question the fundamental law of rituality as symbolic practice. They are aimed, once the true significance of this law is grasped, only at avoiding certain naive interpretations which, under the guise of "science" — ethnology in particular — are led, in connection with the current cultural fashion for the exotic and ancient, to obscure a *fundamental difference in the way rituals are apprehended* in homeostatic societies, that is, those which are comparatively stable and closed, such as

12. See R. Girard, *La violence et le sacré* (Paris: Grasset, 1972) 76–77.

those traditional societies studied by ethnologists and folklorists, and, by contrast, in an open, pluralistic, and ever changing society such as our own.

II. A THEOLOGICAL INTERPRETATION
OF SEVERAL MAJOR COMPONENTS OF RITUALITY

Symbolic practice: this fundamental law governs the various dimensions of all rituality. We will take up four (without pretending to be exhaustive) that clearly show the *concrete modality* according to which the Church sees itself as "radically involved" in the sacraments.

1. *The Symbolic Rupture*

a) The Borderline Nature of Rites (Hetero-topy). A ritual always involves a symbolic rupture with the everyday, the ephemeral, the ordinary. A church, a temple, a high place, a sacred wood, or simply the space around a tree or in the center of the village square, whether it be permanent or temporary — the *place* of religious ritual is always "consecrated," that is, set apart, taken out of its ordinary status as a neutral space by a symbolic marker of some kind (at least a provisional one). In such a way the Hebrews marked off their camp at the base of the mountain at the time of the theophany on Sinai (Exod 19:12). It is the same with *time:* ritual time is lived differently from that of everyday life. The time of the Jewish Sabbath or again of the Christian Sunday is different from that of the remainder of the week; formerly this difference was strongly marked by a whole series of rites which included "Sunday clothes," the prohibition of "servile" work, the ringing of bells, getting together in the village square or at the cafe, a more copious meal . . .

The *objects* or materials used in ritual are equally separated from their usual utilitarian purposes: a golden chalice is used for drinking, exactly like a glass; but it is of such another order that at the extreme, its form and gleaming decorative ornaments scarcely allow its original purpose to show. In the same way our hosts have been so removed from their status as ordinary bread that, now flat, round, and white, they remind us of bread only with great difficulty.

What has just been said concerning the objects or materials, whose ritual purpose may be permanent or temporary, can be said equally of the *agents* of ritual; the "priestly" officials may have, depending on the group or the type of ritual, the status of being permanently "consecrated" or may be only temporarily recognized as socially qualified to carry out such and such a ritual function. But in any case, not just anybody can do just anything. Rituality requires the distribution of roles and specific functions, often linked with rites of purification which allow contact with the "sacred," always regarded as dangerous.

Like the place, the time, the objects or materials, and the agents, ritual *language* is also specific. This may be a "sacred language," such as the special language sometimes revealed during initiation rites or a language that has become more or less dead (Hebrew, Classical Greek, Syriac, Latin, Old Slavonic . . .). However, this may also be the vernacular language but released from its habitual usage either by the statements themselves, more or less rigorously formalized (traditional vocabulary and images, redundancies, a great number of repetitious formulas . . .), or by the particular rhythm and tone of voice, which may repeat and repeat or simply mutter the formulas, may proclaim petitions, jubilations, and thanksgivings loud and clear, or may modulate the pronouncements according to multiple possibilities ranging from a murmur to psalmody to singing.

We could lengthen our list, especially at the level of gesture and posture. The elements mentioned above suffice to indicate the *"borderline nature"* of rites.[13] In effect, they are always in a liminal position, removed from the ordinary and on the threshold of the "sacred." Their place is different from that of the everyday. As thus "hetero-topic" ("placed elsewhere"), they work in a different setting. It remains that we must find the right distance. In what concerns our Christian liturgies, the problem is to measure the symbolic distance between the two extremes of the "too much" and the "not enough."

13. Hameline, "Aspects du rite," 107.

b) Negotiating Between Two Thresholds.

— *"Hieratism"*

There is a threshold of *maximal hetero-topy* beyond which rite cannot function. From being strange, it becomes foreign. In insufficient contact with the expressed or latent cultural values of the group, desymbolized, rite tends to regress to the point where all it can do is appeal to each person's imagination. An entire private phantasmagoria may then unfold at the psychic level, but the symbolism has been deprived of its opportunity for success.

This danger particularly threatens any sensibility too finely attuned to the "sacred" character of the sacraments. Under the pretext of being set apart, they become so *hieratic*, frozen, venerable, and untouchable that they no longer evolve along with the culture and no longer tolerate any spontaneity of expression. It is appropriate at this point to ask oneself what "sacred" or "sense of the sacred" would thus be preserved. "It is the sacred conceived as exterior power and authority, the sacred of a transcendence toward which any proximity would be considered a sacrilegious intrusion," as Vergote describes it. The author continues, "One easily recognizes in this sacred an unmovable authority to which the superego unconsciously transfers its unsettling power." Hence the kinship of this rite with "obsessive ceremonial: rigorous and rigid formalization, isolation from the living forms of the culture, absence or severe reduction of the symbolizing intention, and for many believers a serious anxiety over non-completion of the ritual."[14]

This sort of exaggeration of the heterogeneity of rite is, moreover, nourished by cultic *conservatism*. Following its own programming, of which we will speak below, a rite tends to reproduce itself over generations and even over centuries, according to a process which often has little to do with the original conditions which gave rise to it. Following the American sociologist A. L. Stinchcombe, L. Voyé has shown that ritual behaviors belong to social processes which, born under the pressure of various social factors (economic, political, ethical, religious . . .), tend to *maintain themselves* because the social effects they produce are ex-

14. A. Vergote, *Dette et désir*, 136.

perienced as beneficial, even though they have ceased to maintain contact with the original conditions that created them. There is thus a disjunction between the logic of their production and the logic of their reproduction.[15]

According to the author, traditional Sunday worship is a good example of this. Beyond the "theological" reasons which churchgoers could give at the conscious level, there is evidence of unconscious motives, which derive from various social benefits (such as the desire to incorporate certain values of the elite, especially by aligning oneself with a higher social class which evaluates churchgoing positively) or psychological benefits (a way of managing guilt) and which are in fact more responsible for the maintenance of the custom than the religious reasons one could adduce. Just as the valorization of the raw or the rotten, the cooked or the boiled according to various cultures reveals an unconscious cultural code (C. Lévi-Strauss), just as the kind of photographs taken by amateurs is, in terms of subjects, the angles of perspective, the quality sought in the product, an unconscious expression of a given socio-cultural level (P. Bourdieu), just as the sort of home sought (H. Raymond) or the style of clothes worn (R. Barthes)[16] are themselves, at least statistically, symbols of a given socio-cultural "world," so Sunday churchgoing itself is a symbolic behavior revealing norms and values which are *all the more powerful for being less conscious.* And as, according to Girard, becoming conscious of what he calls the mechanism of victimization leads to a "crisis in sacrifice," so becoming conscious of the psychological or social motives of Sunday practice risks "destroying its efficacy," an efficacy that is often the more firmly ingrained the more its real motives, often interiorized from early childhood, seem self-evident, completely "natural," and thus not open to being questioned.[17]

It is this which explains, at least partly, the discrepancy frequently noted by sociologists of religion between requests to the Church for rites of passage (especially baptism, marriage, and burial) and the content of people's faith. This divorce can be so extreme that a request for a sacra-

---

15. L. Voyé, *Sociologie du geste religieux* (Brussels: Ed. Ouvrières, 1973) 213–218.
16. See C. Lévi-Strauss, *Le cru et le cuit* (Paris: Plon, 1964) Ouverture; P. Bourdieu, et al., *Un art moyen: Essai sur les usages sociaux de la photographie* (Paris: Minuit, 1965); H. Raymond and N. Haumont, *L'habitat pavillonnaire* (Paris: Inst. de Soc. Urb., Centre de Rech. d'Urban); R. Barthes, *Le système de la mode* (Paris: Seuil, 1967). In a more general way, see especially P. Bourdieu, *La distinction: Critique sociale du jugement* (Paris: Minuit, 1979).
17. Voyé, *Sociologie,* 212.

ment can go together with a personal declaration of unbelief;[18] in fact, in this case the request is often made with a greater insistence. This is so because the archaic psychic reactions unleashed by the events of birth, falling in love, and death, as well as the norms of social behavior imposed on each person in these cases by their social milieu, are the more powerful for being latent. It is actually the "sacred" such people seek. Such a "sacred" has a halo of religion, but it is fundamentally "anonymous," related to this latent and free-floating omnipresence, or to this "region of Being": "the ground of the 'there-is' in the depths." Such a sacred is experienced as essentially "inviolable."[19] As a matter of fact, what is behind (although unrecognized) requests addressed to the Church for rites of passage seems to belong to what is experienced as so inviolable that one cannot betray it without betraying oneself and one's socio-cultural "world," both traditional and present. There are, as one says, "things which are simply not done." Not to request marriage in the Church would be, in many cases, to diminish oneself in one's own eyes and in the eyes of one's relatives. It goes without saying that the reception accorded to such requests, if it seeks to be gospel-like, cannot overlook the powerful weight exercised by this "reality" — though this still should not predetermine an automatically positive response . . .

Although conservative by nature, rites undergo *mutations* as do living organisms, mutations which seem to transmit themselves in a hereditary manner, similar to the way genetic traits are passed on, even to the point of occasionally producing a degenerate line. Each mutation in fact tends to become *fossilized* in some way. A rite is made of various sedimentary levels, each one deposited on another. To each generation, the uppermost layer seems obviously alive, and one has an easy time, as the history of Christian liturgy abundantly illustrates, justifying, most often through *allegory,* the layers accumulated earlier: for example, we know how various accessories which originally had a practical purpose, such as the amice or the maniple, became "priestly vestments" that were later justified allegorically by associating them with the virtues or spiritual dispositions the priest, in preparing to say Mass, was to "put on." In the same way, the principal parts of the Eucharistic celebration were submerged under an accumulation of rites, signs,

18. See J. Sutter, "Opinion des Français sur leurs croyances et leurs comportements religieux," LMD 122 (1975) 59–83; Voyé, *Sociologie,* 224.

19. A. Vergote, "Equivoques et articulation du sacré," *Le sacré: Etudes et recherches,* Colloque Castelli (Paris: Aubier-Montaigne, 1974).

objects, and prayers. Having become unrecognizable, the l██
was in the process of being asphyxiated under these too abun██
riches. Revolving in orbit by virtue of its acquired kinetic momen██
tum, impervious to any cultural attraction, the liturgy no longer
spoke to Christians, except perhaps at one remove by invoking an
immemorial tradition: for the Christians of Europe as for the
Bororos of the Amazon or the Azandes of Ethiopia, the ritual symbols had no more justification than a "we don't know why, but
it's always been done this way." For example, who today can
(still?) use as an effective symbol an anointing done on the fly by
a thumb barely moist with oil drawn from a tiny bottle, opaque,
filled with absorbent cotton of a dubious cleanliness, if not just
that "it's always been done this way"? This disease was so griev-
ous that most considered it normal not to understand: Should one
not respect the "mystery" and its "sacred secret"? And was it
not sufficient that the priests, those specialists in the sacred, held
the key to the mysterious functioning of the rites and that they
assured things would go well through their proper, perhaps even
scrupulous, observance of the rubrics? Stuck in the rubrical orbit
of the unchangeable, isolated from the cultural values that nourish
the modern ethos breathed in by everyone, willy-nilly, along with
the air of the time, these liturgical rites, excessively foreign to the
surrounding world, could only become meaningless.

— *Trivialization*
In reaction against this ritual conservatism and in connection
with the valorization of the prophetic aspect of the gospel, there
have recently developed within the Catholic Church movements
gripped with such a passion to "celebrate Jesus Christ in everyday
life" that they also end up, although for reasons opposite to those
of the preceding group, not giving rites a chance to function. For
there is also a *threshold of minimal hetero-topy*, short of which this
opportunity is lost. Trivialized under the excuse of being "relevant"; employing only everyday language, gestures, and objects;
often drowned in a verbiage of explanation and moralistic ser-
monizing, rites become no more than pretexts for doing something
else. People's ideologies are given free rein and often become in
their turn more rigid than the constraint of the ritual programming
they wish to combat.

tation has been the stronger these last decades
mitted lay people and clerics. Perhaps this
itable: when the cultural soup continues to be
se lid has been closed tight, everything ends
e damage is in direct proportion to the pres-
e have been great benefits resulting from criti-
t had become too petrified; we will return to
this later. However, due to a lack of reflection on the nature of
rituality, the liturgy has sometimes been transformed into a mini-
course in theology or a strategy session in protest behavior — all
of which have their importance, but which are better carried on
some place else . . .

Sound ritual requires a minimum of *symbolic distance* with regard
to everyday language, gestures, and attitudes. This distance
should certainly be *negotiated pastorally* regarding various factors:
first, the cultural factor, which seems to require less rupture and
programming than it did formerly for the liturgy to function well
today in Western countries; other factors also, such as the number
of participants (one does not celebrate in a group of ten as one
does in a large crowd), the place (the celebration in an ordinary
room is different from a celebration in a cathedral), the occasion or
practice of the group (a daily Mass will be more flexible, although
not necessarily more devoid of ritual, to spare the participants
from having to subjectively invest themselves too strenuously
every day, than a Sunday Mass or, even more, a major feast), the
average age of the group (children, teenagers, adults), or its dominant ideology . . . The limit beyond which rites can function
properly is not always the same. But it is not by disguising this
limit under a supposedly "natural" spontaneity that one will save
liturgical rituality (What is more cultural and even ideological than
a desperate search for the "natural"? What is more contradictory
than a spontaneity on demand?) Of course, one may use these
procedures for a positive pedagogy of the faith, and it is sometimes necessary to go that route with certain groups: "the sabbath
was made for humankind, and not humankind for the sabbath."
But by doing this we simply put off the problem.

c) A Theological Interpretation of Ritual Hetero-topy. As critical as it
may be with regard to "sacralization" (see above), Christian faith

cannot survive without religion, and therefore without rites. And it obviously cannot evade the anthropological and sociological laws for the functioning of rituals, beginning with the law of the symbolic rupture. Lacking this, the demon of ritualism one pretends to expel returns at a gallop bringing seven others worse than himself, disguised as a dogmatism or moralism more dangerous and no less naive than the religious "magic" one wants to get rid of.

Now, at the heart of its ambivalences, the ritual rupture performs a symbolic function that is extremely beneficial to faith. It creates *an empty space with regard to the immediate and utilitarian*. Inasmuch as it is of a ritual nature, the liturgy is essentially beyond the useful-useless distinction. In itself it is of no didactic usefulness, for it is not a mini-course in theology or a catechism session; of no moral usefulness, for its function is not to "recharge our batteries," or to rally the parish "troops" or an elite shock corps, or on the more affective plane, to foster warm spiritual experiences; of no aesthetic usefulness, for it is not primarily a "spectacle," or even a "feast," in the sense made classic by R. Caillois, among others. Of course, there is also — in fact, there must be — something of the aesthetic, the moral, and the didactic in liturgy. But these empirical elements are not essential to it; a sober liturgy, and thus one with little of the festive about it, may be more useful for bringing about a sacramental connection of the participants with Christ than a celebration where everybody has such "a good time" that it no longer allows this pedagogical rupture without which the sense of the "otherness" of God cannot be made real. That participants find in the celebration something which gives them fresh courage, elements of catechesis that enlighten them, or a theological insight they look forward to pondering afterward is certainly desirable, even indispensable in certain respects: one cannot put life in separate compartments; and besides, these elements, as we have emphasized above, belong to the just claims of the time and the cultural needs without which the liturgy could no longer function at its proper, if different, level. All this is well and good; but it does not change the fact that rituality functions at *another level*, the level of symbol.

Now, at this symbolic level, rituality, by way of the non-utilitarian use of objects, places, language . . . which is proper to itself, effects a decisive *break* with the ordinary world. A space is thus created, a space for breathing, for freedom, for gratuitousness where God may come. Without such a break, the odds are great that the celebration of Jesus Christ will function in fact (and doubtless in all good faith) as an excuse for smug self-celebration. The symbolic rupture allows us the intense experience of the *letting go* of our theological knowledge, our ethical "good works," our personal "experiences" of God — in short, the multiple psychological and ideological ruses we unconsciously deploy to subject the gospel to our own agenda — without which there is no possibility of a true welcome for the graciousness of God.

The less conscious this "letting go," the more it gives structure to our faith. The reason the symbolism of the ritual rupture seems to have such significance is that *we do not master it;* rather, it masters us. In this ritual rupture we do not find a *treatise* on the otherness and graciousness of God, but an *intense experience* of this otherness and graciousness. Such an experience is more decisive in the symbolic "work" it does in us than are discourses, as indispensable as these may be for the critical discernment which must take place to avoid aberrations in practice. One does not require a riotous feast to ritually symbolize satiety at the eschatological banquet, but only a little bread and wine. It is not an everyday drinking glass that one uses for the wine of the reign, but a cup which, without being necessarily gold or encrusted with gems, is clearly something more than an ordinary utensil. For reading the Scriptures as the Word of God, one does not pick up a simple working Bible, more or less grimy, still less a single piece of paper, as if it were enough just to have the written text to satisfy the rubric "reading": the binding, the ornamentation, and the size of the lectionary, as well as the style of the ambo or the pulpit from which the readings are given; the reader's posture and tone of voice — all these are primary symbolic supports for the recognition of the Scriptures as the "Word of God"; they are even *more effective than all our discourses* on this subject, as necessary as these are at the appropriate time. Because an identity is never the fruit of reasoning but the origin of the discourses we make, it is through these symbolic expressions which pervade us — all the more as they operate outside our "reasons" for belief — that each one of us is initiated into the mystery of Christ. To seek to reverse this process under the pretext that it is the plow that does the work and not the oxen is to condemn oneself in advance to sterile efforts with the result that the field of human endeavor will never bear Christian fruit.

As in the various preceding examples, the simple fact of putting one's papers away during a working weekend and placing a table so that it is facing outward, with sufficient spatial distance so that the group does not symbolically (and thus really, at the ideological level) imprison Christ, whom they are going to celebrate, or the fact of decorating this table, even in a relatively simple way, as is suitable in an ordinary room — all this belongs to this "silent language"[20] which speaks, and speaks in an illocutionary way, much more than discourses. That God is the Different, that God's difference, perceived on the symbolic register as the Other, is *Grace* — all this is said "performatively" and *before a word is spoken* through the ritual rupture; all this is said by being done in a symbolic practice where we do not limit ourselves to *speaking about* God's grace (which could be done in more or less empty words), but where we open up, through an effective break with the useful, a space of gratuitousness where God can come. Is ritual hetero-topy ambiguous? Of course! Moreover, this is exactly why the critical practitioner of faith must be constantly vigilant. But what opportunities for structuring the faith are at the very heart of this ambiguity which touches the most human part of our humanity! Well before being formulated in a creed, it is through the mediation of these primary unconceptualized symbolisms that the confession of faith in the otherness and graciousness of God takes place in practice and takes flesh in us.

2. *Symbolic Programming and Reiteration*

a) Ritual Metonymy. According to its Indo-European etymology, the Sanskrit word *rita* means "what is in accord with order."[21] It is in fact characteristic of all religious ritual to be *received from a tradition*. One never invents a ritual; it is, by nature, *programmed in advance*, a trait which by the same token allows it *to be identically*

---

20. E. T. Hall, *Le langage silencieux* (Paris: Mame, 1973) ch. 10 "L'espace parle."

21. L. Benoist, *Signes, symboles et mythes* (Paris: PUF, 1975) 95.

repeated at regular intervals, each year, season, week, new moon, or else at each "season" of human life, at each generation, or for every important occasion in the life of a group. This is, moreover, what the noun or adjective "ritual" indicates in French and English.

Programming is constitutive of the religious rite insofar as one acts there *as the ancestors acted, as the founder* (mythic, historicized, or historical) acted. Even more, one does this *because* they (supposedly) acted this way. Religious rites thus point, like a finger, toward the origin, through the identical reiteration, from generation to generation, of the "same," programmed at the foundation *in illo tempore* ("in those days"). By putting between parentheses the time that separates today from the eponymous ancestor or the historical founder (Moses, Jesus, Muhammad), they function according to the symbolism of *metonymic elision*. They thereby form the prime reservoir of the collective memory of the group. In an anamnestic reimmersing of the group into the primordial time where it was born, ritual erects a barrier against the forces of death which relentlessly threaten to destroy the group's identity and the significance of the world.

Ritual's *regular repetition* has an initiatory effect of the greatest importance. Reiterating the same gestures and the same formulas in identical circumstances and following a fairly regular periodic rhythm, it implants the values of the group into the body of each member, in the end "sticking to the skin" (for here also — here especially — everything is in the "skin") so that the values appear completely "natural." Is *initiation* really anything else than this inculcation of a culture through a slow impregnation? Of course, this process is fraught with serious ambiguities: between initiation into a system of Christian values and initiation into the gospel there is sometimes a large gap. Moreover, ritual programming and reiteration are so booby-trapped that they can easily veer toward all sorts of psychologically pathological or socially alienating conduct: ritualism, attachment to minutiae, a morbid need for purification or expiation, social inertia, conservatism, a defense of the established order, routines . . .

b) A Theological Interpretation of Ritual Programming and Reiteration. It remains that, well managed, ritual programming and reiteration also play an eminently positive symbolic function in the structuring of the faith. Because it is *only* symbolic, the metonymic elision of time, far from filling the distance to the origin, *deepens* it instead. The irreducibility of the absence of the founder (Jesus Christ in this case) is thus manifested, as well as the practical impossibility of our ever recapturing our Christian origin. But, *because* it is symbolic, it brings about a relation of vital communication with this founding origin. Thus, when we do again the supper of the Lord; when we do it again *as* he did it (according to the accounts the gospel traditions deliver to us) and *because* he did it this way; when we take in our hands what he himself took, that is, bread and wine; and when we say again words that are not our own, but his — even more, *because* they are from him and not from us who could nevertheless "translate" them into more comprehensible and poetic language — we do something absolutely primordial for faith: we confess in act the impregnable character of a rite over which we have no power because we perform and live it as having begun in Jesus, the Lord. We thus confess in act that our identity is due to our adhering to him, that the Church exists only by receiving itself from him, its Lord; *we confess in act* what we say with language in the creed: Jesus, the Crucified One, is *our Lord*.[22] We are no longer explaining his lordship theologically, we are living it out symbolically even in our bodies — our own bodies, but also, simultaneously, the social body of the Church. Here again, this process is all the more pregnant in that it works below the level of consciousness, at the pre-reflective level of the symbolic and is not the object of a discourse (as indispensable as this may be in an analytical review conducted at another time),

22. The preceding discussion does not close the door on the possibility of a Eucharistic celebration with *other elements than bread and wine*, in Africa for example. It is a difficult question. Is it bread and wine as such (with their powerful symbolic content in the biblical perspective) or the meal as such (a meal where bread and wine would have essentially a cultural value as a basic food and a festive drink) that Jesus instituted as a sacramental sign of his life delivered up? In any case, it is always through an *act of the interpreting Church* that such a rite is recognized as "sacrament" or that such and such a way of doing things is recognized as "the Lord's Supper." See L.-M. Chauvet, "Sacrements et institution," *La théologie à l'épreuve de la vérité*, CERIT (Paris: Cerf, 1984) 230–232.

but of an action. Indeed, there is here, on the plane of ritual anthropology, a radical involvement of the Church and of the believer, all the more radical because it takes place before and beneath our justifying explanations.

We must add that the *radical dependence* thus confessed is our dependence on *this* Jesus of Nazareth who, on the eve of his death, gathered his friends for a meal of farewell. This ritual programming as confession-of-faith-in-act symbolizes, before any words, the scandalous detour imposed on faith by the humanity and singular story of this human being, executed as a criminal and confessed by us Lord of the world. We grasp, through this detour into the Jewishness of him whom we nonetheless acknowledge as going beyond Jewishness, the importance of the traditional question concerning the institution of the sacraments by Jesus Christ. But we do so here in a concrete manner and from the context where the question arises, that is, from the very act of celebration. The theological discussion on this point will thus consist in translating into a coherent discourse this *impregnable* character of the rite which is already lived symbolically in the celebration. We shall come back to this.

In the same perspective, the ritual programming is the act of the symbolic proclamation of the identity of the Christian group, not only as the unique universal Church of Jesus Christ receiving itself from his grace, but simultaneously as an *apostolic* Church. To do again what our ancestors have done throughout the generations is also, metonymicly, to do again what the first apostolic communities did. Like baptism of water and the words of Matthew 28:19, the Eucharist is not the property of any one particular Christian group, whether in time or space. One can receive it only from a *tradition*. In identically reiterating it throughout the centuries (at least, of course, in its major points), the Church confesses in act its apostolic origin.

c) Pastoral Negotiation. Obviously, this programming is to be negotiated pastorally, avoiding both the "too much" and the "not enough," according to the same factors of place, number, and so on we mentioned above with regard to symbolic distance.

— *"Fixism"*

To the "hieratism" of maximal hetero-topy there corresponds

"fixism," or rubricism, indicative of a too rigid programming. The criticisms that we may address to this too rigorous codification are of the same kind as those mentioned above with regard to the excessive separation between rites and lived experience: a sacred of purely external transcendence which tolerates no proximity under pain of sacrilege and which is only the uneasy projection of an all-powerful super-ego; a conservatism which freezes rites into museum pieces (possibly admirable as well as venerable) and which thus, under the pretext of respect for the "tradition" — we should ask here, "What *tradition?*" just as we asked before "What *sacred?*" — prohibits any creativity (which, as history demonstrates, then finds release outside the celebration); a ritualistic slide toward a repetitive formalism and obsessional neurosis when the rubrics have not been followed to the letter. In brief, a considerable blunting of the salient points of the gospel message and at the same time a cultural desymbolization. It is not necessary to elaborate on these pitfalls at greater length — they have been frequently denounced for several decades, which by the way risks encouraging the opposite excess . . . Let us add that a too rigid programming leads ritual toward intolerance: it excludes those who do not submit to its rigorous rules or who simply will not "conform."

— *Deprogramming*

Conversely, an insufficient programming is equally dangerous. The current that has flowed (must we speak only in the past tense?) in this direction has been fed either by an ideology of "spontaneity" or "naturalism" desirous of finding again, in the wake of the revolutionary activities of the sixties, an innocent "authenticity" beyond institutional strictures judged to be oppressive or by a militant ideology anxious to reinvigorate the liturgy "prophetically" by appealing to "the truth of ordinary life," which would consist especially in the collective struggles against structural injustice maintained by dominant classes. This current of deprogramming carries the risk of a *new intolerance* perhaps more redoubtable than the old. For within ritual too rigorously programmed one may still arrange at least a little space for evasion: one meditates, one says one's rosary, one recites prayers from the missal, all activities more or less on the periphery of the liturgical action itself but about which one feels no guilt because there are many ways of being united "by intention" with what the priest is doing and because one trusts in a rite constructed in some sense to "go by itself" . . . On the contrary, when the programming is inadequate, the level of familiarity necessary for any ritual is too low. One risks generating discomfort, even anxiety, among the participants ("What are they going to ask us to do now?") and, in any case, risks no longer leaving them enough personal space to breathe. Everyone must now submit to the often preachy ideology which has been imposed on rite. The latter can no longer carry out one of its major positive functions (ambiguous in any case, of course): its *protective* function with regard to the investment of subjectivity and permanent attention necessary if each person is to reach *"the"* meaning of the formulas and action for himself or herself. When an ideology takes possession of a rite, which in itself is anti-ideological, it causes the rite to generate a new intolerance which quickly becomes more unbearable than the old. There ensues, in spite of good intentions, a de facto elitism which practically excludes those who are not able to fit the new ideological mould and also a sort of neo-pelagianism in which rite becomes a self-justifying expression of "correct thinking" within the group and the reward for its "good behavior." Under cover of Jesus Christ and the Spirit, it is the group itself which continues to speak itself in the liturgical prayer. The indirect addressee (the group) displaces the primary addressee (God), who serves as an alibi.

When a group deprograms ritual to this degree, it *deprives* the community of what really belongs to it. There are no more reference points; instead, there is a blurring, more or less systematic, of referential vocabulary and traditional actions. Creativity is overvalued without the group's taking into account that because of the simple fact the code is unrecognizable, the discourse, while perhaps decipherable in each of its unit words or phrases, has gone beyond the limits within which it is comprehensible and because of this can no longer be understood. Then the ritual functions just as obscurely as did the Latin of yore, without, however, the familiarity of certain sounds or expressions which people at least "understood" even if they could not have said them . . . When one seizes a rite, no longer respecting its impregnable character, the rite takes its revenge. Thus, once a group is so obsessed by the dangers, very real certainly, of programming that it will allow nothing that is not "spontaneous," 'authentic,'' or "true to life,'' that group is the victim of grave illusions: nothing is more manipulative than power hiding behind the apparently generous but ultimately demagogic extension of "equality," and nothing is more censorious than a libertarian spontaneity which purports to "express itself" truthfully; most often, in fact, what is expressed are only the fleeting feelings and convictions which the group expects. Good improvisation requires the long maturation of tradition sufficiently digested to be presented in a manner suitable to each situation. One does not mistreat rite with impunity. Small, relatively stable groups that frequently celebrate the liturgy among themselves, perhaps everyday, know well, sometimes from bitter experience, how important it is to trust the protective function of rite, especially through the symbolic rupture and programming; otherwise, participants find themselves under an imperious command calling for a permanent personal investment, so that the celebration eventually becomes psycho-socially unbearable.

— *Programming Today*

The criticism we have just leveled against the insufficiency of programming does not by any means take away, of course, nor even minimize, what we said earlier about the reverse tendency. Taking into account the cultural evolution in our Western societies, it seems that, as with the law of symbolic rupture, the law of programming requires *more flexibility* today than in former times. The present situation concerning this point is such that it is desirable, as M. Scouarnec writes, "to consider liturgical programs as *sketches*" on which one may embroider with a fairly free hand, just as was done, incidentally, in the Church of the first three centuries at least.[23] We should use this freedom, not to indulge in an imaginary reconstruction of the "primitive Church" (which is no more possible for us to imitate than the medieval) or in a desire to "modernize," but simply to prevent our liturgical rites from becoming desymbolized and to give them the opportunity to function in a distinctively Christian manner.

To avoid the mediocrity of over-hasty "improvisations" or of a "creativity" not theologically pertinent or insufficiently ritualized, serious work has to take place. The heart of this difficult work lies in rendering meaningful for each assembly the main lines of the celebration and the usual ritual pronouncements, that is, first in *decoding* and then in *reencod-*

23. M. Scouarnec, *Vivre, croire, célébrer* (Paris: Ed. Ouvrières, 1983) 70.

ing the traditional formulas. These will thus be both repeated as far as their ritual statement and their most significant terms or expressions go and then made more explicit in a more contemporary language. Of course, one foresees at once the danger that menaces such an attempt to make explicit: a return to a discursive ''-logy,'' either theological or moral. Now, this decoding must remain, especially in the central sequence of a rite, strongly ritualized: simple formulas, rhythmic, without "explanations," spoken with some solemnity, followed immediately by the action which is their "performative" significance . . . For example: "To follow Jesus Christ, the only Lord, / do you renounce to live under the reign of sin, / under the reign of might makes right, / under the reign of everyone for himself or herself? . . ." "The Church believes in God, Father and Creator. It believes that God gives the earth to all, / that God makes every human being in God's image / and that God thus gives us every human being to love as a brother or sister. And you, do you believe in this God, Father and Creator of the heavens and the earth? . . ."

When we do this, it is indeed the baptism of the catholic, and apostolic Church we are celebrating. We have "invented" nothing which does not belong to the traditional faith of this Church. But we have celebrated it as baptism into this local Church community at this time — a community that is the integral concrete realization of the one Church of Jesus.

3. *A Symbolic Economy of Spareness*

From the ethological point of view, "ritual" actions (in J. Huxley's sense of the word) are adaptive formalizations of behavior favoring an *economy of energy*. One finds this trait also in anthropology: rituality functions in an economical manner. Of course, there is often a profusion of means (multiple objects, formulas endlessly repeated), but it is a profusion of *small means:* through metaphor the victims' blood sprinkled upon the people and the altar becomes the pledge of the covenant with God; through metonymy the entire earth is represented by a few of its fruits.

In the same way, it is the *small amount* of bread or water that is the condition for the operation of the Eucharistic or baptismal symbolism. On the condition, of course, that this "small amount" be not "*too small*," that is, that it constitute a support sufficient for the symbolism to function. The drift of the symbol toward insignificance has played a bad joke on us in the liturgy. However, it is not through a plentiful feast that one will most successfully symbolize the paschal banquet to which Christ invites his people or by mad gambols in a large swimming pool that one will live sacramentally death and resurrection with him. A piece of bread, a simple gesture, a few well-chosen words are all that are necessary. In this way rite protects itself by its spareness against the invasion of a romantic subjectivity desperate for "spontaneous-and-total-expression." In some way it restores "availability" to the self. Kept in check by ritual ascesis, the self can be *available* for the welcome of the Other, and indeed of what the Other wishes to bestow upon it.

This economy of means is theologically a powerful symbolic representation of the *eschatological not yet* of the reign, nevertheless already inaugurated in the Church. Against every species of eschatological impatience, the rite serves to defend us against the ever-recurring dream of a reign without the Church. Its modest discretion protects us from believing we have reached it. Rather, it directs us toward this sense of humor that is the cardinal virtue through which believers adjust themselves to the patience of God. Here again, what is distinctive of rituality is that it causes us to live this humble eschatological sacramentality through the mode of symbolic *practice,* well before we conceptualize it as such and in a manner more radical than in our discourses.

4. *An Indexical Symbolism*

a) Positioning by the Ritual. We said above that the rite is not first of all a matter of mental content but of behavioral index. In this regard, it belongs to what in cybernetics is called "digitality," in contrast to "analogy." *Analogy* is suited to the world of language; one refines an idea; one "modulates" it in various ways. In the domain of faith or ethics, for example, the positions are generally analogical: always in flux, they can be located on a gradual *continuum.* One is more or less believing ("Lord, I believe; help my unbelief!"), just as ethical action is more or less evangelical.

Ritual exists in a regime that is *digital,* indexical, deictic: it *positions.* One cannot be half-baptized, no more than one can make a half-Communion. There is no negotiation at this stage (except interiorly, but we are not on that level at the moment). Like an index, it designates our status to others. This is one of ritual's essential functions, which can be divided into three aspects. First, it *delimits* the group by providing it with symbolic points of reference concerning its identity. Second, it *integrates* individuals within the group; each receives a name there and is assigned a place — nothing more than that place, but every bit that place. Third, it parcels out *different roles* to individuals or to sub-groups, an action that is indispensable to the functioning of the community: whenever power is not allocated explicitly to someone or to several people, it is always there to be grasped by anyone; and the more disguised it is the more easily it is seized and manipulated.

The digital function of rite is probably one of the elements which explain the forceful requests for the rites of passage from the Church, requests largely independent of the degree of belief, as we observed above. In extreme cases, what is requested is only a simple indexical formality: one desires to be recognized as a "Christian," to have a place in the Church, and thus to have the right to request later on a church wedding or a Christian burial. It is a question of being able to wear the *insignia* of "Christianity." *The referent may now be no more than the Christian code*, virtually emptied of content.

b) To Believe and Help Others to Believe. In chapter four we referred to the *illocutionary* dimension of ritual acts of language and, as a consequence, to their performative aim. There, following F. A. Isambert, we said the performative "has all the characteristics of rite, and its performance is exactly of the order of symbolic efficacy." Functioning therefore at another level than that of information, the action or the authoritative discourse which rite is *need not be first understood* in terms of its content in order to be recognized as efficacious; it is enough that it be *recognized as valid*, which implies that the agent be qualified for this role and that he or she carry it out according to the requisite forms. The efficacy recognized as belonging to these authoritative acts obviously does not depend on some secret power in the words themselves, but on the *social consensus* of which they are the coded symbol.

The legitimacy of the ritual agents and the validity of their actions are thus linked directly to the *"symbolic capital"* (Bourdieu) with which they are invested: the group recognizes itself here. This is why "the belief of all, which exists before the ritual, is the condition for the efficacy of the ritual,"[24] and "the first efficacy of rite" is to *"cause people to believe* in the rite itself."[25] To be recognized as true, rite must be socially and culturally acknowledged as *credible.* The real efficacy attributed to it is thus dependent on its *"social acceptability."* One must here "include within the 'real' the representation of the real." We highlighted this with regard to symbolic efficacy: it is "by acting upon the representation of the real" that rites act upon "the real" itself.[26]

This intrinsic (but unacknowledged) connection between ritual and the cultural code is such that V. Turner sees rites as the *warehouses where the "dominant structural values of a culture" are stocked.*[27] From this one understands a little better what archaic mechanisms have triggered the indignation of a certain number of Catholics faced with the liturgical reform of Vatican II. Bourdieu has attempted to analyze these mechanisms. He shows that the expressions of indignation denounce "errors" having to do with the legitimacy of the agents (lay ministers giving communion or guitarists playing church music), the places (first communion in a stadium or prayer in a church where the Blessed Sacrament is not reserved), the language (saying "bread of life" instead of "hosts," addressing God familiarly, or changing words in the Eucharistic Prayer), clothes (a profession of faith in blue jeans or a priest without a chasuble), objects (baskets instead of ciboria or ordinary bread instead of hosts) . . .[28]

Most of the time it is a question of detail. Often these modifications can be easily justified theologically and pastorally. However, and in spite of explanations given in a very pertinent way as regards both the form and the substance of these modifications, these blockages persist. Besides psychological factors which come

24. Bourdieu, *Ce que parler veut dire: L'économie des échanges linguistiques* (Paris: Fayard, 1982) 133.

25. F. A. Isambert, "Réforme liturgique et analyses sociologiques," LMD 128 (1976) 84. In a larger context, see the colloquy of the Ecole française de Rome, *Faire croire: Modalités de la diffusion et de la réception des messages religieux du XIIᵉ au XVᵉ siècle* (Rome: Ecole française de Rome, Palais Farnèse, 1981).

26. Bourdieu, *Ce que parler,* 42, 124, 136.

27. V. Turner, *Les tambours d'affliction: Analyse des rituels des Ndembu de Zambie* (Paris: Gallimard, 1972) 16.

28. Bourdieu, *Ce que parler,* 103–109.

into play here and to which we will return later, it is the social "*acceptability*" of these changes that is in question: no longer corresponding to the representations that one has "always" had of it, the ritual *has lost the symbolic attributes of its legitimacy*. The "error" denounced here concerns the *cipher* or *code* which governs what one traditionally understands as "Catholic" liturgy. This cipher (not acknowledged as such) seems to be grounded especially, as Isambert has observed, in the opposition between the "ordinary" (profane) and the "non-ordinary" (sacred). The "error" which causes such confusion lies in the transgression of this opposition, culturally imbibed as fundamental: the host has become ordinary bread; the altar has been transformed into a table; priests no longer wear certain important insignia of their office (such as the chasuble), while lay people seem to have usurped a role that belongs only to priests. In brief, *the code has been broken*.[29] And when the code is broken, here as in any other language, *people no longer understand ("hear") one another*. You can explain to them as long as you want: each word, each sentence of your explanation will be understood, but none of it will be received.

Now, these reactions, if not invariably of indignation, at least of surprise and regret in the face of the liturgical reform, are far from being peculiar to a small fraction of those who attend church regularly. Sociological surveys show that they belong for the greater part to the mass of people attending "seasonally," representing what is called "popular religion,"[30] who hold on to the "old" lit-

29. Isambert, "Réforme liturgique," 81–86.
30. F. A. Isambert, *Le sens du sacré: Fête et religion populaire* (Paris: Minuit, 1982). This is a fundamental work on the three notions, "popular religion," "feast," and the "sacred" — three terms which "seem to belong together" (p. 14) and the first two of which largely depend on the third which constitutes "the key notion par excellence" (p. 13). They are three terms whose meanings are muddied, often in a polemical way, by a "scholarly elaboration" and a "militant elaboration" (pp. 15–16). The different interpretations to which "popular religion" has given rise, on the one hand in the critical stance of a certain theology and pastoral approach in France, on the other hand in the no less critical approach of liberation theology in Latin America, seem to us extremely significant. See the contributions of S. Galilea, D. Irrarazaval, and J. L. Caravias, *Jésus et la libération en Amérique latine*, ed. J. Doré (Paris: Desclée, 1986), 109–163.

urgy (highly idealized, of course) with all the more nostalgia as they have remained on the fringes during the evolution of the Church. What they primarily demand from the rite is the *reproduction of the most "official" model,* its conformity to the traditional code. This is also often the code of the majesty of an all-powerful and distant God whose protective favors they seek to obtain, a code which originated in the post-Tridentine reform and was considerably reinforced during the Ultramontane period of the last century.[31] The more the liturgical ethos of the priest and lay people most involved in the life of the community is not in strict conformity with this code (which is frequently the case), the further the ritual action's level of credibility is diminished.

c) Theological Interpretation. Here again, one gets a sense of the ambiguities of rite. The positioning which its "digital" nature brings about, through the attribution of identity, status, and role, is essential for the life of the group as well as for that of individuals as subjects. But it happens that one asks no more of it than that. And it can happen that the theological belief in the efficacy of the ritual order is no longer anything else than a sociological belief in the ritual of the established order: what one generously attributes to the gracious action of God is then no more than a religious alibi masking a *demand for conformity to the social order,* "God" becoming simply a cipher standing for this order. No one is safe from this cultic formalism, generally subtle enough not to reveal itself.

Because of the unnuanced positioning that it accomplishes, what is ritual may in practice render blunt the cutting blade of the gospel message, without which, however, the liturgy loses its Christian status. One guesses the temptations which, besides a certain formalism, threaten it. To *delimit* the group in assigning the marks of its identity is certainly indispensable; but this may lead the Church to denature itself by haughtily retiring into its *particularism* when confronted with outside "aggressions" (the world or other religions) or, if the ghetto begins a crusade, by engaging in a militant *proselytism,* whereas the gospel asks it to remain welcoming to the universality of a reign which goes beyond the Church's limits. Assigning *a status and a role* to each person is no

31. Isambert, *Sens du sacré,* 278–280.

less important; but this may lead to a labelling of people, locked forever in their official status, which goes against the gospel, the gospel of grace and mercy always extending to all, whatever their pasts, a chance for conversion and renewal. This same distribution of roles may imprison those who possess power in the *"persona"* of a functionary, whereas the gospel asks that the greatest exercise their power for the service of all. Finally, rituals, which are probably the most conservative of the Church's institutions, risk functioning so "sacrificially" that they no longer assure anything but the *security* of Christians and allow them to forget the violence entailed in a conversion to the gospel.

However, in spite of, or rather at the very heart of these perilous threats of a drift into formalism, the positioning of the Church and, in it, of individuals, effected by what is ritual, has an important theological significance. Here again this significance is not primarily linked to language, but to practice. By inscribing symbolically the marks of the Church's identity on the body of each person, rituals testify to the Christian difference. Rituals testify to it, not as a cut which excludes — the "metaphysical" scheme, we have called it, of a difference represented as competition, distance-separation, and ultimately opposition — but as a placing into communication (see the linguistic "I-You" connection). In this approach, the Church, insofar as it is different, may be received as a *grace* which God gives to Christians and, under a different perspective, non-Christians. Thus, "to believe in the particular grace of love between brothers and sisters and of filiation which we are invited to taste in the Church is for us the path to believing efficaciously in a universal grace of love between brothers and sisters and of filiation — and to working for its manifestation." And "to believe in the universal grace of love between brothers and sisters and of filiation as a promise, offered and accessible to all, is the path to being able to give thanks for this particular grace of love between brothers and sisters and of filiation that Christians are called to live out in the Church."[32]

In imprinting each one with its marks, marks themselves differentiated according to the status one has (catechumen, bap-

32. H. Denis, C. Paliard, P. G. Trebossen, *Le baptême des petit enfants: Histoire, doctrine, pastorale* (Paris: Centurion, 1979) 80.

tized, confirmed, married . . .) or the function one exercises dained ministry, recognized lay ministry . . .), the Church : *itself* in its institutional visibility for what it is, the sacrament or Jesus Christ. There it represents, ex-hibits, proclaims its identity in a radical manner.

5. *Evangelizing Rituality*

a) From the Formal Viewpoint. The preceding observations have shown that rites are inherently so ambiguous that they are capable of producing, from the Christian viewpoint, both the best and the worst. Linked to the w/Word — *non quia dicitur, sed quia creditur* ("not because it is said, but because it is believed"), as Augustine put it when speaking of baptism — and the Spirit, their effective Christianity is compromised when they detach themselves from Word and Spirit to perpetuate themselves simply because of the psychic or social benefits which their mere execution affords. Without dreaming of setting them aside altogether in favor of a contact with the "pure Word" or a direct line to the Holy Spirit, a dream which we have not ceased to denounce, we must still ask the questions: To what "Jesus Christ" do these rites concretely refer? What "dangerous" memorial of him do they accomplish? What model of the Church do they help build for our time? The last part of our work will answer these questions. But it is clear at this point that a sort of *Aufhebung* ("taking up") of rites by the sacraments is required: the latter assume the former, but they assume them in a Christian way only by overcoming them.

From this angle, the vigorous criticisms we have directed toward the current critical of rites, especially its tendency to trivialize and deprogram them, need to be correctly understood. Granted, the theological arguments advanced by this trend are in part only a smoke screen to conceal its more or less conscious ideologies; also, the means chosen to revivify the rites appear to us to have been anthropologically naive, the result of not taking sufficient account of the specific laws governing ritual language; finally, the pastoral consequences of this have on occasion not been happy. But all this cannot obscure the twofold aim of this current of dissent: on the one hand, to restore the vigor of the Christian Word within the liturgy, a vigor noticeably blunted through ritual "fixism" and

conservatism; on the other, to resymbolize these rites, too disconnected from the ambient culture. How can we not agree with this
double goal? This is why, despite its excesses, its deviations, its
naiveté, this dissenting current cannot be placed on a par with the
reverse hieratic current. One cannot simply dismiss them both as
equally wrong.

From the formal viewpoint of the conditions for evangelizing the
rites, we shall put forward three propositions. (1) To evangelize
the rites, against the current of trivialization-deprogramming
which has ignored the laws distinctive of ritual language, it is
necessary that the believer *respect them as rites* and thus not pretend to save them by "using" them as theological or moral conferences — which denatures them. (2) To evangelize the rites,
against the hieratic current, it is necessary that the believer *resymbolize* them and especially take account of the demands for intelligence and comprehension which animate our contemporaries —
especially in the religious domain: even if it is true, as we have
said, that rites do not belong to "-logy" or "discursive reason,"
they still can function well at their properly symbolic and "-urgic"
level only if allowance is made for these demands proper to our
present symbolic system. (3) Finally, to evangelize the rites,
against this same current, it is necessary that *the discerning believer
turn them about* — because faith is not a living faith unless it can
criticize, through the Word received according to the Spirit, the religious and sacred expressions without which it cannot exist. A return to Scripture and to Ethics, explained at length in the
preceding sections, is here the fundamental condition for this
Christianization.

b) From the Material Viewpoint. From the viewpoint of material
"content," the ritual *rupture* is to be evangelized in such a manner
that the otherness of God is manifested not, as in the hieratic approach to the sacred, in opposition to the world, but as holiness
freely communicated to human beings so that they may sanctify
the whole of the "profane." This profane to be sanctified in our
everyday existence is thus not set in competition with the "sacred," no more than Christians should live separated socially from
the rest of humankind or certain moments of life should be reserved for "religion" — even if, as we have seen, marks of

354

differentiation should appear at each of these levels. Evangelizing the ritual *programming* consists essentially in showing the significance of the metonymic connections the rite establishes between the Church of today and Jesus, its Lord. Instead of mechanically reproducing itself, the baptismal and Eucharistic rites should confront the participants with the word and the practice of Jesus of Nazareth, whom in these sacraments they acknowledge to be their Lord. Such a confrontation eventually brings them up against the cross, recalling thereby the dangerous character of the practice to which the sacramental memorial calls them. As concerns the *positioning* through rituality, we have already sketched what its evangelization involves: an openness to the universality of the reign, against the temptation to retreat into a particularism within the boundaries of the Church; conversion and renewal as always possible, against the temptation to reduce people to their status, function, or label; the violent force of the gospel coming to arouse the institutional Church, against its inevitable temptation to fall asleep in the security of a "sacrificial" functioning . . . One sees the picture: such a transformation of rites into sacraments of the Word demands constant vigilance and remains an on-going work.

III. A SYMBOLIZATION OF THE WHOLE HUMAN BEING AS CORPORALITY

By whatever route one approaches them, rites direct us back to the body. The body, let us be precise, is not simply a condition for rites, but their very *place*. If liturgy requires the body, this is not just because, as "matter" substantially "informed" by the soul, the body must necessarily be involved so that its homage to God is total: it is because the body is the stage that gives liturgy its "place." Here, as we can see, what is most "spiritual" in our communication with God, which by its very nature the liturgy aims at, happens in the mediation of what is most "corporeal."

We have previously defined humanity as corporality, a concept that expresses, through the "arch-symbol" of each subject's own body, a threefold relationship: to the cultural system of the group (the social body), to its collective memory (the body of tradition), and to the universe (the cosmic body). This symbolic interrelation comes about differently for each person, depending especially on the history of each one's desire; but each is only the person each is because each is indwelt by this threefold body. It is precisely this corporality which religious rituality symbolizes. We are going to verify this in its three dimensions, cosmic, social, and traditional, and then in its individual dimension which is the stage of each person's desire.

1. *The Symbolization of Human Autochtony*

a) *Elements of the Primary Symbolism.* Like every religious ritual, the sacraments of the Church require the use of *material elements* which represent the cosmic condition of humanity, its "autochtony," its inalienable belonging to the earth, its "being-in-the-world." Water (water of the maternal womb, of the oasis or the rain which gives life, but also water of the flood or of the sea which devastates and drowns), fire (fire which warms and reinvigorates, but also burns and destroys — fire of the Holy Spirit or fire of Hell), ash or earth (earth-mother of our birth and sustenance, but also earth of our grave and our return to dust), bread (white bread of our joys and satisfactions, but also dark bread of our tears and unsatisfied longings), light (light that illumines and reassures, but also blinds and shows our betrayals in broad daylight) . . .: in the liturgy, these elements give up their status as mere objects or subsisting entities in order to *be metaphors of our own existence.* Well before we become aware of these elements or declare what we intend to do with them, they convey to us intimations of our indissoluble marriage to the earth, our original existential condition of *being-in-the-world.*

This autochtony of humanity inseparable from the cosmos is symbolized archaically through the *voice,* whose rituality puts into play all its possibilities: from cries or lamentations, through proclamation, incantation, collective song, exultation, and so on, down to silence — a silence which is the over-fullness of a language reduced to breath . . . This oral language, itself a language of the body, as one can see, a language inscribed in matter (see above), joins with a *gestural* and *postural* language, itself modulated by every possibility of the body: from the trance and the dance, of which there remain only a few traces in the West, like the rhythmic clapping of hands or the discreet rocking of the body that psalmody can produce, through kneeling, prostration, listening, processional walking, the act of chewing, down to recollection — this postural silence that is like the over-fullness of a gesture reduced to the bare "thereness" of the body . . .

If our liturgies are relatively poor in bodily expressions, it remains that these gestures and attitudes (in which we participate not only in executing them ourselves but also in watching the various liturgical actors do them) work on us much more than we are aware because they arise from an ancient store of *sub-ritual schemes* that continually speak to us. We have underlined this fact above, following Vergote: the upright stance, the gesture of sharing (right-left or front-back) the taking in or casting out through the orifices of the body, the opening or closing of the hand, the spot that mars the skin or the washing that cleans it off, are all sub-ritual schemes belonging to the *primary symbolism* inscribed in the contours of the body. This topography is existential so that every "idea" of domination or freedom (upright stance), every ethical consideration (gesture of sharing), every assimilation, up to the most intellectual (taking in), and so forth, pass through the "economy" with which each person invests these corporeal schemes. As the symbolic binding which holds together the outer edges of selfness and thatness, the body "anthropomorphizes" itself into the macrocosm of the universe and "cosmorphizes" itself into a microcosm. It is this permanent osmosis between humanity and its cosmic body the liturgy puts on stage through the materials it uses and the gestures and postures it employs.

We are aware of the great *ambivalence* of the cosmic symbolisms of "nature" and its ever-recurring cycles: a symbolism easily spellbinding and always in danger of regressing toward the wildly imaginary when it is too closely linked to the "good mother" projected into a benevolent nature and too distanced from the law of the father, representing culture and history. Still, it is true that through these materials and objects, through the body, through the architectural arrangements and the plastic arts decorating the sacred space, through the stone of the altar, the wood of the cross or of the seats, the flame of the paschal candle or the fragrance of incense, it is, even before our explicit intentions, the *entire universe* that is celebrated as *creation* in the liturgy.

b) A Theology of Creation.[33] Christian rituality is the *confession in act of God as creator.* It is this through its practical implementation, before any pronouncements that express it. It places the participants "performatively" in a relation of dependence with regard to a *reality* which precedes them. But this reality is not simply that of brute objects; it is a *symbolic* reality, opened up by the word, for it is by God's word that God creates, that is, organizes the original chaos into a "world" (Gen 1). It is a reality that comes about from the beginning as *gift* and because of this cannot be reduced simply to the artisanal model of construction — the creation model — or to the biological model of generation — the "emanation" model — which are the two great paradigms that have fed Western philosophical and religious tradition on the topic of creation. Now, like every gift, the gift of creation is received only through the response of a return-gift: in this case, human *creativity,* charged with bringing the universe into conformity with the Creator's gift, commissioned with rendering it habitable by all, culturally and economically. The Christian notion of creation, irreducible to human creativity (which nevertheless comes from it) but also indissolubly linked to it, thus expresses both human beings' dependence on God as creatures and their responsibility in history for the management of a universe and existence acknowledged as a free gift.

Christian liturgy presents the world as something one may not use in an arbitrary manner: it demands that one make of the universe a world for all, not just for the privileged. It also presents the world to us as something one may not use simply in a utilitarian way. It makes manifest the *symbolic excess* which the real, as created, holds in reserve. Left to its "profanity," thus not sacralized, this world is still off-limits for profanation. The most elementary things — water, bread, wine, and so forth — demand respect.

As a consequence, bread cannot become Eucharist under just any condition. It is not Eucharist when, taken away by an unjust economic system from the poor who have produced it, it has become a symbol of "*de-creation.*" To offer God such bread kneaded with the death of the poor is murder and sacrilege (see Sir 34:24-25). To partake of such bread in Communion is "to eat one's own condem-

33. See the more ample discussion of this topic in our general conclusion.

nation": for in effect, how could one discern in it the body of the Lord (see 1 Cor 11:17-34)? Already long before Paul, the psalmist, speaking for God, condemned all the "evildoers who eat up my people as they eat bread" (Ps 53:5). The theological economy of the cult is inseparable from the social economy of labor. This is what is symbolized in an exemplary way in the *oblation* to God of the bread and wine, "fruit of the earth and work of human hands," a symbol which (see above) does not constitute humanity's final return-gift, but the "sacramental" representation of a return-gift to be made good in the ethical practice of justice and sharing — a symbol expressing reception of the "given" (in the twofold sense) of the universe as "offer."

2. The Symbolization of Sociality and Tradition

a) Rite as "Social Drama." A ritual is never an individual matter — except in its neurotic perversion. This is the postulate of the functionalist school of sociology and ethnology: religious rituals are, in Turner's expression, "social dramas," and their elements are expressions of a group's dominant cultural values (see above). We have shown this with regard to their symbolic efficacy: this is linked to their capacity to *"restore to order"* — the symbolic order of economic, social, political, and ideological values which give the group its identity and cohesion — the elements which first appear incoherent or disturb social harmony. R. Bastide has shown, moreover, that even the "wild sacredness" of possession or trance is, lest it drown in an ever-possible hysteria, in fact carefully regulated, from A to Z (from the ritually guided entrance into the trance, to the withdrawal accomplished according to a gradual and programmed quieting down), by the social group, especially by the "priestly" representatives.[34]

b) An Example: Traditional Initiation and Its Secret. Exorcistic rituals of healing served above to show the social dimension of rites under their aspect of symbolic efficacy. Rites of passage will permit us to better grasp the role of the entire social body in an affair which, however, directly concerns only certain of its members. We choose to concentrate on *initiation rites of the socio-tribal kind*. At the same time we will show that the

34. R. Bastide, *"Le sacré sauvage" et autres essais* (Paris: Payot, 1975) 216.

subjects are spoken as "ancestral" body as much as social body in the ritual metaphors.

We take as an example the ethnic initiation of young males in the Bobo country of Burkina Faso as described by A. T. Sanon.[35]

We find present here the three stages classically distinguished by ethnologists in this sort of initiation: separation from the maternal and feminine world, a time spent apart from the village, and a reintegration, with a new status, into the village. The major symbolism which undergirds the whole of this seven-day period is that of *death-and-regeneration*. In the end it produces a "triple birth": "birth of the *village community* renewed in its foundational values, birth of a *new [male] generation* issuing from tradition, and finally birth of *each [male] member* situated in his generation and in the community according to authentic tradition" (p. 87).

This last birth is apparent in *each male's body*, for this body is the very place where each garners the transmitted "global wisdom," the "terrain where the initiating word is sown by dint of gestures, postures, rhythms, and, if need be, whippings" (p. 82). But this death to childhood and birth to a new status, marked for each by the tests undergone, the learning of the secret language (the *Luo*), the break with the village, then the return to it, in a bowed position at first before returning to an upright posture to dance, are also indeed the business of the *class* of initiates as a whole. This class constitutes an authentic *"communal body"* where "each body is necessary to the bodies of the others. The entire group observes and repeats, moves, surges up, and returns to rest. Body becomes linked to body through the link of tradition that has become living again in the very act of its transmission," especially during the rhythmic learning, almost psalmodic, of the secret language (p. 82). It is only as a member of this collective body that each one can be initiated. And this body, which will have its particular place within the village community, until a new class of initiates succeeds it, understands itself only in its connection to the *village or ethnic body* which, through its young, repeats its *own* passage of initiation. For this passage, done only once, remains for everyone "a permanent status. It will require only a gesture, a phrase, a simple word like *bisla* for each initiate, or an entire class, to again find the proper attitude"; at this point the "sign," as Sanon judiciously notes, "reacquires its symbolic dimension" (p. 92): it introduces one into the order of which it itself is part — in this case, into the order of the values upon which the identity of the group rests, values transmitted during the initiation. Al-

35. A. T. Sanon and R. Luneau, *Enraciner l'Evangile: Initiations africaines et pédagogie de la foi* (Paris: Cerf, 1982) second part. It is to this work that we will refer in the text that follows.

though separated from the initiates, the village community is intensely involved in the whole of the initiating process: not only because it concerns its own children, not only because the entire village lives as though suspended from what is transpiring out there in the forest and prepares actively for the return of its new members, but even more because it is the founding tradition that is being inculcated into the young.

The transmission of such a tradition is not of the order of intellectual knowledge which must be learned by heart. In contrast to us, where culture is "what remains when one has forgotten everything," there is here in some sense nothing to forget, for only that is passed on which can and should endure. But it is passed on by a *pedagogy "within life itself"* (p. 101) where one symbolically does "with one another and through one another" (p. 102) what is said. Is it a matter of learning solidarity? One lives it intensely in the close and constant contact of the initiating process. Is it a question of learning respect for the elders? One lives it through submission to the initiators. Is it a question of learning to venerate the ancestors or the god and to deal with them? One does so in invoking them, in living in their company, in revealing the "secret." Is it a question of learning how to behave in the group, confronted now with sexuality, with death, with different clans and social functions? The entire initiation process is there to inculcate "how to be a man in a way that differentiates man from woman, adult from child, son from father, older brother from younger, one class from another, all the while fundamentally safeguarding their equality as members of a living body" (p. 124). Is it a question of knowing the world? This world is precisely the one "into which I am initiated, my ancestral world, set aside to be my world, my village, my territory, and my country," a world where each one knows "how to locate himself or herself by locating everything else in its proper place" (pp. 117–118).

The knowledge passed on in the initiation is thus a *"knowing how to,"* one of the modalities of which is *"knowing how to speak."* The key skill is being able to adjust oneself to others, to the ancestors (and to the gods), to the world, where one thus learns to *find one's place while situating everything else in its place.* This adjustment, the creation of a world of sense, is the *symbolic act of coherence par excellence* where every element, like a piece from a puzzle or a fragment from a broken vase, can find its meaningful place in the large cultural pattern inherited from tradition. To be initiated is thus to learn the truth, not with the meaning of intellectual exactitude transmitted by science, but with the meaning of *practical discernment* passed on by wisdom. The initiate is one who has so imprinted the foundational values of the group on his body-being that he intuitively knows his place in relation to the various elements of the universe, to the different status and functions of others, and to the supernatural powers with which he has learned to deal. To be initiated is truly *"to enter into humanness"* (p. 125), to come forth into the full humanness proper to a subject. The symbolic efficacy of the initiation resides precisely in the fact that the action of receiving is also, and more importantly, an action of *receiving the self.*

This gracious treasure, which has no other content, as we can see, than the *emergence of the subject,* collectively and personally, finds its major symbol in the "secret." An open secret? Of course, for it is only a matter of showing a mask which "reveals itself while at the same time fully veiling its secret" (p. 95). There is thus a "secret of the secret" (which is the strongest word of the initiation), "that which is not said" and which is *"what everyone knows but which no one speaks"* because it concerns "what is unsaid and unsayable" (pp. 99–100). Even while known by all, it is sayable by nobody because it is nothing other than what the initiation has worked: the *symbolic labor* where, communally and personally, each one has learned his place according to a new knowing-how-to-live in their "world." For the initiate has been given clear sight: the objects in life speak to him; he can confront them without fear of falling victim to the disordered forces of the world; he can orient himself there without fear of getting lost. Following in the steps of previous classes, the entire class of initiates has this sight. All share the same secret which they cannot say because it is not sayable outside the initiating experience where one learns it through the body and which, however, is so much the source of their life that it establishes among them — in their manner of understanding themselves through some species of tree; through such and such social prohibition; through a way of taking one's place in the group or speaking out in public; through such and such a gesture, such and such a word, such and such a rite — the most fundamental solidarity there can be: that of a *cultural identity.* The signs are indeed more and completely other than signs: they are symbols. The secret of the secret is the symbolic transition to this cultural identity that the initiation effects: it is each one's appropriation of the group's system of values.

This much is clear: initiation is a formidable process of the *reproduction of a socio-cultural system;* perhaps the most performative among those humankind has invented. As a consequence, it characterizes in an exemplary way the social drama that imbues every ritual. But at the same time it reveals itself to be burdened with the *ambiguities* of ritual, especially those which relate to its indexical dimension (see above): the subjection of individuals to the group, the difficulty or impossibility for individuals not to be imprisoned by status or function, the isolation of the group in its particularism . . . Moreover, one cannot forget the pathological aberrations which are always possible in the initiating process, especially because of the length and severity of the tests imposed. The Christian conversion of such an initiation rite requires then work of considerable scope.

c) Traditional Initiation and Christian Initiation. This work of *conversion to the gospel* cannot be limited to a mere sprucing up of the facade. It is in the foundations that this change must be accomplished. Here let us speak of but one difficulty among others in such a task. This difficulty is due to the fact that true Christian initiation should balance a *series of paradoxes,* stretched as it is between (1) the transmission of a heritage, and the critical appropriation of the latter by faith; (2) the identification of membership by ecclesial marks, and an openness to the universality of a reign that transcends the Church; (3) a hierarchical transmission of the apostolic tradition, and power exercised as a service by those who initiate others; (4) the necessity of setting an end to the initiation process, an end which, however, never truly arrives in Christianity. This is to say that initiation does not function well from the properly Christian viewpoint unless it remains in an unstable equilibrium: if the first term of each of these paradoxes — that is, the "attestation" aspect — becomes too powerful, Christian initiation risks limiting itself to reproducing a system of values at the hands of the institution; conversely, if the second term — the "contestation" aspect — is too emphasized, the tendency in the West today, Christian initiation risks being rendered impossible because of a lack of sufficient institutional support. In other words, there cannot be a fully satisfying system of Christian initiation. If it turns out to be particularly difficult today as "initiation," it is not sure that it went so well in the past as "Christian," in spite of what we are led to believe. It is instructive, in this perspective, to observe that the Church Fathers of the fourth century, right in the middle of the "golden age" of Christian initiation, bitterly complained about the majority of new converts' adherence to the Christian faith for purely "sociological" (as it is sometimes called today) reasons. It seems that as soon as initiation moves toward a tranquil settling down, it inevitably loses some of its gospel force . . .

What is at stake in these critical reflections is obviously of great importance for a pastoral strategy of Christian initiation. In this strategy, one should not forget the substantial *pedagogical interest* of traditional initiation. Of course, since one cannot transfer an element of one symbolic system into another without its producing completely different effects, there is no question here of transposing the pedagogy of an African initiation into our own culture. Nevertheless, such a pedagogy gives us something to think about. For is not Christian initiation also the handing over of tradition, an act in which the community continues to receive itself? Is it not a process of receiving this tradition through the mysterial mode? Are there other ways of entering into the secret of the "mysteries of the reign" than letting oneself be "taken" by them? It is impossible here to claim to "see" in the sense of "understand": the blind, Jesus declares sharply to the Pharisees, are those who pretend to see-understand, that is, to master a system of the knowledge of God (see John 9:41); these, who think themselves "inside," are really "outside," so much so that "they may indeed look, but not perceive" (Mark 4:11-12). The fruit of initiation into the "mystery of the Reign of God" in Christ cannot be dissociated from the path leading to it: it is thus not a "something," but this path itself as a process of the permanent generation of subjects as Christians. Such an initiating path is from the outset symbolic: "One has understood," writes Sanon, "when one feels oneself grasped from within, concerned, put into a state of participation" (p. 144). We have here perhaps the most typical expression of the test to be shouldered by every subject as such: the impossibility of "taking" without being "taken" (see above). It is the test of mourning, of loss of mastery, of forswearing to finally attain the "Thing," as is shown in exemplary fashion by the secret of the mask. A passage through death so that a new future might become possible. Does not this fundamental symbolism of initiation, lived from beginning to end in the corporality of the subjects, echo, as Paul emphasizes with regard to baptism in Romans 6, the Pasch of the Lord Jesus?

d) The Crisis in Ritual in Our "Critical" Society. The preceding reflection intended to point out, in summary fashion, several aspects of the complexity of the possible connections between a traditional pagan initiation and Christian initiation. This complexity is increased by the difference between a *closed society* and an *open society*. This observation is all the more important here in that we are seeking, through the example of initiation, to show the connection between rituality and human sociality.

The symbolization of this sociality is obviously less characterized in our open and unstable Western society than in traditional societies which are comparatively stable and closed. The "crisis in sacrifice" due to critical suspicion and the growth of cultural pluralism renders our liturgical rites globally much less functional on the social level than they were formerly. Another logic, that of differentiation and competition for equality,[36] has been substituted for the logic of communion in hierarchical stability, which characterizes traditional societies. Unanimity with regard to values assuring social homogeneity has given way to the right to be different

36. J. Baudrillard, *Pour une critique de l'économie politique du signe* (Paris: Gallimard, 1972), especially "La genèse idéologique des besoins," 59-94.

and the demand for autonomy, and this to the point of promoting and even exalting conflict.

Under these conditions, how could initiation — any initiation, inside or outside Christianity — fare but badly? This is why one speaks about it so much today: one speaks about it all the more as it is less practiced and has become the "object" of studies, science, and folklore. If there is still a "spirit of initiation,"[37] it no longer finds a stable institutional home where it can be soundly practiced. When the entire social body is in a state of permanent mutation (or sees itself as such) in its relation to its past, its knowledge, the whole of its heritage, it is obviously not possible to provide a place for stable institutions of initiation — except on the fringes of society, where groups unaccepted by the larger community flourish. *Watered down, the spirit of initiation can no longer give rise to a true initiation.* Into what "world," moreover, could one desire to be initiated when suspicion unavoidably touches every inherited model (moral and religious, especially) and when, notably through the media, one is confronted with a multiplicity of possible models of identification? For lack of adequate symbolic structuring, lack of sufficiently stable points of reference, children, teenagers, and adults find themselves incapable of sorting out this avalanche of political, moral, and religious information and of providing it with a thread of coherence . . .

This does not mean that Christian initiation is irreversibly on the road to extinction. This does mean that we must search for a new model (and that it is already being looked for, occasionally with success,) where, while taking care to maintain and promote in some respects the pole of attestation and institution, one attempts to join it to the pole of contestation and criticism. A difficult tension to maintain, no doubt. But, as we have said, it is this uncomfortable tension, issuing from the gospel itself even before it is aggravated because of our kind of society, that keeps the faith awake and alive.

3. *The Symbolization of the Hidden Order of Desire*

The symbolization of our relation to the same universe, the same culture, the same tradition comes about in an *original way in each one of us,* depending on the unique history of our desire. Like every religion, Christianity is, from this perspective, an attempt to *manage guilt.* Rituality has a very special importance in this area: in its two major schemes, initiation and sacrifice, it has to do, as

37. A. Pasquier, "Recherches pour une initiation chrétienne," *Cahiers Ephrem* 15 (Paris: CNER, 1982).

Vergote has shown, with impurity and debt.[38] We mentioned above several pathological deviations which particularly threaten it. For in setting on stage "the hidden order of desire, of the collective unconscious, of primeval phantasms at once hidden and reactivated in the play of the ritual scenes and the representations of agents and objects,"[39] rituality becomes the place for an intense psychic experience, one favorable to a return of the "repressed."

Thus, even underneath the properly Christian content recognized in *Communion*, the act of chewing, made more intense by the sacrificial dimension that is explicitly associated with it, "cannot help but evoke inescapably ambivalent oral phantasms because these express both the desire to destroy, to kill — aggressiveness, the death wish — and the desire to assimilate, to incorporate, to appropriate, to identify oneself with."[40]

Or again, why some parents insist (and often with a force that disconcerts pastors) on the *baptism of their child* is not due to faith but to unconscious motivations: such a request for a rite is first of all the expression of *archaic mechanisms* that are set in motion by any reminder of *the beginning* and its "mystery." That the child-product they have generated may grow into a son-or daughter-achievement requires of them, in a way more powerful for being unconscious, that the gestures made formerly over them, and before that over their own parents and ancestors, now be made over their own child. A genealogy which, as G. Rosolato has shown, needs symbolic reference to at least three generations[41]—hence the influence of grandparents, especially in the religious domain — can be established in a human, that is, meaningful way only by the symbolic inscription of this word on the child, a ritual word in this case, with which they themselves have been marked at the beginning.

Human birth reveals itself here as something more and other than a simple biological event, and life as more and other than a simple given which one can master. *A debt of existence,* received

38. Vergote, *Dette et désir,* ch. 4 "L'impur et la dette dans le rite."

39. Hameline, "Aspects du rite," 108.

40. J. C. Sagne, "L'interprétation analytique du rite de l'eucharistie," *L'eucharistie,* Profac. (Faculty of Theology of Lyon, 1971) 153-154.

41. G. Rosolato, *Essai sur le symbolique* (Paris: Gallimard, 1969) "Trois générations d'hommes dans le mythe religieux et la généalogie," 59-96.

from elsewhere from an "Other" as a gift, is expressed here in an often unconscious way.[42] On the psychic level this debt itself stirs up phantasms of payment and reparation that are extremely *ambiguous*, like the mythical releasing of the scapegoat, which either "Satan" or "original sin" may represent. The rite thus functions primordially as a tranquilizer against possible evils which might befall the child.

It is worth mentioning in passing that *pastoral practice* will only end in an impasse if, under the pretext of "true faith," it ignores the importance of these unconscious motives or with a wave of the hand dismisses them as "magic." The "truest" faith is still always a human faith, and the truest thing about human life is not necessarily on the level of thought. It remains true that if faith does take account of the primeval symbolism of guilt and the sacrificial scheme which corresponds to it, it is not simply to endorse them, but to convert them to the gospel. Christian baptism requires this reversal which, instead of *discharging* the parents of their responsibility by expelling a satanic victim burdened with their guilt, charges them to *assume symbolically* their debt of existence in the pedagogic task of opening their child to the faith which they profess.

Sacramental symbolism functions necessarily through our most archaic and least-recognizable drives, disguised and distorted as they must be to cross the barrier of censure and manifest themselves to consciousness. However, it is just such a work of the unconscious that, besides the unconscious socio-cultural aspect discussed above, explains why the request for rites of passage *resists so strongly* the assaults of critical doubt and quasi-unbelief, in practice if not in theory, which frequently accompany it. Vergote, for his part, goes so far as to say in this regard: "We believe that the formalism of certain religious practices is due more to this psychological process than to reasons of social order. From this angle of approach, it becomes understandable why the practice of religious rites diminishes when the climate of guilt disappears."[43]

42. Significant in this regard is the choice of a poem by K. Gibran as one of the readings at the baptism of infants: "Your children are not your children, they are sons and daughters of Life itself. . . ." This is a frequent choice by both Christians relatively distanced from the Church and those more committed. . . Thus, something that is normally unconscious breaks through into language.

43. Vergote, *Dette et désir*, 142.

Whatever the merit of this evaluation, the popularity of rites of passage on the practical level, in spite of a theoretical suspicion of their irrationality harbored by the very people who request them, is indeed a symptom of the *ungovernable workings of desire* which are involved here. Yet more indicative is the aggressiveness which comes to the surface, sometimes erupting when the pastoral regulations no longer correspond to the expectations of the petitioners; such outbursts no longer surprise when seen in the light of the analysis we have just given.

Religious rituality inevitably has the function of managing guilt. This is why it *sets on stage the very contradiction which forms desire: "to aspire to what it refuses, to tighten its grip around what it possesses."*[44] For the satisfaction of desire is its death. It lives only to be the "desire of the desire of the Other," according to an indefinite process of incompletion. The essence of human nature is precisely to be opened by an *unsealable breach* and thus to look for quiet without ever being able to find it. This restlessness constitutive of human nature is linked to the *origin,* to this loss of the origin necessarily brought about by the use of language, to this first "partition" from which the subject proceeds to its "parturition" (J. Lacan), and thus to *death,* which is only the reverse side of origin. The drama of ex-sisting is no other than that of the conflict within humankind between Eros and Thanatos. The onto-theological essence of metaphysics can be understood as the attempt, proper to the West since the time of the ancient Greeks, to manage this internal contradiction by another route than that of traditional religions: instead of attempting to fill in the breach — which reopens itself constantly anyway — with myths, rites, beliefs, spirits, and gods, the West has tried to do the same thing with "reasons."[45] But is it not still fundamentally the same trial — that of "melancholy" (see above) — which one has striven to

---

44. Vergote, *Interprétation,* 153.

45. E. Morin, *Le paradigme perdu: La nature humaine* (Paris: Seuil, 1973) 111: "Between objective vision and subjective vision occurs a break which human beings open into a complete rapture filled by myths and rites of an afterlife which in the end integrate death. With homo sapiens, therefore, this duality of subject and object begins, this unbreakable connection and equally insurmountable rupture which, in a thousand different ways, philosophy and religion will thereafter attempt to surmount and deepen."

evade by a different route? Still, religious rites play a particular role in this matter, as we will make explicit now.

4. The Originality of Religious Rites within Human Symbolization

Every human work can be said to express humankind in its entirety, in its relation to a society, a tradition, a universe. Every human work is symbolically the bearer of human desire and its internal contradiction. But every human work is not this to the same degree or for the same reason, and this is true even within the realm of artistic and hermeneutic works (among which are religious works). Religious ritual expression seems to us to be marked by a *twofold characteristic:*

a) The Staging of Corporality as Such. On the one hand, as we have underscored, it is the human *body* itself, with its thousand vocal, gestural, and postural possibilities, which is put on stage as such in its relation to the world, to others, and to the ancestors. It is this "as such" which is relevant here. For it is not only the condition but the very place of the liturgy. The latter is the expression of the human being as a living body, a singular body of desire where the threefold body — cosmic, social, and ancestral — is collected (*relegere*) and interconnected (*religare*) arch-symbolically, a body where the liturgy becomes word.

b) The "Sacred." On the other hand, this staging of human corporality is lived within the religious rite as sacred.

The idea of the *"sacred"* is a difficult notion. A "funnel-concept," Isambert writes, typical of what Bourdieu calls "a mode of substantialist thinking" where, after having passed from the adjective to the substantive,[46] one slides "from the substantive to the substance, from the constancy of the substantive to the constancy of the substance."[47] Thus, in R. Otto and M. Eliade the "sacred" passes from being a logical concept to an ontological reality; that is why, "from all the evidence, there is a theology underlying the work of M. Eliade."[48]

46. Isambert (*Sens du sacré,* 256–257) notes that if Durkheim "little uses the substantive 'the sacred' and prefers instead the adjective (Hubert and Mauss are less reserved on this point)," he still establishes "the bases for an veritable philosophy of the sacred": from "principle-attribute," the sacred becomes "property-object, the principle of every religion."

47. Bourdieu, *Distinction,* 20.

48. Isambert, *Sens du sacré,* 264.

Now, "sacred" is an adjective qualifying things (objects, places, persons, and so on). Taken as a substantive, it does not designate a thing. As Vergote has shown,[49] it is a semanteme which in our culture evokes *depth*, a hidden interiority, a mysterious source, whereas the semanteme "God" evokes *height*, power, majesty; but "depth" can also evoke God, and "height" the sacred. In any case, we are here on a vertical axis. One sees that the sacred cannot be either identified with "God" — even if it directs us toward God — or opposed to the profane. Its opposite is rather what cannot be separated from the simple "horizontality" of existence, what reduces life to a pure biological datum, an interlude between birth and death. The sacred relates, in our culture at least, to what *lies beneath* existence, "the ground of the 'there-is' in the depths" which makes of existence something of an order other than simply a raw given. Every infringement upon this beneath which touches what is most intimate in the life of both the group and the individual can be experienced only as a "sacrilege." Of course, this beneath does not manifest itself as such. It does not even take on consistency except by being projected on a "beyond" (so diversely represented in different cultures that it gives rise, as with us, to a "profane" beyond, such as History, Science, and so forth), itself *mediated* by objects, persons, places, and formulas characterized as "sacred." A capital point: *without these mediations, there is no "sacred"* — no more "beneath" than "beyond." "Neither myth nor rite is an expression of a sacred; they are there first, and if a sacred exists at all, it is because they institute it."[50] The sacred does not explain the rite; the rite instates the holy.

Rites, then, are always connected to the sacred because their function is precisely (depending on their connection with the myths) to be the privileged cultural mediations of institution. In a religious context, they are at the same time the privileged mediation of the relation of human beings with the *divine* or divinized *Other*. This is exactly their second characteristic with regard to the other cultural works where human beings express themselves. Not only do rites make manifest the human subject's body as such, but they present the subject, with the insurmountable contradiction of its desire, to the divine Other, through supplication or jubilation, petition or praise. This *allocutionary* character, which distinguishes rite from all spectacle or religious art, gives it, as it gives the "theological symbol," what D. Dubarle calls an "ana-

49. Vergote, "Equivoques," 478.
50. Ibid., 485.

phoric power":[51] the rite purports to carry the whole human being "upwards." Thus directed, it addresses to the Other, recognized as a partner (superior, of course) in communication, human desire, especially in the familiar "you" (the French "tu") of the allocutionary language of prayer.

Depending on its explicit existential elements, this desire is directed toward obtaining either spiritual goods (pardon, reconciliation, purification, thanksgiving, moral courage . . .) or material goods (health, an abundant harvest . . .), although at times the line between the two is not clear. But desire intends not just these needed empirical objects; beyond them, through them, it is a *"petition"* for the Other that is being formulated. It is desiring human beings as such who bare themselves to the divinity. It is the very drama of their ex-sistence that they present to God. The fact that liturgical prayer is voiced so often as a repetitive cry is significant here: the "Have mercy on us! Have mercy on us!" the "Hear our prayer, grant our request," the "We praise you, we glorify you," the "Alleluias" are all so many prayer-cries directly proceeding from a desire which exceeds in extent and depth the enumerated motifs of petition or thanksgiving and in the end addresses itself *to the Other desired for itself.* At least, Christian prayer orients believers in this direction, a pedagogy aimed at conversion of desire passing little by little from the simple asking for needed objects (material, moral, and even spiritual) to the request for God as such — in gospel terms, the request for the "kingdom of God and its righteousness" (Matt 6:33) and for the Spirit (Luke 11:13).

Liturgical rituality is thus the symbolic expression of the human in its total corporality and as a being of desire. By revealing in full view of the divine Other the whole human being as a body of nature and culture, of history and desire, it "acts out" before the Other the existential anguish of this singular entity which, always in quest of the lost object that would satisfy its desire, still can experience only the non-satisfaction of what it aspires to and which thus learns to see there, painfully, a longing for the Other (named "God" by religions) that expresses itself in its needs.

51. D. Dubarle, "Pratique du symbole et connaissance de Dieu," *Le mythe et le symbole*, S. Breton et al. (Paris: Beauchesne, 1977) 228.

IV. THE CORPORALITY OF THE FAITH

We return, at the conclusion of this reflection on rituality, to a theme already touched on at the end of Chapter Four. The complement that we add here is prompted by the heightened consistency that the preceding reflection on rituality gives it.

1. The Sacramental Difference or the Radical Involvement of the Church in the Sacraments

a) A Fundamental Tension . . . As we have said, rites are capable of producing the best and the worst. Throughout the preceding pages we have pointed out a certain number of *major risks* which threaten them. Hetero-topy, programming, digitality are in effect always prone to favoring a regression into the imaginary. Certainly, rituality does not have a monopoly on such risks. However, because it is so thoroughly human, rituality provides a humus particularly propitious to the germination of such weeds. How many neuroses have been encouraged or maintained by the devout assistance at the "Holy Sacrifice of the Mass," the "theophany" of Communion, the desire to "say everything" in the obscure secrecy of the confessional! How many social and political strategies (the support of established power, the maintenance of cultural or economic privileges . . .) have been served by baptisms or marriages, Masses or confessions used as excuses! How many mystifications have been perpetrated in this area — for the most part completely in good faith!

These psychological and social snares are never entirely avoidable. This is the reason that when one commends the advantages of a less regular practice to break a habit of Sunday attendance that has become mechanical, it is not at all sure one will become a more authentic "believer" or will end up less enslaved to a new social order, to a new mechanical observance, and at last to a new "alienation" from oneself — against such charges one naturally defends oneself, the more obstinately as the "reasons" advanced are the less convincing.[52] Whatever the case here, the risks of the sacramental rites are such that it is not surprising to see them so

52. Vergote, *Religion, foi, incroyance* (Brussels: P. Mardaga, 1983) 281: "On the basis of our research, in any case, we believe we can affirm that there are positive correlations between religious practice and degree of faith."

often the objects of suspicion, even of denigration, in the name of "sincerity" or "authenticity" of faith, or in the name of a boldness (justified as "prophetic") in using the Word.

However, these very risks are also *opportunities* when faith knows how to take advantage of them. It is impossible to escape this tension except, as we have pointed out, by dreaming of a disembodied faith and a miraculous God, in the image of our own ideal selves, whose onto-theological perfections would not be called into question by the *Logos* of the cross. The disconcerting otherness and holiness of this crucified God never shows itself better than in God's withdrawal, through the Spirit, into human corporality. For the sacramental rites, as places in the wholly human — the too human — where grace is bestowed on the significant materiality of gestures, postures, objects, and words which make them up, while not the *only* representation, are still *the most eminent representation of this pro-cession of the divine God within God's re-cession at the heart of what is most human.* And this because of their *specific mode of expression* irreducible to any other. This is why, if the confession of the Word of God in the concrete letter of the Scriptures causes scandal, the confession of this same Word, acting within the "too human" of sacramental gestures, only intensifies this scandal. As we have noted, the evanescence of the "word" in the first case permits us, on the basis of metaphysical logocentrism, to partially blur the body of the written trace and thereby relatively domesticate the scandal in question. But sacraments do not offer this evasion (or offer it less easily): one stumbles against them, as we have said, just as one stumbles against the body . . . And therefore one has applied oneself to find "reasons" of "convenience."

If sacramental rites risk encouraging idolatry and magic, they are nonetheless the confession in act of God's strange otherness. If they risk diverting believers from their tasks in history, they are nonetheless a point of symbolic passage which seeks to be verified in history. If they risk supporting all the clumsiness of the institutional Church, they nonetheless represent the Church, the fundamental sacrament of God, which involves itself in them in a radical manner. *In the last analysis, they crystallize the most profound and irreducible tensions which hold the Church and the faith upright.*

b) Tension Expressed in a Radical Way. Obviously the singularity of the sacraments is not situated at the level of the subjective "intentions" of the Church or of believers. At this level, in fact, the Church is also completely involved in its hermeneutics of Scripture or its ethical witness. The difference lies in the *anthropological modality* according to which the Church's identity as Church-of-Christ attests itself. At the same time, the Church is contested by the sacraments because it is always at some distance from the One whom it announces in them. This modality is *anthropologically unsurpassable.* Unsurpassable in that, as "ritual expressions," they are actions which are performative at the highest level, and not simply ideas; they are practices which are efficacious, and not just didactic discourses; they are symbolic contexts, and not simply discursive developments. We must add this important specification, this pragmatic whole is "received" by the Church as coming from Jesus Christ, as an action of its Lord, an action over which it confesses to have no power (see the following chapter). It is in this way we understand the "absolute" character of the involvement of the Church which, according to Rahner, marks the difference between the sacraments and other ecclesial mediations of the communication of God. This difference, as we see, resides in the *sacramentum* itself, that is, in the wholly human acts of the Church which constitute the *sacramentum,* acts which, structurally involving the Church in its identity as Church of Christ, are received as concrete mediations of the initial involvement of God who here proposes God's self as the gratuitous and gracious gift of "salvation." As a consequence, it is starting from and at the heart of the *sacramentum,* and thus of the *opus operantis Ecclesiae* ("action of the acting Church"), that the *opus operatum* ("efficacious action") of God is to be understood theologically. "We have every right, theologically speaking, to conceive the sacraments as the most radical, the most intense case of the Word of God as word of the Church, here precisely where this word, as the absolute involvement of the Church, is what one calls *opus operatum.*"[53] The various components of the ritual practice we have analyzed — hetero-topy, programming, staging of the body, and so forth —

53. Rahner, *Traité fondamental,* 473.

are for us the concrete anthropological and social mediations of such a "sacramental difference."

What is true of the Church collectively is equally true of *every believer* — at least if we agree to look at it from the viewpoint of the order of ritual, and not that of individual "intentions." The very fact that we receive a sacrament does involve us. It is a step that we take each time. And we cannot "negotiate" at this stage: we either take the step or not; we either make the gesture or not. It is impossible here to play on "analogy": the rite "positions" us, depending on whether we go through with it or not, whether we submit to it or not, in a movement that is more than cerebral, one that requires a follow-through into action. Baptismal immersion, the first *sacramentum* of the Christian, is a good example: the body is completely plunged into the symbolic order proper to the Church, an order metaphorized by water in baptism. In agreeing to submit oneself to the sacramental gesture of the Church, one no longer avails oneself of one's own theological ideas, as incisive as they might be, or of one's own religious feelings, as sincere as they might be, or of one's own ethical accomplishments, as generous as they might be. All this certainly causes us to act, but it is not what is at work in the sacramental rite. Here the self is put at the disposal of the Other whom it can let act in the Church's mediation. The self lets the Other act by performing a gesture which is not from itself, by saying words which are not its own, by receiving elements which it has not chosen. It is indeed the very condition of faith that this symbolizes, it is its being as a believer that the self puts into play, radically, leaving no escape route. And it is precisely in this act of disappropriation that the self is given back to itself.

When everything seems to fail for believers, when the ground of their firmest convictions gives way beneath their feet, when anguish grabs them by their throats as the idea runs through their bodies that perhaps there is no God, what remains for them, so that they are still able, in spite of everything and if it is possible, to communicate with "God," if not their bodies? What else remains for them but their bodies taking in hand what the Church takes up — a little bread and wine — and saying what the Church says — "my body given for you" — taking and saying these as the gestures and words of him whom the Church confesses as its Lord? But when faith has lost every illusion about its good "reasons," when it no longer has anything but the body, then is it not eminently "faith"?

2. *The Enfleshment of Faith*

What does the fact that it is woven together through rites called sacraments tell us about the faith? This was our question at the outset. This fact not only tells us that faith, taking us in our complete humanness, cannot be lived outside the body, outside the group, outside tradition. It tells us much more than that, a "much more" which involves nothing less than the overcoming of metaphysics as we presented it from the perspective of language and, against logocentrism, language inscribed in the empirical resistance of matter possessing meaning. The fact that there are sacraments leads us to say that *corporality is the very mediation where faith takes on flesh* and makes real the truth that inhabits it. It says this to us with all the pragmatic force of a ritual expression that speaks by its actions and works through the word, the word-as-body. It tells us that the body, which is the whole word of humankind, is the unavoidable mediation where the Word of a God involved in the most human dimension of our humanity demands to be inscribed in order to make itself understood. Thus, it tells us that faith requires a *consent to the body*, to history, to the world which makes it a fully human reality.

Chapter Ten

The Sacraments as Instituted

DIALECTICS OF THE INSTITUTING AND INSTITUTED

There is no instituting agency that is not itself instituted. Better still, the most instituting is the most instituted. Such an apparently paradoxical affirmation follows in a straight line from this symbolism which, reversing the representative schemes of what we have called "metaphysics," unmasks metaphysics' false dichotomies: Does not the most spiritual happen in the most corporeal? Is not exterior expression the mediation of interior differentiation? Is not what is closest to subjects precisely what seems to them most distant? And do not humans speak because they are always-already spoken?

If language is indeed the *most powerful* mediation *in instituting* subjects, it is precisely because it is the *most instituted.* It is such inasmuch as it is *"tongue,"* phonetic matter instituted as significant thanks to a cultural delimitation. We emphasized above, in thinking of it as "writing," that here we are dealing with a radical given which precedes each of us and is a law for each within the group and that this law is singular in this, no one ever decreed it as such. This means, we said earlier, that this instituted is not simply one law among others, but rather the original space of all institutions and all culture. Subjects emerge from this primordial subjugation to a language already there. Language set to work in *discourse* or the language act is the instituting mediation of subjects in what is both most social and most singular about them because the formal architecture of their tongue is assumed by each person in a *new* way, an unprecedented event: an event of language.

We attempt here to understand the sacraments theologically according to this dialectics of the instituting and the instituted. In the symbolic order proper to the Church or in the "language game" proper to faith, we can regard them as elements of the Christian mother tongue and language acts bringing about the identity of the Church and the subjects who express themselves in them. The first point, concerning the instituted, will be the subject of the present chapter. The second will be treated in the next.

I. THE INSTITUTION OF THE SACRAMENTS BY JESUS CHRIST: THE CRUX OF THE QUESTION

Among the diverse ecclesial mediations, the sacraments occupy an eminently *institutional* position. They are the Church's indispensable ways of integrating subjects because as an institution it is wholly involved in them. This is why it strictly manages the sacraments, so strictly that it claims all power over them, "save their substance" according to the formula of the Council of Trent. This exception is obviously enormous. We are thus in a paradoxical situation: on the one hand, in calling the sacraments ritual acts which it receives as instituted by Jesus Christ and over the *substantia* of which it declares, by this fact, to have no dominion, the Church attests that *nothing escapes it as much* as these elements because of when they began and from whom they began; but on the other hand, *if nothing is less its own theologically, nothing is more in its power concretely*, for it alone is qualified, in a hermeneutical act at the heart of the faith, to determine the limit of its power over them.[1] Nothing, in sum, is more regulated by the Church than what it recognizes as escaping its dominion. "Decision of the Church, decision of Christ, it is the same thing," said Simon of Florence at the Council of Trent, meaning that Communion *sub utraque* ("under both species") is not given by "divine right":[2] this sort of formula makes us appreciate the scope of the paradox with which we are dealing.

1. The hermeneutics of the doctrine and of the Tridentine canons concerning the sacrament of penance which A. Duval proposes leads him to believe that the fundamental debate for the entire council bore, "in the final analysis, on the sacramental *power* of which the Church is the depository." He explains: "The origin, nature, and extension of the *potestas* in the Church of Christ is without doubt the central problem of the Council of Trent, and perhaps the least studied." A. Duval, *Des sacrements au concile de Trente* (Paris: Cerf, 1985) ch. 4 "La confession," 175–176. See D-S, 1728.
2. On "divine right" at Trent, see A. Duval, 194–202.

It also makes us appreciate the *dangers:* for the ecclesial hierarchy to fix the limits of its power in order to show what is under God's power is in equal measure to sacralize and strengthen its own power. The concealment of its effective power behind a theoretical power attributed to God alone is a strategy heavy with risks of mystifying and manipulating its "mystery."

But the dangers of this inevitable collusion between the expression of truth and the power in expressing it should not conceal the *theological interest* of what is at stake. There is, in this matter, something homologous to language at the anthropological level. Language is the *instituting* mediation of subjects, we have just recalled, inasmuch as it is *always-already instituted,* no member of the group ever having decreed its existence as such at its origin (the reverse of the case with an instrument). Mutatis mutandis, nothing is *more instituting* of the Church in its identity as Church-of-Christ than this *"most instituted,"* the sacraments "instituted through our Lord Jesus Christ" (Trent, D-S 1601), instituted in such a way that no community or believer in the Church, even at the highest level of the hierarchy, could have established. As is the case with language, the Church can regulate their correct usage, but not first produce them. This seems to us the principal interest of the classic question concerning the *institution of the sacraments by Jesus Christ.*

We will not take up here the historical dossier on this question. It is enough to recall that it was not posed *as such* until the Scholastic era although, as Y. Congar has pointed out, the Middle Ages were "much less demanding than we on the institution of the sacraments; they easily admitted an institution that was mediately divine,"[3] a mediately divine that is particularly generous in Bonaventure.[4] For the Scholastics, for example

3. Y. Congar, "L'idée de sacrements majeurs ou principaux," *Concilium* 31 (1968) 25-34.

4. For St. Bonaventure, Christ instituted marriage and penance *confirmando, approbando, et consummando* ("by establishing, approving, and completing"); confirmation and the anointing of the sick *insinuando et initiando* ("by suggesting and beginning"); baptism, the Eucharist, and holy orders *initiando et consummando et in semetipso suscipiendo* ("by beginning and completing and by receiving in himself") (*Brevil.*, p. 6, c. 4, 1). See J. Bittremieux, "L'institution des sacrements d'après saint Bonaventure," *Ephem. theol. lovan.* 9 (1932) 234-252; H. Baril, *La doctrine de saint Bonaventure sur l'institution des sacrements* (Montréal, 1954).

Thomas Aquinas, there is an equivalence between the institution of the sacraments by God ("God," that is, "Christ himself, who is at once God and human," III, q. 64, a. 2, ad 1) and the efficacy of their grace whose source is God alone ("the virtue of the sacrament coming only from God, it follows that God alone instituted the sacraments," q. 64, a. 2). In Scholastic language, to say that God (or Christ as God) is the *institutor* of the sacraments is to say that God is their *auctor*, their creative and operating agent. This is why, even if such an institution in its concrete rules of application passes through the mediation of the Church, the institution remains, through its source, linked to Christ: "Just as the apostles cannot establish another Church, no more can they transmit another faith or institute other sacraments. For 'it is by the sacraments which ran down the side of Christ crucified' that the Church was established" (q. 64, a, 2, ad 3). One sees what is at stake for Thomas: since it is from Christ that the sacraments' efficacy derives, no one else but he, not even the apostles, could have instituted them. He alone, for example, could have instituted confirmation ("not in conferring it, but in promising it"), because he alone could, according to his promise, transmit the Holy Spirit (q. 72, a. 1, ad 1).

After the Scholastics, especially among the Counter-Reformation theologians of the sixteenth century, then later at the time of the Modernist controversy, the question was posed within much too narrow limits. One sought to give historical "proofs" for the institution of every one of the seven sacraments. Much energy was thus expended wrangling over an affair that was as ill-conceived as polemical. Theologians fell victim both to a confusion concerning the epistemological status of the question and to methodological error. To seek to deduce the institution of the sacraments by Christ from historical "proofs" is to place the problem on a terrain not its own and inevitably to demonstrate only what one has decided beforehand. This question is a good example, among others, of bad apologetics using a preconceived interpretation of history based on dogma. At the same time one should distinguish between the method, often inappropriate, with which one sought to resolve the *mode* of the sacraments' institution and the *importance* of the question. What is expressed here is of *fundamental significance:* it bears, as we have shown with Thomas, on the very nature of the sacraments as acts of salvation on the part of Christ himself.

The sacraments are the major symbolic proclamation of the Church's identity. This identity insists essentially on *its dependence on Christ as its beginning and origin.* This is what is *symbolically* at work in the sacraments. This is precisely what is *discursively* developed in the theological — later dogmatic — affirmation of Trent concerning their institution by Jesus Christ. Fundamentally, this institution means nothing else than the identity of the Church as Church *of* Christ, existing only to receive itself from him, as the servant and not the owner of salvation, instituted by an Other and not instituting itself, a gift of the grace of the Father through Christ in the Spirit.

In such a formula (or in another, identical in meaning, *salva illorum substantia*, "save their substance"), the Church is not content with merely saying that in carrying out the sacramental act, it recognizes its dependence on Christ, its Lord. For one could always suppose, as in other mediations of its communion with God, it could itself have invented those acts which express its dependence. It acknowledges itself dispossessed of this very possibility: "Not only," it says in effect, "do I pose an act where I confess myself dependent on Christ, but I confess that I *do not even have the power of inventing such an act*; it is given me as a grace, and I receive it as something instituted which always-already precedes me and which, precisely from the fact I do not have dominion over it and its origin is an *impregnable place*, reveals to me what I am." The sacraments thus refer the Church back to this *empty place* of its Lord which it cannot occupy without destroying itself and can only commemorate. Thus, as we emphasized with regard to the symbolism of ritual programming, whereas sacramental celebration is for the Church the most radical anthropological mediation of its dependence on Christ and consequently the highest confession *in act* of its identity, the affirmation of the institution of the sacraments by Christ is for it the ultimate *discursive* unfolding of what is at stake. We have here a good illustration of the adage *lex orandi, lex credendi*: the *concept* takes up, at its own level, what has been at work in the *symbol*.

Such is the law of faith the institution of the sacraments by Jesus Christ theologically expresses, a law whose complete force is expressed in the symbolic act of their celebration: then, in effect, it ceases to be a mere "idea"; here the believer stumbles on the *scandalous contingency of a ritual* which sets up, in its reality as a programmed given, an insurmountable resistance to any imaginary flight toward a God disconnected from our corporality and historicity. The fact that sacraments are instituted thus forms a *barrier* which frustrates our desire to erase the scandalous empirical nature of *Jesus* of Nazareth as the Christ and Lord, as well as, before and after him, the empirical nature of the letter of the *Scriptures* as the Word of God and of the *Church* as the fundamental sacrament of the reign. However, it is in being shattered upon this *interdict against returning to the origin* that our desire learns to go into mourning for a God who is nothing but the imaginary projection of ourselves and to gradually re-structure itself in a Christian manner. The law of the sacraments is harsh; perhaps it is necessary to have experienced it in all its starkness until we felt the desire to overturn them, in order to realize their significance for the structuring of faith. It is from this perspective, in any case, that we are going to approach the mystery of the Eucharistic body of the Lord.

II. THE EUCHARISTIC BODY OF THE LORD: AN EXEMPLARY FIGURE OF THE RESISTANCE OF THE SACRAMENTS AS INSTITUTED

For the thinking believer there is something particularly scandalous about the Eucharistic presence of Christ. To tell the truth, this does not seem to have always been the case. In the early days of the Church, the stumbling block consisted rather in God's resurrection of Jesus, he who had been crucified for blasphemy against God's law (see above). Now, this very first scandal, decisive for the faith, seems to have partially faded as, with the passage of time, people came to forget its concrete historical and theological significance for the first communities of Jewish origin and as the "theories" of salvation domesticated the *Logos* of the cross. One has the feeling that this first scandal was in a way replaced by that of the presence of Christ in the Eucharist, especially from the twelfth century on, a time where devotion to the Eucharistic presence developed considerably, leading the new theologians, the Scholastics, to scrutinize with every possible intellectual resource the mystery of the real presence. And if not all went as far toward the agnosticism, mixed with mysticism, which Pascal was to express later concerning the Eucharist ("the strangest and the most obscure secret" of the *Deus absconditus*),[5] still all found in it a *challenge to reason* — perhaps the definitive challenge since the conver-

5. B. Pascal, *Œuvres* (Paris: Brunschvicg, 1914) 88–89.

sion of bread into the body of Christ seems to Thomas "more miraculous than the creation."[6]

We will recall first in what terms Scholasticism and the Council of Trent couched this challenge. Second, we will propose an approach by way of symbolism, our major concern being to show how the Eucharistic presence of the Lord is the exemplary expression of the *resistance* of God's mystery to every attempt by the subject to appropriate it. In doing this, we will cast into relief the entire range and content of the sacraments as *instituted*, the subject of the present chapter.

1. Transubstantiation: A Radical Change

The concept of transubstantiation is suited *aptissime* ("in the most appropriate way") for expressing the mode of Christ's Eucharistic presence. The adoption of this adverb by the Council of Trent in its dogmatic enunciations[7] means at least two things. First, the term "transubstantiation" is relevant in the measure in which it expresses the *integrality* of the change or conversion of substance which is effected in the Eucharist. Let us be precise on this point: by deliberately choosing the pair "substance-species," instead of the Aristotelian "substance-accidents," the council deliberately avoided linking the expression of its faith to one philosophy, the Aristotelian, and demonstrated this even though, as E. Schillebeeckx especially has shown, "numerous data enable us to establish beyond the shadow of a doubt that all the council fathers without exception interpreted the dogma in Aristotelian terms."[8] Second, that transubstantiation is a term employed by the Church "in the most appropriate way" means it is *not an absolute* and thus it is theoretically possible to express the specificity of Christ's presence in the Eucharist in a different manner. Such is the hermeneutical task at hand.

a) High Scholasticism. The approach we have just sketched allows us to treat in detail only three points which we consider major for our purpose. What is more, since we find all three clearly affirmed in Thomas' *Summa Theologica*, we will in the main limit ourselves to this work.

6. *ST* III, q. 75, a. 8, ad 3.
7. Trent, canon 2 on the Most Holy Sacrament of the Eucharist, *D-S* 1652.
8. E. Schillebeeckx, *La présence du Christ dans l'eucharistie* (Paris: Cerf, 1970) 50.

— The Change of the Whole Substance

As we indicated in chapter eight, recourse to the Aristotelian conceptual pair of "substance" and "accident" for thinking about Eucharistic transubstantiation, that is, the *conversio totius substantiae* ("change of the whole substance"), in a rational way allowed the great Scholastics of the thirteenth century to react *against the ultra-realism* exacerbated by the first opposition to Berengar and apparent in the profession of faith imposed on him in 1059. The most common situation in the eleventh and twelfth centuries — against which we must understand the resistance of Berengar, the skilled dialectician — was such that because of the absence of a sufficiently refined concept to express the "final reality" of entities, one was forced to conceive the Eucharistic presence in a strongly "sensualist" way; only recourse to the very subtle Aristotelian concept of "substance" would allow theologians to free themselves from this representation.

Thus, for an anti-dialectician like Peter Damien (d. 1072), the *species*, in E. Dumoutet's estimation, "seems to have been analogous to a transparent glass through which, in certain circumstances (which, though miraculous, are no less consonant with the logic of things), it is possible to glimpse the real, bloody flesh of Christ."[9] This was due to the belief in the direct adherence of the *species panis* to the *species carnis*.[10] Lanfranc of Canterbury, one of Berengar's principal adversaries, professed an ultra-realism according to which, as J. de Montclos writes, it would require only a miracle "for the veils (the bread and wine) which cover the flesh and blood of Christ to be taken away and for the flesh and blood to appear as they are in reality." These adhere directly to the "secondary essences" (a frequent expression in Lanfranc) of the Eucharistic species.[11] One sees why Lanfranc sees the *immolatio vera* of Christ taking place in the Mass at the breaking of the bread and in its being chewed at Communion . . .

In clarifying with Aristotle that the *sub-stantia* or again the *sub-jectum* is only pure potentiality to be actualized through its accidents,[12] Thomas

---

9. E. Dumoutet, *Corpus Domini: Aux sources de la piété eucharistique médiévale* (Paris: Beauchesne, 1942) pt. 3, p. 108.

10. J. Geiselmann, *Die Eucharistielehre der Vorscholastik* (1926) 416. In extreme cases, where one goes so far as to deny the separability of accidents from the substance, one reaches the same conclusions as this theologian of the twelfth century: "The whiteness and the roundness cannot be separated from the body, which is also round and white, in such a way that, if the body is not broken, these qualities are not broken either" (ibid.).

11. J. de Montclos, *Lanfranc et Bérenger* (Louvain, 1971) 378.

12. *ST* I, q. 3, a. 6: "Subiectus comparatur ad accidens sicut potentia ad actum; subiectum enim secundum accidens est aliquo modo in actu" ("Sub-

(like others in the thirteenth century) releases it from all the representations by which we are accustomed to characterize accidents: extension, division, locomotion, corruption, taste, color, and so on. The "final reality" of entities is thus neither a "this" or a "that" nor anything which can be attained by sensible cognition. As simply the power to exist by means of its actuation through its accidents, the substance is first a category of the intelligibility of entities: "It offers no footing," writes Thomas, "to any organ of sense or to the imagination, but only to the intelligence, whose object is the essence of things, as Aristotle says."[13] By this fact, *one exorcises every spatial representation* of the Eucharistic presence: only the sacramental sign, made up of accidents which remain unchanged after transubstantiation, can be divided, multiplied, moved, and so on. The reality of the glorified body of Christ, present *"through the mode of substance and not through the mode of quantity"* (the first of the accidents),[14] escapes all of that: Christ present "according to the special mode of the sacrament" is not there "as in a place" nor is he subjected to being moved from place to place.[15] Further, the species are less a *curtain* which hides him than a *sign* which reveals him in the only manner possible, that is, not *in specie propria* ("in his own appearance"), which is possible only in heaven, but *in specie aliena* ("in a different appearance").[16] For such is one of the purposes of the permanence of the species as signs: "The accidents of bread subsist in this sacrament so that it may be *in them that one sees* the body of Christ and not in its own aspect."[17]

— *Outside Any Physicalism*

The novelty of this language (incidentally not linked to Aristotelianism as such because the second profession of faith imposed on Berengar in 1079 already contains the expression *substantialiter converti*[18] and the term *transsubstantiatio* itself seems to have appeared before 1153)[19] does not lie in the ontological affirmation of the presence: this was already clearly af-

---

stance relates to accident as potentiality to act; for substance actuated by accident is in act in some way.")

13. Ibid., III, q. 76, a. 7.

14. Ibid., a. 1, ad 3.

15. Ibid., q. 75, a. 1, ad 3.

16. Ibid., q. 76, a. 8; Bonaventure, *Brevil.*, p. 6, c. 9, 4: the change does not affect Christ "in himself" (*in ipso*), but only in the species (*in eis*). This is why (*Brevil.*, c. 9, 5) Christ is not there *ut occupans locum* ("as occupying space").

17. *ST* III, q. 75, a. 6.

18. D-S 700.

19. J. de Ghellinck, "Eucharistie au XIIe siècle en Occident," DTC 5 (1913) 1287–1293.

firmed by Ambrose and the Greek Fathers. The transformation (as a verb, *metaballo*) of bread and wine into the body and blood of Christ requested by the epicleses of the anaphoras of John Chrysostom or by the one of Cyril of Jerusalem are similar to the *mutatio* of bread and wine by Christ's word found in Ambrose.[20] The novelty consists in the fact that compared with the theology of the pre-Scholastic period, the ontological expression of the presence can be understood only as *outside any physicalism* and any more or less gross representation. Transubstantiation thus has a meaning diametrically opposed to the one often attributed to it.[21] Besides, it consists of a "conversion," that is, a transformation or a becoming and not a succession of two realities; this demands that there be not the annihilation of one substance, the bread, but its transformation into the substance of Christ's body:[22] there is indeed a *becoming* of the bread into Christ's body, and this supposes that one can conceive this becoming as a "conversion from substance to substance."[23] This *conversio totius substantiae* has this singular trait, it is neither a creation nor a simple conversion in the usual sense of the terms: a *creation* implies transition from non-being to being, and in this sense the Eucharist is closer to a conversion; a *conversion* cannot be understood as the radical transformation of substance, and in this sense the Eucharist is closer to a creation. The formula "conversion of the whole substance" stands at the intersection of these two concepts.

— *Sacrificium intellectus*

In the third place, the Scholastic theory of transubstantiation is wholly subordinated to the Church's traditional faith and especially, besides the story of the institution, to its liturgical expression condensed in the formula of Communion so often commented upon by the Church Fathers: "The body of Christ — Amen." We have pointed out the importance of liturgical practice, in this area as in so many others, especially the different marks of respect and veneration during the celebration, until, starting in the twelfth century, new ones developed in the West outside the Mass. It is obviously this concrete weight of *practices*, including — perhaps especially, in certain respects — that of Eucharistic adoration,[24] the Scholastics

---

20. Ambrose, *De Sacr.* IV, 14–16; *De Myst.* 52 (Sources chrétiennes 25 bis, pp. 108–111, 187); Cyril of Jerusalem, *Cat. Myst.* V, 7 (Sources chrétiennes 126, p. 155); Anaphora of John Chrysostom, in A. Hanggi and I. Pahl, *Prex eucharistica* (Fribourg, Switzerland: Universitaires, 1968) 226.

21. Schillebeeckx, *La présence du Christ*, 7–11.

22. *ST* III, q. 75, a. 3.

23. Ibid., q. 76, a. 1, ad 3.

24. Ibid., q. 75, a. 2: for if the substance of the bread and wine subsisted

attempted to account for in framing their theory of transubstantiation. Now, as valuable as the philosophy of Aristotle had been, they saw themselves obliged to break with it and to do so in a frank and deliberate manner. Such was the attitude of Thomas faced with the insoluble problem posed by the permanence of the accidents of the bread and wine without their *subjectum* of inherence, the substance.[25] Wholly conscious that on this point he was contradicting Aristotle, as the difficulties expressed at the beginning of question 77, article 1 show, Thomas saw himself constrained to look for the least inadequate solution possible by having recourse to the first of the accidents, *quantity:* it is presented as the basis of individuation for the others.[26] But one senses what anguish this *sacrifice of the intellect* must have caused a person as sensitive as he was to the requirements of *ratio*.

Our own attempt to understand the Eucharistic presence in all its radicalness, even if it takes a different route from the one used by Thomas and his contemporaries, does not claim any more than they did to account for the mystery of faith. At least we have from the start, because of the symbolic approach we have adopted, renounced the attempt to provide final "reasons" for anything; and our previous discussions show this was not simply a symptom of intellectual laziness. We thus fully embrace Thomas' *sacrificium intellectus*. But we do this *in a manner different* from his.

b) The Principal Limitation of Scholastic Transubstantiation. In canon 3 on the sacraments, the Council of Trent emphasized that the sacraments are not all equal. The canons on the Eucharist describe it in an *eminent* manner: the *sanctissima eucharistia* is a *sacrosanctum* or an *admirabile sacramentum*. By antonomasia, it is even called "the Blessed Sacrament." This is due to the fact that in it "the whole Christ . . . is truly, really, and substantially contained" (canon 1), and this even before its use in Communion as well as after the celebration (canon 4). According to Thomas' terms from the first article of his treatise on the Eucharist, the difference between the Eucharist and the other sacraments is twofold. First, it "contains" Christ himself "absolutely," whereas the

---

after the consecration, "there would be a substance there to which one could not pay the adoration due to God alone."

25. In the same way Bonaventure, *Brevil.* p. 6, c. 9, 5: the accidents remain "without substance" (*praeter subiectum*).

26. *ST* III, q. 77, a. 2.

other sacraments have efficacy only *in ordine ad aliud*, that is, relative to their application to the subject. From this comes the second difference: its first effect (*res et sacramentum*) is *in ipsa materia* ("in the matter itself"), whereas in baptism the effect is *in suscipiente* ("in the one who receives it").[27]

Now, such a statement, even if it does not forget that the final purpose of the Eucharist is the grace of sanctification given to the person who receives it (who is thereby "projected into the mystical body of Christ," according to Bonaventure's beautiful expression),[28] seems *dangerous* to us. In speaking of the "full realization" (*perfectio*) of the Eucharist in the consecration of the matter, inasmuch as the latter contains "in an absolute manner" the *esse* of Christ, one runs the risk of minimizing two capital elements that are linked together. On the one hand, one does not take into account the *human* destination that is implied by the *materia* in question, the bread and wine. On the other, one loses sight of a fundamental aspect of the mystery: the Christ of the Eucharist is the *Christus totus*; the "head" cannot be isolated from the "body," the Church which still remains completely distinct from it. But these two elements cannot be fully taken into account except on another plane than that of metaphysical substance.

No more than his predecessors and contemporaries does Thomas forget that the Eucharist is for the Church. But as we have underlined following H. de Lubac, the "deadly dichotomy," in which the West allowed itself to be imprisoned by reaction against Berengar, between *sacramentum* and *res* provoked an "expulsion" *outside* the intrinsic symbolism of the sacrament of what the Church Fathers considered to be its ultimate reality, specifically, *the Church as the* veritas *of the Eucharistic* corpus mysticum: the Church remains only the *extrinsic* end. If one adds to this evolution the understanding (central for the Scholastic conception of

---

27. Ibid., q. 73, a. 1, ad 3.

28. Bonaventure, *Brevil.* p. 6, c. 9, 6: through a spiritual eating of the sacrament, which consists in "chewing Christ through reflection on faith and assimilating him through the fervor of love," "Christ does not transform [the believer] into himself but rather the believer is transferred into his mystical body" (*non in se transformet Christus, sed ipse potius traiiciatur in eius corpus mysticum*).

the "how" of the Eucharistic conversion) of reality on the model of a metaphysical *substance,* one understands why they were no longer content to take up the language of Augustine, already cited: "If then you are the body of Christ and his members, it is your own mystery that is placed on the Lord's table; it is your own mystery that you receive. . . ." One could only be suspicious of such language, judged insufficiently "realistic." In the perspective of the Aristotelian "substance" as the expression of the *ultimate reality* of entities, one could express the integrality and radicalness of the real presence of Christ in the sacrament only by putting between parentheses, at least during the analysis of the "how" of Eucharistic conversion, its relation to the Church. This is exactly what happens with Thomas: if he strongly emphasizes the connection of the Eucharist to the Church both before and after his analysis of transubstantiation, he puts it *between parentheses* during this analysis. This state of affairs is probably inevitable once one can grasp the ultimate reality of things only under the mode of subsisting entities.

But can one conceive the *esse* of Christ in the Eucharist without the relation of his *ad-esse* to the Church, to the celebrating community, to the believing subjects for whom it is destined? Such is for us the *principal limitation* of the Scholastic work in this domain. Conversely, if one takes into account from beginning to end the *ad* relating to the subjects as constitutive of an *esse* which, being sacramental in nature, can only be *adesse,* can one do justice to the radicalness of what, according to the faith of the Church, is at issue in "transubstantiation" or at least, if one places oneself on another plane than that of substance, to the radicalness of what the prefix "trans-," a bit like a blinking light, constantly recalls? Such is our question.

2. *A Symbolic Approach to the Mystery of the Eucharistic Body of the Lord*

We believe that to express theologically the integral content of the Eucharistic presence, recourse to the concept of "substance" is not the only path possible. Let us attempt to show this.

a) The Ad-esse, *Constitutive of the Sacramental* Esse. We emphasized above that the celebration itself is the natural milieu of every sacramental reflection. This is for us a fundamental principle, which by the way is in accord with the strictest Thomism, for there the sacraments are considered *in genere signi* ("in the genus of sign").

—The Whole of the Celebration

We said in chapter six that it is impossible to understand the Eucharist any other way than as the precipitate of the Scriptures where the living Lord speaks to the assembly over which he presides. The various rites of the Eucharistic celebration are not simply juxtaposed haphazardly; they fit together according to a coherent architectonics, thereby forming a vast structured ensemble which itself must be considered as one great symbol, *a single sacramental whole*. Each element can only be understood as symbolizing with the others, linked together within this whole.

Thus understood, the Eucharistic presence appears as the *crystallization* of Christ's presence in the *assembly* (ecclesia) gathered in his name and presided over by himself and in the *Scriptures* proclaimed as his living word. To stress the truth of this twofold mode of presence is not at all to weaken that of the third, as it seems some have feared. Much to the contrary, the truth of the Eucharistic presence is better recognized the more the truth of these two other modes of presence, which precede it and lead toward it, is taken seriously. The Christ who comes-to-presence in the bread and wine does not suddenly fall "from heaven" (if we are permitted this expression); he comes from the *assembly* — and this is why the grace of the Eucharist is Christ, head *and* body. This is the first scandal of the mystery of faith, which the fixation on that of transubstantiation crowds out of its proper place: these men and these women, all sinners, form the body of Christ, the holy Church of God, who chose "what is low and despised in the world, things that are not, to reduce to nothing things that are" (1 Cor 1:28). Besides, he who comes-to-presence in the Eucharist is the Word of God announced in the Scriptures. This is why Communion is not fruitful unless it is a rumination, according to the Spirit (John 6:63), of the Word, both bitter and sweet (Ezek 2:8–3:3; Rev 10:8-9), which God gives as manna to eat (Deut 8:3). Such is the second scandal of the mystery of faith, in comparison to which that of the Eucharistic presence risks acting as a false scandal: that of the God who was crucified for the life of the world.

From beginning to end the architectural dynamic of the vast *sacramentum* which the whole of the celebration forms forces one to realize that the relational *"for"* belongs to the very concept of the Eucharistic "presence."

— *The Whole of the Eucharistic Prayer*

The same observation must be made with regard to the Eucharistic Prayer. The story of the institution can be understood only as the crystallization of the whole of salvation history in the old covenant and in Jesus (NP 1) and as the anticipation of the Church's future (NP 3). Besides, the story can be told as a living memorial by the ministers only in the Spirit: normally then, it implies an epiclesis. The sacramental "presence" of Christ (NP 2) can thus be understood only *in relation to the twofold memorial* which structures the whole of the Eucharistic Prayer: a memorial of the past in thanksgiving (NP 1) and a memorial of the future in supplication (NP 3). This in no way minimizes the truth of the presence, but obliges us to place it, as C. Perrot puts it, at the midpoint of a "double distance between the yesterday of Golgotha and the future of the parousia": its connection to the parousia keeps it from being reduced to a simple historical evocation of the cross which would equate the Christian meal with Greek funeral rites; its connection to Golgotha prevents it from remaining in the Jewish status of waiting; and the distance between the two crosses out its very truth of presence with the stroke of absence and prohibits us from conceiving it as a "full" presence in the Gnostic manner.[29]

— *The Story of the Institution*

As the focal point of the Eucharistic Prayer, the story of the institution (always to be understood, as we have seen, in its relation with the epiclesis and anamnesis) places Christ's coming-to-presence in this same dynamic of relation. First at the level of the *words* quoted, the "take, eat, . . . drink . . ." and, still more, the *hyper* ("for") are essential to the significance of the action. *Hyper* is neither a simple derivation nor an extrinsic purpose of an *esse* that would be sufficient unto itself. The salvific relation it signifies

29. C. Perrot, "L'anamnèse néo-testamentaire," *Rev. Inst. Cath. Paris* 2 (1982) 33–35.

("for," "for our benefit") indicates that we cannot be content here, under the pretext of "realism," to imagine the reality at issue as the simple *esse* of a subsistent entity; the relation must be conceived precisely as "presence," that is, as *being-for, being-toward*. In other terms, the *esse is constitutively ad-esse*. Moreover, *the gestures* of gift and sharing indicate the same thing, with all the force that one can recognize in these "enfleshed words" which belong to the ritual order. And the *materials* (bread and wine) used here are not deficient in this regard, as we will make clear.

— Bread and Wine, according to the Bible

"In the universe of the Bible, *bread* designates first the one food that none can do without and, as a metaphor, food in general."[30] We thus understand how, with this traditional semantic burden, it could have represented for Jesus, in the "Our Father," the totality of the gifts necessary to us every day and how, at the Last Supper, he could have taken it as the symbol for the greatest of gifts — that of his very life. Likewise, we understand how Jesus, echoing the prophetic and sapiential relation of bread-manna-word of God-eschatological banquet, could have presented himself as being the bread of life.[31] Bread represents at the same time, by metaphor, the primordial *gift of God* and, by metynomy, the whole of the earth and *human work*. It thus binds together "cult" and "culture," incidentally in accord with the common etymology of these two terms in Hebrew as well as in Greek and Latin.[32] In parallel fashion, *wine* carries a biblical richness of equal scope. However, not being necessary for life (in contrast to bread), it introduces "an element of gratuity that intimates no longer mere terrestrial survival, but fullness of life, such as happiness produces."[33] Hence its association with messianic joy.

30. X. Léon-Dufour, *Le partage du pain eucharistique selon le Nouveau Testament* (Paris: Seuil, 1982) 72.

31. Ibid., 297–298.

32. G. Bornkamm, "Latreuô," *Th. Wört. z. N.T.* IV, 58–68. The Latin *colere* and *cultus* mean both the cultivation of the land and of the spirit (*colere artes*) and the worship rendered to the gods (*colere deos*). In Greek, *latris* means a worker's salary and *latreia* and *latreuein* have the same meaning as the Hebrew *'abodal* and *'abad*, which designate not only the service of God (the liturgy), but also manual labor.

33. Léon-Dufour, *Partage du pain eucharistique*, 73, n. 30.

Now, not only did the Scholastics, in their analyses of the "how" of transubstantiation, not take into account this semantic richness of bread and wine in the Bible but they even excluded it in principle since the final reality of entities was identified with their ontological substance. Of course, people will not fail to object that from the metaphysical viewpoint the analysis of the "how" not only can but must leave aside consideration of the end. This objection is pertinent from this viewpoint. But then, it is the entire suit against metaphysics, as we have conducted it in the first part of this book, that is involved here. In any case, it is by no means clear how it is possible to disconnect the "how" from the "for what," or rather from the "for whom," in an area where what is *essentially* at stake for Christ is a *gift* of himself to humankind, a gift so much a gift that he gives it in the form of food and drink. How can one omit from consideration what, by origin and purpose, belongs to *the substantial reality of bread as bread* (and not as a stone or piece of wood, or even water or oil destined to be applied only to the outside of the body) *and thus is destined to be taken into the human body?* It is difficult for us to think of the reality of the gift of Christ in the Eucharist in any other way than as "presence," as "being for," as *ad-esse.*

b) The Essence of the Pitcher and the Bread.

— *The Pitcher according to Heidegger*

Our biblical viewpoint has imperceptibly widened into a *philosophical and anthropological* viewpoint. On this level, the entire approach developed in the first part of this book has emphasized that unless we are ready to reduce the real to what the physical sciences say about it, the *ultimate reality* of an object can never be identified with its physico-chemical components. Can it be identified with their metaphysical *substantia* which has itself nothing to do with physico-chemical components? This is what has been thought traditionally from the Aristotelian viewpoint. But, as we have developed this theme following Heidegger, the representation of the ultimate reality of entities as *hypokeimenon, sub-stratum, sub-jectum* or *sub-stantia* is not at all neutral. This representation is characteristic of a certain way of understanding oneself in the world, a way itself characteristic of a Hellenistic culture which, with considerable mutations, invaded the West and presupposed a *rupture between Being and Language.* We have explained at length why an "overcoming" of metaphysics is now necessary, an overcoming demanded by the historical unfolding of the question of Being in the age in which we find ourselves. Let us recall besides that in placing ourselves on the path of symbolism, we are no longer on the same terrain as that of classical metaphysics, as if we were only giving a new version of it.

What is reality on this *other terrain*, the reality of a pitcher for example — a term that designates here any object for containing liquid used as a drink (a pitcher in the limited sense of the term, a bottle, a jug . . .)? As the film *The Gods Must Be Crazy* shows with humor, a Coca-Cola bottle fallen out of "the sky" (from an airplane) into the territory of a tribe, barely out of the stone age, of the Kalahari can only be perceived as a strange, magical, and ultimately dangerous object which one must go to the end of the world to throw away. It is a fascinating object which, polished, transparent, and shining, glistens in the sun. One can, in blowing across it, make interesting musical sounds; one can also use it as a rolling pin to flatten soft objects . . . But this bottle does not convey anything of "bottleness" to the tribespeople; they have neither the word for the object as such or for the glass of which it is made nor the habit of using such objects. The reality "bottle" can exist only where the *culture* permits one to say its name and imagine the use for which it is essentially destined. It is inseparable from a properly human apprehension, to which, however, it cannot be reduced.

Heidegger has devoted an impressive reflection to the essence of a pitcher.[34] We can summarize what he says in four points.

1) First, the essence of a pitcher cannot be approached by *science* itself. Of course, when science pronounces on the materials, the shape, and the use of a pitcher or when it declares that to fill a pitcher "is to exchange one content (specifically, air) for another" (for example, wine), it "expresses something real and according to which it objectively sets out its procedures." But, Heidegger asks, "is this reality the reality of the pitcher? No. Science never attains anything but what its own mode of expression has admitted at the outset as a possible object for itself. . . . It

34. M. Heidegger, *La chose*, in EC, 199–205.

annihilates this thing which is the pitcher to the extent that it does not admit things as what determines reality. . . . Scientific knowledge had already destroyed things insofar as they are things, long before the atom bomb explosion"; it forgets "the 'thingness' of the thing," which cannot be thought by calculating reason, but only by meditative thought.

2) According to this last, it is a question of permitting the emptiness of the pitcher, shaped by the bottom and sides, to be "its emptiness"; the wine to be not simply a liquid, but indeed wine; and its pouring to be not simply a decantation, but an offering. At this level of thought, the "thingness" of the pitcher "does not reside at all in the matter that makes it up, but in the emptiness that holds." Now, how does this emptiness *hold*? By *taking* what is poured out and *retaining* it within itself. But a third character is essential to the pitcher, one which governs the unity of the two previous ones: a *pouring-out*; for the pitcher as pitcher is shaped to this task of *Ausgiessen*. "The twofold 'holding' of emptiness rests on an 'out-pouring.' " It is of the pitcher's essence to be shaped for this possibility of pouring out.

3) Now, "to pour from the pitcher is to *offer*," according to the twofold sense of *shenken* ("pour" a drink and "offer" it at the same time). So much so that *"what makes the pitcher a pitcher unfolds its being in the pouring of what one offers."* Such a pouring is obviously not simply an act of filling up glasses. "In the poured water, the spring 'lingers.' In the spring, the rocks remain present; and in the rocks, the heavy sleep of the earth which receives rain and dew from heaven. The wedding of heaven and earth is present in the water from the spring. It is present in wine, given to us by the fruit of the vine in which the nourishing substance of the earth and the force of the sun in heaven are entrusted each to the other." *Heaven and earth* are thus present in the being of the pitcher, inasmuch as they remain "lingering" in what one pours out and this offer belongs to its "thingness." The drink that one thus offers is "destined for *mortals*," to quench their thirst, to enliven their leisure time, to lend cheer to their gatherings. Sometimes also, it is offered "in consecration" to the immortal *gods*. Now, "this pouring of the libation as a drink (offered to the immortal gods) is the authentic pouring. In the pouring of the consecrated drink, the pouring pitcher unfolds its being as the pouring which offers." Of course, this dimension of sacrificial offering is not always apparent. It can deteriorate into a "simple fact of filling or pouring out, down to its final degeneration into the common sale of drinks." In this case, there no longer appears this *"gift-giving" which brings the pouring to its fulfillment "in an essential mode" and which the religious libation unfolds.* At least it seems that this "gift-giving" as the essential mode of pouring comes to the fore "insofar as the pouring retains the earth and sky, gods and mor-

tals," which are "present together" in it, "taken in the simplicity of a unique *Quadriparti*."[35]

4) The word that comes immediately to mind with regard to this gathering of the *Quadriparti* is *symbol*. Heidegger does not use it here in his 1950 conference on "The Thing," but in a similar context in a conference the following year entitled "Building, Inhabiting, Thinking." For the essence of a *bridge*, as he shows here following a reflection of the same sort as the one on the pitcher, is to "gather round itself heaven and earth, gods and mortals." Its "thingness" resides precisely in this. This bridge is not first a thing in the sense that it would be first simply a real bridge and then later a symbol in the sense that one would then see in it all we have just discussed. "Inasmuch as it is this thing, it gathers the *Quadriparti*" and it is symbol. "*It is never first a simple bridge and later a symbol*": its "thingness," we would say, happens in no other way than in its symbolic expression.[36] Likewise, the pitcher is essentially a symbol of the Four. *Such is its most real reality: it is never separable from human destiny in its connection with the cosmos, others, and the gods.* The symbol, we observed in chapter four, carries in itself humankind and its "world"; it touches the most real of the subject.

It is clear that such a reality is *of a completely different order* from that of the metaphysical "substance" and is even unthinkable in terms of classical metaphysics, whose internal logic it defies. On this path, one never obtains a final answer; one only enriches oneself with certain glimpses or perspectives which, giving back to human beings the sense of the basic, make them feel the weight of things in their simplicity from which every essential question bursts forth.

— *The Reality of Bread*
Fruit of the sun and the rain from heaven, fruit "of the earth and work of human hands," is bread ever so much bread as

35. See the Dogon basket of which A. Van Eyck writes: "The capacity of a Dogon basket is unlimited because with its round edge and square bottom it is simultaneously basket and granary; at once sun, earth, and cosmic system; at once the millet and the powers that make the millet grow. It seems to me that human beings for whom all things are so unified that one thing can represent everything carry this essential unity within themselves" (*Le sens de la ville* [Paris: Seuil, 1972] 108). This text is quoted by M. Villela-Petit in the collection *Heidegger et la question de Dieu*, ed. J. Greisch (Paris: Grasset, 1980) 86.

36. M. Heidegger, *Bâtir, habiter, penser*, in EC, 180–182.

when it is shared by mortals in a meal which "provides sustenance" (*entre-tient*)? Let us go farther: bread is not a simple composite of nutritive elements. Today we can make pills which have the same nutritive elements as bread and would provide the same number of calories, but no one would claim — unless there is an evolution in language on this point, which is always possible — that such a thing is "bread." Bread is a *socially instituted food* — even if it no longer has the fundamental place and significance in our societies of abundance it once had when the phrases "to earn one's bread" and "to eat one's bread" were enough to evoke the whole of the production-consumption cycle. But just as, according to A. Vergote, the figure of the shepherd "fully retains its symbolic value" even "for Christians far from rural life" because, "contrary to a positivist psychology" or a too naturalistic concept of symbol, "our culture shows us that metaphor and symbol, as transmitted cultural realities, create and maintain their evocative power,"[37] bread still remains a major symbol of food and meal in our societies.

The "sustenance" that the bread-meal allows is not merely biological; it is also, and every bit as much, *symbolic*. If it is socially produced to satisfy hunger, it is also socially instituted as a symbol for what one shares (precisely during a meal), a sharing that concerns the fellowship of subjects in their communal destiny as brothers and sisters in life and death and their communal belonging to one culture. *It is essential for bread to be shared with others in a meal.* When for some reason it is not, it still symbolically recalls that for human beings eating is not reducible to a simple utilitarian act. This is why bread, the bread of a meal, is the *mediation of fellowship as much as of the maintenance of biological life.* It nourishes the "heart" as much as the body.

It happens that it is presented to *God* as the highest word of recognition by humankind: recognition *of* God as God, that is, as the one who makes a gift of bread, and finally of existence itself since bread then functions as an element symbolically representing all creation; and simultaneously gratitude *toward* God. Bread is never so much bread as in the gesture of thankful oblation where it gathers within itself heaven and earth, believers who "hold fel-

37. A. Vergote, *Religion, foi, incroyance* (Brussels: P. Mardaga, 1983) 291–292.

lowship" in sharing it, and the giver whom they acknowledge to be God: in this way a new communion of life is established with God and between themselves. No bread is first of all a simple "real" bread and then only afterwards and under certain circumstances a symbol of this gathering. *All bread is essentially this symbol, even if it is only in the symbolic act of religious oblation that its essence as bread unfolds itself.*

c) The Scope of Our Approach to the Question.

— *Only One Approach*

This symbolic approach is obviously *insufficient* for expressing the significance of the Eucharistic presence. For it does not suffice to say bread is never so much bread as in the religious gesture where it is recognized as a gracious gift of God; it is necessary to say it is never so much bread as in the religious, and more precisely, Christian gesture where, by offering it, the Church recognizes it as the gift of God's very self, as the *autocommunication of God's very self in Christ:* "The body of Christ — Amen!" It is impossible for the faith to side-step this: the bread of the Eucharist (and the wine, of course) is communication of Christ himself in his death and resurrection; it is sacramental mediation, not of simple communion with Christ, but indeed of uniquely intimate union with Christ. The prefix *"trans-"* (in "transubstantiation), we said above, reminds us of the radicalness of what the Church has traditionally believed on this point.

The *sacrificium intellectus* asked here is no less for us than it was for Thomas Aquinas. We will never be able to pass from the offering of bread as a gesture of recognition of God's gracious gift to God's Eucharistic offering as the mediation of the offering of Christ himself. Now, it is indeed the latter that is at issue here, as the offering of the anamnesis, the only true offering of the Church, makes especially clear: it is Christ himself who is offered here in sacrament to God, and it is he who is the thanksgiving of the Church ("we offer you in giving you thanks").

— *The "Response" Is the Path*

Perhaps some feel that the metaphysical logic of substance allows us to advance farther toward understanding this mystery than does the logic of symbol. This impression arises only because this advance is measured by the yardstick of a method whose entire internal logic aims at "summoning" entities. But what may seem a significant, even daring, advance on this level suddenly comes to a stop once, as we have seen, an apparent metaphysical absurdity develops, one which requires appealing to a second "miracle" by which God would support in existence the first of the accidents, quantity, to provide it as a subject of inherence for the others, that is, to have it play the role of a substance (see above). What one seems to have gained in "realism" by advancing in this direction one loses in symbolism, imprisoned as one is in a narrow logic of the real.

We are of the opinion that the path we have followed, although it cannot, any more than the Scholastic path, avoid the scandal of the mystery of faith, nonetheless offers major advantages.

First, with regard to the *sacrificium intellectus*, the *rupture* that the mystery requires does not suddenly interrupt a long, continuous ontological development. This rupture is real, certainly, but it is in harmony with an entire symbolic approach which, in its very rigor, is by nature not dense, not strictly linear one could say, entirely woven *within this fissure* which human beings are in themselves and for others. The *interstices* are necessary so that human beings can breathe, whereas onto-theology has for its secret ambition to cement shut every breach; and the truth needs a rift there to get through.

Second, with regard to the *kind of response* that the path of symbolism allows, we know in advance it can never consist in a definitive solution to a specific problem. For on this terrain the path is always *"transitive"*; the response is the whole journey itself. The response lies, if you will, in the new way of posing the question this journey allows, in another way of allowing oneself to be possessed by the question, and in the displacement the path itself effects in the person asking the question. Whereas the metaphysical route of substance is merely a preparation for one decisive response, *the symbolic path* of connection between earth, sky, gods, and mortals, as constitutive of the reality of bread, *belongs to the response itself:* there is a possible "cor-respondance" between the strange mystery of Christ giving himself as the bread of life and the singular strangeness of humankind coming to its truth when it shares its life as one shares bread.

— Ho Artos Alethinos

Because the mystery of the Eucharistic body of the Lord cannot be expressed on this terrain unless it carries with it the symbolic richness of bread evoked all along the journey, it is clear that to express all its radicalness, not only can one no longer say but one must no longer say, "This bread is no longer bread." On the contrary, such a statement had to be made on the terrain of metaphysical substance since on this level it expressed the necessary implication of the *conversio totius substantiae* formulated dogmatically at the Council of Trent. On the altogether different terrain of symbolism and *due to* the fact it is so different that the verb *"be"* no longer has the same status it had at its origin because the *Sein* is inseparable from the human *Da-Sein* and thus from language, from which it nevertheless remains distinct, to say that "this bread is the body of Christ" requires that one emphasize all the more it is indeed still bread, but now *essential* bread, bread which is never so much bread as it is in this mystery. We find again the biblical language of John 6: This is THE bread, the "true bread," the *artos alethinos* where the truth of bread, always forgotten (*a-letheia*), is revealed: the bread which nourishes human beings in the most human dimension of their humanity is the bread of the *word* and this word where bread comes-to-presence in communicating itself to others is itself, according to the faith, a mediation *where the Word delivered by God in Jesus Christ* to humanity unto death *takes on flesh*. The Eucharistic body of Christ, at this level of thought, is indeed bread par excellence, "the bread of life," the *panis substantialis et supersubstantialis,* as the Church Fathers called it. The *vere, realiter ac substantialiter* ("truly, really and substantially") of the Council of Trent is understood in an *altogether different way* from that of classic onto-theology.

d) Radicalness.

— The Precedence of the Symbolic Order and the Resistance of the Real

One may wonder whether the integration of the subject in what we have said of the "real" does not at the end lead, in spite of everything, to a sort of subjectivist reduction of this real, making our position incompatible with the Church's faith in the "real presence." Here, it is fitting to recall that the real, according to our symbolic approach, resists every attempt at a definitive understanding by the subject. Not coming to a subject except as mediated by language, the real is even, in the last analysis, what is always absent. For the subject the test of the real is precisely the experience of the *presence-of-the-absence:* it is impossible to escape this mediation and thus the symbolic order. Now, *nothing is less liable to a subjectivist reduction than the rules that govern this symbolic order,* for one does not become a "subject" without being *subjected* to them. Such is the *irreducible precedence,* as resistant as writing and the body (Derrida, see above), that *is the law* for all.

In this perspective, *the symbolic order is the most radical mediation of the real's resistance to every attempt at a subjectivist reduction.* Hence, and this is the thrust of our present reflection, one's taking all aspects of the Eucharistic presence into account *does not necessarily require that one conceive it in the mode of metaphysical substance.*

— The Resistance of the Sacraments

To tell the truth, such a reflection concerns not only the Eucharist; it is valid for all the sacraments and even, on a larger scale, for the whole of the faith inasmuch as it is "arch-sacramental" (see above). The obligation to read as the Word of God before the assembly what is set down in the letter of the canonical Scriptures *also* shows the unavoidable obstacle institutional mediations are but outside of which there is no Christian identity. But the metaphysical logocentrism easily erases, as we have said, this mediation of the letter in favor of the "Word." With the sacraments, however, one inescapably stumbles against the empirical nature of the sensible and the body. Now, the implicit logic that governs onto-theology condemns both as a "fall" from ideal internal transparency into exteriority. In spite of the incarnation and resurrection, Christianity has never fully recovered from this suspicion of the body. As a consequence, the sacraments cannot be assumed except grudgingly, even if one goes to great lengths to show their fittingness in a positive way.

Of course, reconciliation with the body is not sufficient for a fundamental reconciliation with the sacraments, but it is the way to it. For, in referring us back to the concrete exteriority and empirical nature of matter, the body, and institutions, the sacraments are the *major figures of the inalienable mediations of a faith which does not exist except as inscribed somewhere.* And perhaps nothing is more difficult than, let us say it again, consenting without resentment to such a condition, for it sets up a barrier before our desire to attain the "thing" and dominate the "real."

— *The Eucharistic Body, the Exemplary Symbolic Figure of This Resistance*

Christ's resistance to every reduction by our "faith" finds in the Eucharist its *radical* expression. This radicalness, expressed in the formula *"body* of Christ," is represented here by both the *exteriority* and the *anteriority* of the significant manner in which the body of Christ gives itself. Here, the body of the glorified Christ is presented to us as *outside* us and *facing* us, as well as *antecedent* to its reception by us in Communion. We have here the *exemplary* symbolic figure of this unavoidable obstacle, the mediations of our relationship to God which we must learn to assume without resentment.

With this mystery of faith, we thus find ourselves in a *paradoxical* situation. On the one hand, of all the affirmations of the faith, the Eucharistic presence of the Lord is probably, precisely because of the anteriority, exteriority, and materiality of the sacrament where it gives itself, *the one most threatened with idolatrous* — even fetishistic — *perversions.* On the other, however, and for the same reasons of anteriority, exteriority, and materiality, it is perhaps *the most radical figure of the prohibition against idolatry* given to the believer. Idolatry, as we have explained, is the reduction of God to the conditions of what we think, say, or experience about God. The object on which it fixes itself may be relatively subtle: even the most apparently refined discourse or concept for expressing God or our relation with God or else the most apparently generous ethical engagement in God's name may serve this function just as well as a statue of wood or stone. In the Bible the Law itself is under the sign of the prohibition against graven images of God because the sin of idolatry as suppression of the difference of God, ignorance of God's radical otherness-holiness, forgetfulness of God (in the sense of forgetfulness that God alone is God) is indeed the fundamental sin of humankind (Gen 3), as it was for Israel at the time of the Exodus. This is to say that the idolatrous temptation to subjugate God by having God permanently available and by "using" God, even for the most "religious" and most "generous" causes, never abandons us.

Now, in its sacramental representation of *material exteriority*, of *anteriority to its use*, and of *permanence* after the celebration, Christ's Eucharistic presence proclaims the irreducibility of God, of Christ, and of the gospel to our concepts, discourses, ideologies, and experiences. It is the great symbol of the prohibition against idolatry. It discloses, even while concealing it, the *difference* of God. Such is the status we have accorded to the "icon": it seeks to allow the invisible divine "prototype" to become visible, even while it emphasizes its "otherness." The icon thus preserves symbolically God's radical difference, but it does so with such a holy reserve that it is always threatened with being distorted into an idol. The abyss separating an icon from an idol is very deep, but very narrow, so narrow that one can easily step from one side to the other if one is not careful. So it is with the sacraments, the most dangerous of the ecclesial mediations of the faith, but nevertheless the greatest among them because it is here the reception of God's gracious gift takes place. So it is, but still more radically, with the Eucharistic presence of Christ, the most threatened with idolatrous perversion among the faith's mediations, however the most exemplary *icon* of the otherness and precedence of Christ, Lord of the Church.

Christ's presence must be fundamentally marked by an *absence* for the "icon" of the Eucharist — a concept here employed in its relation to that of "idol"[38] — to preserve through its own material

38. We are not forgetting that during the acrimonious iconoclastic controversy in the eighth century in the East, the defenders of icons did not want to identify the Eucharist with an icon and this for a twofold reason. First, the iconoclasts maintained that the only icon we have the right to venerate is the Eucharistic body of Christ (an affirmation they based on the anaphora of St. Basil, where in the anamnesis the bread and wine are called the *antitupa* ["antitypes"] of the body and blood of Christ). Second, the Eucharist *is* the body of the Lord, the matter of bread being sanctified and transformed through the Spirit. It is not the same with icons: in the Eastern tradition, they sanctify only by virtue of their relational participation in the hypostasis of Christ, as both St. John Damascene and Theodore of Studios make clear (C. Von Schönborn, *L'icône du Christ*, 226). The Second Council of Nicea, in 787, recognizes this distinction. On the contrary, in our way of approaching the question and in the context of the conceptual distinction we are

consistency and spatial exteriority, against which the faith stumbles, Christ's absolute "difference." Let us be more precise: in the symbolic order, presence and absence are not two complete realities that would be dialectically inseparable, a little like the two sides of a piece of paper — they do not form two countable entities. They are not bivalent, but form one ambivalent reality. Hence, the development that follows does not minimize the radicalness of what we have previously expressed about the Lord's Eucharistic presence, as if we were taking back with one hand what we held out with the other or were seeking in the last analysis to minimize the Lord. *It is the very concept of "presence"* — in what it contains that is essentially symbolic and human at the philosophical level and essentially pneumatological (the importance of the epicleses) and eschatological at the properly sacramental level — which demands the important precision we just announced.

e) A Presence by the Mode of Being Open: The Breaking of the Bread.

— *Presence and Absence*

"Christ is here," we continually say throughout the liturgy. He is here in the assembly united in his name, the Scriptures proclaimed as his Word, the Eucharist done in memory of him. He is here, not like a "thing," but in the gift of his life and his coming-into-presence. The *adesse* of a presence is of a different order from the simple *esse* of a mere thing. The concept of *"coming-into-presence"* precisely marks the absence with which every presence is constitutively crossed out: nothing is nearer to us than the other in its very otherness (see the threefold structure of the linguistic person); nothing is more present to us than what, in principle, escapes us (starting with ourselves). The twofold movement of procession and recession (procession even in recession) we attribute theologically to God, especially in the "paradoxical" revelation of the glory of God in the face of the Crucified, belongs also to humankind; at least our meditation on Heidegger's Being, all the way to its being crossed out, has allowed us to think this.

---

making between idol and icon, an iconic approach to the Eucharist can be completely pertinent.

In this perspective, to take the statement of the faith "Christ is here" in its integrality requires that the representation of the *absence* which the *sacramentum* of the bread and wine supports be as clearly taken into account as the representation of the presence it constitutes. Failing this, one compromises the concept of "presence," and in the Eucharist one compromises the transubstantiation by the Spirit and the Eucharist's eschatological dimension. Thus, the Eucharist seems to us the *paradigmatic figure of this presence-of-the-absence of God* outside of which the faith would no longer be the faith, which holds us upright, watchful, in hope and exacts that we live in love in order to give God this body of humanity and of world for which God has made us responsible. It is by holding us in this "mature proximity to absence" that we receive the word of God as a call and learn to become believers.

— *A Presence Inscribed, Never Circumscribed*

The "here" of the Eucharistic presence, in its signifying, empirical materiality, refers us to the "here" of the faith, duly instituted and duly inscribed *somewhere*. It refers us back to the body — that is, to the historical, social, economic, and cultural determinations, even to the most individual determinations of our desire — as the place where the truth of our faith will come about. Just as language does not dwell in a given person except as institutionalized in a particular tongue, just as the universal does not open to the subject except through its *inscription* in a particular body, so the Word of God cannot make itself understood except as placed in *a* specific body of traditions and writings, down to its ultimate and complete enfleshment, according to the Christian faith, in the *uniqueness* of the human being Jesus of Nazareth. For God is not "nowhere in particular"; God is *somewhere*.[39]

In the Bible this somewhere is first of all the propitiatory seat which, on the Ark of the Covenant, is flanked by the two cherubim with their wings extended and joined. The one whom the psalmist addresses in saying "You who are seated between the cherubim" indeed has a seat there, in this eminently inscribed space; but this space is open, the throne is empty. It is by mode of *open space* that the Glory of God inhabits this place, just as it is

39. In what follows, on the biblical plane, see the fine treatment by J. Pohier, *Quand je dis Dieu* (Paris: Seuil, 1977) 25-31.

by mode of chiaroscuro that God, present in the cloud, present as cloud, accompanied God's people in the desert. The divine presence is actually *inscribed*, but *never circumscribed*.

This is why the great biblical witnesses, once they encounter God, see themselves set on a long wandering journey. Thus Abraham, having left his homeland for another and having reached it after an interminable detour, must exile himself from it and in the end beg a small piece of ground in which to bury his wife; thus Moses does not enter the promised land to which he has led the people; thus this people themselves, once installed in Canaan, must constantly remind themselves of the manna in the desert by dispossessing themselves symbolically, through the offering of firstfruits, of this land which is nevertheless now their own . . . The history of the prophets is itself, from this viewpoint, a faithful repetition of this archetypal history of Israel. Because God is "here" with them, Israel is not condemned to wandering; but because God is "here" with them by mode of "cloud" or open space, Israel sees itself called to a permanent *exodus* — what we have called, finally, with R. Girard, the exodus out of the sacrificial. The goal is never definitively reached since it is the *very fact of being "on the way"* that allows Israel to recognize the "here" of God's presence. Without that, as soon as Israel rests on the presence of its God in the Temple, as on an unconditional guarantee of salvation, the Glory of Yahweh leaves the holy place to go and reside elsewhere (Ezek 8–11; cf. Jer 7).

— *The Breaking of the Bread*

Now, the Eucharistic bread as the "here" of the glorious Lord presents itself as a *closed*, dense reality, without a break. Without a break? But is not this bread destined for the most symbolic opening there is since it is here only *to be broken:* "The bread that we break, is it not a sharing in the body of Christ? Because there is one bread, we who are many are one body, for we all partake of the one bread" (1 Cor 10:16-17). So much so that the great *sacramentum* of Christ's presence is not the bread as such in its unbroken state. Or rather, it is indeed the bread, but *in its very essence*, bread-as-food, bread-as-meal, bread-for-sharing. *It is in the breaking of the bread that its ultimate reality is manifested,* its true essence revealed. As the "he broke it and gave it to them" and the "for you and for all" of the story of the institution indicate, the gesture of breaking the bread is *the symbol par excellence* of the *adesse* of Christ giving his life. The fact that this is itself framed in the liturgy by the gesture where, in the name of Christ, we extend peace to one another and by the coming forward for Communion where, together with others, we commune with Christ himself is particularly expressive on the sacramental level. For the *breaking of the bread* unites symbolically in one action the aspect of *communion between the members* (but "in the charity of Christ"), expressed by the sign of peace, and the aspect of *communion with Christ himself* (but in brotherly and sisterly charity), expressed by the rite of Communion. The breaking of the bread, inasmuch as it is a sharing between members and for their unity of one body broken for all, sacramentally manifests the indissoluble bond with Christ and with others which it joins sym-bolically.

It is thus from *the very heart of the break* that the Eucharist above all speaks. And it is from the hollow of this break that the "spiritual body" (*soma pneumatikon,* 1 Cor 15:44; cf. Rom 8:11) which is the glorified Christ allows himself to be recognized as at Emmaus. This emptiness, *inasmuch as it is for others,* is essential to the *sacramentum:* opening the bread from the inside, it shows that *Christ's presence comes forward through the mode of being open.* Besides, the fact it is essential to such an emptiness to be for *sharing* explains that if it is to be thought non-ontologically, the non-ontology in question is to be understood, not under the category of metaphysical Being, but under that of the *symbolic Other,* with its concrete historical mediations: those of relations with others, beginning with those others whom people have reduced to less than nothing through an economic system which crushes the poorest and a cultural system which makes them scapegoats.

"Be what you see and receive what you are"; we have pointed out how much this symbolic language of Augustine, which demands that Christians give Christ, through their ethical practice, this body of humanity implied by their reception of his Eucharistic body, brings us closest to the mystery. It is indeed the risen *Christ* himself who is received in Communion; but he is received for what he *is,* that is, *gift* from God's very self, only when he is joined to his *ecclesial* body. The symbol requires the radical distinction of the two, but it also requires their indissoluble intrinsic relation. Is not the *res* ("ultimate effect") of the Eucharist the *Christus totus,* Head *and* members?

It goes without saying that the breaking of the bread should regularly be given greater prominence in our celebrations. The emptiness of broken bread belongs in an essential and not an accidental way to the Eucharistic *sacramentum* and, as a consequence, to its very mystery.

The Sacraments as Instituting

A FORGING OF IDENTITY

Through the issue of the theological and dogmatic affirmation concerning the institution of the sacraments by Jesus Christ, we have shown in what sense one can recognize in them the most instituted of ecclesial mediations of our relationship with God. We have presented the Eucharistic body of the Lord as the exemplary symbolic figure of this instituted which always precedes us. It is precisely in those very acts where it recognizes itself as radically instituted by Christ, as existing only as receiving itself from him, its Lord, that the Church attains its identity. The sacraments as instituted are the *instituting* mediation of this identity.

Let us recall incidentally that in our approach *identity* does not depend simply on secondary determinations (such as belonging to such and such a socio-cultural association or such and such a political party) resulting from existential choices of the subject. Identity is the subject existentially; it touches on what is most "real" in the subject. This is why to say that the Church comes into its identity as Church of Christ in the act where it carries out the memorial of Jesus as its Lord, where it does so by involving itself completely in its visibility as an institutional and traditional body is to say that it is engaged *in this act of accomplishing its very essence.* And its essence is nothing else, primordially, than its communion with the Father through Christ in the Spirit. The sacraments institute the Church because they *effect* this relation of communion: communion in a dependence which, from the symbolic viewpoint — because the Church depends upon God for its origin and recognizes this dependence as a gift — is the very condition of its freedom (see the symbolic scheme of communica-

again of filiation). Therefore the task at hand is to theologi-
think of the sacraments as *events of grace.*

. THE TWOFOLD IMPASSE OF SACRAMENTAL THEOLOGY

1. *The Objectivist Impasse*

This first impasse[1] is represented by the *onto-theological model*
whose critical deconstruction we carried out in the first part of this
book, a model which had taken hold of minds and, along with the
catechism learned, until the 1960's, during childhood, still largely
rules them.

This model was presented throughout the first part in sufficient
detail so that we need only highlight its dominant traits here.

A first trait of the objectivist model arises from its representation of the
relation between *Church, Reign, and World.* The Church thinks of itself
as actually or potentially coextensive with the World, to the point that
during the period called "Christendom" to be fully of the world, it was
necessary to be fully of the Church. Thanks to the Church as an institution, the World is open to the beyond of the Reign. And at once in the
World but also in some way above it, the essential apparatus of the
Church, that is, the clergy and sacraments, is situated precisely at the
frontier between the World and the Reign. The passage between World
and Reign is made primarily through them, as through channels, or even
very narrow ducts.

It is easy to understand that what theologians of this persuasion insist
upon when speaking of the *sacraments* — these "sensible signs instituted

1. To speak of an *impasse* is necessarily to make a judgment that is historically and culturally conditioned. This relativity reminds us that Scholastic theology, which we are discussing here as a whole, in virtue of its perfect
coherence with the entire culture and especially with the religious representations of the period, had absolutely nothing about it which we today, speaking
from outside and on the basis of another cultural universe, could characterize
as "erroneous" or even as "less good" than what we propose. To speak of
an impasse in its regard is thus nothing more than to judge it different. Insofar
as it is based at every level (economic, social, cultural) on an understanding of
the world, history, humankind, and God *other* than the one which is familiar
to us and speaks to us, it seems to us no longer transposable into our culture.
Scholasticism is so in the last analysis because the age in which the West
currently finds itself (see Heidegger) obliges us to criticize its unconscious
metaphysical presuppositions. It is at this very fundamental level that it
appears *to us* to be an impasse.

by Our Lord Jesus Christ" — is their capacity to assure such a passage. Their capacity as "signifiers" receives scant appreciation. Attention is fixed on their purpose of producing or increasing grace ("to produce or increase grace"). Hence the massive insistence on their *objective efficacy*. The classic images of this are of an instrument — with the risk of encouraging the representation of grace as a "product," even if a "spiritual" kind — of a cure — with the risk of suggesting a kind of automatic efficacy that will assure the health of the soul, as a medicine procures that of the body — and of a channel — with the risk of implying that the passage through the sacraments is necessary for salvation: may a priest or even an ordinary layperson be "providentially" near by so that a new-born baby might not die without baptism; it is thus saved, or in the contrary case damned (of course with a *damnatio mitissima* ["mildest damnation"], as Augustine says) or consigned to "limbo."

Of course, these images were substantially refined by analogy, as we have pointed out. Nevertheless, historical studies have shown that they massively dominated people's minds and were easily utilized, not necessarily with anyone's Machiavellian intent, by an entire "pastoral practice of fear," in the expression of J. Delumeau.[2] This set of images encourages a strongly *individualistic* representation of the sacraments, as much on the side of the receiving subject upon whom they confer "salvation" as on the side of the priestly agent defined essentially by the inamissible powers received through ordination.

The insistence on objectivity works at the expense of the consideration of the concrete subject. Of course, piety and a good intention are required of the subject so that the sacrament may be received in a truly fruitful manner. But this requirement belongs only to the *bene esse* ("well-being") of the sacrament, and not to its *esse* ("being") itself. In any case it is difficult not to consider significant the fact that in the sixteen chapters on the sacraments in the *Catechism for Use in the Dioceses of France* of 1947, the word "faith" hardly appears, no more than "Church."[3] From the viewpoint of the sacramental nature, the consideration of the subject is

2. J. Delumeau, *Le péché et la peur: La culpabilisation en Occident, XIIIᵉ-XVIIIᵉ siècles* (Paris: Fayard, 1983) especially chs. 8-9.

3. *Catéchisme à l'usage des diocèses de France* (1947). However, there are two exceptions — although they have almost nothing to do with the understanding of the nature of sacraments: q. 194 "Persons who receive baptism commit themselves to believe in Jesus Christ and to follow his commandments, to renounce the devil and sin"; q. 228 "Before taking Communion, I must speak to Our Lord, making acts of faith, contrition, love, and desire." As for the Church, it is mentioned only in connection with baptism, which makes us "children of God and the Church" (q. 187).

reduced to the *simple condition sine qua non* of not putting an obstacle (such as mortal sin or a canonical sanction) to the reception of grace which comes down through the sacramental channel. The sacrament is thus treated from the very outset as an *instrument at our disposal,* as an "ob-ject" God has "placed before" (*ob-jacere*) the human subject to "produce" the graces which the subject needs.

We have explained at length why this productionist scheme, with the subject-object dichotomy accompanying it, appears no longer tenable to us and why, as a consequence, we should conceive the sacraments, not as intermediaries between God and humankind, but as "expressive" mediations of the Church and the believer, in the mode of and within language. As long as one explains their efficacy using the model of metaphysical causality, *one cannot save them except at the cost of the human investment in them.* The history of sacramental theology shows this: one has always been suspicious of taking into account the human within the very essence of the sacraments, so much so that the two sacraments whose "quasi-matter" is the human person (penance and marriage) are those which have given theologians the most trouble. Of course, one never forgets that the sacraments are for the Church and for the faithful or that personal faith is the measure of the fruitful reception of a grace always offered. But it is only in virtue of their *effects,* and not of their very *nature,* that the sacraments require believing subjects to be taken into account.

As A. Vergote rightly says, this classic sacramental theology, "by pushing vertical theocentrism to its limit, deprived the rite of its properly human significance and opened the way for an anthropological recapture of the rite closed to its theological understanding."[4] In fact, recent decades have witnessed the appearance of a lively *reaction* against the quasi-expulsion of the concretely human from the sacraments. The less well controlled, the less sure of its direction the "cultural mutation" going on and, on the other hand, the more securely fastened the lid on the pot where this new culture was brewing, the more vigorous this reaction: the result was a veritable explosion — and not without damage, obviously.

What fostered this current of criticism of classic sacramental theology was a request as profound as it was legitimate: *to reintroduce*

4. A. Vergote, *Interprétation du langage religieux* (Paris: Seuil, 1974) 201.

the concretely human into liturgical celebrations and sacramental discourse. But the circumstances were such that it was easy to go from Charybdis to Scylla. As a matter of fact, one occasionally strayed into a new impasse, the opposite of the previous. However, before things could come to such a pass, Vatican II proposed a path we will call "the middle way." We shall rapidly examine this path before passing on to the subjectivist impasse.

2. *The Middle Way of Vatican II*

In this rapid sketch we will take under consideration only a few of the characteristic traits of the model of Vatican II, those that bring immediate corrections to the elements mentioned in the previous model. Thus, we shall not stop at such important aspects as the return to biblical sources for the liturgy and sacramental theology; the rediscovery of the "memorial"; the revalorization of pneumatology, especially through the epicleses; the theological reemergence of the local Church; and so on. These elements are no less important for our reflection; as a matter of fact, they make up the background without which what will follow could not have seen the light of day.

As before, we will begin with the understanding of the relation between *Church, Reign, and World*. Substantial changes have taken place here: with more than a billion Chinese who are non-Christian — to mention but one group — the Church may no longer consider itself, even relatively, coextensive with the World. Hence the increased importance of the theological category of the reign. Larger than the Church which it exceeds on every side, the reign reminds us that it is not possible to set limits on the Spirit. Vatican II is very clear on this point: "The Holy Spirit in a manner known only to God offers to [all] the possibility of being associated with this paschal mystery," so much so that grace may work "in an unseen way" in the heart of "all [people] of good will."[5] The Church is thus not closed in upon itself, like a fortress exclusively for "the saved"; it cannot understand itself except in osmosis with the World of which it is part and with the reign which, like the small mustard seed, grows slowly in this World or, like leaven, works invisibly in the dough of humanity. It is not itself the reign; however, it is the "sacrament" of it in and for the World, that is, its "sign" as well as its "initial budding forth" "on earth."[6] As

5. *Gaudium et Spes*, no. 22; see *Lumen Gentium*, no. 16.
6. *Lumen Gentium*, no. 5.

sacrament of the reign, it has its own *criteria of identity,* marks that are proper to itself: Scriptures, confession of faith, sacraments — to name only the most important. To be a Christian requires that one at least objectively make these marks one's own. If, on the one hand, one can be saved without belonging to the Church, on the other hand, one may not call oneself a Christian or part of the Church without being differentiated from non-Christians by these marks, beginning with baptism. For the old adage "Outside the Church there is no salvation" there is now substituted a new one "Outside the Church, there is no *recognized* salvation" (Msgr. R. Coffy).

As the major criteria of a Church which, under circumstances of cultural breakup and demographic explosion, most especially needs to manifest its own identity, the nature of the sacraments as *signs* is reclaiming its value. Besides, this valorization is called for by an entire cultural movement demanding that the concretely human be reintroduced into the sacraments. In the wake of Vatican II, it is in any case very clear that their function as a "means," without being ignored, is now subordinated to their quality as signs. In contrast to what one used to think, according to an imprecise theological-pastoral jargon, was derived from a classical theology too "reifying," "punctilious," and "individualistic," one now focuses attention on the truth of the liturgical signs (materials, language) and of the manner of celebrating, a truth that speaks to believers; on the consideration of human experience; on the "diffuse sacramentality" of human existence lived in faith; on the priority of the ecclesial dimension of the sacraments. Thus, one emphasizes that the sacrament of reconciliation is already begun as soon as one seeks reconciliation with one's brother or sister, that the Eucharist cannot be detached from the "sacramentality" (in the loose sense) of the concrete sharing with the poorest, and so on. Further, on the ecclesial level, one vigorously asks: Is the concrete community the living sign of what it celebrates? If it is not a reconciling force in the world, is it not in contradiction to the sacrament of reconciliation it celebrates in the midst of the world? If it is not concerned about the fate of immigrants, for example, what is the meaning of the welcome it extends to the children of these same immigrants when it baptizes them? The sacraments are the proclamation of the Church: they show the world what the Church is and what it is called to become; they challenge the Church at the very moment they affirm it.

This sort of challenge is not without its dangers (we shall examine them later), but it has inspired a substantial *dynamic movement* in pastoral ministry (at least in France) for twenty or thirty years now (and even, in certain milieux, well before that). And this is a good thing. At the same time, and in connection with the return to biblical sources and the restoration of the balance between the Christological and pneumatological principles especially in ecclesiology and sacramental theology, it helps us to revalorize the role of *the whole Church* as the "active subject of the liturgy" (Y. Congar) by virtue of its members' "baptismal priesthood" at the expense of the exclusive control of the clergy and the inflation of "sacerdotal powers."

Through this "middle way," Vatican II thus proposes an important corrective to the earlier objectivist model. That earlier understanding can be represented by a simple linear diagram where the sacraments are placed between God and human beings:

Diagram 1   God $\rightleftarrows$ Sacraments $\rightleftarrows$ Human Beings

Vatican II offers instead a *triangular* model:

Diagram 2

The *exterior* arrows show (*a*) that God is not bound by the sacraments (or the Church as such) to save humankind, and thus that the reign is larger than the Church; (*b*) that the sacraments are the summits of Christian life, the revealing expressions of the action of God's grace in the life of human beings; (*c*) that they are humankind's acts of thanksgiving toward God, an aspect the Scholastic thinkers were certainly aware of but which, for the reasons already pointed out, they scarcely took into consideration in their treatises on the sacraments (see ch. 1).

The *interior* arrows of our second diagram show (*a'*) that God is the operating subject of the sacraments; (*b'*) that the sacraments are the "sources" of the everyday life of Christians, a life where the sacraments must be veri-fied; (*c'*) that this everyday life becomes a "liturgy" which gives glory to God.

The whole problem left open by Vatican II, torn as it was between two theological currents it did not always succeed in harmonizing — the more traditional, the Scholastic and Tridentine, which considers the sacraments "means," and the newer, which insists on their function as expressive signs — is to reconcile the *opposite directions* in which the arrows rotate. We are still left with this *heterogenous* pair, "sign" and "cause," with, however, a new emphasis on the first term. The goal of the present chapter, in fact, is to attempt to open up a path that will allow us to think of the sacraments simultaneously as both "revealers" and "operators."

3. The Subjectivist Impasse

Going beyond this middle way was tempting for the cultural reasons mentioned above. Having pushed "vertical theocentrism" (Vergote) to its extreme, theology now was open, as a reaction, to an anthropological reappropriation of the rites which turned out to be more or less reductive theologically. The subjectivist model also is linked to a specific representation of the relation between Church, Reign, and World. This model has received *varied*, even *contradictory* expressions. The term "subjectivist" we apply to it should be taken to pertain equally to the group-as-subject and the individual-as-subject. What the various movements belonging to this model have most in common is a reaction against the Church-as-institution understood as the "sacrament" of Jesus Christ. We can distinguish *two major types*, each resulting from a different, even opposite, starting point. The first, transconfessional within Christianity, but also easy to detect in the Catholic world, starts from "*below*," that is, from an anthropological demand to reintroduce lived human experience into the sacraments. The second, which we associate especially with the name of K. Barth, starts on the contrary from "*above*" and from a definite theology, that of God's claim upon humankind, a claim that is so transcendent and free it may never be mediated by any human action, even that of the Church through the sacraments.

a) The First Current: Starting from "Below." The reaction against the Church-as-institution can take on an *extremist* form: one absorbs the Church into the Reign. Sincerity tends to become the criterion of truth; generosity or orthopraxis, the criterion of orthodoxy. One hastily calls Christian every person of good will or every good action. The reference to the Holy Spirit — which works in each person and extends beyond the Church as an institution, even to the point that one comes to oppose "charism" and "institution" — is used as an argument all the more convenient as the criteria of discernment are the more fuzzy. The criteria for belonging to the Church are thus erased in favor of a Reign of God rendered present everywhere by the Spirit. Here, we have to do with a new version of Gnosticism which is always resurging.

Another form of this current, much less extremist and of greater interest for us, is the following. This tendency justifies itself loosely as an off-shoot of Vatican II, and it especially recognizes the importance of ecclesial criteria. But instead of receiving these from living tradition, even if its possible pitfalls should be critically unmasked, this group prefers to *give itself its own criteria* of ecclesial "value." Every nuance of this position can be found today. What we criticize here is that some groups have fallen into the trap of gauging the authenticity of one's belonging to the Church by one's adherence to a particular ideology; one tends in this way to imprison the gospel within one's own grid of analysis, which often leads to an attitude of excommunication (in practice, if not in theory) toward the pluralistic Church or toward religion dismissed as "sociological."

The pastorally beneficial challenges to which Vatican II opened the way thus risk being pushed to an extreme one-sided logic. On the *ecclesiological* level, by dint of excessively pressuring Christian communities to be the living signs of what they celebrate, one ends with an elitism which forgets the eschatological condition of the Church and the word of Jesus: "I have come to call not the righteous but sinners" (Mark 2:17). At the level of *Christian anthropology*, by dint of wanting to celebrate what appears "Christian" only when measured against criteria one has developed oneself, by dint of wanting to "celebrate lived experience," one ends by being able to celebrate only those things that have been "validly" experienced (according to the criteria of the group, of course), and one falls into a sort of neo-Pelagianism. Finally, on the *pastoral* level, the demands for admission to the sacraments can be such that one falls into a vigorously selective "Malthusian" rigorism.

Certainly, one can only wish that the sacraments be celebrated and lived as authentically significant expressions of lived experience; and one can only rejoice at a pastoral practice seeking to challenge the community in its words, image, and actions. We in no way dispute the legitimacy and urgency of a pastoral stance which summons the community to conform their actions, the priorities of their decisions, and their organization to the Word they symbolically announce in the sacraments. As a matter of fact, the fruits of such an attitude appear to us considerable. However, by insisting too much, at the level of conscience, intention, and verification through action, on the demand to become what one celebrates, one risks foundering in an *exacerbation of subjectivity* which will end by ruining the very sacramentality one claims to save.

In other words, one tends to forget that the interaction between God, people, and the sacraments goes in both directions. One is keeping in mind *only the exterior rotation* of our second diagram in one's eagerness to emphasize the sacramental dimension of "celebrating lived experience," or more exactly of "celebrating Jesus Christ in lived experience." The sacraments are perceived too one-sidedly as acts of thanksgiving for what God has done and for what God has done in "life." The more one casts into relief their dimension as a "summit," the more one betrays one's suspicion of their aspect as a "source" — precisely, that aspect emphasized in the objectivist model. The tendency (lived out diversely according to the groups or individuals) is to *ignore their dimension of efficacy* (or their function as operators), even to reject all this as "magic." This tendency is consistent with that mentioned above of deciding for oneself the appropriate criteria for belonging to the Church (criteria often highly ideological, under cover of "The Gospel"): one celebrates the action of Jesus Christ in "life," but one has given oneself the criteria for discerning this action.

A twofold criticism seems appropriate here. First, at the properly *theological* level, by what criteria does one affirm, in faith, the action of Christ or the Spirit in lived experience — and thereby acknowledge its aspect of "sacramentality" — and not recognize simultaneously, and even a fortiori (provided, obviously, that one remain critical), this action in the sacramental act where the Church wholly involves itself? Is there not at the very least an inconsistency here? Could it not be objected that one has substituted for the ritual "magic" one seeks to denounce another form of "magic," doubtless more subtle but no less dangerous: that of a totalitarian discourse enforcing everywhere a "sacramental" reading of lived experience? And if one succeeds in explaining why such an interpretation is not necessarily "magical," then one must concede that the understanding of the sacraments as operators of communication with God is not necessarily "magical" either. In short, one may well question the theological consistency of what one has dubbed the "already done" by God in life when one no longer understands the sacraments as anything *but* the celebration of this "already done."

Second, at the *philosophical* level, one substitutes an "existential subjectivism" for the "essentialist objectivism" of the model one is fighting. But one simply exchanges the old intractable problem for a new one, blinded as one is by the idea that subjects are in immediate possession of their lived experience and can thus "express" outwardly the pre-existent interior content *without* this expression affecting that content in any way. According to the Scholastic adage, "contraries are in the same genus." This model, the reverse of the one it wants to denounce, is on the same metaphysical ground. Whereas "essentialist objectivism" was powered by the scheme of *"production," "*existential subjectivism" is powered by that of *"translation"*: instead of being considered as instruments for the production of grace yet to be received, the sacraments are considered as instruments for the translation of grace already given. They remain in both cases instruments by which the substrate-subject (*sub-jectum*) sets in front of itself (*objectum*) its subjective experience in order to "express" it. The nature of the expressive mediation is completely ignored here; we have spoken of it before, we shall return to it later.

b) The Second Current: Starting from "Above" (Barth). One may be surprised to see the name of the great theologian of the Reformed Church mentioned in this context. After all, is not his point of departure the very antithesis of the position we have just been considering? Indeed, it is his acute sensibility to the absolute transcendence of God — *soli Deo gloria* ("to God alone the glory") — and to the sovereign efficacy of God's free word that has led Barth to react against the traditional conception of the sacraments, whereas the preceding current was reacting in the name of the reintegration of human experience into the practice and theology of the sacraments. This starts from below, while Barth begins *from above,* one could say. However, in both cases one ends up erasing the properly instituting dimension of the sacraments, that is, their nature as events of grace, in reaction against the traditional conception which one dismisses as "magic." From below, this erasure is subject to every degree of shading, depending on the groups or the individuals involved; with Barth, on the contrary, this erasure is very clear.

Faithful to his Calvinistic heritage, Barth feels a veritable aversion to anything faintly suggestive of "synergism," that is, to any theology of the "and" which would presuppose or end in a collusion between divine action *and* human action. Such a synergistic collusion is for him the blasphemy par excellence because by presupposing justification comes partly from God *and* partly from humankind, it negates the absolute gratuitousness of salvation. In his work on justification in Barth, H. Küng has clearly shown that "Barth has misunderstood the *cooperari* ['cooperate'] of the Council of Trent": this *cooperari* has nothing of the synergism Barth detects there because human participation also comes from God. "God does everything; but from the fact that God does everything it does not follow that God does so all alone — to the contrary."

One could say that, in the wake of St. Bernard,[7] the decree on justification of the Council of Trent rejected not only the idea that justification would be *ex nobis* ("from us"), but also the idea that it would be *nobiscum* ("with us"), in the synergistic sense of *partim . . . partim* ("in part . . . in part"); however, in doing so, the council wished to emphasize that justification does require that God give it *non sine nobis* ("not without us"). Since what has to be saved is the free will itself, justifying grace is given entirely *in illo* ("in the free will"); since the principle of this salvation is found entirely in grace, it is produced entirely *ex illa* ("from grace"). Thus, in justification the assent of faith is simultaneously everything and nothing. It is *everything* because this assent is required as the condition sine qua non of subjective justification. It is *nothing* because this condition is not a "cause" of justification: faith is not a "work" that would earn it.[8]

"If what you develop in your second part as the doctrine of the Roman Catholic Church is in fact its doctrine, then I must admit that my doctrine

7. H. Küng, *La justification: La doctrine de Karl Barth, Réflexion catholique*, DDB (1965) 310–313; St. Bernard, *De gratia et libero arbitrio* I, 2 and XIV, 46–47: "A Deo ergo sine dubio nostrae fit salutis exordium, nec per nos utique, nec nobiscum. Verum consensus et opus, etsi non ex nobis, non iam tamen sine nobis. . . . Non partim gratia, partim liberum arbitrium, sed totum singula opere individuo peragunt: totum quidem hoc, et totum illa, sed ut totum in illo, sic totum ex illa" ("Without any doubt, the beginning of our salvation comes from God and neither through us nor with us. But the assent and the work, even though they are not from us, are however not without us. . . . Our salvation is not done partly through grace and partly through our free will, but through their individual action they cooperate with one another to produce the whole: free will indeed produces the whole and grace produces the whole, but as the whole *in* free will, thus the whole *from* grace").

8. Council of Trent, *Décret sur la justification* (1547), ch. 8; D-S 1532.

on justification is in accord with it," Barth writes in his laudatory preface to Küng's thesis. This is all well and good. However, that this same Barth shows himself "completely" surprised[9] by this harmony between Roman Catholic doctrine and his own gives grounds for thought. For if we have a right to think, with H. Bouillard, that the disagreement "is certainly much less than Barth believed when he read the definitions of the Council of Trent," still, the same author continues, we should "hesitate . . . to say there is a fundamental agreement between Barth's doctrine on justification and Catholic doctrine."[10] We remain in fact all the more perplexed on this point since in the last volume of his *Church Dogmatics*, not yet written in 1957, the date of the prefatory letter mentioned above, the doctrine of baptism shows an understanding of the sacrament completely different from that developed in the Roman Catholic Church, even opposed to it and, as Barth explicitly recognizes, to earlier, traditional understanding. Now, the all-important point here is the *understanding of the relation between God and human beings in salvation*, that which constitutes the very heart of the doctrine of justification.

After having presented baptism of the Spirit ("God's action") in the first part of his work, Barth presents baptism of water ("human action") in the second. Its "raison d'être" (pp. 53–71) lies nowhere except in the command of Jesus Christ: "It is an act of free obedience to the command of Jesus Christ, an eagerness to recognize the reasonableness and obligatory character of this command." As for its "goal" (pp. 71–105), it is "a movement toward Jesus Christ, in accordance with his command."[11] More interesting from our point of view are the pages devoted to what the author calls the "meaning" of baptism of water (p. 106ff.). It would be "gravely harmful" to seek the holiness of this act "in some divine efficacy that would be, so to speak, immanent within it," that is, "in a work and word of God becoming an event by virtue of what humans want and do when they baptize or are baptized." For then "one does not escape the following *dilemma*": "either" human will and action are "completely dominated" by God's

9. Küng, *Justification*, 12.
10. H. Bouillard, *Karl Barth*, vol. 2 (Paris: Aubier-Montaigne, 1957) 123; see pp. 77–78, n. 6.
11. K. Barth, *Dogmatique* IV, 4 *Le fondement de la vie chrétienne* (pt. 1 "Le baptême d'Esprit," pt. 2 "Le baptême d'eau") (Genève: Labor et Fides, 1969) 105. All future references are to this edition. All translations into English are from this edition.

"which are immanent in them" — in which case "baptism of the Spirit absorbs baptism of water and renders it finally superfluous"; "or" this human will and action become and are "as such" those of God's own self — in which case "it is baptism of water that absorbs baptism of the Spirit and renders it superfluous." In both cases, consequently, "Christian baptism ends up being tainted with Docetism" (p. 106).

The positing of such a dilemma is symptomatic, it seems to us, of a typically synergistic representational scheme. Against the *partim . . . partim* of a *"both* God . . . *and* human beings" whose actions could be added together, Barth poses the dilemma of *"either* God . . . *or* human beings." This is to reject the synergistic scheme while remaining its prisoner by allowing only for either the concurrence or exclusion of the two terms. Does not Barth finally reveal himself here to be in fundamental disagreement with "the Roman Catholic doctrine on justification," which also rejects, but differently, synergism? Or is his presentation of baptism of water, for reasons which would have to be uncovered, truly in disaccord with the agreement he believed to have discerned between his own doctrine of justification and Trent's? In any case, the opposition is unmistakable with regard to baptism; and, as we have just shown, the presentation he gives of baptism is directly dependent upon a doctrine of justification.

This is a radical opposition, on the admission of the author himself: "One must say a *categorical no*" to the sacramentality of baptism as it has been traditionally recognized. "In itself it is neither a mystery nor a sacrament. It is clear that here we are opposed in principle and *ab ovo* ['from the beginning'] to a very ancient and very strong ecclesial and theological tradition, as well as to all its variations" (pp. 106–107). For, as ancient and strong as it may be, such a tradition does not correspond to the New Testament texts concerning baptism. After having examined these on pages 115–132,[12] the author concludes: "In short, taken seriously, all these texts seem in any case to indicate that the act of baptism has a meaning completely other than the sacramental. . . . According to the New Testament, the baptismal act is in all likelihood not to be

12. These are especially Acts 22:16; Heb 10:22; Eph 5:25f.; Titus 3:5; Gal 3:27; Rom 6:3ff.; Col 2:12; John 3:5; Mark 16:16; 1 John 5:5-8; John 19:32-37.

understood at all as a work and word of grace purifying and renewing human beings; in other words, there is no need to see in it a 'mystery' or a 'sacrament,' in the meaning of the theological tradition which has become dominant." Its "meaning" is thus to be sought "in its character as a purely human action responding to the act and word of God" (p. 133).

This position has at least the advantage of being perfectly clear: "Baptism does not accomplish anything: it only *recognizes* and *proclaims* the crisis provoked by God." It *"testifies"* to the crisis. "It is, with regard to Jesus Christ, the human act of obedience which consists in daring to *reflect* God's act of judgment which is in itself God's act of reconciliation. It is thus not the result of a capricious decision. Of course, it is a human action, free and responsible, but precisely in this capacity it does no more than *follow* the justification and sanctification accomplished and revealed by God in Jesus Christ, that is, the purification and renewal of sinful human beings" (pp. 165–166).

In the tradition of Calvin, but even more radically, Barth's sacramental theology unfolds within the domain of *knowledge* and *thanksgiving*. His resounding *Nein!* of 1943 to the practice of infant baptism is obviously in complete harmony with his fundamental principles.[13] Baptism is in no way the operator of grace; it is only the *revealer of the already-there of the grace* granted by God in "baptism of the Spirit." Of the two dimensions of Thomas Aquinas' sacramental theology, the "ascendant" dimension of worship expressing human thanksgiving toward God through Jesus Christ (a dimension unfortunately not used as such in the treatise on the sacraments) and the "descendant" dimension as an instrument (subordinated to God, of course) for the transmission of divine grace, Barth retains only the first, reaching finally, in relation to tradition, a position that one can call a *"non-sacramental theology."* In our last part we will make clearer how this non-sacramental theology, while not necessitated by Barth's trans-Trinitarian presupposition and its implications for ecclesiology and the theology of creation, is at least compatible with them.

13. K. Barth, "La doctrine ecclésiastique du baptême," *Foi et Vie* 47 (1949) 1–50. The same in *Dogmatique* IV, 4.

We thus find in Barth the same "existential subjectivism" we find in the current we have called here "from below," even though the points of departure are opposite. This subjectivism is as onto-theological as the objectivism with which it finds fault; one switches the positions of the terms, but one stays on the same metaphysical ground. Hence, the model becomes as follows:

Diagram 3   God $\rightleftarrows$ Human Beings $\rightleftarrows$ Sacraments

The sacraments (lower arrow) are only the festive translation of the already-there of the grace given by God to human beings in their ethical existence. They act as a spring-board (upper arrow) from which human beings express their gratitude to God for the grace already received. If we look again at the triangle of diagram 2 above, we see that here it works only in a clockwise direction. In spite of appearances, it is as a Scholastic that Barth, in the last analysis, opposes the Scholastic tradition. This is an old story, and both the Protestant and Catholic Reforms have convinced us that we can leave it behind only by changing ground. To substitute an existential subjectivism which tends to sacrifice God's action in the sacraments for an essentialist objectivism which tends to sacrifice human beings' only delays our facing the problem. Theological existentialism postulates a *central subjective consciousness* which supposedly is in immediate possession of its human experiences and then translates them exteriorly in the sacraments as signs of gratitude toward God and does this out of obedience to the command of Jesus Christ. In this perspective, the sacraments are understood not as linguistic mediations which allow the real to become human or meaningful, but as instruments for the translation of an already-existent human reality or as the festive and ecclesial clothing with which one may dress the real. The philosophical criticism we addressed above to the current "from below" is as valid for the one "from above." All this, of course, does not diminish Barth's achievement in writing a very rich essay on worship as *Mitte der Gemeinde*.[14]

14. Ibid., IV, 2, 3 (Genève, Labor et Fides, 1971) (text of 1955) 30, 95–96. See also the beautiful text of Barth in *Connaître Dieu et le servir* (Neuchâtel, 1945) 178, quoted by J. J. Von Allmen, *Célébrer le salut*, 164.

II. THE SACRAMENTS:
EFFECTIVE SYMBOLIC EXPRESSIONS

Getting out of the twofold impasse we have just discussed seems possible to us only from the perspective of the symbolic order. Let us make two things clear. On the one hand, the middle way of Vatican II leads to a balanced sacramental theology, where the sacramental function as "revealer" makes a pair with that of "operator," permitting the arrows in our drawing to rotate in both directions. But on the negative side, as we indicated, this middle way does not attempt — it is probably not, in any case, the role of a council to go into detail — to show in a rigorous manner how the two functions are connected. Or rather, their connection remains that of classical sacramental theology so that if the sacraments' "revealing" aspect plays a more basic role at the pastoral level, their "operating" aspect as means of salvation remains determinative at the strictly theological level. On the other hand, let us remember that to get out of this twofold impasse cannot in any way mean, in our approach, that one has found (finally!) the correct solution. What we can present is one approach to the mystery, and the key to this *approach* is found on the path of this approach.

In understanding the sacraments as "effective symbolic expressions," we are obviously in direct continuity with what we have said about language and symbol throughout the first part of this book. We base ourselves especially on the concept of "expression" and on the notions of the "illocutionary," the "performative," and the "symbolic efficacy of rites." Let us recall, on this last point, the perspective opened up in chapter four. If the rites of traditional religions aim at a verifiable empirical efficacy (for example, healing), they obtain it through the intermediary of a symbolic efficacy, that is, through setting up a new relation between subjects or between subjects and their socio-cultural "world" or both. Now, the end of Christian rites is of another order, beyond the realm of value, one designated by the term "grace." At that time, we suggested — postponing to the present chapter the task of demonstrating it — that this "sacramental grace," because it belongs to the order of the covenant, must be understood from the (intra-linguistic) perspective of symbolic efficacy (the illocutionary instauration of a new relation between persons), even though it cannot be reduced to a simple socio-linguistic mechanism.

Besides the notions we have just mentioned, two points bear upon the development of this approach. The first, already announced, concerns the original character of the ritual "language game," an originality linked especially to its illocutionary modality. Linked equally to this particular modality, the second concerns symbolic efficacy: it must be analyzed as "expression," that is, as an "operation" inseparable from the "revelation" that takes place in it. Let us first, then, develop these two points.

1. *The Language of Faith and the Language of Liturgy as Specific "Language Games"*

The present reflection is based on the studies presented by J. Ladrière on the theory of the *plurality of language games* by L. Wittgenstein, according to whom each time language is brought into play it is according to a concrete modality comparable to a game. Now, every game has its rules. These rules are conventional, but, as we have seen, neither the group nor the individual has been their author; the origin of language always eludes us. In this sense the rules which make up language as game and every language game are not arbitrary: every game is the expression of a *"form of life."*[15] It thus constitutes a system of communication complete in itself and inseparable from the *context* to which it gives "form": "It determines, through the particular form it takes in a determined context, the distinctive quality that characterizes a certain form of experience."[16]

Hence "the meaning of an expression depends on the context, that is, the conditions of its use. There is no one use of language, and therefore there is no one kind of meaning, or as a conse-

15. G. G. Granger, "Wittgenstein," *Enc. Univ.* 16 (1968) 998: in Wittgenstein's mind, this expression "has no affective existential connotation: the feelings that may accompany a language game should be regarded as secondary compared to the game itself and as a possible interpretation. The language game is a form of life in the sense that it is part of a whole behavior of communication and the meaning of symbols is relative to this whole."

16. J. Ladrière, *L'articulation du sens*, vol. 1 *Discours scientifique et parole de foi*, vol. 2 *Les langages de la foi* (Paris: Cerf, 1984). The quote is from vol 1, p. 10. The references in the text are to this work.

quence no one kind of criterion of meaning. For example, there is not just scientific language, and one can not reduce a theory of meaning to what is indicated by scientific practice (I, p. 93). Scientific language, philosophical language, poetic language, religious language . . . *cannot be translated into one another.* And within religious language, ritual language, for example, the primary symbolic language of religious experience, cannot be rendered into theological discourse as such which is a secondary reflective language with its necessary, conceptual apparatus — as indispensable as this speculative reworking may be as an effort at self-understanding required by the very dynamics of the development of faith (II, pp. 169–194).

a) The Language of Faith. As Ladrière stresses, there exists a "language game" so particular to faith that it is untranslatable into another language: "There is a specific modality of meaning in the language of faith," which "must be set in relief within what is specific to it"; as a consequence, we must "allow faith to speak in its own language, in order to understand how it speaks" (I, pp. 235–236).

The language game proper to faith has this characteristic, among other traits of course: it is *self-implicative.* This is to say that here the *illocutionary* dimension is predominant. Certainly it is not the only sort of language which has this property. Every language, we have seen, participates in it to some degree; for it is impossible to speak about anything at all without speaking of *ourselves,* if only in the empty spaces of our discourse (see above). What characterizes the language of faith is that it is constituted by the predominance of self-implication. It arises only according to an illocutionary modality. Making effective the attitudes of consent, trust, commitment, and so forth that it expresses, it has something of the "performative" about it (I, p. 230).

In effect, the speaker necessarily *takes a stand* there, by way of either assent or proclamation, on the statements he or she makes, such as "God is light," "Jesus is the Christ," "this bread is the body of Christ," "baptism is for the remission of sins." By saying "I believe in God," Vergote observes, the believer "gives an expressive form to his or her attitude toward God, and at the same time fulfills this attitude by assuming and confirming it for himself or herself and before God" (as well as before others); "in other words, the believer's statement is expressive and performative."[17]

Because these statements are essentially self-implicative, the reality supported by the referential and predicative functions of the statements of faith cannot be separated from them — although it remains irreducible to them and is precisely expressed as such. Ladrière writes, "Not only does the language of faith not have an explicative function (with regard to sensible experience), but it itself, and it alone, *renders present* the realities of which it speaks. What it speaks about is precisely what is operating within itself," and all this takes place "in the expression that it brings into play" (I, pp. 232–233). The statements "God is Father" or "Jesus is the Christ" can be affirmed only if, *while* formulating these statements, I identify myself as and in some manner become a child of God and a disciple of Jesus Christ. The reality expressed in the statement of faith, specifically here the fatherhood of God and the messiahship of Jesus, itself comes forward *from the fact* that people take a stand in its regard while affirming it: *by* saying it, they give God a body of children and Christ a body of brother-members and sister-members. Christ cannot be alive if none claim to belong to him: his resurrection is inseparable from the witness people — first, those who form the Church — give of him. Of course, it is not faith which makes God Father or Jesus Lord. But the identity of God as Father or of Jesus as Christ and Lord would be reduced to nothing if none named it by confessing it and thus acknowledging themselves *at the same time* as children of God and disciples of Jesus. The language of faith reveals the identity of God as Father and our own identity as sons and daughters, brothers and sisters; and *by* revealing this identity it makes effective the paternity of God, as well as our own filiation and condition as brothers and sisters.

b) The Language of Liturgy. What we have just said applies equally to the different "games" in which the language of faith is diversified: theological language, the language of mystical experience, the foundational language of the origins in the form of a story or of kerygma, ritual language, and so on. But it is clear that the more the language game has the character of testimony, the more the

17. A. Vergote, *Religion, foi, incroyance* (Brussels: P. Mardaga, 1983) 258.

self-implicative modality of faith language becomes evident. This is particularly true of liturgical language.

— *The Illocutionary Modality of Liturgical Language*

The "language game" proper to the sacraments is first of all characterized by its ritual essence. We say "essence" advisedly. Rituality is not simply a festive garment which would clothe discursive theological propositions; on the contrary, it is constitutive of the liturgical statements themselves. It is not simply a "context" for the text, but rather the "text of the text," the essential *"pre-text"* of the text itself. The aim, "-urgic" by nature, of ritual texts (which also include gestures, postures, movement, places, objects, music, decorative elements . . . as well as spoken statements) is pragmatic: the ritual texts seek neither to present an academic explanation or theological hypotheses nor to codify ethical norms nor to transmit information. The efficacious nature which characterizes them is such that their verbal formulations do not act as simple commentaries on an action that would be exterior to them, but as *actions* symbolic in themselves. Whether it expresses praise, belief, petition, desire, or confession . . . , the liturgy is always within a particular kind of language whose unity seems assured, among other things, by its *illocutionary modality*. It is always the establishment of a new relation of place between the community and God which it seeks to accomplish and purports to achieve. And it is always, at the same time, the instauration or restoration of a cohesion among the members of the group, of their mutual reconciliation, of their communion in the same identity which is at work in the act of ritual language: it aims not at discursively thematizing the criteria of the community, but *at constituting* it by enunciating them. The "we" used in the present tense, characteristic of Christian liturgical prayer, even when it is said by a priest (who then acts as the bearer of the "symbolic capital" of the ecclesial assembly), truly functions as the illocutionary agent of the community.

— *The Performative Nature of Sacramental Formulas*

The highly performative character of what are called, in the strict sense, *"sacramental formulas"* belongs to this logic. This is obvious for the "I baptize you," where the gesture makes visible the operative essence of a formula which is eminently a language *act.*

is no less true of what is rightly called the "story of the insti-
n." Granted, no linguistic mark betrays its performative
character. As a story in the third person and in the past tense, it
does not even have the character of a discourse. But the analysis
of it which we have proposed has shown that what, from the
literary viewpoint, appears as the opposite of discourse and the
performative, functions in fact, by virtue of its liturgical pre-text,
as a language act where today's Church is so involved and
"acted" that it "executes" (in the double meaning of the term)
this story in order to make the discourse of the Lord Jesus its own.

As the cornerstones of the architectonic structure of the Christian celebrations, sacramental formulas, with their eminently performative character joining gesture and word to show their
operative goal, are the symbols which are the repositories of the
*illocutionary dimension of the whole of ritual language and, beyond that,
of faith language.* Generally through the ordained minister, the official bearer of its symbolic capital, the Church is completely involved as the "sacrament" of Jesus Christ, that is, as at once
institution and "mystery." It is its very identity it acts out here,
proclaiming symbolically what it is and what it has yet to become.
At the level of language, we have here *the most expressive unfolding
of its essence and truth.*

2. The Symbolic Efficacy of the Sacraments:
Example, the Sacrament of Reconciliation

The preceding development helps us to understand that we can
say nothing about the reality of "sacramental grace" outside the
liturgical expression (the *sacramentum*) the Church provides in its
acts of celebration. This is why, before treating of grace itself, we
must go into the question of effective expression, since in celebrating the sacraments, the Church speaks according to this concrete
modality.

We have helpful reference points for such an elucidation. (1) The
first is linguistic *"expression"*: it is effective because the interior
differentiation that constitutes the subject comes about in expressing itself (which requires an exteriorization). As "an act which is
its own result," expression "is the flesh of an intention born *while*
taking significant form." Expression accomplishes what it signifies,

specifically the subjects in the most real of their connections with themselves, others, the world, God. (2) This is what is at work in the *illocutionary* dimension of language and manifests itself explicitly in the performatives. (3) We have also discussed *symbol* according to this fundamental approach: the human reality of a covenant between subjects which symbol expresses, and, by expressing, effects the human reality of a covenant between subjects. (Marriage provides us with an exemplary illustration of this.)

This approach allows us, we believe, to *escape from the twofold onto-theological impasse* we examined above. The sacraments are not instruments for the *production* of grace since their operation, of the symbolic order, is inseparable from the revelation they bring about. But no more are they simply instruments for the *translation* of a grace that is already there since the revelation they make of it is inseparable from a symbolic labor, new each time, within the believing subject. The scheme of translation is no more valid than the scheme of production. The former substitutes, following a nominalist path, a dictatorship of the subject — who believes itself master of meaning and of its interior experiences — for a dictatorship of the thing the latter imposed following a realist path.

a) The Sacraments as Revealers (insofar as they are operators). That the sacraments are revealers which make symbolically visible what identifies as Christian human existence anterior to them; that consequently they manifest the "already-there" of grace in the experience of faith; that they therefore have an expressive function of *response* to what God has done, and of *gratitude* for what God has done: not only do we not deny all this, but we insist on it. We insist on it first and foremost because this is what the Church expresses in the very celebration of the sacraments. Let us take the example of the *sacrament of reconciliation*. Four important realities are involved.

(1) *The Church:* "To greet one another," as the Ritual says, or to be Church, is to manifest at least two things. On the one hand, as with every sacrament, we have here an event of Church: it is within the ecclesial character shown by the linguistic "we" running through the liturgical action that each one is personally touched by God's pardon. Reconciliation takes place *in the Church*, as the Introduction in the Ritual makes clear, because "the Church, having sinners in its midst, is at the same

time holy and in need of cleansing, and so is unceasingly intent on repentance and reform." On the other hand, this manifests that "penance always therefore entails reconciliation with our brothers and sisters who remain harmed by our sins";[18] as the Ritual makes clear, the penitents are thereby reconciled "at the same time" with God and *"with the Church which they have wounded by their sins."*[19] Rahner has recently reminded us of this "forgotten truth," reconciliation with God (*res sacramenti*) is mediated by reconciliation with the Church (the *pax ecclesiae* as *res et sacramentum*): this, we know, was clearly stressed in the ancient system of reconciliation (see below).[20] Let us add that this "ecclesial" reality is obviously not limited to the beginning of the celebration. It is a dimension that runs through all of it. Moreover, it is especially emphasized in the first part of the reality "Sacrament," as we shall see.

What does this ecclesial dimension of the sacrament show with regard to the sinner's previous lived experience? First of all, it attests that the *"against God,"* the formal component of sin, can never be separated from the *"against others"* (and "against oneself") which is its "material" component. The raw material of sin is the same as that of fault, even if sin requires a theological interpretation of moral fault (see the reality "Word" below). The ecclesial mediation of the relation with God in the sacrament manifests the essential human weight of sin: sin does not directly affect God in God's self, but in God's covenant; it wounds God by wounding others (and thus the sinning subjects themselves) in what is most human in their humanity. One is never a Christian except as a member of a covenant. To sin against God is always to sin in some way *against the Church.* The ecclesial dimension of the sacrament shows that the grace of forgiveness received by sinners in their most personal acts of repentance is not reducible to a purely individual matter: it is mediated by the Church and, as Thomas emphasized in calling contrition and the penitents' other acts "integral parts" of the sacrament (III, q. 90), it is entirely made of sacramentality. Like every grace, that of conversion, as intimate and personal as it may be, has an *ecclesial dimension* and a *sacramental polarity.* The sacrament is the revealer of the human and ecclesial dimensions of both sin and pardon.

(2) *"Word"* (readings, homily, examination of conscience): That reading the Scriptures as Word of God *precedes* the "examination of conscience"

---

18. International Commission on English in the Liturgy, *The Rites of the Catholic Church,* vol. 1 (New York: Pueblo, 1990) no. 3, 5.

19. Ibid., no. 4.

20. K. Rahner, "Vérités oubliées concernant le sacrement de pénitence," *Ecrits théologiques,* vol. 2, DDB (1960) 149–194, especially 188–192.

shows structurally that one can confess one's sin only in confessing "at the same time," according to the expression of the Ritual, the love of God. *Confessio peccati, confessio laudis,* Augustine said, inspired by Ps 51:15-19. The Church does not profess its belief in sin, but in the forgiveness of sin — so much so that none discover themselves to be sinners unless they discover themselves to be *pardoned sinners.* The grace of forgiveness always offered is what reveals sin, just as the prodigal son discovered the true dimension of his sin in the arms of his father. "O happy fault!" the Church sings during the Easter Vigil: the superabundance of grace in the New Adam reveals the abundance of sin in the first Adam (Rom 5). The final authority for judging sin is not our consciences, as necessary as these may be — "I am not aware of anything against myself, but I am not thereby acquitted" (1 Cor 4:4) — but the word of grace and mercy offered in Jesus. Sin is finally revealed only as *taken away.* Thus, the "examination of conscience" becomes a confession of praise at the same time it is a confession of sin to God.

This second reality of the sacrament shows sinners that in their previous lived experiences they could not have recognized their faults as sins unless they had allowed themselves to be challenged *theologically,* in one way or another, by the Word of mercy and that their later remorse could become Christian repentance only when confronted by God's forgiveness always offered in Christ, "up to seventy times seven times." In other words, this dimension of the sacrament reveals what has transformed the repentant sinners' previous lived experiences into lived experiences authentically "Christian."

(3) *"Sacrament,"* which itself contains three elements:

— The first is a *communal* sacramental expression that consists of a common prayer of confession and a common going to the minister of pardon. This point is important: it shows, as the Introduction in the Ritual says, that "the whole Church, as a priestly people . . . intercedes for [sinners]"; thus "*the Church exercizes this ministry of the sacrament of penance* through bishops and priests . . . in the name of Christ and by the power of the Holy Spirit they declare and grant the forgiveness of sins"[21] Moreover, the Church Fathers were perfectly explicit on this point, unfailingly understanding the ministry of reconciliation exercised by the bishop as the expression of the prayer of supplication addressed by the Ecclesia to God.[22] Hence the Augustinian theme of the Church (the local church in

---

21. *Rites of the Catholic Church,* 8–9.

22. It is "while the entire assembly is praying for the sinners" that the bishop, according to the Didascalia of the Apostles (II, 12), imposes hands on them (37); it is in exhorting all the brothers and sisters to be intercessors for

its connection with other churches) as a "stone" or a "dove" that ties or unties, retains or forgives.[23] In short, the celebrating community, as the concrete realization of the Ecclesia is not only the receiver of forgiveness, it plays an *active "ministerial" role* in the reconciliation. It is *by the Church* that one is reconciled to God.

— Within this ecclesial sacramental expression there is a second sacramental element: the *personal* going to the minister of the sacrament, a going that normally concludes with the verbal avowal of sin. This exteriorization sacramentally shows that every conversion to God must pass from the heart to acts.

— The penitent's response to these actions is the sacramental element

---

them to obtain pardon," according to Tertullian (*De Paen.* 9), or again according to Ambrose, it is in requesting "with the tears of the entire people," in seeking "the patronage of the holy people to intercede in their favor," that the sinners are reconciled (39) (*De Paen.* I, 89, and II, 91, trans. R. Gryson, Sources chrétiennes 179).
Compare the purpose of the prayer of absolution according to the *Apostolic Constitutions* VIII, 9: "Return these penitents to your holy Church." Analyzing these texts and various others representative of the Syrian tradition, E. P. Siman concludes "it is always the ecclesial community which prays for the penitents and integrates them back into its communion," even in private penance — an unknown phenomenon, moreover, in the Oriental (Nestorian) Syrian branch and about which there is mention in the Western branch "only from the second half of the twelfth century on." *L'expérience de l'Esprit par l'Eglise d'après la tradition syrienne d'Antioche* (Paris: Beauchesne, 1971) 110–118; the quote is from 117–118.
23. This is an important theme in Augustine: Peter (Matt 16:16-19) as the type of the believer = the Church = the dove of the Holy Spirit which, as the agent of the holiness and unity of the Church, remits sins. From this come these words addressed by the bishop of Hippo to his faithful: "You also bind, you also loosen. Indeed, those who are bound are separated from your community; and because they are separated from your community, they are bound by you. When they are reconciled, they are unbound by you, for you also, you pray for them" (*Sermon Guelf* 16, 2). "These keys are not given to a single human being, but to the whole Church in its unity. . . . The Dove binds, the Dove loosens; the edifice constructed on the rock binds and loosens" (*Sermon* 295, 2). And apropos John 20:22-23: "If the apostles represented the Church in their persons, it is the peace of the Church that loosens sins and separation from the peace of the Church that binds them. . . . The rock binds and the rock loosens; the Dove binds and the Dove loosens" (*De Bapt. c. Don.* III, 18, 23). See A. M. La Bonnardière, "Tu est Petrus: La péricope de Mt 16, 12-23 dans l'œuvre de saint Augustin," *Irenikon* 34 (1961) 451–499.

in the strict sense, where the *minister*, acting as the servant of the Church's action, as the bearer of the assembly's "symbolic capital," pronounces the word of forgiveness. If the Council of Trent affirmed that the word of forgiveness is "like a judgment," it did so first of all to show that what the priest says, as an authorized representative of the Church and in God's name, takes effect *performatively*, in the manner of a word of judgment which acquits or condemns the accused by the simple fact that it is pronounced by a legitimate person and according to a valid procedure. The similarity stops here; all it does is stress the performative nature of the language act in question.

Leaving aside the ecclesial dimension of this reality "Sacrament," of which we have spoken above, let us attend to its intent: forgiveness from God. Here, the sacrament shows that no one owns the power to forgive. No one can pardon who has not already benefitted from pardon. The one pardoning can act only as a witness to a word which comes from further back than the pardoner. Both pardoner and pardoned are thus together, although of course in different positions, *under the third authority* of a pardon which comes from somewhere else, from a *"vacant place"* which is the place of God alone.[24] In the sacrament the priest is precisely the symbolic witness of this vacant place. From this viewpoint, the sacramental request for pardon from the Church and from its minister does no more than unfold the petition for forgiveness made to the one who has been wounded: it manifests, through the symbolic function exercised by the priest, what has taken place; it expresses what has taken place and, by expressing it, by giving it the language of body and word, accomplishes it. It thus reveals the very essence of forgiveness.

(4) *"Thanksgiving"* and *"ethical practice,"* which conclude the celebration, a moment of gratitude toward God for the pardon received: *Laus Dei, ipse cantator* ("praise of God, God the singer"), Augustine further said. This is why the grateful praise of God asks to be verified in the "return-gift" of the concrete practice of reconciliation, justice, and mercy toward others. The sacrament comes into its truth only when we become what we have celebrated and received.

24. "One cannot give pardon without being penetrated by it as by a word which, to bring about rebirth, cuts through whatever impedes openness to the future. Everything happens as though the forgiveness came from a place that can be occupied neither by the one pardoning nor the one pardoned; an empty place that renders possible the free movement of this efficacious word." M. Balleydier, "Essai sur le pardon," *L'aveu et le pardon*, L.-M. Chauvet, M. Balleydier, F. Deniau (Paris: Chalet, 1979) 65.

This last reality shows that every authentic repentance entails, as one of its internal constituents, a resolution to change one's life. Without this resolution, repentance would be no more than a sham.

The fact, repeatedly affirmed by the Scholastics, that sinners are pardoned by God in their very movement of repentance, and consequently well before the sacrament itself, is perfectly consistent with the position we have just expounded. The sacrament is the symbolic manifestation of the elements which make this repentance properly Christian and thus the place of God's pardon. But this repentance is itself not unconnected with the sacrament: it is an "integral part" of it (Thomas). The sacramental celebration shows that the most personal and most "interior" act of conversion cannot "take" except in the Church and is *always-already structured by the ecclesial and sacramental dimension.* For such is the structure of the new covenant that there is grace, to begin with conversion or faith, only in the (actual or virtual) mediation of the Church's sacramentality. *From its very beginning* conversion to Christ is by nature *within the ambit of the Church* (it is never simply as an individual that one converts to Christ, but as an effective or potential *member* of him) and *reaches out to sacramentality.* Obviously, this does not imply that every instance of conversion — neither by right nor in fact — must necessarily end with a request for the sacraments: numerous psychological, historical, social, cultural . . . obstacles may intervene and disturb this process. However, this *does* imply that conversion *fulfills its essence* and comes to its truth in its sacramental expression.

The sacrament thus acts as the *revealer* which makes symbolically visible what has made an anterior human existence also a properly Christian existence. From within a rationalist logic, where faith life and sacramental rites are set in competition, one must unavoidably ask the question, "What need is there for the sacrament if I am already pardoned?" (The extreme of this logic would be to propose that one considers the sacraments the more "useful" or "efficacious," the less one is converted in one's everyday life!) On the contrary, in the symbolic order the sacrament of reconciliation shows its function all the better when it gives flesh to a previous conversion. A sacrament which would not be a revealer of the already-there of grace would only be verging on "magic." However, this function of revealer is possible only *insofar as* it is an operator.

b) The Sacraments as Operators (insofar as they are revealers). Here again, let us say it clearly, if we affirm the efficacious nature of the sacraments, it is not for abstract or a priori reasons, but because of the traditional practice of the Church. A simple consideration of the liturgy of baptism, the Eucharist, or the sacrament of reconciliation leaves no doubt about the Church's intention to *bring about* what the rites express. This claim to being operative belongs to the *sacramentum* itself. To take this *sacramentum* seriously is indispensable: sacramental theology can say nothing about the *res* the faith proclaims except on the basis of the act of celebration. What we are talking about is a ritual act whose specificity we have spelled out. No more than a metaphor can be translated into explanatory language, no more than an illocutionary act (where a subject takes a definite position here and now with regard to others concerning a pronouncement) can be changed to a declarative statement, can religious language, especially ritual language (where subjects take a position with regard to God and others concerning what they say) be rendered into theoretical language. This is to say that *taking seriously the* sacramentum *as the inescapable mediation of every sacramental discourse* commits us to taking seriously the specificity of the illocutionary-performative-ritual language act that makes it up. Lacking this serious consideration, we would no longer know what we are talking about when we say "sacrament." The "non-sacramental" theology at which Barth arrives is, for us, the effect (for reasons which go beyond this discussion) of such a misunderstanding of the *sacramentum*. In other words, to deny the effective nature of the sacraments as "events of grace" (in a sense we will make clear) does not appear tenable to us unless one changes the *sacramentum* itself in its principal expressive moments (words and actions).

However, we must immediately add that the same liturgical practice also shows us that the sacrament as operator is never separate from its symbolic expression: it is *as* revealer it can exercise its function of operator. This "as" is obviously central: acting only through the symbolic mode of revealing expression, the sacrament as operator cannot be identified (even analogically, we believe) with an instrument, and its effect cannot be identified with a finished product. What happens here is not of the physical, moral, or metaphysical but of the symbolic order. This kind of symbolism, we have said, is the most "real." Thus, the death-and-regeneration with Christ in baptism is symbolic. It is not a "real" hidden behind or underneath a verbal-ritual language act which expresses it metaphorically. But neither is it a simple "as if" — a comparison is not a metaphor or symbol — which would dissolve the real into symbolism. It is, according to faith of course, the believer's communion with Christ in his death-and-resurrection. Communion *in sacramento*, that is, communion whose very reality is not separable from the symbolic expression which gives it form, even though it is not reducible to this form. Clearly, the whole problem here lies in the manner in which one thinks of *reality*: it is not of the order of subsistent entities, but of the order of the on-going transformation of subjects into believers.

It is this point that we must now discuss further by evoking "sacramental grace." We shall do so from the perspective opened by our fourth chapter: although not reducible to an intra-linguistic symbolic performance, sacramental grace is still best thought of from this viewpoint.

3. Sacramental Grace

a) In the Wake of the Intra-linguistic. Such is the symbolic efficacy of ritual religious expressions that they bring about an instauration or restoration of *social relationship* between the members of the group *in the name of the absent Third Party* that gathers them — the Ancestor, the God, the Law . . . — that confers on this process of mutual recognition and distribution (or redistribution) of places its "sacred" character. Let us illustrate this general recalling of what we said before by the example of *baptism*. We will consider it first on a strictly socio-linguistic plane, then on a properly theological one.

— *Baptism: A Socio-linguistic Viewpoint*

The ritual enunciation of the formula "I baptize you in the name of the Father and of the Son and of the Holy Spirit" is an eminently performative language act. Pronounced by a legitimate authority (normally, an ordained minister) acting in conformity with prescriptions which are the conditions of the rite's social validity and guarantee the consensus of the group, this language act, as in every rite of passage or institution, "consecrates a difference," as P. Bourdieu puts it; it makes the difference "known and recognized," and thus "it calls it into existence inasmuch as it is a social difference." Symbolic efficacy is "completely real in that it *really* transforms the consecrated persons: it transforms the perception the *other agents* have of these persons . . . and at the same time the perception these persons have of *themselves* and the behavior they believe themselves bound to adopt in order to conform to this perception." So much so that "the indicative mood in this case functions as an imperative. . . . 'Become what you are.' Such is the formula that undergirds the performative magic of every act of institution."[25] In the eyes of all, the baptized persons are really different from what they were before. The rite's symbolic efficacy lies in their *change of status* and, since here description is prescription, in the duty enjoined on them to henceforth *conform their behavior* to this new status. The ritual accomplishes performatively the transition from outside-the-Church to the Church-as-group. All recognize the neophytes as their own. And all may interpret this belonging, in conformity with official doctrine, whatever their own personal adherence through faith to this doctrine, as a filial relationship with the same God named Father — Father of Jesus, the Son — and as a new brotherly and sisterly relationship within the common covenant in which the neophytes are declared henceforth participants.

— *Baptism: A Theological Viewpoint*

If baptismal grace cannot be reduced *theologically* to the symbolic efficacy of a language act, it must still be understood within this perspective. The new relation with God brought about by baptism is in practice inseparable from a new covenantal relation among the people. The absent-present Other, the Third Party witness in whose Name the group is created as the communal "We" of this new covenant which is the Church, has for its name Jesus Christ. By plunging persons into their deaths to make them pass with him to a new life (Rom 6), baptism creates among them a relation

---

25. P. Bourdieu, *Ce que parler veut dire: L'économie des échanges linguistiques* (Paris: Fayard, 1982) 124–127.

of *brotherly and sisterly union,* itself founded on a relation of *filiation* in him, the Son, through the Spirit.

The two aspects are fundamentally connected in Paul. In putting on the same Christ through baptism, Christians become in effect members of this "one new humanity" and this "one body" Christ formed in giving his life so that "the dividing wall" which separates humanity (for Paul, Jew and Gentile) might be destroyed (Eph 2:14-16). Now, through baptism, it is this "new humanity" that comes forth according to the same Paul. We die there to the "old humanity" (the old collective "Adam," the one subject to the reign of sin) in order to put on the "new humanity" (the new collective "Adam" whose "corporate personality" Christ represents). In him, the barriers erected by the Law between the two great parts of humankind are eschatologically abolished: between races (Jew and Greek); between various social classes (slave and free); and between the sexes, the most fundamental of human differences. That Paul has recourse to this baptismal symbolism three times (1 Cor 12:13; Gal 3:26-28; Col 3:9-11) is significant: the baptismal passage from the status of "slaves" to that of *"sons and daughters,"* thanks to the "Spirit of the Son" which God has sent into our hearts and which allows us to cry "Abba! Father!" (Gal 4:6-7), goes hand in hand with the passage to *brotherly and sisterly union* in the name of this same Son.

In baptism this twofold and simultaneous change of relationship with God and others is effected in a *programmatic* manner. Because it is eschatological, it has to be realized in ethical practice. Grace is given as a task to be accomplished. This is why, especially in Paul, the *"dogmatic" indicative* of the "you also must consider yourselves dead to sin . . . in Christ Jesus" is to be joined to the *ethical imperative* of "put to death . . . whatever in you is earthly" (Rom 6:11-12; Col 3:3-5). Baptismal grace thus designates this permanent symbolic work of our conversion by which, through the Spirit, we become believing subjects. Grace concerns this painful *working through* the field of our desire which restores us little by little to the image of Christ and thus makes us different. This baptismal re-creation into the New Adam is the exact reverse of the original "de-creation" in the old Adam: From being the attitude of a slave coveting the privileges of an all-powerful God equally jealous of them (as insinuated by the serpent in Genesis 3:1-5), our desire is turned around into filial gratitude toward the Father. Simultaneously — since the myth of the original transgression shows that to the distorted image of a jealous God there corresponds a distorted image of others — from being a drive to violence towards others, imagined as rivals to be overcome and even killed (Cain and Abel in Genesis 4), our desire is turned around into a covenant between brothers and sisters.

The transition to this new status requires that a real *labor of mourning* take place within us — death to the old humanity — which in all religions is experienced according to the symbolism of the *initiation scheme,* as different as the concrete modalities and cultural representations may otherwise be. Baptismal grace is to be understood theologically according to this initiatory labor of *giving birth* to or re-begetting ourselves according to God's Spirit. For, "without being born from above" (probably the primary sense of the Greek *anothen*) or "without being born again" (its second sense, essential for understanding Nicodemus' objection about the impossibility of entering "a second time into the mother's womb"), that is, "without being born of water and Spirit," "no one can enter the kingdom of God" (John 3:3-5). Baptismal grace has nothing in common with a "commodity" which can be seized, managed, or stored. It is so unlike this that, on the contrary, it is presented symbolically as a labor of childbirth where we learn to receive *ourselves* from God as sons and daughters and thus from others as brothers and sisters.

Jesus' dialogue with the *Samaritan woman* requires us to express ourselves in the same way: God's gift is not a something — as "spiritual" as this might be — which fills a need; it is another way of being and living which hollows out and deepens *"in"* those who drink of this water (the "living water" of the Spirit) the well of their desire and which becomes "in them a spring of water gushing up to eternal life" (John 4:13-15). The same kind of process develops with regard to food: just as he has substituted for the empirical water a "symbolic" water which "one can talk about," but not "manipulate," Jesus now substitutes a symbolic food for the other food of the order of "value" and utility which the disciples have purchased in town (4:8, 31-38). As far as the Samaritan woman is concerned, the reversal of perception is such that her very desire is converted; from being a need, it turns around into a petition, so that at the end of the story Jesus, the initial petitioner, is recognized and asked for himself.[26]

— *Symbolic Labor and Grace*

It seems to us that grace (baptismal grace in this case) is not a "something" to be received (even as a "seed"), but a *self-reception:* a receiving of oneself from God as son or daughter and from others as brother or sister, the two aspects being symbolically distinct but indissolubly linked. We understand it as a *symbolic labor* which penetrates the most real dimension of believing subjects: a fundamental work of restructuring their relation with God and with others. The violence of the affective response toward a God imagined as an overbearing master whose slaves we are is called to reverse itself into a covenant with a Father God from whom we receive, as children, our existence; and the violence of the affective response toward others imagined as potential enemies is called to reverse itself into the recognitions of others as brothers and sisters to love. This kind of conversion is the fundamental task imparted to believers. It is also the most difficult task to achieve, so strongly are we possessed by the nostalgia for a wonder-working God invested with a power which, being ours, makes us want to remain this God's slaves and expiate the pleasure of existing we would have stolen from this God. Like the camel which, according to Nietzsche's aphorism, "desires a heavy burden," do we not often, out of guilt, languish for "the heavy, the still more heavy"?[27] This is precisely why the conversion in question is always in the making. And this permanent task of death to the "old humanity" of violence is a grace, whose symbolic expression par excellence is baptism.

A sacrament is an "event of grace" not because it is a field in which a treasure is buried but because it symbolically ploughs the field *that we ourselves are* and thus renders it fruitful by converting it to the *filiation* and *brotherly and sisterly love* it proclaims to be eschatologically inaugurated in the person whom the Church acknowledges as the Son and our Brother. We understand

26. F. Genuyt, "L'entretien avec la Samaritaine, Jn 4, 1–42: Analyse sémiotique," *Sémiotique et Bible* 36 (1984) 16.

27. F. Nietzsche, *Ainsi parlait Zarathoustra*, "Des trois métaphorphoses" (Paris: Gallimard, Coll. "Idées," 1971) 35.

"sacramental grace" in the perspective of the relation of places between subjects and in the perspective of the recognition effected by language in its illocutionary (and performative) modality. Thus, the paternity of God, the body of Christ, and the temple of the Spirit are rendered effective in our world.

b) A Reality Extra-linguistic Nevertheless. To think of sacramental grace in the perspective of the symbolic efficacy of the illocutionary or performative kind furnishes us with a scheme of theological elaboration that seems to us relatively adequate to what we have said about "grace," but does not constitute *in any way an "explanation"* of this mystery. No more than the Scholastic tradition pretended to explain sacramental grace through causality and instrumentality, do we now pretend to give its ultimate reason. Otherwise, we would postulate a sort of magical power in the words, making use of an energetics much more mechanical and physical than in the productionist scheme we are seeking to overcome.

Besides, as with everything concerning God, from the first we declare grace to be *irreducible* to any explanations. Without this proviso we would reduce the theological to the anthropological, and theology would be only a variant within the social sciences. Now, as soon as God's radical otherness is neglected or erased, God can no longer interest us except as a cultural idea or a cipher for humanity; but one cannot give one's faith to an "idea" or a "cipher" . . . What we are proposing here is in no way a reduction of grace to the socio-linguistic mechanism of symbolic efficacy.

It is one thing to be proclaimed a son or daughter for God and brother or sister for others in Jesus Christ, to be recognized as such by the group, and to be authentically so on the *social* level; it is quite another to be so on the *theological* level of faith, hope, and charity. Who can guarantee, for example, that the baptized (supposed here to be adults) are not dissembling or acting out of self-interest (many theological discussions report such cases to have occurred at certain periods of history) or are not animated by an unconscious desire to escape a crushing feeling of guilt, to expel a satanic "scapegoat," to recover an imaginary innocence by wiping away a stain, intolerable in view of the impeccable image they have of themselves? In other words, who are in a position to judge the truth of their faith and conversion? As a consequence, it is impossible for any of us to pronounce on the effective reception of God's gift — a reception which, as Augustine stressed apropos baptism, is always dependent on faith: *Accipit quisque secundum fidem suam* ("each one receives according to his or her faith).[28] The rite may be perfectly efficacious on the symbolic level of the subject's new status within the Church, without, for all that, this intra-linguistic efficacy being accompanied by an extra-linguistic efficacy concerning the gift and reception of grace itself.

4. *Summary*

In view of what has been said, one may well ask what has been gained by considering grace from the perspective of the symbolic effect of ritual language acts, an effect to which grace is nevertheless irreducible. As a matter of fact, the gain seems considerable to us, and this in three areas.

First, at the level of the discourse about *grace*, we believe that to conceive grace on the symbolic level of the coming-forward of subjects is to place it on a terrain akin to it — that of the non-value — instead of, as in Scholastic tradition and the onto-theology that undergirds it, having recourse to a concept which is from the very first completely foreign to it, like causality.

Then, regarding the *epistemological status* of our discourse, the fact that from the beginning we declare grace to be irreducible, because it is of another order, to everything we can say about it and especially to the symbolic efficacy of language acts in no way disqualifies this discourse. On the contrary, our reflection is *fully conformed* to our way of approaching the problem since we have from the start renounced the claim of giving the ultimate explanation of things.

Last, in proposing this discourse, we are simply carrying out *our task as a theologian:* to render thinkable what we believe, its being granted that this understanding is hermeneutically inseparable from the one we have of ourselves as human beings in the culture of this time. Just like Scripture, which is itself, insofar as it is a witness, already an interpretation, "the response of faith belongs to the very content of revelation."[29] Among the diverse modalities

28. Augustine, *De. Bapt. c. Don.* III, 15.
29. C. Geffré, *Le christianisme au risque de l'interprétation* (Paris: Cerf, 1983) 20.

of this response — prayer, ethical practice, liturgical experience
. . . — theological writing is at once an anamnesis and a prophecy: "It cannot actualize the founding event as a contemporary event except by producing a new text and new historical figures."[30] It is precisely a *"new text"* which, in creative faithfulness to the ecclesial tradition that lives within us, we have attempted to produce here. Not to attempt such a hermeneutical labor in relation to the culture we breathe would be to renege on our task.

Of course, because of the metaphysical tradition which has become part of us, even seeping into our language and, more precisely, into our grammar, it is *inevitable* that we think of grace as an "object" given us by a "subject" God. But thinking something through always involves unmasking the fundamental evidence for what it is: a presupposition. This is theologically true. Consequently, we must continually *counteract* this objectifying scheme, with its implications of causality, instrumentality, and production. Conscious of the limits of this scheme, the *Scholastics* tried to purify it by analogy. This was their way of showing that they were not prisoners of the onto-theological representations within whose framework they necessarily had to think. But even while criticizing these representations, the doctrine of analogy sanctioned their legitimacy; and as a result the theological tradition was built upon them: at that time, one could not think in any other way.

We deem that today we may think in another way by placing ourselves, inasmuch as it is possible, *on another ground* — one always shifting — than that of traditional metaphysics: the ground of the symbolic order. In so doing, we see ourselves as *prolonging* the movement of opening which the great Scholastic tradition, at its best, sought to accomplish in the context of its own age. But in contrast to this Scholastic tradition we are not content to conceive this rupture as a necessary moment *within* the metaphysical context; we attempt to think *starting from* this rupture itself. There is obviously more than a nuance here: another theological thought is seeking to elaborate itself. In any case, such is our way of bringing forth something new from something old. Such is our way of

30. Ibid., 74.

acknowledging ourselves heirs to a great tradition: our task is *to meditate on what this tradition excludes, which nevertheless is what makes it possible,* as it itself shows by taking backward steps through the use of its many qualifications. This is the deepest lesson we have learned from Heidegger: every true advance in thought takes place by moving backward.

A GRACIOUS "LETTING BE"

Dwelling in the symbolic order, grace seems at one and the same time *gratuitous*, that is, always preceding and necessitated by nothing, and *gracious*, that is, irreducible to any demand for justification — thus to any "value" (conceptual, physical, moral . . .). The generosity of Being Heidegger speaks of (*es gibt Sein*) echoes grace. Being and grace are homologous because the way to them, "which sets everything on the way, sets everything on the way inasmuch as this way speaks" and is thus "transitive" and is the attitude of the subject in both cases: an attitude of listening and welcome toward something *ungraspable* by which we are already grasped; a gracious attitude of *"letting be"* and *"allowing oneself to be spoken"* which requires us to renounce all ambition for mastery. What is grace? We will never be able to define it positively as something facing humans which stands by itself. We can express only the symbolic labor of birth which it carries out in us: the labor of the ongoing passage to "thanksgiving" — in this way we come forth as children for God — and to "living-in-grace" — in this way we simultaneously come forth as brothers and sisters for others — which makes us cor-respond to this God who gives grace and is revealed in Jesus.

Part Four

Sacramental Theology and
Trinitarian Christology

Introduction: From Sacramental Discourse to Christological Discourse

The way in which one understands God's action in the eminently human sacramental action of the Church inevitably harks back to the way one understands God's relation with humankind, a relation which in Christianity is necessarily founded on the person whom the Council of Chalcedon has defined as "consubstantial with the Father in his divinity, consubstantial with us in his humanity," there being between the two "natures" neither confusion or change nor division or separation. This is why any theology worthy of its name must achieve *coherence* between its sacramental and Christological discourses. This does not mean that one could simply copy the structure of the Church or of the sacraments from that of the Incarnate Word. Y. Congar has clearly shown "the truth and limits of a parallel" between the two.[1] It remains true that one can infer from a given Christology the ecclesiology and sacramental theology which are consistent with it, and, conversely, a sacramental theology permits us to *determine what sort of Christology is consistent with it.*

As a matter of fact, such a tracing back is traditional. For Ignatius of Antioch, contempt for the Eucharist can only go hand in hand with a docetic Christology.[2] In the same way Tertullian, writing against Marcion, declares that he [Tertullian] has "demonstrated in the Gospel the truth of the body and blood of the

1. Y. Congar, "Dogme christologique et ecclésiologie: Vérité et limites d'un parallèle," *Das Konzil von Chalkedon,* vol. III, A. Grillmeier et al. (Würtzburg, 1954) 239–268.
2. Ignatius of Antioch, *Smyrn.* 7, 1; *Rm* 7, 3 (Sources chrétiennes 10).

Lord" at the Christological level "starting from the sacrament of the bread and chalice."[3] And it is well known that Irenaeus, writing against the Gnostics, states that the Eucharist is the authentic touchstone of Christological and Trinitarian orthodoxy: "For us, our way of thinking is in accord with the Eucharist, and in return the Eucharist confirms our way of thinking."[4]

In a completely different socio-cultural context and following a theological approach very different from that of the Church Fathers, we encounter a similar retracing from sacramental theology to Christology in the Scholastic tradition of the West with regard to a *quaestio* that had become important at that time: that of the *mode of production of sacramental grace*. In chapter one, we called attention to the parallelism between sacramental theology and soteriology equally present in the early Thomas of the *Commentary on the Sentences* and the later Thomas of the *Summa Theologiae*: in the first instance (as with Bonaventure), sacraments play, like Christ's humanity, the simple role of a "disposition" to the reception of the grace of salvation; in the second, an authentic efficacy, subordinated to the divine action, is recognized in both sacraments and Christ's humanity.

It is this connection between sacramental theology and Christology which we will examine in this final part. We will do this in two chapters. Chapter Twelve aims at demonstrating that reflection on the sacraments should take its starting point, not from the hypostatic union as the Scholastic tradition proceeded, but from the *Pasch of Christ* taken in its full scope, that is, from his death (and thus also from his concrete life, without which his death cannot be understood theologically as "death for us") and resurrection, which includes the gift of the Spirit at Pentecost from which the visible Church was born, and the parousia. We will show that such a shift is of considerable significance.

Understood, in this perspective, as symbols of a God who continues to give God's own self a body of world and humanity, the sacraments require us to ask ourselves: *What kind of a God* are we then speaking about if we can recognize in them the gift of God's grace? For to theologically affirm "sacramental grace," that is,

3. Tertullian, "Adv. Marcionem," 5, 8, 3, *CCSL*, vol. I, p. 686.
4. Irenaeus, *Adv. Haer.* IV, 18, 5 (Sources chrétiennes 100).

God's communication with humankind within the wholly human action of the Church, requires, according to us, a subversion of our "simple" onto-theological representations of God. Chapter Thirteen will attempt to elaborate precisely this way of conceiving God as human in God's divinity, starting from the cross.

In this way, we believe, our work will find its *unity*. We have taken as a given received from ecclesial tradition that our condition as Christians is structured through ritual acts in which the Church recognizes events of grace. What *intellectus fidei* ("understanding of the faith") can we impart about this? The elucidation of this fundamental question requires, we have said, that in our reflection we cross the *axis of symbolism*, which permits us a new way of conceiving humankind, with the axis of a *Trinitarian Christology*, which is consistent with the first and opens to us a new way of thinking about God. It is on this last point that our fourth part concentrates.

Chapter Twelve

The Sacraments of the New Pasch

The present chapter aims at showing that the relation between God and humankind in the sacraments is best understood starting not from the hypostatic union, as the Scholastic theologians did (I), but from the Pasch of Christ (II). We will evaluate the consequences of such a shift.

I. SCHOLASTIC SACRAMENTAL THEOLOGY'S POINT OF DEPARTURE: THE HYPOSTATIC UNION

We shall proceed in two stages: first, we shall attempt to show the internal logic which in our opinion exists between, on the one hand, the sacramental theory of Thomas and, on the other, his Christology, pneumatology, and ecclesiology. Then we will go into the implications of this logic for his representation of the relation between God and humankind.

1. Thomas Aquinas: The Internal Logic of the Relation between His Sacramental Theology and the Other Sectors of His Theology

a) His Sacramental Theology, a Direct Prolongation of His Christology. "After the study of the mysteries of the Incarnate Word should come that of the sacraments of the Church, for it is from the Incarnate Word that they derive their efficacy": this is the first statement of Thomas in his "Treatise on the Sacraments" in the *Summa Theologica* (III, q. 60). As this prologue announces, the sacraments are conceived as prolongations of Christology, more precisely, as we shall see, of the hypostatic union.

Of course, from the viewpoint of their *effects*, they derive from Christ's passion: the signs which constitute them are a commemoration of it (*signum rememorativum*); they show the present effects of its grace (*signum demonstrativum*); and they announce its purpose, our future glory (*signum praenuntiativum*).[1] In fact, Thomas constantly repeats, from various viewpoints, that the sacraments *operantur in virtute passionis Christi* ("work by virtue of Christ's passion") and that their efficacy derives entirely from the passion inasmuch as it is the *causa sufficiens humanae salutis* ("sufficient cause for humankind's salvation").[2]

But in its turn such an efficacy is possible only because of the grace of the *hypostatic union*. The "capital grace" of Christ with regard to the Church and to all human beings (III, q. 8) has its foundation in his "personal grace," as *singularis homo* ("a particular human being," q. 7); the latter is directly linked to the "grace of union" (q. 2, a 6). This is why Thomas sees the sacraments entirely as prolongations of the hypostatic union when he no longer considers them under the aspect of their efficacy but in their essence or nature: they are conformed to it, for they "join the 'word' to the sensible thing, just as in the mystery of the incarnation the Word of God is united to sensible flesh."[3] Such a conformation, in Scholastic language, is no simple imitation or exterior tracing; it has an ontological significance.[4] We see this clearly when Thomas analyzes the question of the mode of the sacraments' causality: "The principal cause of grace is God, for whom the humanity of Christ is a conjoined instrument (like the hand in relation to the will) and the sacrament a separate instrument (like a stick, itself moved by the instrument joined to it, the hand). It is necessary then that the power of salvation descend from the divinity of Christ through his humanity until it reaches the sacraments."[5] It would be impossible to conceive of them more fully as *prolongations of the holy humanity of the Incarnate Word*, as *sacramenta humanitatis eius*.[6] Sacramental theology is the exact replica of Christology, and the critical questions one may address

1. *ST* III, q. 60, a. 3.
2. Ibid., q. 61, a. 1, ad 3. Recall that in the *Summa* the *acta et passa* ("actions and sufferings") of Jesus are said to "cause" (instrumentally) the grace of salvation not only "through the modality of merit" but "through a certain efficiency" (III, q. 8, a. 1, ad 1; see q. 49, a. 1, ad 3).
3. Ibid., q. 60, a. 6.
4. On this point, see M. D. Chenu, *Introduction à l'étude de saint Thomas d'Aquin*, op. cit., 86–87.
5. *ST* III, q. 60, a. 6.
6. Ibid., q. 80, a. 5.

to the first come directly from the kind of questions to which one may subject the second.

Considering the Treatise on the Sacraments as a prolongation of Christology has the advantage — and no small one at that — of underlining that the sacraments are *actions of Christ*. But it also has disadvantages. If the "mysteries" of the life of Christ occupy a respectable place in the *Summa* — much more than in recent neo-Scholasticism — they are treated in an *ahistorical* manner, in conformity with the mentality of the age and the technique, as rigorous and precise as it is abstract and impersonal, of the *quaestio-disputatio-determinatio* from which each *articulus* is born. The concrete fabric of Christ's historical life is not taken into consideration as a theologically pertinent place for understanding the significance of his death as a "death for us." Because of this, everything is already over, theologically speaking, in the first part of his Christology, that is, in the *hypostatic union*. The redemption, the major weight of which is essentially borne by the passion and cross (q. 46–50), is nothing more than a consistent, and certainly costly, development of what was already inscribed in the incarnation. As for the *resurrection*, it draws attention for a short while. Moreover, in the medieval Summas, as J. Doré has noted, "it was approached from the primary mystery of the incarnation of the Word in such a way that it appeared much more as the restoration of the Incarnate Word to its proper 'state' (or to what 'it should have been'), hidden for a moment by the humiliations of earthly life freely accepted, than as the advance of the human being Jesus to a new condition, the consequence of a life of fidelity and faith, the culmination of an authentic history of Jesus Christ."[7] No more than the concrete history of Jesus, is his resurrection truly taken into account as the place where the elaboration of Christology finds its principle.

Moreover, one observes that Thomas, in his soteriological part, goes beyond the Gospels and in fact follows, beginning with the passion, the various Christological articles of the Creed.[8] One can then ask oneself why, before treating the sacraments, he has not

7. J. Doré, "La résurrection de Jésus à l'épreuve du discours théologique," *Visages du Christ*, RSR (Paris: Desclée, 1977) 283.

8. Recall the organization of the third part of the *Summa*: (I) *Christology*: (1) the mystery of the incarnation (qq. 1–26); (2) the mystery of the redemption

followed through with this procedure by taking up the third part of the Creed, the part devoted to *pneumatology and ecclesiology*. One of the reasons, without doubt, is that treatises on the Church did not yet exist as such, as we will see. In any case, his failure to take into consideration, in the context of the exaltation of Christ, the sending of the Spirit at Pentecost as the agent of the birth and missionary growth of the visible Church obviously reinforces the ahistorical character of his "Treatise on the Sacraments."

Flowing thus directly out of his Christology — a Christology fundamentally determined by the hypostatic union — his sacramental theology is *static*. It no longer has the dynamism which it possessed in the Church Fathers by virtue of its insertion into the historical movement of the "economy," a movement the Scriptures revealed in "mysteries," mysteries prefiguring that of Christ and the Church and unfolding down to the present, in the breath of the Spirit, as an event of salvation in the sacraments. Scholastic sacramental theology lost this dynamism as a result of the semantic cut which little by little deprived the *sacramentum* of its relation to the biblical *mysterium* from which it originated, a cut made worse by the theory of seven distinct sacraments which had recently been developed. In short, a sacramental theology conceived primarily on the basis of the hypostatic union and, analogically, in the same mode as it, cannot be inserted into the movement of concrete history — as can a sacramental theology conceived on the basis of the resurrection of the Crucified and on the basis of the eschatological enfleshment of the Risen One in the world through the Spirit of Pentecost.

b) A Sacramental Theology Pneumatologically Weak.

— A Precise and Rich Pneumatology

Let us avoid a misunderstanding at the outset. Thomas, to restrict ourselves to him, developed a *precise and rich pneumatology.*

(*acta et passa* of Christ as savior studied in four great moments: (a) qq. 27-39: the entrance of Christ into the world (virginity of Mary, the annunciation to Mary, the birth of Christ, the epiphany to the wise men, circumcision, baptism by John); (b) qq. 40-45: his earthly life (temptations, teaching, miracles, transfiguration; (c) qq. 46-52: his departure from the world (passion, death, burial, descent into hell); (d) qq. 53-59: his exaltation (resurrection, ascension, sitting at the right hand of the Father, power to judge the world). (II) *Sacra-*

We will not stop to consider Thomas' intra-Trinitarian pneumatology. More important for our purpose is the relation between this and *creation*. Proceeding through the mode of will and love, the Spirit is, by appropriation, the principle of everything that emerges from God's free will and love: all of creation (*Contra Gentiles* IV, 20); humankind, which is endowed with reason (IV, 21); and the return of humankind to God (IV, 22). This is why *grace*, without which humankind's return to God is impossible, is to be attributed especially to the Holy Spirit. The mission of the Spirit is in conformity with its procession: "The Holy Spirit is Love. It is thus the gift of charity that makes the soul similar to the Holy Spirit, and it is by reason of charity that one attributes a mission to the Holy Spirit."[9]

Thence, if someone asks what characterizes *principaliter* ("principally") the dispensation of the *new covenant*, what constitutes its *virtus* ("inner force"), Thomas answers, "It is the grace of the Holy Spirit, which is given through faith in Christ";[10] and if a human work receives from God a meritorious efficacy, it is "insofar as it proceeds from the grace of the Holy Spirit" since "the value of the *merit* is determined by the power of the Holy Spirit which moves us toward eternal life and because it is this same Spirit which, "dwelling in humankind through grace," is "the sufficient cause of eternal life."[11] Hence, the space Thomas devotes to the gifts of the Holy Spirit, the beatitudes, and the fruits of the Spirit, all of which contribute to making believers virtuous (Ia-IIae, q. 70).

Under such conditions, we should not be surprised that Thomas' pneumatology extends to the *Church* and the sacraments. "The soul which animates the body (that is the Church) is the Holy Spirit. This is why, after believing in the Holy Spirit, we are required to believe in the holy Catholic Church, as the Creed indicates," writes Thomas in his *Expositio in Symbolum*.[12] Moreover, as he explains further in the *Summa*, is it not preferable to say, in conformity with the most current usage, *credo sanctam ecclesiam*, rather than *in sanctam ecclesiam*? One believes in God; one be-

---

ments: (q. 60-supplement to q. 68). (III) *Four Last Things* (supplement to q. 69-q. 99).

9. *ST* I, q. 43, a. 5, ad 2; *C. Gent.* IV, 21. H. D. Dondaine, *Saint Thomas d'Aquin: Somme théologique I, q. 33-43, La Trinité*, vol. 2 (Paris: éd. de la Revue des Jeunes, 1950) no. 135, pp. 423-453; C. V. Héris, same edition of the *Summa*, *Ia-IIae, qq. 109-114 La grâce* (1961) 387-390; C. Baumgartner, *La Grâce du Christ* (Paris: Desclée, 1963), ch. 4 "La théologie de la grâce selon saint Thomas d'Aquin," 83-104.

10. *ST* Ia-IIae, q. 106, a. 1; q. 107, a. 1. ad 3.

11. Ibid., q. 114, a. 3.

12. *Exp. in Symb.*, a. 9; see Y. Congar, *Esquisses du mystère de l'Eglise*, 59-91.

lieves the Church. If we wish to retain the expression *in ecclesiam,* we must "make reference to the Holy Spirit which sanctifies the Church" so that the meaning may be *Credo in Spiritum sanctum sanctificantem Ecclesiam* ("I believe in the Holy Spirit sanctifying the Church").[13]

With regard to the *sacraments,* Thomas uses equally strong pneumatological expressions, from the viewpoint of the technical concepts employed: "In the person of Christ, his humanity causes our salvation through grace under the action of the divine power which is the principal agent. It is the same in the sacraments of the new law which derive from Christ: grace is instrumentally caused by them and *principally caused by the power of the Holy Spirit who works in them,* according to John 3:5: "without being born of water and Spirit. . . ."[14] And apropos the three baptisms of water, blood, and the Spirit: "Baptism of water derives its efficacy from Christ's passion to which human beings are configured by baptism and also *from the Holy Spirit as first cause.'*[15] Let us quote one more passage, to which we shall return shortly, which concerns the Eastern Eucharistic practice where the epiclesis traditionally plays a major role. Thomas quotes, as an *auctoritas* ("authoritative statement") posing a difficulty, this sentence from St. John Damascene, "It is through the sole power of the Holy Spirit that the conversion of the bread into the body of Christ takes place." The solution: "In saying this, one does not exclude the instrumental power which is found in the form of this sacrament [the words of consecration]. When one says that the artisan alone makes a knife, one does not exclude the power of the hammer."[16] Here again, it is the role of principal agent Thomas accords to the Spirit. Within this ecclesiological and sacramental context, it would be good to quote the entire commentary on John 6. Let us single out this one example: "The unity of the Church is made by the

13. *ST* IIa-IIae, q. 1, a. 9, ad 5.
14. Ibid, Ia-IIae, q. 112, a. 1, ad 3.
15. Ibid., III, q. 66, a. 11; Ibid., a. 12: "The power of the Holy Spirit operates in baptism of water through a certain hidden power; in the baptism of penance through conversion of heart; but in the baptism of blood, it operates by the most intense fervor of love (*dilectio*) and attachment (*affectio*) according to John 15:13: 'No one has greater love than this, to lay down one's life for one's friends.' "
16. Ibid., q. 78, a. 4, obj. 1 and ad 1.

Holy Spirit. . . . The person who spiritually eats and drinks becomes a *participant in the Holy Spirit* by which we are united to Christ in a union of faith and charity and by which we become members of the Church."[17] Here we meet again the Augustine of Treatises 26 and 27 on John's Gospel, many passages of which had become classical maxims as early as the high Middle Ages . . .

— *A Pneumatology Not on a Par However with the*
Christological Principle

How, in view of such texts, can one still maintain that there is a *pneumatological weakness* in Thomas' sacramental theology? Several observations become germane at this point. The first is that Thomas, in his strongest pneumatological texts, does no more than "read" the texts of *Scripture* on this topic, especially those of John and Paul which, together with Acts, accord the Spirit an eminent position. Taking account of such texts as John 3 and 1 Corinthians 10 with regard to baptism and John 6 with regard to the Eucharist, it was unthinkable not to strongly emphasize the role of the Spirit in these sacraments.

On the other hand, in this Thomas did no more than pick up a *common possession* of the Church's great tradition in the West as well as in the East. More exactly, he did no more than pick up the very strong baptismal and Eucharistic pneumatology of Augustine himself, although in Augustine the theme of the Spirit-sanctification of the bread into the Eucharistic body is not as strongly emphasized as the theme of the Spirit-sanctification of the assembly into the ecclesial body.[18] In the same way, the Augustinian theological

17. *Super Evang. S. Ioan. Lectura,* c. 6, lect. 7, 3-5. See M. Corbin, "Le pain de la vie: La lecture de Jean VI par S. Thomas d'Aquin," *Visages du Christ,* RSR 65/1 (1977) 107-138.

18. "Through the coming of the Word, the bread and wine become the body and blood of the Word; through the coming of the fervor of the Spirit, you are cooked and you have become the bread of the Lord" (*Serm. Denis 6,* 1). "Then the Holy Spirit comes, after the water and the fire, and you become the bread which is the body of Christ" (*Sermon* 227). One could thus write with regard to Augustine: "The question of an action of the Holy Spirit on the Eucharistic offering seems totally outside his field of interest," while the action of this same Spirit on the assembly which is becoming the ecclesial body of Christ is, on the contrary, continually set into relief. B. Bobrinskoy, "Saint Augustin et l'eucharistie," *Parole et Pain* 52 (1972) 346-353, quotation from 351; "L'Esprit du Christ dans les sacrements chez Jean Chrysostome et

approach relative to the Church as the sacrament of the unity of the Spirit[19] could not but have affected Scholastic tradition, which in its principles, spirit, and structures "remained dominated by Augustine's theology."[20]

In picking here and there the fruits of this pneumatological tradition, Thomas did nothing more than follow a doctrine very much alive during the high Middle Ages. Is it not *operante invisibiliter Spiritu Dei* ("by the invisible action of God's Spirit") that the sacrament is accomplished, according to Isidore of Seville? He could base himself on a Mozarabic liturgical tradition which, like its Gallican cousin, gave a prominent place to the Holy Spirit even in the Eucharistic prayers, which were in both cases more influenced by the Eastern Syrian anaphoras than by the Roman canon. When in the eighth century the Venerable Bede maintains in his turn that the sacrament is accomplished *ineffabili Spiritus sanctificatione* ("by the Spirit's ineffable sanctification"), he is only expressing the liturgy he was familiar with. Authors all the way down to Peter Lombard and Albert the Great will quote a formula from the *Liber de Corpore et Sanguine Domini* (ch. 4) by Paschasius Radbertus (ninth century) attributed to Augustine: *Sicut per Spiritum sanctum vera Christi caro sine coitu creatur, ita per eundem ex substantia panis et vini idem corpus et sanguis consecrantur* ("As the true body of Christ is created by the Holy Spirit without sexual relations, so by the same Holy Spirit the body and blood are consecrated from the substance of bread and wine"). Moreover, Paschasius has formulas which, by themselves alone, would have been sufficient to avoid

---

Augustin," *Jean Chrysostome et Augustin*, ed. C. Kannengiesser (Paris: Beauchesne, 1975) 247–279. See M. F. Berrouard, *Saint Augustin, Hom. sur l'év. de Jean XVII-XXXIII*, Bibl. aug. 72, homily 71 "L'eucharistie, sacrement de la participation à l'Esprit du Christ," 830–832. *However*, in *De. Trin*. III, 4, 10, Augustine writes, "The consecration that makes of this such a great sacrament comes to it exclusively from the invisible action of the Spirit of God." *Sermon* 8, 3: "Sanctificatio nulla divina et vera est nisi a Spiritu sancto" ("There is no divine and true sanctification except from the Holy Spirit," *Patrologia Latina* 38, 72).

19. The Church as the *societas sanctorum* ("communion of saints") is "the distinctive work of the Holy Spirit" and thus the concrete place of the intra-Trinitarian communion since the Spirit, proceeding from both the Father and the Son *tanquam ab uno principio* ("as from one principle") is the *nexus amborum* ("nexus of both"), their *charitas substantialis et supersubstantialis* ("substantial and supersubstantial charity," *Sur l'év. de Jean*, tr. 14, 9; 105, 3; *De Bapt. c. Don*. I, 17, 26; etc.).

20. Chenu, *Introduction*, 45.

the unfortunate conflict between the East and West over the epiclesis: the consecration takes place *per sacerdotem super altare in verbo Christi per Spiritum sanctum* ("by the priest on the altar in the word of Christ through the Holy Spirit") and *virtute Spiritus sancti per verbum Christi* ("by the power of the Holy Spirit through the word of Christ"); or again this formula Thomas quotes in the *Summa* as from Augustine: *in verbo Creatoris et in virtute Spiritus sancti* ("in the Creator's word and the Holy Spirit's power").[21] Y. Congar provides a whole collection of quotations testifying to the vitality of sacramental pneumatology especially in the ninth century, but also in the eleventh and twelfth centuries and even in so official a text as the profession of faith imposed by Innocent III on the Waldenses in 1208 where the Church is said to celebrate the sacraments *inaestimabili et invisibili virtute Spiritus sancti cooperante* ("by the cooperation of the Holy Spirit's inestimable and invisible power").[22]

Hence, what is surprising in both Thomas' ecclesiology and sacramental theology is not that there are such evocative expressions about the action of the Spirit; it is rather that compared with those concerning Christ, there are *so few*. Certainly, one can cite pneumatological texts, even very beautiful ones, a few of which have an undeniable theoretical weight (for example, with regard to causality). We have done this. But by quoting them one after the other, one risks falsifying the overall perspective.

If statistics have any interest, one cannot help noticing that Christ (the Incarnate Word, the passion of Christ, the priesthood of Christ, the power of the excellence of Christ, and so on) is mentioned in almost every one of the thirty-eight articles of the *"Treatise on the Sacraments"* — and often several times in the course of the same article, a number which altogether easily exceeds a hundred — while the Holy Spirit, outside the few quotations of the baptismal formula, which are not commented upon, is mentioned only five times. Not one of these five, moreover, is the occasion for a pneumatological development.[23] The only passage

21. Paschasius Radbertus, *Liber de corp. et sang. Dom.*, 3 and 12 (*Patrologia Latina* 120:1279, 1310); Thomas, *ST* III, q. 82, a. 5, s.c.

22. *D-S* 793. The pseudo-Augustinian formula of Paschasius recorded by Thomas is also found in this document, *D-S* 794. See Y. Congar, "Le rôle du Saint-Esprit dans l'eucharistie selon la tradition occidentale," *Je crois en l'Esprit-Saint*, vol. 3, op. cit., 320–330.

23. A direct quotation from 2 Cor 1:21 (q. 63, q. 1, s.c.) or from John 3:5 (q. 65, a. 4, obj. 2); a reminder that confirmation is the sacrament of the gift of

which has any force from the viewpoint of pneumatology appears finally in q. 64, a. 3, obj. 1, where, after quoting John 1:33, Thomas emphasizes that to "baptize in the Holy Spirit is to confer interiorly the grace of the Holy Spirit." Let us add that the adjective "spiritual," frequently used, has no pneumatological meaning: "spiritual reality" is the same as "intelligible reality" and is opposed to "sensible reality" (q. 60, a. 4-5); "spiritual power" designates the category of being to which the sacramental character belongs (q. 63, a. 2); and if the sacrament has a "spiritual power," it has received it "by Christ's blessing" (q. 62, a. 4, resp. 3). We are forced to conclude that almost nothing pneumatological balances the massive weight of the Christological principle.

The only mention of the Spirit having a real impact from the sacramental viewpoint in general is found in the "Treatise on Grace"; it is quoted above (n. 14). For baptism we have two, also quoted above (n. 15). For the Eucharist, two quoted above (nn. 16, 21). Of course, the one principle enunciated in these five cases is of capital importance from the theoretical viewpoint: the Holy Spirit is the "principal agent" or the "first cause" of sacramental grace. We take note of this. But how is it that Thomas does not *say a single word about it in his most rigorous analysis of the sacraments in general*, especially when he investigates their essence (q. 60), principal effect, which is grace (q. 62), and cause (q. 64)? Granted, in question 64 on the cause of the sacraments he does repeat many times that "the power of the sacrament comes from God alone," who is their "principal cause" and *institutor*; and this obviously implies the three divine persons since they always operate together in their works *ad extra*. But when he attributes this work of sanctification, by appropriation, to one of them, it is not at first to the Spirit ("gift of sanctification") but to Christ ("author of sanctification"):[24] for him, the Spirit functions more as an "object" than a "principle."

This is why there is no mention of the Spirit throughout the discussion of sacramental causality. It is *"Christ"* who *"produces the*

_____

the Spirit (q. 65, a. 1, c. and ad 4); a refusal to conclude from Eph 4:30 that the sacramental "character" should be attributed to the Holy Spirit rather than Christ (q. 63, a. 3).

24. *ST* I, q. 43, a. 7.

interior effect of the sacraments inasmuch as he is God and inasmuch as he is a human being." Therefore, the *principle* guiding Thomas' sacramental theology from beginning to end is not pneumatological but almost exclusively Christological. The few exceptions we have observed seem a matter of the technique of "reverential presentation": "When St. Thomas in the course of his work meets with the opinions of the Church Fathers, he takes them in and then bends them to his own meaning by interpreting them from the perspective of his system and ideas. Instead of saying that the Church Fathers were more or less mistaken or that he thinks differently from them, he presents them *reverenter* ("reverently"), as he calls this way of operating," a way which had become traditional in Scholasticism since Abelard.[25] Typical of this method is the way he resolves in III, q. 78, a. 4 and q. 82, a. 5 the difficulties arising from the epiclesis in the Eastern Church: the Eastern Church is not wrong; but the Spirit is rendered present only "through the power of Christ whose words the priest pronounces."

We take note here of this *"Christo-monistic" tendency* which, according to Congar,[26] has marked Western theology, especially during the Scholastic era, a bent increasingly stressed after the thirteenth century. This weakness in sacramental theology is, in good part, the price paid for Scholastic insistence on *causality* as the specific trait characterizing the sacraments of the new law. Everything depends on Christ, whose humanity, in virtue of the hypostatic union, possesses a "power of excellence" over the sacraments (separate instruments) and is itself the (conjoined) instrument of his divinity which possesses the "power of authority" (*potestas auctoritatis*) over them; it is "from their institution by Christ that the sacraments derive their power."[27] In them the "power of the Holy Spirit" is subordinated to the action of Christ: *sacramenta humanitatis eius* ("the sacraments of his humanity"). In such a sacramental theology the *Christological principle, constantly af-*

25. P. Mandonnet, quoted by Chenu, *Introduction,* 125.

26. Y. Congar, "Pneumatologie et 'christomonisme' dans la tradition latine?" *Ecclesia a Spiritu sancto edocta,* Mélanges Mgr G. Philips (Paris: Gembloux, 1970), 41–63.

27. *ST* III, q. 64, a. 3.

firmed, has no real pneumatological counterpart. The Holy Spirit is the
object of episodic reflection, on the occasion of confirmation for
example. But no pneumatology is really developed in the "Treatise on Orders."[28] And in that on penance, of the seven references
made to John 20:22-23, only three connect the power to retain or
forgive sins to the "receive the Holy Spirit"; and this is to indicate that (1) the priest acts as "the instrument and minister of
God," (2) without the gift of the Holy Spirit the priest acts validly
but "in an unbecoming way," (3) this word does not imply juridical power but only the power of orders given by Christ.[29] In any
case, this reflection on the Holy Spirit is too sporadic to be a constitutive dimension of his sacramental theology. Pneumatology is
overpowered by the Christological principle of causality; the Spirit
is continually channeled through Christ. This results in a *strongly
institutional* sacramental theology. In our opinion, this is the major
consequence of this mind-set: the insistence on sacramental causality goes hand in hand with a strict adherence of the sacraments
to the hypostatic union and holy humanity of Christ which they
prolong and also, by the same token, with a tendency to over-
emphasize an institution which, endowed with the *potestas* of
Christ, tends to assume control over the freedom of the Spirit.

28. Of course, in *ST Suppl.* q. 35, a. 4, Thomas affirms that "the apostles
received the power of orders before the ascension, when it was said to them,
"Receive the Holy Spirit. . . ." But in q. 37, a. 5, ad 2, he writes that "the
Lord bestowed on his disciples the principal function of the priestly power
before his passion, at the Last Supper," and that "after his resurrection he
passed on to them the secondary function, which consists in binding and
loosing." J. Lécuyer observes: "St. Thomas finds himself, in fact, heir to a
double tradition. The older is favorable to the bestowing of the priesthood on
the apostles on Easter evening. . . . The second opinion, which places the
ordination of the apostles at the Last Supper, appears only in the twelfth century in connection with the opinion that makes of the porrection of the 'instruments' the essential ritual of ordination, an opinion found in Albert the
Great and already in Honorius of Autun" (*Saint Thomas d'Aquin: Somme théologique Suppl. q. 34-40, "L'ordre"* [Paris: éd. de la Revue des Jeunes, 1968]
175-176).

29. *ST Suppl.*, q. 18, a. 4; q. 19, a. 5, obj. 1 and ad 1; q. 20, a. 1, obj. 1 and
ad 1. Let us observe in passing that it is not surprising that the Holy Spirit,
here as in the Eucharist (see above), is often the cause of a "difficulty" at the
beginning of an article — as if it were constantly "upsetting" the "system."

c) A Sacramental Theology Excessively Separated from Ecclesiology.
This third statement, like the two before it, needs first to be nuanced. For Thomas, the sacraments are actions of Christ; he is
their *auctor*. But they are acts of Christ in the Church. Thomas
very frequently calls them *sacramenta Ecclesiae*. To act *in persona
Christi*, one must have such an earnest intention to do what the
Church does that it is described as the intention *facere quod facit
Christus et Ecclesia* ("to do what Christ and the Church does"), the
verb in the singular indicating that the two actions are really only
one.[30] Sacraments are *protestationes fidei Ecclesiae* ("protestations of
the Church's faith"), so that in baptism the minister acts *in persona totius Ecclesiae, ex cujus fide suppletur id quod deest fidei ministro*
("in the person of the whole Church, whose faith supplies what is
lacking in the minister's faith").[31] And although a priest separated
from the Church can validly consecrate the body and blood of
Christ (*res et sacramentum*, "first effect"), it remains that the ultimate *res* ("effect") of the Eucharist is still the *unitas corporis mystici*
("unity of the mystical body").[32] There is no need to multiply
quotations; the ecclesial dimension is almost constantly present in
Thomas' sacramental theology. Then how is it that we are still unsatisfied? There are at least three reasons for this.

The first, due to historical circumstances, derives from the fact
that *treatises on ecclesiology* did not yet exist as such in the thirteenth century. Of course, ecclesiological questions had developed
as early as the twelfth century, but these were in the context of a
Christological question concerning the grace of Christ as head. Because of this, a sacramental theology could not be developed in
relation to ecclesiology.

The second reason is more important. It is due to the major em-
phases of ecclesiology in the thirteenth century. We mention two,
one cast into relief by H. de Lubac, the other by Congar.

As for the first emphasis, let us limit ourselves to recalling the
effect, mentioned above, of the controversy surrounding Berengar:
a "deadly dichotomy" is introduced between the Eucharistic body and
the ecclesial body, the latter losing, as a consequence, its ancient

30. *ST* III, q. 64, a. 8, ad 1.
31. Ibid., a. 9, ad 1.
32. Ibid., q. 73, a. 3.

meaning as *veritas corporis Christi* ("the truth of the body of Christ"). This break is to some extent consecrated by theology with the precise formulation of the distinction between *sacramentum tantum* ("the sacramental sign only") and *res* ("the effect"), on the one hand, and *sacramentum* ("the sacrament") and *res tantum* ("the ultimate effect"), on the other, during the years 1130–1140 in Hugh of St. Victor's *Summa Sententiarum* and *De Sacramentis*, a distinction already perceptible a little before in Alger of Liege and the school of Anselm of Laon. The Eucharistic body is the *res et sacramentum* ("first effect"); church unity, the *res et non sacramentum* ("ultimate effect"). The first is *res significata et significans* ("the reality signified and signifying"); the second, *res significata et non significans* ("the reality signified but not signifying"). With Peter Lombard, this distinction becomes *corpus verum* ("the true body," the Eucharist) = *res significata et contenta* ("the reality signified and contained [in the sacrament]"); *corpus mysticum* (the Church) = *res significata et non contenta* ("the reality signified but not contained [in the sacrament]"). De Lubac comments: "Thus, the ultimate reality of the sacrament, what was formerly the thing and the truth par excellence, is now *expelled from the sacrament. Any symbolism is now only extrinsic:* in the future one will be able to pass it over in silence without damaging the integrity of the sacrament. From the moment it first becomes *corpus mysticum,* the ecclesial body has already been detached from the Eucharist."[33] In this way one will come to speak, in the thirteenth century, of the "mystical body" in an absolute manner, without making any further reference to the Eucharist. "The expression will then come to designate," Congar comments, "the Church as a social body . . . and one will be able to speak of the Pope as a *caput* (*secundarium*), "(secondary) head," of the mystical body: something that would have been impossible as long as the expression retained a Eucharistic reference, for it then designated the body which Christ himself is, of which he is the sole head."[34]

The break is accentuated by the way the question *de Christo Capite* ("on Christ the head"), already treated in Peter Lombard's *Sentences* (III, d. 13), is asked. Towards the end of the twelfth cen-

33. H. de Lubac, *Corpus mysticum*, op. cit., 283.
34. Y. Congar, *L'Eglise, de saint Augustin à l'époque moderne*, op. cit., 168–169.

tury this question will shift and become the treatise *De Gratia Capitis* ("On the Grace of the Head") which the thirteenth century will be familiar with. This change is theologically important, and it seems to have accompanied the change in the meaning of *corpus mysticum*. Indeed, until the middle of the twelfth century and even later, it is the Holy Spirit which, in conformity with Augustinian ecclesiology, is considered the *artifex* ("artisan," Hugh of St. Victor), the efficient agent of the unity of the Church, and not Christ through his grace as the head.[35] Of course, Christ himself is considered the principle and source of the interior riches of his body; but it is the Spirit, the same in the Head and in the body, which makes this communication possible: it is "by participating in Christ's Spirit" (*participans Spiritum Christi*) that "one becomes a member of Christ's body."[36] This is a fully Augustinian doctrine (see above). However, in the thirteenth century one no longer understands things this way: *the "holy humanity" of Christ takes the place of the Holy Spirit as the agent and efficient cause of Church unity.* The fullness of grace which Christ possesses by virtue of the hypostatic union is communicated to the Church through the channel of his holy humanity: "It is necessary that the salvific power descend from Christ's divinity through his humanity down to the sacraments." Thomas could have written equally well "down to the Church."[37] In parallel fashion, as Congar notes, "in the twelfth century one speaks less of the Church's birth at Pentecost; by contrast, the traditional theme, also known in the East, of the Church's birth from the side of Christ on the cross is very frequent."[38]

The third reason is that the Church, for the majority of the Scholastics, rarely evokes the local community, especially the concrete liturgical assembly recognized as the embodiment, particular but still integral, of the universal Church. As we know, the *ekklesia*

35. Hugh of St. Victor, *De Sacr.* I, 6, 17 (*Patrologia Latina* 176:274). Rupert of Deutz: "Quod, cum sint multi, sic per unam fidem unumque Spiritum in unum corpus ecclesiae sunt coniuncti" ("Although many, they are united in the one body of the Church through one faith and one Spirit," *De div. off.* II, 6 [*Patrologia Latina* 170:38]). See Congar, *L'Eglise*, 160–161.

36. Hugh of St. Victor, *De Sacr.* (*Patrologia Latina* 176:417).

37. *ST* III, q. 62, a. 5.

38. Congar, *L'Eglise*, 164, with numerous references in the notes.

in the New Testament was first the local community.[39] Further, in the early Church Fathers this same concrete character of the *ekklesia* was so clearly perceived that they affirmed "forcefully the identity between participation in the ecclesia-assembly and belonging to the Church."[40] During the Scholastic period, for lack of a lively perception of the concrete assembly as the Church, it was practically impossible to emphasize the sacramentality of the Church and to think of the sacraments as based on the Church. The sacraments' ecclesial dimension was always affirmed, but it was no longer perceived as one of their *intrinsically* constitutive elements.

If Thomas succeeded in being original on many points in sacramental theology, he still was not able to correct the course of Scholastic thinking. Having inherited a relatively weak pneumatology in this area, accepting the substitution of Christ for the Spirit as the efficient agent of the unity of the ecclesial "mystical body," and insufficiently sensitive to the concrete sacramentality of the Church-assembly, he contributed for his part to accentuating the institutional trend in sacramental theology.

d) A Sacramental Theology of a Strongly Institutional Kind. There is a coherence between the primacy of the Christological principle in sacramental theology and the theology of the procession of the Spirit *ex Patre et Filio.* Not a necessity, but a coherence (the *Filioque* in Augustine establishes the basis for an ecclesiology of communion). In any case, in the context of established Christendom it is indeed possible that the remark of O. Clément might be pertinent: "The 'filioqueism' . . . which puts the Spirit, as to its very hypostatic existence, in dependence upon the Son, has without a doubt contributed to enhance the institutional and authoritarian

39. *Traduction œcuménique de la Bible,* note on Acts 5:11. See 1 Cor 11:18; 14:23; Matt 18:17.

40. P. M. Gy, "Eucharistie et 'ecclesia' dans le premier vocabulaire de la liturgie chrétienne," LMD 130 (1977), 30. It is within this perspective, the author remarks, that one must understand Ireneaus: "All those who do not flock to the ecclesia do not participate in this Spirit. . . . For where the ecclesia is, there also is the Spirit; and where the Spirit of God is, there also is the ecclesia and every grace" (*Adv. Haer.* III, 24, 1). In the same way Hippolytus, "himself strongly influenced by Ireneaus" (p. 31): "They will be eager to go to the ecclesia, where the Spirit flourishes" (*Tr. Ap.,* 35).

aspect of the Roman Church."[41] This observation can be directly illustrated by one of Thomas' statements in his *Contra Errores Graecorum:* "The error of those who say that the vicar of Christ, the pontiff of the Roman Church, does not have primacy in the universal Church is similar to the error of those who say that the Holy Spirit does not proceed from the Son."[42]

This increasingly institutional emphasis in ecclesiology is illustrated by the growing importance of the *pope's power*, the theological justification for which begins with Gregory VII, finds a first high point with Innocent III (beginning of the thirteenth century), and reaches its culmination in the bull *Unam Sanctam* of Boniface VIII in 1302. The various theories which confront one another, sometimes bitterly, on this subject address a common need: at that time one aspires to an *ideal of unity*, of which the pope would be the capstone, just as one aspires to an ideal of theological synthesis, for which the Summas supply the blueprints. Besides, whether one holds a frankly theocratic or a more nuanced position, it is always a question of "a theology of priestly *power* opposite (and above) royal *power*. In the wake of Gregory VII, papal power becomes an element in the *theological* vision of the Church."[43] It is supreme power, conceived in the twelfth century as *plenitudo potestatis* ("fullness of power"), the holder of which is called *vicarius Christi*. The two notions are ratified by Innocent III: "The supreme pontiff" is "not the vicar of a mere human being, but vicar of the true God."[44] Consequently, he does not hesitate to apply to himself, as pope, what was said of Christ in the treatises on the grace of Christ as head: "The full force of the five senses is located in the head, whereas the members receive only a part."[45] Thus, at least with certain canonists and curialists, papal power becomes "quasi-divine."[46]

Certainly, there is no question here of attempting to derive the entire movement of the theological theses mentioned above from the weakening of pneumatology to the advantage of Christology in sacramental theology or from the progressive detachment of the

---

41. O. Clément, *L'Eglise orthodoxe* (Paris: PUF, 1961) 50.

42. Thomas Aquinas, *Contra Errores Graecorum*, c. 32, par. "Quod Pontifex romanus. . . ." *Opuscula omnia*, vol. 3 (Paris: Lethielleux, 1927) 322. See also p. 303.

43. Congar, *L'Eglise*, 178.

44. *Patrologia Latina* 214:292. See J.M.R. Tillard, *L'évêque de Rome* (Paris: Cerf, 1982) 132.

45. Quoted by Congar, *L'Eglise*, 255.

46. Ibid., 256.

corpus mysticum from its Eucharistic orbit: Gregory VII's papacy occurred before the birth of these theological movements . . . But it is difficult not to notice a family resemblance and an *internal coherence* among these developments. In any case, one observes in the Scholastic tradition a transition from a strongly pneumatological and "sacramental" ecclesiology to a *more institutional and juridical ecclesiology*, a transition theologically fostered by the growing infringement on the Holy Spirit by the holy humanity of Christ and rendered, if not necessary, at least possible by the *filioque*.

Moreover, on the strictly sacramental level this institutional trend is clearly marked in the theology of the *sacrament of holy orders* and in that of the minister's place in the celebration of the Eucharist. The accent placed, especially with Peter Lombard, on the notion of *character, ubi fit promotio potestatis* ("where the conferring of power occurs"), as constitutive of the sacrament of holy orders, is eminently significant. But, for Peter Lombard, the *signaculum sacrum* ("sacred character"), which holy orders is, transmitted not only a *spiritualis potestas* ("spiritual power") but also an *officium* ("office").[47] And, in conformity with the Church's ancient tradition, priests could not validly exercise their *potestas* in the Eucharist if they were under interdict from the Church concerning their *officium*. But the distinction between the *power of orders* and the *power of jurisdiction*, which was progressively introduced from the middle of the twelfth century, led in the end to the recognition of the validity of the exercise of the first without the second, justifying, by the way, the custom of absolute ordinations practiced since the high Middle Ages. Apart from the pastoral charge and insertion into the ecclesial community, priests were thus the holders of the power of orders which they possessed in a *personal and inamissible* way, through their participation in Christ's priesthood. And where is pneumatology in all this? Forgotten, erased, ignored . . .

At the same time, the rite of ordination reverses the relation between the power of the "keys" and the power of confecting the Eucharist which prevailed into the high Middle Ages. During that period, the "priesthood" was still "seen *first as the power of binding and loosing.*"[48] Granted,

47. Peter Lombard, *Sent.* IV, d. 24, c. 13, no. 127.
48. Y. Congar, *L'ecclésiologie du haut Moyen Age* (Paris: Cerf, 1968) 138–151.

470

this pastoral charge was then perceived as more disciplinary than properly evangelizing. But it still supported the ancient tradition: "Since the Eucharist is seen principally as the sacrament of our incorporation into Christ, since it is fruitful and, even according to some, valid only when it is celebrated in the communion of the Church, it pertains in a certain way to the keys entrusted to the Church."[49]

But for the Scholastics the *reversal* has already taken place. It was carried out through the *Pontificale Romano-Germanicum*, a compilation of Gallican and Germanic traditions mixed with Roman elements (completed in Mainz around 960) which, in the service of the Ottos' religious policies, ended by being fully implanted in Rome around 1150.[50] This pontifical thus was *the* authoritative reference for the Scholastic theology of ordination. Now, through the central rite of the porrection of the paten and chalice, "matter" "informed" by the words "receive the power to offer the sacrifice of the Mass . . . ," the Pontifical stresses first of all the power given the priest to *consecrate the Eucharist*. Thomas can then write: "The priest has two functions: the principal one has for its end the *corpus verum* of Christ; the other and secondary one, the *corpus mysticum* of Christ. This second function depends on the first, and not the other way around. Thus, some are promoted to the priesthood and entrusted only with the first function: such are religious who are not charged with the care of souls. One does not expect to hear the law from their mouths; one asks no more of them than to consecrate. . . . Others are called to fill this other function whose object is the mystical body. The faithful expect to hear the law from their mouths. . . ."[51] One could not be any clearer. We also understand why, since the priesthood is constituted essentially by the power to confect the *corpus verum* of the Eucharist, bishops are simply *superiores sacerdotes* ("priests of a higher rank") (ibid.).

Because of this one-sided valorization of the priesthood as the power to consecrate, the Scholastics' attention tends to be concentrated on the action of the priest *in persona Christi*. Of course, as B. D. Marliangeas has shown, this expression, especially in Thomas, is never without some connection with *in persona Ecclesiae*.[52] But the Church in question remains an extremely general

---

49. Ibid., 146–147.

50. C. Vogel, *Introduction aux sources de l'histoire du culte chrétien au Moyen Age* (Spoleto, 1966) 187–203.

51. *ST Suppl.*, q. 36, a. 2, ad 1.

52. B. D. Marliangeas, *Clés pour une théologie du ministère: In persona Christi, in persona Ecclesiae* (Paris: Beauchesne, 1978) 63–146.

entity: the Scholastics hardly think about the local Church, as we have noted; moreover, it no longer intervenes, concretely, in the call and ordination of ministers, leaving the field open for a direct descent from the priesthood of Christ to the ordinand. The notion of *in persona Christi*, which otherwise is a very precious one in that it expresses how priests in their ministry represent Christ, thus suffers an imbalance.

Similarly, we notice the same imbalance in the theology of the Eucharistic Prayer, whose overall unity has been lost in favor of a narrow focusing on the *moment of consecration*. This development, as P. M. Gy has observed, goes "hand in hand with the promotion of efficient causality."[53] Only the words of Christ at the Last Supper belong to the *substantia sacramenti* ("sacrament's substance"); the other parts of the Eucharistic Prayer are there only *ad decorem* ("for embellishment") or *ad solemnitatem* ("for solemnity"). Of course, the majority of theologians after 1170 (the time this new *quaestio* was born) believe that this *substantia* has its proper signification only within the context of the whole prayer and especially the narrative within which Jesus' words at the Last Supper are enshrined.[54] But this is not Thomas' opinion: "The intention [of the priest], in consecrating this sacrament, would cause these words to be understood as pronounced in the person of Christ [*ex persona Christi*], even if the words [this is my body, this is my blood] were pronounced without those that precede them."[55] And if one objects, with Peter Lombard, that the priest actually says, not *offero* ("I offer"), but *offerimus, quasi ex persona Ecclesiae* ("we offer, as if in the person of the Church"),[56] Thomas replies: "In reciting the prayers of the Mass, priests speak indeed

53. P. M. Gy, "Les paroles de la consécration et l'unité de la prière eucharistique selon les théologiens de P. Lombard à S. Thomas d'Aquin," *Lex orandi, lex credendi*, Mélanges Vagaggini, Stud. Anselm. 79 (Rome, 1980) 221–233, quotation from p. 230.

54. If not, as Prévostin judiciously says, there would be no way to understand the representative and ministerial role of the priest: "Tunc sacerdos uteretur illis verbis significative et tanquam propriis, non representative et tanquam Domini" ("In this case, the priest would use these words for what they mean and as his own, not for what they represent and as the Lord's," Ibid., 228).

55. *ST* III, q. 78, a. 1, ad 4.

56. Peter Lombard, *Sent*. IV, d. 13. See B. D. Marliangeas, *Clés*, 55–60.

in the person of the Church, because they stand in its unity [*in persona Ecclesiae, in cujus unitate consistit*]. But in consecrating the sacrament, they speak in the person of Christ [*in persona Christi*], whose place they hold by the power of holy orders."[57] By thus cutting, at the moment of consecration, the *in persona Christi* from the *in persona Ecclesiae*, Thomas pushes to its ultimate consequences the effects of this "*deadly break*" between Christ and the Church born a century before him.

e) Summary. Such is the final position, *not necessary, of course, but logical,* of a sacramental theology which today we consider as having mixed in too one-sided a fashion (1) an instrumental efficient causality understood in such a way that every supplication can only be judged as insufficient for the realization of the sacrament; (2) a Christological principle so valorized as the foundation of this efficiency that pneumatology is undervalued; (3) a connection of this same efficiency to the hypostatic union so direct that the concrete mediation of the Church is largely erased and the power conferred on the priest by ordination, almost entirely cut off from the Church (the "intention," however, remains), becomes a sort of absolute . . . All this, however, does not keep Thomas' sacramental theology from having its high points, unequaled in many areas by the work of other Scholastics.

Even if the relations we have just established between these various elements are not the mere effect of an intrinsic logical necessity (as if such and such a sacramental trait would always be accompanied by such and such a Christological emphasis, Trinitarian position, or ecclesiological tendency), still these relations are surely not the result of pure chance. The prominence given to the hypostatic union, the holy humanity of Christ, the *Filioque*, the Eucharist as *corpus verum* and the Church as *corpus mysticum*, the function of the Pope as the "vicar of Christ" and head of this Church, the definition of the priesthood as the reception of the power to consecrate bread and wine, the power of the words spoken by the priest *in persona Christi* without any other connection with the Church than the intention to do what the Church does — this prominence, in sum, appears to us *symptomatic of a culture, of a new knowledge.* At the outset of this work we outlined this cul-

57. *ST* III, q. 82, a. 7, ad 3. See Marliangeas, *Clés*, 118–122.

ture's major economic, social, and institutional features. The coherence of this Scholastic theological knowledge is assured by an archaic substructure all the more influential for being unconscious, all the more effective in fashioning the culture for seeming to impose itself "naturally."

2. *The Presuppositions of This Sacramental Theology Relative to the Relation between God and Humankind*

The logic that governs Thomas' discourse is rigorously the same in sacramental theology and Christology. Only, as is proper, the first is down one notch (a separate instrument) from the second (a conjoined instrument). The affirmation of God's action in the human action of the Church poses no further fundamental problems once one has accepted the hypostatic union.

The hypostatic union certainly represents a scandal for the faith, a scandal felt the more vigorously by Scholastic tradition because the representation that undergirds it is joined to a spatial scheme of verticality. God's transcendence appears to be naturally the more affirmed and safeguarded, the more this (infinite) distance is regarded as a *separation* (and even an opposition, since God is then represented as what human beings are not). This makes the "miracle" of the incarnation appear all the more impressive since it annuls in Jesus this immeasurable distance. Thus, far from questioning the dominant onto-theological representations of God, the incarnation only *reinforces* them. Of course, on the thematic level, faith in the incarnate Word necessarily gives rise to a new kind of discourse about God and God's salvific relation of love toward humankind. But these new themes do not call into question the fundamental scheme of God's representation, a scheme whose unanalyzed underlying assumptions are "metaphysical," as we have said.

In saying this, we are not forgetting the important developments in Scholasticism devoted to negative theology, analogy, and the Trinitarian presuppositions outside of which the incarnation of the Word would make no sense. However, it is still a fact that, as the plan of the *Summa*'s *Prima Pars* shows, where God is studied first in God's essence and operation (qq. 2-26), then in God's persons (qq. 27-43), and finally as the principle and end of the created universe, the intra-Trinitarian complexity of God is second in relation to the simplicity of God's essence in itself. Of course, it is always as a theologian and not as a simple "philosopher" that Thomas approaches God's being. However, God's being is not conceived from the outset in a Trinitarian manner; it is always the "simple" notion of *Ens supremum* ("supreme Being") one has of God which governs the fundamental scheme of the representation.

For the believing Scholastic, the mystery of Jesus Christ is a scandal, first of all, as the treatises on the incarnation show, because of the question: How is it possible that God could have become human? This question presupposes that one knows *beforehand* what God is. And as a matter of fact, it is precisely because one knows this (even if under the negative mode of "not knowing") that one finds Jesus a stumbling block: Since according to the attributes of super-excellence recognized in God from the outset — God is simple, perfect, infinite, unchangeable, eternal . . . — how is it possible that God has taken on the nature of a human being who is composite; unfinished; finite; subject to generation, development, and corruption? . . . One thus projects a priori on Jesus, from the aspect of his divine nature, all the onto-theological representations that one has about God; the only stumbling block (if we may say so) is the manner in which the union of divine nature and human nature has been possible.

But the Scholastics never go back to the radical question: *What kind of God* are we speaking about if we can say God integrally revealed God's own self in Jesus? Who, then, is God, if we can in truth say of God that God became human in Jesus? Instead of pondering the upheaval in the representations of God demanded by the event of Jesus Christ, and most of all by his death "for us," Scholasticism continued to let itself be guided by these prior representations. Doubtless it could not do otherwise. In a certain way, one knew too well that "Jesus is God" to allow one's notion of "God" to come into question by meditating on the fact that "God is Jesus" — it being understood, incidentally, that this inversion of terms requires that one come back in a second moment to the first formulation: Christology cannot be one-sidedly "from below."

In summary then, as C. Geffré notes, "even if it is true that he [Thomas] very keenly perceives that God, identified with absolute Being, transcends all concepts, is irreducibly Other, it still seems difficult to state that Thomas escapes the fate of Western metaphysics, that is, at least its attempt to explain all of reality starting from a supreme foundation." This is why, "even if it remains a model of theological epistemology," the theory of the divine names developed by Thomas (Ia, q. 13) carries out "a rigorous reduction of the biblical attributes of God, especially those expressed by verbs of action, to the pure actuality of being. . . . In its will to explain, theology-as-science explains the God of Abraham, Isaac, and Jacob starting from something anterior, a certain human experience of the divine, that is, the idea of God conceived as absolute Being. The hermeneutical criterion for knowing which name, biblical or not, is appropriate for God is its agreement with the notion of God conceived as the First Being."[58] This is precisely the approach our last chapter will attempt to overcome.

II. OUR STARTING POINT: THE PASCH OF CHRIST

1. *The Liturgical Tradition*
One of the most fundamental lessons of the Church's liturgical tradition from its earliest antiquity is that the point of departure for sacramental theology is not to be sought in the hypostatic union, but in the Pasch of Christ taken in its full scope (including, as a consequence, the Church or the Christian fact).

a) Baptism and Christian Initiation. Whatever may be the (Christological or Trinitarian) formulas and baptismal symbolism used (a symbolism of remission of sins or purification and gift of the Spirit, of death and resurrection, or else of new birth), it is always to Christ's *Pasch* or its completion at *Pentecost* or both that baptism is referred in the New Testament. Moreover, as G. Kretschmar believes,[59] at the beginning, different Churches probably had their own baptismal rites: this initial diversity, most likely greater than with the Eucharist (which was more firmly ritualized around the traditions received concerning the Last Supper), was little by little reduced and codified around three principal rites (the first two of which were, for a long period, not well distinguished in certain Churches):

58. C. Geffré, *Le christianisme au risque de l'interprétation* (Paris: Cerf, 1983); "Dieu. 2. L'affirmation de Dieu," *Enc. Univ.*, 5:577–580.

59. G. Kretschmar, "Nouvelles recherches sur l'initiation chrétienne," LMD 132 (1977), 7–32.

baptism itself, put into relation primarily with the death and resurrection of the Lord; its completion by a rite linked to the gift of the Spirit; and last, participation at the eschatological banquet. This trilogy which, in certain Churches, may perhaps go back to the apostolic era, gradually imposed itself everywhere. In its exemplary development during the period of the great mystagogic catecheses, it shows that the initial and initiatory process of becoming a Christian lies entirely within the sphere of the resurrection of the Crucified, in which humanity participates, thanks to the gift of the Spirit at Pentecost, a participation itself understood as the eschatological pledge of the advent of a "new creation" in the process of being born. Christian initiation has never been liturgically practiced in any other way than on the basis of Easter-Pentecost-Parousia.

b) The Eucharistic Anamnesis. This is no less true and is perhaps even more striking for the Eucharist. In conformity with Pauline theology where the Lord's Supper is essentially an announcement of "the Lord's death until he comes" (1 Cor 11:26), the anamneses of the ancient Eucharistic prayers never mention the incarnation as such,[60] even though they list in detail the aspects of the mystery celebrated: suffering, death, burial and descent into hell, resurrection, ascension, sitting at the Father's right hand, parousia, and judgment. The incarnation is certainly not excluded: the initial thanksgiving for creation and salvation history is always oriented toward it; but the anamnesis remains silent on this subject of the incarnation, thereby showing that one cannot understand the anamnesis *except by starting from the "paschal mystery"* of Christ, and not from anything anterior to it. This point is all the more significant in that the anaphoras of which we are speaking developed at a time when the Church was fighting heresies which concerned the hypostatic union. Even though theology was polarized on this point, the Church continued, in its liturgical practice, to live the mystery of Christ on paschal ground.

c) The Liturgical Year in the First Three Centuries. We can make the same sort of observation concerning the genesis of the liturgical year. "For the first Christian centuries, Easter is *the feast,* not only the feast par excellence, the feast of feasts, as the martyrology says today, but the only

60. This is true in all the ancient traditions, both the Eastern and Western Syrian, Alexandrian, Roman, etc. The anamneses never make any mention of *Pentecost.* This can be explained as follows: on the one hand, the core of the anamnesis, centered on the death and resurrection of Jesus (Tr. Ap.; Addai and Mari), developed during the fourth century following the Christological article of the Creed; now, in this article, Pentecost is not mentioned — no more, moreover, than in the third article. Besides this, the Spirit is not the object of a memorial, but its power.

feast, beside which no other could exist."[61] From the historical viewpoint, two questions on this subject must be distinguished: that concerning the weekly Easter on Sunday and that concerning the origin of the yearly Christian Easter.

— *The Weekly Easter on Sunday*

The four Gospels agree on this point: it was on "the first day of the week" that Jesus was raised and showed himself to his friends. This unanimous statement probably comes from a theological intention, and even in all likelihood a *liturgical* intention; it was a matter of providing a foundation for the custom, already adopted quite early among the different Churches, of coming together on that day in memory of the risen Lord Jesus. If, in place of its Jewish name ("the first day of the week") or pagan ("the day of the sun"), the Churches sought to substitute a properly Christian expression (*kyriake hemera*, "day of the Lord" or again "the eighth day"),[62] it is precisely because this day, in contrast with the primary meaning of the Jewish Sabbath centered on the rest of God Creator, is essentially the *day of the resurrection* of Christ.[63] In a certain way, one can say that this day, by the very fact that Christians assemble on it, is to time what the bread and wine of the Eucharist, as elements of creation and human work, are to the world and history: a sacrament of the death-resurrection-parousia of the Lord. Christ's Pasch inscribes itself sacramentally in the flesh of the world through the bread and wine, in the flesh of time through Sunday.

The Sunday assembly (an exemplary realization of the *ekklesia*)[64] seems to be an institution almost as old as the Church; in any case, it seems to have been the rule from the foundation of the Churches, at least in pagan territories, since Paul in 1 Corinthians 16:1-2 testifies to its regularity at Corinth and in the Churches of Galatia.[65] Now, this memorial-day

61. I. H. Dalmais, in A. G. Martimort, *L'Eglise en prière: Introduction à la liturgie* (Paris: Desclée, 1968) 218.

62. B. Botte and J. Daniélou, articles cited in ch. 5, n. 26.

63. W. Rordorf, *Sabbat et dimanche dans l'Eglise ancienne* (texts) (Neuchâtel: Delachaux et Niestlé, 1972) xvii.

64. P. Grelot, "Du sabbat juif au dimanche chrétien," LMD 124 (1975).

65. It was on "the first day of each week" that the collection for the Church in Jerusalem was picked up at Corinth and in Galatia. Obviously done during the Christian assembly, "it takes a place analogous to that which the weekly picking up, on the eve of the Sabbath, of the basket for the poor occupied in Judaism" (Ibid., nn. 31–32); C. Perrot, *Jésus et l'histoire*, 296); X. Léon-Dufour, *Le Partage du pain eucharistique selon le Nouveau Testament* (Paris: Seuil, 1982) 26–30.

celebrates "the *whole* of the mystery of Christ," according to its triple dimension as a "memorial of Jesus' *death* and *resurrection*" and as the concrete anticipation of the *final day* — the Lord's Supper being "naturally the climax of the whole celebration."[66] In other words, the Sunday assembly is the celebration of the Lord's Pasch taken in its entire ambit. It is *Easter every Sunday*. And it seems that for a certain time the Church knew no other liturgical cycle than this weekly Easter.

— The Yearly Christian Easter

The question of the origin of the yearly Christian Easter is difficult and still remains controversial among specialists. A summarization of recent research has been done by J. T. Talley, who provides the foundation for what is said here.

"At present, the majority [of specialists] believe the Pasch of the Quartodecimans was the original form of the primitive community's celebration and not a deviation limited to the province of Asia," even if one may continue to think that the celebration's transfer from the fourteenth of Nisan to Sunday could possibly go back "to apostolic times." Whatever the case, it "seems certain" to Talley that the yearly Christian Easter was "born directly from the celebration of Pesach prescribed by the Law"; that it prolonged "this celebration of redemption in memorial and eschatological expectation of the parousia"; and that it thus had for its object "the memory of the passion, the experience of the resurrection, and the wait for the imminent return of him who had been revealed to be the Messiah."[67]

However, it is not historically certain that this yearly Easter was celebrated in all Churches. Thus, the thesis K. Holl presented in 1927, that until about the middle of the second century the yearly Easter was unknown at Rome, where initially *"only a weekly liturgical cycle"* was celebrated, has now become popular again. In any case, "there are at least several scholars of repute who still think that in the primitive community at Rome there was no yearly observance of Easter before this was introduced by Soter about 165 under influence from the East, where the celebration of Easter Sunday, instituted in Jerusalem around 135, spread to Alexandria and from there to everywhere in Hellenistic Christianity."[68]

It is thus possible that, at least in certain Churches, the weekly Easter on Sunday was celebrated much earlier than the yearly Easter. The latter,

---

66. Grelot, "Du sabbat juif," 46.

67. J. T. Talley, "Le temps liturgique dans l'Eglise ancienne: Etat de la recherche," LMD 147 (1981) 29–60, quotations from pp. 30, 34.

68. Ibid., 32–33.

celebrated in a long nocturnal vigil, was in any case just the unfolding of the "only properly Christian feast," that is, the memorial of the death-resurrection-parousia of the Lord Jesus. *This destroys any notion of a simple "anniversary,"* as Tertullian says, "because anniversaries are celebrated only once a year for the pagans; it happens every eighth day for you."[69] What is more, the Christians' weekly celebration, centered as it is on the broken body and spilled blood of Christ, occurs not on the day of Jesus' death, Friday, but on the day of his resurrection, Sunday.

Starting from this nucleus of weekly and then yearly (or perhaps "and yearly") celebrations, it seems the Christian liturgical year began to develop at the end of the second century into *fifty days of joy.* Although this *Pentecoste* also designates the fiftieth day of Easter at the time of Pope Siricius at the end of the fourth century, before this the term signifies the whole of the period of fifty days as *laetissimum spatium* ("the happiest season"). Hence the prohibition against fasting or praying on one's knees "during the whole of *Pentecoste*" as on Sunday, according to Tertullian and others.[70] "What we have here," O. Casel comments, "is the unique day which begins with Easter and continues throughout the *Pentecoste.* The entire duration of fifty days forms, in the faith of Christians, one radiant day."[71] And this *"great Sunday of fifty days,"* as Talley calls it, "is observed everywhere up to now."[72]

To be more precise, let us say that the liturgical cycle in most Churches, at least beginning in the second half of the second century and during the third, included (1) the weekly Easter and (2) the yearly Easter; both celebrated the death and resurrection of the Lord as a single reality while awaiting his second coming.[73] Finally, there was (3) the extension of this

69. Tertullian, *De Idolatria,* 14. Quoted by O. Casel, *La fête de Pâques dans l'Eglise des Pères* (Paris: Cerf, 1963) 42.

70. Tertullian, "De Corona," 3 (CSEL 70, p. 158); *De Baptismo* 19, 2 (Sources chrétiennes 35). In the same way, *Acts of Paul* (quoted by Casel, *La fête de Pâques,* 37-38).

71. Casel, *La fête de Pâques,* 44.

72. J. T. Talley, "Temps liturgique," 38.

73. About 140, the *Epistula Apostolorum* testifies to "the idea, popular in Christian antiquity, according to which the Lord would return during the Easter Vigil or during the *Pentecoste*" (Casel, *La fête de Pâques,* 21). Moreover, this notion had roots in the "eschatological and messianic" interpretation the Jews had given to the rites of Passover "at least since the first century of our era" (R. Le Déaut, "Judaisme," *Dict. de Spir.,* vol. 8 [Paris: Beauchesne, 1974] col. 1515). The author quotes Mekh. Exod. 12:42 as "an article that has the force of law": "It is during Nisan they were liberated, it is during Nisan they will be again." And he adds, "They even came to place the appearance of

yearly Easter into the "great Sunday of fifty days" of the *Pentecoste* commemorating together the resurrection of the Crucified, his ascension, and the gift of the Spirit and anticipating his glorious return, without the Ascension and Pentecost being detached yet as feast days assigned to the fortieth and fiftieth day respectively.[74]

d) Developments in the Liturgical Year from the Fourth Century On. It is only at the very beginning of the fourth century that the fragmentation of the "week of weeks" of the fifty joyous days begins and the adaptation of the liturgical year to Luke's chronology is attempted. This process develops gradually but seems well established in most Churches "toward the end of this century."[75]

— *The Easter Cycle*

(a) The *sacratissimum triduum crucifixi, sepulti, et ressuscitati* ("most sacred triduum of the crucified, buried, and risen," Ambrose and Augustine) is established;[76] (b) the feast of Pentecost on the fiftieth day (with, moreover, a baptismal vigil matching that at Easter); by counting the days backward, (c) the feast of the Ascension on the fortieth day.[77] (d) The primitive Easter fast of one or more days, connected with the "departure

---

the Messiah around midnight, a tradition confirmed by St. Jerome (*Patrologia Latina* 26:184D)."

74. In any case, such is the overall picture A. Chavasse paints in "Le cycle pascal," in Martimort, *L'Eglise in prière,* 1968 edition, p. 694. In the same way, P. Jounel, "Le cycle pascal," in the new edition of *L'Eglise en prière,* vol. 4 (Paris: Desclée, 1983) 45–46.

75. Talley, "Temps liturgique," 37–39.

76. The three dimensions of this triduum still remain fundamentally connected. At the time of Leo, the Roman Church continued to read in its entirety the account of the passion, death, and resurrection of Jesus because that is, as Leo explains, the *totum pascale sacramentum* ("the whole of the paschal mystery," *Sermon* 59, I; Sources chrétiennes 74, p. 128). When all of Thursday came to belong to this triduum, Easter Sunday was excluded; this contributed to the fragmentation of the "paschal mystery." One can guess the theological consequences of this sort of disjunction between the death and resurrection of Jesus.

77. However, this was not carried out in a simple manner. In a first tradition, Pentecost was centered on the universal mission of the Church according to Acts 2; a second tradition, more rooted in Judaism, which connected it with the renewing of the Covenant and the ascent of Moses at Sinai, combined it with the ascension. See R. Cabié, *La Pentecôte: L'évolution de la Cinquantaine pascale au cours des cinq premiers siècles* (Paris-Tournai, Desclée, 1965); Talley, "Temps liturgique," 39.

of the Bridegroom," is first extended, but in a more directly penitential perspective, to *three weeks*, punctuated by the three Sundays of pre-baptismal scrutiny (with their "baptismal" gospels of the good samaritan, the man born blind, and the raising of Lazarus).[78] Then, at some point in the fourth century, it is extended to *forty days* (from the first Sunday of Lent to the beginning of the Triduum): this was, we know, the final period for the doctrinal, moral, and sacramental preparation of the candidates for baptism and, parallel to that, for the reconciliation of penitents (which took place on Holy Thursday).

— Christmas-Epiphany

Finally, it is also in the fourth century that the Christian feast of *Christmas* appears. It is mentioned for the first time by the Chronographer of 354 at the head of the *Depositio Martyrum* written in 336; its origin could go back to 330 in Rome. This *Natale*, celebrated in Rome on December 25, is placed on January 6 in the East under the name of *Epiphania*. In both cases it is a matter of substituting the feast of Christ "sun of righteousness" (Mal 4:2) and "light of the world" (John 8:12) "for that of the *Sol invictus* ['invincible sun'], which was the symbol of the last resistance of paganism," the celebration of the winter solstice falling on December 25 in the West and January 6 in Egypt and Arabia. Moreover, the adoption of this feast was probably encouraged by the dogma of Nicaea of which it was a major liturgical proclamation.[79] From the semantic viewpoint, let us finally emphasize that if *Natale* means anniversary of birth, it also means, in court etiquette, the *glorification* of the emperor, his accession to the throne, his apotheosis. The Greek term *epiphania* especially has this second meaning, and refers to either the triumphal entrance of a sovereign into a city or the beneficial visitation of a divinity on the occasion of its statue's being officially set up in a town. We find *epiphania* applied to Christ in Titus 2:13, a passage read at Christmas Midnight Mass. It is this idea of *manifestation* or *adventus* (a term very close to the preceding ones in the political language of the court) one finds applied everywhere to Christ, in different ways, on December 25 or January 6: at Rome, on December 25, the manifestation of the Word to Israel through the shepherds, then to the nations through the Magi; in the East, besides this double manifestation, there is also that of his messiahship at his baptism and even, in certain Churches, the first sign of the manifestation of his "glory" at Cana (John 2:11). While the West had postponed, as early as the end of the fourth century, the manifestation to the Magi until January

78. A. Chavasse, "Structure du Carême," LMD 31 (1952) 75–119.

79. Jounel, "Le cycle pascal," 91–96; Talley, "Temps liturgique," 41–42, 47–48.

482

6, the East (from 370 in Cappadocia) had returned the double manifestation to the shepherds and the Magi to December 25, keeping only the baptism of the Lord for January 6.

It is clear from all this that *Christmas-Epiphany is understandable in a Christian manner only in its relation with Easter.* Indeed, the very terms *Natale (adventus)* and *Epiphania* refer us back to the triumph of Christ. A paradoxical triumph, certainly, since it manifests itself in the humility of the flesh, but a triumph of the same order as that of the cross seen in the light of the resurrection. Moreover, this relation is indirectly affirmed by the primitive link the East placed between the manifestations of Jesus' childhood and his manifestation at the beginning of his public ministry (*baptism and Cana*): the childhood stories need to be read backward from the ministry, and from the death and resurrection to which the ministry leads. The very pronounced eschatological perspective of *Advent* (end of the fourth century in Gaul, about 550 in Rome) shows the same thing. It is highly significant that in Rome this season begins with the reading of the gospel announcing the parousia of the risen Christ: the Church can wait for Christ, who has already come at Christmas, only by welcoming him as he comes each day in the Word and Eucharist and by anticipating his second coming at the end of time. *The present of Christ cannot be affirmed in a Christian way except within the memory of his past coming and his always "yet to come."*

Thus, in a certain way, Augustine is right when he sees in Christmas only a simple anniversary, a *Natale* at the head of the *Depositiones Martyrum.* He does not accord it the character of a *sacramentum,* a character he reserves uniquely for the feast of Easter: only Easter brings about each year our *transitus* from death to life with Christ.[80] This is to say, at the same time, that the *natale* of Jesus could not be a properly Christian feast if it were not celebrated *in sacramento,* that is, in the memorial of Easter. Moreover, at Christmas the Church celebrates not only the "birth of Jesus" but, as the liturgy says, "the coming of the Lord Jesus." Some fifty years after Augustine, Leo the Great will take pleasure in stressing the sacramental "today" of Christmas as a "mystery."[81] Christmas is not a Christian feast except as bearing the first fruits of the *sacramentum pascale;* it is only from within the "today" of the resurrection that the *hodie Christus natus est* ("today Christ is born") the Church sings at Christmas vespers can be proclaimed.

80. H. Gaillard, "Noël, memoria ou mystère," LMD 59 (1959) 37–70.

81. M. B. de Soos, *Le mystère liturgique d'après saint Léon le Grand* (Münster, 1972) (Liturgiewissenschaftliche Quellen und Forschungen, Heft 34) 22–27; G. Hudon, *La Perfection chrétienne selon les sermons de saint Léon* (Paris: Cerf, 1959) sec. "Le sacramentum de la Nativité," 191–200.

e) A Theological Interpretation of the Data: Easter as the Starting Point. Lex orandi, lex credendi: if it is true that the Church believes as it prays, the liturgy is a place of outstanding theological importance. Now, the Church of the first centuries knew only one feast, Easter. *Even though it had everything, in the Gospels and Acts, to develop from the start a liturgical year* which would have included Christmas, Epiphany, the Baptism, Lent, Holy Thursday, Good Friday, Holy Saturday, Easter, the Ascension on the fortieth day, Pentecost on the fiftieth, and finally the Parousia, *it is theologically significant that it did not do so during the first three centuries.* Instead, it followed Luke's Gospel which locates the ascension on the evening of Easter (Luke 24:50-53) and Johannine theology which suggests Jesus' glorification and ascension at the moment of his elevation on the cross (the verb *hypsoo*), the "handing over of the Spirit" at the moment of his death (John 19:30), and the pouring out of the Spirit on the disciples on the evening of Easter (John 20:22-23); it also maintained the unity of the twofold language of "resurrection" and "exaltation-ascension" found in the diverse primitive traditions and clearly set forth by X. Léon-Dufour.[82] *It is the whole mystery of Christ's Pasch* — death, resurrection-exaltation, gift of the Spirit, parousia — *that is celebrated as a single reality in memorial.* This happens first each Sunday, and then on the yearly Easter.

This unity of the mystery or sacrament was gradually fragmented into different celebrations beginning in the fourth century. R. Taft is certainly right to object to a simplistic representation of this process: one cannot reduce liturgical evolution to a linear passage from a pre-Nicene eschatology to a Constantinian historicism.[83] However, one cannot deny that, making allowances for the different rhythms in different Churches or schools and for periods of reaction, the overall tendency was certainly in this direction.

This process of the liturgical year's development was not without its ambiguities. The major *risk* was to provoke a weakening of the aspect of mystery in any Christian celebration, to forget its eschatological "today" as a memorial to the advantage of the simple

82. See X. Léon-Dufour, *Résurrection de Jésus et message pascal* (Paris: Seuil, 1971) ch. 2.
83. R. Taft, "Historicisme: Une conception à revoir," LMD 147 (1981) 61–83.

idea of an "anniversary" of such and such a moment in the life of Jesus, to overstress its exemplarity to the detriment of its sacramentality, that is, to obscure the properly Christian aspect of the liturgy whose object, the death of the risen Christ, is at once, according to Leo's expression, *et sacramentum et exemplum:* given *in sacramento,* it is the divine grace of salvation (*conferuntur divina,* "divine gifts are conferred"); given *in exemplo,* it requires our human ethical effort of imitation (*exiguntur humana,* "human effort is demanded").[84] Thus, it was the eschatological memorial of the Pasch, that is, the very specificity of the Christian liturgy, which risked being diminished through the progressive distribution of the mysteries throughout the year. The liturgical cycle was threatened with being perceived as nothing more than a great sociodrama celebrating the *anniversaries* of the major stages in Jesus' life or *acting out,* in their proper chronological succession, the various moments of the Pasch.

However, while it risked being the loser in this area, the Church also found *opportunities* for gain in another area. First of all, on the *cultural* plane, it now gathered in a mass of Christians who, during the sociological transition to a fully pluralistic Church where eschatology had lost its original weight of imminence and where martyrdom as a possible fate was no longer present to rekindle the earlier fervor, could only find a weekly or yearly concentration of the entire Pasch too intense for their tastes. Second, on the *theological* plane, by *connecting human time to Christ's time,* the Church restored to concrete history, including its slowness and heaviness, its significance as the place of salvation which a too vigorous eschatology had sometimes blurred. An inevitable development, this process was desirable in many respects, even if it could drift into distortions.

It is clear that theologically the elaboration of a yearly liturgical cycle in Christianity is a perfectly legitimate operation. But to understand what is at stake on this plane, the best method is to begin by forgetting it. Then one remembers that such a cycle is not necessarily required by the Christian identity, as the first three

---

84. Leo the Great, *Sermon 59,* 1 (Sources chrétiennes 74, p. 129); *Sermon 54,* 5 (p. 104); *Sermon 50,* 4 (P. 80–81). Study of *sacramentum* and *exemplum* in de Soos, *Le mystère liturgique,* 78–98.

centuries show. What is required is the ritual memory of the Pasch taken in all its aspects — death, resurrection, gift of the Spirit, parousia — as forming one single mystery, a memorial written in time on each "Day of the Lord."

To take seriously this history of the liturgy (Christian initiation, the Eucharistic anamnesis, the liturgical year) as a *theological place*, to take seriously, with Congar, the fact that "the privileged place for the tradition" of the Church is not the theological or homiletic writings of the Church Fathers, but the liturgical "monuments" the Churches have left us[85] is to be led to elaborate a theological discourse which starts, not from the hypostatic union, but from Easter. Of course, the hypostatic union (or what was so named in the context of the cultures of the fourth and fifth centuries, and later in Scholasticism) is not a secondary matter. But it is second theologically: the liturgical tradition of the Church has read it *backwards*, that is, starting from the resurrection of Jesus, the Crucified. *Moreover, in doing so, this liturgical tradition continued the evangelical tradition.* We know that the primitive kerygma was entirely centered on the announcement of the resurrection of the Crucified. Similarly we know that the most ancient *redactional* cores of our Gospels are the accounts of the passion, developed of course on the basis of faith in the resurrection, and that from there one proceeded, in "increasingly wider concentric circles," so to speak, (until the baptism of Jesus in Mark, his birth in Matthew and Luke, his contemplation as the Word "before" his coming in flesh in John) from Easter toward the incarnation, and not the other way around. The infancy narratives bathe "in the splendor of the resurrection."[86] As for the confessions of faith, whose major context seems to have been the baptismal liturgy,[87] they testify to the same perspective.[88]

85. Y. Congar, *La Tradition et les traditions*, vol. 2 (Paris: Fayard, 1963) ch. 6 "Les monuments de la tradition" (1. La liturgie; 2. Les Pères; 3. Les expressions spontanées du christianisme). The quotation is from p. 186.

86. C. Perrot, "Les récits de l'enfance de Jésus," *Cahiers Evangile* 18 (1976) 6-7.

87. "The confession of Christian faith certainly finds its origin there [in the baptismal liturgies]" (P. Grelot, *Introduction à la Bible: Nouveau Testament*, vol. 5 [Paris: Desclée]) 78.

88. O. Cullmann, *La Foi et le culte dans l'Eglise primitive* (Neuchâtel:

As in many other areas of thought, the question of the point of departure in a theology of the sacraments is all-important. For us this is true in three ways. *To start from the Pasch,* as we have presented it above, and not from the hypostatic union, is first to locate the sacraments within *the dynamic of a history,* that of a Church born, in its historic visibility, from the gift of the Spirit at Pentecost and always in the process of becoming the body of Christ all through history. To start from the Pasch is consequently to be obliged to build sacramental theology not only on the *Christological* but also on the *pneumatological principle.* Finally, apropos the decisive question of the relation between God and humankind, which the traditional affirmation of God's action in the human action of the Church performing its sacramental actions poses in an unavoidable way, to start from the Pasch is to be led to ask oneself, *"What sort of God* are we then talking about if we are able to affirm this?"* Following what we said above, we must proceed here, as in Christology, by moving backward starting from the death and resurrection in order to understand the incarnation. In this way of looking at things, the first scandal for faith is no longer the union as such, without confusion or separation, of divinity and humanity in Christ or its "how," but how it must be with God if we can confess God's full revelation in the human being Jesus, put to death in the name of the very law of God.

2. *The Inclusion of Jesus' Concrete Life in the Easter Mystery*

a) *The Theological Relevance of History.* We have stressed that the Easter the Church celebrates weekly or yearly includes not only the resurrection moment (thus also the exaltation, gift of the Spirit, and parousia), but also the moment of death in its historical reality. In the mystery of Christ, these two moments are inseparable. For the theological significance of the resurrection is connected to the fact that it is the resurrection *of Jesus,* or better, of this Jesus who had been *crucified.* The question we ask is not simply, *"How* could God raise anyone?" Nor even, "How could God raise anyone before the general resurrection at the end of

<hr />

Delachaux et Niestlé, 1963), 2nd pt. "Les premières confessions de foi chrétienne," 68–69, quotation from pp. 68–69.

time?'' These two questions are not relevant from the viewpoint of the Judaism of Jesus' time when the majority believed in the general resurrection on the last day and, through the "taking up" of Elias, Enoch, and Esdras, knew precedents of "anticipation" of the general resurrection. The question asked is inseparable from Jesus' concrete destiny: What does it mean that God raised this Jesus who had been crucified in the name of God's law? *Who, then, is God if God has justified him who was justly condemned for having blasphemed against God's own law? Does God then contradict God? Or, in the end, have we misunderstood God?* The stumbling block, from the viewpoint of Judaism, is indeed this: *the identity of God.*

Hence, Jesus' resurrection cannot be theologically understood from the New Testament viewpoint except by starting with the *historical trial* which condemned him. A double trial: first, a religious trial, for blasphemy against (the law of) God; second, a political trial, for refusal to bend his knee before any political power because in the reign of God announced by Jesus it is the poor who are rulers. Now, this trial is the trial of the *very history of Jesus.* His dying-for cannot be understood except as the expression of his living-for and thus of his concrete manner of expressing in words and manifesting in deeds the newness of the reign of God whose imminent arrival he announces: a reign of grace and of mercy open to all who, in a spirit of poverty, recognize they have no righteousness of their own before God and thus accept to be welcomed by God by welcoming the message of Jesus. Jesus' concrete history, seen as similar to and different from the understanding that his brothers and sisters in nation, culture, and religion had of God and of the relation of humankind to God, is *theologically pertinent* to the understanding of his death and resurrection.

If we do not take into account the empirical history of Jesus within the context of the Judaism of his time, we would not make any fundamental change by starting from the Easter mystery rather than the hypostatic union. We would still remain in the abstract, having to do not with Jesus Christ, but with a semi-Gnostic Christ who, understood outside history (even if one proclaims his incarnation within history), would function in the same way as the ruling and saving gods of the mystery religions. By the same token, his *historical acta et passa* ("actions and sufferings") are to be taken as the sources: without them his death would evaporate into simply one more mythical episodic event and would lose the properly "human" consistency, without which it could no longer have even its soteriological relevance as a "death for us."

b) The Incarnation Interpreted Starting from Easter. Let us proceed further in our progress backward, in the manner of the Gospels themselves: Jesus' *incarnation* itself, as that of the singular human being he was in history, demands to be included within the Easter mystery. "For us and for our salvation, he came down from heaven," says the Creed. Scholastic theology never lost sight of this soteriological, final purpose of the "redemptive incarnation." But just as it put between parentheses the *ad* of the Eucharistic *esse* in the analysis of the how of transubstantiation, as we showed, so it also overlooked this historical "for" in the analysis of the how of the hypostatic union. Now, as in the Eucharist, this *relational "for" is from the start constitutive of the mystery:* Christology can never be separated from soteriology, even when the onto-theological reflection on the "how" is taking place. From that fact, *the very esse of God demands, and from the outset, to be rethought.* Built on the Easter mystery, rather than the hypostatic union, our sacramental theology challenges us *to reach back to our presuppositions about God with a critical attitude* and thus to pose the radical question already announced: *What sort of God* are we then speaking about if we are able to maintain, in faith, that God offers God's very self to be encountered through the mediation of the most material, the most corporeal, the most institutional of the Church's actions, the rites? This is the question to which we shall turn in our final chapter.

Chapter Thirteen

The Sacraments: Symbolic Figures of God's Effacement

SACRAMENTAL GRACE, OR THE ADVENT OF GOD IN CORPORALITY

To theologically affirm sacramental grace is to affirm, in faith, that the risen Christ continues to take flesh in the world and in history and that God continues to come into human corporality. Thus, the body is acknowledged as the place of God, provided we understand the body, as we have done above, to be the arch-symbol in which, in a way proper to each person, the connections to historical tradition, the present society, and the universe — connections which dwell in us and are the fabric of our identity — are knitted together.

Of course, as a rule, it is not in liturgical celebrations that we experience most dramatically our historical existence as the place of God. We have emphasized that in the functioning of the structure of Christian identity, the element Sacrament is only a point of symbolic passage needing to be veri-fied in the element Ethics, and needing to be understood as a response to God's initial gift to us as Word attested in the Scriptures. Consequently, it is quite normal that a concrete ethics — we have called it the "primary liturgy" — of the relation with others through the practice of justice and mercy be experienced as the privileged place of the effacement of God, a place from which springs up, irresistibly, the tragic question ironically put to the psalmist: "Where is he, your God?" "Where is he? He is here . . . He is hung on a cross," speaks a voice deep inside Elie Wiesel standing before a teenager hanged by the SS at Auschwitz. And J. Moltmann, quoting this astounding expression of the theology of the cross spoken by a Jew, continues: "Any other response would be a blasphemy. There cannot be any other Christian response to the question posed by this torture."[1] At any rate, it seems to us that this conforms to this "stumbling block to Jews" and "foolishness to Gentiles" which, according to Paul, the *Logos* of the cross announces (1 Cor 1).

If it is in concrete historical existence, with its excess of evil, that such a scandal is above all embodied, in return, it is in the sacramental celebrations that it finds its major symbolic expression. For, being ritualistic activities, they stage human corporality as such through its numerous expressive possibilities: postures; gestures; voice either speaking or singing, beseeching or rejoicing. And in this way, they "epiphanize" the threefold body — social, historical, and cosmic — which dwells in the believing subject: the Church-as-body (consider the constant "we" of the liturgies and the signification of this "we" as a particular but integral realization of the universal Church); the body of this Church's history and tradition (consider the words and actions repeated and passed down from generation to generation and interpreted as coming from the apostolic tradition); and finally the body of the universe as creation (consider the symbolic representation of the latter through several of its elements, such as bread and wine, water, oil, light, and so forth). Besides, these ritual expressions are by nature essentially pragmatic, aiming at the communication of humankind with God. Hence, on the level of the symbolic structure of Christian identity, where is it more suitable than in these ritual activities called "sacraments" that God should enter into corporality, that God should ask to be inscribed somewhere in humanity, that God's very glory should demand to be given flesh in the world?

This is why we believe that the dogmatic affirmation, according to which the sacraments are events of grace, is inseparable, on the theological plane, from the humanity of God and, on the economic plane, from the sacramentality of history and the world. Faith in the crucified God dares to affirm that in spite of everything, "God is appearing" in humanity, that the "body of Christ" occurs there, according to Paul's expression. The sacraments are the primordial symbolic expressions of what is read in the Scrip-

---

1. J. Moltmann, *Le Dieu crucifié: La croix du Christ, fondement et critique de la théologie chrétienne* (Paris: Cerf, 1974) 319.

tures; but they are so only in order to apply and veri-fy it in ethical practice. Our final chapter thus presupposes (1) that under pain of ending with what we called a "non-sacramental theology," the Church's traditional affirmation that there is a communication from God to humanity in the sacraments — a communication called by the felicitous term "grace" — is firmly upheld (2) but that this sacramental grace can be understood only through the bursting forth of the simple notion of God, a bursting forth into a Trinity that can be adequately conceived only from the perspective of the *Logos* of the cross. We will conduct first a brief survey of Christology (I); then a brief survey of pneumatology (II). Afterwards, we will explain why the relation of God and humankind affirmed in the sacraments ("sacramental grace") requires the subversion of our representations of God as shown in the preceding twofold survey (III). Finally, we will show how, in contrast, the non-sacramental theology of K. Barth appears to us to be consistent with trans-Christological and trans-Trinitarian presuppositions (IV).

I. THE CHRISTOLOGICAL POLE: THE SACRAMENTS, MEMORIALS OF THE CRUCIFIED WHO WAS RAISED

1. *The Crucified God*

a) Four Theses. To begin, let us lay down four general theses.

First thesis: *it is in Jesus, the Christ, that who God is is revealed to us.*

We must remove from this first thesis any pretention, not to universalism, but to the supremacy pridefully assumed by this universalism. To do so, we must specify that it implies neither "the unicity of exclusion," according to which all religious beliefs, except the Christian faith, could be only vain idolatry; nor "the unicity of inclusion," according to which the "germs of truth" contained in various religions would, after going through a "purification," be monopolized by Christianity, which would save them by discerning what is "authentic" in them; nor "the unicity of indifference," according to which the Christian faith, supposedly devoid of anything "religious," would be placed on another plane and as a consequence, would have nothing to either exclude or include from what other religions say.[2]

2. S. Breton, *Unicité et monothéisme* (Paris: Cerf, 1981) 120–131.

What is said about God in Jesus does not belong to anyone, even if only Christians witness to this "saying" of the cross as such; for they witness to it only in recognizing that it precisely does not belong to them, since Jesus "died for all." This Universal requires that there be a Christian Particularity (the messiahship of Jesus would be reduced to nothing if no one proclaimed it), but this Christian Particularity consists in leaving behind exactly what makes it exist.[3] This contradiction, which cannot be resolved in a harmonious synthesis of opposites, finds its symbol in the cross. Thus, the truth of God manifested in Jesus, since it is the truth of the *Logos* of the cross, comes forth only insofar as Christians testify to it in humility. That they testify to this truth requires the Church as its "sacrament"; that they testify to it in humility indicates that whenever they make this truth into an ideological system using universality as a cloak to hide their own desire to dominate, they pervert it.

Second thesis: the God revealed in Jesus is a *God human in God's divinity*, or as E. Jüngel writes, a God who "determines not to be God without humans" to the point that "God's humanity is already part of God's divinity." In any case, according to the author, this is the meaning of the doctrine of the pre-existence of the Son of God identified with Jesus.[4] As an eco-nomic implication of this theo-logy, our "divinization" (a term very ambiguous, as we will see) goes hand in hand with our "humanization," provided these two notions are freed from their merely psychological connotations. We will have occasion to explain what we mean by the humanity of God which we are speaking of here. Let us simply emphasize that in connection with the first, this thesis demands that we stop projecting onto Jesus, on the basis of his "divine nature," our a priori notions of what God is; these are precisely the ones that need to be converted.

Third thesis, which is intrinsically linked to the preceding: *God is nowhere more divine than in the humanity — the sub-humanity — of the Crucified.* Jüngel again, together with Moltmann, has noted this: "For the classic Trinitarian doctrine, the fact that God became human was an event which in no way determined constitutively the triune being of God. . . . One could think of God as

---

3. "Christian faith will thus be all the more distinctive the less it is so" (ibid., 135).

4. E. Jüngel, *Dieu mystère du monde: Fondement de la théologie du crucifié dans le débat entre théisme et athéisme* (Paris: Cerf, 1983) 1:55.

God without having thought of the *crucified* as God. Jesus' death was as little relevant to the concept of divinity as was this man's life to the concept of the divine essence."[5] This last statement reminds us that the cross cannot simply be identified with the terminal moment of Jesus' story: for the reasons stated above, we understand it as the metonymous symbol for the totality of his life and mission, as the summing up or "integral of his existence."[6]

Fourth thesis: such a revelation of God's glory in the disfigured humanity of the Crucified is tenable only if we think of God *in a trinitarian fashion from the outset.* As is well known, this is the central thesis of Moltmann's work, *Le Dieu crucifié (The Crucified God).*[7]

It is significant in this regard that Hegel, wishing to reconcile Christianity and the Enlightenment by expressing what is hidden but at issue in the "manifest religion" — this theological truth that the theologians had forgotten — centered his reflection on "the obscure word" which causes the sorrow of unhappy consciousness: "God is dead." Further, it is significant that he based this thought of the cross on a Trinitarian doctrine (just as this doctrine demands that thought).[8] Even if we must, as Jüngel affirms at the conclusion of his remarkable analysis of this matter, clearly disagree with Hegel (because against Jüngel's central thesis, Hegel is committed to a determining necessity: God has need of humans to become God, just as humans have need of God to realize themselves), still, we should not forget the necessary mutual dependency between the theology of the cross and a Trinitarian theology: Jesus Christ crucified is "the *vestigium trinitatis*" ("trace of the Trinity").[9] God does not exist except through the mode of being open.

b) Jesus' Cry from the Cross: A Christological Culmination. Since our reflection is centered on the revelation, paradoxical in all respects, of God's glory in the humanity of Jesus crucified, we take as the primary place of this revelation the cry — itself highly paradoxical

5. Ibid., 54.

6. Ibid., 2:219.

7. Moltmann, *Le Dieu crucifié,* ch. 6, pp. 225-324. Latin American liberation theology is often written from this perspective. For example, see J. Sobrino, "La Mort de Jésus et la libération dans l'histoire," *Jésus et la libération en Amérique latine,* ed. J. Doré (Paris: Desclée, 1986) 233-290.

8. G.W.F. Hegel, *La phénoménologie de l'esprit,* trans. J. Hyppolite, vol. 2 (Paris: Aubier-Montaigne, 1941) 258-290.

9. Jüngel, *Dieu mystère du monde,* 1:97-153. On the Crucified as the *vestigium trinitatis,* see 2:192-231.

— which, according to Mark and Matthew (Mark 15:34; Matt 27:46), Jesus uttered on the cross, a cry which, according to them, was his only words: "My God, my God, why have you forsaken me?" Here, we are dealing with some sort of climax. But it is a Christological climax or culmination. This means that the cry in question cannot be interpreted in a psychologizing manner or be imagined to stand in and for itself in isolation from the ensemble of evangelical texts and other components of the confession of faith. Without this context, the cry would risk being the occasion for some sort of neurotic, more or less transported rumination . . . We must approach it in a biblical manner.

Now, on this biblical plane, it is significant that the first Christian generations sought to *muffle* the insupportable tone of this cry. X. Léon-Dufour notes: "Various manuscripts did not hesitate to transform the tenor of Jesus' words by replacing them with the following sentence, 'My spirit, my spirit, lo, you abandon me!' It was one way to remove the scandal of an abandonment by God. . . . In any case, it is a fact that Luke replaces the sentence of Jesus with the words of someone full of confidence in God, 'Father, into your hands I commend my spirit.' . . . For his part, John, who has transformed the account of the passion into a triumphal accession to the throne of the cross, presents a Christ who solemnly declares to all, 'Everything is accomplished.' The situation is clear. One observes that as early as the first century, there is a real difficulty in taking literally what Jesus said, 'My God, my God, why have you forsaken me?' "[10] Specialists in Christology, such as Moltmann or W. Kasper, make similar observations. The latter emphasizes that "already within biblical tradition, the fact that Jesus died abandoned by God was considered shocking."[11]

Many of the Church Fathers, both Greek and Latin (these latter, moreover, misled by the incorrect translation of "the words of my groaning" into "the words of my sins," in Psalm 22:1), attempted to remove the scandal in various ways: in this cry, Jesus speaks in the name of sinful

10. X. Léon-Dufour, "La Mort rédemptrice du Christ selon le Nouveau Testament," *Mort pour nos péchés*, ed. X. Léon-Dufour et al. (Brussels: Fac. Univ. S. Louis, 1976) 40.

11. W. Kasper, *Jésus, le Christ* (Paris: Cerf, 1976) 176.

humanity abandoned by God, or it is a dialogue between his human nature and his divine nature . . .

But the biblical interpretation of Jesus' cry requires that it be understood as a quotation of Psalm 22:1. Do we have here an early interpretation of the post-Easter community[12] or the "authentic" words of Jesus?[13] Researchers remain divided on this point.[14] H. Cousin's position seems to us the most consistent: Matthew and Mark's use of Psalm 22:1 "antedates these authors." Quoted in Aramaic in Mark 15:34, it suggests that the Palestinian Christian community "saw there before everything else a *positive* statement: Jesus is the suffering Just One announced by David and the prophets. On the other hand, a Greek Church was likely to be struck most of all by this cry of *despair*. . . . The author [Luke] forestalls this interpretation by suppressing Psalm 22:1 and replacing it with a prayer which would be more acceptable to Greek Christians, 'Father, into your hands I commend my spirit'; this time it is a reference to Psalm 31:6."[15]

Whatever may be the case with this question of "authenticity" — after all a secondary matter — it is more important to inquire whether this cry is to be interpreted in relation to the *whole* of Psalm 22, and especially to its confident conclusion, or not. If yes — and such is the opinion of Kasper, who nevertheless sees here the expression of a state of dereliction — the question of the Crucified conforms to, as Léon-Dufour observes, "an Old Testament literary genre familiar to believers, that of the biblical lamentation, whose aim "is always praise."[16] This last author, however, provides good exegetical clues which "warn us against introducing the psalmist's opinions into Jesus' cry. This cry must be examined

12. Supporting this is the very frequent use of the psalms in the passion accounts (12 times in Matt, of which 4 are references to Ps 22).

13. Supporting this are the criteria of discontinuity with regard to the primitive Church, especially the fact that such a saying did have a scandalous effect and would have probably been poorly understood.

14. M. Gourges, "Les psaumes et Jésus," *Cahiers Evangile* 25 (1978) 56. Moreover, the author presents good arguments in support of both theses (pp. 54–56). Moltmann holds that this saying is "certainly" a very ancient interpretation by the post-Easter community (*Le Dieu crucifié*, 177). Kasper is more reserved: "It could be that this is a very early interpretation of Jesus' death, seen in the light of the resurrection" (*Jésus, le Christ*, 177).

15. H. Cousin, *Le Prophète assassiné: Histoire des textes évangéliques de la Passion* (Paris: J. P. Delarge, 1976) 142.

16. X. Léon-Dufour, *Face à la mort: Jésus et Paul* (Paris: Seuil, 1979) 163; Kasper, *Jésus, le Christ*, 176.

in itself."[17] In this hypothesis, the praise with which every "lamentation" concludes would find an echo, not in Psalm 22:24, but in the centurion's profession of faith, "Truly, this man was God's Son" (Mark 15:39; Matt 27:54).[18]

Moreover, specialists in exegesis and Christology seem to agree on at least three fundamental points.

First, they reject R. Bultmann's hypothesis of a collapse of faith in Jesus. His cry, coming from the psalms, is a prayer: "*My God.* . . ." Even if Jesus dies under a "why?" of incomprehension of God's ways, he still makes this agonizing why into a prayer.

Second, this cry should be understood *biblically* in its relation to Jesus' mission. His death appeared, in Moltmann's expression, as "the death of his cause. This is what is in the first place the unique characteristic of his death on the cross."[19] More precisely, this uniqueness should be interpreted, as Jüngel emphasizes, in relation to the Law, to the conflict of the Law "with itself" which Jesus occasioned and to which he at the same time exposed himself. A victim of this conflict, he dies as a criminal, that is, "cursed" by God, according to the Law (Gal 3:13), abandoned by God. "He who, having abandoned himself to God, had unleashed this conflict now dies the victim of a total abandonment by God."[20] In any case, contrary to Luke, who interprets this moment as that of the just one abandoning himself *to* God, Mark and Matthew seem to present it as an abandonment of the just one *by* God.

But, Jüngel adds, the psalmist's cry taken up by the dying Jesus "can express abandonment by God only because the relation with God is its condition."[21] In fact, exegetes and specialists in Christology emphasize the paradox to which this cry gives expression: an experience of *dereliction*, that is, of abandonment by God,

17. Léon-Dufour, ibid., 153–154.

18. Ibid., 164. This hypothesis would be further supported by the suggestion of E. Jüngel, *Dieu mystère du monde*, 2:232: the *phōnē megalē* ("loud voice") in which the last words of the Crucified One (Mark 15; Matt 27) were said could be understood as *phōnē theou* ("voice of God"). The author invokes especially Ignatius of Antioch, *Philad.* 7, 1.

19. Moltmann, *Le Dieu crucifié*, 174.

20. Jüngel, *Dieu mystère du monde*, 2:220.

21. Ibid.

yet dereliction lived in *faith* — the dark night of faith, whose climactic expression this cry is. From a biblical viewpoint, Léon-Dufour writes: "God lets Jesus die; God has abandoned him to his enemies; God did not deliver him, and his enemies were right to deride him: 'Let God deliver him now, if he wants to' (Matt 27:43 par.). The affirmation is clear: Jesus is in a state of dereliction, the state of death that is, by nature, separation from the living God." At the same time, however, "Jesus proclaims his faith, the certitude that in spite of appearances, God 'leads the dance.' The paradox reaches its climax: the experience of abandonment is simultaneously shouted and denied in a dialogue that proclaims the presence of the One who seems absent."[22] Some specialists in Christology go even farther, and see here an event *within* God's own self: here God is revealed to us, writes Kasper, *"as the One who withdraws precisely within proximity"*; Jesus "thereby became, in this extreme void, a form hollowed out to receive the fullness of God."[23] That God identified God's self with the human being Jesus doomed to death — and this is precisely what the Easter faith affirms — means, writes Jüngel, that "God has identified God's self with the abandonment of Jesus by God," that *"God defines God's self when God identifies God's self with the dead Jesus."* This is a hard thought (see Hegel) "which even Christian theology has continually evaded."[24] Later on, we will hear this again in Moltmann's works.

That Jesus died as "the Abandoned by God," in the expression of this last author, all the while "fully conscious of God's benevolent proximity," does not demand, as he maintains in the perspective of the Lutheran and Calvinist interpretations of the descent into hell, that it should be necessary to go so far as to evoke "the torments of hell."[25] It seems to us that the integrality of the Saying of the cross, uttered in this abandonment, is delimited by two propositions: on the one hand, Jesus has lived *human existence to its very end*, that is, *death*, a death lived in the *silence of God*, who does not even intervene to save the just one from it, a death

22. Léon-Dufour, "La Mort rédemptrice," 42. In the same way in *Face à la mort*, 149–150.

23. Kasper, *Jésus, le Christ*, 177.

24. Jüngel, *Dieu mystère du monde*, 223–224.

25. Moltmann, *Le Dieu crucifié*, 172–173.

which ultimately cannot be justified by any "reason"; on the other hand, this death is linked with the *Law*: in conformity with the Law, Jesus bears in his person the curse of those who are without-God, he the only one who has consistently "allowed God to be God."[26] Thus, in his abandonment, biblically interpreted, it is *God's very being* that is at issue. In any case, this is what the Church's confession of faith shows, the Church represented in Mark and Matthew by the centurion: "Truly, this man was God's Son!"

If God's revelation thus finds its decisive turn in Jesus' cross, if the relation of God and humankind finds its focal point there also (and, only by way of the cross, in the incarnation), this demands that the representation of "God" be lifted to another plane than that of onto-theology. For, ultimately, the latter is always bound to a God used as a "principle of validation of humans by humans"[27] (see Descartes). By its very logic, onto-theology rules out letting God be God. For this letting-be takes "God" away from us: "God is close to us insofar as God is the one who retreats"; and, at the same time, this letting-be takes us away from ourselves: "God is not close to us except through distancing us from ourselves." However, it is such an essential decentering of ourselves that the historical and concrete reality of the cross commands us to carry out.[28]

2. *A Symbolic Meontology*

Even in its most negative expressions, onto-theology can neither think nor express the radical crossing out of "God" which is at issue here. As we have said above (ch. 2), the me-onto-logy (the study of "things that are not") required here cannot be placed in the tradition of apophatic theology. Although apophatic theology leads toward the "learned unknowing" of God, it does so in an atemporal manner, starting from a conceptual logic and once again attributing to God the totality of the perfections of pure Being. But we collide here with the historical scandal of the cross. Of course, Hegel has taught us that the concept can (and even must) be

26. Jüngel, *Dieu mystère du monde*, 2:229.
27. Ibid, 2:227.
28. Ibid, 1:284, 286.

reread as history, and the rereading of the historical Good Friday as the "speculative Good Friday" is a major moment in the dialectic of knowledge.[29] However, we will not follow this path, which remains eminently onto-theological.[30]

Taking into account the scandal of the cross in its historical empiricalness requires a meontology that overcomes the meontology of the negative onto-theology, thus one which springs from another epistemology: the symbolic epistemology of the *Other*, and not the metaphysical one of the most real *Being*. For it is not humanity "in general" (or "human nature") that is here at issue as the place of God's revelation. It is the humanity of *this* Jesus crucified. More precisely, it is this concrete humanity inasmuch as, like that of the *Suffering Servant*, it is "despised," "rejected," held "of no account" by people, to the point that "[its] appearance" is "marred . . . beyond human semblance, and [its] form beyond that of mortals" (Isa 53:2-3; 52:14). This meontology of the dehumanized Servant, reduced to the fringes of animality — like a "sheep that is silent" (53:7) — is taken up again in *Psalm* 22: the supplicant, "scorned . . . despised by the people," is "a worm, and not human" (22:6); he sees himself a prey to wild beasts, surrounded by bulls, by lions, by dogs, reduced to his mere body — a body, moreover, that is no longer anything but the laughable caricature of a body: a body so wasted, so liquified, so melted away that it is already treated as dead by those who divide his clothing (22:17-18). Like the Servant, the psalmist here touches the absolute bottom of the *"nothing" of humanity*. It is impossible to be "humbled" (see Phil 2:8) any further: one more wavering, and the frontier of death, continually brushed against, would be definitively crossed. Like the Servant, broken by human "iniquities" (Isa 53:5), the psalmist is the victim of the bestial forces of hate.

29. See among others, Hegel, *La phénoménologie*, 2:258-290, the discussion of "manifest religion" (or revealed religion).

30. Hegel's dominant idea — the infinite cannot manifest itself except in the finite, thanks to the historical movement by which the finite overcomes and denies itself even unto death (Christ being precisely the great historical and concrete symbol of this movement) — hides a constant threat to the concrete difference between God and humanity; as Jüngel observes, Hegel did not (or did not sufficiently) recognize "in the crucified the human God who is *in equal measure* human and divine by keeping humans from becoming God and liberating them to be fully human and nothing but human" (*Dieu mystère*

And behold, and such is surely the thrust of our two texts, God *acquits* the victim in saving it just beyond (the Servant) or just before (the psalmist) death. At the same time, the eyes of people are opened; they have accused the just one, they have flogged him, they have ranked him with sinners; but the opposing judgment of God unveils the truth: the evil with which they charged the just one is nothing but *their own evil.*[31] It was our sins, it was "the sin of many" that the Servant carried (Isa 53:12). Yes, "the stone that the builders rejected has become the chief cornerstone" (Ps 118:22). As for the suppliant of Psalm 22, this same word is fulfilled at the moment when, suddenly, the suppliant breaks through to praise (vv. 22-27).

As we see, it is impossible to acknowledge God's victory in the just one without *ourselves* being called into question: it is our own evil, it is the sin of the multitude that has condemned Jesus, that has crushed his body and squeezed the blood out of it. The confession of God's glory seen on the disfigured body on the cross goes hand in hand with the unveiling of our own sin: the condemnation of the Just One shows glaringly our own injustice. How can we thereafter speak of God on the basis of the cross without being ourselves implicated down to the very marrow of our desire? A reversal of desire is demanded here, a reversal that would not only confess our own injustice in the very place where we arrogated to ourselves the authority — founded on our claim to be in the right, the right of "God's" very self — to condemn the just one, but also simultaneously confess a God completely other than our infantile desire's God of Marvels, a God all the more easily manipulable "in good conscience" at the service of our ideologies since God's sublime majesty is only the idealized projection of our own megalomania.

---

du monde, 1:146). On the other hand, the teleological logic that guides the Hegelian dialectic toward what Heidegger calls "the parousia of the Absolute," according to a presentation of the movement of consciousness that "begins in the extreme violence of the desire for the parousia" (33), brings us back to onto-theology, or more exactly, shows the essence of metaphysics, including Hegel's, to be an "onto-theo-logy" (M. Heidegger, "Hegel et son concept de l'expérience," *Chemins qui ne mènent nulle part,* French trans. W. Brokmeier [Paris: Gallimard, 1962], especially pp. 245-252).

31. P. Beauchamp, *Psaumes nuit et jour,* 241.

The symbolic meontology evoked above is thereby doubly required: first, because the reduction of Jesus to the sub-human condition of a *mē on* ("non-being," see 1 Cor 1:28; Isa 52:14; Ps 22:6) is not simply the conceptual fruit of a logic of purification in our representations of God, but is rather the *historical* effect of "demonic" forces behind the "good consciences" of human beings; and second, because we are able to "envisage" the Disfigured One on the cross as the visage of God only if *our* own injustice bursts forth in this confession of faith. As a matter of fact, the title "God's Son," given to Jesus by the Roman centurion at the foot of the cross (Mark 15:39; cf. 1:1), a title later favored by all of ecclesial tradition as the exemplary expression of the confession of faith, immediately places us in the field of *symbolism*. The scheme of his filiation will be a guide to us, all the more precious since we take it as expressive of the most fundamental human task: its application to the relation between Jesus and his Father cannot be disconnected from our own implication. As we have seen, this is the way with symbolism: it is impossible to understand without being understood.

3. *The Son and the Father*

Moltmann's central thesis, "the crucified God," is well known: the abandonment of Jesus "involves the divinity of his God and the paternity of his Father which he had brought so close to humankind. . . . The abandonment expressed by the cry he utters as he dies and correctly interpreted in the words of Psalm 22, must thus be strictly understood as an event between Jesus and his Father, that is, an event between God and God. The abandonment on the cross that separates the Son from the Father is an event *within* God's very self; it is a dissension within God — 'God against God' — although, on the other hand, one must maintain that Jesus witnessed to and lived from the truth of God."[32] The *ecce homo,* pointing to the rejected, the cursed one, is thus also an *ecce Deus.* "This is how God is. Nowhere is God greater than in this humiliation. Nowhere is God more divine than in this humanity. . . . What happens to Christ on the cross is something

32. Moltmann, *Le Dieu crucifié,* 176-177.

that happens to God's very self": not a "death of God," but (and only this) a "death *within* God."[33]

a) *The Symbolic Scheme of Paternity and Filiation.* The theological understanding of this intra-divine interpretation of the death of the human being Jesus is possible only if, rejecting the metaphysical scheme of difference (in this case, that between humankind and God) understood as distance and separation, we conceive this difference according to the *symbolic scheme* of otherness. According to this scheme, every *difference* is intrinsically connected to an *identity* or likeness between two realities. Identity and difference are expressed as "belonging to one another," as Heidegger shows.[34] Thus, not like two full realities which would only be in an inseparable dialectical relation (a little like the front and back sides of a sheet of paper) but like two realities, neither of which comes into existence except as *crossed out by the other* (like presence and absence, as we have observed). In such a perspective, difference-otherness is never so fully "realized" as in the relation of identity-likeness with others. Otherness is the symbolic place where all communication can take place, because the other is a subject, and not an object; because, as we have explained, no relation to any object whatever is significant, that is, human, unless the object in question is already invested by the subject, by its desire and culture.

The language act is obviously not only the exemplary place but also the place of origin of such a relationship. We have shown this beginning with the threefold structure of the linguistic person: under the "neutral" agency of the IT which prevents any immediate relation of the speaking subject to the other and to itself, "I" is possible only in its relationship with what is most different, the YOU (the reverse of "I"); and it is precisely from this tear of otherness, impossible to mend, that the likeness and the reciprocity permitting communication are born. According to orthodox Freudian theory, the resolution of the Oedipus complex comes about under similar conditions: to become a son necessitates consent to the loss of the "idealized father" (the all-powerful not "castrated"), that is, consent to the finitude of the father;

33. Ibid., 232–235.
34. M. Heidegger, *Identité et différence*, Q. 1, 257–276.

such a consent marks the recognition of the difference and, at the same time, the likeness between son and father: the "symbolic castration" of the son (as well as that of the father in his psychic processes) simultaneously joins the lack out of which he is born as a subject, his finitude, his mortality, and his (secondary) identification with the father, himself mortal. The son becomes the *"other-who-is-like"* of the father.

We have learned from Heidegger that the Same (*das Selbe*) is not the Equal (*das Gleiche*): "in the Equal, every difference is abolished, while in the Same, differences appear."[35] In the otherness that marks his selfhood, the son is the "same" of the father, but not his "equal" (according to Heidegger's meanings). Language gives out here, exhausted in paradoxes constantly crossed out. J. Derrida has emphasized this, as we have already noted: the impossibility of adequately expressing "in the consistency of the *logos*" how it is with the alter ego (an impossibility which E. Lévinas attempts to escape, but cannot, at least in his metaphors), if, as is right, the two words are taken at the same level and not as adjective and substantive. Is this impossibility not "a sign that thought cuts off its own breath in the area of the origin of language as dialogue and difference"? There is nothing "irrational" about this: this origin is precisely the "concrete condition of rationality," but "there is no way it can be apprehended in language."[36] In this matter, language can only metaphorically turn itself around and thus go back toward its place of origin, the symbol. Psychoanalytic discourse finds here, we believe, its singular and irreplaceable relevance, and this is what has led us to avail ourselves of it to evoke the question of origin through the symbolic scheme of filiation.

To speak about God is inevitably to speak about humans; to speak about the relation of humans to God is inevitably to speak about relations between humans. Furthermore, none of this can be done except on the basis of our humanity (granting, of course, that theology may have something important to say about anthropology). If things are so, why should we not attempt to elaborate

35. Ibid., 280.
36. J. Derrida, "Violence et métaphysique," *L'écriture et la différence* (Paris: Seuil, 1967) 187.

our discourse about the relation between humans and God in Jesus crucified on the basis of the symbolic *scheme of otherness-likeness* that we have just recalled? How can we even do otherwise in what concerns us here if, as we believe to have shown, this scheme, entirely structured by the assent to the "presence-of-the-absence," carries us closest to the human way of "existing"? Let us go farther still: If the Christian tradition has singled out the terms "son" and "father" to name Jesus and the Other who is like him in their identity, how can we possibly avoid such a scheme?

b) The Son Made Perfect. In any case, this scheme opens to us an interesting approach to the mystery of Jesus' death, that is, of its salvific fecundity "for the many." For the character held as *unique* in this death is linked neither to the physical sufferings of the crucified nor to some impressive nobility in his tragic final hours. On the contrary, whereas the deaths of Socrates, of certain Stoics, of many zealots, and of those Christian martyrs, the account of whose "passions" relate their powerful witness in the eyes of their sometimes disconcerted torturers, were "beautiful deaths," Jesus' death was awful and pitiable; he was "distressed and agitated" during his agony (Mark 14:33); he died beseeching "with loud cries and tears . . . the one who was able to save him from death" (Heb 5:7). Now, it is precisely this anti-esthetic dimension that allows us to theologically decipher its singularity: "although he was a Son," continues the Letter to the Hebrews, "he learned obedience through what he suffered" and was thus led to his own *teleiosis* ("perfection," Heb 5:8-9). As we have already noted (ch. 8), this *teleiosis* designates his priestly consecration by the rite (here in metaphor) of "filling the hands"; it thus designates his "being made perfect." Freely consented to in a "docile listening" (*hypakoe*) to the word of the Father, his death thus consecrates his *perfection of Son-in-humanity*, not (in contrast to the ancient high priest) by being snatched from a too close solidarity with humanity, but on the contrary by a *radical plunge into this "all the way to the end" of humanity, which is death*, and a death experienced *in the silence of God*. It is this fraternity with humankind, sorrowfully offered "with loud cries and tears" as a prayer (a sacrifice-prayer according to the current of the spiritualization of sacrifice which we have discussed) and hearkened to by God, that brings him to his perfection as Son.

c) The Other Who Is Like God. This perfection finds its highest theological expression in the cry of Psalm 22:1. Jesus reveals himself to the centurion (the representative of believers) as "Son" by living out his relation to God as to "the One who withdraws precisely within proximity," in Kasper's beautiful expression. Thus, God manifests God's self by withdrawing. It is precisely at the moment when the absence of God is most acute in this Crucified One that the Church acknowledges him to be *the Other who is like the Father.* This, at any rate, is "the image of the invisible God" (Col 1:15) which Mark, Matthew, and the Letter to the Hebrews offer us.

To become a child, we have said, is to learn — but here it is a matter of an apprenticeship that takes place before all learning, of an apprenticeship that happens in the very process of becoming-subject — to recognize others as like us in their very otherness; and, simultaneously, it is to learn to consent to this radical otherness, outside of which there is no likeness. The price of such a consent is high: nothing less than the choice of a freedom that is responsible for the others, the brothers and sisters, an inescapable responsibility from which no others — precisely because they are "other" — can relieve me; nothing less that the handing over of each to himself or herself by and for the Other. To attain filiation and love of brothers and sisters — a task never achieved — requires a costly sacrifice which dismantles the imaginary all-powerfulness to which everything in us tenaciously resorts in order to dispense us, as far as possible, from the courage to be, from the courage to exist in an irreplaceable autonomy.

In dying as the "Abandoned of God," Jesus is *left to himself,* delivered over to his irreducible finitude of being-for-death, to his world, to his enemies, without God intervening to save him, him the Just One. Now, it is in the experience of this total letting-God-be-God, of this *radical difference* of God, so other that God recedes into God's silence — it is there his *likeness* with the Father is fully revealed. We have seen in this his "anti-sacrifice," that of his filiation and of his union with his brothers and sisters: on the one hand, his refusal to "use" God for his own benefit or to play at being God and his consent to let God be God; on the other hand and at the same time, his acquiescence to his fraternal solidarity with humankind, even to an unjust death which had every appearance of a disavowal of his mission.

d) Salvation: Exemplarity and Solidarity. By acquitting everyone's victim through the resurrection — for if he is dead for all, this is only because he was killed by all — God causes the injustice of all to burst forth. Confident of having the right on their side — God's right, God's Law — people believed they were acting justly; they believed they knew how it was with God. But this "knowledge" was nothing more than religious ideology; they purported to act on the authority of the Other, but they were guided only by the desire to justify their own behavior. Lo and behold, the weakness of the Crucified is revealed as the strength of God. This weakness is strength since it reveals to humans their perversity: the evil with which they burdened their victim was in fact *their own evil;* and it is precisely this recognition that is *their salvation,* the salvation of the world.

In view of the fact that humans, all humans, resemble the first Adam who, though made of earth, wished to become like God (Gen 3:5), "was it not necessary" (see especially Luke 24) that there would live in history a *unique subject* who would burst open this idolatrous misunderstanding of God, a misunderstanding itself misunderstood, ignored, disguised behind the facades of religious traditions, theological discourses, ethical justice? But what descendant of Adam could carry out such a subversion? It was necessary, "according to the Scriptures," for God's very self to get involved. Jesus, the Christian faith confesses, is the *new Adam* (Rom 5) "who, though he was in the form of God, did not regard equality with God as something to be exploited, but emptied himself . . . to the point of death" (Phil 2:6-11), so that humans, finally recognizing their injustice, could enter into a conversion which is their salvation.

The fact that this came to pass once within history changes the face of history. Something new has happened within humanity, something which is called "*salvation,*" something which concerns God as much as the world: "the transformation, the crisis, the revolution in the image of God leads to the crisis, the change, in a word, the redemption of the world."[37] To be theologically understood, this "redemption" requires that the two categories of *exemplarity* and *solidarity* be put together. Jesus' example by itself would give us only a model of a prophet or martyr to imitate and would risk delivering us over to the worst of moralizing

37. Kasper, *Jésus, le Christ,* 252.

perfectionism. Conversely, solidarity by itself would veer in the direction of an automatic substitution which would leave us altogether outside the game. Moreover, one has a difficult time understanding how it would be possible to recognize anyone as an example, let alone a unique example, without feeling oneself at the same time in solidarity with that person.

e) God Otherwise. Jesus did not die for an "idea" — not even a new idea of God. Nevertheless, his death implies a "revolution in the image of God." *A bursting open of the simple notion of "God"* is required here. The paradoxical revelation of the glory of God in the disfigured face of him whom humans have reduced to nothing is not tenable unless this simple notion is turned around and made to open itself from within. The crossing out of "God" in the person who died in the *morphe doulou* ("form of a slave," Phil 2:7) has, we have emphasized, a meontological significance, not in the sense of the traditional negative onto-theology, but in the *symbolic and historical* sense because it was the effect of human actions. In this crossing out, it is the humanity of the divine God that is revealed to us. Such a formula should not be understood as a simple metaphor (except to remind us that metaphor touches on what is most "real" in human "existence"). It does not simply mean that God is more human than we, who are so often in-human; it says that God's *esse* cannot be said without being *crossed out by the symbolic Other,* of which the historical other is the concrete mediation. Thus, moving beyond the metaphysical opposition between immutability and becoming, this crossing out says, according to Geffré, that "it is the very nature of God, so to speak, to become other while remaining God" or in Jüngel's words, that it belongs to the *esse* of God to come into the world only "by allowing God's self to be expelled from it,"[38] that is, by coming into the world as God crucified in the name of "God" (the Law), crossed out by humankind. In accord with the Johannine agape, it speaks of God as essentially Gift. Thus, it speaks of God *in another way.*

Being symbolic, this crossing out of God affects us from the out-set by making us liable to criticism. Indeed, it puts into question,

38. C. Geffré, *Le christianisme au risque de l'interprétation* (Paris: Cerf, 1983) 166; Jüngel, *Dieu mystère du monde,* 1:96. The Being of God is in God's "coming."

and in a concrete way, the historical relations between humans who find themselves incapable of tolerating a God who would not be for the good people and against the evil people, who would pay workers who come at the last hour the same wage as those who came at the first, who would throw a feast to celebrate the return of the prodigal who has squandered his inheritance, who would take away from those who do not have and would give to those who do, who would label blind those who claim to see . . . Such a God, insupportable, defying every established order (especially religious) and every good reason (again, especially religious) humans have given themselves cannot but be rejected, expelled, sacrificed. This "blasphemer" does not even have a right to the kind of death accorded the false prophets, stoning: he is robbed of his death by being condemned to the torments reserved for political rabble-rousers and criminals. Our crossing out represents this *historical and symbolic sub-humanity*, and not the meontology of an uncreated Nothingness.

Therefore, it is impossible to separate the divine kenosis from the one that must be carried out in ourselves: our corporality is charged with becoming the place for this kenosis. In our corporality, the most distant is also the closest, the most divine is also the most human . . . Thus we are obliged to give to this God the body of humanity that God asks of us. Corporality is God's place. God, whose being is to "not be" (see 1 Cor 1:18; Phil 2:5-8), reduced to nothing as God has been by humankind, finds God's "sacrament" in those who have themselves been reduced to "not-others."

II. THE PNEUMATOLOGICAL POLE: THE SACRAMENTS, MEMORIALS IN THE HOLY SPIRIT

1. Preface: The Necessity of a Third Term

The Christological dimension of sacramental theology is not theologically acceptable unless it is balanced by a second, pneumatological dimension, and this for two reasons which we shall explain briefly.

The first is that the memorial of Jesus Christ, existential as much as ritual, as a living memorial stirring the (personal and collective) present, is possible only if God takes a hand in it. *Spirit* is the personal name traditionally given to what, *of God,* gives present and future vigor to such a memorial of the past. Lacking this, the memorial would either refer to an ahistorical and mythic Christ or to a Jesus viewed as a mere prophet or an exemplary martyr. In neither case would it be any longer a *sacramental* memory, that is, one implying the involvement of the Risen Crucified in the historical "today" of believers. In order for the past of what is commemorated in the narrative of the institution (of the Eucharist) to be sacramentally given us in the present and to open a future for us, the Spirit must bring it to the memory of the Church. This is why this story, pronounced as a memorial, cannot be separated from the request for the Spirit at the *epiclesis.*

Moreover, seen in the light the cross, God's humanity implies the *difference between "God" and "God,"* in this case, between what apostolic tradition calls the Father and the Son. We welcome these two characterizations as those which have been favored by ecclesial tradition. If then, on the basis of this tradition, we conceive the difference between God and God according to the symbolic scheme of paternity and filiation, we are required to bring in a *third term.*

For as soon as there is a subject, hence language, one is no longer two, but three (the third designating the cultural and social milieux, the symbolic order, the *Other* to whose law both are subjected in order to "understand" one another). This is, of course, valid for the development of the young male human being as a son-subject in relation to his father-subject (the Oedipus complex) — and which we have taken as one example; for "the symbolic order demands the recognition of (and by) the Other, but also . . . the recognition in the Other as the place of the Law."[39]

Hence, if we accept that the terms "Father" and "Son" are, according to ecclesial tradition, especially suitable for characterizing God's and Jesus' identities, their relation *demands* the introduction of a third term: its name is "Spirit." This goes equally, although at a different level of course, for the relation of filiation established by Jesus *between believers and God,* according to Galatians 4:6 and Romans 8:15-16: Is it not, after all, the Spirit that allows them to cry "Abba! Father!" and to recognize that they are no longer

39. G. Rosolato, *Essais sur le symbolique* (Paris: Gallimard, 1969) 118.

"slaves, but free"? Through the Spirit, then, God, as Father and Son, "gets past the ecstatic face-to-face"; besides this "differentiated communion within God," it is also through the Spirit that the opening of this God "to what is not divine" is realized.[40]

2. The Spirit, or God Different

a) The Neuter. It is significant that in contrast to the names Father and Son which come from anthropology, the name "Spirit" comes from cosmology. In the Bible, in fact, this name is linked to a threefold cosmic symbolism. First is the symbol of *space*. As H. Cazelles suggests, the Hebrew *ruah* is most likely connected with the gods of the air and atmosphere in Egypt and at Ugarit. At its origins it designated "this vital space independent of humankind but upon which humankind depends for its life. It is the area between earth and heaven which can be calm or violent. . . . It can be the symbol of emptiness and evanescence, things that humans cannot seize the way they grasp solid objects or dispose of water."[41] Without this *vital space* between God and itself, humankind, lacking *ruah*, could only die. It lives only by maintaining *distance* between itself and God. The paradox of the Spirit is this: it makes one participate in God in the same measure as it maintains God's radical difference. According to Cazelles, such is the work of the Spirit hovering over the primordial waters in Genesis 1:2; "like Shou, the god of the atmosphere in Egypt," it "interposes itself between heaven and earth . . . so that the atmosphere may appear and humans and animals may *breathe*, may become 'breaths of life.' "[42]

40. Geffré, *Le christianisme*, 183. Of course, as the third properly divine term, the Spirit is in *no way deduced from our methodological approach.* Rather, we receive its revelation from the Scriptures on the basis of their interpretation in the Church. But it is no accident, we believe, that the recognition of God as "Father" and of Jesus as "Son" led the Church to confess a third term: the Spirit. This third term was "necessary" *from the viewpoint of* the anthropological symbolism that governs the father-son relationship.

41. H. Cazelles, "L'Esprit Saint dans l'Ancien Testament," *Les quatre fleuves* 9 (Paris: Beauchesne, 1979) 5–22.

42. H. Cazelles, "Esprit et Rouah dans l'Ancien Testament," *L'Esprit Saint dans la Bible, Cahiers Evangile* 52 (1985) 22–24.

The second symbol, *wind* or *breath,* is linked with the preceding and is common in the Bible: a violent wind or cyclone which, associated with the chariot or horses of fire, carries Elijah up to heaven (2 Kgs 2:11) or, taking hold of the prophets and Saul, puts them into a trance (1 Sam 10:6; 19:20-24) or, on the contrary, a gentle breeze which marks the subtle and ungraspable passage of God before Elijah (1 Kgs 19:12-13). Whether violent as the tempest or elusive as the breeze, the Spirit envelops Gideon like a cloak (Judg 6:34); it penetrates certain judges, like Samson with his superhuman strength (Judg 14:6-19); it "enters into" Ezekiel (Ezek 2:2; 3:24), "falls upon" him (11:5), "lifts" him (3:12-14; 8:3; and so on). In sum, it *penetrates* humans like the breath that makes them live: the breath of life (*neshama*) which Yahweh breathes into the nostrils of Adam to make him a living being (Gen 2:7) is interpreted as *ruah* in Psalm 104:29-30 or in Ezekiel 3:5, 6, 8, 10; if Yahweh takes back his breath, it means death. Sometimes this symbolism of the Spirit's penetration to the most intimate depths of humans is evoked through the *oil of anointing* which permeates the bodies of the kings, Saul (1 Sam 10:1, 6) and David (1 Sam 16:13). Penetration by the Spirit is such that even the prophets' bodies become word, with this constant paradox that they can say "Oracle of Yahweh," "Word of the Other" at the very moment when this Word takes hold of them, making of their bodies a living parable.

The third symbol, *fire,* is associated with the "great wind" in the account of Pentecost. Among the numerous, and often opposed, meanings fire can have in the Old Testament (the fire of the benevolent presence of God, the fire of judgment which consumes the evil . . .), there is a particularly prominent one in the theophanies: that of God's *holiness,* of God's otherness, manifested by the luminous cloud of Exodus or the smoke at Sinai. Moreover; the latter is reinterpreted as fire in Deuteronomy (4:12; cf. 5:4). Fire, which no one can seize without being consumed, is the symbol of the absolute otherness of God, whom no one can see without dying (Exod 33:20). This is why it is "from the midst of the fire" that God speaks to God's people at Sinai, just as it is "out of the bush" that God reveals God's name to Moses (Exod 3). But if this fire keeps God apart, it is also the place from which God communicates with humankind. Fire is thus a particularly expressive symbol for the paradoxical twofold function of the Holy Spirit: it is simultaneously the agent of God's *recession* from the world in God's absolute holiness, and of God's *procession* into the world through the communication of God's holiness to humans. "The only way we can think of the Spirit is in terms of this paradox," writes P. Beauchamp. "It is the communication, in an act of unsurpassable quality because it is a divine act, of what is exclusively God's." Like Wisdom, to which it is akin, the same author continues, the Spirit is *attracted by its opposite:* it "shows God's transcendence precisely by touching the extreme limit of God's creation at its most intimate point."[43]

Vital space between heaven and earth, violent wind or gentle breeze, fire which burns without consuming or permits humankind to communicate with God without dying — these various symbols all point toward the radical otherness-holiness of God. The Spirit is God as *ungraspable,* always-surprising, always-elusive; it is the God who cannot be managed, continually spilling over every religious institution; it is the God who is omnipresent, renewing the face of the earth and penetrating to the deepest recesses of the human heart, but at the same time indescribable according to human categories and without an assignable place among human works. Without its own proper name, the Spirit is a kind of anti-name of God. Without a face, it allows itself to be described only through cosmic images (space, wind, fire, and also water in the fourth Gospel). Feminine in Hebrew, it is neuter (*to pneuma*) in Greek, the language that has been most influential in Christian theology.

This *neutral position* is consistent with the Spirit's cosmic symbolism. To designate it, the Council of Constantinople did not hesitate to coin the neologism "the Lordly" (*to kyrion*). God in the Neuter. *Ne-uter:* neither the one nor the other, neither the Father nor the Son, it is their very Difference; and, at the same time, by preserving their difference, it makes possible their communion, just as by preserving the difference of God, it makes possible God's communication with humankind; just as by providing space between humans, it makes possible for them to communicate at Pentecost. It is as the mediator of the difference between God and God that the Spirit is, according to Augustine's theology, the

---

43. P. Beauchamp, *Le récit, la lettre et le corps* (Paris: Cerf, 1982) 131–132.

nexus amborum ("the nexus of the two"), the *charitas substantialis et supersubstantialis* ("the substantial and super-substantial love") of the Father and the Son and that it "proceeds from the Father and from the Son" *tamquam ab uno principio* ("*as from one principle*"),[44] just as it is on the basis of the difference-otherness it establishes that language can forge an alliance between subjects. In God, the Spirit is, in O. Clément's formula, "this mysterious third term which effects a difference without the slightest separation."[45]

b) "The Unrevealed Revealer." The Spirit's neutrality, together with its different cosmic symbolisms, is in the background of the various hermeneutical traditions concerning it. These traditions continually place the Spirit both in the *"beyond" of God* and in the *"before and beneath" of humankind:* the Spirit is God both in God's absolute difference and in God's most intimate communication with humankind, God as the unknown beyond every word and as the inspirer of the unspoken intimations of the truth of every word before all statements and in the fissures of human discourse; God as ex-static opening who is in God's self only by moving out of God's self and who creates human respondents in God's own image — also ex-static — who do not find themselves except by losing themselves; God as the omnipresent, and by that very fact never at humans' beck and call, never under human dominion.

The Spirit has such a paradoxical position that tradition has treated it less as an "object" of knowledge than as the principle of all knowing (or unknowing) of God, less as "revealed" than as *"the revealer."* It is less that which must be theologically pondered than that which makes us able to ponder: homologous to Heidegger's *es gibt* that allows us to "let be," it is the *gift-giving agent* which enables the believer to let God be God and thus to establish a true communication with God. Its function in the economy of Christian life bears less on the contents of thought as such than on the truth that is always to be accomplished in our *attitudes* toward God, that is, on the never fully achieved passage from a re-

---

44. Augustine, *In Io. evang.*, tr. 105, 3 (*PL* 35, 1904). See B. de Margerie, *La Trinité chrétienne dans l'histoire* (Paris: Beauchesne, 1975) 159–172; Y. Congar, "Le rôle du Saint-Esprit dans l'eucharistie selon la tradition occidentale," *Je crois en l'Esprit-Saint*, 3:116–134.

45. O. Clément, *Le visage intérieur* (Stock, 1978) 80–81.

lation of slaves to a relation of children: "And because you are children, God has sent the Spirit of his Son into our hearts crying, 'Abba! Father!' So you are no longer a slave, but a child" (Gal 4:6-7). The Spirit is that which renders possible our filiation in the Son; it is that which attests and sustains it in us, that which enables us to arrive at the prayer of petition and thanksgiving, that which enables us to become "eucharistic people." It is that which gives us the true words to speak about God, that which renders authentic the self-implication which characterizes the language of faith. At the level of believers' language acts, it concerns less their *locutionary* dimension, as objects of discourse, than their *illocutionary* dimension — it "makes possible 'eucharistic' discursive acts," that are carried on by sons and daughters — and their *perlocutionary* dimension — that is, in this case, their dimension of witness.[46] Of course, it is also an object of discourse, as we are making it now. But this object is such that pronouncements about it have relevance only by sending us back to the two other dimensions of language just mentioned: the truth of such an "object" results from its "resolution" into language or its dissemination in writing and, finally, in the body.

There is some truth to Gregory Nazianzus' statement, "The Old Testament preached the Father clearly, and more obscurely the Son; the New preached the divinity of the Son and insinuated that of the Spirit. At present, the Spirit lives in us and manifests itself to us more clearly."[47] There is some truth in the sense that the Spirit, in its fully divine identity, seems almost to escape the very letter of Scripture. The Church Fathers often remarked upon this: although ever present in the Scriptures because it is the principle inspiring the community's selective memory as well as the principle of the Scriptures' conspiring to reveal Christ, still the Spirit holds but little place there. In the letter of the Scriptures, it is as though its place were *vacant*. This place is engraved in intaglio; it is like the blank spaces that permit the "characters" to be both differentiated and connected into words, the words into sentences, the sentences into discourses, the discourses into books,

46. J. Greisch, "Le témoignage de l'Esprit et la philosophie," *L'Esprit Saint*, ed. R. Laurentin et al. (Bruxelles, ed. univ. Saint-Louis, 1978) 90.

47. Gregory of Nazianzus, *Discourse* 31, 26 (Sources chrétiennes 250), the fifth of the "theological discourses."

the books into parts, each endowed with the plenitude of a finished work but whose achieved character is perceptible only because it refers to all the others: "The same Holy Spirit accomplishes the Law and the Prophets, exactly as Wisdom unites them."[48] Finally, the Spirit is the open space that both differentiates and binds together the two Testaments: as *inspirer*, it splits the letter into "figures," not presenting the letter in itself except by opening it to something else than itself, to a new writing; and thus it sets the inspired letter down only as a passage toward something other than the letter. The relation between the two Testaments is the representation of this passage. And it is this same passage which brings about the confluence of the letter's various figures into a single Christic principle of integration.

Thus *the paradox of the Spirit*, stated above, finds its figure in the letter of the Scriptures: present everywhere in the letter in its most historically determined and irreducibly opaque aspects, it is nevertheless absent from it. As the "seal of every letter,"[49] the cross of Christ carries this paradox to its theological culmination: it is "through the eternal Spirit" that Christ "offered himself without blemish to God" (Heb 9:14). Thus, the Spirit is what radically *differentiates* "the One who is the inaccessible origin" from the unique, the "only one" who represents us by coming to occupy the place at the other extreme from God: "the other extreme of the human limit,"[50] that of death in a flesh similar to that of sin, that of the *ecce homo* who no longer has even a human face (Isa 52:14), that of the slave reduced to nothing by humans and dying abandoned by God. And at the same time, the Spirit is what *connects* these extremes, and thereby leads the centurion at the foot of the cross to confess the Other who is like the Father.

"There are no paths toward Wisdom, because all such paths are in her, and this is why one says, 'The beginning of Wisdom is this: Get Wisdom' " (Prov 4:7); this is also why "no sage can boast of being wise." As a "non-knowledge" par excellence, wisdom is "the question of questions."[51] As the pure, gracious gift of

48. Beauchamp, *Le récit*, 131.
49. Ibid., 36.
50. Ibid., 133.
51. P. Beauchamp, *L'Un et L'Autre Testament* (Paris: Seuil, 1976) 120–121.

God, it is the very principle of all knowledge of God. So it is with the Spirit. It is, to avail ourselves of Heidegger's expression (but on an entirely different level from him), "the way which sets everything 'on the way' "; a way which travels, that is, not outside us but within us; a way which is nothing else but the labor of passage, of "passover," which takes place within ourselves; a way which is unending because existing only through its way-making. It is the way of "working through" which, plowing the field that we are, causes us to become sons and daughters: it is "with sighs too deep for words" that the Spirit, in us who "groan inwardly" and are, with all creation, "in labor pains," fashions us in view of our filial adoption (Rom 8:18-28), just as it is through its cries in us that we can say "Abba! Father!" (Rom 8:15-16; Gal 4:6). The question of questions, the Spirit is also beyond all language, the *other side of the letter*, the breath that animates the body. Through it, the Book, expression of the community, comes to its truth: the Spirit inscribes it in the *body* of the community, thus making the community the primary witness of the living God. As has been often remarked, Jesus left no writings. The letter of God, placing a seal on any other letter, is written in his crucified body only insofar as it is crushed to the vanishing point: thus it lets the Spirit come forth. According to John 19:30, in breathing his last, Jesus *paredoken to pneuma* ("handed over the spirit"). Such is his "tradition," so that the letter may pass into the body, according to the promise of the new covenant (Ezek 36:26-28; Jer 31:31-34).

God in the neuter. Blank space of God, anti-name of God, the Spirit is this third term which, while fully of God's very self, works to subvert in us every idolatrous attempt at manipulating God (whether at the conceptual, ethical, or ritual level . . .), and to keep perpetually open, as "the question of questions," the question of God's identity: God crossed out, never so divine as in God's erasure in the disfigured humanity of the Crucified. What can this Spirit whisper to us concerning God, this Spirit who "has every name" and thus is "the only one who cannot be named," if not, as Gregory of Nanzianzus lyrically expresses it, a calling forth within us of "a hymn of silence,"[52] an inarticulate breath, a "sigh

52. Gregory of Nazianzus, *Poèmes dogmatiques*, PG 37:508.

too deep for words" (Rom 8:26), a discourse which breaks down into pure "cries" directed toward the Father (Rom 8:15; Gal 4:6)? As the Difference *between God and God*, the Spirit is simultaneously the very Difference *between God and humankind*. We shall now show that this difference finds a way to inscribe itself in the difference *between humans* and, in each, in this difference between the body and the word from which every subject comes forth.

3. The Spirit, or the Difference of God Inscribing Itself into Human Corporality

We have emphasized this paradox of the Spirit: the Spirit is God as different, unmanageable, always eluding, like the wind which blows "where it chooses" (John 3:8), the control of any knowledge or any institution; at the same time, it is God closest to humankind, to the point of inscribing God's very self into our corporality in order to divinize it. It is God as the most distant and the closest. Better, in order to avoid the ambiguities of this spatial language and to remain within our symbolic approach, it is the very Difference of God never so clearly acknowledged in God's radical otherness as in God's communication with humankind.

Everywhere throughout the Bible there appears this paradoxical impregnation of humans by the all-holy God through the *ruah:* from humankind's creation (Ps 104:29-30; cf. Gen 2:7) to the final resurrection, when the Spirit will restore the dry bones to life (Ezek 37), to the ultimate wedding of God with humanity, when this same Spirit will inspire in the betrothed the eschatological invitation "Come, Lord Jesus!" (Rev 22:17, 20). In between, this impregnation was manifested in the Spirit's bursting forth in the prophets, making their very bodies into the living word of the Other (see above), and in the expectation of the fulfillment of Moses' wish, "would that all the Lord's people were prophets, and that the Lord would put his spirit on them" (Num 11:29). The fulfillment of the promise made to the ancestors lies precisely in the pouring out of the Spirit over all flesh (Acts 2:17-18; Joel 3:1-5) which accomplishes Moses' desire (Acts 2:18). We are going to verify this inscription of the Difference of God in the body of humanity through the Spirit by looking at (a) the Pauline writings,

(b) the account of Pentecost, and (c) the liturgical experience of the Church.

a) Paul. Paul, who can describe the resurrected body in no other way than as "the spiritual body" (1 Cor 15:44), constantly mentions the Spirit's action as a transforming agent of what is deepest in human nature (the passage from slavery to filiation), in the Church, and finally in the whole of humanity and the universe.

At the *personal* level first, the Spirit which "searches everything, even the depths of God" (1 Cor 2:10), transforms "unspiritual" persons into "spiritual" persons, able to interpret "spiritual things to those who are spiritual," able to "discern all things . . . themselves subject to no one else's scrutiny," and thus able to appreciate God's apparent "foolishness" as "wisdom" (1 Cor 2:10-16). This knowledge of the mystery of God which the Spirit teaches from within (v. 13) to the spiritual person is also agape "because God's love has been poured into our hearts through the Holy Spirit that has been given to us" (Rom 5:5). Thus, the Spirit enables those in whom it "dwells" (Rom 8:11) to pass from the status of slaves to that of adopted children (v. 15; see above).

But this participation in the Spirit is not an individual affair; it is done by means of integration into the *Church.* "For in the one Spirit we were all baptized into one body — Jews or Greeks, slaves or free" (1 Cor 12:13). And if it is true that the theme of the "temple of the Holy Spirit" is applied by Paul to each person's body (1 Cor 6:19), it is much more often applied to the body of the Church: "Do you not know that you are God's temple and that God's Spirit dwells in you? If someone destroys God's temple, God will destroy that person. For God's temple is holy, and you are that temple" (1 Cor 3:16-17; cf. 2 Cor 6:16-18). In building Christians, with Christ as the "cornerstone," into a *naos hagios* ("holy temple," Eph 2:20-22), in building them into an *oikos pneumatikos* ("spiritual house") on the "living stone" that is Christ with the goal of making them collectively a "holy priesthood" capable of offering "spiritual sacrifices" (1 Pet 2:4-5), the Spirit makes the Church the place where God dwells in and for humanity and the world.

The Church of baptism "in the one Spirit" is the sign of the reconciliation of Jew and Greek, slave and free, male and female to which *all humanity* is called, the sign of this "new self" which all put on at baptism (Col 3:9-11) and for whose coming into being Christ has given his life (Eph 2:15-16). There is still more: what is destined to be "recapitulated" in Christ goes beyond humanity. In solidarity with it, the *"whole creation"* aspires, as the creation of God, to be "set free from its bondage to decay" and "to obtain the freedom of the glory of the children of God" (Rom 8:21; cf. Isa 55:13; 65:17). Thus, in solidarity with us, "who have the first fruits of the Spirit [and] groan inwardly while we wait for adoption [*hyiothesia*], the redemption [*apolutrosis*] of our bodies" (Rom 8:22-23), the universe as world is itself in the "labor pains" of the salvation Paul calls the coming of a "new creation" and links with the Lord's resurrection and the outpouring of the Spirit.

Thus, the Spirit's proper function is to invest humanity and the universe with the resurrectional power of Christ. For Christ rose not simply for himself, but for us (cf. Rom 4:25) as "the firstborn within a large family" (Rom 8:29; Heb 1:6). It is this "for us" of the resurrection that becomes manifest at Pentecost: through the effusion of the Spirit, humanity is made a participant in the Pasch of the Lord, and is thereby journeying with him, toward the Father. Such is, finally, the gist of Jüngel's thesis: it is "insofar as God is the Holy Spirit" that "God is the mystery of the world. God is such inasmuch as the Spirit is the invisible but powerful relation, on the one hand, of the *Son* of God *visible* as a human being with the *invisible Father* who is in heaven and, on the other hand, of this same Son of God visible as a human being with *ourselves* so that he might draw everyone to himself (John 12:32)."[53] Through the Spirit, the most divine is most secretly inscribed into the world. Such is indeed the *mystery* that the sacraments express *extra nos*.

b) Pentecost. "Not having a mouth, nor a tongue, nor a voice, God decided to produce by a miracle an invisible noise in the air, a breath exhaled in words which, setting the air in motion, giving it a form, and transforming it into fire in the form of flames, like the breath across a trumpet, caused a booming voice to so resound that the most distant people believed they could hear it as easily as those who were closest. . . . A resounding voice from the middle of the fire that

53. Jüngel, *Dieu mystère du monde,* 2:249.

descended from heaven, a voice striking all present with bewilderment, this voice spoke in the dialect familiar to each hearer. Through it, things were said so clearly that they seemed to be seen rather than heard."[54]

This commentary by Philo on the event at Sinai and the Midrash of Rabbi Johanan on Exodus 20:18 ("as it resounded, God's voice divided itself into seventy voices, seventy tongues, so that all nations could understand")[55] show that the Pentecost story is presented to us as a new Sinaitic theophany.

The *fire* of the Spirit makes visible what the *voice* of God (or rather, the voices of God, which are "seen" by all the people, according to Exodus 20:18) makes audible.[56] And what the Spirit makes audible and visible is not only that God speaks every language (Acts 2:9-10; compare with the seventy languages symbolizing totality in the Midrash), but also, by reference to the story of the tower of Babel, of which the account of Pentecost is the reverse, that God cannot be heard except through the intermediary of a variety of tongues.

Babel (Gen 11:1-9) is the myth of humanity refusing the difference of God: to "make a name" for themselves people conceive the idea of building a tower "with its top in the heavens." This is the impurity par excellence; for, as M. Douglas has shown in analyzing "the abominations of Leviticus," any vegetable, animal, or human is impure which transgresses its limits or, in C. Lévi-Strauss' terms, overlaps several classificatory categories. On the contrary, that is pure and holy which holds itself separate, differentiated from the rest, and thus fills its limits without exceeding them.[57] At Babel, the dreamed of and sacrilegious undifferentiation which humans wish to establish between themselves and God is itself the expression of the undifferentiation which reigns among them. Having "one language and the same words," thus speaking back and forth "to one another" as

---

54. Philo of Alexandria, *De decal.* 9 and 11. Quoted in the collection *Une lecture des Actes des apôtres, Cahiers Evangile* 21, p. 25.

55. Ibid.

56. See Isa 2:1, "The word that Isaiah son of Amoz saw . . ." The prophets are "seers"; but the object of their vision is that of their mission: the Word of Yahweh.

57. M. Douglas, *De la souillure: Essai sur les notions de pollution et de tabou* (Paris: Maspero, 1971) ch. 3 "Les abominations du Lévitique."

if to a mirror, inhabiting the same country, they live in uniformity. Now, when the differences, between themselves and between themselves and God (the two are correlative in the text) are abolished, there reigns the totalitarianism of a "phallic" absolute power which, like the tower with its top in heaven, takes itself for the Truth of God's very self and, plugging up every fissure, transforms official discourses into absolute knowledge. Each person is thereafter summoned, under pain of death, to conform to the same ideology. But we know that beneath this regime of *uniform identity* and the parroting of official interpretations, there rumble violence and revolt. God prohibits this sort of undifferentiation. God displaces, gives elbow room, separates, thereby enabling all to breathe, to no longer be short of *ruah,* that is, to come to themselves as subjects in their differences. To the totalitarian reign of the Same, God opposes the symbolic reign of the Other. God's punishment, coming down from heaven to "confuse their language" and to scatter "them abroad from there over the face of all the earth," is the salvation of humankind.

The *anti-Babel* of Pentecost makes clear that the salvation of humanity lies in respect for the *difference.* Respect for the difference-holiness of God, who "suddenly" (Acts 2:2) surprises those who "were all together in one place" (v. 1); who "amazes," "astonishes," and "perplexes" (vv. 7, 12) the crowd of those who represent "every nation under heaven" (v. 5); and who manifests God's self under the symbols of the unmasterable: wind and fire (vv. 2-3), while the "voice" (*phōnē,* v. 6, often translated by "rush") makes itself heard from within these theophanic elements. But also respect for the difference *between humans:* "divided tongues, as of fire, appeared among them" (v. 3); and if all are filled with the same Spirit, it is in order to speak in other languages (v. 4), and so "each one heard them speaking in the native language of each" (v. 6). By creating differences between humans, the Spirit sets up communication between them. By opening up a *lack* between them, it enables them not to fail to meet one another. Just as in opening in each person the absence of God, it enables them not to fail to meet God. The Spirit is thus at the place of our desire. It is the *Openness* in God's very self, the Openness that is constitutive of God's very self, an Openness it inscribes between persons and within each person.

Difference between God and God, establishing their communion (theology), difference between God and humans, establishing their possible communication (economy), the Spirit is this Difference of God taking body (anthropology) in the difference between human subjects — from which springs all reciprocity — and at the same time, within each subject, the difference between body and word — in that place where the body itself may come forth as true word.

c) *The Liturgy, and Especially the Epiclesis.* Faithful to its biblical roots, ecclesial tradition has attempted to discern what is most "spiritual" in God on the basis of what is most "corporeal" in us. This is especially the case in the liturgy. But it is more widely the case in the whole of *Church life.*

Thus, we see that two charisms present a problem for Paul: first, glossolalia, whose practitioners, speaking a word from us to God under the Spirit's influence, risk failing to build the community because their prayer remains incomprehensible; second, prophecy, whose practitioners, speaking a word from God to us under the Spirit's influence, risk uttering extravagant revelations. In order to clarify the prayer of the first and sort out the words of the second, Paul joins to these two defective charisms two other associate charisms: the interpretation of tongues and the discernment of spirits (1 Cor 12:10; cf. 1 Cor 14). Paul emphasizes that every word said in the name of God "must be tested by the way the Church receives it." Through a sort of dialectic of the one and the many, Paul declares that "Christians who, in their diversity, do not untiringly seek unity are not in the Spirit" and, conversely, that "the ecclesial authority which, through an overriding concern for unity, is not open to diversity is not in the Spirit either."[58] Finally, it is the "fruit" produced by the Spirit in existential behavior — love, joy, peace, patience, and so forth — which makes a just discernment possible.

We find the same perspective in the *Didache* (11:8) and also in *The Shepherd of Hermas* (no. 43): the discernment of the Spirit can be done only *tropologically,* on the basis of ethical behavior.[59] The

58. C. Perrot, "L'Esprit Saint chez Paul," *L'Esprit Saint dans la Bible, Cahiers Evangile* 52 (1985) 54–55.

59. *Didache* 11:8: "Anyone who speaks under the inspiration of the Spirit is not a prophet unless that one has the mores (*tropoi*) of the Lord. Thus, one

is the place where the Spirit is verified. As the frequent images used by the Church Fathers show, the Spirit is often referred to as the seal in us of the Word sent out of the Father's mouth or as the point of impact of the Son's ray emanating from the Father's light. God manifests God's self to humankind starting from the Father through the Son in the Holy Spirit, and thus humankind goes back to the Father through the Spirit.[60] Therefore, the Spirit is at the *hinge* between theology and the economy (of salvation), as the Greek Church Fathers of the fourth century (but not only they) especially emphasize.

Hence, the fundamental importance for them of the *liturgical experience as the theological place of the manifestation of the Spirit's full divinity.* Against Macedonius and the Pneumatomachi, they willingly propose arguments drawn from the "divinization" effected at baptism. Thus Athanasius, making reference to *baptism,* says: "If, by the participation in the Spirit, we become participants in the divine nature, a person would have to be stupid to say that the Spirit belongs to created nature and not to God's nature. Because of this, the persons in whom it resides are divinized. If it is able to divinize, there is no doubt that its nature is that of God."[61] The same baptismal argument can be found in Gregory of Nazianzus and Theodore of Mopsuestia,[62] and in Ambrose a similar argument based on *penance.*[63] In Basil, the decisive argumentation in favor of the Spirit's divinity is founded on the liturgical *doxology* ("Glory be to the Father with the Son with the Holy

will distinguish the true and false prophets by their manner of living."
Hermas, *The Shepherd* 43: "Test by their way of life those who possess the divine Spirit."

60. "The road to the knowledge of God thus runs from the one Spirit, through the one Son, to the one Father and, in the other direction, essential goodness, natural holiness, and royal dignity flow from the Father, through the Only Begotten, to the Spirit" (Basil, *Traité du Saint-Esprit* 18, ed. B. Pruche [Sources chrétiennes 17]).

61. Athanasius of Alexandria, *Lettres à Sérapion* I, 24 (Sources chrétiennes 15) 126.

62. Gregory of Nazianzus, *Discourse* 31, 28; Theodore of Mopsuestia, *Homélies catéchétiques* 9, 15, ed. Tonneau-Devreesse (Vatican City, 1949) 237.

63. Ambrose, "Traité du Saint-Esprit" III, 137 (*CSEL* 79:208); *La pénitence* I, 8, 37 (Sources chrétiennes 179) 85; see the introduction by R. Gryson, p. 42, and p. 84, n. 2.

Spirit").[64] *Lex orandi, lex credendi,* the adage we have already discussed, holds especially true for the Holy Spirit since the major theological place for the affirmation of its divinity is the anthropological experience the liturgy affords.

A constant feature of ancient liturgies is their linking the Spirit and the body. Furthermore, in the liturgy, pneumatology integrates not only the body of the Church and those of believers, but together with this body, the matter of the universe as "world." Hence, the traditional importance of the *epiclesis* for the consecration of the bread and wine into the body and blood of Christ, but also, as in the Syrian tradition, for those of the baptismal water and chrism.[65]

This is not the place to review the liturgical and theological dossier of the epiclesis.[66]

First, as Y. Congar reminds us, "even in the Church Fathers belonging to the Western Syrian tradition, among whom we find the most formal epicleses, the invocation designates the entire Eucharistic prayer"[67] (at least sometimes), which implies that the epiclesis cannot be understood except in the context of the whole and that any hint of competition between Christ's action and the Spirit's creates a false problem. Unfortunately, in the twelfth and thirteenth centuries, the Scholastic preoccupation with pinpointing the precise moment of the consecration was to give rise a century later to grave misunderstandings between East and West. These misunderstandings between the Churches have been almost entirely cleared up, as the bilateral and multilateral accords between them as well as the recent texts of *Faith and Constitution* show.[68]

Second, in the epicleses, the Spirit is always the *agent of the incorporation* of the risen Christ into the Church and into the elements of the sacra-

64. Basil, *Traité du Saint-Esprit* 1, p. 109: "How one can say 'with' the Holy Spirit, I shall now, with its aid, explain."

65. E. P. Siman, *L'expérience de l'Esprit par l'Eglise d'après la tradition syrienne d'Antioche* (Paris: Beauchesne, 1971) 227–229, "Tableau comparatif des épiclèses des trois principaux mystères."

66. See the entire dossier, with a full bibliography, in Congar, *Je crois,* 3:294–341; Siman, *L'expérience de l'Esprit,* 214–244.

67. Congar, ibid., 295.

68. J. E. Desseaux, *Dialogues théologiques et accords œcuméniques* (Paris: Cerf, 1982); *Foi et constitution,* "Baptême, eucharistie, ministère" (Paris: Centurion-Presses de Taizé, 1982) (document called "de Lima") nos. 14–18 "L'eucharistie, invocation de l'Esprit." Catholic opinions concerning this document can be found in *Istina* 1982/1 and *Irenikon* 1982/2.

ments (water, chrism, bread and wine). Let us make clear, however, that even from the fourth century on, when the strength of the verbs indicating the Spirit's action on the elements is accentuated ("manifest," "sanctify," "make," "change"), the epiclesis' aim always remains the sanctification of the subjects through their participation in the elements thus consecrated: it is always for the *Church* and, in it, for the believing subjects that the Spirit transforms the gifts, never for the gifts themselves. This is as true of baptism and the anointing of the sick as it is of the Eucharist. In this perspective, it is significant that the Spirit is the operating agent of the threefold body of Christ: his historical body, born of Mary, overshadowed by the Spirit (Luke 1), and spiritualized into a glorious body; his sacramental body (first epiclesis); and his ecclesial body (second epiclesis).

In the liturgy, the Spirit clearly appears as the *agent of the Word's burial in the flesh,* more precisely, after Easter, as the agent of the *disappearance* of the Risen One into the flesh, which is thus sacramental, of humanity and the world. In the biblical as well as liturgical perspectives we have just sketched, the Spirit indeed represents, as Barth writes, "the moment of the appropriation of God by humans."[69] The Spirit, "the secret God," as Clément suggests, is "not itself a face, but the revealer of faces, not the holy Face, but the holiness of every human face, God who disappears into the properly personal existence of human beings."[70] As *the moment of the appropriation of God in what God has that is most divine by humankind in what it has that is most human,* the Spirit has the mission of raising up for the Risen One a body of humanity and of world. Through it, he who was raised now raises others. Under the Spirit's breath, the Word becomes our word: a word which comes closest to the truth when it wells forth in the very fissures of our discourses or murmurs in a hymn of silence; then, indeed, the word touches us to the quick and is at one with our bodies. The Spirit is the agent of this *enfleshment of the word.* However, this is not to be taken in the extreme sense of an enfleshment which would be imagined as closing up every fissure between body and word. The identity between body and word effected by

69. Conversely, the Son represents "the moment of the appropriation of humankind by God" (K. Barth, *Dogmatique* I, 1, 2 [Genève: Labor et Fides, 1969]) 165.

70. Clément, *Le visage intérieur,* 81.

the Spirit is symbolic; it rigorously maintains the difference between the two. This is why the major criterion for the discernment of the Spirit lies in the capacity of the subject truly inhabited
by it to bear testimony to the Other — which, for Christians, always requires an ecclesial verification.

   d) The New Scriptural Body of God. Thus, the Spirit is the agent of
a new inscription of the Word. This word, as we have said, is the
Logos of the cross, that is, the Word of the divine tri-unity as buried in the bitter end of humanity which is death. It is this
unheard-of saying of God as God crossed out in the sub-humanity
of a "less than nothing" which the Spirit brings to the Church's
body and to each Christian's body.

   As word, this *Logos* of the cross cannot have the full consistency
of a concept (*Be-griff*). This is why Heidegger, substituting for the
"names heard since metaphysics began: *glossa, lingua,* tongue, language," calls what is signified by the word "the Saying" (*die
Sage*), which means "the saying and what the saying says, together with what is to be said."[71] The word does not come forth
except as fractured, just as the Word of the cross is fractured,
even when this Word is expressed, as it should be, starting with
the resurrection. For the resurrection creates a *tear* in the fabric of
language. One cannot speak of it without leaving open the interstice which both separates and unites opposites: flesh and spirit,
to appear and to disappear, to touch and not to touch, presence
and absence . . . Of these interstices, the open tomb is the great
metaphor. The resurrection is the absolute breach, the pure ir-
reparable difference. But it makes speech and life possible precisely because of this breach. Where meaning is walled in, the
word is no longer possible. Thus the resurrection refers us back to
this *dictum* of the cross, this "Thing that the cross proposes,"
which, as we said above, does not set up "new divine attributes
which would overthrow the former ones" (those of the most real
Being), but stresses "the necessity of a change of *attitude.*" The
Logos of the cross, opening "another space" than that of the concept, is also the manifestation of the "'cross of language'": it can

---

   71. M. Heidegger, *Acheminement vers la parole* (Paris: Gallimard, 1976) "Un
entretien de parole," 131-133.

be said in neither Hebrew nor Greek, and yet it condemns us to speak these languages by turns.[72]

The Spirit is precisely the agent that makes possible the expression of the crucified Word by removing it to another space than that of the concept: the space of the conversion of attitudes, the space of the *body*. Hence, the primary mediation of God's revelation in Christianity is no longer only that of the cosmos and seeing or even that of the word of the Law and hearing, but, recapitulating these two and particularly the second in a sort of *"Aufhebung"* ("revocation"), that of the body and living. Moreover, such a return to the Word in order to unfold it into corporality, and especially into ethical *practice*, was written in the Book itself as we have emphasized (see Ezek 36; Jer 31). Thus, the baptism of the Holy Spirit (Acts 1:5) at Pentecost can be understood, according to the Christian hermeneutics of the Scriptures, as the fulfillment of "what God promised to our ancestors" (Acts 13:32-33). For it was written that the people's historical practice from which the Book was born was to become the new scriptural space for God's revelation. It was written that the body was to become the living letter of God traced by the Spirit's hand. In any case, this is the way Paul understands things, "taking his inspiration from the texts of Jeremiah (31:32) and Ezekiel (11:9; 36:26) concerning the new covenant, without following them or quoting them."[73] Paul needs no other letter of recommendation to authenticate his apostleship than the very existence of the Corinthian community: "You yourselves are our letter, written on our hearts, to be known and read by all; and you show that you are a letter of Christ, prepared by us, written not with ink but with the Spirit of the living God, not on tablets of stone but on tablets of human hearts" (2 Cor 3:2-3). The "new covenant," not that of the letter (which "kills") but that of the Spirit (which "gives life," v. 6), comes about precisely in this *passage from the letter to the body through the Spirit.*

Of course, the letter of the Book remains, marking the impregnable place of our Christian origin. Even for Paul, the opposition

---

72. S. Breton, *Le verbe et la croix* (Paris: Desclée, 1981).

73. M. Carrez, "La Deuxième Epître aux Corinthiens," *Cahiers Evangile* 51 (1985) 21.

of *gramma* ("letter") to *pneuma* ("spirit") does not in any way imply the erasure of the letter. Carrez writes, "In Paul's mind, there is no Spirit which does not take form and express itself through a text."[74] But Scripture would be the letter that kills if it did not go back through the Spirit to its living source in order to make the Church as a body its place of truth. In conformity with this program prescribed by the Book and symbolized by the liturgy, God's revelation demands that the Word be made flesh in the actions of Christians, just as it was made flesh in Jesus Christ. The *sign* of the letter comes into its truth when it becomes the *symbol* of the body: Christ cannot be announced unless the letter of the cross, which the apostolic tradition deposited as a testament in the Book, pervades believers' existences and becomes a testimony. Where human beings give flesh to their confession of the Risen One by following him on the way of the cross for the liberation of their brothers and sisters (and thus for their own as well), there the body of Christ comes forth. Of this body, the Church is the eschatological promise in and for the world.

This command to believers to incorporate the book in their ethical practice finds its great *symbolic expression* in the marking of the body by the *sacraments*.

In the Pauline literature, the inscription of the Spirit's gift in each person is done by the *baptism* "in the one Spirit" (1 Cor 12:13) as well as, in a context that is probably baptismal, by *the anointing and the seal of the Spirit:* "But it is God who establishes us with you in Christ and has anointed us, by putting his seal on us and giving us his Spirit in our hearts as a first installment" (2 Cor 1:21-22).[75] This anointing and marking "with the seal of the promised Holy Spirit" (Eph 1:13; cf. 4:30) are probably to be understood in a metaphorical sense, since this was the case for Jesus himself at his baptism in the Jordan according to the Gospels: anointed by the Spirit, he was thus designated — in the tradition of the king's anointing (1 Sam 16:13), then, after the Exile, of the high priest's anointing (Lev

74. Ibid., 22.

75. See the in-depth analysis of J. R. Villalon, *Sacrements dans l'Esprit* (Paris: Beauchesne, 1977) 78–200, of this text and the following. The sacramental interpretation of the "unction" and the "seal" was common among the Church Fathers. In any case, these two biblical images have been translated both in the East and West by two symbolic gestures: anointing and signing. (B. Botte, "Le vocabulaire ancien de la confirmation," LMD 54 [1958] 19).

4:3; Exod 30:22-23), and especially of the prophet's metaphorical anointing (Isa 61:1-2; cf. Luke 4:17) — *messiah-christos* and "son" of God (see Ps 2:7). Even if the testimonies relating to the use of the anointing with oil and of the signing or seal (*sphragis, signaculum, character*) at the baptism of Christians do not go back farther than the beginning of the third century (Tertullian, *De bapt.* 7; Hippolytus, *Tr. Ap.*, 21), it is possible that this use itself dates back to an earlier time since the metaphors of the anointing and of the seal are widely attested.[76]

In any case, the gift of the Spirit has taken the form of an inscription and *marking* on the neophyte's very body. This marking has the twofold function of authentication (the seal is the stamp used to attest the authenticity of a document) and of indelibility. Thus, walking in the footsteps of Jesus on whom "God the Father has set his seal" (John 6:27), the baptized are authenticated in their identity and their mission of disciples of Jesus. Just as circumcision was for Abraham "the seal of the righteousness that he had by faith while he was still uncircumcised (Rom 4:11), the signing in the form of the cross made on the foreheads of the baptized is the indelible mark (the "character") of their membership in Christ through the Spirit. This symbolic engraving of the letter of Christ (that of the cross) by the Spirit on the initiates' very bodies makes visible and inaugurates what becoming Christian means: to veri-fy this *sacramentum* in day by day ethical practice by becoming in their corporality a living "letter of Christ" (Paul, above).

The body — better, corporality in the sense we have given this concept — is the *new place of the letter which the Spirit inspires*. This is, again, the paradox of the Spirit: it inscribes the radical difference of the holy God on what is most human in the human body. If it attracts the world to the Risen One, it is by hiding the latter, in his spiritualized body, in the world. If the faces of the most despised persons are the holy face of the Risen One in his humiliated condition, it is because the Spirit erases him by immersing him in humanity. The Spirit, neutral, faceless, nameless except

76. The rite of the laying on of hands which, according to L. Ligier, "the East once had, like Rome," was everywhere combined with that of the anointing with scented oil (except among the Byzantines who used only chrism). This cannot be a surprise, given the rich biblical tradition of anointing in connection with the coming of the Spirit (*La Confirmation* [Paris: Beauchesne, 1973] 101).

for the names drawn from cosmic symbolism, is the agent of the divine God's concealment in Jesus' personal body, in the body of history the Church gives him, and joining these two bodies, in the symbolic body of the Eucharist in which the body of Jesus is given only to be veri-fied in the Church's body, as our analysis of the Eucharistic Prayer has shown.

Our anthropology of the most spiritual coming forth in the most corporeal, of the arch-writing being, in its sensible materiality itself, the concrete mediation of the word, and finally, of the body being the unavoidable arch-symbolic place where the subject's truth comes to be, finds its properly theological expression in the pneumatological vein we have just followed. *The corporality constitutive of human beings is the place of God.* In the last analysis, this is what we learn about the faith and about Christian identity from the fact that their fabric is made of rites which the Church calls sacraments. They are the Spirit's work.

III. THE SACRAMENTS: PLACES OF GRACE

1. *The Trinitarian Subversion of Our Representations of God*

a) Subversion. Moltmann is right: "A radical theology of the cross cannot give a theistic answer to the question of the dying Christ. It would do away with the cross."[77] That God should not be "any more divine than in the humanity [of the Crucified]" is only tenable if we overthrow "the simple notion of God."[78] The scandal expressed here is certainly difficult to bear, not just at the level of our conceptual thinking about God — which is already difficult enough — but more so at the level of the conversion of desire and attitudes that it demands of us.

However, this kind of scandal is not new: recall that of *Mark and Matthew's communities* when confronted with this dying Jesus whose only words are a lament over his abandonment and who is acknowledged by the centurion, who "saw that in this way he breathed his last," as "God's Son." And, we have mentioned the various ways in which this harsh cry was toned down in certain manuscripts. We should also mention Paul's inner turmoil and

77. Moltmann, *Le Dieu crucifié*, 259.
78. Ibid., 233 and 231.

radical transformation, which he confides to us in Philippians 3:7-14, as he discovers that "Christ redeemed us from the curse of the law by becoming a curse for us . . . in order that . . . the blessing of Abraham might come to the Gentiles" (Gal 3:13-14). How could this "crucified messiah," "foolishness to Gentiles," not be a "stumbling block to Jews" (1 Cor 1:23)? It is this same scandal of the "crucified God," but now dressed in dogmatic terms, that the *Second Council of Constantinople* (553) expresses: "He who was crucified in the flesh is . . . One of the Trinity" (can. 10).

"It is only as the action of the Trinitarian God that the scandal of the cross can be endured by the believer," writes H. Urs von Balthasar.[79] And, as Kasper echoes, "The cross can be interpreted only as the renunciation by God of God's very self."[80] To the Son's abandonment of his own will to his Father there corresponds a sort of impotence in the Father's renouncing all power of domination over his Son. Now, starting from the "simple notion" of God and all of God's essential attributes as Supreme Being, classic onto-theology could not conceive the magnitude of this self-renunciation of God. Of course, it did express well the newness of the Christian God revealed in Jesus in relation to the theodicy of the "philosophers." But it still continued to lead this God back to God's *pre-Trinitarian* representation as the Supreme Being: "God of identity, of self-fulfillment, of perfection which is not disturbed by the slightest otherness, of self-sufficiency and self-contemplation." Lastly, in its effort at speculative thinking, classic onto-theology ignored, as Geffré again notes, "the difference between religious language, which is that of invocation, and philosophic language, which is that of attribution," constantly attempting to reduce the first to the second, unable to understand that renouncing the God of philosophy does not in any way entail rejecting thought itself.[81] As we know, it is precisely Jüngel's project to show that, on the contrary, such a renunciation is the way to a rigorous conception of the living God's very being.

Because of its presuppositions, classic theology inevitably projected onto Jesus, on the basis of his divine nature, a pre-

79. H. Urs von Balthasar, "Le mystère pascal," *Mysterium salutis*, vol. 12 (Paris: Cerf, 1972) 133, and *Pâques: Le mystère* (Paris: Cerf, 1981) 133.

80. Kasper, *Jésus, le Christ*, 251.

81. Geffré, *Le christianisme*, 180–184.

Trinitarian representation of God. By dint of repeating that Jesus was God (and the battles of the first centuries on the Trinitarian and Christological fronts gave it good reasons for constantly emphasizing this), classic theology came to the point of forgetting that such an affirmation demanded *a new way of thinking about God*. This forgetting was doubtless inevitable. For this new way of thinking implied, as Jüngel expresses it, that "the God produced metaphysically" would have to perish "because of God's very perfection." Congenitally linked to "the negative evaluation of what is ephemeral," to the devaluation of what becomes (*genesis*) in favor of what stays (*ousia*, see our analysis of the *Philebus* in ch. 1), onto-theology could push its criticism of God's image (but with what strength!) only toward the unthinkable.[82] It could maintain the radical difference of God only by schematizing it spatially as distance, and eventually as opposition. Then, God was defined as what humanity is not (eternal, perfect, unmoving, unchangeable . . .). We have severely criticized this onto-theo-logical notion.

b) A Work of Mourning within Ourselves. This does not mean that it is simple to think of God's humanity in the field of the symbolic. We have been warned by Heidegger: one does not let go of metaphysics as easily as one sheds an opinion; "overcoming" it involves more than crossing it out with a stroke of the pen; it involves making the voyage anew but now in the reverse direction, back to the overlooked essence of metaphysics, which means that we turn it around by our criticism, even as it continues to dwell in us. For us, symbolism represents this turning around. Symbolism is precisely the very impossibility of completing our thinking process, *grasped* by it *as we always-already are* as subjects together with our "world." But this impossibility makes us able to think; this difference makes us able to live; the bread of absence nourishes us. Symbolism holds us under the law of this *oportet transire* ("one must go beyond") which S. Breton advisedly borrows from Meister Eckhart and which denounces the "error" of believing we will have finished with "passing" once the sublime point of the "nothing par excellence" is attained. The "one must" it imposes upon us is this unachievable task where "our God, in God's pas-

82. Jüngel, *Dieu mystère du monde*, 1:317–320.

sage through language, becomes the accomplice of the lightness of our transits" and where "our negations are, before anything else, the irony of a 'distance taken' and constantly reiterated."[83] According to Jüngel's fundamental thesis, such is the theological task that can cor-respond to a God, whose being is in the coming," in the very act of God's coming.[84]

That we must steadfastly remain in the presence of the absence of God; that we read the radical image of the presence of absence in the face of the crucified; that this requires in us the witness (*summatureo*) of the "Spirit of God" which, joining itself to our spirit, leads us to renounce the "spirit of slavery" in order to draw us forward to the "spirit of adoption" (Rom 8:14-16): all this cannot become the object of a simple theological knowledge, even in its "negative" variety; all this comes to us only by way of kenosis. Moreover, the introductory verse of the Christological hymn in Philippians (2:5-11) expresses this: the announcement of the divine kenosis cannot be disconnected from its fulfillment *in us*. The *Logos* of the cross demands that we give a body in ourselves, through a travail of mourning, to the divine meontology. The theological act is thereby urged to come to its truth, that is, to become witness. Such is precisely the "transitive" way which symbolism opens up to us. Theologically, this is the work of the Spirit.

Consequently, the God "above us," cannot be spoken of in a Christian way except on the basis of the God "among us." Of course, as a study by A. Vergote has especially made clear, the representation of God as "above" us (or at the origin of the deepest element in us, which pertains to the vertical scheme) seems unavoidable, connected as it is to the primary symbolism of our upright posture[85] and thus belonging to this "existential topography" that structures

83. S. Breton, "Les métamorphoses du langage religieux chez Maître Eckhart," *Dire ou taire Dieu, RST* 67/3-4 (1979) 74-75.

84. Jüngel, *Dieu mystère du monde,* 2:250, 265. For the author it is a matter of a Trinitarian movement wherein God, as Father, comes from God; as Son, comes toward God; as Spirit, comes as God (250-265). In what follows Jüngel explains why "developing these fundamental concepts about the Being of God is the task of narrative theology" (pp. 266ff.).

85. A. Vergote, "Equivoques et articulation du sacré," *Le sacré: Etudes et recherches,* Colloque Castelli (Paris: Aubier-Montaigne, 1974).

the human subject.[86] Moreover, it is intensified by twenty-five centuries of this metaphysical tradition which, onto-theological by nature, has constantly projected the *hypokeimenon* ("substance") of entities onto a divine summit that holds and founds them. Now, the Saying of the cross twists this scheme, which nonetheless is inalienable.

Our necessary statements are thus intrinsically marked with the "sign of contradiction": the "Thing" that the cross pro-poses can be said only in the always open space which separates and links Greek and Hebrew, without being able to have them meet halfway. Now, it is precisely by keeping this fissure open that we can let the mystery speak itself and at the same time let ourselves be spoken within it.

The *indicative* mode of the God crucified in the form of a slave does not tolerate being mastered by a science. Its Word can be expressed only as a "categorical *imperative* of life and action"[87] which makes it happen among us. To the work of mourning this demands, the obligation of an ethical activity which gives body to this God is simultaneously joined. This practice gives privilege of place to the exercise of justice and mercy where we have recognized the "liturgy of the neighbor," a spiritual sacrifice making effective in daily life this *multi unum corpus in Christo* ("the many are one body in Christ") symbolized by "the sacrament of the altar" (Augustine). The ethics of "living-in-grace," primarily with regard to those whom humans have reduced to the state of slaves, is the place of veri-fication, the *veritas*, of the filial "giving thanks" of the Eucharist.

The subversion of "God" is not first of all a simple matter of concept — even if, of course, conceptual discourse is a necessary moment of criticism in this matter. It requires the passage *from discourse to body*. This passage, where the body of our desire, our history, and our society becomes the place of the truth of our *word*, is the work of the Spirit. This divine third term is rigorously necessary if we are to be able to confess the humanity of the Crucified as the revelation of the very face of God. It is in the Spirit

---

86. A. Vergote, *Interprétation du langage religieux* (Paris: Seuil, 1974) ch. 4 "La déhiscence verticale."

87. Breton, *Le verbe et la croix*, 154.

that God's fatherhood makes itself effective in the world by raising up for itself a body of sons and daughters. It is in the Spirit
that God, in Jesus, effaces God's very self inside humanity. God
open. Open within God's self: the Spirit is the very difference
that renders possible the communication between God and God,
Father and Son. Open to the world, to the point that God cannot
be adequately conceived without the world: the Spirit is the very
difference which makes it possible for God to take on an eschatological body in humanity. This is what the sacraments symbolize.

2. Sacramental Grace

"Humanity speaks of God. Now, corporality traces the fundamental word, the only one humanity can understand. . . . The
body creates the place of God where humanity will be able to
recognize God; it formulates a language in which humanity will
be able to hear the mystery. It is in espousing the mystery of humanity that the mystery of God takes on a body in humanity."[88]

In the midst of the world the mystery of the Church and, at the
heart of the Church, the mystery of the sacraments are the great
symbols of this mystery of God taking flesh in humanity. The
sacraments are the primary symbol of God's mystery since they
are the fundamental proclamation of the sacramental "essence" of
the Church in its institutional visibility; and they are the radical
symbol of God's mystery since they bring to the body the Word
which through the Spirit gives life to the Church, the Word
whose fulfillment is their very purpose (they are "-urgic" by nature). However, two conditions are required to make it theologically tenable that God takes on the eschatological body the
sacraments symbolize.

First, *God must be thought of according to corporality.* It is this possibility we have verified in our twofold survey of Christology and
pneumatology. The fact that we can confess the very glory of God
in the sub-humanity of him whom human beings have reduced to
less than nothing revolutionizes every representation of "God."
The crossing out thus executed over the majestic *Esse* of "God" is
the trace of an historic and symbolic meontology which leads us

88. Y. Ledure, *Si Dieu s'efface: La corporéité comme lieu d'une affirmation de
Dieu* (Paris: Desclée, 1975) 66–67.

to think of God in God's mystery as the One who is "crossed out" in humanity by the Spirit and who thus gives to the former the possibility of becoming the "sacramental" place where God takes on a body. For the reasons given above, the sacraments — and always primarily baptism and the Eucharist, which are the two paradigms among them — are precisely the major symbolic "expressions" of God's effacement through the Spirit in the flesh of the world, which thus becomes sacramental.

Second, such an embodiment must be conceived in the order of *grace*. From the symbolic viewpoint, grace is both beyond every object, since it is outside the field of value, and before and beneath all subjects, since the latter, as believers, can never precede it: on the contrary, they proceed from it, unable to receive themselves from it except in a continual genesis of their identities as children-for-God and as brothers-and-sisters-for-others in Christ.

The two conditions given are necessarily linked; the *theological*, and even dogmatic, *affirmation of "sacramental grace" is simply the concrete unfolding of the general affirmation of the world as the eschatological place of God* and of the "body of Christ" in genesis through the Spirit. Without the second affirmation, the first would lose its relevance, reduced as it would be to an element imaginarily isolated from the symbolic totality found in the Christian interpretation of history and the universe. But without the first affirmation, the second would risk evaporating into thin air. Of course, the concrete affirmation of the world and of the body as the place of God is not verified just in the sacraments, as the second part of this work has emphasized. But it is indeed in them that this affirmation finds its *primordial symbolic expression*. Their recognition as "places of grace" would lose its relevance if they were not "revealers" of the fact that God takes on an eschatological body in humanity. But this taking on of an eschatological body would in turn risk being emptied of any effective significance if it did not find concrete places to become crystallized. As symbolic "operators" of "grace," the sacraments are precisely these primary concrete places. The stumbling block which they place in our way — the stumbling block of an entirely "material" mediation by the body, by an institution, and by the cosmos in our "spiritual" relationship with God — discloses for us another, much more fundamental, stumbling block, one which everything in us is bent on forgetting, one which is implied in our numerous affirmations, explicit or not, about the "here" of the presence and action of God, Christ, and the Spirit in prayer, the communication of the word among believers, and ethical action. However, the irrepressible power of "logocentrism," which pervades us, hides from us a piece of evidence we should normally find blinding, namely, that these affirmations also come to us through the body. However, their purely verbal mediation of expression dulls the edge of scandal; and habit eventually renders them so believable that we readily accept them as self-evident!

In conclusion, our *fundamental difficulty* lies, not in the affirmation of "sacramental grace" as such, but in what this presupposes, specifically, the humanity of the divine God revealed in the scandal of the cross, a scandal which is irreducible to any justifying "reason" and continues to work upon us when we dare to "envisage" the disfigured ones of this world as the image of our crucified Lord and thereby to transfigure our tragic history into a salvific history. Such "foolishness" finds its most compelling expression in the affirmation of the sacraments as places of grace.

IV. A COUNTERCHECK: THE NON-SACRAMENTAL THEOLOGY OF KARL BARTH

We have already mentioned Barth, this giant of contemporary theology. He himself has emphasized that the categorical "No" with which he denies the sacramentality of baptism, that is, its nature as a mediation of an event of grace, collides head on, *de principe et ab ovo* ("by principle and from the beginning"), with what he recognizes as being "a very ancient and very strong ecclesiastical and theological tradition"[89] which, however, according to him, is in contradiction with the New Testament. Now, a theology worthy of the name, we have noted at the beginning of this last part, should have a sacramental theology consistent with its Christology, its Trinitarian doctrine, and its ecclesiology. It is this *de facto consistency* (we do not say consistency in principle) in Barth which we would like to outline as a countercheck.

In systematically contradicting classic sacramental theology, Barth shows his almost visceral fear of calling into question God's free and gratuitous sovereign action by having it enter into "synergistic" cooperation with the human action the Church performs in the sacraments. Now, one

89. Barth, *Dogmatique* IV/4, pp. 106–107.

wonders how it is that the Christocentrism which is such a prominent feature of his theology did not carry him past this fear.

In fact, his *Christology* already bears within itself, at least in its general tendency and in certain of its expressions, his non-sacramental theology. Barth's one-sided insistence on the divine initiative minimizes the role of humanity even in Christ himself. Hence, his tendency to understand "the Word made flesh" as "the Word living in the flesh" and to favor a formula such as "God in the flesh" where the human nature of Christ is "the clothing, the temple, and the organ of the Son of God."[90] As H. Bouillard puts it, for Barth, God's action assumes "so exclusive a position that the God made human seems to be absorbed back into it and the human conduct of Jesus appears then as only a veil concealing the unique divine action."[91] This logic leads to an almost exclusive use of the language of substitution in soteriology: the "for us" is repeatedly translated as "in our place." In short, the author of the *Dogmatics* "tends to see in Jesus Christ only the event produced by divine action: God who hides God in God's opposite in order to act alone, *in the place* of humanity."[92] Hence, Urs von Balthasar asks, is the cross anything else than a "monologue of God with God," "a nightmare without any reality"?[93] Without any reality, to the extent that the incarnation and the cross of Christ are not "truly conditioned by sin, but by his self-denial decided upon from all eternity."[94]

This line of thought leads H. Zahrnt to observe: "Unexpectedly, Barth, the strict theologian of revelation, locates his point of view not below, but above revelation, not in time, but in eternity." Despite appearances, "his true point of departure is not the event of the incarnation, but the pre-existence of Christ." "Not only is everything decided upon from eternity, but even already realized there; what happens in time is merely the execution of God's original decision." Human history is nothing more than the context or stage where this "salvation history" is played out. It is not taken into account for itself, but only (like creation, see below) from the perspective of the grace of salvation. Strictly speaking, nothing really happens in salvation history: what has already happened in the gratuitous election in Christ, made from all eternity, simply unfolds. "With Barth, then, the incarnation is not a really new event, a new intervention of

90. H. Bouillard, *Karl Barth*, vol. 2/1 (Paris: Aubier-Montaigne, 1957) 122.

91. Ibid., 118.

92. Ibid., vol. 2/2, p. 292.

93. H. Urs von Balthasar, *Karl Barth: Darstellung und Deutung seiner Theologie* (Cologne, 1951) 380.

94. Ibid., 255–256.

God, but merely the new *clothing* of what already existed before: for Barth, 'The Word was made Flesh' means 'The Word took on flesh.' "[95] Indicative of this interpretation is his formula: "It is the Word who speaks, who acts, who wins the victory . . . the incarnate Word, certainly, therefore . . . the Word in the flesh and by the flesh — but the Word *and not* the flesh."[96]

Hence the paradox: there are few theologies that speak so much of events and history, and yet there are few theologies where so little takes place on the properly historical plane. That the Word of God is sovereign, that this Word gathers in Christ the entire unfolding of human history, no Christian would dispute; and one is thankful to Barth for having expressed this with a force and a genius perhaps unequalled in our time. But has not Barth, perhaps without noticing it, slipped behind the mirror? Bouillard concludes his long study of Barth with this observation, "What bothers us the most is precisely that Barth has somehow placed himself in God's unique vantage point (that of the God who speaks in the Bible), in order to contemplate God's work from that vantage point." It is because he gives in to this temptation, it seems, that his theological discourse on the Word of God "has the trappings of a gnosis fallen from heaven."[97]

Let us go farther in this direction. We know that Barth, departing from any theology that begins with the *De Deo Uno*, speaks a language intended to be Trinitarian and Christological from the start: Trinitarian, in the sense that God's being, coinciding with God's action, is posited at the outset as God's "being to the extent that God loves" and God's "being in freedom" (*Dogm.* II/2), which cannot be conceived except on the basis of God's "three manners of being" (*Dogm.* I/1); Christological, in the sense that God's free election, which dominates Barth's entire perspective and contains "the Gospel *in nuce*" ("in a nutshell"), has no other principle, content, or term than Jesus Christ (*Dogm.* II/2). Now, and for the same reasons of supra-temporality as those advanced above, such a discourse presupposes a reference, doubtless overlooked, to a pre-Trinitarian God. We agree with Breton (see ch. 1) that with Barth, there always secretly presides an "eminent Self" behind this willing and loving of God, who through grace predestines God's creatures in Christ. This is why, even while developing a theology of the humanity and suffering of God (even to making God in the Son bear our reprobation in our place) from his rigorous thought concerning "God in Christ," Barth has, so to

95. H. Zahrnt, *Aux prises avec Dieu: La théologie protestante au XXe siècle* (Paris: Cerf, 1969) 147-149.

96. Barth, *Dogmatique* I/2, p. 149.

97. Bouillard, *Karl Barth*, vol. 2/2, p. 300.

speak, stopped in mid-course along this path: the cross of Jesus is indeed the revelation of God, but it is not, strictly speaking, an event in God. A sort of "trans-Christological reserve," in the words of Moltmann, permits Barth in the last analysis to avoid a total identification of the hidden God with the revealed God. The same author adds that this is why Barth "in a curious way . . . thinks in a manner which is too theological and insufficiently Trinitarian. In making again and again, and correctly, the point that God was in Christ, that God's self was humiliated, that God's self was on the cross, he uses a simple notion of God not yet developed in a Trinitarian way."[98] In short, he conceives God in a "pre-Trinitarian" and "trans-Christological" way. Moreover, could it have been otherwise, when one considers his supra-historical perspective? The "simple notion" of God which he keeps in reserve does not enable him to make a statement like "the Word *and* the flesh" without his seeing it as flawed by the synergistic sacrilege . . .

The same permanent fear of creating a mixture of God and humanity is found in Barth's *ecclesiology*. Of course, Barth reacts powerfully against liberal theology's minimizing the mystery of the visible Church. He insists "it is in the Church and through the Church that one comes to the faith," to the point that the Church is "the accessible place and the available instrument of grace."[99] In spite of the force of this last statement, he does not intend to recognize the Church as having any role of active participation in salvation. To avoid synergism, he is obliged to limit the Church's "instrumental" role: it is no more than a *passive* tool in God's hands. For, as A. Dumas has noted, it is "the doctrine of election which constitutes the central element of Barth's theology of the Church." This Church exists "independently from the fall." This author, in his turn, discerns in this ecclesiology "an ahistorical unfolding which God accomplishes within God's self, to humanity's benefit certainly, but outside it: a great intra-Trinitarian action even down to its manifestation in Jesus Christ's rejection and election in our place." However, he notes in the "very old Barth" an effort to balance his ecclesiology by giving the Church and humankind their own "*active* part in salvation history." He detects this tendency in the section of the *Dogmatics* (IV/4) which we have analyzed with regard to baptism, inasmuch as the "baptism of water" requires that "human beings commit themselves to God" in response to the "baptism of the Spirit" where "God turns toward humanity." But as we have explained above, it seems to us that this "correction" changes nothing fundamental. It is only, as Dumas has commented, that "the old

98. Moltmann, *Le Dieu crucifié*, 230.
99. K. Barth, *L'Eglise* (Genève: Labor et Fides, 1964) 49–50 (text of 1927).

Barth worries that sacraments might be conceived as a confused mixture of two freedoms (that of God, which convokes, and that of humanity, which responds) when one attributes to them the virtue of communicating grace."[100]

The fact that Barth cannot conceive the action of God in active human mediation (by Jesus-as-human: "the Word and not the flesh"; by human beings-in-the-Church: a merely passive instrument) is also implied by his theology of *creation*. Many commentators on his work have noted this. We are grateful to him for having reminded us that creation is a mystery of faith and that, as such, it should not be considered as a sort of independent entity belonging to theodicy, but as one phase in the unfolding economy of grace (*Dogm.* III/1). But, has he not gone too far? Envisaged not from the temporal viewpoint but from that of the eternal election, creation does not precede redemption; it proceeds from it. As Barth himself admits, it is reduced to being no more than "the production of the space where the history of the covenant of grace must be played out," no more than "the theater and setting, . . . foreseen in the eternal election of Jesus Christ," of salvation history. Then we wonder: Is there any room left for a (relative) autonomy of creation? Do the world and history still have their own consistency? It seems not. Indeed, for Barth, the universe, humankind, and history are understood only by analogy with God, with Christ as the point of departure. Of course, what we have here is not the *analogia entis* ("analogy of being"), continually rejected, but the *analogia relationis* ("analogy of relation"), which is also *analogia revelationis* ("analogy of revelation") or *analogia fidei* ("analogy of faith"): an analogy revealed by God and which can be received only through faith in Christ. Hence R. Prenter's statement: "If the unity of creation and redemption is to be made visible to the believer through analogical exegesis, it is then necessary that the analogy of redemption constitute the *being* of the created world. In other words, the proper function of created existence is to produce an image of redemption. . . . Thus, an unmistakably Platonic aura envelopes the world of creation this exegesis presents. The world, in some sense, must not be 'itself'; *it finds its 'true being' only in the significance of redemption.*" In other words, we have here "a certain Docetism concerning creation." As Bouillard comments, this is a judgment "doubtless too severe," but a judgment "one cannot entirely put aside."[101]

---

100. A. Dumas, "L'Eglise dans la théologie de Karl Barth," *Les quatre fleuves* 5 (Paris: Beauchesne, 1975) 57–69.

101. Bouillard, *Karl Barth*, vol. 2/1, pp. 193–194. The same judgment is given by Zahrnt, *Aux prises avec Dieu*, 123–125, 137–138.

Thus, one senses in all the sectors of Barth's theology this deeply ingrained impossibility of conceiving God's gracious action and free human action at the same time without competition or synergism understood as an addition. We recognize here a *typically metaphysical presupposition:* God's transcendence can be understood only according to the vertical scheme involving distance from and, ultimately, opposition to humanity. This presupposition itself depends on an onto-theological *"simple notion"* of God; despite appearances, Barth thinks in a pre-Trinitarian and trans-Christological modality. It is not our purpose to challenge the "orthodoxy" of Barth's Christology. Neither do we wish to say that his non-sacramental theology is the unavoidable consequence of his Christology. We simply maintain that there is a coherence between a tendency in his Christology — a tendency which is, if not "Nestorian," at least spontaneously "anti-Monophysite," as with Calvin, and which leads him to disconnect, as far as this is possible in the context of the tradition inherited from the Councils of Ephesus and Chalcedon, the divinity of Christ from his humanity — and his position on the non-sacramentality (in the traditional sense) of baptism. The Word in and through the flesh . . . but the Word, and not the flesh. We may conclude that the dimension of what we have called sacramentality is lacking at every level in Barth's thought, and not just in the area of Christology.

CONCLUSION

1. *Sacramental Grace and the Humanity of the Divine God*
   a) Barth had good reasons to be critical of classic sacramental theology on the pastoral level (excessive sacramentalism) as well as on the properly theological level (a "productionist" model which, even when purified by the use of analogy, did not sufficiently take into account the subjects with their ethical experience and which fostered what we have called the "sacrificial regime"). However, his criticism is too strongly based on onto-theological presuppositions (a pre-Trinitarian notion of God and an instrumentalist conception of the mediations of the relationship between humankind and God) to be pertinent. It results, in fact, in a sacramental theology which, since it is inoperative, loses most of its interest. Barth certainly expresses an important dimension of baptism when he underlines its character as a grateful response by humans for the justification which God has already bestowed upon them. But by taking into account only this one dimension,

he can no longer justify the baptism of water and its holiness except as the Church's obedience to a command from its Lord. Seeking to understand their faith, theologians then wonder: What does such a command mean? What significance did the first Christian communities attach to the baptism of water if Matthew (28:19) places the command in the mouth of the Risen One himself? Barth gives no response to this query; he withdraws behind the "Word of God" as behind an absolute thing fallen directly from heaven. Moreover, he cannot do otherwise, convinced as he is a priori that the baptism of water cannot be an event of salvation — otherwise, God's sovereign liberty would be, in his eyes, gravely compromised. As we have said, and in spite of appearances, Barth responds to Scholasticism as a Scholastic. He has in no way overcome the metaphysical dualism between the "natural" and the "supernatural."

b) The sacraments lose the essential of their interest if their dimension as "revealers" of God's grace, which is the foundation of Christian ethical practice, is not complemented by their dimension as "operators" and hence events of grace. However, the emphasis on this second dimension can free itself from the productionist scheme — which Barth rightly criticizes — only if we "overcome" the metaphysical view of the world (characterized by instrumentality and causality) and move into the symbolic (characterized by the mediation through language and symbol, where "revealer" and "operator" are indissolubly linked insofar as they are homogeneous). In this symbolic perspective, the relation of God and humankind is conceived according to the scheme of otherness which transcends the dualistic scheme of nature and grace undergirding classic onto-theology. Such a scheme requires that God, on the one hand, and our relation to God, on the other, be expressed from the start in the mode of being open.

In what concerns *God,* the present chapter has just shown that the *Logos* of the cross authoritatively orders us to turn the simple notion around and in that way develop a conception of God manifesting God's self as God precisely by refusing to be God. It is impossible to speak about this God in any other way than as human in God's divinity, and it is impossible to speak about the humanity of this divine God without at the same time letting ourselves be spoken according to an essentially transitive way of thinking.

Along the same lines, the *relation of God to us* needs to be treated, not as an object to which a value can be assigned, but as an unceasing symbolic labor by which the Spirit works in us in view of our own birth into filiation and love for brothers and sisters. This is what we have shown by the concept of "grace." "Sacramental grace" expresses how God renders effective within history God's divine paternity by raising up for Christ a body of children and brothers and sisters. In this way the essential humanity of this divine God finds its exemplary symbolic "expression" in the sacraments.

2. *The Equipoise of the Christological and Pneumatological Principles in Sacramental Theology*

In the preceding chapter, we argued for a sacramental theology in which pneumatology would be considered a principle on a par with Christology. We outlined the concrete consequences which follow. Obviously, the present chapter does no more than reinforce this position.

One must be careful not to swing from a "Christo-monistic" to a "pneumato-monistic" emphasis. Without sufficient attention to its *Christological* principle (that of its particularity as an institution), the Church would veer toward the universalism of a kingdom which, lacking criteria of identity, could not differentiate itself from all people of good will and, consequently, would have nothing to communicate to them from the perspective of Christian particularity; at the same time, the sacraments could not but be open to all who are animated by "the Spirit," without the check of institutional criteria of discernment.[102] Conversely, without sufficient attention to its *pneumatological* principle (that of its openness to the universal), the Church would veer toward the particularism of a group narrowly attached to its marks of identity; and participation in the sacraments would be subjected to strict rules of orthodoxy and "purity," rules which continually threaten to sink liturgy in legalism. It is by means of the universality of the Spirit,

102. J. Moltmann goes too far in this direction (*L'Eglise dans la force de l'Esprit: Une contribution à l'ecclésiologie moderne* [Paris: Cerf, 1980] 319–322).

surpassing any institution, that the Christic particular can find a way to ground its claim to the universality of the "for all"; but it by means of the particularity of Jesus Christ — inscribed in the Jewishness of this one man and of the history of Israel, Jewishness which alone gives meaning to his "Christness" "according to the Scriptures" — that the pneumatological universal can avoid evaporating into the illusions of everyone's good intentions and sincerity, that is, dissolving the singularity of Christian identity.

3. *The In-between Time*

The irreducible tension between the universal of the Spirit and the particular of Jesus Christ which affects the sacraments is nothing else, in the last analysis, than the expression of the *eschatological* contradiction that defines the Church's identity.

The sacraments symbolize this contradiction first inasmuch as they are a memorial of Jesus Christ. They are not a memorial of *Jesus*: this would be a memorial without an eschatological future, and its past would be limited to the remembrance of a fine example (the most beautiful, the most noble, the holiest person, perhaps) of a prophet and martyr. Nor are they a memorial of *Christ* only: this would be a memorial without a properly historical past, and its future would evaporate into a mythic "other world." As a memory of *Jesus Christ*, the sacramental memorial avoids the "two excesses" which threaten the Christian theology of history. First, an *eschatological* excess which, emphasizing one-sidedly the "absolute discontinuity" between "profane" history and "salvation" history (Barth, Bultmann, Urs von Balthasar), ends, in this last author, in a sort of "apocalyptic paroxysm of delight" where "history is no longer anything but the 'exterior stage' on which the drama of salvation is played out." Second, an *incarnational* excess which, showing an exaggerated "evolutionary optimism" (Teilhard de Chardin, certain political theologians), tends to minimize the eschatological rupture, that is, to reduce eschatology to a teleology.[103] Against the first current, the Christian memorial stresses the engaging ethical *exemplarity* of the history of Jesus, the Christ, all the way to the martyr's gift of his life; without this history, his Christic identity and his salvific function would vanish

103. Geffré, *Le christianisme*, 198–200.

546

into an atemporal myth. Against the second, the Christian memorial upholds the gratuitous *"sacramentality"* of his Pasch "for us men and women and for our salvation"; without this sacramental Pasch, his exemplarity would not fundamentally differ from that of all prophets and righteous martyrs. Thus, the sacraments speak of the eschatological *in-between time.*

·

Sacrament: Creation, History, and Eschatology

Our project at the outset was to develop a fundamental theology of sacramentality which would permit a global reinterpretation of Christian existence. Obviously, this project included a possible reinterpretation of the world as creation. But this undoubtedly important dimension of Christian existence has been the object only of allusions here and there: the present work became so extensive that it did not allow for the inclusion of the intended chapter on this topic. As we conclude, we would like to briefly show the direction in which such a study could be carried out.

Two main schemes seem to have dominated Western philosophic and religious tradition on the subject of creation.[1] The *artisanal* scheme of fabrication, on the model of Genesis, had the advantage of freeing the Creator from the bonds of necessity and of highlighting the free and deliberate character of the Creator's work; but, by identifying the first "principle" with the "cause," it had the drawback of too narrowly fashioning the Creator on the human model and also of depicting the world in too static a manner as a finished product. The *biological* scheme of generation, or alternatively that of the diffusion of light from its source, a scheme on the model of emanationism, had the advantage of disconnecting the creative principle from the concept of cause and thus of promoting a dynamic understanding of creation as always in the process of realization; but it had the drawback of too closely linking this creation to a sort of internal necessity of the divine principle. Of course, every gradation between these two models has existed.

1. S. Breton, "Création. 2 — La création dans les synthèses philosophico-religieuses," *Enc. Univ.*, 5:44–66.

These are clearly complementary models, and yet probably never fully reconcilable. They are also doubtlessly unavoidable models, stemming as they do from the psychological impossibility of evading questions about the origin of everything. But, to think is to learn to ask questions and thus to go beyond what at first appears to be spontaneous and undeniable evidence — knowing all the while that such an "overcoming" is as impossible to achieve as the schemes of the primary symbolism which dwell in us (in this case those of a cause or a source at our origin) are inescapable.

Now, according to the Bible, God creates by God's *word:* "God said . . . and it was so" (Gen 1). This verbal modality locates from the outset the divine work in the symbolic order, neither in the order of causality proper to a finished product nor in the order of derivation of essences according to the their degree of participation in the first principle. Thus, such a modality opens the ontological through the symbolic: Being is marked with the stamp of the Other. Inasmuch as it is created, the world of entities is posited as a *gift* from the start. Theologically, the world is confessed as creation insofar as it is marked by the word; and this word makes the world come forth immediately as an offer. Moreover, this is the function of the forbidden tree in Genesis 2–3. This prohibition does not jealously reserve for God a quantitative portion of the world, as if God feared human competition — precisely contrary to what the serpent insinuates by depicting a God as evil and jealous as itself. The prohibition does not have the calculating value of a subtraction; it has a symbolic value: *everything* is yours; but never forget that all this is a *gift*. Without the prohibition, there would be no gift. The biblical point of creation is in this gift. This gift is *gratuitous,* necessitated by nothing, preceding all existence, forbidding humanity under pain of "sin" the pretention of going back to its origin, of establishing itself in existence, or of founding its world by itself. The gift is *gracious* as well, irreducible to any consideration of worth or any calculation, always in excess and, consequently, impossible to justify by any ultimate "reason." There is no scientific answer to the question, "Why is there something rather than nothing?" Creation bespeaks an irreducible *precedence.* It is a *positive* precedence, erecting a barrier against every exacerbation of subjectivity which would pretend to reduce creation to human creativity. But this positive aspect, because it is linked to the word (of God), is not simply the factual aspect of a finished product; thus, it calls humanity to *make a "world"* out of the universe which it receives, to make throughout history a livable world, that is, a world where each person can find his or her proper place.

From the biblical viewpoint, creation calls upon human creativity, to which, however, it cannot be reduced. This is why the act of creation by the divine word is an act of *differentiation*. God creates by putting order, and thus free space, in the primordial chaos, by establishing difference. Difference between light and darkness, heaven and earth, and so on. A difference that culminates on the sixth day with this fundamental difference which is the sexual difference, beyond the realm of value or calculation. This difference belongs to the "image of God" since humans are said to be created in this image as a couple, as "male and female" (Gen 1:27); since creation is not good until *ish* ("man") discovers *"the other like itself"* in an *ishah* ("woman," Gen 2:18-24). This difference is metaphorically inscribed as a lack, lack-in-being, in Adam's flesh through the removed rib. This difference cannot be assumed without a distancing from the parents who gave birth and must now be left behind (Gen 2:24). And this threefold anthropological difference (with regard to oneself, the rib; with regard to others, the sexual difference; with regard to one's origin, the taking leave of one's parents) sends us back to and finds its meaning in the holiness-difference of God who creates by withdrawing from the world (an event solemnized on the seventh day), of which, as we have seen, the forbidden tree is the symbol.

The term "gift" unites the two aspects of creation, as distinct as they are indissociable: first, the positive reality of an unavoidable precedence; second, the calling stamped in this reality by the word, a calling addressed to humans in order to have them assume this reality in a creative way so that all may find their places and live in this universe organized into a "world." Thus, we have the pure *contingency* of the real which is simply here and which the notion of creation designates as neither "made by" (the artisanal scheme of "working upon") nor "resulting from" (the emanation-like scheme of "participating in"), but purely and simply as "here." Such a "hereness" is accessible only to a meditative approach. By its very nature, it is outside the scope of scientific thought, which shows that creative action cannot be placed on a par with anything — this is the point of creation *ex nihilo* — and that to think of it is impossible without the astonished questioning of this apparent evidence and this apparent banality that "there is" something at all, and not nothing — an astonished questioning which bestows on the real an altogether different face. This "there is" is something "posited." But this "posited" comes forth — and this is the second aspect — only as "given" (see Heidegger's *es gibt*). Because it arises from the word, the "hereness" is *"donation."* This gift is not added, in a logically second step, to a somehow preexisting real; it is constitutive of this real in its very coming forth, a little like a question or a problem that begins to exist when it is enunciated. Thus, theologically, to call upon human responsibility in history belongs to the notion of creation.

At bottom, what the doctrine of creation proposes (it is the proposal of possibility, not the necessity of evidence) is *the opening of a word.* Faced with a future plunged into the uncertainties of pure chance, together with the constraining determinations of a teleology (or an archeology), the theology of creation proposes the emergence of a responsible word. To confess creation is to attain freedom: the given of the universe is received as an offer.[2]

The major expression of this offer made to humankind, thus regarded as free and responsible, is that of the *offering* to God. The "reception" of the world as creation, that is, as "gift," implies the "return-gift" of the offering. Thus, the confession of creation is itself charged with *sacramentality.* It is in the "sacrament-mystery" of the oblation that the "mystery" of creation finds its "expression" (in the strong sense of this word). "Blessed are you, Lord, God of all creation / Through your goodness we have this bread to offer, / which earth has given and human hands have made." Making visible the gesture of presenting the gifts at Mass, this formula, inspired by the Jewish table blessings, is the way faith confesses in action that God is creator. This gesture of disappropriation is the concrete mediation of the

2. A. Dumas, *Nommer Dieu,* ch. 15 "La création, par-delà le hasard et l'évolution," 275–287.

appropriation of the world as "given," as offered as a present and in the present to the responsible freedom of humans.

Sacramentality arises only at the intersection of these two dimensions, cosmic and historic, evoked by the oblation of the bread as fruit both of the earth and of human work. Without the earth, there is no work; but without the work, the earth is not "matter." The bread is Eucharistic matter only as a link between the cosmos and history. But this link-relation, implied by the notion of creation, is ambivalent: it is able to give rise to a "decreation" as well as to the unfolding of the creation.[3]

As the symbolic representation of all that feeds humans, bread is heavy with their "death" in their work.[4] Death unto life. For, once digested, it turns death into life, it denies this death to give life to life. Now, when it is not consumed by those who have produced it, it becomes bread of death. When an unjust economic system takes away from the poor the bread they have made, when it distributes it only to those who are economically well off, it makes of the bread a symbol of "de-creation"; thus it de-sacramentalizes it. *Bread cannot become Eucharist under just any condition.* "Like one who kills a son before his father's eyes is the person who offers a sacrifice from the property of the poor. The bread of the needy is the life of the poor; whoever deprives them of it is a murderer." (Sir 34:24-25). To offer God this bread kneaded from the death of the poor is a sacrilege. To partake of this bread stolen from those who produced it is to eat "judgment against [oneself]": it is impossible to discern the body of the Lord, namely, this sacramental body where the Head and the members are indissolubly joined together (1 Cor 11:17-34). The psalmist, speaking in God's name, accuses all those "evildoers who eat up my people as they eat their bread" (Ps 53:4). To pretend to eat the body of Christ unto life, when in fact this bread, taken from the mouths of the poor, is the bearer of death, is to condemn oneself. The theological economy of the sacramental cult is inseparable from the social economy of labor.

3. For original sin as "decreation," see X. Thévenot, *Les péchés, que peut-on en dire?* (Mulhouse: Salvator 1983) 25–49.

4. See E. Dussel, "Le pain de la célébration: Signe communautaire de justice," *Concilium* 172 (1982) 89–101.

Sacraments present the world to us as something we may not use in an arbitrary fashion; they demand that we make of reality a "world" for all, and not simply for the well-off. They also present the world to us as not reducible to a simple object at our disposal, which we may exploit for purely utilitarian purposes. They manifest *the symbolic excess* which the real, inasmuch as it is created, holds in reserve. They reveal to us the "sacramentality" of the world as creation. In virtue of its profane nature, therefore not sacralized, this world contains a prohibition against profanation. The most elementary things — water, bread, wine . . . — demand "respect."

This *respect*, which is a distancing, a detachment from an all-devouring utilitarianism, opens up the opacity of the real. It opens it by way of the word. Only the human word of creativity can make it cor-respond to the divine word of creation which sets it down as "ordered" — if it is true that this creative word authoritatively commands chaos to set itself in order so that it may ultimately be hospitable to humankind. Because it is created, the real has a distinct existence; commerce with it requires respect for this "distinctness." Creation speaks of the world as "fissured," irreducible to its positive opacity, which, however, resists. Creation is "position," but position *fractured by the word* which "sets it in order." To be responsible for creation is to open it, just as one opens the dense wholeness of a loaf of bread in order to share it. This is why, as the Eucharistic Prayers show, the breaking of the bread is the memorial of the gesture and historic deeds of Jesus sharing his life like bread and also the memorial of the creative deed of God through the "Word through which [God] made the universe" (beginning of the second Eucharistic Prayer).

Sacraments do not refer us back to *salvation history* without at the same time referring us back to *creation*, just as, biblically, the latter is unthinkable without the former, beyond which it nonetheless extends: it is the God of Israel, the God of the Covenant, the God of history who creates the world, according to Genesis. Sacramental memorialization, focused on Jesus' Pasch, would lose all historical texture (and would thus be comparable to the Greek myths of savior gods) if it did not include the history of Israel. But in its turn, the history of Israel, in its particularity, cannot be acknowledged as salvation history except against a background of universality. This is why the biblical tradition, beginning with the historical creation of Israel as God's people through the desert experience, came to enlarge this historical particularity into a cosmic universality. Such a widening of perspective was necessary if the God of Israel was to become the God of all peoples and all things. It was necessary if Israel, while remaining Israel, was to become universal.[5] It was necessary if the promise was to expand to include all nations and, finally, if the Christic universality of this singular Jew who was Jesus was to be affirmed. The confession of creation was born from the impossibility of "Israel only."

The "profane" (that is, the natural) state of the world and of history is thus recognized as the *possible sacramental place* of a sacred history. Therefore, this profane state demands to be treated with respect, as we said above. Not in order to be sacralized — which would take away its autonomy — but in order not to be profaned by being used in an arbitrary and utilitarian way. To treat the world as an offer, an offering to others, thus to make of it a "house" open to brothers and sisters where all can find their places: such is the ethical implication, in its universal economic and political dimensions, of this recognition of creation in the Eucharistic gesture of offering; such is the practical exigency of the *tua ex tuis tibi offerentes* of the ancient anaphoras (see above), the reason why, precisely, the anamnestic oblation to God of Christ (who takes flesh in elements representing by metonymy creation and human history) finds its culmination in the gesture of the bread broken for the life of all. Sacraments are the *great symbolic places* which attest that the recognition of the grace of creation and the exigency of a counter-gift are inseparable: humankind is commissioned to offer God this return-gift throughout history by ordering this world in such a way that it cor-responds to its primordial divine plan. Sacraments are *indispensable* symbols, if it is true that the ritual "language game," "-urgic" and pragmatic by nature, represents what is required of such a recognition (of the grace of creation): the passage from language to body, from word to practice.

5. P. Beauchamp, *L'Un et l'Autre Testament*, (Paris: Seuil, 1976) ch. 3 "Les sages," especially 116–118.

However, the "sacramentality" of the "profane" must not make us forget that the risen Lord, who takes flesh in it through the Spirit, still bears the marks of the wounds of his death. *Eschatology*. On the one hand, that it is the Lord of glory who eschatologically takes flesh in the world precludes this split between "profane" history and "salvation" history, a split which causes eschatology to drift into "eschatologism." This split is characteristic of theologies of redemptive "rupture," where creation, insufficiently respected in its autonomy, finds meaning only in redemption. But, on the other hand, that the Lordship of Christ remains that of the humility of the cross and that it is incarnated in the tragic condition of the disfigured ones of history — who thereby become our judges (Matt 25:31-46) — precludes an evolutionist interpretation implying continuity between "profane" history and "salvation" history. This is an interpretation characteristic of the excessively "naturalistic" theologies of history, where eschatology tends to be confused with a teleology.[6]

Thus, sacraments speak of the eschatological *in-between* time. It is the time of an "already," but qualified by a "not yet." If this were not so, we would reduce the reign to a mere "otherwise" (not even evident at that!) of this world. It is the time of a "not yet," but shot through by an "already." If this were not so, we would reduce the reign to an "other world" without relation to this world. Sacraments are the bearers of the joy of the "already" and the distress of the "not yet." They are the *witnesses of a God who is never finished with coming:* the amazed witnesses of a God who comes continually; the patient witnesses, patient unto weariness at times, of a God who "is" not here except by mode of passage. And of this passage, the sacraments are the trace . . .

6. C. Geffré, *Le christianisme au risque de l'interprétation* (Paris: Cerf, 1983) ch. 9 "Eclatement de l'histoire et Seigneurie du Christ," 189-208.

Index of Authors

Sanon, A. T., 360–362, 364
Saussure, F. de, 143
Schelling, F. W., 122
Schillebeeckx, E., 383, 386
Schubert, K., 246
Scouarnec, M., 345
Sendler, E., 217
Serapion, 275
Shepherd of Hermas, 523–524
Siman, E. P., 434, 525
Simon, A., 303
Simon of Florence, 378
Siricius, 480
Smith, P., 208
Sobrino, J., 494
Soos, M. B. de, 483, 485
Soter, 479
Sperber, D., 125
Stevenson, K., 276
Stinchcombe, A. L., 332
Sutter, J., 334

Taft, R., 484
Talley, J. T., 479–481, 482
Tarby, A., 269
Teilhard de Chardin, P., 546
Tertullian, 199, 211, 214, 259, 434,
    449–450, 480, 530
Theodore of Mopsuestia, 524
Theodore of Studios, 403
Thévenot, X., 552
Thomas Aquinas, 7, 8, 9–21, 27,
    30, 31, 37–40, 44, 70, 164, 309,
    380, 383, 384–390, 423, 436, 450,
    453–476
Thurian, M., 232
Tillard, J.M.R., 469

Tinland, F., 147
Todorov, T., 30, 121–122, 205
Trebossen, P. G., 352
Trent, council of, 295, 311, 379,
    381, 383, 387, 400, 420, 435
Turner, V., 115, 116, 137, 139, 349

Ushte, T., 116

Valéry, P., 151
Van Eyck, A., 396
Vanhoye, A., 249, 255, 298
Vasse, D., 97, 147
Vatican II, council, 171, 184–185,
    214, 268, 328, 413–416, 417
Vaux, R. de, 191, 194, 242, 243
Vergote, A., 91, 98, 123, 148, 174,
    179, 302, 315, 328, 332, 334, 357,
    366, 367, 368, 372, 397, 412, 416,
    427–428, 534–535
Vignaux, P., 293
Villalon, J. R., 529
Villela-Petit, M., 396
Vogel, C., 310, 471
Von Allmen, J. J., 226, 232, 257,
    282, 321, 424
Von Rad, G., 201, 203, 230
Von Schönborn, C., 218, 403
Voyé, L., 332–333

Wiesel, E., 490
William of Auvergne, 16
Wittgenstein, L., 426

Yerkes, R. K., 241

Zahrnt, H., 539, 542

Index of Subjects

fundamental mediation, 171, 182
fundamental mediation, diagram,
172
gift of grace, 185–186
See also Ecclesia
Cognition, 124, 127–128
See also Recognition
Consent to loss, 170, 177
See also Presence of the absence
(Index of Phrases)
Corporality
of faith, 152, 376
place of God, 264, 531
place of rites, 355
See also Body
Creation
by God's word, 549
charged with sacramentality, 551
explained by artisanal scheme of
production, 548
explained by biological scheme
of generation, 548
gift implying a return-gift, 551
irreducible precedence of, 549
Crisis in ritual, 238–239, 364–365
Crucified God, The
four theses, 492–494
Moltmann's thesis, 502–504
Cult
Christian, an eschatological
memorial, 239–240
Christian vocabulary of, early,
254–259
Christian vocabulary of, second
century, 257–259
Jesus' attitude towards, 244–247
Jewish, an historic-prophetic
memorial, 229–234
theological difference between
Jewish and Christian cults,
250–252
theological difference, diagram,
253

Deadly dichotomy, 294, 388, 465–468

Descartes' dualism, 34–36
Deuteronomy 26:1-11, analysis of,
234–237
Difference of God, 518, 521
Difference-otherness, scheme of,
92, 94–95, 503
"Digitality," 347
Divine God, 59, 61
Dualism, 144

Easter
as tear, break, 247–249
metaphor of the tear, 248–250
weekly, on Sunday, 478–479
yearly, 479–481
Ecclesia
local assembly, 184
place of the Bible's truth, 210
See also Church
Emmaus, story of, 161–162, 167
Entities, 26, 47
as events, 50
See also Ontological difference
Epiclesis, 523–527
Eschatology, 239–240
defining Church's identity,
546–547
in-between time, 546–547, 555
Esse and *adesse*, 389–390
Heidegger's pitcher, 393–396
Ethics, 179–180
return-gift of ethical practice,
277, 279
See also Return-gift
Eucharist
Augustine's view of, 292
Berengar's view of, 293–294,
384, 388
Council of Trent, 293
Medieval debates, 292–297
paradigmatic figure of the
presence of the absence of
God, 405
Paschasius' view of, 13, 293
Ratramnus' view of, 293

symbolic process characteristic
of, 272–281
symbolic process, diagram, 278
See also Breaking of the bread;
Sacramental Causality in
Thomas Aquinas; Transub-
stantiation
Eucharistic ethics, according to
Irenaeus and Augustine, 311–315
Eucharistic Prayer
crystallization of salvation
history and parousia, 391
too exclusively centered on
consecration in Thomistic
theology, 472
Eucharistic Prayer Number 2,
268–272
Narrative Program, 268
Narrative Program, diagram, 269
Eucharistic presence, crystallization of Christ's presence in the
assembly and Scripture, 390–391
Scripture, 390–391

Faith
arch-sacramentality of, 154–155
corporeal by nature, 152, 372, 376
"ecclesial" and "theological," 183
expressed in a life of witness,
164–166
language of, 427, 428
"necrotic" temptations against,
173–176
passage to, 3 key texts, 162–166
trial of, *see* Consent to loss
Foundational events, 202–204

God
"simple" notion of, to be burst
open, 508, 531, 543–544
what kind of, 66, 225, 450, 475,
487, 489
See also Crucified God
Grace, 60, 108–109
a non-thing, non-value, 45

a receiving of oneself from God,
442
gracious and gratuitous, 108, 446
irreducible to explanations, 443
sacramental, 536–538

Heidegger's criticism of
metaphysics, 26–36
Heidegger's *Sein* and *Dasein*, 43, 54
Hermeneutics, 66–67, 142 (n. 41),
195–197
Holy Spirit
agent of the Word's burial in
the flesh, 526
and Christ's resurrectional
power, 520
difference between Father and
Son, 513–514
difference of God inscribed into
corporality, 518–520
fire, 513
holding small place in Scripture,
515–516
neuter, 511
paradox, 516
third term, 510
unrevealed revealer, 514
vital space, 511
wind or breath, 512
Hypostatic union
felt as a scandal by Scholastic
tradition, 474
point of departure for Scholastic
sacramental theology, 453

I, you, it, 93–95, 503
Idol and icon, 216–220, 403
Idolatry, 216–217, 402
Incarnation, interpreted from the
resurrection, 489
Initiation
death and life, 97–98
difficult in Christianity, 363–364
in closed societies, 359–363

Jesus' abandonment on the cross, 494–499, 506–507
  an event *within* God's very self, 502
Jesus' life and death
  kenosis, 301–302
  Paul's interpretation of, 297
Jesus' temptation to use God, 299
Jewish identity, 283
  offering of the firstfruits, 283–286
  offering of the firstfruits, diagram, 285
Journey
  response to mystery, 398–399
  work of journeying itself, 54

Knowledge, Thomistic theory of, 32

Language, 30–34, 55–58
  Aristotle's view of, 30
  as "writing" or "(arch-) writing," 141–143
  Augustine's view of, 30–31, 33–34
  constructing the real into a world, 40
  creative expression, 88–92
  creative power, 92
  declarative and performative functions of, 131–132
  humans always-already spoken, 57
  instrument in classical metaphysics, 33
  it is language that speaks, 55
  "language acts," 130–135
  "language games," 42, 325, 426–430
  letting oneself be spoken, listening, 58
  locutionary, illocutionary, perlocutionary, 132–135
  mediation, 87, 90
  naming and labelling function of, 56

phonemes in, 113
poetry, 57
summoning and calling function of, 56
traditional view of, 89
Last Supper stories, 198–199
Letter of Scripture
  divided into "letter" and "figure," 216
  historical reality of, 215
Letter to the Hebrews, 249–250, 255–257, 297–298, 505–506
Letting-be, 51, 53, 60, 300, 446
Lex orandi, lex credendi, 214, 381, 484
Liturgical Year
  first three centuries, 477–481
  fourth century on, 481–487
Liturgy, illocutionary language of, 428
Logocentrism, 528
  criticism of, 143–145
  erasing the mediation of the letter, 401
  favoring voice over letter, 143–146
Logos of the cross, 69, 502, 527–528, 537

Manna, 44–45, 237
  figure of God's gracious gift, 222–223
Mass priests, *see* Sacerdotalization
Mediation, 84–109
  of symbols, 82
"Melancholy," test of, 79
Memorial, 231
  Passover, paradigm of, 232–234
  See also Ritual memory
Memory, two levels: memorization and commemoration, 233
Meontology, 74, 499–502, 509, 545
  See also Negative theology
Metaphysics, criticism of, 26–45
Metaphysics, overcoming, according to Heidegger, 47–63
Mode of being open, 404, 405, 407, 544

Sacramental theology
as a dimension of the whole of theology, 159
Christological and pneumatological principles of, 545–546
classical, 7–45
middle way of Vatican II, 413–416
middle way of Vatican II, diagram, 415
objectivist model of, 410–413
subjectivist model of, approach from "above," 419–424
subjectivist model of, approach from "below," 416–419
symbolic approach to, 9
See also Barth's sacramental theology; Thomas Aquinas' sacramental theology
Sacrament of reconciliation, 420–436
Sacraments
as instituted, 379
as instituting, 409
Christological pole of, 492–508
effective symbolic expressions, 425
eminently institutional, 378
events of grace, 410
expressing submission to the Other, 375
frustrating desire to erase empiricity, 382
great symbolic places, 554
indispensable symbols, 554
in sacramento: basic sacramental "representation," 291
major figures of the mediations of faith, 401–402
mediations, not instruments, 110
memorials in the Holy Spirit, 509–531
memorials of the Crucified who was raised, 492–508
obligatory points of passage, 281–282
operators, 437–438, 544
originality of, 321
places of grace, 531–538
pneumatological pole of, 509–531
precipitate of the Scriptures, 220
productionist scheme of representation of, 21
radical involvement of the Church in, 321–323
referring back to salvation history and creation, 553
referring the Church to the Lord's empty place, 381
remedies, 11–12
revealers, 431–437, 544
signs, 13–15
stumbling blocks, 153, 537
symbolic figures of God's effacement, 490
traces of God's passage, 555
transitions between Scripture and ethics, 265
wholly human acts of the Church, 374
Sacred
difficult notion, 369
reversed, not denied, 262
Sacrifice
anti-sacrificial trends, 240–244, 259
"farewell to sacrifices," 258, 260
Girard's thesis of, 303–306
notion to be used with care, 290–291, 315
of communion, 310–311
of expiation, 310–311
"progressive exodus away from sacrifices," 305
spiritual 254–255
Sacrificium intellectus, 386, 398, 399
Scandal of the cross, as action of the Trinitarian God, 532, 538
Scripture
"born of the liturgy," 190
chewing the book, 222–227
the liturgical assembly, place of, 200, 210
sacramental in essence, 213–216
See also Bible
Semio-linguistic theory of the text

567

Index of Phrases

This index lists phrases and quotes that constantly recur throughout the book and serve as leitmotifs.

Augustine's formula concerning the Eucharist, 291–292, 389, 407

Body of world and humanity, 75, 83, 87, 187, 189, 261, 289, 405, 407, 428, 509

"It is the way which sets everything on its way and it gets everything on its way inasmuch as it is a speaking way" (Heidegger), 47, 54, 98, 446, 517

Language, culture, and desire, 40, 41, 42, 43, 85, 86, 535

Presence of the absence, 62, 63, 74, 98, 307, 404, 405, 534

Reduced to less than nothing, 69, 74, 219, 407, 500, 502, 527

"Something facing human beings which stands by itself" (Heidegger), 30, 49, 53, 82, 240, 446

Step backwards, 8, 50, 53, 73

The most "spiritual" happens through the most "corporeal," 141, 146, 531

"Thing that the cross proposes," 70, 527, 535

"To hold ourselves in a mature proximity to absence" (Heidegger), 58, 62, 75, 405

Transparency of the self to itself, to others, and to God, 34, 44, 94, 141, 144, 154, 307

P 336. Liturgy — too constrained
re action today